SONORA YAQUI LANGUAGE STRUCTURES

SONORA YAQUI LANGUAGE STRUCTURES

John M. Dedrick and Eugene H. Casad

The University of Arizona Press

Tucson

The University of Arizona Press
©1999 The Arizona Board of Regents
First Printing
All rights reserved

This book was edited, designed, and typeset by the Summer Institute of Linguistics.

♾ This book is printed on acid-free, archival-quality paper.
Manufactured in the United States of America

04 03 02 01 00 99 6 5 4 3 2 1

Library of Congress Cataloging-in-Publication Data
Dedrick, John M., 1910–
Sonora Yaqui language structures / John M. Dedrick and Eugene H. Casad.
p. cm.
ISBN 0-8165-1981-1 (cloth : alk. paper)
1. Yaqui language—Grammar. I. Casad, Eugene H. II. Title.
PM4526 .D44 1999
497'.45—dc21
99-006866

British Library Cataloguing-in-Publication Data
A catalogue record for this book is available from the British Library.

This volume is dedicated to

Ambrosio Castro
(1894?–1953)

whose
gift of story telling
delighted me through the years
and whose generosity
in sharing his language with me
makes this description
much more colorful
than it otherwise
would have
been.

kat kapée hé'ée, čukúise'e 'aúnee
"Don't drink coffee, it will make you turn black."

kía háin tala-sáalaika híba ná'a hí'inee
"No matter how black it is, I will keep on drinking it."

kaibu=nee 'íntok 'á'a sú'utóhinee,
'ela'aposu=nee 'áamak 'ó'omúknee
"I'll never stop drinking it, even though I die of old age because of it."

lúula yéh-te'utáhtia bó'obítnee
taa čukúiba'áta kaítanee
"He may wait till high noon, but there won't be any coffee."

CONTENTS

Foreword
   by Eloise Jelinek xix
Preface xxi
Abbreviations xxiii

PART I: INTRODUCTION

Introduction 3
  1.0. Setting 3
  2.0. Yaqui linguistics 3
  3.0. Yaqui sociolinguistics 8
  4.0. Yaqui culture 12
  5.0. Yaqui history 15
  6.0. The present work 18

Phonology 21
  1.0. Introduction 21
  1.1. Phonemic inventory 21
  1.2. Surface contrasts 21
  1.3. Consonant allophones 22
  1.4. Vowel allophones 24
  1.5. The phoneme /b^w/ 24
  1.6. High and low tones vis-à-vis stress 25
  2.0. Paradigmatic phonological relations 26
  2.1. Vowels 26
  2.2. The distribution of consonants within syllables 27
  2.3. Syllable types 28
  3.0. Morphophonemics 28
  3.1. The echo-vowel -'V 28
  3.2. The pitch shift (penultimate stress) 29
  3.3. Dropping intervocalic /l/ and /r/ 30
  3.4. Velarization of the grooved fricative /s/ 30
  3.5. Two palatalization processes 30
  3.6. Glide reduction with **-u/-wi** 30
  3.7. Metathesis 31
  4.0. Patterns of reduplication 31
  5.0. Euphonic fillers and postpositional bases 32
  5.1. Inventory of postpositions 33
  5.2. Observations 33
  6.0. Some features not yet dealt with 35

PART II: SENTENCE TYPES

Basic sentence structure 39
  1.0. Introduction 39
  2.0. Word order 39
  3.0. Introducer elements 42
  4.0. Topic 43
  5.0. Focus constructions 44

vii

Particles and clitics 47
    1.0. Introduction 47
    2.0. Subject clitics... 47
    3.0. The emphatic clitic =**su** 47
    4.0. The deictic expletive =**bʷan**...................................... 51
    5.0. The expletive =**san**.. 52
    6.0. The dubitative particle =**kun** 53
    7.0. Negatives... 54
    7.1. The pausal negative **'é'e** 54
    7.2. The negative imperative **kát** 54
    7.3. The basic negative **káa** 55
    7.4. The variable scope of **káa**....................................... 56
    7.5. Clitic sequences with **káa** 59

Be/Have/Do 63
    1.0. Introduction 63
    2.0. Be 63
    2.1. The main verbs **'aáne** and **'aáyu** 63
    2.2. The "posture" verbs... 64
    2.3. The imperfective participle -**ka** 65
    2.4. The many-faced modal morpheme **mači** 66
    2.5. The adverbial **maís/mai-si**...................................... 70
    2.6. The existential -**taka** 70
    2.7. The appelative -**tea** 71
    2.8. The remote appelative **N + -roka** "to say to be" 72
    3.0. Have 73
    3.1. The main verbs **'aáne, hpʷee**, and **'áttea** 73
    3.2. More about **maáči** 74
    3.3. The possessive verbal suffixes -**ek** and -**ka**................. 74
    4.0. Do 75
    4.1. The main verb **yáa** 76
    4.2. The main verb **hoóa** 76
    4.3. The agentive suffix -**leo**....................................... 77
    4.4. The intentive suffix -**'u** 77

Nondistinct argument phenomena 79
    1.0. Introduction 79
    2.0. Unspecified subjects and objects 79
    2.1. The unspecified plural object marker **yee-**...................... 79
    2.2. The unspecified inanimate object marker **hi'i-**.................. 80
    2.3. The unspecified animate subject or object marker **né-**........... 82
    3.0. Reflexive objects 83
    4.0. The passive suffix -**wa** 85

Questions... 89
    1.0. Introduction 89
    2.0. Yes/No questions... 89
    3.0. WH–questions 90
    4.0. Complex WH-forms with =**sa** 93

Imperative sentences 97
    1.0. Introduction 97
    2.0. Pragmatic aspects of imperatives 97

3.0. Morphology of the imperatives 97
3.1. Positive imperatives........................... 97
3.2. Negative imperatives 99
4.0. Verbs of speech and the modal imperatives............ 100
4.1. The suffix **-sae** 100
4.2. The suffix **-tebo**............................ 102
4.3. Other modal imperatives 103

Comparative constructions........................... 105
1.0. Introduction 105
2.0. Comparisons of equality 105
2.1. Postpositional comparisons of equality 105
2.2. Other postpositional constructions 108
2.3. Comparisons of equality: the adjectives............ 109
3.0. Comparisons of inequality 110
3.1. The ambiguity of inferiority comparisons 110
3.2. The meaning of **če'a** 112
4.0. The superlative degree of comparison 114

PART III: WORD CLASSES

Noun morphology 119
1.0. Introduction 119
2.0. Compound nouns............................. 119
2.1. Phonological characteristics of compounding......... 119
2.2. Derived nouns 120
2.2.1. The abstract **-wa**............................ 120
2.2.2. The "passive" abstractivizer **-wa-me**.............. 120
2.2.3. The agentive nominalizer **-me**.................. 121
2.2.4. The agentive suffix **-reo** 123
2.2.5. The nominalizer **-ri**.......................... 123
2.2.6. The collective suffix -**raa** 124
2.2.7. The rare suffixes **-i, -ia** and **-laa** 125
3.0. Layering................................... 126

Noun inflection 129
1.0. Introduction 129
2.0. Major inflectional processes..................... 129
2.1. Accusative marking 129
2.1.1. Extensions of **-ta**............................ 130
2.1.2. Possessive **-ta** as subject of a relative clause 130
2.1.3. Use of **-ta** as a postpositional base................ 131
2.2. Plural marking on nouns 131
2.3. Accusative marking: the collective................. 133
2.4. Accusative marking on adjectives and quantifiers 133
2.4.1. Accusative marking on attributive adjectives........... 134
2.4.2. The accusative **-k** with **-béna** "like" 135
3.0. Minor inflectional processes..................... 136
3.1. **N + -la** diminutive/affectionate..................... 136
3.2. The prior state **-tu-ká'u** "used to be, now deceased" 136

Verb morphology................................ 137
1.0. Introduction 137
2.0. The possessive suffix **-ek**....................... 137

- 3.0. The causative **-te** 138
- 3.1. Causative **-te** with nouns (*intransitive*) 138
- 3.2. Causative **-te** with adjectives 139
- 4.0. The verbalizer **-tu** 139
- 4.1. The past durative with **-tu** 139
- 4.2. The antecedent state: **-tu** with **-ka'u** 140
- 4.3. Inceptive **-tu** 140
- 4.4. The days of the week and **-tu** + **-k** 140
- 4.5. Transitive **-te** vs. intransitive **-tu** 141
- 4.6. The matrix predicate use of **-tu** 142
- 5.0. The intentive postposition **-'u** 142
- 6.0. The causative **-tua** 143
- 7.0. A miscellany of derivational suffixes 143
- 7.1. The processual **-oa** 143
- 7.2. The quotative **-tea** 143
- 7.3. The participial **-taka** 143
- 8.0. The connective **-ti** 143
- 8.1. A basic syntactic property of **-ti** 143
- 8.2. The connector morpheme role of **-ti** 144
- 8.3. The connective **-i** with the verb **-'éa** "to think" ... 145
- 8.4. In V1 **-ti-** V2 constructions 146
- 8.5. Noun + **-ti** + **ia** + suffix combinations 146
- 8.6. Contractions of **-ti** + **X** 147

Adjective morphology 149
- 1.0. Introduction 149
- 2.0. The stative adjectives 149
- 2.1. Adjectives derived with **-la** 149
- 2.2. Adjectives derived with **-la** + **-i** 150
- 2.3. Adjectives derived with **-li/-i** 150
- 2.4. Adjectives derived with **-i** 151
- 2.5. Adjectives with an **-i** and **-ia** alternation 151
- 3.0. The directional adverbial **-i** 151
- 4.0. The adverbializer **-si** 151
- 5.0. Syntax 153
- 5.1. Overview of the morphology 153
- 5.2. The singular forms 153
- 5.3. Reduplication of adjectives 154

Compounds 157
- 1.0. Introduction 157
- 2.0. Noun compounds 157
- 2.1. Noun + noun = noun 157
- 2.2. Locational noun compounds 158
- 2.3. Body-part noun compounds 158
- 2.4. Abstract noun compounds 159
- 2.5. Noun + adjective or verb 159
- 3.0. Verb compounds 160
- 3.1. Verb + verb = verb 160
- 3.2. Noun + verb = verb 161
- 3.3. Aspectual verb compounds 161
- 3.4. Verb + suffix = verb 163

Possessive constructions 165
   1.0. Introduction 165
   2.0. Morphology 165
   2.1. The possessive clitics............................. 165
   2.2. Marking of the specified possessor 165
   2.3. The possessor suffix **-wa**......................... 166
   2.4. The emphatic possessive suffixes................... 167
   3.0. Syntax 169
   3.1. The possessive verbal suffix **-ek** 169
   3.2. Possessive marking on relative clauses 169
   3.3. Structuring the domain of possession............... 170

Postpositions 173
   1.0. Introduction 173
   2.0. The simple spatials 176
   2.1. The goal-oriented **-u/-wi** 176
   2.2. The internally bounded **-po** "in" 178
   2.3. The areal **-ku** "in, on" 180
   2.4. The proximal contact **-étči** "on" 181
   2.5. The positional **hika-** "the top of X" 183
   2.6. The limiter **-táhtia** "until"....................... 185
   3.0. The associative postpositions 186
   3.1. The instrumental **-e** (SG)/**-mea** (PL) 187
   3.1.1. The singular **-e** 187
   3.1.2. The plural **-mea** 188
   3.2. The accompaniment **-make/-mak**.................... 189
   3.3. The proximative **-náapo** 190
   3.4. The reflexive **-násuk** "middle" 191
   4.0. The **-be** postpositions............................ 193
   4.1. The spatial **-beas\beasi** 193
   4.2. The positional **-bépa** "over" 194
   4.3. The positional **betuk/-tuk** "underneath" 195
   4.4. The source-oriented **bétana/-tana** 196
   4.5. The positional **-bé-wit-či** "beside" 198
   4.6. The benefactive/causative/purposive **-betčí'ibo**.......... 198
   4.7. The simulfactive **-béna** 200
   4.8. The ubiquitous **-bíča/-bičáa**...................... 201

Demonstratives 203
   1.0. Introduction 203
   2.0. The paradigmatic sets 203
   2.1. The basic demonstratives.......................... 203
   2.2. The pausal singular forms 203
   2.3. The plural forms 204
   2.4. Nominative versus accusative plural................ 204
   3.0. Singular nominal demonstratives 205
   3.1. Use as postpositional bases 205
   3.2. The source of the **-e** forms 206
   4.0. Syntax 207
   4.1. Demonstratives and sentence types 207
   4.2. Demonstratives in discourse....................... 210

Adverbial demonstratives 213
   1.0. Introduction 213
   2.0. The semantic parameters 213
   2.1. The distance parameter 213
   2.2. Degrees of specificity 213
   2.3. The directional forms with **-i**. 214
   3.0. Usages in given situations 214
   3.1. The proximal forms. 214
   3.2. The **-n-** forms 216
   4.0. The **wa-** forms 217
   5.0. The **'áma** series of adverbs. 218
   6.0. The adverbial **'omó-tči** "off to one side" 220
   7.0. The manner adverbs. 220
   8.0. Temporal adverbs. 222

Quantifiers 223
   1.0. Introduction 223
   2.0. The inventory. 223
   3.0. Some semantic properties. 223
   4.0. Use as modifiers 224
   5.0. Nominal properties. 225
   6.0. Predicative usages of quantifiers 227

Numerals 229
   1.0. Introduction 229
   2.0. The cardinal numbers. 229
   2.1. "One" is more than "one" 229
   2.2. **Wépul** is only "one". 230
   2.3. The compound numeral terms 231
   2.4. The ordinal numbers 232
   3.0. Derived forms 232
   4.0. Syntax of the numeral constructions 233

Adjective constructions 235
   1.0. Introduction 235
   2.0. Form 235
   3.0. Syntax 235
   3.1. Strings of attributive adjectives 236
   3.2. Functioning as heads of noun phrases 236
   3.3. Accusative marking on adjectives 236
   3.4. Objects and possessors. 237
   3.5. In discontinuous constructions 238
   3.6. Degrees of comparison. 238
   3.7. Adjectives and adverbs 239

Definite pronouns 241
   1.0. Introduction 241
   2.0. The nominative forms 241
   2.1. The independent forms. 241
   2.2. The subject clitics 242
   2.3. Subject clitic sequences 242
   2.4. Subject pronoun + **-ik** and **-im** 243
   3.0. The emphatic reflexive subject pronouns 243

    4.0. Direct object pronouns 244
    5.0. Possessive pronouns 245
    6.0. Reflexives 246
    7.0. Objects of postpositions 247

Indefinite pronouns, obliques and adverbs 249
    1.0. Introduction 249
    2.0. Positive indefinites 249
    3.0. Negative indefinites 252

PART IV: VERB STRUCTURE

Verb stems 257
    1.0. Introduction 257
    2.0. The three major verb classes 257
    2.1. Intransitive verbs 257
    2.2. Transitive stems 258
    2.3. Transitive/intransitive verbs 261
    3.0. Phonologically modified forms 262
    3.1. Transitivity changing suffixes 263
    3.2. Reduplication 263
    3.3. Vowel and consonant gemination 265
    3.4. CVC reduplication and consonant gemination 265

Incorporation 269
    1.0. Introduction 269
    2.0. The manner adverbial **báa-** 269
    3.0. The adverbial **bát-** 269
    4.0. The locative **náas-** 270
    5.0. The adverbial **nát-** 271
    6.0. The reciprocal **náu-** 271
    7.0. The incorporated unspecified human object **yee-** 272
    8.0. The locative adverbial **yéeu-/yéu-** 273

Syntactic marking 277
    1.0. Introduction 277
    2.0. Pronominal marking 277
    2.1. Subject marking 277
    2.2. Object marking 278
    2.3. Unspecified object marking 279
    2.3.1. Inanimate unspecified **hi'i-** 279
    2.3.2. Unspecified animate subject or object **né-** 281
    3.0. The passive **-wa** 283
    4.0. Number agreement 283
    5.0. Subordination 283
    6.0. Causative suffixes 284
    6.1. The causative suffix **-tua** 284
    6.2. Derivational usages of **-tua** 287
    6.3. The applicative suffix **-ria** 289

Inflectional and derivational affixation 293
    1.0. Introduction 293
    2.0. Adverbial affixation 293
    2.1. The adverbials **-sime** (SG)/**-saka** (PL) 293

SONORA YAQUI LANGUAGE STRUCTURES

   2.2. The andatives **-se** (SG)/**-bo** (PL)........................ 295
   3.0. Volitional notions... 296
   3.1. The desiderative **-bae**...................................... 296
   3.2. The heightened desiderative **-pea**.......................... 298
   3.3. The indirect desiderative **'íi'aa**........................... 299
   4.0. The modal suffixes... 303
   4.1. The subjunctive mode **-'ea-n**................................ 303
   4.2. The past subjunctive **-ka + -'ea-n**.......................... 305
   4.3. The presumptive **-le**.. 305
   5.0. The tense markers... 307
   5.1. The future tense marker **-nee**............................. 307
   5.2. The future passive **-naa**.................................... 309
   6.0. Tense/aspect marking.. 310
   6.1. The perfective aspect suffix **-k**............................ 310
   6.2. The imperfective participle **-ka**............................ 312
   6.3. The remote stative **-i (-ka + -i)**............................ 315
   6.4. The past continuative **-n**................................... 318
   7.0. Aspectual marking... 320
   7.1. The inceptive aspect... 320
   7.2. The cessative aspect **-yaáte**................................ 322
   7.3. The completive aspect marker **-su**......................... 323
   7.4. The suffix **-oa**... 325

Overall verb structure.. 327
   1.0. Introduction... 327
   2.0. The grammaticalization path................................. 327
   2.1. Compound verbs... 327
   2.2. Derivational suffixes... 329
   2.3. The adverbials forming compounds.......................... 332
   3.0. The transitivity classes...................................... 334
   3.1. Intransitive verbs.. 335
   3.2. Transitive verbs.. 335
   3.3. Multitransitive stems.. 336
   3.4. Prefixes and proclitics....................................... 338
   4.0. The verbal suffixes and their class ordering................. 339
   5.0. The suffixal position classes................................. 340
   5.1. First and second position suffixes........................... 341
   5.2. Problematic orderings near the stem......................... 346
   5.3. The intermediate position suffixes........................... 347
   5.4. The final position suffixes................................... 353

PART V: COMPLEX SENTENCES

Coordination.. 359
   1.0. Introduction... 359
   2.0. Coordinating conjunctions................................... 359
   2.1. The introducer **'íntok**...................................... 359
   2.2. Juxtaposed conjuncts.. 360
   2.3. Marked with postposition **-mak**............................ 363
   3.0. Adversative sentences....................................... 363

Complement clauses 365
  1.0. Introduction 365
  2.0. The governing verbs and position of the complement 365
  2.1. The capacitative **'áa**. 365
  2.2. The mental activity verb **'éa** 367
  2.3. The speech act verb **hiía** 372
  2.4. Other speech act verbs................................... 372
  2.5. Onomatopoetic complements 373
  3.0. Marking of complements 374
  3.1. The existential **'aáne** "be, do"........................ 375
  3.2. The quotative **-tea** 375
  3.3. The imperfective participial **-ka**...................... 375
  4.0. Embedded questions....................................... 376
  4.1. Embedded Yes/No questions 376
  4.2. Embedded WH-clauses...................................... 377

Relative clauses. 379
  1.0. Introduction 379
  2.0. Subject relative clauses 379
  2.1. Kinds of subject relative clauses 379
  2.2. Formation of subject relative clauses 380
  2.3. A historical note on relative clauses 381
  3.0. Object relative clauses.................................. 382
  3.1. The morphology of object relative clauses................ 382
  3.2. Regarding relative pronouns.............................. 383
  4.0. Oblique relative clauses................................. 384
  5.0. Headless relative clauses 385

Adverbial clauses 387
  1.0. Introduction 387
  2.0. Two kinds of adverbial clauses 387
  2.1. Locative adverbial clauses 387
  2.2. Temporal clauses 388
  2.3. A "while" clause marking simultaneity 389
  3.0. Irrealis adverbial relations 391
  3.1. Temporal "if" clauses 391
  3.2. "If" and "because" clauses 392
  3.3. Conditional "if" clauses................................. 392
  4.0. "Without" clauses 394
  4.1. Counterfactive clauses with **-ean** and **-o** 395
  4.2. Simulfactive clauses..................................... 395
  4.3. "Because" clauses 397
  4.4. Manner clauses 397

PART VI: A YAQUI TEXT
Habiel Mó'el: "Gabriel Sparrow's Narrow Escape"............. 401

REFERENCES 409

TABLES

1. Sonora Yaqui phonemes 21
2. Contrast of /w/ and /u/ 23
3. Contrast of /y/ and /i/ 23
4. Vowel combinations 26
5. Bound postpositions 33
6. Negative + subject clitics 59
7. Indefinite pronouns used as interrogative pronouns 91
8. Interrogative pronouns formed with =sa 91
9. Comparative constructions 105
10. Comparisons using adjectives 109
11. Verbalizers 137
12. Case marking of nouns and adjectives 153
13. Yaqui postpositions 173
14. Pronominal objects of postpositions 173
15. Pronominal bases with -u/-wi 177
16. Pronominal objects with -táhtia 186
17. Pronominal bases with -make 189
18. Pronominal bases with náapo 190
19. Pronominal bases of násuk 192
20. Personal pronominal objects with -biča 202
21. Singular demonstratives 203
22. Singular pausal demonstratives 203
23. Plural demonstratives 204
24. Singular nominal demonstratives 205
25. Demonstrative postpositional objects I 206
26. Demonstrative postpositional objects II 206
27. Categories of Yaqui deictics 213
28. Proximal deictics 215
29. Series of 'áma- adverbs 218
30. Deictic manner adverbs 220
31. Morphemically simple quantifiers 223
32. Morphemically complex quantifiers 223
33. Basic cardinal numbers 229
34. Compound numerals—the teens 231
35. Vigesimal number system 231
36. Derived Adverbs—X times 232
37. Adjectives with final -i 235
38. Independent subject pronouns 241
39. Reduced independent subject pronouns 241
40. Subject clitics 242
41. Accusative/possessor pronouns 243
42. Emphatic reflexive pronouns 244
43. Reduced reflexive pronouns 244
44. Independent direct object pronouns 245
45. Direct object clitics 245
46. Possessive pronominal clitics 246
47. Reflexive pronouns 246
48. Postpositional object pronouns 247

49. Negative indefinites 252
50. Intransitive suppletive verb stems 258
51. Reduplicated intransitive verb stems 258
52. Transitive verb stem alternates 259
53. Closed syllable reduplication pattern 265
54. Reduplicated forms of **yó'o** 266
55. Imperfective stems versus perfective **-ka** 311
56. Compound verb constituency 327
57. Manner verbs in compounds 327
58. Yaqui verbalizing suffixes 330
59. Adverbials as compounding elements 332
60. Modal suffixes 340
61. Adverbial suffixes 340
62. Tense/aspect suffixes 340
63. Subordinating suffixes 340
64. Yaqui suffix position class order 341
65. Subjects of relative clauses as possessors 382

FOREWORD

This description of the Sonoran Yaqui language is an invaluable contribution to the study of the Uto-Aztecan language family, one of the largest and most widely distributed of the language families of Native North America. In aboriginal times, this language family extended from middle America to what is now the northwestern United States. The material collected here represents the life work of the senior author, John Dedrick, who lived and worked among the Yaqui of Sonora for more than twenty years, and who acquired an impressive knowledge of the language and culture. Dr. Eugene Casad, the second author of this volume, who has done extensive research on other Uto-Aztecan languages, has aided in the organization and presentation of the material from a comparative perspective.

The material included is organized according to established grammatical tradition, in a format that will prove convenient for scholars pursuing historical and comparative studies as well as synchronic linguistic analysis. There is a wealth of material of interest to those linguists interested in such current theoretical questions as functional and lexical categories: for example, the sections on auxiliary verbs and the well-documented information on voice, aspect, and other features of verbal inflection from both morphological and lexical perspectives, providing the reader with useful data for particular lines of linguistic inquiry.

Each grammatical point is illustrated by example sentences that are distinguished by their naturalness and cultural relevance. Many of the example sentences are citations from texts and narratives, and there is a complete text appended to the volume that provides a sample of connected sentences in a natural context.

The volume includes very useful sections on quantifiers and adverbial and deictic particles in the language, material that is often given inadequate attention in reference grammars. This work promises to be an invaluable aid in future research on Uto-Aztecan and is a contribution that scholars interested in this language family and cultural area will find indispensable.

Eloise Jelinek
Department of Linguistics
University of Arizona

PREFACE

Documenting the indigenous languages of the world is a worthwhile and satisfying task—one that also requires dedication and diligence and is greatly facilitated by a love for the language under study and an enthusiasm for its intricacies and beauty. All of the above characterize John Dedrick's attachment to the Yaqui language as spoken in the community of Estación Vicam, Sonora, Mexico, and his profound identification with the Yaqui people.

In the first place, this descriptive grammar would not have been possible without the cooperation and generosity of both the leaders of the Vicam community and the people who belonged to the community. They accepted the presence of John and Mary Jane Dedrick and helped them to learn to speak Yaqui and taught them many things about Yaqui culture and beliefs. Particular details of the roles carried out by specific Yaqui language consultants are given in the Introduction. We would like to give them all a most warm **di¢s e'em chiokoe**.

My own role has been that of editor and coauthor, beginning sometime in 1982, about the time that I was finishing my graduate studies at the University of California at San Diego. Doris Bartholomew, who was then the Linguistic Coordinator for the Mexico Branch of the Summer Institute of Linguistics, appointed me to be a linguistic consultant to Dedrick. This wound up being a 14-year working relationship that has been both challenging and rewarding. In a very special way Ronald W. Langacker of the University of California at San Diego has been instrumental in helping to bring this grammar to fruition. First, he introduced several of us to the marvels of Uto-Aztecan in a 10-week workshop held at Ixmiquilpan, Hidalgo, in the spring of 1976. Later he supervised my writing of a Cora grammar sketch. His outline of Uto-Aztecan structure underlies the organization of this present work.

We would also like to acknowledge the support and expertise of two colleagues, Eunice Pike and David Tuggy. In the late 1970s Eunice worked through the Phonology section with Dedrick. Then in November 1996, David Tuggy read through both the Introduction and the Phonology section and made a number of insightful and helpful suggestions.

A number of people have worked on keyboarding data and revisions during these years. At the beginning Margot Finkestyn and Helen Campbell keyboarded the original 500 pages of rough manuscript that I received from Dedrick. I subdivided Mr. Dedrick's 19 files into 55 files that corresponded to the sections and subsections of Langacker's outline of Uto-Aztecan language structures.

The next several years saw a variety of shuffling and sortings of the data and the addition of several Yaqui texts to the data base. At an early stage of the project, Gary Simons wrote a small program for me that allowed me to extract flagged sentences from a text and output them to distinct files. This added to the available data that we could then incorporate into the grammar for making additional descriptive statements. By June 1991, the manuscript began to look like a descriptive grammar. John would read and either approve or veto the descriptive statements that I made about the data, add his own statements, and correct typos. This back and forth revision and comment work continued until mid 1995.

During the last year, both Emily Stairs and Louise Schoenhals have overseen the copy editing work. Emily has also prepared the formatted version for the Ventura Publisher system and has sent me three or four rounds of questions, the answering of which has helped us straighten out a myriad of editorial inconsistencies and has made this present version immensely more readable. Dedrick and I are deeply indebted to Emily and Louise for their nice work on the final manuscript. We are also profoundly indebted to Eloise Jelinek of the University of Arizona, who, in spite of ill health, read through the entire manuscript carefully and made numerous detailed comments throughout, comments that have significantly improved the final product. Finally, I would like to thank the Directorate of the Mexico Branch of the Summer Institute of Linguistics for both giving me their vote of confidence and allowing me time to do the work that was needed in bringing this descriptive work to completion. And I assume responsibility for any errors that might remain.

Eugene H. Casad
Tucson, Arizona
January 30, 1997

ABBREVIATIONS

The following abbreviations are used for identifying the morphemes that occur in the examples cited throughout this work.

ABL	*Ablative*	INST	*Instrumental*
ABS	*Absolutive*	INTERR	*Interrogative*
ACC	*Accusative*	INTR	*Intransitive*
ADJ	*Adjective*	IZR	*Intransitivizer*
ADV	*Adverb*	LOC	*Locative*
AGT	*Agentive*	MAN	*Manner*
AJR	*Adjectivizer*	NEG	*Negative*
APL	*Applicative*	NOM	*Nominative*
AVR	*Adverbializer*	NP	*Noun phrase*
AZR	*Abstractivizer*	NZR	*Nominalizer*
CAU	*Causative*	PAST	*Past tense*
CMP	*Comparative*	PAU	*Pausative*
CND	*Conditional*	PCN	*Past-continuative*
CPL	*Completive*	PL	*Plural*
CNJ	*Conjunction*	POS	*Possessive*
COM	*Commitative*	PPL	*Participializer*
CON	*Connective*	PRE	*Presumptive*
CTX	*Counter expectation*	PRF	*Perfective*
DAT	*Dative*	PRO	*Pronoun*
DEM	*Demonstrative*	PSV	*Passive*
DIM	*Diminutive*	Q	*Question*
DIR	*Directional*	QNT	*Quantifier*
DSD	*Desiderative*	QUA	*Qualitative*
DUB	*Dubitative*	QUO	*Quotative*
EMP	*Emphatic*	RCIP	*Reciprocal*
EQ	*Equality*	RDP	*Reduplication*
EV	*Echo vowel*	RFL	*Reflexive*
EXP	*Expletive*	SG	*Singular*
FUT	*Future/Potential*	SJV	*Subjunctive*
GM	*Gemination*	SPEC	*Specified*
GND	*Gerundial*	STAT	*Stative*
HL	*Highlight*	STOP	*Cessative*
HRT	*Hortative*	TRN	*Transitive*
IMP	*Imperative*	TZR	*Transitivizer*
INC	*Inceptive*	VR	*Verbalizer*
INDEF	*Indefinite*	UNSPEC	*Unspecified*
IN:DSD	*Indirect desiderative*		

PART I: INTRODUCTION

INTRODUCTION

1.0. Setting

Yaqui is a southern Uto-Aztecan language of the Tara-Cáhitic subgroup, which includes Tarahumara, Guarijio, Yaqui, and Mayo (Langacker 1977:5; Heath 1977:26; Miller 1980:2, 26, 31). Yaqui and Mayo are very closely related, and speakers of these two languages can communicate with one another quite readily (cf. Escalante 1990:16). Less significant dialectal variants occur within Yaqui itself.[1] The Yaqui language and culture are becoming better known through the writings of the Yaqui people themselves as well as through the studies of professional scholars: linguists, ethnographers, and historians. In what follows, we survey briefly some of the most salient of these studies. For more detailed information and other points of view on Yaqui phonology and grammar the reader should consult the references.

The majority of the Yaqui are located in the southern part of the state of Sonora, in Mexico. They now number possibly in excess of 30,000.[2] Several significant communities of Yaqui speakers also live in the state of Arizona, having moved north from Mexico during the excesses of the regime of Porfirio Díaz in the late nineteenth century and in the early years of this one (cf. Spicer 1981:80–82).[3]

2.0. Yaqui linguistics

The earliest known description of Yaqui/Mayo is given in the *Arte de la lengua Cáhita, por un Padre de la Compañia de Jesus*. This was probably compiled by members of the Jesuit society prior to 1650.[4] In 1737 a version was printed in Mexico City by Francisco Javier. This version was later edited and published in Mexico City in 1891 by Eustaquio Buelna. It contains morphological, lexical, syntactic, and grammatical information and some phonological data. The linguistic forms it cites compare remarkably well with those of contemporary Mayo.

Internal evidence suggests to Dedrick that several people were involved in the compilation of the linguistic data that has been incorporated into this description and that the collecting of these data may have begun as early as 1533. In spite of the word "un" in the title *Arte de la lengua Cáhita por un Padre* there is also a catechism at the end of the grammar and dictionary which is attributed to "un padre," who is identified as Tomas Basilio (?–1650?) on page 236 of this work. Buelna attributes the grammar (and dictionary?) to Juan B. de Velasco (1562–1613). The dedicatoria of the grammar uses such archaic Spanish forms as **Santissimo** *most holy*, **passos** *advances,* **charidad** *charity*, **throno** *throne*, **rethoricas** *rhetorical*, **Fee** *faith*, **debaxo** *below*, **dexe** *permits* and so on (pp. 1–3), whereas the dedicatoria to the Catechism does not. Within the grammar, the orthography used for citing Cáhita forms varies considerably, from **muquuc** *died* (p. 7) to **mucuc** *died* (p. 13), **cotzeye** *asleep* (p. 16) to **coche** *sleep* (p. 156), **tuuriua** *is liked* (p. 22) to **turisi** *very* (p. 31) (for **tu'u-ri-wa** and **tu'u-ri-si**, respectively). The orthographic variation also reveals the presence of hispanicized forms alongside of native forms, as in **ateuacatecamta** *maker of heaven* (p. 35) and its modified counterpart **ateuacatecanta** *maker of heaven* (p. 238); i.e., the nasal plus stop sequence **m-t** corresponds to the hispanicized sequence **n-t**. These are just a few of the examples of the many kinds of variations that Dedrick has found in Buelna. This, of course, suggests that the original material was collected throughout a fairly long span of time and was compiled by a number of contributors.

---

1 Particular examples of the dialect variants that do occur are discussed in López and Moctezuma 1994.
2 This figure is based on the 1990 Census.
3 In contrast to his extensive and long-time contact with the Yaquis in Sonora, Dedrick's contact with the the Yaquis in Arizona has been limited and sporadic. His impression is that the Yaqui spoken in Arizona is basically the same as that spoken in the Rio Yaqui area of Sonora, but that it has "a leaner vocabulary" with a fair number of Spanish and English borrowings. For example, Molina's forms **Bwikam** *songs* and **Hiakim** *the Yaqui homeland* (Evers and Molina 1987) are probably idiolectal variants for **bwiíki-m** *songs* and **hiák-bwíaraa** *Yaqui homeland*.
4 Dedrick would like to acknowledge his appreciation of and indebtedness to the Jesuit fathers who compiled this work. They have made available to present day students of "Cáhita" a very valid, relevant and ample body of information on this language.

Following the publication of an article in the *International Journal of American Linguistics*, Vol. 43, No. 2, Dedrick received the following communication from Andres Lionnet in August 1977: "Tratandose de Buelna, me permite señalarle que la atribucion al P. J. B. Velasco es probablemente erronea. Parece que Buelna no vio el frontispicio de la obra original que califica al autor como 'misionero de mas de treinta años, en la provincia de Sinaloa', lo que no fue Velasco, pero si Tomas Basilio, a quien el bibliógrafo Emile Riviere atribuye la obra."[5]

Be that as it may, Dedrick still feels that his observations above are valid and that the most important matter is to ascertain the earliest date at which the data was collected as a source of relatively unacculturated Cáhita.

The oldest known reasonably extensive body of Yaqui written during the immediate postcolonial period is found in what are called "The Bandera letters." This material consists of eleven handwritten letters that were written between July 1, 1830, and November 8, 1832. They were either addressed to, or in some way concerned, the Yaqui leader "Juan de la Bandera," who led an attempt to expel the Mexican goverment and install an imperial indigenous order based on the ideals of Moctezuma.

The late Edward H. Spicer located these letters in the Hubert H. Bancroft library of the University of California at Berkeley. He sent photocopies of them to Dedrick, who first deciphered them and then retranscribed them phonemically and translated them. Reproductions of the letters themselves, Dedrick's phonemic transcriptions, his literal and free translations, and several related appendices are all contained in this work (Dedrick 1985).

Later studies in Yaqui linguistics cover both the phonology and the morphology, as well as syntax and semantics. There are also several studies of contact phenomena and bilingualism. Chronologically, phonology is represented by research carried out by Johnson (1940), Fraenkel (1959), Crumrine (1961), Burnham (1988), and Hagberg (1988, 1993).

In Dedrick's own words, "Jean Johnson's manuscript 'El Yaqui' is the earliest phonemic analysis of the Yaqui spoken in the Yaqui River area that I know of and was of considerable aid and benefit to me. This unpublished manuscript was drafted in 1939 or 1940. Johnson is entitled to credit for all the data, analyses and teminology in my description that concurs with his. He personally presented me with pre-draft copy #4 of this paper when I first began to study Yaqui. I accept responsibility for the material in which our findings and analyses do not agree."

The first published account of Yaqui phonology is given in Gerd Fraenkel's "Yaqui Phonemics," published in 1959 in A*nthropological Linguistics*, Vol. 1, No. 5. Fraenkel shows a phonemic inventory of 19 consonants and five vowels (1959:11). Stress is said to be phonemic, and its alternative patterning is stated in terms of a moraic analysis. Single vowels are one mora in length, and long vowels are interpreted as sequences of two like vowels, each of which is one mora in length. Pairs of unlike vowels are said to be one mora in length. Thus, in clusters of a non–high vowel and a following high vowel, the high vowel is said to have no moraic value (1959:8).

Fraenkel finds that Yaqui has both inherently stressed morphemes and inherently nonstressed ones (1959:10). He describes stress placement in isolated words in the following terms: monosyllables are all stressed, bisyllabic words may be stressed on either the first or the second syllables, or even on both. Trisyllabic sequences have two stress patterns: monomorphemic words with either an initial long vowel or an initial V'V syllable show the pattern CV(C)VCV. Other kinds of trisyllabic sequences show the pattern CV(C)VCV (1959:11).

A few of Fraenkel's distributional statements do not seem to cohere. For example, in section 2.2.1., he notes, "All bi-consonantal clusters are possible in Yaqui" and claims that there are no restrictions whatsoever against any sequences of kinds of consonants. Yet five lines later he notes (a) that the only consonant clusters to be found in Yaqui occur in word medial position, i.e., there are no word initial or

---

5 "With regard to Buelna, let me point out that it is probably erroneous to attribute it to Padre J. B. Velasco. Probably Buelna never saw the frontispiece of the original work, which describes the author as 'missionary to the province of Sinaloa for more than 30 years.' This was not true of Velasco, but it does fit Tomás Basilio to whom the bibliographer Emile Riviere attributes the work."

word final clusters. He goes on to note that fully half of the Yaqui consonants occur as the first member of a cluster and that none of the labialized stops or the fricatives occur in this position (1959:12).

The final two sections of this paper treat vowels and their allophones and two types of juncture, pausal and nonpausal (1959:15–16).

A second, more comprehensive treatment of Yaqui phonology is found in Lynn S. Crumrine's 1961 work titled *The Phonology of Arizona Yaqui with Texts*. It is based on her 1958 M.A. thesis and is Number 5 of the Anthropological Papers of the University of Arizona, published by the University of Arizona Press.[6]

Crumrine begins by noting that "The phonology presented here is that of an Arizona dialect of Yaqui as spoken by Refugio Savala and Fernando Suarez of Pascua, Arizona." (1958:1). She goes on to describe the procedures that she used for collecting the data. These included the use of drawings designed to elicit certain kinds of responses, as well as the use of short English sentences used to elicit translation equivalents and even the use of a three-dimensional model of a house and its yard in order to elicit information about directional and relational concepts for her morphological analysis (1958:4).

Crumrine's analysis lists 15 consonant phonemes (1958:7) and five vowels (1958:11). She presents much of her analysis in terms of what she calls "macrospans" (1958:12). These are units bounded by terminal junctures which serve as carriers for one or more intonational patterns that may occur within that span (1958:14). In contrast, microspans are sequences of vowels bounded by a plus juncture. Such junctures may either precede the vowel, follow it, or do both (1958:15). For Crumrine, any segmental vowel may carry a tone (1958:15).

Crumrine describes Yaqui intonational patterns in terms of five allophonic levels of pitch (1958:14) and discusses Yaqui phoneme sequences in terms of contrastive syllable patterns (1958:16–19). Her statements about consonant clusters are made solely in terms of actually observed sequences without making any higher-level generalizations of the kind found in Fraenkel. Her statements on vowel clusters are in accord both with Fraenkel's work and with the description that follows in the present work. Crumrine also describes some of the morphophonemic processes operative in Yaqui (1958:21). She closes her study with a short discussion of the limitations of her methodology, and proposals for further research (1958:22).

Second-generation studies of Yaqui phonology include those of Jeffrey Burnham and Larry Hagberg, both of which are published in the volume *In Honor of Mary Haas*, edited by William Shipley (1988). In "Mayo Suprasegmentals: Synchronic and Diachronic Consideration" (pp. 37–51) Burnham investigates aspects of the suprasegmental phenomena of Mayo that have not yet been adequately described. This includes stress, pitch/tone, and vowel and consonant length. Burnham relates the Mayo data to the broader field of southern Uto-Aztecan and considers both diachronic and synchronic facts in framing his conclusions. Hagberg presents an alternative analysis of similar phenomena in "Stress and Length in Mayo" (pp. 361–375). This is a formal account of the Mayo system for marking pitch and stress at both the word and phrase level. Hagberg also describes the differences between phonemic vowel length and rule-governed length determined by stress. This theme is developed in more detail in *An Autosegmental Theory of Stress*, Hagberg's 1993 University of Arizona Ph.D. dissertation.

Grammars and studies of particular domains of Yaqui grammar include, in chronological order, those by Kurath and Spicer (1947), Johnson (1962), Lindenfeld (1973), Escalante and Jelinek (1988), and Escalante (1990), as well as a variety of other papers by Jelinek.

The first description of Yaqui grammar published in this century was that given in Kurath and Spicer (1947) in a work that they titled *A Brief Introduction to Yaqui: A Native Language of Sonora*. It was Number 15 in the University of Arizona's series of Social Science Bulletins. The authors intended their work to be a "popularized" treatise suitable for educated laymen as well as for linguists in general and especially for comparative purposes. The orthography they employed was an adaptation of the International Phonetic Alphabet. (Preface pp. 5–6)

---

[6] The page numbers given in the following paragraphs are based on the copy of the M.A. thesis that Casad located in the Special Collections section of the University of Arizona library in early September 1995.

Kurath and Spicer gratefully acknowledged the valuable assistance they received from Refugio Savala, Lucas Chaves, and Jesús Juan Ujllolimea. Ujllolimea was a native Sonoran Yaqui, while the other two spent most or all of their lives in the United States.

This work contains eight sections as follows: "Introduction" (pp. 7–11), "Classification of Yaqui" (pp. 11–17), "Yaqui Sounds" (pp. 17–24), "Yaqui Word Formation" (pp. 24–31), "Yaqui Sentence Structure" (pp. 32–34), "Yaqui Vocabulary" (pp. 34–36), and "Texts" with a word list (pp. 36–46).[7]

In the "Introduction," they discuss the distribution of the Yaqui population. The Yaqui defeat in 1887 caused many to flee to the United States and elsewhere. Many were also deported to Yucatan. At the time that Kurath and Spicer wrote, about 10,000 Yaquis were living in their homeland in the lower Yaqui River valley. There had been a gradual returning to their homeland during the 20 years prior to this. The Yaqui spoken in Hermosillo or Tucson was considered to be as "pure" as that spoken in Torim or Pótam. Kurath and Spicer noted that current Yaqui, due to circumstances, contains many words "borrowed" from Latin, Spanish, and English. Yet its basic features are relatively little affected.

In this same chapter, they review the previous 400 years of Yaqui history, with special attention to the influence of the Jesuits (1617–1767) because of the introduction of wheat, metal tools, horses, cattle, etc., all of which resulted in numerous additions to the Yaqui vocabulary. In addition, they provide data on the post-Jesuit and the republican periods. A summary of the Yaquis' struggle to remain in their own territory and the development of some literacy based on the Spanish alphabet conclude the section.

In the "Classification of Yaqui", Kurath and Spicer compare the relation between the Indo-European Language Family and its Germanic and Italic submembers to the relation between the Uto-Aztecan family and its Cáhita-Ópata-Tarahumara submembers. The relationship between Yaqui (Cáhita) and Papago (Ópata) is held to be comparable to that which holds between Swedish and Italian.[8]

In "Yaqui Sounds", the authors describe the Yaqui phonemes and illustrate them with contrastive pairs. From two frequency charts, based on a Yaqui text of "roughly four hundred words" (p. 20), they tallied the count of consonant initial syllables and that of vowel initial syllables to determine that **h** and **t** are the most frequent initial consonants; **i, e,** and **a** are the most frequent initial vowels. A frequency count of all the phonemes revealed that **a, m, u, i, e, n, t, m, s, k** occurred most frequently in that order. The "trigrams" **a'a, i'u,** and **u'a** are listed as being the most frequent and are said to be those "which give the language its essential character" (pp. 17–24).

In the chapter titled "Yaqui Word Formation", Kurath and Spicer deal with words, as both free and bound forms, and discuss the categorization of languages, as being "analytic" (virtually no bound forms) or "synthetic" (many bound forms). Yaqui is classified as "synthetic." No words with fewer than two syllables were found. The following are the most common syllable patterns for Yaqui words: (1) CVCV, (2) CVCCV, (3) CVCVC, (4) CVCVCV, (5) CVVCV, and (6) CVCVCCV. They provide Yaqui examples of words for each of these patterns.

Later in this chapter, they cite the 9 most common noun suffixes and the 25 most common verb suffixes. They go on to illustrate some of the usages of these and attribute certain meanings to them, but also indicate their uncertainty about some of these meanings, pointing out that other meanings are only approximations. Several verbal suffixes may follow a given stem in Yaqui and some affixes only occur in final position: e.g., **-o** *if, when* and **-k** *perfective*.

Giving further detail, they list the paradigm of the possessive pronouns. Two sets of "object pronouns" are prefixed to the verbs **noóka** *to speak* and **bíča** *to see*.[9] Paradigms for free and bound subject pronouns are also given. The section concludes with the examples **inkarimpo** *in my houses* and **ne'aunook-taitek** *I began to speak to him*.

---

7   The volume of linguistic material on Yaqui that has been published subsequent to 1947 leaves this treatise somewhat dated.
8   This latter comparison is questionable, however, because Swedish is a Scandinavian language and Italian is a Romance one. Both Yaqui and Papago (= Tohono O'odham) are southern Uto-Aztecan languages and come from two distinct coordinate groupings (cf. Langacker 1977:6).
9   Actually, these pronouns are in the dative case for **noóka** and in the accusative for **bíča**.

In the chapter "Yaqui Sentence Structure," Kurath and Spicer note that the "usual order of words in the sentence is as follows: (the actor)(the object, result, or condition of the action)(the action)" or "subject, object, and predicate." They illustrate this with six declarative sentences and go on to compare semantically "simple quality" sentences (e.g., **wiykit čukui** *the bird is black*) with "modifier" constructions (**čukui wiykit** *black bird*) as distinct from the actor/action type. But this order is not rigid, and native speakers often use other arrangements for effective eloquence and to influence others, a talent useful in leadership.

They note some similarities between Yaqui and English, such as the marking of singular and plural for nouns. They also point out some distinctions not made in English, as in the case of many intransitive verbs in Yaqui where there is one verb form for a singular subject and a different form for a plural subject. The "to be" concept has different forms to differentiate between locative positions such as *be standing, be seated, be located within a general area*, and *be lying down*, among others, which "require much effort for mastery by outsiders." They also consider the similarities of the usages of the tenses in the Yaqui and English verbs.

In their discussion of "Yaqui Vocabulary," they note that "The Yaqui language at present seems to be in a state of vigorous growth" (p. 34). The reason for this is the result of their tumultuous history. The dispersal of the Yaquis in 1887 forced most of them to learn other languages, predominantly Spanish. The Yaquis' ability to adapt has been one of the strongest factors in the continued usage of their language. As is typical of Mesoamerican languages, the tradition of borrowing dates back to the Yaquis' earliest contact with the Spaniards (cf. Karttunen 1985). The earliest borrowings show the greatest phonological modifications. For practical purposes these may now be considered to be native vocabulary. Later borrowings show less phonetic modification, but some substitutions of phonemes still occur, as **p** for **f** in **pohporo** *match* and **l** for **d** as in **Lios** *Dios*. The verbalizing **-oa** (from **hoóa** *to do, to make*) may be affixed to Spanish infinitives as a base to which other verbal suffixes may be added: e.g., **pensaar-oa-n** *he was thinking*.

The bulletin ends with a section titled "Texts" and a word list. Six texts in Yaqui, with interlinear glosses in English, and a free translation are presented in this section. They include (1) The Origin of Tobacco, (2) A Wedding Sermon, (3) A Conversation, (4) A Tongue Twister, (5) A Bear Song, and (6) A Drinking Song.

Johnson's grammar, titled *El Idioma Yaqui*, was edited and published posthumously in 1962 by the Instituto Nacional de Antropología e Historia, Departamento de Investigaciones Antropológicas in Mexico City. Johnson was killed in military action in North Africa in 1943. His grammar is based partly on the 1940 manuscript mentioned above and partly on other data that he had recorded. It represents a good solid analysis of Yaqui grammar and also contains considerable text material.

Lindenfeld's *Yaqui Syntax* (1973) is one of the few attempts that was ever made to apply the framework of Transformational Generative Grammar to an Amerindian language. Lindenfeld covered the main outlines of the Extended Standard Theory model, including phrase structure base rules, several common transformations, and the formation of relative clauses, nominalizations, subordinate clauses, and coordinate sentences in Yaqui.

Professor Eloise Jelinek of the University of Arizona has published a number of articles on Yaqui grammatical structure, several of them coauthored with Fernando Escalante, as in the 1988 paper titled "'Verbless' Possessive Sentences in Yaqui," published in the volume *In Honor of Mary Haas: From the Haas Festival Conference on Native American Linguistics*, edited by William Shipley. This is a formal analysis of both the perfective suffix **-k** and the possessor suffix **-ek**, which the authors equate and to which they assign the underlying morphemic shape of **-ek** (Jelinek and Escalante 1988:416). They also conclude that the Yaqui possessive **-ek** belongs to the class of tense/aspect/modal markers and that the process of marking possession is not a part of verb derivation, but rather is a syntactic process involving noun incorporation (1988:426–427). In this volume we give a different analysis of these two prefixes (cf. VERB MORPHOLOGY, p. 145 and POSSESSIVE CONSTRUCTIONS, p. 178).

Fernando Escalante's *Voice and Argument Structure in Yaqui*, a University of Arizona Ph.D. dissertation (1990) represents the first doctoral dissertation on Yaqui linguistics written by a native speaker of the Arizona Yaqui language. It was supervised by Professor Jelinek. It includes an introductory chapter that touches on questions of both pitch and accent as well as on bilingualism. Other chapters, all full of well-described data, cover such topics as argument structure in simple sentences, voice in a variety of sentence types, complex verbs including direct and indirect causatives, dative constructions, and applicative and possessive sentences.

3.0. Yaqui sociolinguistics

Studies of contact between the Yaqui language and Spanish include those by Johnson (1943), Spicer (1943), Dozier (1956, 1967), Diebold (1964), Lindenfeld (1971), and Dedrick (1977).[10]

In his 1943 article "A Clear Case of Linguistic Acculturation," published in the *American Anthropologist*, Johnson asserts that although acculturation has been "clearly defined in its relation to certain cultural phenomena," in the sphere of linguistics "it has not been defined or illustrated" (1943:427). He opens his case by discussing diffusion, acculturation, borrowing, loan words, and other theoretically related matters. This is followed by information about the Yaqui people and their language on which Johnson based his notion of "a clear case of linguistic acculturation."

He cites the normal structure of a postpositional phrase, for example **'ín-'áčai betčí'ibo** *my-father for*, and says that Yaqui bilinguals "frequently" change the word order of such phrases to something like the following: **betčí'ibo 'ín-ačai** *for my-father*. He goes on to state that these "alternate constructions are applied to the entire set of Yaqui postpositions" (p. 432).[11]

Johnson lists a set of Yaqui personal pronouns to which the bound postposition **-u** *to, toward* is attached and states that this set is "extremely atypical" (p. 433). Following this, he deals with "the relative particle **'áet** *for him, to him, of which... etc.* and concludes that **'áet** is unique...a...recent and atypical innovation" (ibid.) He closes his discussion with the claim that "these forms do not occur in Buelna's grammar" (p. 434). Contra Johnson, Buelna does cite complete paradigms for **né-u** and **'áe-t**, as well as paradigms for the bound postpositions **-mak** *accompaniment*, **-bépa** *above*, **-pat** *at the time of*, and several others. These can be found in Buelna on pages 16, 25, 38, 47, 72, 87, 98–99, and 293–294, to cite just a few examples.

In his 1943 article, "Linguistic Aspects of Yaqui Acculturation," Spicer contextualizes the borrowing process that has influenced the Yaqui language in a variety of ways. The data for this article were collected in the Yaqui villages of Arizona in 1936–1937 (1943:410n.1). Spicer notes that modern Yaqui has a large number of Spanish loanwords and states that this paper should be regarded only as an introductory statement (ibid., p. 410).

Yaquis have experienced, "to use Linton's suggested terminology, both directed culture change and sociocultural fusion" (ibid.). The principal era of contact with Spanish was from 1617 to the end of the eighteenth century. Even by the end of the seventeenth century, the Yaqui towns were sufficiently hispanicized to serve as chief bases for supplying missionaries like Kino (ibid.).

When thrown into the cross-currents of mestizo culture, the Yaquis were already a strongly hispanicized people. A major result has been the extensive borrowing of words from Spanish (1943:411), a decidedly one-sided proposition (1943:412). These borrowings have primarily involved nominal expressions, although a good number of verbal expressions have also been borrowed. Some of the more common verbal expressions include **pásiyaaloa** (< Sp. pasear), **beláaroa** (< Sp. velar), **pensáaroa** (< Sp. pensar), **necessitáaroa** (< Sp. necessitar), and **kombiláaroa** (< Sp. convidar). Yaqui has also borrowed some conjunctions such as **si** *if*, **o** *or*, and **pórke** *because*. For the most part, however, Spicer limited his attention to the description of borrowed nominals (1943:412).[12]

Spicer provides a number of tables to show that for terms designating domestic utensils, social organization, and ritual objects, about 65% of the vocabulary is derived from Spanish. He cautions,

---

10 I have recently become aware of additional studies of Yaqui linguistic structures that I have not been able to bring into this discussion; this includes the study by Martínez Fabián, 1994, among others.
11 Dedrick comments on this as follows: "In well over 30 years' contact with Yaquis, I have never heard, nor do I have in any text any example of an inverted postpositional phrase like **betčí'ibo 'ín-'áčai**."
12 All these particular borrowings are also common to Nahuatl (David H. Tuggy, personal communication, November 26, 1996).

Introduction 3.0.

however, that this figure does not hold up for all domains of vocabulary. He also notes that although the Arizona Yaqui demonstrate high bilingual proficiency with Spanish and appear to use both Spanish and Yaqui with equal ease, they nonetheless keep the languages distinct.

In Table 1, "Words Used to Designate Material Objects in an Arizona Yaqui Household," Spicer shows that of a total of 41 items, 27 are Yaqui modifications of Spanish, 4 are Yaqui-Spanish combinations, and 10 are native Yaqui (1943:414).

In Table 2, "Kinship Terminologies of Six Yaqui Males," the respondents were arranged in six columns grouped according to decade intervals to indicate their ages. The surprising result of this study was to discover that all age groups used native Yaqui terms for the nuclear family, i.e., father, mother, sister, and brother, etc. However, for non-nuclear relations, all groups except those over 50 years of age used Spanish kinship terms, rather than Yaqui ones (1943:415).

In Table 3, "Arizona Yaqui Ceremonial Sponsor Terms," Spicer gives a list of the Yaqui terms for *godfather, godmother, godson, goddaughter,* i.e., the *compadre, comadre* relations. Yaqui equivalents are listed under two columns, for male and female speakers, respectively, i.e., the *compadre, comadre, padrino,* and *ahijado* relations.

In Table 4, he summarizes the "Names and Titles in Yaqui Ceremonial Societies." These include the following: (1) **fariseo**, (2) **matačín**, (3) **kábayum**, (4) **maéhto**, (5) **bkiyohtei**, (6) **kopária**, and (7) **wó'i**. Under each of these categories are additional terms for leader, second in command, flagbearer, and ordinary member (1943:419).

Finally, in Table 5, "Some Important Ritual Terms," Spicer lists a number of ritual terms, including **'áanimam** *soul,* **'ánkelwaatam** *guardian angel,* **'itóm 'áe** *Virgin Mary,* **Maríasantísima** *Holy Mary,* **'itóm 'áe wadalupana** *Virgin of Guadalupe,* **'itóm 'áčai** *our Father,* **lios, dios** *God,* **'itóm yaučíwa** *Jesus,* **santo** *saint,* and **kus 'itóm 'áe** *holy cross* (1943:419).

An additional topic that Spicer treats in this paper is "Sound Shifts and Chronology" (1943:420). He notes that Spanish has several phonemes that do not occur in Yaqui. These include **d, f,** and **g**. In word initial position, Spanish **d** generally becomes **l** in Yaqui, e.g., **lomínko** (< Sp. domingo). In word medial position, Spanish **d** becomes either **r** or **l** or **n**, e.g., **juúras** (< Sp. Judás), **sabala** (< Sp. sábado). In word final position, Spanish **d** becomes **n**, e.g., **tírinan** (< Sp. Trinidad). Spanish **f** became **p** in all environments, e.g., **póhporo** (< Sp. fósforo), **kapée** (< Sp. café).

Yaqui does not have initial consonant clusters. Thus the **r** of Spanish **cr-** and **tr-** clusters falls out in borrowings into Yaqui, e.g., **kus** (< Sp. cruz), **tíikom** (< Sp. trigo). Likewise, Spanish medial clusters beginning in **s** change to **h**-initial clusters in Yaqui borrowings, e.g., **maéhto** (< Sp. maestro). The initial **r** in Spanish medial clusters drops out in Yaqui loan words, e.g., **pueéta** (< Sp. puerta). Yaqui also suffixes the plural marker **-m** to borrowings from Spanish, e.g., **loónam** (< Sp. lona), **'aínam** (< Sp. harina).

Spicer considers that all of the loans that reflect the phonological modifications illustrated above are early borrowings and were introduced into Yaqui before the beginning of the nineteenth century. He observes, however, that many Spanish loans required no phonological modification to fit Yaqui patterns, and in these cases, one simply cannot tell whether a borrowing was early or not.

Spicer comments on the semantic aspects of these borrowings in the section "Cultural Processes" (1943:423). He notes, first of all, that the majority of these loanwords have been the names of items that the Spanish and the Mexicans introduced into the Yaqui culture. He observes that "Yaquis borrowed words just as readily as they accepted new cultural elements" (1943:424). With respect to ritual and social terminology, Spicer comments that it is "reasonably certain" that there were similar institutions in the aboriginal culture but that, nonetheless, new terms were adopted in these cultural domains. Part of the adoption process, however, involved adapting the Spanish concepts to Yaqui ideals. This entailed both widening and narrowing the meanings of the borrowed terms. For example, the Yaqui godparent/godchildren system includes a much wider involvement of kin relations than does the Spanish system. On the other hand, the Yaquis were not aware that their term **Monaaha** actually was a borrowing of the Spanish word that referred to the Aztec monarch. Spicer closes his article with a number of conclusions he deduced from the discussion of the data described.

In a pair of articles Edward P. Dozier also discussed linguistic acculturation as evidenced by Yaqui vocabulary. Here we summarize Dozier's 1964 article titled "Two Examples of Linguisti Acculturation: the Yaqui of Arizona and the Tewa of New Mexico," published in *Language in Culture and Society*, which was edited by Dell Hymes.

Dozier examines both sociocultural and linguistic aspects of languages in contact, much in the spirit of Dieboldəs article "Incipient Bilingualism," which is found in the same volume. Dozier characterizes the Yaqui response to Spanish contact as an amalgamation of Spanish and Yaqui elements such that one can no longer distinguish Yaqui traits from Spanish traits (1964:509). His account of Yaqui linguistic structure is based on Johnson (1943) and Spicer (1943). His claim that the Yaqui language is an amalgam such that Yaqui elements and Spanish elements are thoroughly integrated is correct, if understood properly. Although it is true that Spanish influences are found in the Yaqui lexicon, morphology, and syntax (cf. Dozier 1964:516), as this grammar will show, quite a variety of borrowings from Spanish are nonetheless clearly detectable in the linguistic structure of Yaqui.

In her 1971 article "Semantic Categorization as a Deterrent to Grammatical Borrowing: A Yaqui Example," published in *International Journal of American Linguistics,* Vol. 37, Jacqueline Lindenfeld sought to pinpoint the limits within which one language can borrow grammatical patterns from another one.

This article demonstrates how risky it is to use elicited material to document what is held to be natural, conventionalized usages of grammatical patterns. On the one hand, the thesis that "semantic categorization" is a "deterrent" to grammatical borrowing certainly seems to be valid. For the arena in which to test this thesis, Lindenfeld chose simple comparative constructions as her Yaqui examples. She tried to find out how Yaqui expressed comparative concepts such as "more than," "the same as," and "less than." Her language consultant composed the sentences given in (1)–(4).

(1)(a) hu o'óo če'a hume haamúčim beppá bʷe'u
     that man more those women above big

  (b) hu o'óo húme haamúčim benásya bʷe'u
     that man those women like/as big

  (c) émpo kaá húme ili uúsim benásya tutú'uli
     you not those little children like/as pretty

  (d) im kuúna če'a káa neé beppá yó'owe
     my husband more not me above old

Sentences (1)(a)–(d) are all understandable in Yaqui, but their construction is a bit unnatural. It is likely that the language consultant accommodated himself to the word order of the corresponding Spanish constructions to some extent. The closest idiomatic translations of these sentences into English are given in (2)(a)–(d).

(2)(a) That man is bigger than those women.
  (b) That man is big like those women.
  (c) You are not pretty like those little children.
  (d) My husband is not older than me.

Semantically, sentence (1a) is a comparative of superiority, sentence (1b) is a comparative of equality, sentence (1c) is a comparative of inequality of quality, and (1d) is a comparative of inequality of quantity.

Lindenfeld concludes that whereas Yaqui has a structure for indicating comparisons of superiority, it does not have one for indicating comparisons of inferiority. In short, so the account goes, whereas Spanish has a binary system for indicating two kinds of comparisons, Yaqui has only a single grammatical construction for marking comparisons.

The problem here has to do with both structure and the lexicon. From the structure of sentences (1)(a)–(d), one can only assume that her language consultant has tried to follow as closely as possible the word order of the elicitation language in which these sentences were presented. These sentences draw only on three lexical items, i.e., **če'a** *more,* **-bépa** *above,* and **béna-sia** *like,* in order to express comparative notions. Yaqui is really not quite that impoverished lexically.

For sentence (1a), Lindenfeld appears to have assumed that **čé'a** means *more* and **-bépa** means *than*. Actually both are just comparatives, with **čé'a** modifying the adjective and **-bépa** the noun in the same phrase. Taken together, their meaning comes closer to that of the English comparative suffix -er in words such as bigger, smaller, fatter, thinner.

For all practical purposes, the structures of English and Spanish comparisons of superiority and inferiority are identical, as illustrated in the schemata of (3)(a)–(b).

(3)(a) NP1 is more X than NP2.
 (b) NP1 is less X than NP2.

Yaqui can express the concept "less than" in a phrase such as **čé'a káa-huébena** *more not-much*. Thus, sentence (1c) could have been expressed in the form given in (4a). Usually, however, this sentence would have a different word order, that shown in (4b). In either case, these sentences are acceptable, understandable Yaqui and are comparatives of inferiority, and can be glossed in two different ways.

(4)(a) 'émpo čé'a káa-tutu'uli húme'e 'ili 'uúsi-m-bépa
  you more not-pretty those little child-PL-above
  You are not as pretty as those little children. (i.e., less pretty)
 (b) 'émpo, húme'e 'ili 'uúsi-m-bépa čé'a káa tutú'uli
  you, those little kid-PL-above more not pretty
  You are more ugly than those little children. (i.e., uglier)

In trying to generate a literal equivalent for the concept "less than," Lindenfeld's source has coined the phrases **káa X béna-si** *NEG X like-ADV* and **káa X -bépa**, which mean *not like X* and *not more than X*, both of which express only dissimilarity.

For expressing the concept of equality, Yaqui has a variety of terms including **nánna'ana** *identical to X, equally as X, the same as X*; **nánanča** *equally, the same as*; **nanaú-wit** *simultaneously*; and the postposition **-wit** *together with*. Sentences (5)(a)–(c) illustrate these patterns.

(5)(a) húu'u hóan 'íntok húu'u beétu nánna'ana-k béttea-k
  that John and that Bob same-ACC weight-have
  John weighs the same as Robert.
 (b) húu'u Hóan 'íntok húu'u beétu nánanča b^{w}é'u
  that John and that Bob equally big
  John is the same size as Robert.
 (c) húu'u 'uúsi 'íntok huú'u tren nanaú-wit 'áma yépsa-k
  that boy and that train simultaneously-with there arrive-PRF
  The boy and the train arrived there simultaneously.

For comparatives of superiority, inferiority, and equality, the following formulae may be considered typical.

(6)(a) Comp$_{sup}$ = NP1$_{nom}$ + NP2$_{acc}$-bépa + čé'a + ADJ
 (b) Comp$_{inf}$ = NP1$_{nom}$ + NP2$_{acc}$-bépa + čé'a + káa-ADJ/antonym
 (c) Comp$_{eq}$ = NP1$_{nom}$ + 'íntok + NP2$_{nom}$ + nánanča/(nánna'ana) + ADJ

Numerous examples of all these constructions are given in COMPARATIVE CONSTRUCTIONS, pp. 105–110.

In his 1977 article "Spanish Influence on Yaqui Grammar?" published in *International Journal of American Linguistics*, Dedrick addresses issues discussed in two previous works in Yaqui linguistics, the 1943 paper written by Jean Johnson, published in *Anthropological Linguistics* and titled "A Clear Case of Linguistic Acculturation," and Jacqueline Lindenfeld's 1971 *IJAL* article "Semantic Categorization as a Deterrent to Grammatical Borrowing: A Yaqui Example." As mentioned above, Dedrick corrects some of Johnson's statements about data actually cited by Buelna, and he provides additional data to further bolster Lindenfeld's point about the factors that impede grammatical borrowing.

4.0. Yaqui culture

There is a quickly growing body of ethnographic writings about aspects of Yaqui culture, some of which was partially or entirely authored by Yaquis themselves. Among the more accessible of these are Fábila (1940), Rosalío Moisés, Holden Kelly and Curry Holden (1971), Savala (1980), Spicer (1940, 1956, 1980), and two volumes by Evers and Molina (1987, 1992).

In his 1954 monograph *Pótam: A Yaqui Village in Sonora*, Edward Spicer examined the relations between economics, social organization, and religion as found in a rural Yaqui village in Sonora, Mexico. He encapsulated the cultural integrity of the Yaqui in the following terms: "The Yaqui Indians, natives of Sonora in northwestern Mexico, are notable among non-Yaquis who know them on three accounts. They were the last North American Indians to be regarded by white men as a serious military threat. They are at present among the most widely scattered of North American groups. They have retained their own ethnic distinctness almost wherever they are found in Mexico or the United States (1954:1)."

Pótam was the second in a projected series of four volumes. It was preceded by *Pascua, A Yaqui Village in Arizona* (1940). The *Pascua* study concerned a small community of Yaquis who had settled near Tucson. It was primarily an analysis of the relations between economics, social organization, and religion. The study *Pótam* applied a similar approach to those Yaquis living in the aboriginal homeland (1954:2). The study of the Pascua community focused on conflicts resulting from "the splicing" of Yaqui and Anglo-American cultures and how the Yaquis maintained their own social organization and culture while concurrently participating in the American wage system (ibid.). The content of the two volumes that were never published was later incorporated in Spicerəs 1981 magnum opus *Cycles of Conquest*.

Data for *Pótam* were gathered by Spicer and his wife. Their contact with Pótam extended over a 10-year period, starting in December 1939. Research for this volume began January 1942 and continued until April 1947. Of a total of 7 months, only a little over 5 months was spent in residence in Pótam (1954:3).

Subsequent to entry into Yaqui territory in 1617, for convenience of administration, the Jesuits organized a scattered population into 8 town centers along the lower course of the Yaqui River. From east to west these were Kó'okorim, Báhko'am, Tórim, Vicam, Pótam, Raáhum, Wíibisim, and Belém (1954:15). During the late nineteenth century, the main channel of the Yaqui River shifted sharply below Pótam, leaving Raáhum, Wíibisim, and Belém with an insufficient supply of water. Subsequently, most of the inhabitants had to abandon these sites, and many of them settled in Pótam (1954:16–18).

"Pótam territory" seems to be a band about 8 miles wide at the mountains and running about 25 miles southward. It includes individual farmhouses and the villages of Oroz, Laatico, Labores, La Misa, Hupsitakateka'apo, Béene Tekolai, Saáni, and Cuesta Alta. These are regarded as full members of the Pótam community. In 1954, they numbered about 3700 individuals.

Among those living in Pótam, Spicer noted 259 who claimed no Indian ancestry and spoke of themselves as Mexicans. These consisted of the personnel at the Mexican Army post, the storekeepers, the baker, and those who were engaged in other specialties. The 14 stores that were then operative sold cloth, hats, shoes, coffee, sugar, meat, soda pop, saddles, and canned goods (1954:12–15). The Spicers noted that there seemed to have been a solid basis of common understanding, as well as cordial personal friendships, between the Yaqui and Mexican residents of Pótam (1954:108).

The indigenous population of Pótam was not homogeneous with respect to physical types, places of origin, or cultural behavior. The principal cleavage was between the "Aguileños" and the other three groups, the Santiamé'a people, the Merida people and the Vera Cruz people. The "Aguileños," also known as the "tame batallion," fought for the Mexicans against the Yaquis in 1927. However, Spicer found no antagonism between them and the other groups during his time of research there. The Santiamé'a people regard themselves as descendents of the original founders of Pótam. Their namesake leader, Santiamé'a, returned to Pótam some time prior to 1915, fought against Obregón's troops, and achieved the status of captain in the Yaqui Military Society. The Santiamé'a people live in typical Yaqui houses around the southeastern boundary of Pótam. The other three groups live in their respective "barrios" in the part of Pótam that is organized into blocks (1954:18–38).

Introduction 4.0.

Notwithstanding, there is for the majority of the Yaquis "one world of social relations, beliefs, and standard of conduct" which is quite distinct from that of the majority of the Mexicans (1954:21), many of whom say they "have no religion" and regard Yaqui religious activities as "fanatical" (1954:109).

Throughout the larger settlements "armed Yaqui and Mexican soldiers have faced each other daily, since 1927, but there has been no fighting" (1954:9–10). The people of Pótam often visit Guaymas or Ciudad Obregón for shopping or recreation. Some visit Magdalena in northern Sonora to attend the yearly festivals of St. Francis Xavier and seek cures there.

Most adults spend most of their time in almost identical occupations, as far as economic activities are concerned. Most of the differences are in connection with ceremonial activities.

The highest degree of cultural specialization is in connection with ceremonial activities, which manifests about twenty specialties for men and five for women. This is indicative of the areas which Yaquis have chosen to elaborate. These are based on religious, political, and military interests, "while economic production remains relatively separate from all three. The agricultural techniques are not reinforced by the ceremonial activities." "This lack of relation between the economy and the religion is one of the striking features of Yaqui culture" (1954:54).[13]

Yaquis regard their government as independent of the state-municipality organization of Sonora. The Yaqui government is based on the medieval European concept that the political and military elements are ultimately in the service of the religious authorities. This strongly influences their system of government (1954:55). The extent to which this is rooted in preconquest tradition remains a question.

There are five **yá'uram** (spheres of authority): civil (the village government), military, church officials, fiesta, and **kóhtumbre** (1954:65–68). The **puéplo yoówem** (village elders) and **puéplo kobanáom** (governors) oversee the day-to-day village government. They deal with disputes, thefts, land, and property problems. For example, in 1942, the head sacristan's wife accused him of having sexual relations with another woman. An account of the trial is given on pages 98–99 of *Pótam*.

The Yaqui Military Society is distinct from the Mexican Army organization. Their sphere is that of warfare (defense or aggression) and ceremonial activities. Because there has been no fighting since 1927, most of their activity is ceremonial. They also act as members of the governing councils (cf. 1954:67–72).

Whereas the Jesuits had originally set up a traditional church hierarchy, this changed radically after they were expelled in 1767. In effect, the Yaqui **maéhto** became the chief church official and has always had a sacristan as his assistant. The **maéhto** has charge of the church building and the images. He carries out all his activities in complete independence of the Roman Catholic church. Some Yaquis may occasionally desire the services of a Catholic priest to baptize a baby or to perform a marriage ceremony, but such a choice is an individual option. Otherwise the Yaqui system is totally self-sufficient.

The Fiesta Organization consists of the Fiesteros and includes the services of the **Páhko'olam** at weddings and special saints' days (1954:72–78). The **Kóhtumbre Yá'uraa** (Traditional Authorities) function only during Lent, with all other authorities inactive from Ash Wednesday through Holy Week. These consist of two groups, the **Kabayeeom** (the Blue Flag group) and the **Paiseeom** (< Sp. Fariseos) and **Hurásim** (< Sp. Judeos), who together constitute the **Chapayékam** (the Red Flag group) (1954:88–93).

With the help of Adolfo de la Huerta in 1919–1920, construction of a church was begun, but not completed. It has a concrete floor and burnt adobe brick walls and roof and is nearly 200 feet long (1954:79). Summarizing all of the above discussion, Spicer noted that "Pótam might properly be called a theocracy" (1954:95). Spicer also noted that the supernatural beliefs regarding their symbols and rituals are distinctive for Yaquis and that it is very difficult to present it all coherently. The ideal procedure would be to select a dozen or so representatives from different segments of society (ibid.).

As an example of their terminology, Spicer cites the concept "Our Mother." The Yaquis employ a general mother term **'itóm 'áe**, *our Mother,* which is applied to all female images that go by the name

---

13 This last statement reflects Spicer's conclusion, but this is in an area that is very difficult to evaluate. Even those who participate because of a "manda" made in some emergency assume that failure would bring disaster, and conversely, compliance contributes to overall well-being, of which "economic production" is a part.

of Mary. It is also applied to the crosses used in the ceremonies. The "Guadalupana" is the Patroness of the Soldiers and is second in command. Mary exercises her power only for good. The Lord Jesus Christ is a curer, regarded as a stern, harsh disciplinarian. His power is not for the general good, but rather is used only for healing (1954:117–118). Yaquis occasionally refer to the sun as **'áčai taá'a** *Father Sun* and the moon as **malá meéča** *Mother Moon*, although they no longer seem to deify the sun and moon as they did aboriginally (1954:124–125).

Yaquis customarily have their babies baptized as soon after birth as is reasonably possible. At baptism, a child becomes a "Cristiano," that is, a human being. Babies who die before being baptized are not considered human and cannot be buried in a cemetery. The categorization of the world into the "sacred" versus the "profane" is further reflected in their ritual system by the fact that the "Blue Fiesteros" are considered "baptized," whereas the "Red Fiesteros" are considered "not baptized."

The foregoing deals with the contents of *Pótam* through chapter 7. The rest of the chapters of the book bear the following titles: "Ceremonies," "Patterns of Ritual," "Orientations of Yaqui Culture," and "Cultural Integration." These aspects of the culture are thoroughly documented and described under their corresponding headings. Had this study been carried out in any of the other eight **pueplom**, the contents of the description would have been essentially the same. The exception would have been Vicam Estación. As the railroad station, Vicam Estación is also the commercial center of Yaqui territory, and its inhabitants are almost entirely Mexicans.

In contrast to the Yaquis at Pótam, the Pascua Yaquis were a minority group in a predominantly Anglo-Hispanic community and were under the constraints of the American wage system. Conversely, the ratio of non-Yaquis to Yaquis in Pótam was so small as to constitute an exclusively Yaqui environment for all practical considerations. For economic purposes they were self-employed and so were free to give whatever time and attention to ceremonial matters they chose. Predictably, ceremonial and ritual activities occupied a greater proportion of their time and efforts than would seem to be necessary to pragmatists.

Ceremony and ritual are topics to which we now turn in summarizing the works of Evers and Molina. Evers and Molina met in 1974 and have been working together since that time (1987:8). They have coauthored several works, two of which we discuss in this section.

The first of the two volumes edited by these two authors is called *Yaqui Deer Songs/Maso Bwikam: A Native American Poetry*. It was published as Volume 14 of the Sun Tracks series by the University of Arizona Press in Tucson, Arizona, in 1987. Finding that they had some things to say together, they wrote both volumes in part with the editorial "we," whereas finding that they had other things to say as individuals, they wrote other sections of the volumes in the first person.

This volume is organized into the following chapters: "Prologue," pp. 3–6; "Yopo Nooki: Enchanted Talk", pp. 7–34; "Yeu a Weepo: Where It Comes Out," pp. 35–72; "Senu Tukaria Bwikam: One Night of Deer Songs," pp. 73–129; "Maso Me'awa: Killing the Deer," pp. 130–180; and "Epilogue", pp. 183–186.

Evers and Molina link their account to the role of Yaqui tradition, which prescribed the deer dance and deer singing as part of the ritual to be performed before starting out on the deer hunt (1987:18).

From prehistoric times the deer has been an important source of meat, skin, bone, and antlers for food, clothing, and tools, respectively. The deer's keen eyesight, sense of smell, hearing, and speed are its means for self-preservation. Deer hunting for the Yaquis and their neighbors in the western desert was neither a sport nor a luxury, but rather was a necessity. Any device that brought results was employed. All was fair game. Both Evers and Molina, as well as the Dedricks, were told of the use of carefully concealed snares being set in deer-runs as late as the 1940s. These were often quite effective.

Confidence in the efficacy of imitative magic also dates back into prehistory. This likely means that deer dance rituals have been practiced for millennia. In the early 1940s, the Dedricks were told that some Yaquis still practiced the rituals prior to a hunt, but they never personally observed this and were therefore unable to confirm it. Dedrick's conclusion at this point is identical to that expressed by Evers and Molina, that on the contemporary scene, the Yaqui seem to make no direct connection between the deer dance and the hunting of deer in the field (1987:18).

The Evers and Molina volume is dedicated to Don Jesús Yoilo'i (Jesús Alvarez Vasquez), who was born in Pótam "around the turn of the century." A visa issued April 4, 1952, listed his birth date as December 24, 1904 (1987:201 n.12). The songs translated for this volume came from several singers, but the primary one was Don Jesús Yoilo'i (1987:13).

Evers and Molina describe their visits into Yaqui country in Mexico and the United States to make contacts with many Yaquis to record and transcribe deer songs. A considerable portion of the book deals with these experiences. On one occasion, they visited a Yaqui drum maker's home and made a deal to trade a Stetson hat for the drum he was working on. Then, when the drum was finished, the hat did not fit. No deal. Maybe later.

Deer songs are usually sung by three men. Deer singers may know as many as 300 or more deer songs (1987:82), but, in a given **pahko** *fiesta,* 18 to 20 is the usual number and at most not more than 50. I counted 67 songs in this book, but this count is not precise. The songs are written in "Yopo Nooki: Enchanted Talk." They "describe a double world" conceived of as "here" and "over there" in the **sea ania** *flower world.*

"From the point of view of the **saila maso** and the other living things with whom he shares the **sea ania**, Yaqui deer songs tell a continuing story of life and death in the wilderness world of the Sonoran desert" (1987:8). They are from a living tradition that dates past the time of the first contact with Diego de Guzman.

The coauthor, Felipe Molina, is himself a lead deer dancer. He plays the **hirukiam** *notched sticks*. At his home in Yoem Pueblo, he encourages the children of the neighborhood to practice the parts of musicians and deer dancing.

The second volume produced by these two authors is titled *Hiakim: The Yaqui Homeland* and was published in 1992 as a special issue of the *Journal of the Southwest*. This work consists of the presentation and explication of a text written in both Yaqui and in Spanish by a Yaqui elder, Don Alfonso Flores Leyva. The text, which Don Alfonso calls a "testament," relates to a complex series of events that are said to have taken place when the world was new.

The authors explain how they came into possession of the "Testamento" and some of the problems they ran into before being able to publish it (1992:1–2). They then quote from an "anonymous expedition report" in which, referring to Diego de Guzman's first encounter with the Yaquis, the Yaqui were described as being "the fiercest fighters in the New World." Sustaining Edward H. Spicer's references to the Yaqui as an "enduring people," they comment that the "Testamento" may be regarded "as a contribution from a long...Yaqui tradition of cross-cultural interpretation" (ibid.:3–5).

The first third of this book is an orientation and general commentary. As in *Yaqui Deer Songs*, Evers and Molina make alternating entries (pp. 3–46). A holograph, a transcription, and a translation of the "Testamento" are given (pp. 74–101). This work also contains maps by Donald Bufkin and photographs by David Burkhalter (pp. 47–72) Another section includes photographs from the 1940s, taken by Rosamond Spicer and contains a discussion from Edward H. Spicer's "Preliminary Report on Pótam" (pp. 107–128). The book ends with a series of photographs taken by Burkhalter in the 1980s (pp. 129–138).

5.0. Yaqui history

The history of the Yaquis from the late preconquest period to the present is covered primarily in the works of three authors: Buelna (1891), Hu-DeHart (1981, 1984), and Spicer (1981). All three give well-documented accounts of the earliest contacts with the Yaquis by Europeans.[14] Because Buelna, Spicer, and Hu-DeHart all worked from much of the same source material, their accounts understandably overlap in many places in their coverage of Yaqui history. Spicer's 1981 book *Cycles of Conquest* is the *sine qua non* of historical studies on all the indigenous cultures of the American Southwest and northwestern Mexico. However, because Hu-DeHart deals more specifically with the Yaquis than either Buelna or Spicer, her account is somewhat easier to recapitulate; thus, much of the following summary of historical events is based on her work.

---

14 Dedrick could find no documentation in Fabila's account on pages 70–79. One could get the impression that Fabila himself was an eyewitness to the events he is describing.

To begin, Spicer notes the tone of early Yaqui interactions with the Spanish in the following terms: "The Yaquis...resisted armed intrusion in their territory from the first, and were so successful that they were able to set their own terms for the entrance of the missionaries" (1981:46).[15]

October 4, 1533, is the date of Diego de Guzman's first contact with the Yaquis. Buelna records, however, that on the expedition's way north, in Tamazula on the Sinaloa River, they had seen swords, daggers, and other artifacts that could not have been indigenous and, on their return, they were able to "confirm their suspicion" that other "cristianos" had been there before them. "en su vuelta en Teocomo, vieron en poder de una índia un pedazo de capa de Londres, y preguntandola...sacaron la verdad... que unos extranjeros habían llegado en una embarcación a la boca del rio de Sinaloa y teniendo necesidad de bastimento saltaron a tierra en número de quince á veinte, se internaron siguiendo por sus orillas los rastros de la gente del pais, arribaron de esta manera á los pueblos, donde por el hambre y el cansancio se descuidaron, y en la noche, dormidos, fueron muertos por los naturales" (Buelna, Introducción, XL, XLI).[16]

The local people then killed the few Spaniards that remained aboard the ship, and no one was left to report the incident. And that was the sad fate of Captain Diego de Hurtado and his crew, who the previous year had been sent north by Hernán Cortés to explore the northern coast. There seems to have been little activity in the northwest from that point on until the end of July 1591. At that time, the first of the Jesuit fathers arrived in Culiacan. Their names were Gonzalo de Tapia and Martín Pérez (Buelna, XXXIX—XLI).

In 1599, Captain Don Diego Martinez de Hurdaide came to Culiacan, where he remained until his death in 1626. Hurdaide consolidated control of the indigenous population all the way up to the country of the Mayos but was not able to subjugate the Yaquis. He made three different attempts but was badly beaten back on each occasion. However, the Yaquis themselves voluntarily "surrendered" to the Spaniards and asked for peace. This peace was celebrated on April 25, 1610 (Buelna, LIII—LIV).

Hu-DeHart's book *Missionaries, Miners and Indians: Spanish Contact with the Yaqui Nation of Northwestern New Spain,* 1533–1820 is succinct, thorough, relatively objective, and amply documented.[17] The missionaries are the Jesuits who were in Yaqui country from 1617 to 1767. The Indians are principally the Yaqui. The miners are colonial Spaniards of northwestern New Spain for whom the Yaquis provided a transient, rotating work force. Crucially, the political philosophy of the Jesuits was irreconcilably opposed to that of the secular Spaniards.

Unquestionably, the Jesuits brought about some radical and permanent changes in Yaqui culture. Some of the changes were obvious, i.e., the introduction of horses, cattle, and wheat, the use of metal and the trade of blacksmithing, new musical instruments, and so on. Other changes are not easy to codify and assess even though they affected Yaqui religious beliefs and practices.

Beginning outside of Yaqui country, the Jesuits carried out their missionary efforts among related language groups in the area of the Fuerte River. Of the estimated 100,000 people who constituted these groups, the Jesuits counted some 40,000 converts by the year 1606. Hu-DeHart appears to support Buelna's characterization of the authorship of the *Arte de la lengua Cáhita* when she comments that Padre Juan de Velasco was already working on it by that time and that he may even have visited the Mayo people as early as 1605 (1981:25).

The initial successful contact with the Yaquis was carried out from the already established Mayo mission by an experienced missionary, Father Andrés Péres Rivas, and his companion Fray Tomás Basilio, the other known main figure in the compilation of the *Arte*. They started out on Ascension Day, May 20, 1617 (1981:21). According to their account, Father Péres Rivas discovered a conspiracy against

15 This seems to have stipulated only priests and not Spanish colonists in general.
16 "On their return to Teocomo, they saw in the possession of an Indian woman a piece of cloak from London. They inquired of her about it and thus obtained the truth of its origin: some strangers had come into the harbor at the mouth of the Sinaloa River. Because they had need of replenishing their supplies, some 15 or 20 of them disembarked there. They proceeded inland along the banks of the river following the footprints of the local populace. Thus they arrived in the villages, where, because they were so tired and hungry, they got careless and fell asleep. In the night while they were sleeping, the people killed all of them."
17 Hu-DeHart also notes that "another common spelling for **Yaqui** is **Hiaqui**" (1981:15).

them by some of the Yaqui shamans and their associates. Their handling of this unrest must have been impressive, because very few missionaries ever brought this issue up again (1981:31–32)

However, the matter of the propriety of religious observances is an area in which it is difficult to deal with matters objectively. Both Spicer and Valenzuela take issue with this last statement by Hu-DeHart. Spicer, for example, describes the following concerning Juan M. Valenzuela in Pótam: "Despite a very practical and direct approach and manner, he impressed me as living in some world which I knew very little about. He was a mystic. I more or less unconsciously felt this from the first and gradually found abundant evidence to back up the impression. His eyes were not bright and burning, but rather dim and burning. They were definitely looking off somewhere, clouded by the passage from our world to the other one. We sometimes said, as we sat around in the big room at Pótam (that is, Bets, and Roz and I),[18] that we had the feeling that maybe Juan was sitting in the rafters up there looking at us and listening to what we said. Bets took to calling him the Brujo and that stuck; we were all thinking of him as the Brujo by the time we left. That nickname is merely an indication of the feeling of unearthiness which he gave rise to in all of us." (1954:6–7; also in Evers and Molina 113–114)

In short, Hu-DeHart's own account implies quite a long, drawn-out and tense state of competition between the Jesuits and the Yaquis for political and religious domination.

The Jesuits began by quietly getting themselves settled in among the Yaquis and setting themselves up as the supreme religious authority in the mission area (1981:36). Given that their relationship with the Yaquis can be characterized as a long and hard fight to "keep the Yaquis in perpetual tutelage" (1981:31), it is clear that the Yaquis managed to retain their own worldview and cultural patterning to a large extent, a point that the Jesuits obviously missed, as shown by their insistence on treating the Yaquis "as immature wards" (1981:52).

The secular Spaniards of the area were convinced that the Yaquis "were ready to become tax-paying subjects" (1981:64). Both the Jesuits and the secular Spaniards were at least partially mistaken. As things subsequently developed, the main motivation of the Yaquis seems to have been a tenacious will to maintain their own language, culture, and territory. The Yaquis were characteristically very flexible and ingenious in meeting and coping with new situations. This served them very well (1981:59).

In her 1984 sequel to *Missionaries, Miners and Indians*, which she called *Yaqui Resistance and Survival: The Struggle for Land and Autonomy*, Hu-DeHart chronicles the experiences of the Yaqui people from 1821 to 1910. This time period saw the status of the Yaqui nation switch from that of some-time conquerors, under Juan de la Bandera, to that of virtual annihilation under the presidency of Porfirio Diaz.

The scenario involved two peoples with two different worldviews, bringing two different sets of values to bear on a common set of problems: who was to control the land, the water, the labor power, the community itself—the Yaqui? or the Mexican? The struggle between the two was continuous and often violent.

There were several prominent Yaqui leaders during this time period. Juan Ignacio Húsakame'a, was also known as "Juan de la Bandera." His principal activities were carried out between 1825 and 1832. He was executed on January 7, 1833 and was followed by José Maria Leyva, who was also known as **Káa hé'eme** (*lit.* "the one who does not drink"). He was born in 1837 and was executed on April 25, 1887. He had received some military training and had also participated in some military action. He was able to take advantage of the struggle for power in Mexico City, and under his leadership, the Yaquis were able to control their own territory for ten years. This came to an abrupt end, however. In the overall program to bring an end to anarchy on both the regional and the national level, the regime of Porfirio Diaz "also destroyed the Yaqui state by military force" (1984:8).

The subsequent Yaqui leader was Juan Maldonado, who was also known by his Yaqui name **Teta kó'om Bíakti** *stone turned downward*. It is not known when he was born, but he was killed in 1901. As he gained influence, he came to be held in high regard. Beginning rather inauspiciously, Maldonado spurned the Mexican government's peace treaty of 1887 and led about 400 men and their families into

---

18 "Bets" refers to Ruth Warner Giddings, who, at that time, was associated with the University of Arizona and was researching Yaqui folklore literature. "Roz" refers to Mrs. Rosalind Spicer.

the heart of the Sierra Bacatete "Bamboo Rock" (1984:119). "Juan Maldonado...el más querido y noble de todos los gobernantes indios, por su lealtad y pureza de alma" (Fábila 1940:8).[19]

Valuable to the regional economy as laborers, Yaquis were categorized as *broncos* and *pacíficos*. But with time, it became evident that the *pacíficos* had an important part in the sustenance of the *broncos*. Nonetheless, the *broncos* were finding it increasingly difficult to subsist.

When the Mexican authorities seemed willing to meet Yaqui terms, Téta Bíakti agreed to sign a peace treaty. The signing ceremony was carried out at the railroad station of Ortiz on May 15, 1897. But the treaty did not cover the guarantees that Téta Bíakti had expected, so he returned to the mountains. Two of his former lieutenants, Loreto Villa and Espinosa, capitulated to the Mexican authorities.

What followed shortly afterward was one of the most valorous, but also one of the most bloody and disastrous battles in Yaqui history (Hu-DeHart 1984:148). In January 1900, General Lorenzo Torres, with over 1000 men, including Captain Villa and 82 Yaquis, attacked the fortress at **Masó Kóba** *deer head*. The Masó Kóba massacre took place on Jan. 18, 1900.[20] It began at about 10 in the morning and lasted until sunset. About 400 men, women, and children were killed, and many more were taken prisoner (Spicer 1981:81; Fabila 1940:99).

The disaster at Masó Kóba did not extinguish the Yaqui struggle for autonomy in their homeland. Once again, Téta Bíakti resumed the leadership of Yaqui military organization and initiated a hit-and-run style of guerilla warfare (1984:143–144). Colonel Garcia Peña, under General Torres, committed so many troops and exerted such tight control over escape routes and water holes that many Yaquis were captured and deported. The dissidents still refused to surrender and were able to replenish their supplies with the help of the pacificos. Nonetheless, within a year, the government had succeeded in reducing their following to around 300 people (1984:149).

A further major setback for the Yaquis came six months later when Loreto Villa stalked and killed Téta Bíakti at Masó Kóba. At that time, Téta Bíakti had not even recovered from the wounds he received at the January battle (Fábila 1940:100).

The loss of Téta Bíakti decidedly dampened Yaqui activism. Nevertheless, the Yaquis had not lost sight of what they valued most: autonomy in their homeland. Neither had the Mexican government abandoned their goals, and the most intense campaign to acheive those governmental goals still lay ahead (1984:154).

After Téta Bíakti's death, no other Yaqui claimed the title of captain general. There was still a small group of Yaquis led by Luis Espinoza that was unwilling to come to terms with the Mexican government, and that group was, to be sure, one to be reckoned with (1984:197). That faction might also have been destroyed if the Mexican Revolution of 1911 had not terminated the Diaz regime. As it was, it can be seen from the above summaries that the last twenty years of the 1821–1910 segment of Yaqui history was the most significant in demonstrating the tenacity of the Yaquis' devotion to their homeland. And it is eminently clear that the Yaquis were never interested in anything other than controlling their own lives on their own land. They never took their struggle into the surrounding Mexican towns, and they did not cause a significant number of casualties among either the Mexican military or the civilian populations (1984:202).

Technically Hu-DeHart's account of Yaqui history ends with this "cliff hanger." However, the book includes an epilogue (pp. 205–219) in which she gives a fairly comprehensive overview of the following period between 1910 and the 1980s with the promise of more to come.

6.0. The present work

Turning back to the contents of this present work, Dedrick began the study of the Yaqui language in Tlaxcala, Tlaxcala, Mexico, in October–November 1940 with retired Captain Ignacio Nieves and Sergeant Jesús Valenzuela as language consultants. In December 1940, the study was continued in Vicam Estación, Sonora, where Dedrick maintained residence until recently. Almost thirty years of the intervening time were spent living in Vicam. Extensive contact with the Yaqui and constant exposure to the language were

---

19 "Juan Maldonado...the most beloved and nobel of all the Yaqui governors because of his loyalty and upright spirit.
20 Sebastian Gonzalez Hiyyokamé'a was there. At the time he was an eight- or nine-year-old boy.

maintained through medical aid and literacy work. Primers, simple readers, pamphlets on health, and the New Testament have been published during the time there.

In addition to Nieves and Valenzuela, a number of other Yaqui speakers have served as language helpers. For about three years beginning in 1941, Ambrosio Castro (about 47 years of age at that time) helped in language learning and analysis by providing Dedrick with a variety of interesting folklore texts, as well as with a detailed autobiographical sketch. Much of the description in this sketch is based on data gathered from Ambrosio Castro in these early years. Castro's autobiographical material was typed by Dedrick as Castro dictated it.

In addition to the texts given by Castro, several other native authored texts have also contributed data for the linguistic description contained in this volume. One was anonymously authored by a Yaqui schoolteacher. Another, written by a local Yaqui, embodied a complaint that he had against several other Yaquis.

In November 1963, a seventy-year-old retired army officer, Captain Sebastian Gonzales Hiyyokame'a,[21] allowed Dedrick to record on magnetic tape an autobiographical account, the contents of which he gave in response to questions Dedrick asked him. In March 1974, Jesús Ozuna, then about 30 years of age, recorded on tape a short autobiographical sketch.

In 1951–1952 and again in 1958–1959, Jesús Robles Alvárez (Vega Alvárez)[22] (about 25 years of age when he started) helped in the translation of the New Testament. From 1964-75, Jose Maria Romero E. (beginning at some 19 years of age) helped to complete the translation. He also worked with Dedrick on a dictionary and provided endless explanations of the data and illustrated numerous usages of words and constructions through the years.

This grammatical description is organized along the same lines as a series of grammatical sketches edited by Ronald W. Langacker (cf. Langacker, ed., 1977–1984). The outline was devised by Langacker as a result of ten years of study and comparative work on the languages within the Uto-Aztecan family. Although it is clearly not the only way that Uto-Aztecan grammatical data can be presented, it is an outline that Casad has found supremely useful in his own research on the Cora language, another southern Uto-Aztecan language spoken in northwestern Mexico. The emphasis of this grammar, of course, is to provide readers with a clear and comprehensive description of the major grammatical patterns of this marvellous language and their usages.

---

[21] Dedrick does not know what rank, if any, Sebastian Gonzales held in the Mexican Army. Yaquis and local residents frequently referred to him as "Capitan Sebahti." He probably held that rank in the Yaqui Military.

[22] Robles Vega Alvárez told Dedrick that his fatherəs surname had been Vega but that after their return to Yaqui country, having been abandoned, he adopted the surname "Robles" when he started attending Mexican school in Vicam Estación, "just because he liked the sound of it."

PHONOLOGY

1.0. Introduction

In this section of the grammar we present an overview of the surface contrasts signalled by the phonemic system and discuss briefly a number of phonological and morphophonemic processes that are commonly observed to operate in the grammar of Sonora Yaqui. The discussions are geared to describing the data themselves rather than attempt to substantiate any particular theory of phonology.[1]

1.1. Phonemic inventory

The consonants of Sonora Yaqui can be divided into the classes of voiced and voiceless stops, affricates, fricatives, nasals, laterals and semivowels. The points of articulation relevant to the phonemic system are labial, alveolar, alveo-palatal, velar and glottal. In addition, there is a voiced, labialized, bilabial stop /b^w/. These contrasts are summarized in Table 1 below. Contrasts are also found in tone, primary stress, and secondary stress.

Consonants

	Lab	Alv	Al-pal	Vel	Glottal
Stops vl.	p	t		k	'
Stops vd.	b				
Stops vd. labialized	b^w				
Affricates			č[tš]		
Fricatives		s			h
Nasals	m	n			
Semivowels	w		y		
Lateral		l			
Flap		r			

Vowels

	Front	Central	Back
High	i		u
Mid	e		o
Low		a	

Table 1. Sonora Yaqui phonemes

1.2. Surface contrasts

The labials /**p, b, b^w, m, w**/ contrast in word initial position pre-tonically and in medial position post-tonically as follows:

Initial		**Medial**	
pémta	*he spurs a horse*	bépa	*above*
bémta	*he anoints*	kába	*egg*
bá'awa	*juice*		
b^wá'awa	*it is eaten*	hí'ib^{w}a	*eating*
mána	*he places (a plate)*	káma	*squash*
wáate	*others*	naáwa	*root*

The alveolars /**t, n, s, l, r**/ contrast as follows in both word initial and word medial positions:

---

[1] In analyzing the phonology of Yaqui, much attention was paid to the speech of mothers in talking to their children. Mothers' speech in these circumstances tended to be more deliberate, uncontracted, and clearly articulated.

	Initial		Medial
tata	*hot*	wáta	*willow*
náya	*to light a fire*	baáne	*to irrigate*
sápte	*to make a wall*	tuúse	*to grind*
ló'i	*crippled* (diminutive)	momóli	*to mature*
ró'i	*crippled*	tú'ure	*to like*

The grooved fricative /s/ also contrasts with /h/ in word initial position and in post-tonic position intervocalically:

	Initial		Medial
seéka	*armpit*	tuúse	*to grind*
heéka	*wind*	tóha	*to bring*

The alveopalatals /č, y/ contrast intervocalically and post-tonically, as follows:

	Initial		Medial
čé'e	*to nurse*	'áčai	*father*
yé'e	*to dance*	máya	*to stone*

The alveo-palatal affricate /č/ also contrasts with /t/ in word initial position preceeding the high front vowel /i/ as well as in word medial position preceding post-tonic /a/:

| číiwe | *to shell corn* | waáča | *to dry out* |
| tíiwe | *to be ashamed* | waáta | *basket* |

The velar /k/ and the glottals /', h/ contrast both word initially and word medially in post-tonic syllables:

	Initial		Medial
ké'e	*to bite*	baáka	*reed*
hé'e	*to drink*	tóha	*to bring*
'é'e	*no*	baá'a	*water*

The vowels /i, e, a, o, u/ contrast as follows:

wií'i	*thread*	weé'e	*bledo (an edible weed)*
teéka	*to lay flat*	taáka	*fruit*
baá'a	*water*	buú'u	*much*

1.3. Consonant allophones

The voiceless stops /p/, /t/, /k/ tend to have zero to slight aspiration in all positions. /k/ moves front or back according to the position of the vowel that follows it.

Bilabial /b/ has been heard as [b] [ƀ] and [v]. It is most likely to be pronounced as a stopped [b] at a syllable juncture where it follows any consonant. Otherwise it is pronounced generally as a bilabial fricative [ƀ] word initially or word medially. The postulation of the English-like labiodental [v] seems to be idiosyncratic. Castro is the only one who has used it, to Dedrick's sure knowledge.

The voiceless alveopalatal affricate /č/ [tš] has been heard on occasion as freely fluctuating with [¢]=[ts], but this is a rare allophone, e.g., ['átšai] ~ ['á¢ai] *father*.

The alveolar nasal /n/ becomes backed to [ŋ] before the velar stop /k/, the layngeal /h/ and the labiovelar /w/.

nénka	[néŋka]	*to sell*
bínwa	[bíŋwa]	*long time*
bʷán-hapte	[bʷáŋ-hapte]	*start to cry*

The laryngeal fricative /h/ may vary from a glottal fricative to a very light velar one. Generally, /h/ assimilates to the point of articulation of the following vowel, having a somewhat more perceptible degree of friction in the back positions. But nowhere does Yaqui /h/ have the degree of friction associated with Spanish /j/.

| híta | [híta] | *thing* |
| hoóka | [xoóka] | *seated* |

The liquid /r/ occurs only as a single flap.

| ríhu'utiam | [řího'utiam] | *rattles* |
| kári | [káři] | *house* |

The two semivowels /w/[2] and /y/ are non-syllabic and clearly contrast with their syllabic counterparts in two syllable sequences. The two apparently non-occurring sequences are *wu and *uo.

Single syllables: (a) wa, we, wi, wo, *wu
(b) ya, ye, yi, yo, yu

Two syllables: (a) ua, ue, ui, *uo, uu
(b) ia, ie, ii, io, iu

The contrasts between each semivowel and its corresponding disyllabic sequence are given in Table 2 and Table 3 below.

Semivowel		**Disyllabic**	
wa		ua	
wáta	*willow*	túa	*indeed*
we		ue	
wépul	*one*	húe	*with that*
wi		ui	
b^wíse	*to grab*	buísek	*went to scold*
wo		uo	
wó'i	*coyote*	(no example)	
wu		uu	
(no example)		luúla	*straight*

Table 2. Contrast of /w/ and /u/

Semivowel		**Disyllabic**	
ya		ia	
yáha	*to arrive: PL*	anía	*help*
ye		ie	
yépsa	*to arrive:SG*	inien	*this*
yi		ii	
'íiyíi'i	*this one here*	miíka	*to give*
yo		io	
yoéme	*mestizos*	hiókoi	*pardon*
yu		iu	
yukú	*rain*	tíu	*shame*

Table 3. Contrast of /y/ and /i/

---

2 Apparently due entirely to the influence of Spanish phonology, /w/ is frequently pronounced as [gw] or as [g] before back vowels, e.g., Crumrine, in *The Mayo Indians of Sonora*, (p. 157) gives **go'i** for *coyote*. But Buelna's grammar does not even list **g** in the vocabulary/dictionary at the end of the book, and on page 215 gives **Huoi** *coyote* so that the word was probably pronounced **wó'i** at that time.

1.4. Vowel allophones

The phoneme /e/ varies with [ɛ] which tends to occur in the following environments:

(1) In any closed syllable:

pétta	[pɛtta]	to make an incision
bépʷa	[bɛpʷa]	to be hit
betčí'ibo	[bɛtčí'ibo]	for

(2) When a glottal stop /'/ occurs between two /e/s:

'é'e	['ɛ'ɛ]	no
ké'e	[kɛ'ɛ]	to bite
wéye'etea	[wéyɛ'ɛtea]	to say it moves

(3) In a geminate cluster following the high tone:

| néene | [néɛne] | I |
| béeba | [béɛba] | he hits |

Otherwise it is pronounced as close [e] as in

| téeka | [téeka] | sky |
| seé'e | [seé'e] | sand, and so on. |

The phoneme /a/ becomes [æ] in an unstressed syllable ending in a velar stop.

| yá'awak | [yá'aw'k] | it was made |

The phoneme /o/ may vary slightly toward [ɔ] in the vicinity of velar consonants.[3]

| boó'o | [boó'o] | road |
| boó'o-k | [boóɔ'-k] | to have a road |

The phoneme /u/ seems to be uniformly pronounced as a back rounded [u] among the middle aged and younger Yaquis. In Dedrick's earlier contacts he sometimes transcribed an [o] from some of the more elderly Yaqui speakers for what was a /u/ phoneme to the younger, e.g., **kólopti** for **kúlupti** *suddenly*.

1.5. The phoneme /bʷ/

We treat the phonologically complex [bʷ][4] as a unit consonant phoneme because it functions as the onset to syllables, whereas the superficially similar [pʷ], [tʷ] and [kʷ] do not. These latter three sequences occur only across syllable boundaries within words. In short, our findings do not agree with Johnson's interpretation of this phenomenon (cf. Johnson 1962:2–3).[5]

Typically, /bʷ/ begins with a voiced bilabial stop which is held until some pressure builds up in the oral cavity prior to its release as a labialized offglide to the following vowel (accented or not). This phoneme does not occur with great frequency, but it is definitely contrastive with Johnson's formulation.

---

3 In certain intonational patterns (e.g., anger) both /é/ /á/ and /ó/ have been heard as [ɔ].
4 Yaqui /bʷ/ can be shown to be a reflex of Uto-Aztecan /*kʷ/. Note the following reflexes of the corresponding Proto-Uto-Aztecan forms (cf. Voegelin, Voegelin and Hale 1962:75; 133–1344; Langacker 1977:22).
    (Yq) **bʷiika** > PUA *kʷiika *sing*
    (Yq) **bʷiita** > PUA *kʷiita *excrement*.
5 Johnson described phonetic [bʷ] as being a phonological phenomenon resulting from an unaccented syllable /bu/ being followed by any accented vowel (V[+accent]), i.e., /bu/ + /V[+accent]/ > [bʷV[+accent]. Thus, the form /buá'e/ > [bʷá'e] *to eat*. In his earlier transcriptions Dedrick followed Johnson's analysis of this phenomenon, but by 1943 Dedrick had been obliged to revise his analysis as discussed above. Crumrine does not list a phoneme **bʷ** in her list of "consonant phonemes", nor on the phonetic chart she gives on p. 3. On p. 10 she has **bué'ituk** and **bo'etuk** for **bʷé'ituk** *because*. In texts in the appendix she has transcribed the word **há'abʷek** *standing* (pl.) (or a derived form) in three different ways, e.g., **há'abukámta** (this may be a typographical error) p. 23, **náu há'abʷeka**, p. 25, and **há'abuek**, p. 26. Johnson's formulation also fails to account for words such as **buúe** *to scold* and **buúa** *to wrap around* which should somehow become **bʷúe** and **bʷúa**, which is certainly not the case.

In fairness to Johnson, we note that he himself recognized exceptions to his own rule (Johnson 1962:2, para. 4) which can be expressed schematically as follows: (bu + V[+stress] > (b^w + V[+stress]).

The combination bu + V[+stress] occurs in a two syllable configuration in contrast with b^w + V[+stress] occurring as a one syllable configuration.

'áman 'á'a buí-sek	(buí = 2 syllables) [bu.í]
there him scold-went	buísek = buí-se-k *scold-go*-PRF
he went there to scold him	
'áman 'á'a b^wísek	(b^wí = 1 syllable) [b^wí]
there him grabbed	b^wísek = b^wíse-k *grab*-PRF
he grabbed him there	

The phoneme /b^w/ commonly occurs as the onset of high-toned syllables in word initial position.

b^wá'e	*to eat*	b^wéhe	*to dig*
b^wíse	*to grab*	b^wiíka	*to sing*
b^wiíkim	*song(s)*	b^wíta	*excrement*
b^wiía	*land, earth*		

It also occurs in word medial position, as the onset of post-tonic syllables.

| 'átb^wa | *to laugh at* | 'étb^wa | *to steal* |

Note that in the cases as above, where /b^w/ occurs word medially with the high pitch falling on the preceding syllable, so that /b^w/ itself is followed by an unaccented vowel, Johnson's formula would predict *'**átbua** and *'**étbua**, which are incorrect.

1.6. High and low tones vis-à-vis stress

There are two contrastive pitches in Yaqui, high pitch, marked by an accent /´/ and low pitch, which is unmarked. On vowel clusters a sequence of high-low or low-high is heard as a down-glide [V́V̀] or an up-glide [V̀V́].

Low pitch has two principle variants, low pitch [ˋ] which occurs preceding pause, and mid pitch [-] which occurs elsewhere. In a series of syllables between a high pitched syllable and a prepausal low pitched syllable, the mid-pitched syllables are not all identical. They drop gradually from a pitch just below high pitch to one just above low pitch.

The following are typical examples of pitch contrasts:

(1) (a) yóoko	*ocelot (tigre)*	(3) (c) téeka	*sky*
(b) yooko	*tomorrow*	(d) teéka	*to lay it flat*
(2) (a) 'á'a wíuta	*to wave it*	(4) (a) b^wíčia	*worm*
(b) 'á'a wiúta	*to wear it out*	(b) b^wičía	*smoke*

The question still to be decided is whether or not stress is also intrinsically a part of this phenomenon. In general, stress is not prominent (except for emphasis). Pitch is a characteristic of individual lexical items and is contrastive. In some words closed low-toned syllables immediately preceding or following a high-toned syllable seem to carry stress:

(5) (a) wásuktia	[wá**suk**tia]	*year*
(b) betčí'ibo	[**bet**čí'ibo]	*for*
(c) tekípannoa	[tekí**pan**noa]	*to work*

Perhaps spectrographic analyses will have to be made for more conclusive evidence.

There is also a secondary stress which occurs in longer words or phrases and sentences, usually at two or three syllable intervals, as a feature of the rhythm group.

['e"téhota "hé "híkkahíbaeka "'áet we"áma]
I went there, wanting to hear the news.

["te' "wa'et "'a'm "hu'k-"sa'ka'a'nee'eti'ia]
We'll take them by that way.

Primary stress is marked with ["], preceding the stressed syllable; secondary stress is marked with accent on the syllable nucleus e.g., [á]. Stress placement also obeys certain morphophonemic rules given later. Johnson seems to consider pitch and stress to coincide. Lindenfeld (1971) gives only passing notice to intonational "phrases" (1971:6).[6]

2.0. Paradigmatic phonological relations

In this section we describe the basic patterns by which vowels are distributed into the nuclei of syllables, the patterns by which consonants are distributed into the onsets and codas of syllables and the inventory of syllable types in the phonology of Sonora Yaqui.

2.1. Vowels

The vowel is the nucleus of the syllable and is relatively uniform in its value throughout, a single short vowel being one mora in duration. Yaqui has syllable timed rhythm rather than stress timed rhythm. There are no diphthongs in which two vowels combine into a single mora. Vowels have been found in all possible combinations and as many as four vowels may occur in sequence, though this is rare, e.g., **láuti** *quickly*, **láaautia** *very slowly*. All vowels may occur in either stressed or unstressed syllables anywhere within the word. All the vowel combinations that occur in Yaqui are presented in Table 4. Long vowels are indicated along the diagonal.

	i	e	a	o	u
i	ii	ie	ia	io	iu
e	ei	ee	ea	eo	eu
a	ai	ae	aa	ao	au
o	oi	oe	oa	oo	ou
u	ui	ue	ua	uo	uu

Table 4. Vowel combinations

The words given below illustrate each vowel combination left to right. In order of occurrence they are as follows:

wií'i	*thread*	hí'ohtei	*written*	kaíta	*nothing*
'iníe	*with this*	weé'e	*bledo (edible weed)*	'áe	*mother*
bíakta	*to turn over (tr)*	'éa	*to think*	baá'a	*water*
hiókoe	*to pardon*	'éo'o-te	*to be nauseated*	naáo	*corn-cob*
híunee	*will say*	néu	*to me*	náu	*together*

nóite	*to visit*	huíwa	*to be sorry*
tecóe	*bad luck*	húe	*with that*
hoóa	*to do*	túa	*indeed*
boó'o	*road*	basó'ou	*when he goes for greens*
'óo'ou	*man*	muú'u	*owl*

---

6 The problem of pitch-stress has been recognized by, but not yet been conclusively dealt with by other investigators. Crumrine says: "The incompleteness or tentativeness of phonemic solutions, such as those regarding tone, should be emphasized. I have revised my own conclusions on them several times. (1961:1)." Fraenkel says: "In isolable words tone differences have been noted which were not treated in this paper. A discussion with Kenneth Hale...revealed that our results, at variance in these cases, were conditioned by the fact that he was listening for tone while I was listening to stress.... Hale's tentative idea was to assign these tone differences to what he said may be termed dictionary stress (1959:17 n.4).

2.2. The distribution of consonants within syllables

All consonants may occur syllable initially. Each word in Yaqui begins with a consonant. The glottal stop /'/ is the most common word initial consonant.[7] For example, the phoneme count for a single page of text (from the story *Yóo páhko'ola The enchanted paschal dancer*) shows the following: /'/ = 43 occurrences; /k/ = 18; /h/ = 17; /t/ = 12; /n, y, w/ = 11 each; /b/ = 9; /s/ = 4; /m, l, č/ = 2 each; and /b^w/ = 1.

Consonant clusters occur only across a syllable boundary and may be geminate or heterorganic. Consonant clusters never occur word or syllable initially in native words. When a voiced consonant follows a voiceless consonant across a syllable boundary, there is an open transition between the two consonants, as in the following examples:

bátwe	[bát^{æ}wə]	river
'óhbo	['óh^{æ}bo]	blood
tékwa	[tek^{æ}wa]	meat

In Mayo, this open transition is precluded by pre-voicing of the preceding voiceless consonant: e.g., **bátwe** > [bád^{æ}we] *river*.

The only consonants that may occur as syllable codas or in word final position are /p, t, k, s, h, m, n, l/.

sép	at once	két	also
-mak	with	káuwis	fox
-beah	beside	'uúsi-m	children
weáma-n	was walking	tópol	gopher
mótčik	bat		

We have found only two cases in which a glottal stop /'/ occurs regularly as the second member of a consonant cluster. This combination takes place only across morpheme boundaries, and in conjunction with the subjunctive morpheme -**'éa**, and the non-coreferent desiderative morpheme **'íi'aa** following the negative **kát**.

| 'áman sím'éa-n | he ought to go there |
| 'á'abo kát'ii'aa-wa | it is desired that they come here |

All consonants except /b^w/ and /r/ may occur as geminates, (including /'/, /w/, and /y/). Note that /tč/ is the geminate form of /č/).

náppat	from here on	mábbeta	to continually receive
'áttea	property	mékka	far
híssaa	to scatter	'é''e	no (emphatic)
'ámmani	way off yonder	'ánnee	will be
'ilítči	very small	háwwoi	stretched out
yéyyena	to smoke excessively		

Where gemination occurs, the articulation is prolonged. Historically, gemination in Yaqui resulted from stress placement such that a consonant syllable coda of a stressed syllable was lengthened (cf. Voegelin, Voegelin and Hale 1962:46). In contemporary Yaqui, certain forms with geminate consonants result from reduplication and represent a subsequent round of grammaticalization that confers more than simple phonological status to the geminate. Note the following three-way contrast between an unreduplicated stem, a reduplicated one in which the reduplication indicates habitual mode and a second reduplicated stem with a geminate as part of the reduplication process. In this case, the reduplication signals intensity of the process in view.

---

[7] Johnson consistently recorded initial /'/. Fraenkel, Crumrine and Lindenfeld are not consistent in this regard, sometimes transcribing it, and sometimes not, e.g., see Fraenkel 1959:10, Crumrine 1961:15, and Lindenfeld *International Journal of American Linguistics* 37.1:8.

hí'i-b^wa	*he is eating*
b^wa-b^wá'e	*he eats habitually*
b^wáb-b^wa'e	*he's a real glutton*

2.3. Syllable types

The syllable patterning of Yaqui may be described as: CV- or CVC- word initially, and -CV-, -CVC-, -V- and -VC- word medially and finally. The bisyllabic sequences CVCV and CVVCV are very common word patterns:

CV[+high pitch]-CV		CV[+high pitch]-V-CV	
hí-nu	*to buy*	té-e-ka	*sky*
bú-sa	*to awaken*	bé-e-te	*to burn*
kó-če	*to sleep*	wá-a-ta	*to want*

CV[+high pitch]-CV-CV		CV[+high pitch]C-CV	
lú-'u-te	*to terminate*	bát-te	*nearly*
té-'i-te	*to stumble*	táh-te	*to touch*
sí-ki-li	*red*	yép-sa	*to arrive*
yó-'o-we	*to be old*		

CV-V[+high pitch]-CV		CV[+high pitch]-CVC	
wi-í-'i	*thread*	té-put	*flea*
te-é-ni	*mouth*	wé-pul	*one*
mu-ú-ke	*to die*	té-kil	*work*

The above schemas reflect the most common patterns. The longer words do not seem to follow any uniform types.

CV[+high pitch]-CVC-CV-V
wá -suk -ti -a   *year*

CV[+high pitch]C-CV-CV
hík -ka -ha   *to hear*

CV-CV-CV[+high pitch]C-V-V
te -ki -pán -o-a   *to work*

3.0. Morphophonemics

Several morphophonemic processes are particularly salient among the phonological patterns of Yaqui. These include the epenthesis of an echo-vowel, the shift of high tone under affixation, the loss of liquids in intervocalic position, the velarization of the grooved fricative /s/, the palatalization of /s/ in other environments, the related depalatalization of /č/, glide reduction and the development of "euphonic fillers" or connector elements.

3.1. The echo-vowel -'V

The epenthesis of an "echo-vowel"[8] is a very common process in Yaqui. This epenthetic vowel serves as a suffixing or compounding agent. When a word ending in a vowel is followed by an affix, or is compounded with an element that begins with a consonant, a glottal stop and a copy of the stem final vowel may be inserted before the added element. Note, for example, the Yaqui forms of the following personal names, all borrowed from Spanish.

Liíli	*Lilly*	Luúpe	*Lupe*
Hoána	*Janie*	Lupélto	*Rupert*
Beétu	*Bert*		

---

8 I am indebted to the late Maurice Swadesh for the term echo-vowel (personal correspondence and elsewhere).

When the the suffix **-téa** *to be named, be called* is added to those names that end in a vowel, a glottal stop followed by a rearticulated echo-vowel is inserted and they take on the following forms:

        Lilí-'itea   Lupé'-etea,
        Hoána-'atea   Lupélto-'otea
        Betú-'utea, respectively.

No echo-vowel is inserted at the end of those proper names that terminate in a consonant, e.g., Hóan-tea *He is called John*.

The echo-vowel appears with different parts of speech (nouns, verbs, etc.) under a number of derivational and syntactic patterns. The following example illustrates the echo-vowel rule occurring in the second layering of a derivational process that operates on a concrete noun **hamut** *woman*, first turning it into **haámučia** *wife* and then into **haámuiča'araa** *woman-chaser*.

    haámuč-ia + **-raa** ABS   becomes   **haámuč-ia-'araa** *woman chaser* (idiom)
    b^{w}áse *to be ripe* + **-teko** CND becomes   **b^{w}asé'eteko** *if it is ripe*
    hatčíni *a way or manner* + **-kun** becomes   **hatčíni'ikun** *in whatever way*

In some cases, the insertion of the echo-vowel appears to be morphologically determined. For example, the bound postpositions **-po** LOC *in* and **-u/-wi** *to, toward* occur only in their basic -CV and -V or -CV forms when they follow substantives. On the other hand, they have the phonological shapes of -'Vpo, and -'u respectively when they attach to verbs that have become substantivized. Semantically, when used with nouns they are basically locative in nature, with **-po** meaning *in* and **-u/-wi** *toward*. The following are typical examples:

    kári   *house*   kári-po   *in the house*
    káuwi   *mountain*   káuwi-u   *toward the mountain*

But when they occur with verbs, the locative concepts are practically lost and they take on the grammatical meaning imperfective participle. These suffixes are dealt with more fully in INFLECTIONAL AND DERIVATIONAL AFFIXATION, pp. 312–314.. The locative meanings are only occasionally in focus in many contexts, for example, those relative clauses that include a possessor clitic as the introducer of the clause (cf. RELATIVE CLAUSES, pp. 382–383).

    siíka   *to go*   siká-'apo   *(in) going*
    hípwe   *to have*   hípwe-'u   *(to) having*

3.2. The pitch shift (penultimate stress)

Although its position in a word is not predictable, high pitch (which is often accompanied by either primary or secondary stress) frequently falls on the first or second syllable of a word. There is, moreover, a morphophonemic process which affects the placement of high pitch. When the first syllable of a word has a geminate vowel nucleus and the high pitch occurs on either of the vowels, the addition of a suffix to the word results in the loss of one of the geminate vowels or the simplification of a cluster and the shift of high pitch to the following syllable. For example: **'oó'ou** *man* plus **-im/-m** *plural* becomes **'o'ówim** *men*; **wiíkit** *bird* has the plural form **wikítim** *birds*. The same morphophonemic process occurs when **'áma** *there* follows words with the phonemic shape described above. For example: **waáte** *others* becomes **waté** and **'aáne** *to be* becomes **'ané-** in the following sentence.

    humé'e waté   'áma 'ané-me
    those   others there being-ones
    the others who are over there

This process frequently results in pairs of words contrasting only in terms of pitch placement. For example:

    'áma káteka   *(it) being located there, there located*
    'áma katéka   *(while they were) travelling over there, there travelling*

kátek *to be located* plus the gerundizing suffix **-ka/-a** results in **káteka**. This same suffix added to **kaáte** *to be travelling (pl.)* results in **katéka** (following the morphophonemic rule of shortening and stress shift). Similarly, **buísek** *went to scold* contrasts with **bʷísek** *he grabbed it*.

On the one hand, the verb stem **buúe** *to scold, bark* plus **-i** NOM, plus **-se** *to go* plus **-ka** PRF results in the form **buísek**, whereas the stem **bʷíse** *to grab* plus **-k** PRF results in **bʷísek**.

3.3. Dropping intervocalic /l/ and /r/

Yaqui has a marked tendency to drop intervocalic /l/ and /r/, whereas Mayo tends to retain them. Thus Yaqui **bóohtia** *to have diarrhea* corresponds to Mayo **bórohtia**, Yaqui **'áa** *to be able to* corresponds to Mayo **'ára**, and the Yaqui desiderative verbal suffix **-bae** corresponds to the Mayo form **-baáre**.

In the examples that follow, the first form is the one most commonly used in Yaqui, although the second form is heard occasionally:

    baái / baáli   *fresh, cool*
    saé'ečiam / saré'ečiam   *lungs*

In a few instances, Yaqui shows a three way contrast between the versions: that without any form of the laryngeal, that with intervocalic /l/, and that with intervocalic /r/.

    sikíi / sikíli / sikíri   *red*
    čukúi / čukúli / čukúri   *black*

3.4. Velarization of the grooved fricative /s/

An /s/ becomes /h/ before a stop consonant.

    káuwis *fox* + -ta ACC   >   káuwih-ta   *fox*-ACC
    waása *field* + -po LOC *in*   >   wáh-po   *in the field*

Notice that the second example reflects the same process of shortening and tone shift cited above. In this case, only the long vowel of **waása** shortens; also the word final **a** drops and the grooved fricative of the stem softens to /h/.

3.5. Two palatalization processes

Two consonants undergo a process of palatalization. In the first place, the grooved fricative /s/ may become /č/ following a /t/.

    ket *also* + -su EMP   >   ket-ču   *also then*
    waé-t *on that* + -su EMP   >   waé-t-ču   *on that one*

Secondly, the stop **-t** becomes **-č** when followed by the high front vowel /i/. One may postulate **-či** as an earlier final syllable which now alternates with **-t** as the ending of some words, e.g., the semantically identical forms **nét** and **neétči** *on me* alternate freely. Note also: **wíikit** *bird* and **wiíkičim** *birds*. Here the **-či** ending occurs only with the plural suffix **-m**, but it is reasonable to postulate an earlier singular form ***wikítči**. Additional examples can be found on other nouns ending in **-t**.

3.6. Glide reduction with -u/-wi

As mentioned above, **-u** and **-wi** alternate somewhat freely as the final syllable in some words, e.g., **néu/neéwi** *to me* alternate freely. The longer form with **-wi** is more likely to occur in final position in an intonational phrase or at the end of a sentence.[9]

    né-u yépsa-k   *He came to me.*
    né-wi yépsa-k   *He came to me.*

---

9 For the **t/tč** and **u/wi** variations see POSTPOSITIONS, p. 169, 174.

3.7. Metathesis

Metathesis occurs in Yaqui, though less commonly and notably than it does in Mayo, e.g., **báhi/ báih** *three*, **málon/mánol** *chipmunk*.

4.0. Patterns of reduplication

The most simple pattern of reduplication in Yaqui involves the straightforward reduplication of the initial CV- in a stem.

Base Form	Reduplicated	Gloss
kóče	ko-kóče	*sleep*
hínu	hi-hínu	*buy*
sáka	sa-sáka	*go:PL*
'útte'a	'u-'útte'a	*necessary*

Some stems with long vowels in the initial syllable nonetheless reduplicate with a simple CV- initial syllable. All of these also have a high tone on the first orthographic vowel.

káa-te	ka-káa-te	*build a house*
wáa-ta	wa-wáa-ta	*want*
náako	na-náako	*get drunk*

Certain CV'V stems and stems with a nasal coda in the first syllable also reduplicate with a simple CV- initial syllable.

| yó'owe | yo-yó'owe | *be grown* |
| bámse | ba-bámse | *to hurry* |

A second set of stems with a long vowel in the initial syllable both reduplicate with a simple CV- pattern and shorten the long vowel of the stem. In this case these forms all have a rising high tone on the initial long vowel of the bare form.

miíka	mi-míka	*to give*
teébe	te-tébe	*to be tall*
noóka	no-nóka	*to talk*

Other classes of stems reduplicate with a CVC initial syllable. In two cases, the offset segment is a laryngeal, either **h** or a glottal stop /'/. CV'V-CV stems reduplicate as in the following two examples.

| lú'u-te | lú'u-lú'u-te | *to finish* |
| té'i-te | té'i-té'i-te | *to slip* |

Notice that in the two examples above, both the stem initial syllable and the reduplicated syllable carry high pitch/stress. In the following examples, it turns out that the reduplicated syllable is not stressed when the syllable coda is **h** or the stop consonant **t**.

| táh-te | tah-táh-te | *to touch* |
| bát-te | bat-bát-te | *nearly* |

Finally, there are a few polysyllabic forms that reduplicate the initial CV- of a word medial syllable.

| tekípanoa | tekí-pa-panoa | *to work* |
| naámuke | naá-mu-muke | *to get drunk* |

Forms like **tekipanoa'** from nahuatl **téki** *work* + **-panoa** *to pass* are more difficult to account for. The reduplicated form is **teki-pa-pánoa** *work repeatedly*.

In one case, an entire CVCV word gets reduplicated. In the process, an echo-vowel gets inserted between the stem and its following reduplicated form. This is the only case of following reduplication that we have noted to date.

    sáka > sáka-'a-sáka   *go:PL*

Besides assuming a variety of forms, reduplication in Yaqui serves a multiplicity of functions in the grammar. These are discussed later in VERB STEMS, pp. 263–264.

Stem reduplication will require more study, but data so far seems to indicate that it functions as a variant of initial syllable reduplication. The "middle syllable" reduplication occurs on a "modifier/head" type of word in which the first syllable of the verbal component is reduplicated. For example the nominal **naámu** *cloud* forms a compound with the following verb stem **muúke** *to die*. The resulting form **naa-muúke** means *to be drunk* and shows the reduplicated form **naa-mu-múke**, which means *to be drunk repeatedly*.

5.0. Euphonic fillers and postpositional bases

Functioning in a manner analogous to echo-vowel epenthesis, any one of the connecting elements **-a**, **-ta**, **-e**, **-be** or **-le** may occur following a noun, a verb nominalized by the suffix **-ame/-me/-m**, a pronoun, or a demonstrative stem in a construction with a following postposition. In certain cases, at least, these elements serve as a base for attaching a following postposition, with no other function as far as we have been able to determine.

These elements occur in the singular forms only. None affect the meanings of any of the component morphemes with which they are in construction, although there may be a subtle semantic difference between constructions that involve the use of a connecting element and those that do not employ one.

Dedrick's own experience in using the language leaves him with the distinct "feeling" that a "filler" is more apt to be used with expressions that designate animate entities than with those designating inanimate ones; in particular, Dedrick thinks that **-be** is more apt to be used with a human, than with a non-human reference. If adequate check could be made for verification, it might show that in a past era "Cáhita" morphologically distinguished animate vs. inanimate, human vs. non-human classes, and perhaps respectful vs. neutral attitudes and that these syllables are remnants of "lost" or desemanticized morphemes.

As shown by the two sentences below, when the postposition **-u** *to, toward* is added to **maála** *mother* and **Hóan** *John*, the bases **-be-** and **-ta-** are suffixed to the nouns.

'ín Malá-be-u   né wáate   Hóan-ta-u   né wáate
my-mother-BASE-to I remember   John-BASE-to I remember
I remember (to) my mother.   *I remember (about) John.*

The connector **-le** can be used to link a demonstrative pronoun with a postposition as in the sequence consisting of **'iníi'i** *this* + **-béna-k**, with the meaning *to be similiar to*-ACC.

'iní-le-béna-k   né wáata
this-BASE-like-ACC I want
I want one like this.

The connector **-a** links an action nominal with an instrumental postposition in the example below.

tékil *work* + -e *instrumental.*

'á'a tékil-a-e
it work-BASE-INST
by means of his work

Two distinct forms of the PLURAL marker are used with expressions indicating movement toward a settlement.

kári-m + -u
house-PL toward
toward the houses

kári-m-me-u   né wéye
house-PL-BASE-to I go
I am on my way to the houses.

The suffix **-ta** ACC/POS often occurs in its function as a suffix; at other times, it seems to function as a connective or as a postpositional base.

Hóan *John* + -betí'či-bo *for*
'iníi'i Hóan-ta-betí'čibo
this John-ACC-for
This is for John.

5.1. Inventory of postpositions

The following inventory presents the entire set of bound postpositions that figure in constructions of the form X-CON-POS.

-e(sg.), -mea(pl.)	INST	*with*
-tči/-t(sg.), metči/-met(pl.)	LOC	*on, at*
-u/-wi(sg.), -meu/-mewi(pl.)	LOC	*to, toward*
-mak/-make	LOC	*with*
-be-(wa)as	LOC	*behind, beside*
-be-tana	ABL	*from, regarding*
-be-tuk	LOC	*under*
-be-wit	LOC	*together*
-be-pa	LOC/CMP	*above, more*
-naá-po	LOC	*next to*
-be-tí'čibo	CNJ	*for, because*
-be-na	CMP	*like*

Table 5. Bound postpositions

Of the above postpositions, **-u** *to*, **-bena** *like*, and the instrumental **-e** may also occur in other analogous positions without the postpositional bases. Examples:

'á'a tékil-a-e   *by means of his work*
'á'a malá-ta-u   *to his mother*
káuwis-e-u   *to the fox*
'á'a tekó-be-u   *to his boss*
'á-le-béna   *like him*

Note also that the instrumental and the two locatives meaning *on, at* and *to, toward*, respectively, all share an initial syllable **-me-**, which is inserted between the plural marker of the object of the pronoun and the postposition itself. This is illustrated by the following pair.

(a) haámut-či   (b) haámutči-m-me-tči
    woman-on   woman-PL-CON-on
    on the woman   *on the women*

The locative postposition **-po** *on, at* is nearly identical in meaning with **-tči/-t** *on, at* and sometimes used interchangeably, but is not included in the above list because none of the syllables treated here have been found before **-po**.

5.2. Observations

(1) The postpositional base **-le** is used with singular personal pronoun or singular demonstrative stems for attaching the comparative **-bena** *like*. This construction results in the following paradigm:

né-**le**-béna   *like me,*
'é-**le**-béna   *like you*
'á-**le**-béna   *like him*
'í-**le**-béna   *like this one*

Dedrick has also heard the expression **'itó-le-béna** *like us,* but it is not typical and appears to represent a case of paradigm leveling. The more usual form is given below.

> bémpo 'itó-béna-si noóka
> they us-like-ADV talk
> *They talk just like us.*

(2) The ACC/POS morpheme **-ta** is used as a base for attaching the **-ame/-me/-m** nominalizing suffix (singular only). It also functions as the base for attaching any of the complete set of postpositions to a postpositional object.

> 'áma weáma-m-**ta**-make   *with the one walking over there*
> 'áma káteka-m-**ta**-e   *by means of the one located over there*

The use of **-ta** with most noun forms reflects its role as an accusative marker, which within Uto-Aztecan is a common base for attaching postpositions. Yaqui **-ta** serves as the base for attaching all of the following ones to noun roots: **-mak/-make, -be-(wa)as, -bétana, -betuk, -bewit, -naápo, -bepa, -bena, -betí'čibo**.

> hóan-**ta**-make   *with John*
> kári-**ta**-béas   *behind the house*
> bát^we-**ta**-bétana   *from the river*

(3) **-e** occurs between a noun ending in a consonant, and the postpositions **-tči/-t** and **-u/-wi**.

> 'á'a tékil-**e**-u   *to his work*
> húe káuwis-**e**-tči   *on the fox*

It also occurs between the third person pronominal stem **'á-** and all the bound postpositions except **-u, -mak, -wit** and **-béna**.

> 'á-**e**-t né weáman   *I was walking on it*
> 'á-**e**-waas ne kóptek   *I forgot about him*
> 'á-**e**-tuk kátek   *it is located under it*

(4) The element **-a** is used between a noun ending in a consonant and the instrumental suffix **-e** (dissimilation)

> 'á'a tékil-**a**-e   *by means of his work, and so on*

The third person pronominal stem **'a-** is linked by **-a** to the postpositions **-mak** and **-wit**.

> 'á-**a**-mak   *with him*
> 'á-**a**-wit   *at the same time as he*

(5) The connective element **-be** obviously is, or has been a morpheme. It is probable that the **be** of **-be-(wa)as, -be-tana, -be-tuk** and **be-wit** is its source historically, and that its "euphonic" or connective use reflects the end stage of its grammaticalization which began as a third person singular object pronoun ***pɨ** (cf. Langacker 1977a:52; 1977b).

What must be pointed out, however, is that the usages of the connective elements are not always the same from speaker to speaker, particularly in the cases of **-a, -ta,** and **-be**. For example, any of the following three expressions may be used to say "he gave it to his mother".

> 'á'a malá-u   'á'a mińka-k,
> his mother-to it give-PERF
> 'á'a malá-**ta**-u 'á'a mińkak
> 'á'a malá-**be**-u 'á'a mińkak

The variation in usage of these elements even extends to individuals. For example, the following examples have been selected from texts told by the same author. The first illustrates the use of the connective **-be-**, the second the use of **-ta-**, and the third involves no connector at all.

'á'a tekó-**be**-u siíka   *he went to his boss*
hitébi-**ta**-u lúula   *straight to the healer*
hú'upa-u sumá'awak   *was tied to a mesquite tree*

6.0. Some features not yet dealt with

There are still a number of features of Yaqui phonology that deserve more attention than we are prepared to give to them at the present. Two of these features are: incorporation of Spanish phonemes in the loanwords used, and intonational patterns with their connotative values in particular sentence types such as questions and emphatic affirmations or negations, as well as in those expressions encoding attitudinal postures such as surprise, disgust, scolding, and so on.

The overall subject of the influence of Spanish on Yaqui phonology requires much more research in its own right than we are prepared to do at present and warrants a special paper. Informally, we recognize three types of Yaqui, (1) conservative Yaqui spoken generally by older members of the tribe, women and children, (2) various degrees of mixing structural patterns, and inclusion of Spanish lexemes, and (3) a tendency toward a "staccato" type of rapidly spoken Yaqui in which the items under (2)(b) above are more noticeable. This latter is used by younger male Yaquis who have more contact with nationals.

Regarding the phonemic inventory of Yaqui, it is obvious that the nature of that inventory has been affected by contact with the Spanish language and culture. Many of the earlier lexical borrowings from Spanish were modified phonetically to conform to the basic Yaqui phoneme system, the earlier borrowings being more radically modified than the later ones. These earlier lexemes are now so completely incorporated into the Yaqui language that they may be considered to be native Yaqui. Spicer 1943 is as good a treatment on this subject as one needs for general orientation. Thus, it is clear that in a few instances, certain Spanish phonemes must be included in the contemporary Yaqui phonemic inventory because of Spanish lexemes which are now completely incorporated into native Yaqui and commonly pronounced as in Spanish. However, the assimilation of some of these distinctions is not without exception in the lexicon of Yaqui. Even such an early borrowing as **Liós**, from the Spanish **Dios** *God* can still be heard either as [liós] or [diós].

Finally, Spanish pronunciation patterns are beginning to influence the phonology of Yaqui in a number of other ways. These include pressure on the Yaquis to shorten geminate vowels, eliminate the glottal stop /'/, and assimilate the nasals /m/ and /n/ to the point of articulation of a following consonant according to the assimilation patterns of Spanish, e.g., -**n** + **p** = **mp, -m** + **-t** = **nt, -m** + **k** = **nk**).

This latter effect is seen clearly when one compares certain forms found in the Bandera letters with contemporary forms. Thus, the **'émči** of one hundred years ago is now **'énči**. Also **'ótamkauwi** *bones, mountain* is sometimes heard as **'otánkauwi** though contemporary Yaqui has no trouble per se with combinations such as -**mt**, -**mk**, -**np**, and -**nk** (cf. Dedrick 1989:*ms*).

For practical purposes Fraenkel and Crumrine have adequately treated the overall patterning of Yaqui intonation. Special patterns emerge in cases where emotions such as anger or excitement are involved, e.g., a scolding pattern emerges with the following characteristics: louder speech, higher pitch, stress more marked and rhythmic[10] and all with slight to heavy pharyngealization, and a tendency to pronounce /á/ /ó/ and /ú/ as [ɔ]. There is also a "ceremonial" patterning in which "liturgical" type of monotone is employed in greetings and sermons. Dedrick has not yet made as careful a study of these matters as is fitting. Preferably examples of all of these intonation patterns should be recorded on tape, transcribed and described.

There are a few words about whose pronunciation there is some uncertainty, e.g., **hóyok/hówok** *poison*, which suggests the possibility of a former rounded front (ï) vowel which has been lost but now shows up as a /y/, a /w/, an /í/, or a /u/.

---

[10] Stress is meant here to represent loudness and a more tense articulation.

PART II: SENTENCE TYPES

BASIC SENTENCE STRUCTURE

1.0. Introduction

In this section we discuss the structure of simple positive declarative sentences. More complex sentence structures, including negative sentences, are described in later sections of this work.

2.0. Word order

In describing the word order of simple sentences in Yaqui, we concern ourselves primarily with the position of subject, indirect object and direct object nominals or phrases with respect to the main verb in a sentence. Yaqui is a verb final language, that is, in simple intransitive sentences, the subject nominal comes first; the predicate adjective or intransitive verb stem follows, as can be seen in examples (1)–(3). This is a pattern general to Uto-Aztecan, but most consistently seen in the northern languages (Langacker 1977:24).

(1) tékil né-u 'aáyu-k
    work me-to be-PRF
    There is work for me.

(2) wépu'ula-i-ka híba bé'ee
    one-STAT-being only lack
    There is only one missing.

(3) tá'abwi-ka-su 'áma yépsa-k
    different-being-CTX there arrive-PRF
    It was a different (person) who came.

The rich use of postpositional phrases also marks Yaqui as a verb final language. In particular, postpositional phrases serving as indirect objects occur preverbally, as illustrated in example (4).

(4) 'ámani 'ámeu-u 'á'a téuwaa
    there them-to it tell
    He detailed it all to them.

The strength of the verb final order is shown in example (5). A complex locative phrase consisting of a locative adverb and a following postpositional phrase further elaborated on by a negative locative adverbial phrase all occupy first position in the sentence. Next comes a noun phrase with an attributive adjective and finally comes the intransitive verb of position.

(5) hunáma'a 'áme-u káa mékkaa bwé'u báu-ba'á-m máne-k
    there them-to not far:away big lake-water-PL lay-PRF
    There not far from them was a lake.

As suggested by example (5), locative phrases generally occur in preverbal position. Additional examples of this are given in sentence (6) and in the second clause of sentence (7).

(6) káuwis 'íntok póčo-'o-kun-bíča-u búite-k
    fox and woods-EV-to-site-to run-PRF
    And the fox ran to the woods.

(7) hunáman yéu-sií-ka húči hú'upa-po kibáke-k
    off there out go-PRF again mesquite-in enter-PRF
    He came out on the other side and entered the mesquite thickets again.

The word order in simple transitive clauses is to some degree, flexible. In general, both the subject and the direct object occupy one of the first two positions in the sentence, whereas the verb is placed in sentence final position. For the most part, Yaqui tends to avoid stringing nominals together; usually a pronoun will serve to mark one entity or the other, only one overt nominal marking either subject or object.

Examining the basic structure of the Yaqui declarative sentence in more detail, the primary features are as follows. The subject may be marked by a noun or a pronoun or by (zero). The indirect object and the direct object must both be marked in the accusative case. These are usually pronouns. The absence of a stated subject in any utterance is understood as third person singular.

(8) nabó-ta b^wá'e
    tuna-ACC he:eat
    He is eating a cactus apple.

(9) kaábe-ta hiníle
    no:one-ACC he:fear
    He fears no one.

Yaqui occasionally does allow two overt nominals in a single declarative clause. Sentence (10), taken from the story of Gabriel Sparrow, shows this pattern clearly. Sentence (11) shows a simple animate noun as subject in sentence initial position, the direct object is a derived compound noun functioning as head of a relative clause. It is followed by a manner adverb and all of these constituents are followed by the verb.

(10) hunáa'a yá'u-raa hunáka'a hámut-ta nok-ria-k
     that   chief-ABS that:ACC woman-ACC speak-APL-PRF
     Those authorities defended that woman.

(11) taáwe tótoi-'asó-'o-la-m   káa-mo-móli-m   híba tu'u-re
     hawk   chicken-children-EV-DIM-PL not-RDP-mature-ACC   only good-VR
     The hawk likes only tender young chickens.

In sentences (12) and (13) the subject noun phrase occupies first position, and the direct object, in second position, is marked by a demonstrative pronoun and an indefinite pronoun, respectively.

(12) lolá-ta   'asóa-m   'inika'a   'ábači-róka-n
     lola-POS children-PL   this:ACC   brother-call-PCN
     Lola's children called this person "brother."

(13) haámuč-im   kaíta   náya-'a-máči
     woman-PL   nothing   burn-EV-have
     The women have no wood/fuel.

Yaqui appears to have functional principles such as heavy NP movement. In sentence (14), for example, a complex object noun phrase occurs in sentence initial position, whereas the locative adverbial phrase **'áma**, which normally occupies sentence initial position occurs immediately preceding the verb. In example (15) a participial manner clause occurs as the first constituent which has a final verb, but it is then followed by a postpositional phrase that designates the goal of the event. This prepositional phrase is itself modified by a manner adverb and appears to be shifted to sentence final position in order to keep things straight communicatively.

(14) baá'a-m   hai-ti-mači-m   'áma   wo'o-ta-k,   húu'u hámut
     water-PL   soil-PPL-seem-PL   there throw-VR-PRF that   woman
     The woman threw out dirty water there.

(15) 'usí-ta   pú'a-te-ka   wée, hitébii-ta-u   luúla
     child-ACC carry-VR-PPL   go   doctor-ACC-to   straight
     She went, carrying the child, straight to the doctor.

Direct objects are more closely tied semantically to the Yaqui verb than adverbials and indirect objects. This is shown clearly by example (16) in which a locative adverb occurs sentence intially and is followed by a postpositional phrase that marks the indirect object of the verb **téuwaa** *to tell*. The 3rd person singular direct object clitic **'á'a** immediately precedes the verb in this sentence.

(16) 'ámani   'áme-'u   'á'a téuwaa
     there   them-to   it   tell
     He detailed it all to them.

Commonly, one of the two nominals used as subject or direct object is marked by either a positive or negative indefinite pronoun. In the following examples, this indefinite pronoun serves as the direct object.

(17) 'í'an né híta hóo-mači
now I thing do-have
I have things to do today.

(18) née kaíta-e mó'i-ti-máčí
I nothing-INST plow-PPL-have
I don't have anything to plow with.

(19) hunáma čé'a mačí-si 'á-u 'á'a téuwaa-k
there more clear-ADV him-to it tell-PRF
He explained it to him more clearly, there.

Both the subject and the direct object may be marked by pronouns. In their positioning within the sentence, these pronouns mirror the preverbal positioning of full nominals as illustrated by example (20).

(20) 'án=a'a téa-k
I=it find-PRF
I found it.

In Yaqui noun phrases, adjectives agree in number and case with the nominals that they modify. Yaqui does not have grammatical gender nor any pronouns that distinguish biological gender. Attributive adjectives usually follow the nouns that they modify. In many cases, they come to be used syntactically as heads of noun phrases. As such, they are marked in the accusative when functioning as direct objects, as in examples (21)–(22).

(21) wó'i-m kía-k tú'ure
coyote-PL delicious-ACC like
coyotes like delicious food

(22) tómi-ta 'ilíiki-k maáčuk-ta-ka
money-ACC little-ACC grasp-VR-PPL
and receiving just a tiny bit of money

Adjectives may occur in a discontinuous construction with the nouns that they modify. In example (23) the adjective **sebé-ka** *being cold ones* is participial in form and contrasts with a strictly attributive adjectival form, which is **sébe-soódam** *cold sodas*.

(23) sodá-m 'íntok sebé-ka 'áma 'aáyu-k
soda-PL and cold-being there be-PRF
And there are sodas, cold ones, there.

Adverbs often precede predicate adjectives. In the first clause of sentence (24) a quantifier precedes the predicate adjective, whereas in the second clause, a temporal adverb is in clause initial position, preceding an attributive adjective.

(24) tú'isi yó'o-we haíbu tosái-m čáo-boa-k
very old-VR now white-ACC:PL chin-hair-VR-has
He is very old, he now has white whiskers.

Likewise, quantifiers precede their head nouns as shown by sentence (25).

(25) huébena-m húya-m há'abwe-ka-'apo ne ho'aa-k
many-PL tree-PL stand-PRF-where I house-have
I live where there are many trees standing.

As the examples above suggest, frequently indirect objects and direct objects are marked in sentences by pronouns. For the most part, noun phrases that correspond to these occur only elsewhere in the wider discourse. Because of number and case agreement, there is little chance for ambiguity. In those utterances in which overt noun phrases are used concomitantly with those pronouns that correspond to them, some kind of discourse related functions such as topicalization or focus is involved. In example (26) the noun phrase **huu'u hóan** is an emphatic way of specifying precisely who is designated by the preposed third person pronoun **'aápo**.

(26) 'aápo huu'u hóan 'a'a ya'a-k
he that John it did
John himself did it.

3.0. Introducer elements

Various expletives, adverbials and conjunctions occur in first position as sentence introducers, that is, in those sentences illustrating "neutral" word order, which is probably not the most frequent word order statistically. The expletive **béha** *well* introduces sentences (27)–(28). It also serves as a base for the emphatic clitic =**su** in both sentences and shows a third person plural subject clitic as part of the introducing complex in (27).

(27) béha=su-m   kaábe-ta   yó'ore-ka   'ám 'á'a yáa-ka-i
     well=EMP-they no:one-ACC respect-PRF they it do-PPL
     Well, they did it because they don't respect anyone.

(28) béha=su ta'á-'áman wée-k
     now=EMP sun-there fall-PRF
     Well, the sun set.

Contrasting manner adverbs introduce the sentences in (29)–(30). Finally, the common conjunction **'íntok** *and* introduces the rest of sentence (31).

(29) 'inían né 'ení   né-sauwe-k
     thus   I you:ACC UNSPEC-command-PRF
     That's how I commanded you.

(30) hunúen hiía, 'á'a mé'e-tébo-bae-ka-i
     thus   say   him kill-IMP-DSD-PPL
     He said that because he wanted to give orders to kill him.

(31) 'íntok si'ime-m-meu 'áu bít-tébo-su-ka,   úkula 'íntok nee-wi
     and   all-PL-to   RFL sight-IMP-CMP-PPL after and   me-to
     And after he had revealed himself to all the others he revealed himself to me.

The introducer **pues** *well* has been borrowed into Yaqui from Spanish. In the following example, the borrowed conjunction is followed by the Yaqui introductory affirmative particle **heéwi**.

(32) púes heéwi senyóres-im 'áali-m bát-naáte-ka 'itóm puéplo prinsipal 'aali-m.
     well yes   sir-PL   sir-PL first-beginning our town   principal sir-PL
     well, yes sirs, gentlemen, beginning with the principal authorities of our town

The use of **púes** above is probably a reflection of the usage of "pues" in Spanish, since the Yaqui equivalent **beha** is not used discourse initially.

Castro's stylistic introducer for the different folk tales he told was **'iníi'i** *this* or **'iníi'i há'ani** *this perhaps*. Functionally, this is equivalent to the English formula "once upon a time," but semantically it it is more like "I don't know if this is true or not."

(33) 'íníi'i há'ani bemé-hámut mása'asai-'i-tea
     this   perhaps virgin-woman St.:Michael's:blossom-EV-named
     Perhaps this happened. There was a young girl named Saint Michael's Blossom.

(34) 'íníi'i yóo-páhko'olaa-ta   'etého-i
     this   enchanted-festal:dancer-POS tell-PPL
     This is the story of the Enchanted Pascal Dancer.

The standard conjunctions used to introduce successive sentences in a discourse include **'íntok** *and* as illustrated in sentence (35), **táa** *but* as in sentence (36), **húnak** *then* as in sentence (37), and **čukula** *later* as in sentence (38). They express a variety of notions such as simple concatenation, adversative, and immediate and remote temporal succession.

(35) 'íntok né káa hú'unea híta-betčí'ibo 'á'a b^{w}án-sí-sime-'u
     and   I   not know   thing-for   her cry-RDP-go-GND
     And I do not know why she went along crying.

(36) táa 'á'a híkkahi-nee yá'ut-ta 'éa-'u
but it hear-FUT chief-POS will-GND
But you must obey the wishes of the authority.

(37) húnak, húi húya-u kibák-ek
then again woods-to enter-PRF
Then he entered the woods again.

(38) čúkula 'íntok 'ém bo'ó-u kíkte-nee
afterward and your road-to stand-FUT
Afterward you can resume your trip.

Other introducers such as **bʷé'ituk** *because* illustrated in example (39) and **hunúen** *thus* in example (40), express causal and resultative notions as the logical progression of a given argument.

(39) bʷé'ituk 'amú-reo-ta 'á'a wéye-'e-bétana téa-k
because hunt-NZR-ACC his go-EV-from find-PRF
Because he noticed a hunter coming in his direction.

(40) hunúen sí'ime wée-m-ta 'áma kiíma-k
thus all go-NZR-ACC there put:in:PL-PRF
Thus, he put everything in there.

4.0. Topic

Deviations from word order, along with other kinds of morphological and syntactic patterning, allow a wide range of semantic structurings for several different functional ends. One common process is topicalization, i.e., a foregrounding of the primary entity that the sentence is about. In Yaqui, a topicalized noun occurs in sentence initial position, often preceding the conjunction **'íntok.**

(41) mása'asai 'íntok 'á'a téa-ka 'ínen té'e-ka 'iním 'émpo wée 'ín-hápi
St. M's Bloom and him see-PPL thus say-PRF here you go my-father
And, Saint Michael's Bloom, noticing him, said: "Is that you, my father?"

(42) káuwis 'íntok, pócho'o-kun-biča-u buíte-k
fox and woods-to-site-to run-PRF
And the fox ran toward the woods.

(43) 'áapo 'íntok 'ehéa-ta-bétuk taáwa-k
he and ironwood:tree-ACC-under remain-PRF
He stayed under the ironwood tree.

When two nominals occur in a single sentence, one is usually selected as topic and placed in sentence initial position, whereas the other is backgrounded to follow the verb. In example (44) the direct object is fronted whereas the indirect object is backgrounded.

(44) hi'ohte-ta 'áma tóha-k kobanaó-ta-wi
paper-ACC there bring-PRF governor-CON-to
He took the paper there to the governor.

In addition to direct and indirect objects, instrumental phrases may also be fronted during topicalization as illustrated by example (45).

(45) 'inía-e 'itóm tekil-a-e 'itépo itó-'anía
this-INST our work-CON-INST we RFL-help
By means of this work of ours, we earn our living.

Locations may also be topicalized. Both subject clitics as shown by sentence (46) and coordinating conjunctions as in sentence (47) serve as topic pivots for locative phrases.

(46) wasá-m-me-u né weáma-n
field-PL-CON-to I walk-PCN
I was walking to the fields.

(47) bátwe 'íntok 'áma 'áe-béas bó'oka, tú'i-si yú'in ba'á-ka-i
river and there him-front lie good-ADV much water-VR:PPL

kanóa-reo-m-me-wi 'úhbʷána waí-tána 'áu tóhi-ne-sae
boat-AGT-PL-CON-to beg other-side RFL take-IZR-order

The river was there in front of him with a lot of water; he begged the ferrymen to take him to the other side.

Finally, temporal adverbs can also be topicalized or placed in focus. In sentence (48) **í'an** designates the highlighted existence of a change of state, i.e., the present situation contrasts with the former one that the speaker was mentioning.

(48) 'í'an 'íntok hiókot 'ané-ka wéama
now and suffer be-PPL walk
And now he walks with difficulty.

5.0. Focus constructions

Yaqui can indicate focus on a particular individual by means of a cleft-like construction that is more highly marked than the usual fronting process used for topicalization. A common purpose of such focus constructions in Yaqui is to contrast one entity with another. In sentence (49), **Hóan** is placed in focus to single him out from an indefinite list of other people who might have been responsible for some action. On the other hand, in sentence (50) the event itself is placed in focus to signal exactly what John did in contrast to a whole list of other possibilities.

(49) Hóan hunáa'a-tu-ka-n huu'u 'a'a yáa-ka-me
John that:one-VR-PPL-PCN that:one it do-PRF-NZR
It was John who did it.

(50) húu'u Hóan, 'áapo 'au béeba-k
that John he himself hit-PRF
That John, he hit himself.

Kinship terms and pronouns are commonly put into focus position in Yaqui sentences as illustrated by sentences (51)–(52) respectively.

(51) 'itóm 'áe-be-u noóka-k
our mother-CON-to speak-PRF
He spoke to our mother.

(52) 'áapo 'íntok 'ehéa-ta-bétuk taáwa-k
he and ironwood:tree-ACC-under stay-PRF
And he stayed under the ironwood tree.

Entire constructions can be brought into focus. For example, the entire dependent clause of sentence (53) is fronted and put into focus. On the other hand, procomplements may occupy focus position, as seen in sentence (54).

(53) 'usí-ta pú'a-te-ka wée hitébii-ta-u luúla
child-ACC carry-VR-PPL go doctor-CON-to straight
She took the child straight to the doctor.

(54) 'ínen-po béha ču'u-ta-u hiía-k
thus-in well dog-ACC-to sound-PRF
In that way he talked to the dog.

Yaqui also employs a pair of clitics in order to signal focus on particular constituents within a sentence or discourse. These are the deictic clitic, =**bʷan,** illustrated in sentences (55)–(56) and the emphatic clitic, =**san,** found in sentences (57)–(58). In these examples =**bʷan** is used to put the focus of attention on discrete entities, inanimate in sentence (55) and human in sentence (56).

(55) 'í'i=bʷan sísi'iwooki née 'ae-t mám-te-k   haíbu nók-nee
     this=EXP iron   I   it-on hand-VR-PRF now   speak-FUT
     This particular piece of metal, if I put my hand on it, it will talk (telegraph key).

(56) náya-ka kápe   hoóa 'inii'i=bʷan maria flooreh-tea
     fire-PPL coffee make this=EXP   Maria Flores-called
     Lighting a fire, she made coffee. This particular woman was called Maria Flores.

In semantic contrast to =bʷan, =san draws the listeners' attention to the manner in which an event is realized as illustrated by sentence (57) or to the location where it takes place as in sentence (58).

(57) hunúen-tu-k=san 'émpo 'iníán 'á'a yá'a-nee
     thus-VR-PRF=EXP you   thus   it   do-FUT
     Since it is that way, you will do it thus.

(58) hunáma=san béha sí'ime-ta hu'uneiyaa-nee
     there=EXP well all-ACC   know-FUT
     Well, at that particular place, you will know everything.

PARTICLES AND CLITICS

1.0. Introduction

The framework of Yaqui discourse is largely organized by a number of particles and clitics that carry out diverse highlighting and contrasting functions. Topicalization processes introduce participants, emphatic particles signal major turning points in the discourse, and polarity notions highlight contrasts in a variety of domains. In this section, we present an overview of the usages of Yaqui particles and clitics.

2.0. Subject clitics

Subject clitics, which ordinarily appear in second position in the sentence, serve as reference points for preposing and highlighting topics and thus attach to a wide range of grammatical elements which can be employed to signal to the hearer what the rest of the sentence is all about. In the following example, a second person singular subject clitic attaches to a topicalized locative adverb.

(1) 'áman=e'e   noi-ti-sae-wa
    there=you   go-PPL-IMP-PSV
    You are ordered/asked to go there.

Subject clitics commonly attach to the NEGATIVE **ka-**. In the following conjoined sentence, a second occurrence of the subject clitic occurs following the expletive clitic =**san** in the second clause. The sequence of the conjunction and the expletive clitic serves as a complex constituent to which =**ne** attaches.

(2) kán=ne 'áa   noóka 'íntok=sán=ne nín-waáke[1]
    and=EXP=I   tongue-dry
    I can't talk, and my tongue is dry.

Subject clitics also combine with following object pronoun clitics to form a Subject-Object clitic sequence.

(3) 'án=a'a téa-k
    I=it   find-PRF
    I found it.

3.0. The emphatic clitic =su

This clitic is used in a number of ways. Among other things it signals emphasis, focus or attention on some entity or situation, and may even express counter-expectation. It can be glossed by varied expressions such as *well, now, indeed, you see, so, really,* and *then*.

The emphatic clitic =**su** is to be distinguished from the verbal suffix **-su** completive. The two can be easily differentiated because the emphatic =**su**, attaches to a variety of parts of speech and is often the final element of that phrase. It only takes a restricted number of suffixes. On the other hand, the completive suffix **-su** exclusively occurs within the verb-complex. In example (4) emphatic =**su** highlights a sentence initial nominalized adjective.

---

[1] Yaqui shows a clear contrast between the unreduced sequence **kaa née**, given in the following example, and the reduced **kan=ne** of this example. This appears to be mostly a matter of deliberate speech, with a slight bit more prominence on the negative, versus fast speech and less prominence on the negative.

(i) káa née 'áe-t   hú'unea 'íntok=san née káa 'á'a yeéka
    not I her-on know   and=EXP   I not her control
    I don't know about her, and furthermore, I have no control over her.

(4) tá'ab^wíka=su 'áma yepsa-k
    different=EMP there come-PT
    It was another person who came there.

Emphatic =**su** does occur with verbs, but it can almost always be distinguished from completive -**su** by its order in the verb word. Emphatic =**su** always occurs as the final morpheme in the complex. It follows the participial suffix -**ka** in example (6) and it even follows the temporal and conditional suffix -**o**, as seen in examples (5) and (7).

(5) pá'aria-po 'á'a wé'ma-o=su   wó'i   počo'oria-betana wee
    open:space-in his walk-when=EMP coyote woods-from   come
    When he was walking in an open space, a coyote came out of the woods.

(6) láau-láu-ti   wéye-ka=su mékkaa yebíh-nee
    RDP-slowly-CON go-PPL=EMP far   arrive-FUT
    By keeping on moving slowly, one arrives far away.

(7) tutuka-biako-o ne koče-o=su   woó'o   née ke'e-ka
    last:night-when I sleep-when=EMP mosquito me bite-PRF
    Last night, while I was sleeping, mosquitos bit me.

As seen in example (8), emphatic =**su** can cliticize to nouns.

(8) áčai-wa-i-m   lemóonio-m-po téuwaa-wa-o 'á'a yoémia-wa-im=su čé'a hunúen
    father-POS-PL demon-PL-in   call-PSV-if his child-POS-PL=EMP more thus

téuwaa-naa
call-FUT:PSV
If the father is called a demon, much more will his children be so called.

Various kinds of adverbs may also be marked with emphatic =**su**. In example (9) =**su** attaches to the temporal adberb, **híba** *always,* whereas in example (10) it attaches to the manner adverb, **húnen** *thus,* that makes reference to the content of the following clause.

(9) tómi híba=su   hunaa'a-taka-i
    money always=EMP that-being-ABS
    Money is what really matters.

(10) 'ae-t čá'a-ka   tét-tene húnen=su 'itóm lót-ta-k   wáa'a paarós
     it-on follow-PPL RDP-run thus=EMP us   tire-VR-PRF that jackrabbit
     We were running after it, but the jackrabbit tired us in this way.

As mentioned in PHONOLOGY, p. 30, when preceded by a morphemic sequence ending in **t**, such as the postposition -**met** *on* as is the case in example (11), the postposition -**t** *on* as in example (12), or the conjunction **két** *also* as in the third example here, the clitic =**su** is modified to the shape =**ču**.

(11) hunám-met=ču 'ánkeles-im kimú-pea
     those-on=EMP angel-PL   enter-DSD
     Angels desire to enter into those things.

(12) wáe-t=su   >   waétču
     that-on=EMP   *Well, on that one...*

(13) két=su   >   kétču
     also=EMP   *Well, also...*

Finally, emphatic =**su** can attach to pronouns, as in examples (14)–(17). In examples (14) and (15) it attaches to the third person singular **'áapo** *he,* in example (16) it attaches to the second singular **'émpo'** *you,* and in example (17) it attaches to the second plural **'emé** *you all.*

48

(14) 'á'a mám-po 'aáyu-k 'áapo=su yó'o-taka-i 'áapo=su nésauwe
his hand-in is-PRF he=EMP old-being-ABS he=EMP commands
It is in his hands, he is the authority, he gives the commands.

(15) 'áapo=su 'inían hiía-k čé'ewa-n=su tú'i wáa'a híta yée-mík-áme
he=EMP thus sound-PRF much:more=EMP good that thing people-give-NZR
He himself is the one who said, giving things to people is much better.

(16) 'émpo=su két hunálen=su tú'u-wa-m-po náah-kúak-te
you=EMP also thus=EMP good-ABS-NOM-in all:around-turn-VR
You, likewise, occupy yourself in good deeds.

(17) 'emé=su yeká-ka 'á'a hú'uneiyaa
you:PL=EMP control-PPL it know
You (yourselves) know it exceedingly well.

To highlight noun phrases whose initial constituent is a demonstrative adjective, emphatic =**su** attaches to the demonstrative and not to the head noun. In example (18), =**su** also functions as an interrogative marker.

(18) háu-sa hó'aa-k húu'u 'ém 'ásoa —húu'u=su
where-INTERR house-have that your child —that=EMP
'ém maára wáa'a=su 'ém 'uúsi
your daughter that=EMP your boy
Where does your child live? —your daughter? your other boy?

In the following examples, emphatic =**su** serves as the base for attaching subject clitics onto various kinds of sentence introducers, including expletives as shown in examples (19)–(20) and indefinite pronouns as in (21). In its use with the indefinite pronoun **kaíta**, it seems to carry the force of counter expectation.

(19) béha=su=m kaábe-ta yó'ore-ka 'ám 'á'a yáa-ka-i
well=EMP=they no:one-ACC respect-PRF they it do-PPL-PPL
Well, they did it because they don't respect anyone.

(20) béha=su ta'á 'áman wéče-k
now=EMP sun there fall-PRF
Well, the sun set.

(21) kaíta=su=ne 'éa
nothing=CTX=I think
I don't have any opinion.

Emphatic =**su** also attaches to a variety of adverbs, including the concessive adverb **'éla'apo** *no matter if* as in example (22), the procomplement manner adverb **húnen** *thus* in example (23), the locative adverb **hunáma** *at that particular location* in example (24), and the temporal adverb **'í'an** *right now* in examples (25)–(26).

(22) 'éla'apo=su=ne 'áa-mak 'ó'o-muk-nee
no:matter=CTX=I it-with old-die-FUT
It doesn't matter even if I die of old age with it.

(23) húnen=su=te 'a'a su'u-toha-k
thus=EMP=we it release-bring-PRF
So we left him and went away.

(24) hunáma=su nehpo né-sau-ta mám-po mák-wa-k
there=EMP I UNSPEC-order-ACC hand-in give-PSV-PRF
I was given the command at that place/time.

(25) 'i'an=su=te   'a'a hu'uneiyaa
     now=EMP=we   it   know
     Well, now we know it.

(26) nee 'a'abo   'enči   haría-k   'i'an=su   'em mam-po   taáwa-k
     I   over:here you:ACC hunt-PRF now=EMP   your hand-in remain-PRF
     I came over looking for you. Well, it's in your hands now.

The adverbial **čé'ewan**, a slightly stronger form of **čé'e** *more*, serves as a base for =**su** in a number of circumstances. In (27), it seems to augment a basic comparative of inequality, imparting the meaning "very much more" to the entire construction.

(27) če'e-wan=su   tú'ii wáa'a híta   yee-mi-mika-me,   'á'a
     more-CTX=EMP   good   that thing people-RDP-give-NZR it
     mabet-'ea-'a-ka=su
     receive-think-EV-PPL=EMP
     It is better to give things to people than to receive things.

The basic augmenting of a quantity throughout a temporal duration is illustrated in examples (28)–(30). Notice in (28) that emphatic =**su** does serve as the base for attaching a subject clitic, a pattern also found in examples (19)–(22) and (25). In all these cases, the subject clitic has in its scope all the structure that follows it in each sentence.

(28) čé'e-wan=su=ne   'ili   hú'unea
     more-CTX=EMP=I   little know
     I am getting to understand a little better.

(29) čé'e-wan=su   tú'ii 'etého-ta né-u   wée-tua-sime
     more-CTX=EMP   good   talk-ACC   me-to go-CAU-go
     He is carrying on better and better conversation with me.

(30) čé'e-wa=su   búiti-sime karíl-ta   bʷíh-bae-ka-'éan
     more-CTX=EMP   run-go   train-ACC grab-DSD-PPL-SJV
     He ran faster and faster, hoping that he could catch the train.

A different use of **čé'e-wa=su** is seen in example (31), which gives a perfective view of things, i.e., throughout a certain past duration, one state of affairs was in effect. At a given point in the past, however, a new state of affairs was instituted, a state which continues to the time of the speaker's utterance.

(31) hunáma naáte-ka   Lióh-ta   čé'e-wan=su   yó'ori-si-wa
     there begin-PPL God-ACC   more-CTX=EMP   revere-ADV-PSV
     Beginning at that time, God was held in much more reverence.

The clitic =**su** occurs in a special construction with the verbal suffix -**'éa** (subjunctive mode "to think to, ought to") to give the comparative meaning "A instead of B," or "A rather than B," and so on. In some usages, the idea of an alternative is couched in moral terms, as in example (32)

(32) 'é-t   'áu-ka-m-ta   tá'aru-k   tú'ii-nee, káa sí'ime 'ém
     you-on   be-PPL-NOM-ACC   lose-PRF   good-FUT   not all   your

     takáa   kóp-'éa-'a-ka=su
     body   lose-ought-EV-PPL=EMP
     It is better to lose a member rather than to lose all your body.

The usage of **'éa** *su* frequently carries some degree of counter expectation on the part of the speaker. Also, often associated with the idea of unexpectedness, is the additional idea of inappropriateness, as evidenced by the examples in (33)–(37). Note also that a variety of morphological elements may occur between the subjunctive **'ea** and the emphatic =**su**. In (33) the intervening morpheme is the postposition -**'apo** *in,* whereas in (34) and (35) the imperfective participle -**(a)ka** intervenes.

(33) húnuen-po béha Liój-ta yéh-te-'éa-'apo=su 'au yéeča
thus-in well God-POS sit-VR-ought-NZR=EMP RFL place
So that it is that he sits where God ought to sit.

(34) 'iníme'e 'á'a súal-'éa-'a-ka=su hu-hu'ena-si híu-taite-k
those him believe-ought-EV-PPL=EMP RDP-evil-AVR sound-begin-PRF
Instead of believing him, these people began to speak very evilly.

(35) seénu-k káačin 'áa hume'e yee-nau-tu-tu'u-te-m-meu
one-ACC no-way able those people-together-RDP-good-CAU-PL-to
nok-nee, 'ito-bena-si lioh-ta yoemia-m-meu nók-'éa-'aka=su
talk-FUT us-like-AVR God-ACC children-PL-to talk-SJV-PPL=EMP
One should not go before the judges when he ought to talk with God's children about it.

(36) táa 'emé'e hunúen 'án-'ea-'a-ka=su 'ála emé'e, kaa-tu'ii-k
but you thus be-ought-EV-PPL=EMP indeed you not-good-ACC
bó'o-hóoria
road-make (*practice*)
But you, who ought to be living good like that, actually are practicing evil.

In (37) =**su** marks the unexpectedness of an inappropriate choice for leadership.

(37) túa 'á'a suale-ka taáwa-k túa wáka'a kaa-tu'ii-k
indeed him believe-PPL remain-PRF indeed that-ACC not-good-ACC
bó'o-hóo-ria-m-ta=su wáka'a kaa-tu'ii-k
road-make-APL-NZR-ACC=CTX that:ACC not-good-ACC
bó'o-hoo-ria-m-ta=su yeu-pua-ka 'á'a yá'ut yaa-k
road-make-APL-NZR-ACC=CTX out-choose-PPL him chief make-PRF
They actually trusted him, the very one who had done that evil thing; they chose the one who did that evil thing and made him chief.

4.0. The deictic expletive =b^{w}an

The deictic clitic =**b^{w}an** can be glossed as "well!," "you see!," or "this particular X." It is often translated into Spanish as "pues." This clitic attaches to any part of speech to which attention is called and is only one of several ways that Yaqui has for marking focused elements in discourse (cf. BASIC SENTENCE STRUCTURE, pp. 44–45). In examples (38)–(40) =**b^{w}an** attaches to a demonstrative which is in the attributive position preceding the head noun in a noun phrase.

(38) 'í'i=b^{w}an sísi'iwooki née 'ae-t mám-te-k haíbu nók-nee
this=EXP iron I it-on hand-VR-PRF now speak-FUT
This particular piece of metal, if I put my hand on it, it will talk (telegraph key).

(39) náya-ka kápe hoóa 'inii'i=b^{w}an Maria flooreh-tea
fire-PPL coffee make this=EXP Maria Flores-called
Lighting a fire, she made coffee. This particular woman was called Maria Flores.

(40) 'inika'a=b^{w}an, Liós mukí-aa-m-násuk 'á'a tóbok-ta-k
this:ACC=EXP God die-NZR-PL-among him raise-VR-PRF
God raised this particular one from among the dead.

As example (41) shows, Yaqui also permits the clitic -**b^{w}an** to occur on the head noun in a phrase of the form demonstrative + noun.

(41) hunáa'a pueeta-'a=b^{w}an 'inen téa-k-ame 'uhyoóli
that door-CON=EXP thus call-VR-NZR beautiful
That particular door, that is called beautiful.

In example (42) -b^w an attaches to the coordinate conjunction **táa** and serves to highlight the contrast between the initial clause of the sentence (not given here) and the clause introduced by the adversative conjunction.

    (42) táa-'a=b^wan   'ii'i 'ámbroosio káa suá-k-am-ta-béna-si
        but-CON=EXP this Ambrose   not wise-VR-NZR-ACC-like-AZR
        ...but, in spite of this, this Ambrose, like someone without any sense...

5.0. The expletive =san

The expletive =**san** is also used with all parts of speech. It is often used by the speaker to highlight a particular entity within eyeshot, as in examples (43)–(45), or to draw attention to a particular topic as in example (46). In all these sentences =**san** attaches to a demonstrative.

    (43) bakótči-m 'áma rehte huname=san kurúes-im-tea
        snake-PL there go:PL these=EXP kurues-PL-are:called
        There are some snakes going over there, these are called "kurues."

    (44) húu'u=san baá'a sio'o-ti   búite
        that=EXP water burble-CON run
        Well, the water is burbling as it goes.

    (45) 'ín puúsi-m béete 'íme=san   náka-m súka-sió'o-te
        my eye-PL burn these=EXP ear-PL hot-hurt-VR
        My eyes are burning, these ears are painfully hot.

    (46) hunáa'a=san kóba-taka   sí'ime-m né-sauwe
        that=EXP   head-being all-ACC UNSPEC-command
        That one is the head, he commands everyone.

In example (47) =**san** attaches to a temporal adverbial demonstrative that introduces an immediately following event evoked by a prior circumstance stated in the preceding clause. In example (48) =**san** registers the speaker's strong surprise at an unexpected result.

    (47) 'o'óm-te-k   húnak=san hú'una 'órden-ta nénka-k
        anger-VR-PRF then=EXP evil   order-ACC sell-PRF
        He got angry, and right then he gave an evil command.

    (48) táa née 'á'a sóba-o=san   kába'i húba-táite-k
        but I   it broil-when=EXP horse smell-begin-PRF
        But when I began to broil it, it smelled like horse meat.

In its deictic usages, it can often be glossed as "well" or "you see," as in example (49).

    (49) naíki mét-ta   wée-o=san, húme=san 'abaí-m   'áma háp-nee
        four month-ACC go-when=EXP those=EXP roasting:ears-PL there stand-FUT
        After four months, you see, the roasting ears will be standing out there.

In its weaker senses, =**san** registers mild and pleasant surprise on the part of the narrator as illustrated by example (50). Sometimes the degree of counter expectation is no more than simple irony as in example (51).

    (50) húme'e wóki-m=san káa bétte-si   bó'o-hóa
        those   foot-PL=EXP not heavy-AVR travel
        even those feet were travelling lightly

    (51) né kaíta   yuúma-k 'ín čú'u=san hi'-'ib^wa-k
        I nothing attain-PRF my dog=EXP IZR-eat-PRF
        I didn't get anything; my dog, however, ate.

A higher degree of pleasant unexpectedness can be signalled by the use of =**san** with the comparative adjective **čé'a** *more* as in sentence (52). This combination is conventionally construed as meaning *fortunately*.

(52) táa čé'a=san 'éa-ka,   káa bemúča-'a-wa-k
     but more=EXP think-PPL not whip-EV-PSV-PRF
     But fortunately for you, you weren't whipped.

The final use of =**san** is to highlight explanatory material. In this case the degree of counter expectation is minimal as shown in sentence (53). The illocutionary force is more like that of a slightly emphasized assertion. In sentence (54) the attachment of =**san** to the coordinating conjunction **íntok** shows that the second clause in the sentence is the highlighted one. In other words, =**san** is often a functional equivalent of English contrastive stress.

(53) hún-tuk=san   bʷaána
     even-VR=EXP   cry
     That is why she is crying.

(54) káa née 'áe-t   hú'unea 'íntok=san née káa 'á'a yeéka
     not I her-on know   and=EXP I not her control
     I don't know about her, and furthermore, I have no control over her.

The use of =**san** on the adverbial **humák** in sentence (55) signals the highlighted indefiniteness on the part of the speaker as to the actual number of entities included in the count.

(55) hák-sa búsan-takaa-tu-ka-n   humák=san máa húnen 'ée-wa-či
     where-Q six-body-VR-PPL-PCN perhaps=EXP seem thus think-PSV-on
     Perhaps, somewhere around a hundred and twenty, at least that is what is thought.

Yaqui may use =**san** to highlight both manner as in sentence (56) and temporal notions as in (57).

(56) hunúen-tu-k=san 'émpo 'inían 'á'a yá'a-nee
     thus-VR-PRF=EXP you   thus it do-FUT
     Since it is that way, you will do it thus.

(57) hunáma=san béha sí'ime-ta hú'uneiyaa-nee
     there=EXP well all-ACC   know-FUT
     Well, when we get there, everyone will know.

As one would also expect, =**san** may be used to highlight individual participants in the events in view, as in sentence (58).

(58) 'ite 'á'a bʷíse-k   'émpo=san 'á'a híkkahi-nee 'á'a témae-k-o
     we him seize-PRF you=EXP   him hear-FUT   him ask-PRF-when
     We arrested him, even you will know (the truth) (why we are mad) if you question him.

In contrast to =**su** and =**bʷan**, the clitic =**san** can serve as the base for attaching the plural marker **-im**.

(59) káte='em 'ám mámmate   humák huni=san-im Liós
     not-you them pay:attention maybe-even=EXP-PL God
     'usí-a-ri-m   humák huni=san-im bé-behe'eri-m
     child-ABS-ABS-PL maybe-even=EXP-they RDP-enemy-PL
     Don't pay any attention to them; maybe they are God's children, maybe they are devils.

6.0. The dubitative particle =kun

A possible contrast between counter expectation =**su** and dubitative =**kun** is that the usages of =**su** apparently presuppose something that should have been the case, but turned out not to be, whereas the usages of =**kun** apparently presuppose that something should not be the case, but in fact does turn out to be the way things are. In sentence (61) for example, the speaker did not expect the addressee to turn out to be a Roman citizen, in sentence (62) the speaker did not expect to find the work finished, and in sentence (63) the speaker did not expect his/her addressee to actually know the person in question.

(61) 'áa'a temáe-k 'émpo-'o=kun romáano
him ask-PRF you-EV=DUB roman
He asked him, "Are you really a Roman?"

(62) béha-'a=kun 'án-su-a-k
well-EV=DUB be-CPL-PSV-PRF
So, you have finished!

(63) 'áa tú'u=kun, 'émpo 'á'a tá'aa
ah good=DUB you him know
Oh, good, then, you do know him?

Questions may also be based on the unexpected state of affairs. In these cases, **=kun**, with the appropriate echo-vowel, attaches to the WH-word as shown in sentences (64)–(66).

(64) hátčini-'i=kun 'emé'e bató'i-m
what:way-EV=DUB you-PL baptized-PL
In what way then are you baptized?

(65) híta-'a=kun 'áma 'áayu-k
thing-EV=DUB there be-PRF
What is the problem then?

(66) híta=sa-'a=kun=s=e'e híp^wee-ka, kaíta mabét-laa
thing=Q-EV=DUB=Q=you have-PPL nothing receive-PPL
How can you have anything, having received nothing?

7.0. Negatives

Grammatical categories are often quite complex and the Yaqui negative is no exception. At least three morphemes are employed for signalling a variety of speaker intentions. These include the pausal **'é'e**, the negative imperative **kát**, and the multipurpose **káa**. All these are discussed in the following sections.

7.1. The pausal negative 'é'e

The pausal form of the negative, which is used for answering yes/no questions, is **'é'e** *no*. Sentences (1)–(2) illustrate the typical use of **'e'e** in conversation. The first speaker opens with a Yes/No tag question, which the second speaker answers in the negative.

(1) hai=sa 'émpo 'áman wée-bae há'ani
how=INTERR you there go-DSD maybe
Do you plan to go there?

(2) 'é'e né káa 'áman wée-bae
no I not there go-DSD
No. I don't plan to go there.

The pausal negative **'e'e** can also be construed as highly topicalized, in that it makes a denial that may range in force from a comforting statement as in sentence (3) to a stern admonition as in sentence (4) or warning as in (5). This variation in force is communicated only by the tone of voice and general mein of the speaker.

(3) 'é'e kaita wée-nee
no nothing go-FUT
No, nothing will happen.

(4) 'é'e ém pusi-m káa hunú-ka'a bit-nee
no your eye-PL not that-ACC see-FUT
No, your eyes will not see that.

(5) 'é'e kaíbu-'ee 'ém 'éa-'u-mak yéu-wée-nee
no never-you your think-GND-with out-go-FUT
No, you will never succeed with your plan.

7.2. The negative imperative kát

The form **kát** *don't* is used for expressing normal negative imperatives and occurs in sentence initial position in this construction. In the second position, Yaqui places a number of different constituents. In intransitive imperative clauses, the verb immediately follows the negative as illustrated by sentences (6)–(8).[2]

(6) kát wóm-wómte
    not RDP-be:afraid
    Don't be frightened.

(7) kát tóo-wássaa
    not dust-scatter
    Stop raising dust.

(8) kát na-náse
    not RDP-turn:aside
    Don't turn aside.

In conventionalized expressions, an adverb serving as complement to the verb may occur in second position as in sentence (9). Manner adverbs may also occur immediately after the negative **kat** as is the case in example (10).

(9) kát suá-ti   hiía
    not annoy-AVR sound
    Be quiet.

(10) kát húnen 'aáne
     not thus practice
     Don't do that.

Direct object nouns and pronouns also occur in second position, showing clearly the Yaqui verb final sentence pattern as in sentences (11)–(12).

(11) kát=a'a piike'
     not=her milk
     Don't milk her.

(12) kát née 'ómta saái čúu'u
     not me scold brother dog
     Don't scold me, brother dog.

Finally, negative imperative clauses may be strung together in giving a complex injunction as is done in sentence (13).

(13) kát kapée hé'ee kát waká-ba'á-ri-ta b^{W}á'e kat b^{W}ia-po yéehte
     don't coffee drink not meat-fresh-NZR-ACC eat don't ground-on sit
     Don't drink coffee; don't eat fresh-meat; don't sit on the ground.

Yaqui allows the use of multiple negatives in a sentence. The pausal negative **'e'e** form is often used to heighten the force of the negative imperative, which is marked by the sentence initial form **kát** *not*. In this construction, the pausal negative is placed before the clause that is introduced by **kát**. A common instruction from a father to a child is given in sentence (14). Strong pleas are also framed with this form of the double negative, as sentence (15) illustrates.

(14) 'é''e kát húnen 'aáne
     no not thus do
     No! Don't do that!

(15) 'é'e nabóli kát née b^{W}ab-b^{W}á'e
     no grandfather not me RDP-eat
     No, Grandfather, do not eat me.

Castro, Dedrick's first language associate, gave him the form: **'ólo no**, which he said was the response a person might give if asked to do something he didn't want to do, meaning "I don't want to." He has not heard it used by anyone else.

7.3. The basic negative káa

The basic verbal, adjectival, or adverbial negative form is **káa** *no, not*. Generally, it is placed ahead of whatever it negates, with its differential placement in a sentence correlating with distinct implications. For example, sentences (16)–(17) are typical. In each case, **káa** has its scope over the verb and serves to tell either what someone does not do as in sentence (16), what is not taking place as in sentence (17), or what did not happen to someone as in sentence (18).

---

2 Arizona Yaqui differs slightly here, using the singular form **kaate** and its plural counterpart **kaatem** as in (i)(a) and (b). (Eloise Jelinek, personal communication)
    (i) (a) kaate b^{W}iika   *Don't (you) sing.*
       (b) kaatem b^{W}iika *Don't (you all) sing.*

(16) 'áapo káa tékipanoa
    he not work
    He does not work.

(17) híba káa sukáu-bae 'ii'i taéwai
    just not warm-DSD this day
    This day just doesn't want to warm up.

(18) wáa'a mó'el káa máhhae-k
    that Mo'el not be:afraid-PRF
    Mo'el didn't get scared.

In simple clauses, **káa** functions to negate the entire proposition. It often occurs sentence initially as in sentences (19) and (20), but may also serve as the grounding grammatical unit for preposing a topicalized noun phrase as it does in sentence (18), a topicalized pronoun as in sentence (16), or a preposed adverbial as in sentence (17). In complex sentences, **káa** follows a clause introducer as shown in sentences (20) and (22) or a subordinate clause as in (21) but otherwise occurs clause initially unless special purposes determine placement elsewhere.

(19) káa 'áu wóm-ta-k
    not RFL be:scared-VR-PRF
    He didn't let himself be afraid.

(20) káa 'áa nétane teén-ek táa káa noóka
    not able beg mouth-has but not speak
    He can't beg; he has a mouth, but can't talk. (said of a dog)

(21) 'encí hióko-le-ka káa 'enčí bép-su-k
    you:ACC pity-VR-PPL not you:ACC whip-CPL-PRF
    They didn't whip you because they felt sorry for you.

(22) 'á'a beéba-k táa káa 'á'a mé'aa-k
    it hit-PRF but not it kill-PRF
    He hit it, but didn't kill it.

7.4. The variable scope of káa

While often it is the verbal concept that is being negated, there is considerable freedom in the placement of **káa** which connotatively negates whatever part of speech immediately follows it. This feature is a bit more difficult to specify but the following sentences may be used to illustrate connotative differences that differ only in the placement of **káa**. In sentence (23) by placing **káa** in sentence initial position, the speaker implies to the hearer that "others may do so, but you must not." On the other hand, by placing **káa** in front of the procomplement as is the case in sentence (24), the speaker implies "you should not do it that way, but rather do it some other way." Finally, by placing **káa** in front of the verb as is illustrated in sentence (25), the speaker highlights the absolute prohibition of doing something in a particular way. In short, both the immediate context and stress and intonation patterns are important cues for the appropriate understanding of the usages of **káa**.

(23) káa 'emé'e hunúen 'án-nee
    not you:PL thus do-FUT
    You must not do that (thus).

(24) 'emé'e káa hunúen 'án-nee
    you:PL not thus do-FUT
    You must not do that.

(25) 'emé'e hunúen káa 'án-nee
    you:PL thus not do-FUT
    You must not do that.

Differential semantic affects also correlate with scope inversion as it relates to the placement of the negative with respect to certain adverbials. For example, if the adverbial **tua** *indeed* falls under the scope of **kaa** *no,* the speaker may be indulging in an understatement, as he does in sentence (26). On the other hand, a vastly different meaning results when **káa** falls under the scope of **túa** *indeed,* as in sentence (27). The combination of **káa** *not* and **'alléa** *happy* forms an antonym which means "to be sick, angry or upset."

(26) káa túa 'á'a 'alléa-'u née 'etého-ria-k
    not truly his happy-GND me tell-APL-PRF
    He told me he was a bit sad.

(27) túa káa 'á'a 'alléa-'u née 'etého-ria-k
    truly not his happy-GND me tell-APL-PRF
    He told me that he was very angry.

Sentences (28)–(31) provide more examples of scope inversion. Although one could gloss the first two sentences the same, the speaker is signalling very different things when he/she uses them. In sentence (28) the speaker is implying that someone simply does not want to go someplace, whereas in sentence (29) the person does not want to go to a particular place, but he/she is willing to go somewhere else. The second pair of sentences also may be glossed identically, but in sentence (30) the implication is that the person doesn't want to go by foot but he might be willing to go by some other means. But in sentence (31) he/she is simply unwilling to go afoot without any implication of his/her willingness to go by some other mode of travel.

(28) káa 'aman wée-bae
    not there go-DSD
    He doesn't want to go there.

(29) 'áman káa wee-bae
    there not go-DSD
    He doesn't want to go there.

(30) wokí-m-mea káa wée-bae
    foot-PL-INST not go-DSD
    He doesn't want to go afoot.

(31) káa wókí-m-mea wée-bae
    not foot-PL-INST go-DSD
    He doesn't want to go afoot.

Differential placement of the negative can shade the meanings of sentences in other ways also. For example, the meanings of sentences (32) and (33) differ in that the placement of the intensive adverb **túa** in front of **káa**, which in turn has its scope over **'á'a bičak** *he sees it*, underscores the failure of the interested party to see something, whereas the placement of **káa** in sentence initial position in sentence (33) with **túa** in its scope implies that he/she saw some entity but that the perception was not a clear one at all.

(32) túa káa 'á'a bíča-k
    indeed not it see-PRF
    He sure didn't see it.

(33) káa túa 'á'a bíča-k
    not indeed it see-PRF
    He didn't see it very well.

The final set of examples of differential meaning due to differential placement of the negative **káa** in otherwise lexically identical sentences is given by examples (34)–(36). In this case example (35) differs from (34) because in (35) the speaker is negating the nominalized adjective meaning "joy," with the result that what the interested parties will experience is the antonym of "joy," i.e., both the speaker and those to whom he refers will experience sorrow. This meaning is determined by the conventionalized meaning of **kaa + 'alléa**, which form a single unit of the Yaqui grammar. Sentence (36), on the other hand, simply affirms strongly and unambiguously that the interested parties will not experience a particular pleasure with the speaker without implying that they might experience some other pleasure with him/her, whereas sentence (34) does carry the implication that they might experience some other pleasure with the speaker.

(34) bémpo káa né-mak 'allée-wam-ta bít-nee
    they not me-with happy-NZR-ACC see-FUT
    They will not experience this joy with me.

(35) bémpo né-mak káa 'allée-wam-ta bít-nee
    they me-with not happy-NZR-ACC see-FUT
    They will experience sorrow with me.

(36) bémpo né-mak 'allée-wam-ta káa bít-nee
    they me-with happy-NZR-ACC not see-FUT
    They will not experience this joy with me.

The unmarked form **káa** holds its scope over participial phrases, as illustrated in sentences (37) and (38).

(37) néhpo káa yó'o-ta-ka-i há'iyeo-m-mak   we-wé'ama-n
I   not old-being "mescaleros"-with RDP-walk-PCN
When I was a child, I used to go around with the "mescaleros."

(38) mékka-ekuni káa nú'u-ka-i   káa tóme-ka-i
far-to   not food-having not money-having
We went very far away. I went without food and without money.

In conjoined sentences **káa** may negate either clause. In sentence (39) it negates the second clause, occurring immediately after the coordinating conjunction. In sentence (40) the negative follows the topicalized subject demonstrative of the second sentence in a pair of juxtaposed sentences.

(39) lúula   yéhte-su-k hiba   káa súka-bae
straight sit-CPL-PRF always not warm-DSD
It is already past noon, and even so, the day does not want to get warm.

(40) 'á'a himučak-tia   hunáka'a káa né-u   téuwaa
him buried-he:said that-ACC not me-to tell
"They buried him," he said. He had not told me about that.

Negative questions are also possible. In (41) a WH-question is framed as a negative one by using **kaa** to negate the entire verb complex.

(41) habé=sa 'i'an káa 'á-u   wáati-nee
who=Q now not it-to remember-FUT
Who will not remember these things?

The next three examples illustrate the contrast between **káa** in its initial position. In sentence (42) its scope is over a derived adjectival form, in (43) it is following a topicalized noun phrase, and in (44) it is following a preposed postpositional phrase.

(42) káa kop-tá-mači
not forget-VR-seem
unforgettable

(43) áapo=su káa yée-yó'ore-ka-i
he=EMP not people respect-PPL-PPL
Though he himself does not respect people.

(44) bʷia-ta-bétuk   káa mo-móye
dirt-ACC-under not RDP-decay
They do not decay under the soil.

Because the meanings of adjectivals vary so much, the effect of **káa** on a following adjective is not strongly predictable and may be anything from the weakening of its meaning to the formation of an antonym. The meaning of **káa** and **bʷé'u** found in example (45) is straightforward, as is the combination of **káa** with the quantifier in example (46). The force of the negative in example (47) is to turn the adjective **tú'ii** *good* into its antonym "bad." Likewise in example (48) the combination of **káa** with the adjective meaning "tough" results in the antonym "tender." Whether we have an antonym or not is unclear in example (49), although it is fully natural to construe a "not a long road" as being "a short road."

(45) káa bʷé'u húu'u kári
not big that house
That house isn't big.

(46) káa huébena húme'e yéu-pú'a-ri-m
not many those out-pick-NZR-PL
Not many are chosen.

(47) káa-tú'ii yée-sú'a-wame
not good people-kill-NZR
Murder is bad.

(48) káa-momólim tú'u-re
not-tough-PL good-VR
He likes the tender ones.

(49) káa teébe húu'u boó'o
not long that road
It isn't a long road.

Generally, **káa** negates or weakens the force of adverbials. Thus the implication of **káa tókti** in example (50) is that partial destruction was the actual case. The implication of the negative in examples (51) and (52) is that the person moving along a pathway is not expending much energy in that motion.

(50) káa tókti nasón-tu-k
 not totally damage-VR-PRF
 It wasn't totally destroyed.

(51) káa láuti yepsá-k-ame b^wá'a-naa
 not quickly arrive-PRF-NZR eat-FUT:PSV
 The one who doesn't get there quickly, will be eaten.

(52) káa 'ú'ute wéye húu'u 'uúsi
 not strength go that child
 The child is not going fast.

To summarize, Yaqui employs the negative to form antonyms as in sentences (26)–(27): **allea** *happy*, **kaa allea** *sick, upset, angry*. Such antonyms in Yaqui are not always easy to identify. In the cases of sentences (47) and (48), the pairs **tú'ii** *good*, **káa-tú'ii** *bad*, and **momóli** *tough* and **kaa-momóli** *tender* are among the few forms we have found so far for those sets of opposites. We have arbitrarily adopted the practice of hyphenating those words in which the antonym is formed by the use of **káa**. However, **b^wé'u** *big* and **káa b^wé'u** *not big* are not antonyms in the narrow sense of the term since there is the form **'ilitci** *small* which is the antonym of **b^wé'u**. However, **b^wé'u** and **káa b^wé'u** do designate opposite extreme values of a continuous scale that takes its meaning from the particular domain in which it is employed, e.g., the domain of tangible objects. Thus in many contexts, **káa b^wé'u** does encode the meaning "small." Likewise, pairs like **láutia** *quickly* and **káa láutia** *not quickly* in some contexts function as the antonyms "early" and "late," but in other contexts they simply mean "quickly" and "not quickly."[3]

7.5. Clitic sequences with káa

The negative particle **káa** coalesces with following subject clitics, giving a full paradigm of Negative-Subject Clitic sequences. The set of forms in Table 6 shows that third person singular is unmarked.

NEG=*I* (EMP)	ka=nné	NEG=*we*	kát=té
NEG=*you*:SG	kát=e'e:IMP	NEG=*you*:PL	kát=e'em
NEG (*unmarked*)	káa	NEG=*they*	kát=ím
+ indefinite	káa		
(+ EMP)	kát		

Table 6. Negative + subject clitics

The following sentences illustrate various of the Negative + Subject Clitic sequences. Sentence (53) illustrates the negative with a first person singular subject clitic. The emphatic form **kat** is used with non-first person subjects, as is seen in sentences (54)–(55). The second person singular forms used with **kat** in these two sentences have imperative force.

(53) káa=nee yumá'i-k téuwaa 'ó'oben
 NEG=I complete-ACC tell although
 Although I can't say everything (speak completely).

(54) née mukú-k-o kát=e'em hi'osia-ta née sewá-tua
 I die-PRF-when NEG=you:PL paper-ACC me flower-cause

 kát=e'em wi'i-tá née wikóh-tua
 NEG=you:PL fiber-ACC me belt-cause
 When I die, don't put paper flowers on me, and don't put a fiber belt on me.

---

3 A somewhat dubious antonym was developed in the translation of the New Testament, i.e., **hurío (-yoém-raa)** *Jew(ish nation)*, and **káa-hurío(-yoém-raa)** *gentiles*.

(55) kát=e'em   'álala'a-te-m-ta   'éa
     NEG=you:PL   falter-VR-NZR-ACC   seem
     Don't be indecisive.

These sentences also show that the use of **kat** is not just restricted to imperative sentences. Thus its use in sentences (56)–(59) is in declarative sentences. In sentences (56) and (59) third person plural subjects are involved, whereas a first person plural subject is illustrated in sentence (57).

(56) waté   née tó'o-tét-ten-nee kat=im   née máhta-bae
     others me   leave-RDP run   not=they me   teach-DSD
     Some run away from me, they don't want to teach me.

(57) kát=te   bit-wa-k
     not=we   see-PSV-PRF
     We were not seen.

(58) hipeta-m né né-nenka kat=im   béhe'e
     mat-PL   I RDP-sell not=they expensive
     I sell mats, they are not expensive.

(59) hóo'o'o-ti-ko-kóče   kat=im 'ó'obe húme maomeom
     snore-CON-RDP-sleep   not=they lazy those acrobats
     They were snoring up a storm; it isn't that those acrobats were lazy.

In addition to the negative-subject clitic sequences, there are actually a number of contracted forms that involve the negative. For example, the form **káak** represents a coalescence of the bimorphemic sequence **ka-hak** (NEG + **hak**) *not somewhere*. The resulting combination means "nowhere," as can be seen in sentence (60).

(60) káak   baásu-máči
     not:where   cross-able
     There is no place to cross the river.

An additional coalescence that involves the negative **káa** pairs it with the concessive adverb **húni'i** *even*. The resulting configuration is **kaúni** *not really* as in sentence (61).

(61) senú két 'áu 'áawe-le-nee   kaúni   'áawe-ka-i
     one also RFL know:how-think-FUT   not-really know:how-PPL-PPL
     A person might think that he is able to do it, when he really is not (able to do so).

In negative comparative phrases, there is a potential for ambiguity with regard to the placement of **káa**. If the comparatives **čé'a** *more*, or **-bépa** *above, more* are negated, the result while grammatically correct, is ambiguous, resulting in a phrase meaning "not more (than)" which is not the equivalent of "less (than)" since it may well imply "just as much as."

For the concept of "less (than)" an antonym is used. Often an antonym is produced by negating an adjective. This can be illustrated by the expressions given in sentences (62)–(64).

(62) 'iníi'i čé'a tú'ii   (64) 'iníi'i čé'a káa-tú'ii
     this   more good   this   more not-good
     This is better.   *This is worse.*

(63) 'iníi'i káa čé'a tú'ii
     this   not more good
     This is not better.

Yaqui does not have grammatical constructions for the expressions "more than" or "less than". These are communicated by using "positives" or "antonyms". Sentence (63) is a perfectly acceptable sentence, but simply states that "X is not better than Y." On the other hand sentence (64) is "less good" than whatever is being compared in sentence (63). When negated, the conjunction **'íntok** *and, again, also* may mean "no more" or "never again" as in sentence (65).

(65) húu'u káuwis káa 'íntok póčo'o-ku hó'a-pea
that fox not and woods-in live-DSD
The fox didn't want to live in the woods any longer.

The negative indefinite pronouns (discussed in more detail in INDEFINITE PRONOUNS, p. 252–253) are formed by combining **káa** with **hábe** *a person*, **híta** *a thing*, **háčin(i)** *a manner*, **hákun(i)** *a place*, and **háibu** *now* (66).

(66) kaábe   *no one*
     kaíta   *nothing*
     kaáčin(i) *in no way*
     kaákun(i) *nowhere*
     kaíbu   *never*

BE/HAVE/DO

1.0. Introduction

As is typical for Uto-Aztecan languages, Yaqui employs a number of stems, suffixes and grammatical constructions to convey the notions "be," "have," and "do." Furthermore, individual stems and suffixes exhibit polysemy ranging throughout all of these categories.

2.0. Be

"Be" verbs comment on various states of existence vis-à-vis reality as the speaker perceives it. They range in specificity from designating simple existence to indicating particular configurations that entities assume when they occur en situ. We can call such verbs "epistemic verbs." In the following section we discuss the schematic verbs **'aáne** and **'aáyu'/'aú**, a set of "posture verbs," the participial suffix **-ka**, the many faced morpheme **-mači**, the adverbial **mais/maisi**, the existential **-taka**, the appelative **-tea**, and the remote appelative **-roka**.

2.1. The main verbs 'aáne and 'aáyu

The verbs **'aáne** and **'aáyu**, with its shortened form **'áu-** are difficult to gloss. The existential verb **'aáne** shows a broad range of uses, both in its basic form and in its reduced forms **'án** and **'ané**. In short, **'aáne** seems to carry the general concept of "being in the vicinity of," "being engaged in some activity," or "being found in a particular state or condition." The locative usages of **'aáne** are illustrated in examples (1)–(3).

(1) kaáčin=te waé-tána 'an-née
no:way=we there-side be-FUT
There's no way we can get to the other side.

(2) 'émpo káa hú'uneiyaa-n 'iním 'ín 'ané-'u
you not know-PCN here my be-GND
Didn't you know that I was here?

(3) tuká-ne húya-u 'aáne-n
yesterday-I woods-to be-PCN
Yesterday I was in the woods.

The existential **'aáne** shows clear processual usages, in contrast to the stative usages described above. The idea of engaging in some kind of activity is illustrated in sentences (4)–(5). In such cases, **'aáne** can be glossed as "do."

(4) haí=sa 'émpo 'aáne-n
how=Q you be-PCN
What were you doing?

(5) haí=sa=ne túa 'áme-'u 'ané-ka 'ám 'át-túa-nee
how=Q=I indeed them-to be-ing them laugh-CAU-FUT
What in the world can I do for them to make them laugh.

haí=sa 'án-nee 'ínepo née káa 'ám sáuwe
how=Q be-FUT I I not them command
But what can I do? I don't order them.

The circumstantial usages of **'aáne** are illustrated in sentences (6)–(8).

(6) hióko-t 'ané-ka weáma
misery-on be-PPL walk
It is with difficulty that I walk.

(7) haí=sa 'a-'án-wa wá'ami
how=Q RDP-be-PSV off:there
How are things going off yonder?

(8) 'áapo 'obí-si 'aáne
he stress-AVR be
He is very busy.

The shortened form of **'án** occurs as the base of a postposition in a more complex postpositional structure that functions as a subordinate adverbial clause in example (9).

(9) hióko-t   'án-po ne híapsa
    misery-on be-in I   live
    I am barely able to survive.

The main verb **'aáyu** seems to be a kind of "stative" as in examples (10) and (11), but sometimes may be glossed as "to have," as in sentences (12) and (13). The variants **'aáu-/'áu-** are elided forms.

(10) sodá-m 'íntok sebé-ka   'áma 'aáyu-k
     soda-PL and   cold-being there be-PRF
     And there are cold sodas there.

(12) tékil né-u 'aáyu-k
     work me-to have-PRF
     I have work. or *There is work for me.*

(11) hiák-nokí 'áu-sú'uli 'itó-t 'aayu-k
     yaqui-word RFL-alone us-on be-PRF
     We spoke only Yaqui.

(13) bácia sakobai-po   'aáyu-k
     seed watermelon-in have-PRF
     The watermelon has seeds in it.

Examples (14)–(15) illustrate the use of **'au**, a reduced form of the verb **'aáyu** *be*.

(14) 'ín kóba-po huébena-ka 'áu-ka-n   tú'u-wa-ta
     my head-in much-being be-PPL-PCN good-NZR-ACC
     There used to be a lot of goodness in my head.

(15) 'ín kóba-po balí 'éeria 'aú-ka-n
     my head-in fresh thought be-PPL-PCN
     There were pleasant thoughts in my head.

The epistemic verb **bé'ee** *to be absent* in Yaqui indicates the lack of something as illustrated in example (16).

(16) wepu'ula-i-ka   híba bé'ee
     one-STAT-being only lack
     There is only one missing.

A somewhat different slant on things is given by one Yaqui existential expression that means "to live." As shown by example (17) this expression includes an incorporated noun to which a form of **-ek** *to have* is suffixed.

(17) hunámani bibá-hímaa-ri-wi   yoéme 'áma
     off:yonder cigarette-throw-NZR-to man   there

     hó'a-k-an   pahkó'olaa-taka-i   táa tú'i-si polóobe
     house-have-PCN festal:dancer-being-PPL but very-AVR poor
     Off yonder in Discarded Cigarette Butts, there used to live a man who was a ritual dancer for the Pascal fiesta, but he was very poor.

Yaqui retains to some degree the use of juxtaposition for indicating certain kinds of equational statements. In this case we can say that "be" is marked by zero, as seen in example (18).

(18) 'iníi'i yóo-páhko'olaa-ta   etého-i
     this   enchanted-festal:dancer-POS relate-PPL
     This is the story about the Enchanted Feaster.

2.2. The "posture" verbs

Yaqui also has a set of "posture" verbs, which can be glossed "be" in general terms. More specifically, these verbs convey notions such as "to lie stretched out," "to lie spread out like a sheet," "to be sitting," or "to be standing." As we have discussed above, the general locative verb **aáne** *be*, illustrated again in sentences (19) and (20).

(19) huébena wásuktia wéye 'ím né 'ané-ka-i
many year go here I be-PPL-PPL
I came here a long time ago.

(20) wá'ema-m-bétana 'áma 'án-wa
Guaymas-PL-from there be-PSV
People from Guaymas were there.

The verb stem **mane** designates entities that are spread out horizontally throughout two dimensions like a lake or an ocean, as illustrated in sentence (21).

(21) hunáma'a 'áme-u káa-mékka b^{w}é'u báu-ba'á-m máne-k
there them-to not-far big lake-water-PL lay-PRF
There not far from/to them was a lake.

The verb stem **hoka** designates entities which are construed as being in a sitting position. A typical example is shown in sentence (22).

(22) yoím 'íntok huébena-ka 'á-u hoká-a 'á'a bít-ču
mexicans and many-being it-to sit-PPL it see-COM
And a lot of Mexicans were around it staring at it.

Yaqui uses the verb stem **kikte** to talk about objects that can stand up (23).

(23) tú'i-si káa 'áa yé'e 'íntok káa 'áa 'etého kía tené-ka kík-nee
very-ADJ NEG able dance CNJ NEG able converse only mouth-having stand-FUT
He was not able to dance well, and he was not able to tell stories very well; he would just stand there with his tongue in his mouth.

A different view of standing is employed in the use of the verb stem **kéča,** as illustrated by sentence (24). This transitive verb may be glossed as "to place in a standing position."

(24) 'áman yéu-kéča-'a-wa-k báhi pahkó'a-m haíbu sumá'i-taka 'áma yé'ee-n
there out-stand:SG-EV-PSV-PRF three feaster-PL now tied-being there dance-PCN
He was taken to where he was to perform, where three "tied" Pascal Dancers were already dancing.

2.3. The imperfective participle -ka

The imperfective participle **-ka** is very productively used in a variety of ways. Often it marks subordinate clauses and can be glossed "being," as it is in sentence (25).

(25) hunáa'a búite-m-ta-béna-ka noká-m-ta ho-hóa
that run-NZR-ACC-like-being word-NZR-ACC RDP-make
That pen, being like a running thing, makes words.

In many of the usages of **-ka,** its meaning is quite schematic and may even be left untranslated, especially when it occurs in attributive adjective constructions such as those illustrated in sentences (26)–(29).

(26) yoóko yoéme búsani-ka 'á'abo 'é-u yáhi-nee
tomorrow men six-being over:here you-to arrive-FUT
Tomorrow six men will come over here to you.

(27) nokí káa-tú'ii-ka né-u yuúma-k
word not-good-being me-to reach-PRF
I got some bad news.

(28) kía háin tala-sáala-i-ka híba n=á'a hí'i-nee
only much shiny-black-PPL-being always I=it drink-FUT
No matter how black it is I will keep on drinking it.

(29) bát^{w}e mayóa-či baáka b^{w}éere-ka yó'o-tu
river edge-on carrizo big-being grow-VR
Tall carrizos are growing by the river.

Strings of adjectives marked by **-ka** may modify a single noun in a sentence, as illustrated in sentence (30).

(30) bakóči-m tú'i-si te-tébe-ka bᵂéere-ka 'áma réhte
snake-PL good-AVR RDP-long-being big-being there walk
Big long snakes were moving there.

In another one of its uses, **-ka** may function to derive adverbial clauses, such as shown in examples (31) and (32).

(31) 'uhyoí-ka kúp-te   (32) 'állea-ka
beautiful-being eve-VR   happy-being
It is a beautiful evening.   *happily*

The schematicity of its meaning allows **-ka** to apply to possessive constructions such as those illustrated in examples (33)–(35). Such usages may represent the convergence of the meaning of **-ka** with the possessive suffix **-ek** (cf. section 3.3. of this chapter), which is seen in example (33) and may influence the meanings of sentences (34)–(36).

(33) čána čukúi-ka sikíi-m puús-ek
chanate black-being red-PL eye-have
The chanate, being black, has red eyes.

(34) hunáka tené-ka k'u-ta bᵂá'e
that:ACC mouth-having mescal-ACC eat
With that mouth he eats baked agave.

(35) wáa'a 'ilí 'uúsi 'áma ho'aa-k-ame 'ée-bépa
that little child there house-PPL-NZR you-above

'ilítci-ka húni'i haibu nok-ta tá'aa
little-being even now word-ACC know
The little boy who lives over there, even though he is smaller than you, he already knows how to read.

(36) áape-la hó'aa-ka kó'okoe wétče-k kaábe 'á'a bítča-k
he-alone live-PPL sick fall-PRF no:one him see-PRF
Because he was living by himself, he got sick and no one took care of him.

The standard of the comparison in comparative equative constructions is also marked by **-ka** as sentence (37) illustrates. This is also true in other kinds of equative constructions, for example those involving adjectives such as that given in example (38).

(37) čé'a húni'i tú'ii sí'ime-m-bépa tú'ii-ka
more even good all-PL:ACC-above good-being
It is better, it is the best of all.

(38) 'áapo káa neu 'á'a téuwaa tá'abᵂí-ka né-u 'á'a téuwaa
he not me-to it tell different-being me-to it tell
It wasn't he who told me, it was somebody else.

2.4. The many-faced modal morpheme mači

The form **maáči** is basically a stative verb meaning "to be visible," "to give off light," "to appear," "to seem to be," and so on. However, it has both nominal and adverbial forms and is also used extensively as a suffix attaching to different parts of speech, displaying a complex network of somewhat different, but related, meanings.

In the following two predicative usages, **maáči** can be glossed "be." These predicative usages show a contrast between one form with a long vowel in example (39) and another form with a short vowel in example (40). In example (39) however, **maáči** functions as a main verb without any phonological or morphological encumbrances, whereas in example (40) the form **máči** is the second element in a compound stem. As noted in COMPOUNDS p. 158, vowel shortening is a common effect of the compounding process.

(39) haí=sa   maáči   húu'u 'ém sá'awa
     how=INTERR appear that   you sore
     How does your sore seem to be? or
     How is your sore?

(40) káita-e   mó'iti-máči
     nothing-INST plow-appear
     There is nothing with which to plow.

Buelna, p. 19, glosses **mači** as "-able/-ible," making the following comment about the modal usages of **mači**: "que siempre son pasivos, se forman... añadiendo... machi al presente de pasiva... **buauamachi** *comestible*, **houamachi** *factible* **nocuamachi** *decible*, **cahibouamachi** *no se puede tejer*.[1]

In sentence (41) **mači** is used twice. In its first occurrence, it is used as a stative verb. In its second occurrence it appears as a nominalization which is the second element in a Noun-Noun compound.

(41) 'í'an tua   maáči   táhi-mači-ria-ta   ká=t=a'a   wáata mečá-bili
     now indeed   light (bright) fire-light-NZR-ACC   not=we=it   want moonlight
     It is real light now, we don't need firelight; there is moonlight.

In other contexts, **mači** functions as a nominal, meaning "daylight," "moonlight," or "firelight," i.e., illumination in general. The combination of **kaa-** negative + **mači** has the conventionalized meaning "darkness." this is illustrated by examples (42) and (43).

(42) káa-mačí-ku   káte
     not-light-in travel-PL
     They traveled in the darkness.

(43) haíbu káa-maáči
     now   not-light
     It is now dark.

In its most concrete predicative usages, **mači** functions as an intransitive verb meaning "to appear" or "to come to light" as in sentences (44)–(45) and as a transitive verb meaning "to reveal X" or "discover" as in sentence (46).

(44) 'éme'e 'á'a hú'uneiyaa wáka'a   káa-yé-'a-mačí-a-'íi'aa-m-ta
     you-PL it   know   that-ACC   not-out-him-appear-VR-IN:DSD-NZR-ACC
     You know the one who doesn't want him to appear.

(45) sáawea yeča-k   haíbu=su tá'ab^{w}i-si   mačí-ka   karpá-m-me-u wéama
     trousers put:on-PRF now=EMP different-AVR   appear-PPL   tent-PL-to   walk
     He put on other trousers and walked to the tent, now appearing totally different.

(46) 'itó-u yé-'a-mačí-a-k   'enčí-m 'a'a hoá-'u
     us-to out-it-appear-VR-PRF your-pl its do-GND
     He revealed to us that you did it.

In many cases, Castro would translate **mači** as either "provoca" or as "dan ganas de," e.g., **b^{w}á'a-máči** *eat-appear* "da ganas de comer." The modal meaning of **mači** with a motion verb is illustrated by example (47).

(47) bát^{w}ee b^{w}é'uu-'u-téa ká-ak   yéu-baa-su-maáči
     river big-EV-QUO   no-where out-cross-COM-appear
     They say that the river is up; apparently there is no place to cross it. or
     They say that the river is up; there appears to be no place to cross it.

In certain of its usages, **mači** has the clear sense of "have." However, **mači** is typical of modals and is hard to translate in many specific cases. In sentences (48), (49), and (50) were the meanings "doable," "plowable," and "burnable." To make sense, one would expect these sentences to be impersonal and the pronominal forms to be in the dative. One would also expect the plural noun form in example (50) to be

---

1 "[They]... are always passives, [and] are formed by adding **machi** to to the present passive... **buauamachi** *edible*, **houamachi** *doable*, **nocuamachi** *sayable*, **cahibouamachi** *it can't be woven*" (Buelna 1891:19).

functioning as an object of a postposition. The use of the subject pronoun clitics in sentences (48) and (49) and the definite plural subject noun in sentence (50) shows that these sentences are not impersonal at all and that the "-able" gloss is inappropriate here. Instead, the appropriate gloss in these instances is the existential meaning "have."

(48) 'í'an né híta hóo-mači
now I thing do-have
I have things to do today.

(50) haámuč-im kaíta náya-'a-máči
woman-PL nothing burn-EV-have
The women have no firewood.

(49) née kaíta-e mó'i-ti-máčí
I nothing-INST plow-PPL-have
I don't have anything to plow with.

The semantics of **-máči** are not always predictable. For example, sentence (51) does not mean "He is able to talk a lot (but who knows whether or not he'll say a thing)," which is the meaning one would expect if **mači** really meant "able." What it actually means is that there are many things this person will say when he/she has a chance.

(51) huébena-k nók-máči
much-ACC talk-"able"
He has a lot to talk about.

There is also a causative use of **máči**, in which it can be glossed as either "do" or "make" in example (52).

(52) kókko-wame káa-tú'íi bʷan-máči
die-PL-NZR not-good cry-make
Death is not good, it makes one cry.

The capacitative use of **máči,** in which it can be glossed "-able," represents a more attenuated version of the causative. In sentence (53) for example, **máči** reflects the continued registry of the impression of someone on another person's mind.

(53) káa-kóp-ta-máči
not-forget-VR-"able"
One doesn't want to forget (him/her/it).

In sentence (54) we have a clear instance of **máči** used in the sense of one's being able to carry out successfully the activity in which he/she is engaged, i.e., searching for a house. This is likely the prototypical value for the capacitative.

(54) kári-ta né haíwa hák-sa né túa 'á'a téu-máči
house-ACC I hunt where-INTERR I really it find-"able"
I am looking for a house; where can I find one?

The capacitative use of **máči** in example (55) reflects the idea of potential success in a given endeavor, whereas that in example (56) carries the idea of moral responsibility. Two different usages of **máči,** the capacitative and the existential, are illustrated in example (57). Finally, sentence (58) gives a capacitative use of **máči** in which inherent characteristics of a fruit are the instigative cause of its being desirable for food, i.e., one can eat it because it is so good.

(55) tú'u-wa-ta 'áma 'emo téu-máči-le-ka-i
good-NZR-ACC there RFL find-"able"-think-PPL-PPL
Because you thought that you would find what was good for you there.

(56) híttoa káa-báa-tá'aru-máči
medicine not-once-lose-"able"
The medicine should by no means be lost.

(57) húu'u hitása bʷá'a-máči káa-nanáu-mači-ka 'áma 'aayu-k
that thing eat-"able" not-same-appear-PPL there be-PRF
There were all kinds of different edible things there.

(58) túa kía híba bʷá'a-maáči
indeed delicious always eat-"able"
It's really delicious; you could eat it anytime.

Many usages of **máči** can be characterized as existential usages. In these cases, **máči** takes adverbial, adjectival or stative verb complements, as illustrated in sentence (59).

(59) té náu-'etého-nee súa-si-maáči-k híkkah-i-maáči-k,
we together-talk-FUT wise-AVR-appear-ACC hear-PPL-appear-ACC

tá'ee-mači-k káa kúh-ti-mači-k téuwaa-nee
know-appear-ACC not anger-PPL-appear-ACC speak-FUT
We will now talk together (about that which is) of intelligence, worth listening to, worth knowing, not irritating.

In sentence (60) **máči** takes a derived adverb **nák-si** *lovingly* as its complement and in sentence (61) it takes a reduplicated derived adverb, also marked with the adverbial suffix **-si**. On the other hand in sentence (62) it takes a derived adjective marked by the qualitative **la-**.

(60) kríhto-ta-bétana nák-si-maáči-m (62) musá'a-la-maáči
Christ-POS-from love-AVR-"able"-PL   pleasant-AVR-appear
those whom Christ loves   *It is very funny/pleasant.*

(61) tú-tu'u-li-si-maáči
RDP-good-PPL-AVR-appear
It is very beautiful.

Other kinds of constituents may also serve as complements to **máči**. In sentence (63) for example, the negative **káa** in construction with the procomplement **húnen** serves as the complement of **máči**.

(63) 'ilí híta-taka káa-húnen-mačí-ka 'itóm musá'a-la yáa-k
little thing-being not-thus-appear-PPL us pleasant-ABS do-PRF
A little thing that didn't seem that way played a trick on us.

Reciprocal adjectives may also serve as complements of **máči**, as seen in sentences (64) and (65).

(64) káa nanáu-mačí-k téuwaa
not alike-seem-ACC talk
(He) talks about all kinds of different things.

(65) húu'u nánnaa-mačí-raa káa nanáu-mačí-ka
that set:fire-appear-ABS not alike-appear-PPL
There was quite an assortment of ridiculousness.

Finally, more nominal elements such as demonstrative pronouns may enter into the structure of the complement of **máči**. In sentence (66) the nominative demonstrative form **huná'aa** is incorporated into the complement structure via an echo-vowel connector, the verbalizer **tu-**, and the participial **ka-**.

(66) túa né káa 'á'a huná-'a-tu-ka-'a-mačí-le-ka
indeed I not him that-EV-PPL-CON-EV-appear-think-PPL
I surely didn't think that he was the one.

Frequently, existential **máči** is linked to verbal complements via the connector **-ti-**, as illustrated by sentences (67) and (68).

(67) 'akí-sóo-'o-ku sebíi-po 'áman-i káa 'áa 'áma réh-ti-mačí-ku 'áman wée
pitahaya-thicket-EV-in cactus-in by-there not able there walk-PPL-appear-in there go
He went through the pitahaya thickets and chollas, places that didn't seem passable.

(68) baá'a-m   haí-ti-mači-m   'áma wo'o-ta-k   húu'u hámut
     water-PL dirty-PPL-appear-PL there throw-VR-PRF that   woman
     The woman threw out dirty water there.

2.5. The adverbial maís/mai-si

As an adverb derived by attaching the suffix **-si,** the morpheme **mači** acquires an extended meaning of "clear" when it is used in the logical or intellectual domain, as in example (69).

(69) hunáma čé'a mačí-si   'á-u   'á'a téuwaa-k
     there   more clear-AVR him-to it   tell-PRF
     He explained it to him more clearly, there.

The adverbial form **maí-si** seems to be a contraction of **maáči** plus **-si,** the adverbializing suffix. The derived adverb has the generalized meaning "in this manner," but retains a partly separate identity. Dedrick had earlier conjectured that **mai-si** might be a variant of **mačí-si.** But it turns out that both may be used in the same construction, and **mačí-si** generally has the meaning "clearly," while **maí-si** means "in this manner," as in example (70). In short, they both have independent status in Yaqui grammar and may well represent different paths of grammaticalization of common elements.

(70) wiíru   b^wé'u bétte-mai-si   né'e
     buzzard big   heavy-manner-AVR   fly
     The turkey buzzard flies "heavily."

The semantics of **maí-si** overlaps with that of **máči** in a variety of its usages. In sentence (71) for example, **maí-si** is used in an existential sense of "to be." On the other hand, in example (72) **maí-si** can be glossed as "able." Its existential meaning comes out in the usage illustrated by example (73), whereas a more generalized meaning of manner is seen in sentence (74).

(71) húme   baá'a-m   káa 'iné-maí-si   sébe
     those water-PL   not feel-appear-AVR   cold
     The water is unendurably cold.

(72) naíki-mét-ta   wée-'e-san   'ábai-m   b^wá'a-maí-si   háp-nee
     four-month-ACC   go:SG-EV-EXP roasting:ear-PL   eat-able-AVR   stand:PL-FUT
     In four months there will be delicious roasting ears standing out here (from these stalks).

(73) haí=sa   maí-s=e'e   hi'i-b^wa-k
     how=INTERR   manner-AVR=you   UNSPEC-eat-PRF
     How was your meal?

(74) baáwe 'uhyolí-si   'amé-beah   bó'o-ka, bít-ču-maí-si
     ocean beautiful-AVR   them-front lay-PPL   see-CMP-manner-AVR
     There was the ocean lying beautifully before them, a sight to stare at.

2.6. The existential -taka

The existential **-taka** can be glossed as "being" or "existing in a particular state of affairs." This suffix is used with nouns, pronouns, attributives, and participials. Most commonly **-taka** predicates the status of someone as seen in examples (75) and (77). It also indicates the quality of material designated by a given noun as in example (76). Finally, it indicates category membership as is the case in example (78).

(75) hunáa'a-sán   kóba-taka   si'ime-m   né-sauwe-me
     that:one-EXP   head-being all-PL   IZR-command-NZR
     That one, being the head, is the ruler of all.

(76) sísi'iwooki sisi'iwók-táka   noóka
     metal   metal-being   talks
     It is metal, being-metal, it talks.

(77) 'áma ho'aa-k-an   pahkó'olaa-taka-i
     there house-have-PCN festal:dancer-being-PPL
     He lived there because of being a festal dancer.

(78) si'ime 'enči   nák-nee   haámuč-im-taka 'o'ówi-m-taka kaábe bé'ee-ka
     all   you:ACC love-FUT woman-PL-being man-PL-being no:one lack-PPL
     Everyone will love you, men, women, lacking no one.

The combination of **-taka** with a pronoun results in an emphatic personal pronoun. Examples (79) and (80) give instances of its use with a first person singular subject pronoun.

(79) hunáka'a yéu-weye-o   'inepo-táka 'áma 'aáne-n
     that:POS out-go-when   I-being   there be-PCN
     I myself was there when that happened.

(80) néhpo-taka húni'i lú'u-ti-nee
     I-being   even end-PPL-FUT
     Even I myself will waste away.

A similar strengthening of the salience of the role of a constituent in the semantic structure of a sentence is seen in the augmentative use of **-taka** with clitics in example (81) and quantifiers in (82).

(81) bʷé'ituk néhpo túa-taka   húnen 'emó-u hiia   (82) 'intok si'ime-taka húni'i
     because   I   indeed-being   thus you-to say   and   all-being   even
     Because I truly tell you so.   *and even everyone*

In examples (83)–(85) **-taka** suffixes to derived adjectives that reflect the last stage of a change of state.

(83) puh-báhiya-táka   húni'i bʷaána
     face-swollen-being even   cry
     Her face is swollen from so much crying.

(84) kúta pú'ato-m báksia-taka   mo-móbe-laa-čá'a-ka
     wood plate-PL washed-being RDP-face:down-PPL-suspend-PPL
     The washed wooden plates were lying face down.

(85) sép kóčo-k   bʷé'ituk yumia-taka wée-n
     at:once-sleep-PRF because tired-being go-PCN
     He slept at once, being very tired.

A very common usage of **-taka** is its occurrence with participials. This, in fact, may be its statistically most frequent use. In sentence (86) **-taka** is suffixed to the verb **mačúk** *to grasp* via the ubiquitous connective **-ti-**. In sentence (87) it suffixes to the participial **-laa**.

(86) bʷáaro-m senú mačúk-ti-taka   mámni sentáabo-m   (87) lót-ti-laa-taka   ne wée
     green-PL one grasp-PPL-being five cent-PL   tire-PPL-PPL-being   I   go
     A bunch of greens is five cents.   *I am very tired as I go along.*

Nominalized verbs may occur as the base for **-taka** as seen in sentence (88). This construction may be viewed as a heightened existential, i.e., "the existing one being in X state."

(88) bakót kó'oko-si 'aú-la-taka   húya-u kibák-ek
     snake pain-AVR be-NZR-being wood-to enter-PRF
     The wounded snake entered the woods.

2.7. The appelative -tea

The appelative **téa(n)** *to be named X* or *to be called X* and the verb **téa/téu** *to discover, to find* are superficially the same, but they are readily distinguishable from their behavior in broader contexts, i.e., by the distinct kinds of complements that they occur with. Note the following contrast between sentences (89) and (90).

(89) hai=sa   'émpo tea-k
    how=INTERR you name-have
    What is your name?

(90) 'án-a'a téa-k
    I- it   find-PRF
    I found it.

The morphemic structures are quite different in the two examples given above. The first consists of the nominal form **tea** *name* in construction with one form of the possessive suffix **-ek.** The second example contains the verb **tea** *to find* followed by the perfective suffix **-k.** The suffix **-tea** is commonly used with proper names and in such cases the constructional meaning may be glossed as "his/her name is X." Example (91) is typical.

(91) 'áapo hóan-tea
    he   John-be:named
    His name is John.

A distinct constructional meaning is invoked when the proper noun **-tea** is put into a relative clause. In this case **-tea** is preceded by both a reduced form of the agentive nominalizer **-ame** and the accusative suffix **-ta**, typical diagnostics of relative clause status in Yaqui. The constructional meaning is "the one who is called X."

(92) 'usi-hámut-ta   ne hariu-si-sime matilede-'e-tea-m-ta
    child-woman-ACC I hunt-RDP-go   matilede-EV-name-NZR-ACC
    I am looking for a girl named Matilde.

Further examples of the vowel alternations preceding **-tea** can be found in PHONOLOGY p. 27–28 where the usage of the echo vowel was given. Note also that accusative marking occurs on all of the constituents that designate the complement of "look for," whereas the nominals that serve as the complements of **-tea** are not so marked, i.e., ***matilede-ta-tea** is an impermissible form. Also note the incorporated noun in the second half of (93).

(93) widobro-'o-téa-ka   kobanáo-tu-ka-n
    Huidobro-EV-name-having governor-VR-PPL-PCN
    One named Huidobro was governor.

In examples (94)–(96) **-tea** serves as a quotative marker, taking an entire sentence as its complement. This evidential use anchors the source of information to the shared knowledge of the community and allows the speaker to avoid taking personal responsibility for the statement that he/she makes.

(94) 'émpo káa téa-tua-ri-'i-tea
    you   not name-CAU-PPL-EV-QUO
    It is said (they say) that you are not named.

(95) 'áu   bamíh-tua-me   láuti muk-née-'e-tea
    him-RFL hurry-CAU-NZR soon die-FUT-EV-QUO
    They say that one who hurries will die soon.

(96) yó'o-taka huni'i póčo'o-ku weáma-'a-tea
    old-being even woods-in walk-EV-QUO
    They say that even though you are old, you live/walk in the woods.

2.8. The remote appelative N + -roka "to say to be"

In contrast to the appelative **-tea** which is linked to the time of speaking, Yaqui employs the evidential **-roka** to relate the content of a statement to states of affairs temporally removed from the time of speaking, i.e., either past or future. Generally **-róka** *to say to be* is used with verbs but in sentences (97) and (98) below, it is used as a kind of a verbalizer meaning "to call or designate someone as being in a particular kinship relationship."

(97) lolá-ta   'asóa-m 'iika'a   'ábači-roka-n
    Lola-POS children-PL this:one:ACC big:brother-QUO-PCN
    Lola's children called this fellow "Big Brother."

(98) née két 'á'a 'áe-rók-nee
    I   also her mother-QUO-FUT
    I will also call her "mother."

Several instances of its usage show that -roka has its source in a main verb. In sentence (99) -roka takes a complement and is linked to the verb stem **noí** *come* by the connector -ti- in the common V1-ti-V2 construction. In sentence (100) -roka is in construction with the incorporated derived noun **hínko'o-laa** *a race*. In sentence (101) -roka suffixes directly to the motion verb **wée** *to go:SG*. Morphologically, the usage in (101) is the most semantically transparent suffixal usage that we have observed thus far. The example given in sentence (102) shows an echo-vowel intervening between -roka and the verb stem **yéča** *to place standing up*. This would appear to represent the logical end in the grammaticalization of **roka** as a main verb to -roka as a suffix.

(99) 'á'abo   'itó-u noí-ti-roka
    over:here us-to come-PPL-QUO
    He says that he is coming to visit us.

(100) 'itápo 'íntok náu   hínko'o-laa-rok-nee
    we   and   together race-PPL-QUO-FUT
    And we will say that we are going to run a race.

(101) hó'aa-raa-po náa-búuh-ti   wée-róka-n
    home-ABS-in on-through-AVR go-QUO-PCN
    He said that he was going on through the villages.

(102) sí'ime 'úb^Wan-ta 'ém mám-po yéča-'a-roka
    all   plea-ACC   your hand-in put-EV-QUO
    He says he is going to put all requests in your hands.

3.0. Have

The notion of "have" is handled by both main verbs and suffixation in Yaqui. The main verbs include **'aáne**, **híp^Wee**, and **'áttea**. The suffixes include **maáči**, **-ek**, and **-ka**.

3.1. The main verbs 'aáne, híp^Wee, and 'áttea

In example (1) the main verb **'aáne** occurs in construction with the nominal **hiókot** *suffering*, in this case taking on the extended meaning "to have."

(1) 'í'an 'íntok hiókot 'ané-ka wéama
    now and   suffer be-PPL walk
    And now he walks with difficulty.

The main verb **híp^Wee** has two phonological variants, **híp^Wee** and **hípu'u**. This verb is used to designate one's personal belongings in general as in examples (2) and (3) or to designate discrete possessed objects as in example (4).

(2) yú'in ne híta híp^Wee   (4) lántanaas-im né két híp^Wee
    much I thing have   banana-PL   I also have
    I have lots of things.   *I also have bananas.*

(3) 'iníen né sí'ime-m náu   hípu'u-bae
    thus I all-PL   together have-DSD
    I want to keep them all together in this way.

In addition, Spanish usage has influenced Yaqui as in the expression of certain abstract concepts, e.g., wisdom, in which the concept is conceived of as being possessed, e.g., **súawata híp^Wee** *he has wisdom*. But I do not believe this is "native" Yaqui since the way to say "he is wise" would be **'áapo súa-wa-ek**.

The verb **'áttea** *one's possessions* is frequently used of clothing as in examples (5)–(6).

(5) táa 'í'an té náu 'á'a 'attea-k
    but now we together it have-PRF
    But now we both own it together.

(6) 'ín 'áttea-mak ne káa tiíwe
    my possession-with I not ashamed
    I am not ashamed of my clothing.

3.2. More about maáči

As we have noted above, the highly flexible **maáči** is also used in the sense of "have." This represents the grammaticalization of an implication of the meaning "appear" that often attaches to **maáči**, i.e., if nothing appears in one's memory, then he/she has nothing to draw on for giving an answer to someone.

(7) húu'u 'uúsi kaá-čin 'á'a yoopna-mačí-ka, 'ínen hiía
    that child no-way him answer-ADJ-PPL thus said
    The boy, not having any idea what to answer, said...

In the following sentences, **mači** is used in the sense of "have" in one clause and the verb **bit** *to see* is used in the metaphorical sense of "to experience" in the other clause.

(8) wáka'a kó'oko-si mačí-k bém bít-ne-'e-po
    that-ACC pain-AVR have-PRF their see-FUT-EV-NZR
    the suffering that they will experience

(9) tá'ab^wi-si mačí-m né bít-laa
    different-AVR light-PL I see-PRF
    I have seen a different kind.

3.3. The possessive verbal suffixes -ek and -ka

Yaqui draws on two derivational verbal suffixes for expressing possessive relations. These are **-ek** and **-ka**, morphemes with distinct historical roots, but with overlapping meanings and sometimes homophonous shapes.

The conceptual categories BE, HAVE and DO are notoriously mixed together in the history of the Uto-Aztecan languages (Langacker 1977:39, 43). This merging of categories is probably nowhere seen better in Yaqui than in the pair of derivational suffixes **-ek** and **-ka**.

The suffix **-ek**, which most commonly signals the notion "have" in Yaqui, is in certain contexts homophonous with the highly polysemous participial **-ka**. In examples (10) and (11) **-ek** suffixes to the body part noun **puúsi** "eye." In these two examples, we can construe the possessive relationship as an inalienable one. Sentences (10) and (11) also illustrate the use of both the participial **-ka** and possessive **-ek**. Usually the usages of **-ka** and **-ek** are readily distinguishable, as these examples show clearly, with **-ka** suffixing to adjectives and **-ek** suffixing to body part nouns.

(10) wépul-ka-tána tósaim puús-ek
     one-being-from white-PL eye-have
     He has a white eye on one side.

(11) čána čukúi-ka sikíi-m puús-ek
     black bird black-being red-ACC:PL eye-has
     Though the blackbird is black, it has red eyes.

The suffix **-ek,** and its allomorph **-k** are very productively used with nouns to form possessive statements with the meaning "to have X." A typical example in which the possessed item is a domestic animal is given in example (12).

(12) húu'u Hóan b^wé'uu-k kába'e-k
     that John big-ACC horse-have
     John has a big horse.

Note that in example (12), the combination of **kaba'e** *horse* with **-ek** *to have* results in the predicative construction "to own a horse" and has the phonological form **kába'e-k**.[2] Similarly, the body part noun **woki** *foot* drops its final vowel when suffixed by possessive **-ek**, as illustrated in example (13).

(13) 'ahaa n-ačai   o'olaa   tu'i-si   n=am yi'i-pea
     aha my-father ancient good-ADV I=them dance-DSD

   taa nee kaa=tu'ii-m   wok-ek.
   CJN I   NEG=good-PL foot-have
   "*Aha! my revered father, how I wish I could dance to that music, but I just don't have good legs.*"

A clear usage of **-ka** with the meaning "have" is given in sentence (14). Note that in this usage, **-ka** is suffixed to the body part **bʷási** "tail" by means of a connector vowel **-a**.

(14) sambáyo bʷási-a-ka   née wómta-k wíča-pú'i   tené-ka   né-u bit-ču
     fluffy tail-CON-having me scare-PRF sharp-point mouth-having me-to stare
     A thing with a fluffy tail scared me; a thing with a tiny pointed mouth stared at me.

We provide additional usages of **-ek** and **-ka** with further discussion of their morphemic status in VERB MORPHOLOGY, pp. (137–138).

One interesting aspect of the meaning of the participializing suffix **-ka** shown by sentence (15) is that it acts like a stative verb when affixed to adjectivals, and as a verbalizer meaning "having" when affixed to nouns.

(15) húnen á'a 'éa-o=su   hunáma'a téh-po   yóo-číba'ato   tósai-ka,
     thus his think-when=EMP there   cave-in enchanted-goat white-being

   čúkui-ka   tána-la   bʷási-a-ka, káa 'awá-ka   kía tét-tebe-m   náka-k
   black-being curve-ADJ tail-have-EV NEG horn-having only RDP-long-PL ear-having

   tét-tebe-m púh-sé'ebe-k   bátte bʷíia-u   núki-m hímse-ka   'á-u yéu-búite
   RDP-long-PL eye-lash-having nearly ground-to reach-PL beard-having him-to out-run
   As he was going along with these thoughts, a black and white enchanted goat, hornless, with his tail curved over his back, with long ears, very long eyelashes, and a beard that reached nearly to the ground, came running out toward him.

4.0. Do

The concept of "do", or more specifically "make" may be expressed in Yaqui by the main verbs **yáa/yá'a-** *to do, to make* and **hoóa** *to make*. Also related to this domain of the grammar are the causative suffix **-te** *to make*, (as in **kaa-te** *to make a house*), the agentive **-reo/-leo** *a doer*, and the intentive **-'u** *to go to do X, to go for X*.

---

[2] Interestingly enough the constructional meaning "to own a horse" carries over into all of the tense/aspect combinations, as seen in the following forms. (Data from Eloise Jelinek.)
   kába'i-bae   *is going to have a horse*
   kába'i-ne   *will have a horse*
   kába'i-su-kan *used to have a horse*
   kába'i-mači   *should have a horse*
   kába'i-'ean   *should have had a horse*
The question arises as to why all these mean "have a horse," even though there is no sign of possessive **-ek** in them. The answer we give is that the conventional construal of the construction is that the connection between a man and a horse is typically one of ownership which carries over into all the tense/aspect choices the speaker has at his/her disposal. From a strictly formal account, the fact that there is no trace of possessive **-ek** in all of the above forms argues that the **-ek** in example (12) is actually the perfective suffix, and is not a possessive at all in this context. We view it otherwise, however.

4.1. The main verb yáa

The main verb **yáa** takes both indefinite pronouns and specific nouns as its object and applies to both abstract and concrete entities. The indefinite pronoun **híta** serves as an incorporated object noun in sentence (16).

(16) kée   'é'e híta yáa
 not:yet you thing do
 You haven't done a thing yet.

Discrete object nouns marked by **-ta** frequently occur with **yáa** and represent the prototypical transitive clause construction, as illustrated in sentences (17)–(20).

(17) 'enčí sík   ne tá'ab^w i tékil-ta   yá'a-nee
 you go:PRF I different work-ACC do-FUT
 When you go, I will do different work.

(18) 'íka'a   né-sau-ta   née yá'a-ria
 this:ACC IZR-order-ACC me do-APL
 Do this chore for me.

(19) 'iníka'a 'ánia-ta yáa-k-ame
 this:ACC world-ACC make-PRF-NZR
 the maker of this world

(20) 'aásoh-ta né-t   yáa-ka   póčo'o-kun weám-bae
 garlic-ACC me-on make-PPL woods-in   walk-DSD
 I put garlic on me because I want to walk in the woods.[3]

In sentence (21) the accusative form of a demonstrative pronoun functions as the direct object of **yáa**, whereas in sentence (22) an incorporated concrete noun assumes that function within the verb of the relative clause. Note also that incorporated object nouns in Yaqui are not marked with the accusative suffix **-ta**.

(21) hái=s-ea-ka-i   'émpo hunúka'a yáa-k
 how=Q-think-PPL-PPL you   that:ACC do-PRF
 Why did you do that?

(22) béa-m   né-nenka súpe-yá'a-ri-ka-i
 skin-ACC:PL RDP-sell shirt-make-PPL-PPL-PPL
 He sells skins that have been made into shirts.

4.2. The main verb hoóa

The second main verb that Yaqui uses for these kinds of concepts is the verb **hoóa** *to do, to make*. The usage of **hoóa** to mean "to make" is clearly evident in example (23). Here the incorporated noun is actually the subject of a passive clause. The noun **kúnwo** actually designates the material from which the passive subject is made and can be viewed as filling a SOURCE role, but it is unmarked in Yaqui.

(23) kúnwo wíko'o-hóo-wa
 (a tree) bow-make-PSV
 Bows are made of "kunwo" wood.

The schematic meaning "do" is illustrated by the use of **hoóa** in sentences (24) and (25). Example (24) also illustrates the incorporation of an indefinite pronoun into the verb complex. In example (25) **hoóa** is the first verb of a double verb compound.

(24) Liós 'áa híta hoóa   (25) 'í'ani né túa   kaíta   hóo-máči
 God able thing do-exist   today I indeed nothing do
 God can work miracles.   *There is absolutely nothing for me to do today.*

---

3   A little bit of cultural knowledge makes this statement clear, i.e., the Yaquis say that garlic will repel rattlesnakes.

A more abstract causative meaning of **hoóa** is given in sentence (26). In this instance, we can gloss **hoóa** as "to bring upon X." In this sentence the condition brought upon the Yaqui nation is expressed in a postpositional phrase, whereas the indirect object **hiáki** *Yaqui* is marked in the accusative.

(26) 'íka'a   hiáki-ta   hióko-t   hóo-su-k
     this:ACC Yaqui-ACC misery-on do-CPL-PRF
     They brought much misery upon the Yaqui nation.

In WH-questions, the direct object of **hoóa** is fronted to immediately follow the WH-word. The direct object noun is itself marked with the accusative **-ta** and then the question marker =**sa** is attached as a postclitic to the accusative noun, as seen in sentence (27).

(27) híta   tékil-ta=sa   'émpo 'áa   hoóa
     thing work-ACC=Q   you   able do
     What kind of work can you do?

4.3. The agentive suffix -leo

Other means that Yaqui employs to signal the concept of "do" include the agentive suffix **-leo**, which has the alternate form of **-reo** and can be glossed as "a doer." Typical usages are illustrated in sentences (28) and (29).

(28) húme'e kanóa-reo-m   bát^{w}e mayóa-t   'aáne-n
     those   boat-AGT-PL   river   edge-on   be-PCN
     The boatmen were at the river's edge.

(29) húu'u kuču-leo b^{w}é'u kúču-ta   'á'a mikka-k
     the   fish-AGT big   fish-ACC   him   give-PRF
     The fisherman gave him a big fish.

4.4. The intentive suffix -'u

Adverbials also relate to the Yaqui elements that signal "do." In particular, Yaqui employs the suffix **-'u** to convey the meaning "go to do X," as in sentences (30)–(31). This suffix attaches to incorporated nouns and is the grammaticalized version of an erstwhile bound postposition that possibly meant "off there at X location." This is illustrated in greater detail in VERB MORPHOLOGY, p. 135?

(30) basó-'u-k   húu'u péipe
     grass-go:do-PRF   that   Philip
     Philip went to get grass.

(31) yokó=ne   kékke-'u-bae
     tomorrow=I   cut:wood-go:do-DSD
     I am going to go cut firewood tomorrow.

NONDISTINCT ARGUMENT PHENOMENA

1.0. Introduction

This section concerns grammatical phenomena that are grouped together under the rubric "Nondistinct Argument Phenomena." This term refers to the way that Yaqui signals the marking of unspecified subjects and objects, reflexive objects, and passive and impersonal sentences. All these kinds of sentences are used to talk about situations in which both a subject and an object are participants in the conceptual scene to which the sentence structure is being related. Nevertheless, these sentence types do not highlight the difference between these two potential arguments of the verb, but rather they highlight the lack of any contrast between the entities serving as subject and object. Yaqui, and Uto-Aztecan in general, does this in a variety of ways, ranging from situations in which the subject and object are identical to the case in which neither the subject nor the object is particularly salient to the characterization of the conceptual scene associated with the meaning of the sentence.

2.0. Unspecified subjects and objects

The first set of morphemes that we discuss are the markers for unspecified subjects and objects. The specific morphemes in the group include **yee-** "unspecified plural human object," **hi'i-** "unspecified inanimate object," and **ne-** "unspecified human subject or object."

2.1. The unspecified plural object marker yee-

Yaqui retains traces of markings for unspecified objects at various points in its grammar. One of these is found in the use of **yee-** to indicate unspecified human objects, conventionally construed to designate people in general. This is illustrated by examples (1)–(6). The corresponding Mayo form is **yore-**, meaning "relating to people in general." Historically, this object marker is probably derived from **yoéme** or **yoréme** *a person*.

(1) 'áapo kía yée-mahtá-bae
he just people-teach-DSD
He just wants to teach people.

(2) miísi yée-súke
cat people-scratch
A cat scratches people.

(3) híta téuwaa-ka húni'i yée-'át-tua-nee
thing say-PPL even people-laugh-CAU-FUT
Anything he says makes people laugh.

(4) yée-yó'ore
people-respect
He respects people.

(5) ču'ú yee-buúe
dog people-scold
A dog growls at people.

(6) 'únna-m hita yée-bʷá-bʷá'a-ria
much-PL thing people-RDP-eat-APL
They eat a lot of people's things.

Occasionally **yee** is still used as a free form. In example (7) **yee** occurs in sentence initial position, immediately preceeding the matrix verb **'aa** *be able to do X*, but it is actually the direct object of the embedded verb **bai-tat-ta'aa** *to deceive*. This contrasts with the more common bound form given in example (8).

(7) yée 'áa bai-tát-ta'áa
people able cool-RDP-know
He is a deceiver.

(8) tú'ii bo'ó-t yée-puh-te-tua-me
good road-on people-eye-VR-CAU-NZR
the one who causes people to "see" the good road

A surface ambiguity between **yee-** *people* and **yeu-** *outside* can arise when either of these combine with a following pronoun. Both forms shorten to **yé-**, as by the process represented in example (9).

(9) yée 'ám-máka > yé'am-máka   *he gives them to people*

2.2. The unspecified inanimate object marker hi'i-

The inanimate unspecified marker **hi'i-** has a reduced form **hi-** and is the most productive of the unspecified object markers that Yaqui employs. It generally indicates that someone is performing some kind of action on "things in general." A common effect of its use with transitive verbs is to lower the degree of transitivity inherent to the composite verb. Thus in many contexts it carries out the role of an intransitivizer. This prefix is probably a reduced form of the indefinite pronoun **hita** *a thing*.

A restricted number of transitive verbs can be marked with the inanimate unspecified object marker **hí'i-**. These verbs include **béeba/bép-** *to hit*, **bwá'e** *to eat*, **číke** *to sweep, brush*, **čoóna** *to strike*, **čó'ilaa** *to lasso*, **kó'a/kó'o-** *to chew*, **má'ako** *to chop*, **múhe** *to shoot someone*, and **ná'ikia** *to separate*.

The use of **hí'i-** with a verb precludes the use of an overt direct object nominal or pronoun. In many cases, the meaning difference between the verb in its fully transitive usage and its usage with **hí'i-** is transparent. Thus the transitive usage of **čó'ila** means "to rope X, to lasso X," as in example (10). In its nominalized form, it is both marked with the shortened variant **hí-** and the passive suffix **-wa** and can be translated "roping," as in example (11).

(10) kábá'i máhhai-m-ta   né čó'ila-k
     horse fear-NZR-ACC I   rope-PRF
     I roped a wild horse.

(11) waká-kóau ne weáma-n bʷé'uu-si hi-čó'ilaa-wa
     cow-pen   I walk-PCN big-AVR IZR-rope-PSV
     I was there in the cow pen; roping was going on in a big way.

The transitive stem **béeba** in its transitive usages can be glossed "to strike X, to hit X," as in example (12). In its intransitive usages with **hí-**, it can be glossed simply "to hit" or "to hit at," as in example (13).

(12) kúta-e   'á'a béeba húka'a bakót-ta
     stick-INST it hit   that:ACC snake-ACC
     Hit that snake with a stick.

(13) húya-m-násuk   hí-bép-síme-n
     brush-PL-among IZR-hit-go:SG-PCN
     He was striking out as he went through the bushes.

The transitive usages of **kó'a/kó'o-** give it the meaning "to chew X" as in example (14). Its intransitive usages with **hí-** can often be glossed as "to chew" or "to masticate" as in sentences (15)–(16).

(14) yoi-sána-ta   kó'a-síme-n
     Mexican-cane-ACC chew-go-PCN
     He was going along chewing sugar-cane.

(15) mékka-'a-ria-t   wéye-ka hi-kó'o-sime
     far:NZR-EV-APL-on   go-GND IZR-chew-go
     He went along chewing off in the distance. (chewing roasting ears)

(16) bóa-yáhu-yáhu-ti   hi-kó'a
     wool-RDP-ripple-CON IZR-chew
     The hair on his back ripples in rhythm as he chews his cud.

The verb **čoóna** is ordinarily glossed as "to strike or to slap someone" when it is used transitively as in sentence (17). When nominalized, **čoóna** is marked with the unspecified object prefix **hi-** and can take the accusative suffix **-ta** when used as a direct object as shown by example (18).

(17) tení-t   'á'a čó-čón-tébo-k
    mouth-on him RDP-hit-IMP-PRF
    He commanded him to hit him in the mouth.

(18) Liós 'é-t   'á'a nót-ta-nee   'inika'a hi-čón-ta
    God you-on it return-VR-FUT this:ACC IZR-slap-ACC
    God will pay you back for this slap.

In its usages with an overt object nominal, as in sentence (19), the verb stem **číɾke** can be glossed as "to brush." In its intransitive usages with the unspecified object marker **hí-**, **číɾke** conventionally means "to sweep" as in sentence (20). The unspecified object marker comprises one element in the derived nominal form **hičikía** *brush, broom*. Finally, a more specialized meaning "to comb the hair" arises when **číɾke** is compounded with the object noun **čón,** as is the case in sentence (21). This latter verb takes the reflexive clitic.

(19) hímsim-mea sí'ime púhba-t 'á'a čike
    beard-INST all   face-on him brush
    He brushed him in the face with his beard.

(20) maála 'obí-si   'aáne kári-po hí-číke
    mother busy-AVR be   house-in IZR-sweep
    Mother is busy, she is sweeping in the house.

(21) húu'u hámut 'áu čón-číke
    that woman RFL hair-comb
    That woman is combing her hair.

Note that with **hi'i-** the verb stem **b^{w}a'e** indicates eating in general, in sentences (22)–(23), and that there is no specification whatsoever of what food item is involved. The use of an unspecified object marker precludes marking for a direct object also, but with causatives, both a direct object clitic and the prefix **hi'i-** can occur together when they designate conceptually distinct entities such as the one given something to eat and the entity given for consumption as in sentence (23). Examples (24)–(25) illustrate prototypical transitive uses of this verb with compound nouns marked with the accusative **-ta**.

(22) 'á'a hó'aa-u siɾka,   hí'i-b^{w}á-betčí'ibo
    his house-to go:SG:PRF IZR-eat-for
    He went to his house to eat.

(23) 'á'a hi'i-b^{w}á-tua-k
    him IZR-eat-CAU-PRF
    He fed him.

(24) kúču-bák-ta   né b^{w}á'a-ka
    fish-stew-ACC I eat-PRF
    I ate some fish stew.

(25) bémpo wáka-bák-ta   b^{w}á'ee
    they beef-stew-ACC eat
    They are eating beef stew.

In its transitive use, the verb **má'ako** means "to chop X down" as is illustrated in example (26). In its usage with **hí'i,** it simply means "to chop" as shown in example (27).

(26) b^{w}é'u húya-ta má'ako-k
    big   tree-ACC chop-PRF
    He chopped down a big tree.

(27) née 'áa hi-má'ako tép^{w}a-m-mea
    I   able IZR-chop axe-PL-INST
    I know how/am able to chop with an ax.

In sentence (27) the role of **-m-** to mark accusative plural may also be that of functioning as the base for attaching the instrumental postposition. However, its function here is not crystal clear because the nominal **tép^{w}am** *axes* is conventionally taken as a plural noun.

The examples (28)–(29) show that the result of passivization of a verb places **hi'i-** in the role of unspecified subject. There are two verbs in sentence (28), **kót-ta** *to break* (*transitive*) and **béeba** *to hit* (*transitive*). Possibly, a better equivalent would be: "The horse's leg was broken because of being hit so hard."

(28) kába'i mám-kót-ti   hi-bép-wa-k
    horse leg-break-PPL IZR-hit-PSV-PRF
    A horse's leg was broken from being hit.

(29) áapo húka'a   kába'i-ta máma-m kót-ta-k
    he   that:ACC horse-POS leg-PL break-VR-PRF
    He/it broke the horse's leg.

With an overt subject noun, the verb **ná'ikia** means "to separate into distinct groups." This usage is given in sentence (30). With an overt object nominal, it means "to divide" or "to break X into pieces" as it does in example (31). When it is marked with **hí'i-**, **ná'ikia** means "to count," as in example (32).

(30) húme'e híaki-m   'áman   ná'iki-m-te-k
     those Yaqui-PL there   divide-NZR-VR-PRF
     The Yaquis separated there. (i.e., *scattered; broke up into separate groups*)

(31) 'itépo 'itó náu   tóha-k,   páan-im ná'iki-m-te-bae-ka
     we   RFL together come-PRF   bread-PL divide-NZR-VR-DSD-PPL
     We came together in order to break bread.

(32) senú-takáa   hi-ná'ikia-wa-'a-po
     one-body (20)   IZR-divide-PSV-EV-GND
     When counting, it is twenty.

2.3. The unspecified animate subject or object marker né-

The unspecified object marker **né-** is used to designate people or living things. It has a very limited distribution. In our data, **sáuwe** *to command, to order*, **haás** *to follow*, and **ne-hun** *to invite* are the only transitive verbs we have identified with certainty that use this prefix.

The examples below show the verb **sauwe** taking a direct object in sentence (33) and a reflexive object in sentence (34). In neither case does it carry the prefix **ne-**; this morphological contrast strongly suggests that **ne-** retains synchronic status as an unspecified object marker, albeit one that has largely fallen into disuse.

(33) haí=sa=ne   'án-nee, 'ínepo ká='am   sáuwe
     how=INTERR=I   do-FUT   I   NEG=them   command
     What can I do, I do not command them?

(34) née=káa yá'u-ra-k,   ínepo 'íno sáuwe
     I=not chief-ABS-have   I   RFL   order
     I am under no one's authority, I govern myself.

In its intransitive usages with **ne-**, **sáuwe** conventionally means "to rule" or "to govern," as in sentence (35). It also has a nominalized form that is marked with ne- and means "orders" as in sentence (36).

(35) woi-takáa   wásuktia-m-po   'áma né-sau-pea-n
     two-body(40)   year-PL-in   there UNSPEC-order-DSD-PCN
     He was wanting to rule there for forty years.

(36) bo'ó-t   hapté-ka   né-sáu-ta   yáa-k
     road-on stand-PPL UNSPEC-order-ACC   do-PRF
     Taking to the road, they carried out the orders.

The stem **haáse** means "to follow" when it is used transitively as in example (37). When used with the unspecified animate object prefix, it has the conventional specialized meanings of "to track someone" or "to track animals" as in example (38).

(37) senú-k   wók-háa-sai-wa-'a-te-k-o
     one-ACC foot-follow-IMP-PSV-EV-VR-PRF-if
     if I am ordered to follow someone

(38) née 'áa   né-h-ha'ase
     I   able UNSPEC-RDP-follow
     I am able/know how to track (animals).

Example (39) below shows a passive form of the transitive verb stem **ne-hun-** *to invite*. This may be cognate with Guarijío **uhúla-ni** *to send him, to give him an order*, Tarahumara **hu-rá** *to send*, and the Eudeve **hurán** *to send* (cf. Miller 1988:89, no. **hu**-13). Both semantic motivation and historical phonological motivation exist for this identification of these forms with Yaqui **hun.** In addition, Mayo has the attested form **né-hune** *to invite* (Larry Hagberg, personal communication). The passivization of this stem, marked with the unspecified object marker **ne-**, again shows how an unspecified object marker can come to have the meaning of "unspecified subject."

(39) kó'okoi-m-po b^wé'úu-si páhkó-baa-wa-o 'áman né-hun-wa-k.
Cocorit-PL-in big-AVR feast-DSD-PSV-when there UNSPEC-invite-PSV-PRF
When there was going to be a big feast in Cocorit, he was invited there.

A possible alternate morphemic shape **nat-** occurs only with the stem **témae** *to question* in sentence (41). The transitive counterpart is illustrated by example (40). Here **témae** has a reduplicated stem, indicating plurality of the subject.

(40) 'emé'e káa 'ím hák 'á'a bít-laa-tí 'ám te-témae-k
you:PL NEG here somewhere him see-PPL-CON them RDP-ask-PRF
"You all have not seen him anywhere around here, have you?" they asked them.

(41) née káa hú'unea b^wé'ituk né káa nát-temae-k
I NEG know because I NEG UNSPEC-ask-PRF
I don't know, because I didn't ask.

3.0. Reflexive objects

The prototypical reflexive sentence designates a situation in which the subject and object are identical, i.e., the subject of the sentence engages in some action which is directed toward himself, as in sentences (42)–(45).

(42) káa 'áu wóm-ta-k
not RFL be:scared-VR-PRF
He didn't let himself be afraid.

(43) 'áu yó'ori-tébo
RFL respect-CAU
He causes himself to be respected.

(44) 'áu bamíh-tua-me láuti mú-nee-'e-tea
RFL hurry-CAU-NZR quickly die-FUT-EV-QUO
It is said that one who hurries himself, will die soon.

(45) hunáme béha 'ée-béas hoóte-k 'emó hiák-yáa-ka-i
those then you-front stand:PL-PRF RFL yaqui-make-PPL-STAT
Those are the ones who stood in front of you, having made themselves into Yaquis.

First person singular reflexive objects are marked by the pronominal form **'íno** as in example (46).

(46) née=káa yá'u-ra-k 'ínepo 'íno sáuwe
I=not chief-ABS-have I RFL order
I am under no one's authority, I govern myself.

Example (47) involves an interesting variety of coordination in which the suffix **-bae** on the verb of the second clause is construed as also holding within its scope the verb of the initial clause. This is substantiated by the way that Castro translated it into Spanish. In sentence (48) the reflexive clitic in first position in the clause serves as a base for attaching a following subject clitic.

(47) 'á'a tá'aa-ka 'á-e 'íno 'anía-báe   (48) 'inó=nee bam-sí-biča
it know-PPL it-with RFL help-DSD   RFL=I hurry-AVR-see
I want to know it and help myself with it.   *I am in a hurry.*
[Castro: "aprender y ayudarme con ello."]

As previous examples have illlustrated, third person singular reflexive objects are marked by the pronoun **'áu**. An additional use of this with an applicative verb is given in example 49).

(49) káa 'áa 'áu nók-ria
not able RFL talk-APL
He is not able to speak on his own behalf.

First person plural reflexive objects are marked by the pronoun **'íto.** Emphatic pronouns may also accompany reflexive pronouns in these sentences, as the example in (50) shows.

(50) 'itépo hú'ena-m-po 'ito-biča.
we evil-PL-in RFL-see
We are experiencing hard times.

Second person plural reflexives are marked by the reflexive pronominal form **'émo** as in example (51).

(51) kát 'émo tíu-tua
not RFL shame-CAU
Don't be ashamed.

Third person plural reflexives are also marked by the reflexive pronoun **'émo.** Typical examples are given in (52)–(54).

(52) híta 'émo huiwa-le-ka réhte-me 'íntok
thing RFL feel-think-PPL walk:PL-NZR and
'emó habé-le-ka tat-ta'ab^w i-mak kúakte
RFL someone-think-PPL RDP-different-with turn
People who go around thinking that they are offended, and because they have a high opinion of themselves, they turn to others.

(53) tú'u-wa-ta 'áma 'emó téu-mači-le-ka-i
good-NZR-ACC there RFL find-seem-think-PPL-PPL
Because they think that they will find there that which is good for them.

(54) 'emó hábe-le-me
RFL someone-think-NZR
those who think they are great

The notion "reciprocal" is inherently plural. In Yaqui, the reciprocal is marked somewhat differently than ordinary plural reflexives. In some cases, a form of the reciprocal pronoun **nau** *together* is used along with an ordinary subject clitic as in sentence (55). The ordering of the reciprocal pronoun and the subject clitic seems to be rather free in Yaqui. For example, in sentence (55) the subject clitic precedes the reciprocal, and in sentence (56) it follows it.

(55) té náu-'etého-nee súa-si-maáči-k híkkah-i-maáči-k
we together-talk-FUT wise-AVR-seem-ACC hear-PPL-seem-ACC

tá'ee-mači-k káa kúh-ti-mači-k téuwaa-nee
know-seem-ACC not anger-CON-be-ACC speak-FUT
We will now talk together (about that which is) of intelligence, worth listening to, worth knowing, not irritating.

(56) náu te bít-ču-su-k
together we see-CMP-CMP-PRF
We have now met again.

The reciprocal pronoun **nau** may occur as the only marker in the sentence. In such cases, it may well be glossed "together."

(57) wóh-naiki pueplo náu yáha-ka, 'á'a pahkó-ria-k.
two-four town together arrive:PL-PPL him feast-APL-PRF
All the eight towns, coming together, participated in the burial ceremonies for him.

(58) wána=te pá'aku 'á'a kečá-'a-nee   'itépo=te 'íntok náu-hínko'ola-rók-nee
there=we outside him stand-EV-FUT we=we and together-race-QUO-FUT
We will stand him off yonder, and we will say that we are going to run a race.

The reciprocal pronoun may occur in the reduplicated form and may even mark oblique relations. In example (59) it functions together with the negative to indicate that the topics of X's discussion are not all the same by any means.

(59) káa na-náu-mačí-k   téuwaa
not RDP-RCIP-appear-ACC talk
He talks about all kinds of different things.

Finally, the reciprocal **nau** may serve as the pronominal base for the postposition **witči**. The different forms of **nau** have very different semantic results for such postpositional phrases. The simple combination of the two, i.e., **náu-witči** means "simultaneously" whereas the complex form **nán-nau-witči** means "evenly."

Reflexive marking is used to indicate a wide range of extensions from the prototype in Yaqui. One such extension involves the use of the third singular reflexive marker **au-** to attach to the adverbial base **su'uli** *alone* to give the emphatic meaning "only" as seen in sentence (60).

(60) hiák-nokí 'áu-sú'uli 'itó-t 'aáyu-k
yaqui-word RFL-alone us-on be-PRF
We spoke only Yaqui.

4.0. The passive suffix -wa

The passive suffix **-wa**, marks prototypical passive subjects, among its various roles and is used very frequently. The subjects that it marks may be either definite or indefinite, in the case of impersonal sentences. Sentences (61)–(64) show that Yaqui passives often mark overt subjects that are both specific and definite.

(61) muúni 'íntok béhnabee b^{w}íh-wa-ka sú'a-wa-k
Muuni and Bernabe seize-PSV-PPL kill:PL-PSV-PRF
Muúni and Bernabe, having been seized, were killed.

(62) 450 hiákim te'opo-po táya-'a-wa-k
450 yaquis church-in burn-EV-PSV-PRF
Four hundred fifty Yaquis were burned to death in a church.

(63) wáaria-bétana 'é-u bíttua-wa-k   nehpo 'áman=e'e
guard-from you-to send-PSV-PRF I there=you
nói-ti-sae-wa   ne-mák wée-nee
go-CON-command-PSV me-with go-FUT
I have been sent from the "guardia"; you are ordered to go there, you will go with me.

(64) hunáka'a hí'osia-ta hunáman 'á'a b^{w}íh-wa-ka-'apo   'á'a 'ú'aa-wa-k
that:ACC paper-ACC there his sieze-PSV-PPL-GND him take:away-PSV-PF
The paper was taken away from him, there in the place where he was seized.

In example (61) the narrator gives the specific names of the victims, whereas in example (62) he tells us which group of people were killed. In sentence (63) the passive **-wa** is used with a first peson singular subject in the first clause and a second person singular subject in the second clause. In this instance, both the interlocutors in a single speech situation are singled out by the use of the passive. In example (64), on the other hand, the narrator singles out a specific inanimate entity.

Frequently the passive subject is definite, but not overt; the identity of the subject is known from context as seen in examples (65)–(68).

(65) hunáma béha temái-wa
 there well question-PSV
 He was questioned there.

(66) hú'upa-u sumá-'a-wa-k yokó-ria-po mé'e-wa-k
 mesquite-to tie-EV-PSV-PRF next-day-in kill-PSV-PRF
 It was tied to a tree, the next day it was killed.

(67) kée hú'unee-wa
 not:yet know-PSV
 It is not yet known.

(68) bʷé'ituk-im 'étbʷá-nú'u-wa-k
 because-they steal-take-PSV-PRF
 because they were betrayed

Passive **-wa** occurs frequently with the desideratives **-baa** and **-pea** as well as alone to result in a meaning that almost has to be expressed in English with the third person plural pronoun "they." This is the way that Yaqui typically marks impersonal sentences with indefinite agents, as examples (69)–(70) show.

(69) haísa híu-wa hitá-sa túa 'etého-wa
 how sound-PSV thing-INTERR indeed talk:about-PSV
 What's the word; what is being talked about?

(70) nássua-wa-k-o
 fight-PSV-PRF-when
 when "they" fought (lit.: *when there was fighting*)

Passive impersonal situations can also be construed as only potentially occurring. Typical examples are given in sentences (71)–(73). Present tense usages of these impersonals are often glossed with an editorial "they" as subject, as is done in example (72) or with a presentative "there is going to be X activity, as in example (73).

(71) káa-tú'ii-k kóba-ka wee-nee hák 'ó-'ómti-tua-wa-k-o
 not-good-ACC head-having go-FUT where RDP-anger-CAU-PSV-PRF-when
 A person is apt to do something foolish when he is angry.

(72) nassua-baa-wa
 fight-DSD-PSV
 They are going to fight.

(73) péuti-baa-wa
 butcher-DSD-PSV
 They are going to butcher.

Yaqui also allows passives to be strung together in a single sentence. In the sequence of clauses in example (74), the first one is impersonal, whereas the others show passives in which the passive subject is incorporated into the verb, a pattern often called "antipassive."

(74) wátak-ti-wa nu'ú-te-wa bočá-tu'u-te-wa ba'á-nu'ú-m čá'abʷa-wa
 prepare:to:leave-CON-PSV food-VR-PSV shoe-good-VR-PSV water-carry-PL patch-PSV
 They are making preparations for leaving, food is being prepared, shoes repaired, canteens patched.

(75) hunáma béha hiókoi-wa-ka yéu-waák-te-k
 there well pardon-PSV-PRF out-stride-VR-PRF
 Having been pardoned there, he went on his way.

In sentence (75) the subordinate clause is active intransitive, but has no overt subject. The subject's specific identity is established in an earlier sentence in the text from which this sentence was taken. The following clauses of sentence (76) then present this participant as a prototypical passive subject.

(76) 'áma yepsá-ka tebóte-k yóopna-wa-k mabét-wa-k kúta-t
there arrive-PPL greet-PRF answer-PSV-PRF receive-PSV-PRF wood-on put-PSV-PRF
When he arrived there, he greeted them, was answered, was received, and was seated on a wood stool.

Both the impersonal and the prototypical passive usages are illustrated in example (77). Note that the subject of the impersonal passive clause, i.e., fiesta making, is not equivalent to the subject of the second passive clause, i.e., the enchanted Paschal Dancer.

(77) háksa wée-ka-i kó'oko'i-m-po b^wé'uu-si
somewhere go-PPL-PPL chile-PL-in big-ADV

pahkó-baa-wa-o 'aman ne-hun-wa-k
feast-DSD-PSV-when there UNSPEC-invite-PSV-PRF
Well, at some time back then, when there was going to be a really colossal feast in (the town of) Chile Peppers, he was invited to take part.

The sequence of the completive suffix **-su** and the passive suffix **-wa** frequently results in the configuration **-sua,** as can be seen in examples (78)–(80).

(78) páhko ramáa-ta yéča-'a-su-a-k-o pahk-o'a-m
feast shade-ACC stand-EV-CMP-PSV-PRF-when feast-elder-PL

náu béep-su-a-k-o páhkó'a-m naáte-k
together strike-CMP-PSV-PRF-when feast-PL start-PRF
When the ramada for the feast was completed, when the "pascolas" were all brought together, the fiesta started.

(79) wáme'e 'asúka-bákim páhko-po káa nénki-su-a-ka-me tiénda-m-po nénki-wa-k
those sugar-cooked feast-in not sell-CMP-PSV-PRF-NZR store-PL-in sell-PSV-PRF
The candy that had not been sold during the feast was sold in the stores.

(80) kétwoo hí'i-b^wá-su-a-k kétwoo hi'i-b^wá-su-k-a'u lu'u-te-k
early IZR-eat-CMP-PSV-PRF early IZR-eat-CMP-PRF-PPL end-VR-PRF
It was all eaten up early this a.m.; that which was all eaten up early is now all gone.

The passive suffix does not reduce when it assumes a secondarily stressed position in a following "foot," as it does in example (81).

(81) nák-su-wa-k=ane
love-CMP-PSV-PRF=I
I have been loved.

QUESTIONS

1.0. Introduction

In this section, we discuss the linguistic patterns that Yaqui utilizes in forming both yes/no questions and WH-questions, i.e., those requesting information about who, what, how, when, where, and why. Basically, Yaqui employs three primary strategies. These include the use of an interrogative intonational pattern, the use of interrogative particles and pronouns, and the use of adverbials as tags.

2.0. Yes/No Questions

The interrogative intonation pattern used for Yes/No questions consists of a rising pitch contour on the last phonological phrase of the sentence, as seen in examples (1)–(3). In contrast, the declarative sentence tends to have a lower final phonological phrase pitch contour with a slight downglide at the end. Except for this, corresponding declarative and interrogative sentences have the same structure in terms of word order and lexical material. Thus, placing final intonation on the sentence of example (1) would result in a sentence with the declarative meaning "he saw it."

(1) 'á'a bíča-k
　　it　 see-PRF
　　Did you see it?

(2) 'á'a wáata húka'a sákobai-ta
　　it　 want　that:ACC watermelon-ACC
　　Do you want that watermelon?

(3) mása'asai　'íntok 'á'a téa-ka　'ínen té'e-ka　'iním 'émpo wée 'ín-hápči
　　S. M.Flower and　him see-PPL thus say-PRF here　you　go　my-father
　　And, S. M. Flower, noticing him, said: "Is that you, my father?"

The minimal interrogative pattern utilizing intonation is quite commonly employed in forming Yes/No questions. Yaqui usage often omits any overt signalling of the addressee by a clitic or pronoun; the "you" subject is inferred, much in the same way that it is for imperatives, which often do not mark overtly a "you" subject. However, as sentence (3) shows, a second person addressee may be signalled by the use of independent pronouns, along with vocative forms, at the speaker's choice. Generally, Yes/No questions elicit simple responses, although, naturally, additional observations or related comments may be expected.

Yaqui appears to have several forms of tag questions, in which some sentence final form serves to catch the hearer's attention as a strong cue for eliciting a response. Tag questions are a common second type of Yes/No questions which Yaqui forms by appending an adverbial to a simple Yes/No question marked with the interrogative intonation pattern. The three most common adverbials used in tags are **há'ani** *perhaps*, **há'ako** *maybe*, and **hewí** *yes*. These are illustrated by sentences (4)–(6). These adverbials appear to contribute different degrees of certainty to the sentences in which they are used. Thus, in using sentence (4) or (5), the speaker does not normally expect either a "yes" or a "no" answer since he/she is expressing a significant degree of doubt.

(4) 'á'a hínu-k　há'ani
　　it　 buy-PRF perhaps
　　You bought it, didn't you?

(5) tóo-čiha'a-ku　yéu 'ám tóha-k-ame　há'ako
　　dust-scatter-in　out them bring-PRF-NZR maybe
　　Might it be the one who took them to the desert?

(6) ketúni bínwa　yúk-ne-m-ta-béna,　hewí
　　still　long:time rain-FUT-NZR-ACC-like yes
　　It looks like it is going to rain for a long time yet, doesn't it?

On the other hand, the use of the general affirmative particle as in sentence (6), signals that the speaker does expect a "yes" answer. The probable answer would be that given in sentence (7).

(7) híba   tua
    always indeed
    It sure looks that way.

Yaqui also has two ways for forming negative tag questions. In example (8) the negative notion is encoded by use of the negative indefinite pronoun **kaábe** *no one*. In example (9) the negative particle **káa** is used and holds its scope over the entire first clause of the sentence. Both of these questions would normally be answered in the negative.

(8) 'émpo kaábe-ta hiníle hunúen 'á-u   híu-nee-ka-i
    you   none-ACC fear   thus   him-to say-FUT-PPL-PPL
    Aren't you afraid of anyone, talking to him like that?

(9) 'émpo káa 'á'a hiníle hunúka   'á-u   teuwaa-nee-ka-i
    you   not him fear   that:ACC him-to say-FUT-PPL-PPL
    Aren't you afraid of him, having said that to him?

More complex forms of Yes/No questions in Yaqui are formed by combining the patterns given above with the indefinite interrogative pronoun **haisa** *what* (cf. Langacker 1977:52). In both sentence (10) and (11), an overt second person singular independent pronoun is used. (Note also the contrast between sentence (3) given earlier, and sentence (11) here). As seen in sentence (12), **haísa** can also be used with tag questions.

(10) haí=sa   'empo sukau-bae táhi-m-mewi
     how=INTERR   you   warm-DSD   fire-PL-to
     Do you want to warm yourself by the fire?

(11) haí=sa   'émpo hunáa'a há'ako
     how=INTERR   you   that:one maybe
     Are you that person, perhaps?

(12) haí=sa   hunáa'a káa 'intok 'á'abo noiti-nee   há'ani
     how=INTERR   that:one not again here   return-FUT maybe
     Will he perhaps never come back here again?

A rare form of the Yes/No question pattern is given in example (13) in which the question is introduced by the particle **hán=sa.**

(13) hán=sa 'áma hó'aa-k   há'ani
     how=Q   there house-have maybe
     Does he, by any chance, live there?

Yaqui did not seem to originally use alternative questions, but rather this pattern seems to have been borrowed from Spanish. Thus, the use of the Spanish conjunction "o" may occasionally be heard in sentences such as (14):

(14) haí=sa   haíbu siíka   'óo ketúni 'ím 'áane, há'ani
     how=INTERR   now   go:PRF or still here be   maybe
     Has he gone, or is he still here?

3.0. WH-questions

Whereas Yes/No questions are directed at eliciting a simple affirmation or denial of some state of affairs, WH-questions seek to elicit specific information about personages, locations, reasons, times, and ways of carrying out activities. WH-questions are frequently marked, at least in part, by indefinite pronouns. There are four indefinite pronominal forms in Yaqui from which all the current interrogative pronouns have been formed (cf. INDEFINITE PRONOUNS, pp. 249–253). These are given in Table 7.

Questions 3.0.

    hábe   *a person* (*any person, some person*)
    híta   *a thing*
    háčin(i)   *a manner*
    hákun(i)   *a place*

Table 7. Indefinite pronouns used as interrogative pronouns

The pronouns **háčin(i)** *manner* and **hákun(i)** *a place* have the alternate reduced forms **hái** and **hák** derived via a process that that dropped out **č** and **k** to produce these reduced forms. The locative **hákun(i)** also has a contracted form **haú**. We base this on the observation that we have been unable to find any other forms in Yaqui grammar which would otherwise account for **hái** and **hak**. The rare form **hán-** illustrated earlier in sentence (13) is apparently another reduced form based on **háčini**.

Both **hačín-sa** and **haí-sa** mean "how/what?", but the form **haí-sa** is the most frequently used.

(15) haí=sa 'áme-u hiía-k húu'u Hóan
    how=Q them-to say-PRF that John
    What did John say to them?

(16) hačín=s=am 'án-nee húme'e polóobe-n
    what=Q=they do-FUT those poor-PL
    What can those poor people do?

(17) hák=sa hó'aa-k húu'u Hóan
    where=Q house-have that John
    Where does John live?

(18) haú=sa 'émpo siíka
    where=Q you went
    Where are you going?

Two more forms derived from **haí-** are **haí-ki-(k)-sa** *how much?* and **hai-kí-m-sa** *how many?* Both of these draw on an indefinite morpheme **-ki**, which is also found in Cora (cf. Casad 1984:198). The form **haí-ki** may well have been reanalyzed into a single morpheme **haíki-** meaning "a quantity, an amount." It now functions to question the quantity of both subject and object nominals, as seen in examples (19) and (20).

(19) haíki-m=sa 'áman sáha-k
    amount-PL:ACC=Q there go:PL-PRF
    How many went there?

(20) haíki-k=sa béhe'e húu'u sákobai
    amount-ACC=Q cost that watermelon
    How much does that watermelon cost?

Yaqui commonly strings questions together, in which case the clitic **-su** is used as a sort of coordinate conjunction to form a complex question as in sentence (21).

(21) hák=sa hó'aa-k húu'u 'ém 'áčai
    where=Q house-have that your father

    húu'u=su 'ém saila húu'u=su 'ém 'ákkoo
    that=Q your brother that=Q your sister
    Where does your father live? and your brother? and your older sister?

The indefinite pronouns given earlier in Table 7 are the basic set from which the interrogative pronouns are formed by adding the interrogative clitic =sa. This results in the set of forms given in Table 8.

    habé=sa   *who?*
    hitá=sa   *what?*
    hačin=sa   *how?*
    hakún=sa   *where?*

Table 8. Interrogative pronouns formed with =sa

Yaqui does not have a form for "which." This concept requires the use of a circumlocution such as "between these two, what do you want?"

The usual word order in WH-questions, as in Uto-Aztecan in general, is with the interrogative pronoun in sentence inital position. Examples (22)–(30) illustrate usages of each distinct WH-word.

Sentences (22) and (23) present typical usages of **habé=sa** *who*. The content of the question in (22) utilizes an equational statement formed by simply juxtaposing a WH-word and a demonstrative pronoun. The content of example (23), on the other hand, is a negative question built on a transitive clause.

(22) habé=sa hunáa'a
    who=Q that
    Who is that?

(23) habé=sa 'í'an káa 'á-u wáati-nee
    who=Q now not it-to remember-FUT
    Who doesn't remember it these days?

Examples (24)–(28) illustrate typical usages of **hitá=sa** *what?* The information being requested ranges from the maximally general in sentences (24) and (25) to the very specific in sentences (26), (27), and (28). Note that the indefinite **hita** does not take the accusative suffix **-ta** when it designates a direct object, but in contrast, the indefinite human pronoun **habe** does take the accusative as later examples will show.

(24) hitá=sa 'empo ho-hóa
    thing=Q you RDP-do
    What are you doing?

(25) hitá=sa 'áman 'aáyu-k
    thing=Q there be-PRF
    What is there?
    What is going on over there?

(26) hitá=sa 'émpo hínu-bae
    what=Q you buy-DSD
    What do you want to buy?

(27) hitá=sa bítču
    thing=Q stare:at
    What is he staring at?

(28) hitá=sa túa néhpo 'enčí b^{w}á'a-tua-nee
    thing=Q indeed I you:ACC eat-CAU-FUT
    What in the world can I give you to eat?

Examples (29)–(31) illustrate queries regarding location as shown in sentence (29), manner as shown in (30), and time as in (31).

(29) hakún=sa tekipánoa
    where=Q work
    Where does he work?

(30) haí=sa maáči húu'u 'ém sá'awa
    how=Q appear that you sore
    How does your sore seem to be? or *How is your sore?*

(31) hakwóo=sa yépsa-k
    when=Q arrive-PRF
    When did he come?

Subject clitics are often attached to WH-words as in sentence (32). Notice that the question marker =**sa** shortens to =**s** before vowel initial subject clitics as happens in sentence (33).

(32) haí=sa=te 'án-nee
    how=Q=we do-FUT
    What/how shall we do?

(33) haí=s=e'e 'emo bíča
    how=Q=you self see
    How are you?

WH-questions may also be strung together in normal conversation as in example (34).

(34) hita=sa 'áma 'aáyu-k habé=sa né-u tebóte
    thing=Q there be-PRF who=Q me-to greet
    What is going on there, who sends greetings to me?

Topicalization can override the normal WH-word order so that the topicalized noun takes sentence initial position. This is illustrated by sentence (35).

(35) 'ii'i boó'o hakun-bičáa=sa wée
    this road where-site=Q go
    Where does this road go to?

To enquire about one's welfare, a Yaqui usually asks whether or not one is sick. But occasionally, the expression given in example (36) may be used. The standard greeting is given in example (37).

(36) haí=s=e'e 'émo bíča
    how=Q=you RFL see
    How are you doing?

(37) kétči alléa
    still happy
    Are you well?

4.0. Complex WH-forms with =sa

In addition to the use of the suffix =**sa** QUESTION to form the interrogatives **habésa, hitása, hakúnsa,** and **haísa** from the corresponding indefinite pronouns, Yaqui employs this suffix as one member of more complex interrogative constituents, which include a variety of constituent types that occur following a basic WH-root and preceding =**sa.**

For expressing the concept "when", Yaqui has developed a rather circuitous phrase. Yaqui already had the verbal suffix **-o,** which can mean either "when" or "if," as in sentences (38) and (39).

(38) 'enčí 'áman weáma-o ne 'enčí bíca-k
     you:ACC there walk-when I you:ACC see-PRF
     I saw you when you were walking there.

(39) 'enčí 'á'a wáata-o 'á'a hínu-nee
     you:ACC it want-if it buy-FUT
     If you want, you will buy it.

The reduced forms **hák-** and **haí-** combine with two distinct verbal expressions to yield complex WH-forms meaning "when" and "why", respectively. These are of the form **hakwóo=sa** *when*, and **hai-s-áaka/haisáakai** *why*. It turns out that the complex form **hak-wóosa** *when?* derives from **hák-wéye-o=sa** (*lit.* where-go-when=Q). Mayo uses the subordinate form **ha-wey-o** *when* and the interrogative form **ha-wée-su** *when?*, for which there is no evidence that the temporal/conditional **-o** is part of its morphology (Larry Hagberg, personal communication.). Both Yaqui **hak** and Mayo **ha** are related historically to a demonstrative pronoun. Synchronically, Yaqui **hak-wóo=sa** may now be considered to be an unanalyzable independent form.

Notice from the differential position of =**sa** in these two complex forms that their grammaticalization has followed two distinct compositional paths, as suggested by examples (40) and (41). The probable expanded morphemic sequence of the grammaticalization chain is given at the left of the formula and the present phonological form is given at the right.

(40) hák-wéye-o=sa   >   hakwoo=sa
     where-go-when=Q   *When?*

(41) haí=sa 'éa-ka-i   >   haí=sa-akai
     how=Q seem-PPL-STAT   *Why?*

Examples (42) and (43) are typical of the usages of these two complex WH-constituents.

(42) hakwóo=sa yebíh-nee   (43) haí=s-aa-ka hunúen 'aáne
     when=Q   arrive-FUT   why=Q-be-PPL thus   do
     When will he arrive?   *Why is he doing that/thus?*

Besides attaching to indefinite pronominal bases, =**sa** may also attach to a variety of postpositional phrases and compound nouns marked by the accusative **-ta**. For example, the indefinite pronoun **habé** *who* in example (44) is marked with **-ta** accusative, which in turn serves as a base for attaching the postposition **-u** *toward*. On the other hand, the postposition **-po** *in* attaches directly to the WH-word **háčin** *how* in example (45) without any intervening connector element.

(44) habé-ta-u=sa hú'ena-k yá'a-la   (45) háčin-po=sa 'iníi'i-tu-nee
     who-ACC-to=Q evil-ACC do-PPL   how-in=Q   this-VR-FUT
     Whom has he harmed?   *In what way can this happen?*

Examples (46)–(48) illustrate compound WH-words in which constituents other than postpositions are employed. Sentence (46) includes a reduced form of the manner adverb **maísi,** to which is attached a second person singular subject clitic. Sentence (47) on the other hand, calls on an abstract noun **tekil** *work,* marked with the accusative **-ta,** whereas in (48) a plural inanimate noun forms part of the WH-constituent.

(46) haí=sa maí-s=e'e   hi'i-bʷa-k
     how=Q manner-AVR=you IZR-eat-PRF
     What kind of a meal did you have? How was your meal/dinner?

(47) híta-tekíl-ta=sa   'émpo 'áa hoóa
     thing-work-ACC=Q   you   able do
     What kind of work can you do?

(48) haíki-muní-m=sa   'émpo hípʷee
     how:many-bean-PL=Q   you   have
     How many beans do you have?

For questioning locational concepts, **hák=sa** and **hakún=sa** are about equally common in usage, but they mean slightly different things; **hák=sa** appears to designate a relatively fixed location and can often be glossed "where" as in example (49); **hakún-bíčáa=sa** designates the direction toward which something is headed and may be glossed "to where" as in example (50), and the form **hakú'ubo=sa** means "from where?" as in sentence (51). This difference in meaning is partly due to the use of distinct postpositions in these complex WH-words. In sentence (50) the use of **-bíča** correlates with the notion of direction toward a location away from the speaker's location, whereas the use of the postposition **-bo** in (51) correlates with the notion of direction toward the speaker's location at the time of the speech-act.

(49) kári-ta   né haíwa hák=sa   né túa   'á'a téu-máči
     house-ACC I   hunt where=Q   I   really it   find-able
     I am looking for a house, where can I find one?

(50) 'íi'i boó'o hakún-bíčáa=sa wée
     this road   where-site=Q   go
     Where does this road go?

(51) hakú'ubo=sa   'émpo wée
     from:where=Q you   come
     Where have you come from?

WH-words formed with an indefinite pronoun and the suffix **=sa** may form additional distinct kinds of complex interrogative structures by taking either a verbal complement or a postpositional phrase as its adjunct. In example (52) the verb **'ea** *think*, marked with the imperfective participle **-ka**, is in construction with the WH-word **haísa**. The postposition **-bena** *like* can be used with the indefinite pronominal WH-form **hitá=sa** to indicate the idea of the speaker's focus on a particular reason for something. Note that in example (53) the entire complex WH-word is marked with the accusative **-k**.

(52) haí=sa 'éa-ka   'áman siíka húu'u Hóan
     how=Q think-PPL   there went   that John
     With what thought in mind did John go there?

(53) híta=sa-béna-k   'emé'e 'áe-tána huíwa
     thing=Q-like-ACC   you:PL him-from   feel
     What is it that you are upset/angry at him about?

The reduced form for "why?" has been derived from a combination of the form **haí=sa** *how?* and the verb **'aáyu-k** *to happen, to be* as in example (54), or the related form **'ayú-ka-i** as in (55).

(54) haí=sa 'aáyu-k   (55) haí=sa 'ayú-ka-i
     why=Q be-PRF   why=Q be-PPL-PPL
     Why?, What happened?   *Why? What caused it?*

The form in example (56) has undergone further reduction to **hai-s-áaka(i)** as shown earlier in sentence (41). But the postpositional **-betčí'ibo** *for, because,* and the unreduced verbal form **'éa-ka** *thinking,* are also very frequently used with **haí=sa** in the sense of "why" as seen in sentences (56) and (57).

(56) haí=sa-betčí'bo 'émpo 'á'a wáata
    how=Q-for   you   it want
    Why do you want it?

(57) haí=sa-'éa-ka   'áman siíka húu'u hóan
    how=Q-think-PPL there went that John
    Why did John go there?

For a cleft type answer in which the intransitive verb **hu'unea** *to know* would be used, the possessed gerund with the locative suffix **-t** *on, at, about* would also be employed, as seen in (58).

(58) 'á'a yebíh-nee-'u-t   ne hú'unea
    his arrive-FUT-GND-on I know
    I know when he will arrive.

This sentence is ambiguous, however, and a more typical expression could be used which employs a complex temporal WH-word structure as in example (59):

(59) ne 'áe-t hú'unea híta-taéwai-tči 'á'a yebíh-nee-'u-tči
    I it-on know   thing-day-on   his arrive-FUT-GND-on
    I know the day he will arrive on.

In current Yaqui usage, however, all of the basic forms are frequently heard in embedded questions. In such constructions, the interrogative **-sa** gets bleached of its meaning. Examples (60)–(64) are taken from various native texts or from the translation of the New Testament.

(60) 'emé'e hú'unea haísa tú'isi 'itóm híapsa-k-a'u
    you:PL know   how   well   our   live-PRF-GND
    You know how well (good lives) we lived among you.

(61) hunáman 'émpo téhwaa-tu-nee hitása 'ém hóo-nee-'u
    there   you   tell-PSV-FUT what   you do-FUT-GND
    There, you will be told what you are to do.

(62) bempó'im-meu haísa 'a-u   yéu-siká-m-ta   sí'ime-ta teuwaa-k
    them ACC-to how   him-to out-go-NZR-ACC all-ACC   tell-PRF
    He told them all that had happened to him.

(63) hunáma'a háksa   baká-túu'u-ku   tó'e
    there   somewhere carrizo-thicket-in lie:down:PL
    They slept there somewhere in a carrizo thicket.

(64) háksa-wée-kai   kó'oko'i-m-po bʷé'uu-si pahkó-baa-wa-o
    somewhere-go-PPL   pepper-PL-in   big-AVR   feast-DSD-PSV-when
                        (place name)
    Somewhere about that time, when there was going to be a big feast in Cocorit…

In examples (60)–(64) above, **haísa, hitása,** and **háksa** have been written as unit words because they are used as relative pronouns, whereas in their interrogative usages, the clitic =**sa** retains morphemic status. However, examples (65)–(67) show that the relative pronouns do not need to be used in expressions that are analogous to them. Thus, there is no form **haísa** in example (65), no **hitása** in (66), and no **háksa** in (67). This may suggest that the use of relative pronouns in these contexts is a relatively recent development in Yaqui, motivated by the use of relative pronouns in Spanish. However, the usages of the Yaqui relative pronouns is fully consonant with the grammatical patterns of other Uto-Aztecan languages (cf. Langacker 1977b:51–52).

(65) sí'ime-ta wáka'a bo'ó-t 'á'a bíč-k-a'u, hióko-t
    all-ACC that:ACC road-on his see-PRF-GND pain-AVR

    'á'a 'án-su-ka-'apo 'áman 'áme-u 'á'a téuwaa
    his be-CMP-PRF-GND (manner) them-to it tell
    He told them all that he had experienced on the trip, all the misery he had gone through.

(66) 'iníme'e káa-hú'unea-ka húka'a bém hoá-u 'á'a hoóa
    these:people not-know-PPL that:ACC their do-GND it do
    These people do not know what they are doing.

(67) húm makó'očin-ta wée-k-a'u bʷé'u hó'aa-raa-tu-ka-n
    there guamuchil-POS stand-PRE-GND big house-AZR-VR-PPL-PCN
    There, where the guamuchil tree is standing, used to be a big town.

IMPERATIVE SENTENCES

1.0. Introduction

Yaqui does not have a morphologically unified set of imperative forms within its verb system as do languages like Spanish and Greek. Both morphological and suprasegmental characteristics, as well as pragmatic factors interact in intricate ways and must be jointly described in order to account for the usages of Yaqui imperative sentences.

2.0. Pragmatic aspects of imperatives

The conceptual scene related to the use of imperative sentences includes two persons within a speech-act setting such that the primary speaker conveys to the other person in the setting an order, command, or request to perform some action.

Commands, orders and requests are usually given verbally and in a face to face setting. Imperative sentences typically call on the basic verb form unmarked for any particular tense, as is common in Uto-Aztecan (cf. Langacker 1977b:53). In written communication on the other hand, there are several ways to order someone to do something.

The context of the speech-act and the tone of the voice, when spoken directly to an addressee, determine the degree of urgency attached to carrying out the instructions conveyed by an imperative sentence. The general intonational pattern employed in imperative sentences consists in the speaker's using relatively more acoustic intensity in the total utterance with heavy sentence stress on the verb and a higher than normal overall pitch contour. This results in a pattern that conveys relative degrees of sternness, which may be communicated by the mein as well as by the intonation. A given utterance such as (1) below may be anything from a suggestion to an urgent command, depending on who says it and how it is said.

(1) bín=á'abo wéye
   this:direction=here go
   Come here.

3.0. Morphology of the imperatives

Yaqui imperatives may be either positive or negative and this distinction is clearly marked morphologically, as data in the next two sections show.

3.1. Positive imperatives

Positive imperatives are generally marked overtly by one of the suppletive clitic forms =**ma** SG and =**bu** PL. They may be used for making requests or commands. Typical examples of the usage of singular =**ma** are given in (2)–(5). In particular contexts, as the usages in examples (2) and (3) show, we gloss these morphemes as HRT. In other contexts we gloss them as IMP.

(2) bín-a'abo wéye=ma
   this:direction-here come=HRT:SG
   Come here.

(3) 'itóm 'áma tóha=ma-tí 'áu hiía húu'u gringo
   us there take=HRT-CON him-to say that gringo
   "Take us there," the gringo said to him.

The suppletive nature of this clitic pair and certain of their usages suggest that Yaqui -**ma**/-**bu** represent semantically extended versions of a Proto-Southern Uto-Aztecan desiderative suffix pair, which itself was grammaticalized from the suppletive verb meaning "to die" (cf. Langacker 1977:149).[1]

---

1 The Cora correspondents to =**ma**/=**bu** are the desiderative suffixes -**mi'i** (SG) and -**ku**, respectively.

The placement of =**ma** within the quotative statement appears to be flexible. Examples (2) and (3) above suggest that it is commonly placed on the main verb of the quoted clause, but that is not always the case as sentences (4) and (5) suggest.

(4) néhpo 'áman bít-tua-wa-k nóolia=ma-t-ia   húu'u Hose-maria 'á-u mámte-patči
    I   there sent-PSV-PRF hurry=HRT-CON-say that Jose-maria him-to hand-upon
    "I was sent there. Hurry then," Jose María said to him extending his hand.

(5) 'emó mám-sú'u-tóha-k,   nóolia=ma, bamsé-ka wée-tí 'á-u   hiía
    selves hand-release-PRF hurry=HRT quickly go-CON him-to say
    They released their hands, "Hurry now, get going," he said to him.

In example (4) =**ma** attaches to a derived adverb which is the complement of the main verb of speaking in the matrix clause, whereas in (5) the same derived adverb which takes the imperative =**ma** is the first main constituent in the quotative complement.

Plural imperative forms are marked by the clitic =**bu**. Note that in example (6), the directional adverb is not marked with the imperative, but the main verb of the clause is so marked.

(6) bín=a'abo   katé='em=bu
    this:direction=here come=you:PL=HRT:PL
    Come here.

Sentence (7) shows two uses of =**bu**. In the first clause it attaches to the hortative adverb **nóolia** *hurry*, and in the second clause it suffixes to the temporal adverb **béha** *now*.

(7) nóolia=bu húu'u wó'i 'áme-u   bit-čú-ka 'áme-t
    hurry=HRT that coyote them-to looking them-on

    čá-čae-k   béha=bu ténne='em
    RDP-yell-PRF now=HRT run=you:PL
    The coyote looked at them, "Now," he yelled, "run."

(8) híba=bu   'íi'i 'émo-betčí'ibo
    take=HRT this selves-for
    Take this, it is for you.

Although subject marking is usually absent from Yaqui imperatives, in heightened imperative forms the second person singular and plural pronouns may be attached to the verb. Typical examples are given in sentences (9)–(11).

(9) bín=a'abo   wéye='e   (11) hapté='em=bu
    this:direction=here come=you   stand=you=IMP:PL
    You, come here.   *Stand up. (plural)*

(10) kíkte='e=ma
     stand=you=IMP:SG
     Stand up. (singular)

Notice that the singular form given in example (9) does not carry the clitic =**ma**, but that of (10) does, as well as the plural form of example (11). When there is both a subject clitic and an imperative clitic, the imperative marker follows the second person subject clitic, as can be seen in sentences (10) and (11).

Examples (12) and (13) show the contrast between the unmarked plural form of the imperative for a suppletive intransitive verb and the marked form with a second person plural subject suffix.

(12) bín=a'abo   kaáte   (13) bín=a'abo   katé='em
     this:direction=here come:PL   this:direction=here come:PL=you:PL
     You (plural), come here.   *You (plural), come here.*

Ordinarily, =**ma** and =**bu** are used as hortatives. This is illustrated by examples (14) and (15)

(14) hánte=ma
    let's go=HRT:SG
    Let's (you and me) go.

(15) hánte=bu
    let's go=HRT:PL
    Let's (all of us) go.

Note that the use of =**ma** and =**bu** to mark both imperatives, as in (10) and (11), and hortatives, as in (14) and (15), suggests that these two grammatical categories are not rigidly distinct.

3.2. Negative imperatives

Negative imperatives are formed by placing the emphatic negative **kát** *don't* into a construction with a bare verb stem. The negative **kat** is related to the more general negative **káa** *no, not* (cf. PARTICLES AND CLITICS, pp. 54–55). Examples given (16) and (17) are typical.

(16) kát húnen 'aáne
    don't thus   do
    Don't do that.

(17) kát suá-ti   hiía
    don't annoy-AVR sound
    Be quiet.

In example (16) the negative is followed by a procomplement and a form of the verb "be." In example (17) **kat** is followed by a Verb Complement + Verb Clause. In both cases, everything in the sentence to the right of **kat** is within its scope.

When the strong negative **kat** is used in a sentence, the addressee is understood to be the subject unless other grammatical features force a different interpretation. Whether or not a sentence with **kat** employs a second person subject pronoun, the sentence itself is usually construed as carrying an imperative illocutionary force, as seen in examples (18)–(21).

(18) kát tóo-wássaa
    not dust-scatter
    Stop making a dust.

(19) kát kapée hé'ee čukúi-s=e'e 'áu-nee
    don't coffee drink black-AVR=you be-FUT
    Don't drink coffee, it will make you turn black.

In example (18) there is no overt subject, analogous to the formation of singular imperatives in Indo-European languages, for example. In example (19) the second person singular subject pronoun cliticizes to the derived manner adverb in the explanatory clause that follows the negative imperative and not to the imperative verb stem, as one might suppose. In other situations, the subject pronoun may cliticize to the strong negative, as seen in sentence (20).

(20) kát=e'em 'álala-'a-te-m-ta 'éa
    not=you:PL fickle-EV-VR-NZR-ACC think
    Don't be indecisive.

In sentences such as (21) below, **kat** seems to have a portmanteau role of marking a negative imperative sentence and helping to form an indefinite adverbial phrase.

(21) 'í'an naáte-ka kát haíbu ta'á-po bakót-ta béeba
    today begin-PPL not now sun-in snake-ACC hit
    Beginning today, never hit a snake any time.

Finally, in example (22) **kat** is used to mark a strong entreaty or injunction. The entreaty itself is marked by an introductory negative **'é'e**.

(22) 'é'e, n-abóli kát=née b^{w}a-b^{w}á'e[2]
    no my-grandfather NEG=me RDP-eat
    No, my friend, don't eat me.

As has been noted in PARTICLES AND CLITICS, pp. 59–60, **kát** is also an emphatic "no." Examples (23)–(25) are typical.

---

[2] The form **n-abóli** represents a reduction from the fuller possessed form **'ín habóli.**

(23) hípeta-m né né-nenka kát=i'im béhe'e
 petate-PL I RDP-sell not=they expensive
 I'm selling petates, they're not expensive.

(24) kát=i'im sáawea-ka yéu-ténne-k
 not=they trousers-having out-run-PRF
 They ran out (of the water) without their trousers (on).

(25) woó'o-m tú'isi buú'u, kát=i'im née ko-kót-tua
 mosquito-PL very many not=they me RDP-sleep-CAU
 There were lots of mosquitos, they wouldn't let me sleep.

4.0. Verbs of speech and the modal imperatives

In addition to =**ma** and =**bu,** Yaqui exploits a variety of sources for modal imperatives, e.g., syntactic and morphological patterns that are selected to convey close to the same illocutionary effect as standard imperatives. Two of these are -**sae** and -**tebo** and they both find their grammatical sources in a pair of main verbs. Yaqui uses both -**sae** and -**tebo** for direct strong commands. Yet both of these suffixes display a range of usage that varies from the force of a direct command to what may be very close to being a desiderative. More generally, the modal imperatives of Yaqui actually subsume a wide range of values from the imperative to the exhortative and the optative. In addition to these two, Yaqui also draws on the speech-act verb **noóka** *to speak* and the future tense suffix -**nee** for use as modal imperatives.

4.1. The suffix -sae

The suffix -**sae** is a reduced form of the verb **sáuwe** which can be variously glossed as "to order," "to command," and "to tell X to do Y." This verb may occur with the unspecified object marker **ne-**. In particular, the verb **nésae/nésauwe** *to command, order*, may also be used by those in authority to overtly signal to the hearer that what follows is a command. In ordinary narration, the use of these two verb forms simply indicates that some kind of a command was given, as exemplified in examples (26) and (27).

(26) né 'é-t né-sauwe, bamsé-ka 'iním yéu-wée
 I you-on UNSPEC-command hurry-PPL here out-go
 I order you to leave here at once.

(27) 'inían né 'enčí né-sauwe-k
 thus I you-ACC UNSPEC-command-PRF
 That's how I commanded you.

The use of -**sae** to mean "to plead" is illustrated in sentences (28) and (29), both of which also illustrate its usage as a main verb.

(28) kaábe né 'áma 'ám nána-'a-sae
 no:one me there them put-EV-order
 No one ordered me to put them there.

(29) 'ilí haíki ta'á-po 'áma 'ám tawá-sae-ka, 'á-u 'úhbʷána-k
 little many day-in there them stay-ask-PPL him-to plead-PRF
 They pleaded with him, asking permission for them to stay there for a few days.

(30) mansanó-ta 'á'a te-téhwa, 'á'a bʷá-'a-sae
 apple-ACC her RDP-show it eat-EV-tell
 He showed her an apple and told her to eat it.

Note that in sentences (28) and (30), it combines with its complement via and echo-vowel connector. Sentence (30) also illustrates the use of -**sae** with a more neutral meaning of "tell someone to do X."

Sentence (31) illustrates the use of the intransitive verb form **ne-sae** functioning as the rightmost element in a Verb-Verb compound.

Imperative Sentences 4.1.

(31) máyo kanóa-reo-m-mewi 'úhbʷána waí-tána 'áu tóhi-né-sae.
Mayo boat-AGT-PL-to plead other-side RFL take-IZR-ask
He pleaded with the Mayo boatmen. He asked them to take him to the other side.

As a number of the preceding examples suggest, the semantics of **-sae** predispose it to take a verbal complement. Such complements are often embedded in the main verb by the participial connector **-ti,** as illustrated in example (32). In many of its main verb usages, **-sae** has emotively strong meanings such as "to order" or "to implore," as seen in examples (32) and (33).

(32) 'áman=e'e nói-ti-sai-wa
there=you go-PPL-IMP-PSV
You are ordered/asked to go there.

(33) hiókot 'á-u hiía-k, 'á'a bʷá'a-sae húnak té káa kóko-nee-'e-tea
pain him-to say-PRF it eat-IMP then we not die:PL-FUT-EV-QUO
She implored him, she asked him to eat it, "then we won't die," they say.

On the other hand, sentences (34) and (35) illustrate usages of **-sae** with the more neutral meaning of "to ask."

(34) 'enčím née 'ám 'é'eria-sae
you-PL me them guard-IMP
I ask you to guard them for me.

(35) née 'enčí haríu-sae 'á-u='e-e hí'ohte-sae-wa
me you-ACC hunt-IMP him-to=you write-IMP-PSV
He asked me to look you up, you are requested to write to him.

Both the semantics of the construction in which **-sae** occurs and the morphology of that construction reflect the main verb source of **-sae.** For example, when the passive suffix **-wa** attaches to **-sae,** it restricts its scope to **-sae** and does not affect the meaning of the verb that serves as the complement of **-sae,** as illustrated by examples (36)–(38).

(36) senú-k wók-háa-sae-wa-'a-te-k-o
one-ACC foot-trail-IMP-PSV-EV-PRF-when/if
when ordered to trail/track someone

(37) 'itépo 'á'a 'usíwa-m, 'á'a yó'ori-sae-wa
we his child-POS-PL him respect-IMP-PSV
We his children are ordered to revere him.

(38) sí'ime-m bélle'eka-tana bʷís-sae-wa
all-PL:ACC everywhere-from sieze-IMP-PSV
They are ordered to sieze everyone everywhere.

In sentence (36) for example, the one doing the tracking is the passive subject of **-sae.** The object of the tracking is marked by the accusative indefinite **senú-k** *one*-ACC. In example (37) the children are the passive subject of **-sae,** whereas the object of their reverence is marked by the third person singular pronominal object clitic **'á'a.** Finally, there is no overt passive subject in example (38), which can be construed as an impersonal sentence.

In many of its usages, **-sae** is tightly bound to the verb-like or adverb-like element that precedes it and that falls within its scope. This pattern is sanctioned by the patterns that Yaqui has for forming compounds that include verbs as one element. The compounding pattern in turn leads to the suffixal usages of **-sae.** These usages still maintain the semantics of the main verb usages. Examples (39) and (40) show it having the meaning "to order."

(39) káa 'ám Liós-im-t-ia-ka kaábe-ta 'ám yó'ori-sae
not them God-PL-CON-say-PPL no:one-ACC them revere-IMP
Saying that they were not gods, he ordered that no one worship them.

(40) 'áman née tekipánoa-saí-wa-t-iia húu'u
    there I   work-IMP-PSV-CON-say that
    I was ordered to work there, said that one.

The third person singular subject of the complement of **-sae** is marked by the third person singular accusative clitic **'a'a,** as seen in sentences (41)–(43).

(41) 'á-u   'úhb^Wana 'áman 'á'a wée-sae-ka-i
    him-to plead   there him go-IMP-PPL-PPL
    He begged him, asking him to come there.

(42) káa téta-koa-u   'á'a kibák-sae
    not rock-fence-to him enter-IMP
    They told him not to enter the field.

(43) 'ilí haíki   ta'á-po 'ám 'a'a tawá-sae-ka   'á-u   'úhb^Wána-k
    few how:many day-in there he remain-IMP-PPL him-to plead-PRF
    They begged him, asking/telling him to stay there for a few days.

4.2. The suffix -tebo

The suffix **-tebo** encompasses both causative (cf. INFLECTIONAL AND DERIVATIONAL AFFIXATION. p. 303) and imperative uses, as well as a variety of related main verb usages. Parallel to **-sae** in a number of ways, **-tebo** clearly has usages as a main verb that takes a variety of nominal and clausal complements. It may usually be glossed as "to cause to do X", or "to command to do X." Causative usages, involving the compound stem **tóhi-tebo** *leave*-CAU are illustrated by examples (44) and (45).

(44) ná'ikim 'ám tóhi-tebo-k   (45) Haohóm-meu 'émo tohi-tebo-k
    scatter them bring-IMP-PRF   Haohome-to RFL leave-IMP-PRF
    He caused them to be scattered.   *They caused themselves to arrive in Haohome.*

The reflexive form of **-tebo** in a compound with **sik-** *to cut* means "X gets himself a haircut," as illustrated by sentence (46).

(46) 'áu   siká-'a-tebo-k
    RFL cut:hair-EV-IMP-PRF
    He got a haircut.

The most general pattern with **-tebo** is for it to mean "to order X to do Y," as illustrated by examples (47)–(49). Many of these usages can be viewed as compound verbs in which the first verb is the complement of **-tebo.** This complement verb may be reduplicated, as seen in example (47).

(47) 'asúka-ta tu-túh-tebo-ka   dulse-ta   yáa-k
    sugar-ACC RDP-grind-IMP-PPL   candy-ACC make-PRF
    Ordering them to grind sugar, he made candy.

Nominal adjuncts to the complement verb may be marked by direct object clitics as example (48) shows. They also may be marked by accusative nouns with **-ta** as in (49). Finally, they may only be realized sub-lexically, as seen in (50), in which there is no overt direct object of the complement of **-tebo,** which is itself a compound verb **sák-túh** *to grind parched corn*.

(48) hunúen hiía, 'á'a mé'e-tébo-bae-kai
    thus   say   him kill-IMP-DSD-PPL
    He said that because he wanted to give orders to kill him.

(49) 'asúka-ta tu-túh-tébo-k
    sugar-ACC RDP-grind-IMP-PRF
    He ordered that sugar be ground up.

(50) waté sák-túh-tébo
    others roast-grind-IMP
    And others give an order to prepare "pinole."

A passive object of the complement of **-tebo** may be marked by a reflexive pronoun. Sentence (51) is a typical example of this. Postpositions may also be used to mark a passive object of the complement of **-tebo**. In example (52) the postposition **-meu** *to* serves this function. In (53), the third person plural object pronoun clitic **'am** is used to designate the passive object of the complement of **-tebo**.

(51) burú-m takéa-ka Haóm-meu-táhtia 'emó tóhi-tébo-k
   donkey-PL rent-PPL Haome-to-until   RFL take-IMP-PRF
   Renting donkeys, they gave orders to be taken to Haome.

(52) húme'e té'opo-po yoó'owe-m-meu čái-tébo-k
   those   temple-in GM-elder-PL-to call-IMP-PRF
   He ordered that the temple elders be called.

(53) tómi-ta   mabéta-ka 'ám sú'u-tóhi-tébo-k
   money-ACC receive-PPL them release-bring-IMP-PRF
   Having received money, he gave orders that they be released.

Finally, as is common with causatives like **-tebo,** the meanings of its combination with other elements is highly unpredictable, although at least in part motivated by the meanings of the morphological chunks. Thus the combination of **bíča** *to see* with **-tebo** means "to reveal oneself to X" when used with a reflexive pronoun clitic, as exemplified in example (54).

(54) 'íntok sí'ime-m-meu 'áu bít-tébo-su-ka   čúkula 'íntok née-wi
   and   all-PL-to   RFL sight-IMP-CMP-PPL after and   me-to
   And after he had revealed himself to all the others, he revealed himself to me.

4.3. Other modal imperatives

Other modal imperatives found in Yaqui include the use of the verb of speaking **noóka** *to talk to X* (or a similar construction with the indirect object construction built on a postpositional phrase of the form ...(X)...-u (in preverbal position) is frequently used as a kind of modal imperative. This is illustrated in sentence (55), which is used as a kind of polite suggestion for somebody to do something. On the other hand this verb can also be used to catch someone's attention, as illustrated in sentence (56).

(55) 'iníme'e 'enčím   'ám yó'ori-tá'aa-nee-'e-betčí'ibo té 'emó-u noóka
   these   you-PL-ACC their respect-know-FUT-EV-for   we you-to speak
   We are telling you (instructing you) to know how to respect these men.

(56) haí=sa   káa híkkaha há'ani né 'é-u   noóka
   how=INTERR not hear   maybe I you-to speak
   Don't you hear, I'm talking to you.

The suffix **-nee** FUT/POT can also be used as a modal imperative. This is illustrated by the following passage from Sebastian González Hiyyókame'a's autobiographical sketch. Examples (57)(a)–(c) give the setting for the use of this modal imperative which is exemplified in example (57)(d).

(57)(a) húme'e pelóon-im 'áman née bítču-k
     those bald-PL   there me see-PRF
     The Mexican soldiers had discovered me.

   (b) née bočá-čúkte-k
     I   shoe-cut-PRF
     My huarache strap had broken.

   (c) béha née to'o-sáha-k húme'e yoéme
     well me leave-go-PRF those Yaquis
     Well, the Yaquis (that were accompanying me) ran off.

(d) táa née: káuwi-u   ténni-nee ʼóm-mee tí   né ʼáme-u hiía
    but I   mountain-to run-FUT man-PL CON I them-to say
    but I: "Run to the mountains, men," I said to them.[3]

A very common relayed imperative (sometimes more imperiously executed by the relaying brother or sister than by the originator) is given in example (58).

(58) malá ʼé-u   čaáe
     mother you-to call
     Mamma is calling you.

---

[3] The "Sebahti" paragraph above was taken from a much longer historical text that we are preparing for publication in another work. It illustrates a common kind of modal imperative.

COMPARATIVE CONSTRUCTIONS

1.0. Introduction

Yaqui comparative constructions can be divided roughly into comparisons of equality, comparisons of inequality, and superlative comparisons of inequality. The comparison may be either positive or negative and, as the data in this section show, the means that Yaqui employs for expressing such comparisons involve complex relationships between syntax, morphology and semantics.

The Yaqui comparative is basically an equative sentence in which A, in relation to B, is either superior to, equal to, or inferior to B. In structural terms, NP1 and NP2 are juxtaposed, but the nominals are marked differently depending on the kind of comparison being made. For comparisons of equality (EQ) that employ postpositions, the postposition takes an object marked in the accusative. For comparisons of equality with the reciprocal **nánanča,** both NPs are marked in the nominative and are followed by a form of the reciprocal pronoun and an adjective. For comparisons of inequality, either comparisons of superiority (SUP) or inferiority (INF), NP1 is marked in the nominative, whereas NP2 is in the accusative. In these constructions, the accusative noun is the postpositional object of **-bépa,** which is followed by the adverb of quantity **če'a** *more* and an adjective. Grammatical formulae that express these kinds of relationships are given in Table 9. The first two are comparisons of equality whereas the final two are comparisons of inequality.

$$\text{CMP}_{eq} = \text{ADJ/CL NP1}_{ACC} = \text{Postposition}$$
$$\text{CMP}_{eq} = \text{NP1}_{NOM} + \text{'íntok} + \text{NP2}_{NOM} + \textbf{nánanča/nánna'ana} + \text{ADJ.}$$
$$\text{CMP}_{sup} = \text{NP1}_{NOM} + \text{NP2}_{ACC}\text{-}\textbf{bépa} + \textbf{čé'a} + \text{adj}$$
$$\text{Comp}_{inf} = \text{NP1}_{NOM} + \text{NP2}_{ACC}\text{-}\textbf{bépa} + \textbf{čé'a} + \textbf{káa}\text{-ADJ/antonym}$$

Table 9. Comparative constructions

2.0. Comparisons of equality

Yaqui employs a variety of constructions and lexical items to signal comparisons of equality. These generally involve semantic notions such as "be similar to X," "be like X," "be the same as X," "be of the same quality as X," or "be of the same amount as X." A very common way to mark comparisons of similarity or equality is by means of the postposition **-béna**.

2.1. Postpositional comparisons of equality

Yaqui has several comparison of equality constructions that employ postpositions. These include **-béna** *like, similar to X, as if,* as well as **-wit** *on,* and **-'étči** *on, at.* Both grammatical properties and semantic content suggest that the postposition **-bena** has as its diachronic source an intransitive verb meaning "seems like." This postposition (as well as its reduplicated form **-bé-béna**) can be attached to the following kinds of postpositional objects: nouns marked in the accusative case, nominalized phrases, pronouns, adjectives, and verbs. Unlike most of the other postpositions of Yaqui, **béna** takes a variety of noun, adverbial and verbal suffixes. For example, at times, it can be verbalized with **-e**.

When **béna** takes a noun as its object, the noun is marked with the accusative **-ta,** as illustrated in examples (1) and (2). The entire construction that includes **-bena** may function in several ways in Yaqui grammar. This is evidenced from the fact that **-béna** itself may be marked with the accusative **-k,** as seen in (2). The object of **béna** ranges from prototypical animate nouns as in example (1), to discrete inanimate nouns as in (2) and on to more abstract versions such as nominalizations of various kinds as in (3). Note that in example (3) **béna** is marked for plural subject.

(1) híta húni'i téuwaa-ne peíko-ta-béna
 thing even say-FUT parrot-ACC-like
 He will say anything, like a parrot.

(2) neó'okai yoí-kusía-ta-béna-k hía-wa-ek
    mockingbird Mexican-flute-ACC-like-ACC sound-has
    The mockingbird has a note like a flute.

(3) yoká-'a-ta-béna-m mása-k
    paint-EV-ACC-like-PL wing-have
    It has wings that look as if they were painted.

The postpositional object of **béna** can actually be a complex linguistic expression such as that seen in example (4). In this example, **béna** has within its scope everything to the left of it, i.e., **wáme'e tú'u-nokí-m** *those good words*. In turn **béna** is marked with the plural morpheme which both makes **béna** agree in number with **nokím**, but also serves as a base for attaching the following instrumental postposition **-mea**. A similar example of a linguistically complex expression serving as the postpositional object of **béna** is given in sentence (5). Here **béna** attaches to a preceding accusative **-ta** and carries no other marking. There is also no overt copula in this example. Instead, **béna** seems to function as the copula. This suggests to us that semantically, **béna** is more like a stative adjective than anything else.

(4) wáme'e tú'u-nokí-m-béna-m-mea káa 'enčím baí-tá'aa-naa-'a-betčí'ibo.
    those good-word-PL-like-PL-INST not you:PL:ACC fresh-deceive-FUT:PSV-EV-for
    That you may not be deceived by what seem to be good words.

(5) 'á'a kobáwa káa-kobá-ka-m-ta-béna wáa'a yoéme b^{w}é'ituk huébena-k 'ée-sime
    his head not-head-VR-NZR-ACC-like that man because much-ACC think-go
    It was as if that man didn't have a head because he was thinking so much.

In sentence (6) the standard of comparison is the projected cause of a sensation, i.e., one feels bloated if he eats fish stew. Notice here that the postpositional object is a nominalized clause that is marked with the accusative **-ta**.

(6) kúču-bák-ta né b^{w}á-'a-ka-m-ta-béna pótti héelai
    fish-stew-ACC I eat-EV-PPL-NZR-ACC-like bloat nearly
    I feel somewhat bloated as if I had eaten fish-stew.

Frequently, the construction in which **béna** occurs functions as an adverbial of manner. In such cases, **béna** is marked with the adverbial suffix **-si**, as seen in examples (7)–(10). This is another bit of evidence for considering **béna** to be some kind of a predicate adjective.

(7) 'ám b^{w}álkote tutú'uli-si táho-'o-ta-béna-si
    them soften pretty-AVR cloth-EV-ACC-like-AVR
    He tans them beautifully, like cloth.

(8) tútubiak-béna-si-a
    last:night-like-AVR
    like last night

(9) tápla-kári b^{w}éha'i-ta-béna-si ba'á-bépa čá'a-si-síme
    board-house gourd-ACC-like-AVR water-on float-RDP-go
    The boat floated on top of the water like a gourd.

(10) kaákun nóitek-am-ta-béna-si
     no:where go-PRF-NZR-ACC-like-ADV
     like someone who wasn't going anywhere

Other verbal markings on **-béna** substantiate this. Among such markings are the participial **-ka** illustrated in example (11) and the future **-nee** shown in example (12). The polysemy of **-béna** is further illustrated in these two examples. In example (11) **-béna** can be glossed as "being like X;" whereas in (12) it can be glossed as "look like X."

(11) káa wéye-m-ta-béna-ka
     not go-NOM-ACC-like-PPL
     being like a nonmoving thing

106

(12) húnak 'íntok hú'ub^wa yó'o-tu-m-ta-béna-nee
    then and just   grown-VR-NZR-ACC-like-FUT
    Then he will look just like a youth.

When it takes verb-like structures as its postpositional object, **-béna** may be preceded by a connecting echo vowel, depending on the phonological shape of the verb stem. In turn, it may be adverbialized by the suffix **-si**, as in examples (7)–(10) above and in (13). With a manner procomplement as its object, **-béna** may require the connector **-tu-** as in example (14) without any additional marking.

(13) batéa-po   kóče-'e-béna-si   mú'ila kík-síme
    washbowl-ín sleep-EV-like-AVR glumly stand-go
    (A cockroach) goes around glumly in the washbowl like it was asleep.

(14) hunúen-tu-béna
    thus-VR-like
    It seems like it is that way.

When it takes quantifiers and adverbs as its postpositional object, **-béna** typically occurs with the suffix **-si,** as seen in examples (15)–(16).

(15) wépu'ulai-béna-si té náu   kát-nee
    one-like-AVR   we together go:PL-FUT
    We will go together like one person.

(16) hó'aa-ra-m-tu-ka'u-m   kaíta-tu-k   húči-béna-si   húa-soó'o-ku   taáwa-k
    home-ABS-PL-VR-former-PL nothing-VR-PRF again-like-AVR wood-thicket-in remain-PRF
    The village that had been there, disappeared; it became a wood thicket as it had been before.

With procomplements of manner and demonstrative pronouns, **-béna** may take various other markings, including the general locative postposition **-ku,** as in examples (17) and (18). With a demonstrative pronoun **-béna** can also be marked with the accusative **-k,** as is seen in example (19). And the ubiquitous adverbial suffix **-si** also comes into play in these semantic domains as shown in example (20).

(17) 'inílen-béna-ku née yéu-tómte-k
    thus-like-in   I   out-born-PRF
    I was born in a place like this place.

(18) 'ámani háksa-béna-ku
    there somewhere-like-in
    there in some unknown place

(19) 'iníle-béna-k né wáata
    this-like-ACC I want
    I want one like this.

(20) yée-sú'a-wame   'ále-béna-si   wáa'a 'étb^wá-wa-me   káa 'á'a tú'ure
    people-kill-ABS   thus-like-AVR that   steal-PSV-NZR   not it   like
    Murder, and likewise theft, he does not like.

When it takes a predicate adjective as its base, **-béna** may function as a copulative verb, as in example (21). In this case **-béna** carries no suffix, as was also true in examples (5) and (14).

(21) tú'ii-béna 'íi'i kári
    good-like   this house
    This seems like a good house.

The alternation between marking **-béna** with the adverbial **-si** and marking it with the accusative **-k** is consistent for those constructions in which **-béna** takes pronouns as its objects as in examples (22)–(24).

(22) née káa 'áme-béna-k 'éa
     I   not them-like-ACC think
     I do not think like they do.

(23) kaá-be né-le-béna-si   'áu   'áawe
     no-one me-CON-like-AVR RFL know:how
     No one knows how to do it like I do.

(24) 'ála   húnak-o 'emó-béna-si   'á'a téuwaa-nee
     indeed then-when you:PL-like-AVR it   say-FUT
     Then indeed, I will be able to say it like you do.

In summary, **-béna** is used as comparative of equality in a wide variety of syntactic contexts and semantic domains. It has numerous conventionalized usages of which a relatively ample sampling is given here.

2.2. Other postpositional constructions

The postpositions **-wit** *on* and **-etči** *on, at* take as their postpositional object either the reflexive **nau** or some one of its morphologically related forms such as **na-náu** RDP-*together*. In its temporal use, the postpositional construction **na-náu-wit** means "simultaneously, at the same time," as illustrated by examples (25) and (26).

(25) náu-wit   máa-m-mea   wáka-pipi-m b^{w}ise-ka hi-pi'ike
     together-on hand-PL-INST cow-teat-PL seize-PPL IZR-milk
     Seizing the cow's teats simultaneously with both hands, he milked.

(26) boré'eko-m na-náu-wit-či   na-náu-wit   'á-u   yáha-k
     ram-PL   RDP-together-simultaneously-on RDP-together-on him-to arrive-PRF
     The rams arrived to where he was, at exactly the same time.

The postpositional construction **naál-etči** and its alternate form **naár-etči** are used to signal the concept "the same amount." Sentence (27) is a typical example.

(27) húu'u čeéma 'íntok húu'u Hosée naár-etči-m   b^{w}íia-k
     that Chema and   that Jose same-amount-PL land-have
     Chema and Joseph have the same amount of land.

The postposition **-wit**, along with some of its morphologically related forms such as **-witči, bé-wit, béas, béwas,** and **-was**, basically signals some kind of "simultaneity." In particular cases, it is often glossed "on" or "with." Both meanings, of course, relate to some kind of associativity between entities in physical, logical or conceptual space. For example, when it is also used with pronouns or demonstratives, it takes on the extended meanings of "in the same location," "at the same time," or "of the same quantity or quality" depending upon the particular context and the pronoun or demonstrative serving as its object. In sentence (28), for example, its related form **-bewit** has the meaning "is the same size as." On the other hand, in sentence (29) **-wit** means "of the same quality."

(28) húu'u Krésénsia bátte   'áa-wit wéye 'Estér-ta-béwit
     that Cresencia almost her-with goes Esther-ACC-with
     Cresencia is almost the same size as Esther.[1]

(29) húme'e 'ánkeles-im-mak   káa 'áme-wit 'á'a hú'unakte-ka
     those angel-PL:ACC-with   not them-with him create-PPL

     če'a   kó'om 'á'a tawáa-k
     more   down him to:place-PRF
     He did not create him the same as the angels, he made him lower than they.

---

[1] This example is interesting because the first use of **-wit** does not carry the syllable **be-**, which Langacker reconstructs as a third person singular object pronoun ***pɨ**, which has become reanalyzed as part of the postposition in Yaqui (cf. Langacker 1977: "The syntax of Postpositions in Uto-Aztecan." (IJAL). The second use of **-wit** does occur in company with **be-**, which in this context, could well be an anaphoric use in which it refers back to the postpositional object of the first occurrence of **-wit**.

The following usages of the related form **-be-wi-tči** *parallel to, along side of, simultaneously* illustrate clearly the spatial usages of **-wit**. These are the grounds for the extensions of **-wit** into other domains. The spatial sense of **-bewitči** illustrated by examples (30) and (31) is "off to one side of X."

(30) hunáman báhkoam-bewitči hú'upa-sóo'o-ku   'ámani
there   Bacum-beside   mesquite-thicket-in there
He went there alongside (off to one side) of Bacum, through the mesquite thickets.

(31) mó'očim-me-u   héela yáhi-nee   mó'očim-bewitči
Los:Mochis-CON-to nearly arrive:PL-FUT Los:Mochos-beside
They will arrive nearly to Los Mochis, alongside of Los Mochis.

In sentence (32) the meaning of **-wit** is extended into the domain of time, with the resultant meaning of "at the same time."

(32) máakina kumi'ipo-bétana wéeka   'áa-wit   'áma yépsa-k
machine Cumipas-from   traveling him-with there arrive-PRF
The train, coming from Cumipas, got there at the same time as he did.

2.3. Comparisons of equality using adjectives

In addition to the postpositional constructions discussed above, Yaqui also draws on several adjectives (each signifying exact equalness or identicalness) to convey the concept: "A is the same as B." The structure of these expressions is usually in one of two forms given in Table 10.

NP1 and NP2 + ADV$_{eq}$ + V or ADJ

NP2 + ADV$_{eq}$ + V or ADJ

Table 10. Comparisons using adjectives

Other structures are possible however. In certain constructions, the notion of equality is expressed lexically. In particular, Yaqui commonly expresses the notion of similarity through several related adjective forms that are built on the Yaqui reflex of the Proto-Uto-Aztecan reciprocal pronoun *na. The related forms **naáre-/naále-/nálle-** *the same* (amount, quantity, or size) are seen in examples (33) and (34). The forms refer to amounts of money in example (33) and a given quantity of bread in (34). In sentence (35) **naáre** refers to physical characteristics within the abstract domain of measure.

(33) tómi yéu-wó'ota-wa-k   si'ime naáre-ki-k   mák-wa-k
money out-throw-PSV-PRF all   same-AVR-ACC give-PSV-PRF
The money was brought out, each one was given the same amount.

(34) páani-m hám-ta-ka   yée   'ám mi-mik-táite-k   si'ime-m nallé-ki-m mińka-k
bread-PL break-VR-PPL people them RDP-give-begin-PRF all-ACC same-AVR-PL give-PRF
Breaking the bread, she began giving it to the people, she gave each one the same amount.

(35) 'á'a tebéawa hiká-u-biča 'intok 'á'a b^{w}ékawa naáre-pán-ia-ka-n
its length up-to-site and its width   same-VR-PPL-PPL-PCN
Its height (lit. length upward) and its width were exactly the same.

The form **naare** has a temporal use in which it can be glossed as "at the same time" as seen in example (36).

(36) naáre-'emu hapté-ka   yéu-ténne-k
same-in   stand:PL-PPL out-run-PRF
Standing up in unison, they ran away.

One reduplicated form **nánanča** designates members of the "same class." It also is used to designate distinct entities that share the same quality as in example (37) or distinct events that are carried out in the same manner as in example (38).

(37) káa si'ime ték^{w}a nánanča ték^{w}a
    not all   meat   same   meat
    Not all meat is the same.

(38) nánanča 'itó=te nák-nee
    same   RFL=we love-FUT
    We should all love each other the same way.

When used to indicate entities who are viewed as enacting patient or object roles, the reduplicated reciprocal adjective has the form **nánna'ana** and retains the meaning "same type" as in examples (39)–(40).

(39) náu   tekipánoa-n b^{w}é'ituk nánna'ana-k tékil-e-kan
    together work-PCN because same-ACC   work-have-PCN
    They worked together because they had the same skills.

(40) húme'e nánna'ana-k éa-me   'áma yáha-k
    those same-ACC   think-NZR there arrive:PL-PRF
    The ones who were of the same opinion came there.

Buelna lists these adverbials as conjunctions. Curiously, he does not seem to provide much data on comparatives. On page 123, under the heading "De las conjunciones," he says in paragraph 360: "Pónense con nombres de adverbios muchas, que verdaderamente son conjunciones, con que se traban y atan las oraciones en varios sentidos; y aunque algunos son verdaderos adverbios, no se han segregado aqui..." (Buelna 1891:123–124).[2]

However, on the same page there is paragraph 363 in which he says, "**Nanamtza** es adverbio, significa igualmente, esto es, de una misma manera..."[3]

This form is cited on p. 219 in his "Diccionario" in the following terms: "**Nanamtza**, conj. —Igualmente, por iguales partes..."[4]

There may well be other data on comparatives in the overall description of the grammar of "Cáhita" which I have overlooked. But this one form is the only one listed technically as a comparative of equality.

3.0. Comparisons of inequality

In Yaqui, comparisons of inequality range in meaning along a scale from "inferior to" through a point on the scale that can be characterized as "similar to (but not exactly like)" to "superior to." In the prototypical comparative of inequality construction, two entities, often noun phrases, are related in a comparison such that one entity is the ground of the relation, commonly called the standard of comparison, whereas the other one is the topic or target of the comparison. Adjectives and verbs are typically the lexical classes used for specifying the domain within which the comparison is being made. The postposition **-bépa** *above* must be attached to nominal functioning as the standard of the comparison. This nominal must also be marked for the accusative case. The adjective **čé'a** *more,* will be used in conjunction with **-bépa** as will be explained later.

3.1. The ambiguity of inferiority comparisons

Yaqui comparative of inferiority constructions are systematically ambiguous, a point that Lindenfeld noted (1971:9). They mark only inequalities, but do so in one of two ways. In short, the semantics of Yaqui inequalities displays a systematic patterning of preciseness of meaning attached to the comparative construction, depending on whether it is a positive or a negative comparison. The positive ones have only a single constructional meaning; the negative ones have two. Thus, "not more than" can mean either "the

---

2   "They fall together with many kinds of adverbs, which really are conjunctions, with which they link or tie together the sentences with one another in a variety of ways; and although some of them are really adverbs, they have not been grouped together here as such." (Buelna 1891:123, Item 360)
3   "**Nanamtza** is an adverb, it means æequally,' that is, æin the same manner'." (Buelna 1891:123.)
4   "**Nanamtza**, conj. — 'Equally, in equal portions...'" The contemporary form of this 'conjunction' is **nánanča**.

same amount as" or "less than," whereas "not less than" can mean either "the same amount as" or "more than."

To be more specific, when the negative **kaa** precedes the postposition **-bepa** in a comparison of inequalities construction, the resulting sentence is ambiguous, as seen below in sentence (41).

(41) 'ii'i kaa hume-bepa tu'ii
this not those-above good
This is not better than those.

To say "this is not better than that" in Yaqui can mean either that it is just as good as or it is worse than that. Where Yaqui attributives do not have antonyms such as **bʷé'u** *big* in contrast to **'ilítči** *small*, an antonym may sometimes be formed by preceding the attributive with the negative **káa**, as illustrated by examples (42) and (43).

(42) tú'ii   (43) káa-tú'ii
good, lawful   NEG-good
                           bad, illegal

As one begins the study of Yaqui, it would appear, as Lindenfeld 1971 concluded, that Yaqui can say "more than," but not "less than." However, this turns out to be illusory due to our own conceptualizations. In fact, in Yaqui the terms **čé'a** *more* and **-bépa** *above*, either alone or in combination, are used to express comparisons of inequality, as in examples (44) and (45).

(44) 'émpo čé'a huébena-k ta'áa-me
you more much-ACC know-NZR
you who know more

(45) tekipánoa čé'a 'i'an-po-bépa húni'i 'á-et hiapse-ka čé'a-bépa
work more now-in-above even it-on live-PPL more-above
work, being much more diligent (about it) than you are now

In such constructions, the concepts of "superior to" versus "inferior to" are set in contrast to one another and are expressed by the use of antonyms. In particular, the notion "less than" is often signalled by the combination of **čé'a** and an antonym of the quality with respect to which the comparison is being made, as evidenced by examples (46) and (47).

(46) wáa'a 'ili 'uúsi 'ée-bépa 'ilitči-ka-i
that little child you-above small-be-PPL
that little boy who is smaller than you (i.e., *less big*)

(47) hunáa'a 'itóm saila čé'a káa-yó'owe
that:one our little:brother more not-old
Our little brother there, is a bit younger. (i.e., *less old*.)

Examples (48) and (49) show the contrast between a "more than" and a "less than" comparison in which the negative is used to derive an antonym from the positive grade of an adjective.

(48) čé'a húni'i tú'ii   (49) čé'a húni'i káa-tú'ii
more even good   more even not-good
It is even better.   *It is even worse.*

In framing her argument for her 1977 paper, Lindenfeld chose as her Yaqui examples simple comparative constructions. She concluded that whereas Yaqui has a structure for indicating comparisons of superiority, it does not have one for indicating comparisons of inferiority. Thus, whereas Spanish has a binary system of indicating two different kinds of comparisons, Yaqui was said to have only a single device for marking comparisons.

A closer examination of Yaqui comparative constructions shows that the case is not quite so simple. To begin, sentences (50)–(53) are some of the Yaqui sentences that Lindenfeld used to substantiate her point.

(50) hu 'o'óo čé'a hume haamúčim beppá bʷe'u
that man more those women above big

(51) hu 'o'óo húme haamúčim benásya bʷe'u
that man those women like/as big

(52) 'émpo kaá húme ili 'uúsim benásya tutú'uli
you not those little children like/as pretty

(53) 'im kuúna čé'a káa neé beppá yó'owe
my husband more not me above old

It should be obvious that these sentences are not identical semantically. I have organized them according to the following categorization: Example (50) is a comparison of superiority, (51) is a comparison of similarity, (52) is a comparison of inequality or inferiority, and (53) is a comparison of inequality of quantity. To begin, one could offer the following English sentences as proper translation equivalents of examples (50)–(53).

That man, as compared to those women, is bigger.
That man is big like those women.
You are not pretty like those children.
My husband is not older than me.

For practical purposes, however, we will use translation equivalents such as "bigger than," "the same as," "less than," and "younger than" in rendering such sentences into English.

In a similar vein, Spanish "tan...como" may well have prompted the use of **benásya** as the marker for the comparative of equality in sentence (51). The Yaqui word **béna** basically means "like," "resembles," or "as." It can also be glossed as "the same as" in particular contexts, but its use does not imply exact likeness. In this construction it is marked by the adverbializing suffix **-sia**, which has a shorter variant **-si**.

Overall, with respect to examples 50)–(53), the composer of the sentences seemed to be modelling the Yaqui sentences according to the rules of forming the comparative construction in Spanish in so far as Yaqui will allow and still be understandable. It is specifically in this regard that semantic categorization is the deterrent. Although **čé'a** does mean "más" (*more*), **bépa** *above* does not mean "que" (*than*) in these constructions. At a loss for a single Yaqui generic term meaning "menos" (*less*), the person who provided the examples for Lindenfeld apparently improvised **káa...bénasia** and **káa... bépa** on the spot.

Yaqui does not construct its comparative sentences on the "más...que," "tan...como," and "menos...que" patterns of Spanish. Lindenfeld may have been mislead by the Yaqui words **čé'a** *more* and **-bépa** *above*, assuming that they correspond to "more" and "than." They do not. In comparative constructions, **čé'a** modifies the adverb and **-bépa** marks the substantive involved. They complement each other semantically in these constructions, and in meaning approximate the English comparative suffix "-er" in words such as "larger" and "smaller."

3.2. The meaning of če'a

With respect to the meaning of **če'a** itself, it is instructive to consider its usages in contexts other that the comparative construction. In sentence (54), for example, **če'a** marks a zone of increase from a low point on the temperature scale. In example (55) **če'a** indicates the expanse of a virtual path heading downwards beginning from a point on the verticality scale in the domain of the topography. And in example (56) **če'a** is used to indicate an augmentation of mental acuity, i.e., expansion in the domain of the field of knowledge.

(54) kó'om kúak-te-o-biča čé'a sébe-nee
down turn-VR-CND-site more cold-FUT
As the sun gets lower, it is going to be colder.

(55) čé'a kó'om héela tóo-kóba-po ketúni kó'om biča
more down almost bull-head-in still down site
a little further down, on down from "bull-head" mountain

(56) čé'a-wa=su=ne 'ili hu'unee
more-VR=EMP=I little know
Little by little I'm learning.

The basic idea of specifying an increasing quantity of something within a given domain, allows **če'a** to function in the grammar in various ways, including that of playing a role in the comparative constructions. In sentences (57)–(59), for example, **če'a** functions within the domain of discourse to augment the strength of one's assertions and conclusion.

(57) 'í'an čé'a waté moá-'a-téa
now more others tassel-EV-QUO
In fact, they say some are even putting out tassels.

(58) 'inepo čé'a kumi'ipa-u biča wée
I more Kumipau-to site go
In fact, I am going to Kumipas.

(59) hunáka'a hámut-ta nók-ria-k táa čé'a=san 'éa-ka káa bemúcha-'a-wa-k
that-ACC woman-ACC speak-APL-PRF but more=EMP think-PPL not beat-EV-PSV-PRF
They defended the woman, but, fortunately for him, he was not beaten.

Yaqui comparative notions may be expressed either with or without **čé'a** *more*, as a comparative of superiority or inferiority with NP1 and NP2. The following are some patterns for forming comparative constructions.

In forming implied comparisons, in which the standard of comparison is left unspecified, **čé'a** is obligatory, as in example (60).

(60) 'iní'i čé'a tú'ii
this more good
This is better.

In forming explicit comparisons, the speaker may highlight either the topic of comparison or the standard of the comparison. If he highlights the standard of the comparison, he may do so by attaching the postposition **-bepa** to the nominal or the demonstrative that designates that standard and preposing it to both **čé'a** and the adjective that specifies the content of the comparison. In this case, **-bepa** is followed by **čé'a,** as in example (61).

(61) 'iní'i hunáe-bépa čé'a tú'ii
this that-above more good
This is better than that.

If the speaker wishes to highlight the contrast itself, then the noun phrase designating the standard of comparison occurs in its normal post-predicate position as in example (62).

(62) 'iní'i čé'a tú'ii, húnae-bépa
this more good that-above
This is better than that.

Actually, there is not a great deal of connotative difference between sentences (61) and (62). To make a marked difference, more would depend on the intonation of the utterance.

In its most neutral word order, the Yaqui comparative of inequality construction consists of the topic of comparison, followed by the target of comparison expressed as the postpositional phrase X + **-bepa,** in its turn followed by the relevant adjective or verb stem. The quantifier **čé'a** does not occur in this version of the construction as illustrated in example (63). Its absence suggests that in the more elaborate versions, **-bépa** and **čé'a** reinforce one another.

(63) 'iní'i hunáe-bépa tutú'uli
    this that-above pretty
    This is prettier than that.

Notice that in this comparative of inequality construction, the demonstrative form **húnae** serves as object of **-bepa** in examples (61)–(63) instead of the accusative form **hunáka'a,** which I would have expected in that context and which does occur in example (64). In addition, **hunáe** in example (65) is in the attributive position to **kári-ta-bépa.** In short, **hunáe** is often used as a sort of absolutive, or unmarked, form of the demonstrative but it can also be used attributively in these comparative constructions. In example (66) the postpositional object of **-bepa** is a third person singular pronoun and refers backwards to the subject noun phrase **hunáa'a 'uúsi.**

(64) 'ini'ii hunáka'a-bépa če'a káa-tú'ii
    this that:ACC-above more not-good
    This is worse than that.

(65) 'ii'i kári hunáe kári-ta-bépa če'a bʷé'u
    this house that house-POS-above more big
    This house is bigger than that house.

(66) hunáa'a 'uúsi 'ée-bepa 'ilitči-kai haibu nók-ta ta'aa
    that child you-above small-being now word-ACC know
    That child, who is smaller than you, already knows how to read.

4.0. The superlative degree of comparison

The construction consisting of the quantifier **si'ime-m** *all*-PL:ACC + **bepa** *above* is used to convey the notion of the superlative degree of comparisons, as illustrated by example (67).

(67) Kahro-magno-tu-ká'u 'inim bʷia-po si'ime-m-bépa yó'o-ta-ka-i
    Charlemagne-now-deceased here earth-in all-PL-above superior-CAU-be-PPL
    Charlemagne was the supreme king on earth.

Sentence (68) which draws on **če'a** shows how a prototypical comparison of inequality and the superlative degree can appear as conjoined structures in a heightened comparative of inequality construction.

(68) če'a húni tú'ii si'ime-m-bépa tú'ii-ka-i
    more even good all-PL:ACC-above good-be-PPL
    This is even better, it's better than all of them.

Buelna correctly says the following with respect to superlatives: "No tiene esta lengua comparativo, ni superlativo, que se forma de positivo, como la latina;" (Buelna 1891:45, Item 143)[5] Nevertheless, he still lists **cheua (če'ewa)** as an adverb of comparison. Subsequently, in items 143–146 on p. 45, he lists a number of adverbials which he considers to be superlatives of these. In contemporary Yaqui, several forms of the adverb of comparison **cheua (če'ewa)** are still used. These include **če'e-wa-su,** given in examples (69)–(71).

(69) če'e-wa=su=ne 'ilí hú'unea
    more-VR=EMP=I little know
    More and more, I am understanding a little.

(70) née 'íntok če'e-wa=su 'á'a tú'u-ri-síme
    I CNJ more-VR=EMP it good-VR-go
    And I was enjoying it more and more.

---

[5] "This language, unlike Latin, has neither the comparative nor the superlative, which are formed from the positive grade." (Buelna 1891:45, Item 143)

(71) čé'e-wa=su búi-ti-sime bʷé'ituk káril-ta ku-kúh-híkkaha-k
    more-VR=EMP run-PPL-go   train-ACC RDP-whistle-hear-PRF
    He ran faster and faster, because he heard the train whistling.

The use of a morphemically more complex sequence **če'e-wan-su** is illustrated by sentence (72). There seems to be no significant difference in meaning between this and the shorter **če'e-wa=su** in examples (69)–(71).

(72) Lióh-ta téa-m čé'e-wa-n=su   yó'o-ri-si-wa
    God-ACC name-PL more-VR-CON=EMP revere-ABS-AVR-PSV
    God's name was being revered more and more.

In addition to the above two contrastive sequences, Yaqui has a reduplicated form of **čé'a** which is used when there is a conceived object that is being produced with increasingly high quality through time as seen in example (73).

(73) 'áapo 'íntok če-čé'e-wa=su   tú'ii 'etého-i-ta   né-u wée-tua-síme
    he   and   RDP-more-VR=EMP good talk-NZR-ACC me-to go-CAU-go
    He went on telling me better and better stories.

A slightly different construction involves the use of the emphatic counter expectation particle **=san** with **čé'a** *more*. In the following example, **čé'a=san** is the object complement of the participialized verb **-'éa** *to think*, which registers the normal expected state of affairs which is negated in the main clause of the sentence (74).

(74) táa čé'a=san-'éa-ka   káa bémuča-'a-wa-k
    But more=CTX-think-PPL not whip-EV-PSV-PRF
    But fortunately for him, he was not whipped.

Another version of the superlative is the use of the suppletive verb **muúke/kókko** *die* SG/PL to express an extreme degree of the physiological state of thirst, as the examples in (75) and (76) show. Another interesting aspect of (76) is that the use of the postposition **-e** INST indicates the source of the sensation described by the sentence.

(75) ba'á-e   ne muúke   (76) ba'á-e   té kókko
    water-INST I die:SG   water-INST we die:PL
    I am exceedingly thirsty. (dying of thirst)   *We are dying of thirst.*

There are probably other ways to compose descriptive phrases to express the superlative degree. For example, in (77) the negative **kaa** functions along with the non-finite verb **'áa** *be able* with a following stative verb.

(77) káa 'áa támačia-tu
    not able measure-VR
    immeasurable

The most common way to express the superlative degree of comparison, however, is by means of the accusative form of the quantifier "all" in a variety of constructions that involve the postposition **-bepa** *above*. The simplest of these is given in sentence (78).

(78) si'ime-m-bépa nák-su-a-k
    all-pl-above love-CMP-PSV-PRF
    He was loved more than all.

The postposition **-bepa** in these superlative constructions may itself carry additional morphemic material. In sentence (79), for example, it is further marked by the following postposition **-t** *on*.

(79) si'ime-m-bépa-t   'á'a weám-nee-'u
    all-PL:ACC-above-on his walk-FUT-GND
    He will have supreme authority over everyone. (lit., he will walk on top of all of them)

The entire positional phrase may be verbalized. In such cases it functions as the complement of the verbalizing **-tu** and this structure is then participialized with the suffix **-laa,** as illustrated by sentences (80) and (81).

(80) 'áapo si'ime-bépa-tu-laa si'ime 'áet hiapsa
he, above-over-be-PRF:PPL all him-on live
He is above all, everyone lives because of him.

(81) 'áapo si'ime-bépa-tú-laa
he above-over-be-PRF:PPL
He has become above everyone (in location and power).

PART III: WORD CLASSES

NOUN MORPHOLOGY

1.0. Introduction

The word classes of Yaqui include nouns, pronouns, demonstratives, verbs, adverbs, adjectives, and particles. In this section we begin to describe the properties of Yaqui nouns. On the one hand, nouns in Yaqui have no phonological characteristics per se that set them off from other parts of speech. Their syllabic patterning follows that of Yaqui words in general, e.g., CVCV, CVCVC, CVVCV, CVVCVC, as evidenced by the forms in examples (1)(a)–(j).

(1)(a)	téta	*stone*	(f)	hamut	*woman*
(b)	téeka	*sky*	(g)	tékil	*work*
(c)	baá'a	*water*	(h)	yá'ut	*leader*
(d)	hékkaa	*shade*	(i)	káuwis	*fox*
(e)	wásuktia	*year*	(j)	wásuk	*year*

On the other hand, nouns make up a considerable segment of Yaqui vocabulary and they do have their fully distinctive semantic and morphological properties. In this section we discuss some of the most salient of these morphological properties. In addition to the basic forms, Yaqui vocabulary contains numerous derived nouns as well as compound nouns which are formed by a variety of processes. These compounds may be broadly categorized as Noun + Noun, Noun + Verb, and Noun + Adjective compounds. Finally, Yaqui employs several different kinds of suffixes to derive nouns from verbs and adjectives.

2.0. Compound nouns

The Noun + Noun compounds given in examples (2)(a)–(c) can all be characterized as Modifier-Head constructions since characteristics of the second noun are what determine the overall meaning of the compound. Moreover in each case, the semantic relation between Noun1 and Noun2 is metonymic, i.e., a kind of Part-to-Whole relationship. Thus, a feather is a part of a bird's wing in example (2)(a), a sweet tasting viscous fluid we call honey is produced by bees in (2)(b), and fingers are extensions from the palm of the hand in (2)(c).

(2)(a)	mása	*wing*	+	boóa	*fur*	>	masá-bóa	*feather*
(b)	muúmu	*bee*	+	bá'a-wa	*juice*	>	mumú-bá'awa	*honey*
(c)	máma-n	*hand*	+	pusía-m	*eye-s*	>	mám-pusíam	*fingers*

2.1. Phonological characteristics of compounding

Compounding also has its phonological characteristics. In all three cases above, one of the members has a longer phonological form in its uncompounded state and loses this length when it enters into the compound. Thus the long vowels of **boóa** *fur* and **muúmu** *bee* are realized as short vowels in their respective compounds in (2)(a)–(b). High tone also shifts to the second syllable in the compound form of (2)(b). Finally, the CVCV syllable structure of **máma** *hand* shortens to **mam** in the compound of (2)(c). However, as later examples will show, not all compounds involve phonological shortening of some member in a compound.

Other patterns form compound nouns composed of a Noun + Derived Adjectives or Noun + Derived Verb. Typical examples of this are given in (3)(a)–(c). In example (3)(a) the noun is the direct object of **baáki** *cooked*. The compound, consisting of the word **naposa** *ashes* + **baáki** *cooked* is conventionally taken to refer to "hominy." A similar compound is used to express the idea of "candy" in (3)(b). The compound in (3)(c) is composed of a subject noun, an intransitive verb, and a nominalizing suffix. It graphically characterizes the concept lightning as the rain sticking out its tongue.

```
(3)(a) napósa    + baák-i      >   napó-báki
       ashes      cook-STAT        hominy
   (b) 'asúka    + baák-i-m    >   'asúka-bakim
       sugar      cook-STAT-PL     candy
   (c) yúku     + bé'ok-te + -ia > yúku-bé'oktia
       rain      stick out tongue  lightning
```

Yaqui commonly uses compounding as a favorite means for coining place names, as the story of Gabriel Sparrow given in Part VI reveals.

2.2. Derived nouns

Nouns may be derived from adjectives, verbs, or other nouns by means of several different suffixes. These include **-wa** ABSTRACT QUALITY, **-wa-me** ABSTRACT + NOMINALIZER, **-reo** AGENTIVE, **-ri** PASSIVE, and **-raa** COLLECTIVE.

2.2.1. The abstract -wa

A limited number of adjectives may take the suffix **-wa** to derive an abstract noun which denotes the quality designated by the adjective itself. Thus, the abstract suffix **-wa** is functionally equivalent to English **-ness,** as examples (4)–(6) illustrate.

```
(4) tú'i/tu'u-    good       >   tú'u-wa     goodness
(5) káka          sweet      >   káka-wa     sweetness, candy
(6) kía           delicious  >   kía-wa      flavor
```

A derived noun with **-wa** can function in the grammar just like an underived noun, as seen in (7), where **káka-wa** means "candy."

```
(7) káka-wa      tuká       yá'a-wa-k
    sweet-QUA    yesterday  make-PSV-PRF
    Candy was made yesterday
```

2.2.2. The "passive" abstractivizer -wa-me

A second kind of nominalization is derived by the use of the bimorphemic suffix sequence **-wa-me**. The source of this sequence is the passive suffix **-wa** and the nominalizing suffix **-me**. Because it seems to be used much more frequently to derive abstract nouns and very rarely results in nominalizations having the meaning of "one who is...", I treat **-wame** as a unit.

In some contexts, this suffix is used as a functional equivalent of the abstract **-wa,** as in example (8). Semantically, it adds the schematic meaning "being in a state characterized by the presence of X" to the noun that it derives.

```
(8) naámu    cloud    >   namú-wame   cloudiness
```

Sentence (9) illustrates this derived nominal in focus position in a complex sentence.

```
(9) namú-wame  káa-tú'ii,  tásia-ta     yé-te-u       nun-nu'upa
    cloud-QUA  not-good    cough-ACC    people-VR-to  RDP-bring
    Cloudiness is not good; it brings coughs to people.
```

Semantically, however, **-wame** differs from **-me** in that it seems to usually imply a change of state, as in example (10) or the result of some purposeful action as in examples (11)–(13). The use of a nominal formed with **-me** does not carry any such implication.

```
(10) 'alléa        to be happy       >   'allée-wame   happiness
(11) sú'a         to kill (pl. obj)  >   sú'a-wame     murder
(12) kókko/kóko   to die (pl. subj)  >   kókko-wame    death
(13) 'étbʷa       to steal           >   'étbʷa-wame   theft
```

Usages of the derived nominals of examples (11) and (13) are both illustrated in sentence (14).

(14) yée-sú'a-wame 'ale-béna-si wáa'a 'étbʷa-wame káa-tú'ii
people-kill-ABS it-like-AVR that steal-ABS not-good
Murder and likewise theft are bad.

Notice however, that Yaqui does maintain contrastive forms in which **-wa** still retains its passive meaning. This is clear in the nominalized form given in example (15)(b).

(15)(a) sú'a-wame *murder* (b) sú'a-wá-k-ame *those who were killed*

2.2.3. The agentive nominalizer -me

The two classes of nominalizations discussed above designate concepts like the inherent qualities of specific entities or categories of events. In contrast, the third kind of nominalization that we turn to now, places salience on the agent who is involved in an event. The agentive nominalizer **-me** actually has a variety of morphemic alternates with the shapes **-ame, -me,** and **-m.** It can often be glossed as "the one who" or "those who," as illustrated by examples (16)–(18).

(16) húu'u 'áma hó'aa-k-ame
that there house-VR-NZR
the one who lives there

(17) húme'e húya-m, káka-si ta-táka-me
those tree-PL sweet-AVR RDP-fruit:bear-NZR
the trees that bear sweet fruit

The meaning "the one who does X" is clearly seen in example (18), where it designates the singular subject of the motion verb **wéye** *to go.*

(18) wéye *to go, be in motion* > wéye-me *one who is going*

The use of the nominalization **wéyeme** *the one who is going* is illustrated in sentence (19), where it functions as the direct object of the verb **bíča** *to see.* Notice that the nominalization suffix **-me** reduces to **-m** with the addition of the accusative suffix **-ta.** This shortening does not take place, however, when **wéyeme** functions as a subject noun, as in sentence (20).

(19) húka'a 'áma wéyém-ta bíča-k
that:ACC there going-ACC saw-PRF
He saw the one who went there.

(20) wáa'a wéye-me hí'i-bʷá-bae-ka wéye
that go-NZR IZR-eat-DSD-PPL go
The one who is in motion is looking for food.

Transitive and causative verbs also commonly enter into nominalizations and function as subject nouns (21) with different semantic roles. Sentence (22) shows a nominalization functioning as a reflexive subject nominal.

(21) bamíh-tua (b) bamíh-tuá-me
hurry-CAU hurry-CAU-NZR
to cause to hurry *one who causes to hurry*

(22) 'áu bamíh-tua-me láuti múk-nee-'e-tea
self hurry-CAU-NZR quickly die-FUT-EV-QUO
It is said that one who hurries himself, will die soon.

Applicative forms of Yaqui verbs are also nominalized, as seen in examples (23)–(25).

(23) wásuk-te *to attain/to be X years* > wásuk-te-me *one who attains.. years*
(24) wáme'e 'ilí 'uúsim kée woói wásuk-te-me
those little children not:yet two year-VR-NZR
little children not yet two years old
(25) nóite *to go somewhere, visit* > nóite-me *one who visits*

Nominalizations with **-ame** often function as objects of postpositions, as seen in sentence (26). This example is also a fully independent sentence, which again illustrates the predicative character of the postposition **-béna** (cf. COMPARATIVE CONSTRUCTIONS, pp. 105–109 and POSTPOSITIONS, pp. 200–201).

(26) kaákun   nóite-k-am-ta-béna-sia
     nowhere go-PRF-NZR-ACC-like-AVR
     He was like someone who was not going anywhere.

When a nominalization serves as a modifier of a noun which is the object of a postposition, the postposition attaches to the modifying nominalization, as seen in sentence (28).

(27) bʷáána   *to cry* > bwaná-me   *one who is crying*

(28) húe hámut-ta   bʷáná-m-ta-mak   siíka
     that woman-ACC cry-NZR-ACC-with go:SG:PAST
     He went with the woman who was crying.

Note that Yaqui forms agentive nouns with **-me** with the same mechanisms that it uses to form relative clauses that modify a head noun that is co-referential with the subject of the relative clause. Nouns formed with **-me** may function in any of the grammatical roles such as actor, agent, patient or goal. The morphologically simplest nominalizations are those in which **-ame** attaches to a bare verb stem, as seen in examples (29)–(31). More generally, however, as those examples attest, Yaqui verbs in any tense or aspect form may be nominalized.

(29) hé'ee   *to drink*   > hé'ee-me   *drinker*
(30) taáka   *to bear fruit*   > taká-me   *fruit bearer*
(31) bʷáse   *to ripen, to mature* > bwáse-me   *one who is ripening*

Many nominalizations with **-ame** are built on verb stems that are derived or otherwise morphemically complex. In (33) for example, the verb stem **yáa** *to make* is marked with the participial **-ka** before it gets nominalized. In example (34), the verb stem **hé'ee** *to drink* is also marked with the participial **-ka,** indicating one who habitually does something.

(32)(a) yáa/yá'a- *to do, to make* > yáa-ka-me   *maker*

(33) Liós 'iníka'a 'ánia-ta   yáa-ka-me
     God this:ACC world-ACC   make-PPL-NZR
     God, the maker of this world

(34) ba'á-súkam hé'e-ka-me
     water-hot   drink-PPL-NZR
     someone, anyone, one who drinks hot water

Nominalizations with **-ame** may also be used to modify a nominal elsewhere in the sentence. In sentence (35) the modifying nominalization is actually a nominalized adverbial clause.

(35) wáme=san húya-m   kía-m   ta-táka-me   wín-huba-si   bʷá-bʷáse-me
     DEM=EXP   tree-PL delicious-PL:ACC RDP-fruit-NZR   fragrant-smell-AVR   RDP-ripe-NZR
     the trees that were bearing delicious fruit which was ripening fragrantly...

The contrast between a bare verb and its nominalized form is illustrated in examples (36) and (37). The nominalization may be related to the stem in more than one way. For example, the nominalization in example (36) is a lexical passive, whereas that of example (37) is an agent.

(36) lú'ute   *to come to an end, be used up* > lú'ute-me   *that which is used up*
(37) nénka   *to sell*   > ne-nénka-me *a seller*

Example (38) shows both a Noun-Verb compound and two different nominalizations and the intricate way in which they can interrelate in a single complex sentence. The compound **'asúka-báki-m** *candy* is a Noun-Verb compound marked in the plural and serving as subject of the sentence. The first nominalization is built on the intransitive applicative stem **lú'ute** *to come to an end*, which is marked with the perfective suffix **-k**. It is the heart of a negative relative clause which modifies the subject of the sentence. Finally, the second nominalization is actually in apposition to the first one and it is built on the reduplicated stem of the verb **nénka** *to sell*.

(38) 'asúka-báki-m   káa lú'ute-k-ame   páhko'-apo káa né-nenki-su-a-k-ame
     sugar-cooked-PL   not use:up-PRF-NZR   feast-in   not RDP-sell-CMP-PSV-PRF-NZR
     the candy that was not used up in the feast, which had not been completely sold

Example (40) illustrates a simple nominalization functioning as the head of a subject relative clause. The verb stem itself, as shown in (39), is a common loan from Náhuatl and the nominalization built on it is fully transparent semantically.

(39) tekípanoa *to work* > tekipanoa-me *worker*

(40) tú'i-si   tekipánoa-me bú'uu-k   kobá'a-nee
     good-AVR   work-NZR   much-ACC   earn-FUT
     He who works well will earn a lot.

The negative **kaa** is preposed to form nominalizations that convey notions such as "uncooked" or "without."

(41) káa-mantéka-ka-me bʷá'ee
     not-lard-VR-NZR   eat
     He eats the ones without grease.

2.2.4. The agentive suffix -reo

The agentive suffix **-reo**, and its alternate form **-leo**, suffixes to both nouns and verbs to form a nominal with the generalized meaning "one who customarily does X," as in example (42).

(42) 'aámu *to hunt* > 'amú-reo *a hunter*

This suffix has probably been derived from the Spanish **-ero/-era**, e.g., "lavar" *to wash* > "lavadero" *a laundry*. I am not aware of having seen it in Buelna. It very possibly could have entered Yaqui through the borrowing of Aztec words such as in example (43), which contrasts with the nominalization given above in example (39).

(43)(a) tekipánoa   (b) tekipánoa-reo
        to work   *worker*

The fact that nominal forms derived with the form **-leo** designate either agents carrying out typically female roles or activities directed to children suggests that it is a diminutive form of the agentive suffix **-reo**.

(44) hí-paksia *to wash (intransitive)* > hí-paksia-leo *wash-woman, washer*
(45) 'uhú'u *to take care of (children)* > 'uhú'u-leo *a nurse, maid*

A small number of object nouns take the suffix **-leo** to designate an agent whose activity involves the object noun in some way or another. In examples (46), the object noun **kúču** *fish* serving as the base for the nominalization is an animate noun and is typically small in size relative to the agent. Thus, the l-form of the nominalization suffix used here may well be construable as a diminutive. On the other hand, in example (47), the object noun **kúta** *wood, pole* may be quite large relative to the the woodcutter.

(46) kúču *a fish* > kúču-leo *a fisherman*
(47) kúta *a piece of wood* > kúta-reo *a woodcutter*

2.2.5. The nominalizer -ri

Finally, there is the rare nominalizing suffix **-ri**, which seems to be inherently passive in its meaning. While this suffix seems to be a participializer, it also functions as a kind of nominalizer. This is clearly seen in example (48). The possessive term **'attea**, meaning "one's possessions" is conventionally construed to mean "women's clothing" when it carries this suffix. The functional utility of a variety of nominalizing suffixes is seen in the way that Yaqui allows a simple stem such as **yoéme** *person* to participate in distinct nominalizations that mean quite different things. Thus the nominalization **yoémia** *child* contrasts semantically with **yoémiari** *descendents* and with **yoémraa** *people, the Yaqui nation* given below in example (52).

(48) 'áttea *one's possessions* > (hamut) 'átte-ri *(women's) clothing*
(49) yoém-ia *a child* > yoém-ia-ri *descendents, etc.*
(50) tá'aru *to lose* > (bem) tá'aru-ri *what (they) lost*

A nominalization with **-ri** can, like other nominalizations, be subject to further morphological development. In (51) for example, the **-ri** nominalization is marked for plural.

(51) húme'e 'áman bíttua-ri-m
 those there send-NZR-PL
 the ones who were sent there

2.2.6. The collective suffix -raa

The suffix **-raa** can be construed as a collective, its function being that of extending the attribution of some property from a single individual to a set of individuals, or from a restricted area to a broad one. As the following examples show, **-raa** rather productively suffixes to both animate and inanimate nouns as well as to some abstract nouns and to some derived nominals with a wide variety of semantic consequences. The examples in (52) present a straightforward use of the collective: a single Yaqui is a **yoéme**, and the entire group of Yaquis as a people is **yoémraa**. Similarly, the chief spokesman for the Yaqui community is a **yá'ut**. The use of the collective suffix with this root extends the idea of authority to an entire group of people associated with the chief spokesman.

(52) yoéme *a person, a Yaqui* > yoém-raa *people, Yaqui nation*
(53) yá'ut *a chief* > yá'u-raa *the authorities*

Some of the usages of **-raa** result in derived nouns with meanings that are based on some rather abstract characteristics of the entity being described, meanings that are motivated, but not necessarily predictable. This can be considered to be the grammaticalization of some kind of implication extracted from the meaning of the underived root. In example (54), for instance, the root **'uúsi** *a child*, when used with **-raa,** comes to have the meaning "the innocents." The derived form takes its meaning from a primary perceived characteristic of young children. The usage of **-raa** in example (55) gives an even more attenuated meaning. Whereas **haámučia** means "a female," the derived form **haámučia'araa** does not mean "womankind in general," but rather designates a kind of male member of the species, a Yaqui Don Juan who is always on the lookout for a woman.

(54) 'uúsi *a child* > 'usi-raa *innocents*
(55) haámučia *a female* > haámučia-'araa *woman chaser*

Sentence (56) provides clear evidence for the meaning of (55) given above since there is a clearly specified plural male subject involved.

(56) 'o'ówi-m haámut-čia-'a-raa-m
 man-PL GM:woman-NZR-EV-AZR-PL
 The men are women chasers.

The use of the collective **-raa** as it applies to physical regions is seen in examples (57) and (58). From (57) we see that **b^{w}iía** means "land." It implies nothing whatsoever regarding ownership. On the other hand, the collective form **b^{w}íaraa** means "territory, country" and this clearly implies some kind of control and possession on somebody's part. Likewise, in example (58) the form **hó'aa** *domicile* implies some kind of ownership, but this is restricted to a single house. The collective form **hó'araa** extends the implied ownership throughout an entire area where houses are densely clustered.

(57) b^{w}iía *land* > b^{w}ia-raa *territory, country*
(58) hó'aa *domicile* > hó'a-raa *a village*

Less productively, **-raa** suffixes to verbs to derive the base for a nominalization with **-me**. Both of the following examples result in a nominal with a pejorative meaning. The nominalization in example (59) is built on a reduplicated stem to indicate that the sentence has a plural subject, whereas that of (60) is built on a compound verb stem consisting of an adverb and a motion verb.

(59) noóka *to speak* > nón-noka-'ara-m *babblers*

(60) réhte *to walk* > náah-rehté-'eraa-m *vagabonds*

Adjectives also serve as bases for **-raa** in deriving abstract nouns. Semantically, the resultant meaning is often equivalent to that of **-wa** described above. In other instances, the abstract noun designates some effect due to the state designated by the adjective. In example (61) the nominalization **bú'uuraa** is built on the adjective stem **bú'uu** *many*, with the resultant meaning of "a multitude."

(61) bú'uu *much, many* > bú'uu-raa *a multitude (of people)*

Frequently, the meaning of nominalized adjectives is based on some perceptual characteristic of an entity. For example, (62) reflects the reification of a quality of something pleasing to the beholder's eyes. A psychological quality is designated by the nominalization **obéraa** in example (63), whereas example (64) places the speaker's attention on the result of an effective illuminating agent.

(62) 'uhyoói *beautiful* > 'uhyói-raa *beauty*

(63) 'oóbe *to be lazy* > 'obé-raa *laziness*

(64) maáči *to be visible* > mačí-raa *light*

Following the patterns we have already observed for other nominalizations of Yaqui, those nominals formed with **-raa** function in numerous ways in Yaqui grammar, including carrying out the roles of subjects, objects, incorporated nouns, and locative nouns. Examples (65)–(70) are typical. To begin, a **-raa** nominalization functions as the comment in the equative (or topic-comment) sentence given in sentence (65). The topic slot is filled by a nominalization in **-me**.

(65) pusí-m-mea yée-wa-me   kía 'usí-raa
     eye-PL-INST play-PSV-NZR just child-AZR
     Flirting with the eyes, it was only a thing of children.

An incorporated **-raa** nominalization is illustrated in example (66). It is incorporated into a kind of possessive statement as shown by the use of a form of the suffix **-ek**.

(66) née-káa yá'u-ra-k   ínepo 'íno sáuwe
     I-not   chief-NZR-have I   RFL   order
     I am under no one's authority, I govern myself.

Examples (67)–(69) show **-raa** nominalizations that serve as objects of a postposition.

(67) sí'ime hó'a-ra-m-met   siíka   (69) bu'úu-raa-ta-nasuk
     all   house-NZR-PL-on went   much-NZR-POS-amidst
     He went to all the homes/villages.   *in the midst of the multitude*

(68) nót-te-k-amme   bém b^{w}ía-ra-u lúula
     return-VR-PRF-they their land-NZR-to straight
     They returned straight to their land.

The final example illustrates a **-raa** nominalization that is head of a Quantifier-Noun Noun Phrase.

(70) sí'ime yoém-ra
     all   yaqui-NZR
     all the people

2.2.7. The rare suffixes -i, -ia, and -laa

The suffixes **-i, -ia,** and **-laa** which basically are participializers, occur with very limited distribution as nominalizers. The nominalizations themselves relate to the verb stem in a variety of ways. In example

(71) for example, the verb **'etého** is a speech-act verb and its nominalization is the perceived result of a given speech-act. The pair of nominalizations given in examples (72) and (73) are built on verb stems that designate an instrumental noun and a discrete, but unspecified entity, respectively.

 (71) 'etého *to converse* > 'etého-i *a story, an account*

 (72) hí-číke *to brush, to sweep* > hí-čik-ia *a brush, comb, broom*

 (73) čiktu *to be lost* > číktu-laa-ta *that which was lost* (ACC)

There is also the suffix **-ria** which seems to be a kind of abstractivizer. In example (74), it functions to turn the word meaning "day" into its opposite, i.e., "night." In example (75) **-ria** takes an adverb meaning "far away" and derives a form meaning "in the distance."

 (74) tuúka/tukáa *yesterday* > tukáa-ria-m *night*

 (75) mékkaa *far away* > mékka-'aria-t *in the distance*

3.0. Layering

Layering is quite common in Yaqui, i.e., verbalized nouns become renominalized, and nominalized verbs become reverbalized. This mechanism, in part, allows for grammatical structures that are single words to encode sufficient semantic content that turns them into minimal relative clauses, i.e., this is the point at which syntax and morphology interface. The particular verbalization process that feeds into the highest level nominalization gives a particular semantic flavoring to the whole structure. The first of these consists of the use of the possessive suffix **-ek** and its related allomorphs. Semantically, the nominalization means "the one who has X."

 (76) 'ópoa-k-am-ta né 'á'a biča-k
   tear-have-NZR-ACC I her see-PRF
   I saw her while she was crying.

 (77) tutú'uli-k hékkaa-k-am-ta-u yepsa-k
   beautiful-ACC shade-have-NZR-ACC-to arrive-PRF
   He came to a tree having a beautiful shade.

 (78) káa-mantéka-ka-me b^{w}á'ee
   not-lard-have-NZR eat
   He eats the ones without grease.

A second verbalization process utilizes the causative suffix **-te** *to make*. The nominalization that results from suffixing the proper form of **-ame** generally means "the one who makes X."

 (79) kári-te-k-ame
   house-VR-PRF-NZR
   the one who made the house

An epistemically remote nominalization is derived by suffixing **-ame** to a nominal verbalized by the connecting suffix **-tu-** and the composite **-ka'u** *formerly*. The resulting nominal is generally construed as meaning "the one or ones who used to exist." Frequently **-ame** reduces phonologically to the single nasal **-m**, as it does in examples (80) and (81). This makes it homophonous with the plural suffix **-m**. Context, however, usually resolves the ambiguity.

 (80) si'ime húme'e hó'aa-ra-tu-k-a'u-m
   all those house-AZR-VR-PRF-GND-NZR
   all those houses that used to be there

 (81) si'ime húme'e bát-kát-ria-m-tu-k-a'u-m
   all those first-go:PL-ABS-PL-VR-PRF-GND-NZR
   all the "ancestors"

Finally, **-ame** may be suffixed to a noun that has functions as the complement of the quotative **-tea**. The resulting nominalization, in this case, means "the one who/that which is called X," as in sentences (82) and (83).

(82) kopáal-im-téa-m-ta   'á'a miika-k
     copal-PL-call-NZR-ACC him give-PRF
     They gave him something called copal.

(83) matilde-'e-tea-m-ta   né haiwa
     matilde-EV-called-NZR-ACC I look:for
     I am looking for a girl named Matilde.

Nominalizations formed with **-ame** can be the bases for attaching postpositions. For example, a nominalization of the form **V + -ame** serves as the base for attaching the postposition **-béna**, which in turn is marked with the future suffix **-nee**. The overall construction has the schematic meaning "the one who will become like X." This is illustrated by sentence (84).

(84) húnak 'intok hú'ub^{w}a yó'o-tu-m-ta-béna-nee
     then and just:now grow-VR-NZR-ACC-like-FUT
     Then he will be like a youth.

A very productive nominalizer in Yaqui is a syntactic process by which a gerund or participial is construed as a possessed abstract entity. Any of the forms that indicate possession may be used, as well as any of the following participializers: **-i, -ri, -laa, -(a)'u/-Vwi, -'Vpo**. Various possessive markers are illustrated in examples (85)–(89). The examples (85) and (86) employ the first person singular possessive prefix **'ín**.

(85) 'ín 'etého-i
     my converse-PPL
     what I say (my speech)

(86) 'ín wáata-'u-ta=ne   tómi-e   hínu-nee
     my want-GND-ACC=I money-INST buy-FUT
     I will buy what I want with money.

Third person singular possessors are indicated for the nominalizations given in examples (87) and (88), but they differ in that a specific possessor nominal is present in the construction in (87), whereas an emphatic third person singular possessor pronoun, marked with **-ik** is employed in (88).

(87) Jóanta   yá'a-ri
     John-POS do-PPL
     what John did (John's doing)

(88) 'ím tawá-nee 'áapo-'ik nót-te-'epo-táhtia
     here stay-FUT he-POS   return-VR-GND-until
     It will stay here until he returns.

Finally, sentence (89) illustrates an unpossessed nominalization marked with both the nominalizing suffix **-laa** and the accusative suffix **-ta**.

(89) 'áapo húka'a   čík-tu-laa-ta   téa-k
     he   that:ACC lose-VR-PPL-ACC find-PRF
     He found the one that was lost.

All these constructions are described more extensively in RELATIVE CLAUSES, pp. 379–385.

NOUN INFLECTION

1.0. Introduction

Yaqui shows very productive processes for marking nouns that serve as indirect and direct objects. It also registers a consistent contrast between singular and plural number on nouns. However, it has essentially lost the absolutive marking that is common in other Uto-Aztecan languages. As Langacker (1977a:94–95) shows, the Proto-Uto-Aztecan absolutive suffix **-ti** was followed by the active participle **-a** in Yaqui. These two suffixes fused to become **-ta** and became an accusative singular marker. Less productively, Yaqui marks diminutives of proper nouns. It also marks the category "used to exist" for nominals or "deceased" for proper names or kin terms. For ease in presentation, we assign the inflectional data of Yaqui to two classes, major inflectional processes and minor inflectional ones.

2.0. Major inflectional processes

The major inflectional processes of Yaqui relate to the marking of subjects, objects, and indirect objects. As the following discussion shows, accusative marking in Yaqui serves for more than simply highlighting the direct object or the indirect object. Particular extensions include the marking of possessors and marking for the subject of relative clauses. Other major inflectional processes relate to the marking of plural and collective subjects.

2.1. Accusative marking

The suffix **-ta** in its basic usage, indicates accusative singular case. The following examples of **-ta** show it in its role of marking different kinds of accusative singular nouns or entities that can be treated syntactically as direct objects. Example (1) illustrates the use of **-ta** to signal a prototypical human direct object. Edible fruits are also good candidates for direct object marking, as seen in example (2).

(1) yoém-ta 'áman nánke-k
person-ACC there meet-PRF
He met a man there.

(2) nabó-ta bʷá'ee
tuna-ACC eat
He is eating a tuna.

(3) 'ámman káu-kobi'i-ku né ku'ú-ta ... bit-laa
off:there mountain-corner-in I agave-ACC... see-PPL
I have seen an agave off there in the mountain.

Yaqui also marks discrete inanimate objects with **-ta,** as illustrated in sentence (4).

(4) 'áapo kári-ta 'enčí 'á'a yá'a-ria-'ii'a
he house-ACC you:ACC him make-APL-IN:DSD
He wants you to build a house for him.

Abstract nouns such as **tékil** *work* and nominalized verbs such as **'úhyoria** *beautiful things* and **hí'ohtei** *paper* are also marked with **-ta,** as seen in examples (5)–(7).

(5) tá'abʷi tékil-ta yá'a-nee
different work-ACC do-FUT
He will do a different work.

(6) 'úhyo-ria-ta ne-u noóka-k
beauty-NZR-ACC me-to speak-PRF
He spoke beautiful things to me.

(7) hí'oh-te-i-ta mabéta-k
paper-VR-NZR-ACC receive-PRF
He received a letter.

Yaqui also treats nominalized clauses as direct objects syntactically by marking them with **-ta,** as shown by sentence (8).

(8) 'á'a súale-k, húka'a káa-tú'ii-k bó'o-hóo-ria-m-ta-su
him believe-PRF that:ACC not-good-ACC do-NZR-ACC-EXP
Well, they believed that one who did wrong.

The indefinite pronoun **kaábe** *no one* may also be marked with the accusative. Example (9) is typical.

(9) kaábe-ta hiníle
no:one-ACC fears
He is afraid of no one.

2.1.1. Extensions of -ta

Other usages of **-ta** show an extension of the accusative that is common in Uto-Aztecan languages, i.e., the accusative is also used to mark a third person singular nominal possessor as in examples (10) and (11). Perhaps the original semantics involved the concept of a substantive "possessing" the action of a verb. In possessor + possessed object noun phrases, **-ta** suffixes to the attributive noun in a role that is functionally equivalent to the use of "-'s" in English.

(10) Hóan-ta huúbi (11) María-ta kuúna
John-POS wife   Maria-POS husband
John's wife   *Mary's husband*

Possessor nouns that are the ground of comparison for a comparative construction, as in sentence (12), are also marked with **-ta**.

(12) kowí-ta wee-la-'apo bétčei teene-k
pig-POS go-NZR-GND curved mouth-have
He had a curved mouth like a pig's

2.1.2. Possessive -ta as subject of a relative clause

The possessive suffix **-ta** also marks the subject nouns of relative clauses and temporal clauses. Such clauses can often be glossed as "X's doing," indicating that Yaqui relative, temporal and circumstantial clauses are at the nominal end of the Noun-Verb spectrum. Lindenfeld characterized this use of the accusative as one kind of "dependency marking." (1973:53–61). A temporal dependent clause with the subject marked in the accusative is given in sentence (13), whereas a dependent locative clause with the subject **baa'á** *water* marked in the accusative is given in example (14). Finally, example (15) illustrates a dependent circumstantial clause in which the place name is marked in the accusative.

(13) ta'á-ta yéu-yéh-te-k né béha wák-nee
sun-POS out-sit-VR-PRF I well dry-FUT
When the sun comes out, I'll get dry.

(14) ba'á-ta kó'om-siká-'apo
water-POS down-go-NZR
where the water goes down

(15) Sonóora-ta mám-po wéče-ka-'apo
Sonora-POS hand-in fall-PPL-GND
the fall/conquest of Sonora

In example (16) both the object of the main verb "see" and the object of the embedded verb "eat" are marked by the accusative **-ta**. Notice also that the object of "see" is also the subject of the relative clause and that the nominalized verb which modifies **bobók** *frog* is also marked with **-ta**.

(16) behák née bakót-ta bobók-ta bwá'e-m-ta né bíča-k
just:now I snake-ACC frog-ACC eat-NZR-ACC I see-PRF
I just saw a snake eating a frog.

Relative clauses in Uto-Aztecan serve as both subjects and direct objects in sentences. Yaqui is no exception. The nominal serving as head of a direct object relative clause is marked with **-ta,** as is the clause itself. If there are two conjoined relative clauses in the sentence, as is the case in example (17), both clauses are marked with accusative **-ta**.

(17) bémpo 'usí-ta   kó'om-wéče-k-a'u-ta   híapsa-m-ta   tóbok-ta-k
     they child-ACC down-fall-PPL-GND-ACC live-NZR-ACC lift-VR-PRF
     They lifted up alive the boy who had fallen down.

2.1.3. Use of -ta as a postpositional base

In an even more semantically attenuated version, possessive **-ta** serves as a base for attaching a postposition. In examples (18) and (19), **-ta** is the base for attaching **-beah** *by*.

(18) hú'upa-ta-béah   né 'á'a 'éu-su-ria-k
     mesquite-POS-by I it   hide-CMP-APL-PRF
     I hid it for him by the mesquite tree.

(19) húu'u káuwis ču'ú-ta-béah   wéye-n
     that fox   dog-POS-front   go-PCN
     The fox was on the other side of the dog.

Occasionally, an echo-vowel is inserted between **-ta** and the noun to which it attaches, as seen in example (20), for instance.

(20) bʷéha-'a-ta-bena-si...   čá'a-si-síme
     gourd-EV-POS-like-AVR   suspend-RDP-go
     It went floating like a gourd.

In examples (21) and (22), **-ta** is the base for attaching the postposition **-bétuk** *underneath* to its nominal object.

(21) 'áapo 'íntok 'ehéa-ta-bétuk   taáwa-k
     he   and   ironwood-POS-under remain-PRF
     He stayed beneath the ironwood tree.

(22) bʷé'u hú'upa-ta-bétuk   kátek
     big   mesquite-POS-under located
     He is under a big mesquite.

Other postpositions for which **-ta** serves as a connecting base include **-u** *to*, **-násuk** *in the middle of*, and **-či** *on*. These are illustrated in examples (23)–(25).

(23) počo'o-ria-bétana wée hobé'eso-ta-u lúula
     woods-NZR-from   go ram-POS-to   straight
     Coming out of the woods, he went straight to the ram.

(24) 'enéro-ta-násuk   wé-o   'á'abo noite
     January-POS-mid   go-when here   come
     He comes here in the middle of January

(25) 'ilí búu-hámut-ta-či   yéča-'a-wa-k
     little donkey-woman-POS-on   put-EV-PSV-PRF
     It was put on a little donkey.

In sentences with nominals serving as direct and indirect objects, respectively, both nominals are marked with the accusative **-ta.** Sentence (26) is a typical example.

(26) hú'u hóan betú-ta   lipró-ta   miíka-k
     that John Bert-ACC book-ACC   give-PRF
     John gave Bert a book.

2.2. Plural marking on nouns

Most noun stems can take either singular or plural forms. There are only a few inherently plural nouns, e.g., **náka-m** *ear*-PL, **máma-m** *hand*-PL. Whereas the nominative-accusative distinction is clearly marked for singular forms in Yaqui, the situation is not so clear for the plural forms in which the same morpheme

-im, alternating with **-m** marks all of the following: nominative plural, accusative plural, and possessive plural.

The use of **-im** to mark nominative plural is illustrated in sentences (27) and (28).

(27) wó'i-m   kía-k   tú'ure
    coyote-PL delicious-ACC like
    Coyotes like delicious food.

(28) 'o'ów-im 'á'abo kaáte
    man-PL this:way come
    Men are coming over here

The nominalization in example (29) suggests that a reduced form of the Proto-Uto-Aztecan actor nominalizer ***-ame** has fallen together with the Yaqui plural morpheme. Notice that the notion of plurality may also in part be signalled by the reduplication in this example.

(29) nón-noka-'a-ra-m
    RDP-talk-EV-ABS-PL
    babblers

For plural or mass nouns that serve as objects of postpositions, **-m** also serves as a postpositional base, as can be seen in example (30).

(30) tečó-m-po   né   kaíta   'ínne'a
    elbow-PL-in I nothing feel
    I don't feel anything in my elbows.

In certain contexts, **-im** clearly marks accusative plural. Example (31) illustrates a protypical plural direct object human noun.

(31) 'o'ów-im   bíča-k
    man-ACC:PL see-PRF
    He saw the men.

The Yaqui sentence in (32) uses the expression meaning "to kill bees" as a metaphor for collecting honey. This is an interesting parallel to the Cora use of the plural form of **sára** *bee* to designate "honey."

(32) mumú-m   káa sú'a-bae
    bees-ACC:PL not kill-DSD
    He does not want to "kill bees"

In plural direct object noun phrases of the form Attributive Adjective/Quantifier + Noun, both the modifier and the head noun are marked with **-im,** as seen in sentence (33)

(33) huébena-m   húya-m   há'ab^{w}e-ka-'apo ne ho'aa-k
    many-ACC:PL tree-ACC:PL stand-PRF-where I house-have
    I live where there are many trees standing.

Yaqui incorporates body part nouns into verbal constructions meaning "X possesses Y." Body parts such as **čáo-boa** *chin whiskers* are inherently plural. When inherently plural incorporated body parts occur with a modifying adjective in the clause, as is the case in example (34), the adjective itself is marked with the plural **-im.**

(34) tú'isi yó'o-we haíbu tosái-m   čáo-boa-k
    very old   now   white-ACC:PL chin-hair-VR-have
    He is very old, he now has white whiskers.

Quantifiers, which can function as head nouns in their own right, are marked with **-im** in the accusative plural. Typical examples are given in examples (35) and (36).

(35) sí'ime-m   tekípánoa-bit-róka
    all-ACC:PL work-see-QUO
    He says that he wants to see everyone working.

(36) sí'ime-m-bépa   tu'ii-ka
    all-ACC:PL-above good-being
    the best of all

The plural marker **-im** is also used to indicate the plurality of the subjects of relative clauses, as in example (37) as well as those of adverbial clause as in (38).

(37) húme'e yoéme-m hóa-'u
those man-ACC:PL do-NZR
what the men did (the men's doing)

(38) waébas-im lú'uto-'epo-táhtia
guayaba-ACC:PL end-NZR-until
until there were no more guayabas

2.3. Accusative marking: the collective

Both the accusative singular **-ta** and the plural marker **-im** may occur together suffixed to the same nominal. In such cases, as illustrated in sentence (39), the combination indicates a group or company of people accompanying the one to whose name it is attached.

(39) húme'e sebáhti-ta-im 'áman kaáte
those Sebastian-POS-PL there go:PL
Sebastian's family is going there.

When the group consists of only two people in a conjoined noun phrase, the double marking occurs only on the second member of the pair, as can be observed in example (40)

(40) húme'e páplo 'íntok siláh-ta-im
those Paul and Silas-POS-PL
Paul and Silas's group

Most Yaqui verbs that become nominalized show their nominalized status by means of a nominalizing suffix (cf. NOUN MORPHOLOGY, pp. 119–126). However, there is a small set of nominalized verbs that appear to have no nominalization suffix, at least when the nominalized verb is used in the accusative. Curiously, all four of the verbs in examples (41)–(45) belong to the domain of verbal or written communication. Two of them given in examples (41) and (42), **hí'oh-te** *to write* and **tebó-te** *to greet*, are marked with the verbalizing suffix **-te**, which comes historically from Proto-Uto-Aztecan *ti. The present day nominal status of these two forms suggests that the particular *-ti from which **-te** derives was the Proto-Uto-Aztecan absolutive suffix.

(41) née hí'oh-te-ta mabéta-k
I write-VR-ACC receive-PRF
I received a letter.

(42) tebó-te-ta né 'á-u tóhi-'i-se-k
greet-VR-ACC I her-to bring-EV-come-PRF
I have come to bring her greetings.

The nominalizations **sau-ta** *an order*, **uh-bʷán-ta** *a plea*, and **'etého-ta** *a talk, a story* are marked with the accusative **-ta**, which is also related historically to the Proto-Uto-Aztecan absolutive *-ti, which came to have the shape it does by fusing with a following older accusative suffix **-a** (cf. Langacker 1977a:95). Typical usages of these are illustrated in examples (43)–(45).

(43) 'íka né-sau-ta née yá'a-ria
this:ACC IZR-command-ACC me do-APL
Carry out this order for me.

(44) 'íka uhbʷán-ta née yá'a-ria
this:ACC plea-ACC me do-APL
Do me this favor.

(45) 'etého-ta súa-si-mači-k téuwaa-nee
talk-ACC smart-AVR-like-PRF tell-FUT
He will deliver a sophisticated discourse.

2.4. Accusative marking on adjectives and quantifiers

Quantifiers and nominalized adjectives also take **-ta** when functioning as heads of direct object noun phrases. Example (46) shows **-ta** marking a quantifier. In example (47) it attaches to a nominalized adjective, and in (48) it marks an indefinite pronoun.

SONORA YAQUI LANGUAGE STRUCTURES

(46) 'í'an senú sí'ime-ta   'á'au-nee
     now   one   all-ACC   ask:for-FUT
     Now, a person will ask for everything.

(47) tú'u-wa-ta   'áu   hariu-ria-nee
     good-NZR-ACC   RFL   hunt-APL-FUT
     He will search for goodness for himself.

(48) habé-ta   mamáto-bae-'e-tek   'emó   suúa
     someone-ACC   imitate-DSD-EV-if   RFL   guard
     If you want to imitate someone, be careful.

2.4.1. Accusative marking on attributive adjectives

When adjectives are in the attributive position with a direct object nominal, they are marked by the suffix **-k,** as illustrated by example (49). Normally, attributive adjectives follow the nominals that they modify, as in both of the following examples.

(49) tómi-ta   'ilíiki-k   maáčuk-ta-ka
     money-ACC   little-ACC   grasp-VR-PPL
     and receiving just a tiny bit of money

(50) yoém-nók-ta   huébena-k   né-u   téuwaa-taite-k
     yaqui-word-ACC   many-ACC   me-to tell-begin-PRF
     He began to tell me a lot of Yaqui words

Sentence (51) shows a construction in which each of three elements of a complex direct object noun phrase reflect a form of accusative marking. The first element is the accusative form of a demonstrative pronoun, the second is a negative adjective phrase marked with accusative **-k**, and the third is a nominalization marked with **-ta**.

(51) 'á'a súale-ka   taáwa-k   wáka'a   káa-tú'ii-k   bó'o-hóoria-m-ta=su
     him believe-PPL   remain-PRF   that:ACC not-good-ACC   road-make-NZR-ACC=EMP
     They kept on believing that "good for nothing," anyway.

As example (52) shows, the attributive adjective can be discontinuous from the head noun.

(52) čú'ú-ta   née b^{w}é'uu-k   nún-nu'ub^{w}a-n
     dog-ACC   I   big-ACC   RDP-carry-PCN
     I was carrying along a big dog.

Adverbs modifying nominalized adjectives may also be discontinuous from their head, as can be seen in example (53).

(53) tú'isi née káka-k   b^{w}á'a-b^{w}asa   néhpo
     very   I   sweet-ACC   RDP-cook   I
     I cook/make very good/sweet candy.

The order in which the discontinuous segments of the noun phrase occur in a sentence is variable. Whereas the head noun occurs first in sentence (52) followed by its modifier, in the first clause of sentence (54), the quantifier occurs first and its head noun follows the verb

(54) wépu'ulai-k   'á'a téhwaa-k   hunáka'a   taká-ta   káa 'á'a b^{w}a'a-nee-'e-bétana
     one-ACC   her   show-PRF   that:ACC   fruit-ACC   not it   eat-FUT-EV-from
     He showed her one fruit and told her that she should not eat that one.

Attributive adjectives may also precede the nominals that they modify. In example (55) the adjective **tuú'uli-k** precedes a nominalized noun that functions as the object of a postposition, whereas in example (56) the attributive adjective precedes an incorporated noun compound that is the possessed object. These two examples reinforce the point that we made earlier that accusative marking and possession are intimately related in Yaqui.

(55) tuú'uli-k hékkaa-k-am-ta-u yépsa-k
   pretty-ACC shade-VR-NZR-ACC-to arrive-PRF
   He came to one that had a beautiful shade.

(56) tú'isi túurui-k tén-béria-k
   very thick-ACC mouth-lip-have
   He has a very thick upper lip.

2.4.2. The accusative -k with -béna "like"

The accusative **-k** is also used for marking the postposition **-béna** *like* in the construction seen in example (57), which like (56) has an incorporated body part noun in the verb.

(57) 'iníle béna-k né híapse-k
   thus like-ACC I heart-have
   That is the kind of heart I have.

A predicate adjective serving as a modifier to an incorporated body part in a possessive statement is not only marked with the accusative **-k,** but the accusatively marked form itself may then be the base for attaching a subject clitic. Example (58) shows a pair of instances of this in a conjoined Modifier-Head construction.

(58) tú'ii-k='e'e kóba-k bali-k='e'e híapse-k
   good-ACC=you head-have cool-ACC=you heart-have
   You have a good head and a nice heart.

Example (59) illustrates a pair of modifiers, the first a quantifier, the second a compound adjective. Both are marked with accusative **-k** to agree with the accusative form of the demonstrative pronoun **wáka'a** *that one.*

(59) wáka'a hú'ena-k kó'oko-si-mačí-k bém bít-nee-'epo
   that:ACC evil-ACC painful-AVR-appear-ACC their see-FUT-GND
   the evil and painful experiences that they will see

In example (60) the quantifier occurs as a full noun phrase in its own right. It is marked with the accusative **-k**. Relative clauses which have predicate adjectives as their verbs are also marked with **-k,** as seen in example (61).

(60) bʷé'ituk huébena-k 'ée-síme
   because much-ACC think-go
   because he was thinking a lot of things as he was walking along

(61) née híta-bʷa'a-ka káa né-u tú'ii-k
   I thing-eat-PRF not me-to good-ACC
   I ate something that wasn't good for me.

Examples (62) and (63) show the alternate morphemic shape **-ik** for the adjectival accusative.

(62) né-u 'á'a 'á'awa yumá-'ik tóme-k-o
   me-to it ask enough-ACC money-have-if
   Ask me for it, if you have enough money.

(63) uusí-ta 'ilítči-héela-ik pú'ak-te-k
   child-ACC small-almost-ACC carry-VR-PRF
   She was carrying a somewhat small child.

The final example, sentence (64), shows a single direct object derived noun marked with **-ta** followed by a string of modifying predicate adjectives, each marked with the accusative **-k.**

(64) 'etého-ta suási-maáči-k híkkahi-maáči-k tá'e-maáči-k
talk-ACC wise-seem-ACC hear-seem-ACC know-seem-ACC

káa-kúhti-mačí-k té náu 'etého-nee
not-anger-seem-ACC we together talk-FUT
We will talk talk that is intelligent, good to hear, good to know, and not inflammatory.

3.0. Minor inflectional processes

Several additional semantic notions are coded onto Yaqui nominals by less productive inflectional processes. These notions include that of diminutiveness and affection, as well as that of prior state.

3.1. N + -la diminutive/affectionate

Certain classes of nouns and proper names may be marked with a suffix **-la** to dennote affection or diminutiveness. In example (65) **-la** suffixes to a proper noun. In (66) it suffixes to a kinship term.

(65) Hóana *Jane* > Hoána-la *Janie*

(66) 'iníi'i 'itóm 'usí-la
this our child-DIM
this little boy of ours

The diminutive suffix **-la** precedes the plural **-m** when both occur together in the same word, as can be seen in example (67).

(67) taáwe tótoi-'asó-'o-la-m káa-mo-móli-m híba tu'u-re
hawk chicken-child-EV-DIM-PL not-RDP-mature-ACC only good-VR
The hawk likes only tender young chickens.

An **r** occurring either word initially or word medially may be replaced by an **l** to also signal diminutiveness. In example (68), this is done with a proper noun, whereas in example (69), the change is applied to a derived human noun.

(68) Heríipe *Philip* > Helíip *little Philip*

(69) ró'i *a crippled person* > ló'i *the crippled little person*

In some cases, an **-l** may be inserted intervocalically for marking the diminutive, as in (70).

(70) Holána *Janie*

3.2. The prior state -tu-ká'u "used to be, now deceased"

The suffix (or suffix sequence) **-ka'u** may be attached to nominals to indicate the prior existence of something that no longer occurs or to indicate that the person being referred to is deceased. In example (71) **-ka'u** is suffixed to a derived noun. In example (72) on the other hand, it is suffixed to a verbalizer that attaches to an incorporated human noun.

(71) bát-kát-ria-m-tu-ka'u-m   (72) wáa'a hámut-tu-ka'u wakáh-tu-k
first/front-go:PL-ABS-NZR-VR-former-PL   that woman-VR-former cow-VR-PRF
those who were/used to be (ancestors)   *The one who had been a woman became a cow.*

Our final example shows a conjoined subject in which one part of the pair precedes the verb and the other part follows the verb. Both conjuncts are marked with **-ka'u**. Although all the instances of **-ka'u** contain the verbalizing **-tu,** since **-tu** occurs by itself apart from **-ka'u,** we assign both morphemes independent morphemic status.

(73) wáme'e hó'aa-ra-m-tu-ka'u-m kaíta-tu-k wáa'a hiák-ya'u-raa-tu-ka'u-m
those house-ABS-PL-VR-former-PL nothing-VR-RF that yaqui-chief-ABS-VR-former-PL
The former houses and the former Yaqui authorities disappeared. (lit. became nothing)

VERB MORPHOLOGY

1.0. Introduction

In this section, we discuss those grammatical elements that derive verbs from nouns or from other classes of constituents. The verbalization of substantives and adjectives is a very active process in Yaqui. The inventory in Table 11 summarizes the elements that are involved in such derivations and suggests the range of meanings attached to them.

-ek	to have, to own	'áa + -tu	able + to be/do
-te	to be, to do, to make	-oa	verbalizes Spanish loans
-tu	to be, become	-tea	to call, to name
-'u	verbalizes nouns to be/do	-taka	be, being
-tua	to cause	-ti	Participial; Connector

Table 11. Verbalizers

In what follows, we discuss the morphology and semantics of each of these derivational elements, give examples of their typical usages, and cite cross references to where fuller discussions of certain of these may be found.

2.0. The possessive suffix -ek

The suffix **-ek** has both a shortened allomorph **-k,** which is homophonous with one form of the perfective and a participialized form **-ka**, homophonous with another form of the perfective, but is clearly distinct from it.[1] This suffix is also discussed in BE/HAVE/DO, pp.72–74, therefore we provide only a few illustrative usages of it here. Examples (1)–(3) illustrate its various morphological shapes, **-ek** in (1), **-ka** in (2), and **-k** in (3).

(1) čána čukúi-ka sikíi-m puús-ek
 chanate black-being red-PL eye-have
 The chanate, being black, has red eyes.

(2) widobro-'o-téa-ka kobanáo-tu-ka-n
 Huidobro-EV-name-having governor-VR-PPL-PCN
 One named Huidobro was governor.

(3) húu'u Hóan b^{w}é'uu-k kába'e-k
 that John big-ACC horse-have
 John has a big horse.

When **-ek** is attached to a substantive, the resultant construction is one in which the subject of the clause is the possessor of the item named. This is a very productive pattern in Yaqui. The entities that can be possessed include typical things like houses illustrated in example (4) and body parts in examples (5)–(6). More tenuous relations are also construed as "possessive" in Yaqui. Typical associations, such as that of a tall object and the shadow it casts fall into this category. This is illustrated by (7).

(4) 'áapo tú'ii-k kár-ek
 he good-ACC house-has
 He has a good house.

(5) sámbayo b^{w}ásia-ka née wómta-k
 fluffy tail-having me scare-PRF
 A thing with a fluffy tail scared me.

(6) tú'isi túurui-k tén-béria-k
 very thick-ACC mouth-lip-has
 He has very thick lips.

(7) sawá-yóhte-k, káa náppat hékkaa-k
 leaf-fall-PRF not longer shade-has
 The leaves fell, it no longer has/gives shade.

---

[1] All three of these morphemes are probably related historically, but the contemporary patterns in which they participate reflect three distinct paths of grammaticalization. All this relates to contemporary Yaqui in another way also, i.e., the range and variety of tense and aspect markers that occur with **-ek** in Arizona Yaqui is different to some extent from that of the tense/aspect markers that occur with **-ek** in Sonora Yaqui (Eloise Jelinek, personal communication. September 1, 1997).

Possession of money and the relation of a tree to the fruit that it bears are also expressed by suffixing **-ek** to the appropriate noun, as seen in examples (8) and (9). Money, of course, is not inherently possessed, but the fruit of a tree can easily be construed as enjoying an "inherently possessive" relationship.

(8) 'á'a 'a'áwa, 'á-u yumá'i-k tóm-eka-'a-teko
it ask:for it-to enough-ACC money-have-EV-if
Ask for it if you have enough money.

(9) bʷá'a-mači-k taáka-k
eat-ADJ-ACC fruit-have
It has enticing fruit.

Constructions with **-ek** can be used instead of the possessive adjective construction in which the possessed object is marked in the accusative case. The contrast between the two is illustrated by examples (10)–(11). This is a very common alternative construction.

(10) 'áapo 'á'a kár-ek
he it house-has
It is his house.

(11) hái-sa 'émpo simó'o-tea-m-ta hápč-ek
how-Q you Simon-name-NZR-ACC father-have
Is a man named Simon your father?

3.0. The causative -te

There are at least three different functions of the causative suffix **-te**. First, certain verb stems take **-ta/-te/-ti** as alternate transitive, intransitive, and participialized forms of that stem. This sets up verb paradigms like the one in example (12).

(12) wóm-ta *to frighten something* (transitive)
wóm-te *to be frightened* (intransitive)
wóm-ti *frightened* (participialized)

The second function of **-te** concerns certain adjectivals that take **-te** as a transitive verbalizer, e.g., the adjective **tú'u** *good* > **tú'u-te** *to fix or repair something*. In its third function, **-te** suffixes to incorporated nouns, with the resultant meaning "to do X" or "to make X."

Verbalizing causative **-te** *to make, to do, to act upon* has to be distinguished from the intransitive verbal suffix **-te** of the **-ta/-te** suffix pair that distinguishes transitive and intransitive verb stems. Although causative **-te** most generally verbalizes substantives, there are cases in which it attaches to adjectives. Many of these adjectives and adverbs end in **-i**, or **-li**, or **-la**.

3.1. Causative -te with nouns

Typical intransitive usages of **-te** are found in its role in deriving verbs from incorporated body-part nouns such as "stomach" with the resultant meaning "to be born," as seen in example (13). Another option is to draw on an incorporated temporal noun such as "year" to derive a verb meaning "to last a specified period of time," as in example (14).

(13) yéu-tóm-te
out-stomach-VR
to be born

(14) kia woói-m wásuk-te-k hiba
just two-ACC year-VR-PRF only
It only lasted two years.

When **-te** suffixes to nouns, the result is a semi-transitive sentence with a wide variety of semantic outcomes, many of which are highly lexicalized. In example (15) the combination of **kári** *house* with **-te** means "to build a house." On the other hand, the combination of **-te** with the body part noun **woóki** *foot* means "to track animals," as in sentence (16).

(15) káa-te-k 'ámmani 'intok hunúen káa-te-ka 'áman hó'aa-k
house-VR-PRF off:yonder and thus house-VR-PPL there live-PRF
He built a house way off yonder, and so having built it, he lived there.

(16) née 'áa wók-te
I able foot-VR
I am able to track animals.

Even when **-te** combines with incorporated body part nouns, the resultant conventional semantic value is often unpredictable. For example, the combination of **mámam** *hand* with **-te** means "to extend the hand towards someone." as can be seen in sentence (17).

(17) nóolia=ma ti hiia 'á-u mám-te-patči Hambró'osio két 'á-u mám-te-ka
hurry=HRT so sound him-to hand-VR-upon Ambrosio also him-to hand-VR-PRF
"Hurry then," he said, extending his hand to him. Ambrose also extended his hand to him.

With items of clothing, the derived verb consisting of a body part and the verbalizer **-te** is conventionally taken to mean "to put on X by inserting body part Y." Examples (18) and (19) are typical.

(18) sáawea yéča-k, tá'ab^{w}im-m-po wók-té-ka kárpa-m-me-u weáma
pants remove-PRF different-PL-in foot-VR-having tent-PL-CON-to walk
He took off his trousers, put on another pair and went to the tent.

(19) súpe-m-po kóba-te
shirt-PL-in head-VR
to put on a shirt

3.2. Causative -te with adjectives

When the verbalizer **-te** is suffixed to an adjective, the result is a causative meaning "to bring about such and such state" with respect to a given entity. The semantics of examples (20) and (21) is relatively transparent. In example (22) **-te** sufixes to the Yaqui affirmative particle **hewi** *that's right*. The applicative suffix then attaches to this combination, with the resultant meaning of the whole construction being "to affirm something to X."

(20) tú'u-te (22) 'iní'i 'usí 'íntok sép 'á'a hewí-te-ria-k
good-VR   this child and at-once it yes-VR-APL-PRF
to repair, to make good   *And this boy affirmed it at once.*

(21) b^{w}álko-te
soft-VR
to soften, to tan leather

4.0. The verbalizer -tu

The verbalizer **-tu,** which is variously glossed as "to be," "to become," "to be turned into" is used very productively with both nouns and adjectives. It typically indicates some change of state, as it does in sentence (23). In example (24) it indicates a remote past result, whereas in (25), it designates a remote past state of affairs or quality.

(23) wét-la-tu-ka-n (25) 'áa-nokí'iči-a-tu-k
fall-PPL-VR-PPL-PCN   able-lie-NZR-VR-PRF
It had fallen down.   *It was just a lie.*

(24) húmak húnen čúp-ia-tu-ka-n
perhaps thus fulfill-NZR-VR-PPL-PCN
Perhaps it was so destined (for me).

4.1. The past durative with -tu

The use of **-an** "past durative" with **-tu-ka,** as seen above in example (24), signals a salient durative aspect to a state located in the remote past, i.e., "It was in a state of being." In example (26) the use of **-tu-ka-n** with the incorporated kinship term **wéeri** *sibling* signals a remote past kinship relation. In (27), on the other hand, **-tu-ka-n** indicates a remote past change of state.

(26) náu wéeri-m-tu-ka-n (27) 'au pót-ta-laa-tu-k-an
together sibling-PL-VR-PRF-PCN RFL swell-VR-PPL-VR-PRF-PCN
They were brothers/sisters.   *He had swollen himself up.*

4.2. The antecedent state: -tu with -ka'u

The use of **-ka'u** *now deceased, used to be (but no longer exists)* with **-tu** in example (28), shows how Yaqui can form a complex noun via successive rounds of morphological derivations. This is suggested by the multiple occurrence of the PLURAL morpheme **-m** as well as the use of **-tu** as the base for attaching **-ka'u** in the final round of the derivation of the nominalization in this example.

(28) bát-kát-ria-m-tu-ka'u-m
front-go:PL-ABS-PL-VR-former-PL
those who were/used to be (ancestors)

4.3. Inceptive -tu

Frequently, when **-tu** combines with a preceding noun, it can be glossed as "become" or "turn into" as seen in examples (29) and (30).

(29) wáa'a hámut-tu-ka'u   wakáh-tu-k
that woman-VR-former cow-VR-PRF
The one who had been a woman became a cow.

(30) 'émpo béha, 'i'an toró-tu-nee
you well today bull-VR-FUT
As for you, today you will become a bull.

In some of its usages, **-tu** can be glossed as "to come about," as in (31) where it indicates the emergence of a state of tranquility, and in (32) where it gives a functional equivalent to the English change of state "become X."

(31) mámni wásuktia-m-po páah-tu-k
five year-PL-in peace-VR-PRF
There was peace for five years.

(32) pa'aku káa-tú'ii tóokos-yu-nr=mme
outside not-good dust-VR-FUT=they
Outside is not good, they will become dusty.

In other usages, **-tu** indicates a variety of changes of state, both those that come about suddenly, as in example (33) and those that arise from purposeful intent exercised over a long period of time, as in (34).

(33) muúku-k bʷičia-tu-ka-i   (34) émpo haibu hiáki-tu-su-k
die-PRF worm-VR-PPL-PPL   you now Yaqui-VR-CMP-PRF
He died, having become wormy.   *You have now completely become a Yaqui.*

The verbalizer **-tu** may suffix to indefinite pronouns, resulting in a construction with the meaning of "ever." In example (35) **-tu** suffixes to both the indefinite human pronoun **hábe** and the inanimate indefinite pronoun **híta**.

(35) kia 'á'a hábe-tu-k   húni'i 'intok kia 'á'a hita-tú-k   húni'i
just it someone-VR-PRF even and just it thing-VR-PRF even
No matter whoever or whatever it is.

The expression formed by suffixing **-tu** to the negative indefinite pronoun **kaita** *nothing* means "to disappear," i.e., "become nothing," as illustrated by (36).

(36) wáme'e hó'aa-ra-m-tu-ka'u   kaita-tu-k   wáa'a hiák-ya'u-raa-tu-ka'u
those house-ABS-PL-VR-former nothing-VR-PRF that yaqui-chief-ABS-VR-former
The former houses and the former Yaqui authorities disappeared (i.e., became nothing).

4.4. The days of the week and -tu + -k

The Spanish terms for the days of the week require the addition of **-tu** plus the perfective suffix **-k** if one wishes to refer to a specific day. Two examples are given in (37) and (38).

(37) lominko-tú-k
    Sunday-VR-PRF
    Sunday

(38) lunéh-tu-k
    Monday-VR-PRF
    Monday

More abstract temporal notions are also coded by combining -tu with temporal adjectives. In such cases -tu can be glossed as "be" or "elapse," as illustrated by example (39). The combination -tu-k generally means "it happened" or "it was." This is shown in example (40).

(39) čúubaa-tu-k-o
    moment-VR-PRF-when
    after a moment

(40) hállepan-tu-k
    right:away-VR-PRF
    it happened in a moment

Verbalizing **-tu** has additional grammaticalized usages in which it seems to have gotten largely bleached of its change of state meaning. In sentence (41) for example, -tu attaches to the procomplement **inílen** *thus* and the meaning of the combination approximates "be this way", with the specifics spelled out by the following verb phrase.

(41) 'inílen-tu-k káa-wótti 'emé'e
    thus-VR-PRF not-agitated you:PL
    Therefore you should be calm.

Both usages of -tu in example (43) designate a change of state, as does the use of -tu in sentences (43) and (44). Example (44) also shows multiple occurrences of -tu in a single word corresponding to two distinct layers of morphological compositions. This example also carries the implication that the person who stood up was no longer crippled.

(42) 'ínepo 'á'a bíča-k náamukia-tu-k-o wečía-tu-ka-n
    I   him see-PRF drunken-VR-PRF-when fallen-VR-PPL-PCN
    I saw him when he was drunk, he had fallen down.

(43) hiáki 'á'a múhu-ka 'á'a ró'i-tu-k
    Yaqui him shoot-PPL him crippled-VR-PRF
    A Yaqui shot him and crippled him.

(44) wáa'a ró'i-tu-laa-tu-ka'u   kúpti kikte-k
    that cripple-VR-PPL-VR-former quickly stand-PRF
    The one who had been crippled stood up at once.

4.5. Transitive -te versus intransitive -tu

With some stems, the suffixes **-te** and **-tu** function in a kind of active/passive, or transitive/intransitive, verbalizing relationship. For example, the stem **nasón** *damage* takes either **-te** or **-tu,** with rather distinct semantic results. The transitive use of **nasón** with **-te** is shown in sentence (45).

(45) 'émo suúa híta='e   nasón-te-nee
    RFL guard thing=you damage-VR-FUT
    Be careful, you will damage something.

In contrast to the transitive form marked by **-te** in sentence (45), sentences (46) and (47) show two ways of producing the same passive concept, i.e., with **-te-wa,** as in (46) or with **-tu,** as in (47). In example (48) the suffix **-la** heightens the durative aspect of the stative relation signalled by **-tu.**

(46) húu'u tú'ii boó'o nasón-te-wa-k
    that good road damage-VR-PSV-PRF
    The good road was damaged.

(47) kó'om né čép-te-ka   wók-po nasón-tu-k
    down I jump-VR-PPL foot-in damage-VR-PRF
    When I jumped down, my foot was hurt.

(48) tamú-laa-tu-ka-n   'íntok wépe'e-po nasón-tu-la
     daze-PPL-VR-PPL-PCN and hip-in   damage-VR-PPL
     He was dazed, and his hip had been damaged.

Additional examples of the way that Yaqui employs distinct suffixal combinations to highlight the different construals of an objectively similar situation is seen in its use of the future passive suffixes, where either the future passive **-naa,** or the future **-tu-ne,** may be used. The use of **-naa** in (49) backgrounds the effective agents of the event while foregrounding the patient as subject of the sentence. The use of **-tu-nee** in sentence (50) highlights the future change of state.

(49) 'íntok yó'o-raa-ta   bíča-po 'emé'e yéu-weiya-naa
     and   old-AZR-ACC sight-in you:PL out-carry-FUT:PSV
     And you will be brought before the authorities.

(50) 'ábai-m   háp-nee, 'íntok čúkula báči-tu-nee
     roasting:ear-PL stand-FUT and   later   corn-VR-FUT
     Roasting ears will stand out, and later they will become corn.

4.6. The matrix predicate use of -tu

The highly schematic meaning of **-tu,** allows it to function in many roles. One particularly interesting case is its use in the schematic pattern consisting of **'áa** *be able* plus an embedded verb marked by **-tu.** The meaning of the overall construction can be glossed as "to be do-able," or "to be possible." The verbs to which **-tu** suffixes can range from the highly schematic **hoóa** *to do*, illustrated in example (51), to highly specific verbs of perception as in (52) and those that describe psychological states as in examples (53) and (54).

(51) 'áa hóo-tu   (53) káa 'áa 'á-u   nók-tu
     able do-VR   not able him-to talk-VR
     It can be done.   *He won't take advice.* [lit.: he cannot be talked to]

(52) 'áa bit-tu   (54) hunáa'a 'uúsi 'áa sáu-tu
     able see-VR   that   child able command-VR
     It can be seen; it is visible. *That boy is obedient.* [lit.: can be ordered]

5.0. The intentive postposition -'u

The combination of a noun with the intentive suffix **-'u** is conventionally taken to mean "to go to perform some action on X." Typical examples are given in (55)–(57).

(55) baáso > basó-'u   *to go for grass*
     grass   grass-go:to
(56) kékke > keké-'u   *to go for fuel/wood*
     fuel, wood wood-go:to
(57) beéa   > beá-'u   *to skin an animal, to pare a vegetable*
     skin/peel skin-go:to

This construction is a particularly interesting parallel to the use of prefixal **uu-** in Cora to indicate the same kind of meaning, both with verbs and incorporated nouns (cf. Casad 1982:349–350; 1993:629–631). In each case there are emergent semantic properties of the overall linguistic unit that suggest that the meanings of these Noun + **-u** forms are based on the grammaticalization of one or more implications, i.e., in order to do something at a distal location, one must first go there. Notice also that the relationship between the noun and the overall meaning varies considerably from case to case. In examples (55) and (56), the action is that of going off to a place to collect grass to be used for thatch or to cut firewood and bring it back, whereas in example (57) the action is that of removing the skin off a dead animal or that of paring the skin off a vegetable.

Some of the combinations of the adverbial **-'u** with a nominal base have taken on highly conventionalized and unpredictable meanings, as in example (58), in which the combination of **heéka** *wind* plus **-'u** does not mean "to go to a windy place", or "to catch wind in your sails" but rather "to catch wind" in the metaphorical sense of "to be crazy."

(58) heéka   >   heká-'u   *to be crazy*
     wind   wind-go:to

6.0. The causative -tua

The causative suffix **-tua** most commonly is a type of auxiliary verb meaning "to cause to." But in limited instances, it also verbalizes nouns. In the case of nouns that designate articles of clothing, the combination of the noun and causative **-tua** means "to put on X (an article of clothing)" as illustrated in example (59). Additional examples of this construction can be found in SYNTACTIC MARKING, pp. 284–287.

(60) 'á'a súpe-tua-k
     him shirt-CAU-PRF
     They put a shirt on him.

7.0. A miscellany of derivational suffixes

The derivational suffixes vary widely in their range of productivity within Yaqui grammar and in the generality of the patterns that they instantiate as well as in their placement along the lexical to syntagmatic status as symbolic units. In this section, we illustrate the word level suffix **-oa**, the quotative **-tea** and the participial **-taka**.

7.1. The processual -oa

The suffix **-oa** may be derived from Yaqui **hoóa** *to do, to make*. It is affixed to Spanish infinitives to verbalize them. A typical example is given in (60). Further discussion is given in INFLECTIONAL AND DERIVATIONAL AFFIXATION, pp. 325–326.

(60) tómi-ta   'á'a pi-píaar-oa-k
     money-ACC him RDP-loan-VR-PRF
     They loaned him some money.

7.2. The quotative -tea

The quotative suffix **-tea** carries the general meaning "they say" or "is named." This is illustrated by example (61). Additional examples of this are given in BE/HAVE/DO, pp. 71–72.

(61) kóopal-im-tea-m-ta   'á'a miíka-k
     copal-PL-call-NZR-ACC him give-PRF
     They gave him something called copal.

7.3. The participial -taka

The suffix **-taka** is actually a participializer with the general meaning of "being." Example (62) is typical. For a more complete discussion of this suffix (cf. BE/HAVE/DO, pp. 70–71).

(62) sisi'iwóok-taka noóka
     iron-being   talk
     It is iron, it speaks. (telegraph sounder)

8.0. The connective -ti

The morpheme **-ti** is the past participial form of the verbalizing suffixes **-ta/-te** described earlier and illustrated in example (12). This suffix is also used very extensively as a kind of a connective. How it came to get used for both requires an intricate historical explanation and ample exemplification.

8.1. A basic syntactic property of -ti

To begin, the Yaqui connector -ti fits the apodosis condition discussed in Hale (1983:304; 310). This reflects its earlier status as a absolutive suffix on nouns in Proto Uto-Aztecan times, (cf., Langacker 1977:78). For example, it suffixes to the honorific term **'áčali** *sir* in sentence (63), to the kinship terms **nabóli** *grandfather* in example (64), and to the verbalized **saira-k** *to have a younger brother* in example (65).

(63) Liós 'é'em=čanía 'áčali-ti 'á-u hiía
God you:PL=help sir-CON him-to say
"Good morning, Sir," he said to him.

(64) kétči 'alléa nabóli-tí 'á-u hiía húu'u wó'i
still happy grandfather-CON him-to say that coyote
"How are you, grandfather?" the coyote said to him.

(65) n=á'a saíra-k-ti té'e-ka húu'u kúču-reo
I=him young:brother-have-CON say-PRF that fish-AGT
"He is my younger brother," said the fisherman.

In other contexts, **-ti** can suffix to a human noun, as it does to **'oó'ou** *man* in sentence (66). It also suffixes to the adjective **tú'i** *good* in sentence (67). In both cases, these lexical items are the last word in a quotative complement clause. In example (68) on the other hand, it suffixes to the adverb of manner **čólak** *sideways*. Finally, in example (69) **-ti** suffixes to a minimal quotative complement, the single affirmative form **heéwi**, which constitutes the speaker's entire utterance.

(66) húnak 'íntok káa 'itó-u pútti-nee húu'u 'óo'ou-ti hiá-ka sékká'ana kíkte-k
then and not us-toward shoot-FUT that man-CON say-PPL other:side stand-PRF
Having said thus, "Then that man won't shoot at us," he changed sides with him.

(67) 'áa két tú'i-ti 'á'a yóopna-k
ah still good-CON him answer-PRF
"Oh, I'm fine," he answered him.

(68) táu-táu-táu-t-ía-ka=su koóni čólak-ti čépte-ka
caw-caw-caw-CON-say-PPL=EMP crow sideways-AVR jump-PPL
"Caw caw, caw" says the crow as he lopes along sideways.

(69) heéwi-ti híu-pat kíkte-k
yes-CON say-upon stand-PRF
Immediately upon saying yes, he stood up.

8.2. The connector morpheme role of -ti

Most commonly, Yaqui **-ti** links a word or a phrase that serves as the verbal complement to the verb that follows **-ti**. Typical complements include onomatopoetic expressions, direct quotations, and the linguistic content of mental act verbs. Finally, **-ti** is also a kind of adverbializer with some adjectival forms.

In its use as a quotative complementizer, **-ti** marks a wide range of structures including onomatopoetic expressions like those given in (70) and (71).

(70) ró'o ró'o ró'o ró'o-ti jé'e
RDP RDP RDP slurp-CON drink:water
He slurps water like a bunch of oxen.

(71) táu-táu-táu-t-ía-ka=su koóni, čólak-ti čépte-ka
caw-caw-caw-CON-say-PPL=EMP crow sideways-AVR jump-PPL
"Caw caw, caw" says the crow as he lopes along sideways.

Direct quotations almost always precede the verb and are marked by the connective **-ti,** which is suffixed to the last lexical item in the quotative complement. Sentences (72) and (73) illustrate this word order. They also show that the quotative complement marked by **-ti** can be separated from the following matrix verb by adverbs as in sentences (72) and (73), or by pronouns as seen in (74) and (75).

(72) née kaábe-ta bít-laa ne-tč-é'em hiókoe-ti húči té'e-ka
I no one-ACC see-PPL me-on-you pardon-CON again say-PRF
"I ask your pardon, but I haven't seen anyone," he said again.

(73) 'áa tú'u-kun 'émpo 'á'a tá'aa-ti húči té'e-ka
ah well-then you him know-CON again say-PRF
"Well, good then, so you know him," he said again.

(74) Liós 'e'ém-čanía 'áčali-ti 'á-u hiía
God you:PL-help sir-CON him-to say
"Good morning, sir," he said.

(75) Liós 'e'ém-čiókoe-ti 'á'a yóopna-k
God- you:PL-have:mercy-CON him reply-PRF
"Good morning," he answered him.

Yaqui can put pairs of quotative complements into a single complex sentence. Example (76) has a phonologically reduced form of **-ti** in the first clause, as well as an unreduced one in the second clause. This is a common way of marking indirect discourse. Additional examples of the role of **-ti** to help indicate indirect discourse are given in (77) and (78).

(76) 'áma 'áu tekipánoa-báe-'e-t-iá-ka 'áma yéu-hí'i-b^wa-báe-'e-ti-ía
there RFL work-DSD-EV-CON-say-PPL there out-IZR-eat-DSD-EV-CON-say
Saying that he was wanting to work, he wanted to eat there.

(77) 'áapo 'áu 'á'a maára-k-ti-ia tebóte-ta né 'a-u tohí-'i-se-k
he RFL her daughter-have-CON-say greetings-ACC I her-to bring-EV-come-PRF
He says that she is his daughter, I come to bring her his greetings.

(78) tebóte-ta két 'áu 'alléa-'a-tí-a-ka née téhwaa-k
greeting-ACC also RFL happy-EV-CON-say-PPL me tell-PRF
He told me to tell her that he was happy.

8.3. The connective -ti with the verb 'éa "to think"

The connective **-ti** also serves to mark the complements of the mental-act verb **'ea** *to think that X, to consider X to be Y, to assume X*. The complements themselves are at the verbal end of the spectrum. Many of them reflect hypothetical situations, as can be deduced from the glosses of examples (79)–(81) and the use of the future tense prefixes **-nee** and **-naa**.

(79) 'itóm híapsi yolé-'enée-'e-ti-'éa-ka-i
our life escape-FUT-EV-CON-think-PPL-PPL
because we thought our lives would be saved (that way)

(80) humák húni'i 'áme-násuk téu-na-ti-'éa 'áapo
perhaps even them-among find-FUT:PSV-CON-think he
because he was thinking that perhaps he would be found among them.

(81) 'émpo 'á'à yá'a-nee-ti ne 'éa
you it do-FUT-CON I think
I think that you will do it.

The use of **'ea** and the the epistemic distance of the conceptual content of its complement does not require, however, that only the future tense be employed. The following two examples are framed in the past. In sentence (82) **'ea** is marked with the participial **-ka** and the verb in its complement is marked with the perfective **-k**. In example (83), on the other hand, **'ea** is marked with the past continuative **-n**. The verb in the complement clause is marked with the perfective **-k**.

(82) née 'íntok 'áme-u nétane-k 'á'a wáka-tékwa-t-ea-ka hiókot 'á'a nétanek
I and them-to beg-PRF it cow-meat-CON-think-PPL pitifully it ask:for
I really begged them for it because I thought it was beef.

(83) 'enči=ne yebís-su-k-t-ea-n
you:ACC=I arrive-CPL-PRF-CON-think-PCN
I thought that you had already come.

8.4. In V1 -ti- V2 constructions

The third use of **-ti** in Yaqui is a grammatical parallel to a number of other Uto-Aztecan languages, in particular Cora, Huichol, Nahuatl, and the Tepiman languages. These constructions consist of a broad class of verbs that function in the slot preceding **-ti** and a member of the class of motion verbs, psychological predicates, and aspectual verbs which serve in the slot following **-ti**. With motion verbs, for example, the entire construction means "to go along doing X." Typical examples are given in (84)–(87). The motion verb **-sime** *to go along a path* is illustrated in examples (84) and (85).

(84) héno-m-po   né-t   wíhu-'u-ti-síme
     shoulder-PL-on me-on lean-EV-CON-go:SG
     He went/goes leaning on my shoulder.

(85) húa-m-po-bétuk   behúk-ti-síme
     tree-PL-in-under duck-CON-go:SG
     He went ducking under the brush/trees.

More specific motion verbs with **-ti** as the complementizer are given in examples (86) and (87). In both cases, the complement verb is reduplicated. This reduplication reflects a form of iconicity in the grammar with the conceptual situation associated with their use.

(86) bóa yahú-yahú-ti-kaáte
     hair RDP-wool:bounce-CON-go:PL
     Their wool bounces (ripples) as they go.

(87) bóa hút-hút-ti   yéu-réhte
     wool RDP-snatch-CON   out-walk:PL
     Their wool is snatched off as they go through (the thicket).

Another non-quotative pattern associated with the connector use of **-ti** consists of a manner complement and the passive form of a transitive verb, as in sentences (88)–(91). In this pattern the second verb in the sentence is not tightly bound phonologically to **-ti**, but rather **-ti** fits the protasis condition noted for Tohono O'odham in Hale (1983:304, 310). All of these examples show that the complement marked by **-ti** is an adverbial of manner clause. As in the examples above, the verbs in these clauses are frequently reduplicated. The one exception here is the compound verb **kóba-wiu** *to shake the head* in example (91).

(88) hú'upa-u   kút-kút-ti   sumá-'a-wa-k
     mesquite-to RDP-firm-CON tie-EV-PSV-PRF
     It was tied securely to a mesquite tree.

(89) woó'o-m   wóho-wóhok-ti   yée-ké-ke-me
     mosquitoe-PL RDP-pierce-CON   people-RDP-bite-NZR
     mosquitoes that bite people full of holes

(90) túa   née hám-hám-ti   híapsi-po wánte
     indeed I   RDP-break-CON   heart-in ache
     My heart is really breaking.

(91) 'ám bíča-ka kóba-wíu-ti   táite-k
     them see-PPL head-shake-CON   begin-PRF
     When he saw them, he began to shake his head.

8.5. Noun + -ti + ia + suffix combinations

Further evidence of the tendency for **-ti** to bracket with the grammatical element that immediately precedes it is seen in those constructions that attach further verbs and their suffixes to **-ti**. In these constructions, both preceding and following elements are tightly bound phonologically to **-ti**. The preceding element is either a verb or a noun, whereas the following elements consist entirely of more closed class morphological elements. In sentence (92) the verb **-ia** *to say* is cliticized to **-ti,** which itself suffixes to the preceding kinship term **nabóli** *grandfather*. In example (93), the preceding element is the proper noun **Lios,** marked for plural. The following element is again the verb **'ia** *to say.* In this instance, **ia** is marked with the imperfective participial **-ka.**

(92) heéwi, tú'i-si née tebaure-ka wée nabóli-ti-ia húu'u wó'i
yes good-AVR I hungry-being go grandfather-CON-say that coyote
"Well, I am hungry today, grandfather," said the coyote.

(93) káa 'ám Liós-im-t-iá-ka kaábe-ta 'ám yó'ori-sáe
not them God-PL-CON-say-PPL no:one-ACC them ship-IMP
Saying that they are not gods, he orders people not to worship them.

As suggested by examples (92) and (93), among others, considerable contraction takes place between **-ti** and several of the elements that follow it. In particular, the vowel "**i**" of **-ti** is elided when it is followed by a verb form beginning with the syllable **hi** or with an initial front vowel. Crucially, Yaqui grammar maintains a consistent difference in usage for uncontracted forms and their contracted counterparts. This difference is determined by the rhythm or cadence of the utterance in which it occurs. In all cases, either form may be used without causing any essential change in meaning.

8.6. Contractions of -ti + X

The final set of examples that we cite here illustrates the contrast between uncontracted forms of **-ti** and a following sequence of morphemes and the corresponding contracted forms. The contrast between **-ti-hia** and **-t-ia** is given in examples (94)(a) and (b).

(94)(a) húnak 'íntok káa 'itó-u pútti-nee húu'u 'óo'ou-ti hiá-ka sékká'ana kíkte-k
then and not us-toward shoot-FUT that man-CON say-PPL other:side stand-PRF
Having said thus, "Then that man won't shoot at us," he changed sides with him.

(b) káa tuá 'au 'alléa-t-ia-ka née 'eteho-ria 'á'a
not really RFL happy-CON-say-PPL me tell-APL him

hí-muča-k-t-ia hunáka'a
IZR-bury-PRF-CON-say that:one:ACC
He said that he was not very happy, he said that they buried that one.

The examples in (95)(a) and (b) illustrate the contrast between the unreduced **-ti-hía**, seen in example (95)(a), and its contracted counterparts **-t-iía** and **-t-ia**, illustrated in (95)(b).

(95)(a) kétči 'alléa nabóli-tí 'á-u hía húu'u wó'i
still happy grandfather-CON him-to say that coyote
"Hello, grandfather," the coyote said to him.

(b) káa 'emó hí-'ib{^W}a-nee káa 'emó hí'i-ne-'et-iía híta tá'ab{^W}i wée-m-ta
not RFL IZR-eat-FUT not RFL drink-FUT-CON-say thing different:thing go-NZR-ACC

húni'i káa 'emó yá'a-nee-t-ia papló-ta mé'e-su-k hú'ub{^W}a-ti-híu-wa
even not RFL do-FUT-CON-say Paul-ACC kill-CPL-PRF then-CON-say-PSV
They are saying that they will not eat, will not drink, nor do anything else, until Paul is killed, that is what is being said.

Examples (96)(a) and (b) give a closely matching pair of sentences that employ the sequence **-ti-hiu + -X** and its counterpart **-t-iu +X.**

(96)(a) heéwi-ti híu-pat kíkte-k
yes-CON say-upon stand-PRF
Immediately upon saying yes, he stood up.

(b) 'emé'e yumá'i-si 'á-et 'emó 'á'a híkkahi-bae-t-íu-nee
you-PL total-AVR it-on RFL him hear-DSD-CON-say-FUT
You will say that you want to completely obey him.

SONORA YAQUI LANGUAGE STRUCTURES

(97) húni'i káa 'emó yá'a-ne-'e-t-ia papló-ta mé'e-su-k hú'ub^wa-ti-híu-wa
even not RFL do-FUT-EV-CON-say Paul-ACC kill-CPL-PRF then-CON-say-PSV
They are saying that they will not drink anything else until Paul is killed, that is what is being said.

The final example shows the use of the uncontracted sequence **-ti-'éa** and its contracted counterpart **-t-ea.**

(98)(a) húba-táite-k 'á-e ne 'éo'o-ti-'éa-ka 'á'a hímmaa-k
stink begin-PRF it-with I nausea-CON-think-PPL it throw:away-PRF
It began to stink, and nauseating me, I threw it away.

(b) mé'e-báa-wa-n táa 'éu-su-k née 'ínta=a mé'e-su-wa-k-t-éa-n
kill-DSD-PSV-PCN but hide-CMP-PRF I and=it kill-CCPL-PSV-PRF-CON-think-PCN
It was to have been killed, but it hid itself completely, I thought that it had been killed.

148

ADJECTIVE MORPHOLOGY

1.0. Introduction

Based on their morphological and semantic properties, there appear to be at least four classes of adjectives in Yaqui. Some adjectives are basic in the sense that they are monomorphemic and are not derived from any other class of grammatical elements. Semantically, many of these adjectives appear to be more like stative verbs. This is based on both their meanings and the kinds of contructions in which they occur. Functionally, Yaqui adjectives may serve as modifiers to nouns or they may serve as the predicates in descriptive clauses. In either case they undergo a number of morphological processes including reduplication and suffixation. Among the affixes that they take is the Adverbializer **-si.**

2.0. The stative adjectives

The class of adjective suffixes used for marking the stative include **-la, -li, -i,** and, apparently **-ia.** It is possible to distinguish the adjectival **-i** suffix from the participializing verbal suffixes **-i** and **-ia,** although these participialized verbs may themselves become adjective-like in function.

2.1. Adjectives derived with -la

The suffix **-la** "singular" is actually quite complex semantically, i.e., it has several different effects when suffixed to different kinds of adjective stems. Examples (1)(a)–(g) that follow show that **-la** operates on abstract adjectives, verbs, and even a demonstrative, to derive adjectives with an even more abstract meaning. In these usages it serves as a sort of classifier. These examples also show differing degrees of morphological transparency. Some are clearly related to other forms of a distinct morphological class, whereas others are not related to any other obvious form in the Yaqui lexicon. Some may well reflect borrowings. Thus, **lóbo-la** *spherical* may be derived from the Yaqui predicate adjective **róbbo-i** *it is spherical* or it may be borrowed from Spanish **bola** "ball shaped."

(1)(a) lóbo-la *spherical* (ADJ) < róbbo-i *spherical*
 (b) kówi-la *curled* (STAT)
 (c) bemé-la *new* (noun) < beéme *a girl*
 (d) húne-'e-la *alone, exclusive* (DEM) < húnen
 (e) lútu-la *straight* (ABS noun) < lutú'u *truth*
 (f) béta-la *flat* (ADJ)
 (g) kóni-la *encircling* (verb) < kón-ta *to surround*

In context, a derived adjective with **-la** may serve as an appositional noun as in example (2), which also illustrates the use of juxtaposition as a device for marking coordinate structures. In this case, two subordinate clauses are being conjoined. Note also that the use of **-laa** in the adjective **musá'alaa** designates a category of sayings, and not just a single utterance.

(2) béha 'áme-u 'etého-táite-k musá'a-laa 'áme-u hiá-ka háh-haana 'áme-u hiá-ka
 well them-to relate-begin-PRF witty-ADJ them-to say-PPL RDP-risque them-to say-PPL
 Well, he began to talk to them, saying witty things to them, and saying risque things to them.

The suffix **-la** can also be used to derive adverbs from adjectives, as seen in example (3).

(3) 'á'a kon-tí-su-ka 'á-u 'éka-la čá'a-tú-ka tópa-t 'á'a siíse-k
 him circle-PPL-CPL-PPL him-to oblique-AVR hang-VR-PPL belly-on him urinate-PRF
 Having finished circling him, raising its body semi-sideways the goat urinated on his belly.

Examples (4)(a)–(d) show that **-la** suffixes to posture adverbs to form a set of distinct directional adverbs.

(4)(a) móbe-la   *face up*
  (b) 'átta-la   *face down*
  (c) péta-la   *face down*
  (d) sutu-la   *squatted position*

Example (5), in an almost unbelievable string of Yaqui metaphors, illustrates the use of the derived posture adverb **atta-la**.

(5) 'ám 'át-tua   sí'ime yoém-raa kóba-e   háapte-ka-i   'átta-la
    them laugh-CAU all   person-AZR head-INST stand:PL-PPL-PPL face:down-AVR

    wát-wát-te-ka   'aáče
    RDP-pile-VR-PPL laugh
    He made them laugh; it was as though all the people were standing on their heads and rolling over one another with laughter.

Sentence (6) invokes the temporal domain by the use of the derived adverbial **čúkula** *afterwards*. This is now a frozen form since there is no independent root **čúku**.

(6) 'ámman   yúmhó'e-nee čúkula   'íntok 'ém   bó'o-u kíkte-nee
    off:yonder rest-FUT   afterward CNJ   your:PL road-to stand-FUT
    You can rest off yonder, and afterward you can resume your trip.

Yaqui may also mark person and number of the direct object or patient on a derived adverb marked by **-la**. Examples (7) and (8) are typical.

(7) húči 'áe-kóni-la   sik-áa ho'á-t   'íntok 'á'a siíse-k   'íntok
    again him-circle-AVR go-PPL back-on CNJ   him urinate-PRF CNJ

    čobé-t   'á'a siíse-k   wók-ohó'o-ku
    buttocks-on him urinate-PRF leg-calf-on
    And having gone around him, it also urinated on his back and urinated on his buttocks and on the calves of his legs.

(8) 'áe-kowi-la   bó'o-ka=ne   kóče-n
    it-around-AVR lie:SG-PPL=I sleep-PCN
    I was sleeping curled up around it.

2.2. Adjectives derived with -la + -i

A second class of Yaqui adjectives is marked by both the adjectivizer **-la** and the stative **-i,** which occurs widely in Southern Uto-Aztecan. Examples are given in (9)(a)–(c).

(9)(a) tápsio-la-i   *thin (as paper)*
  (b) ná'u-la-i   *narrow*
  (c) wépu-'ula-i   *one (only)*

2.3. Adjectives derived with -li/-i

A third class of stative adjectives overlaps with the above set in that the stative **-i** occurs either by itself or fused with **-la** with the resultant shape **-li**. There appear to be both **-li** and **-i** forms of the same adjective, which simply reflects the Yaqui tendency to drop intervocalic **l**'s and **r**'s, as described in the chapter on PHONOLOGY, p. 30. For example, whereas the adjective form **tutú'u-li** *pretty* occurs only with the suffix **-li**, the adjective **'uhyóo-li** *beautiful* occurs with a functionally equivalent form **'uhyóo-i**. A second example of an adjective that is marked only by **-li** is **'ámma'a-li**, which can be glossed variously as either "precisely" or "small." Several more examples of adjectives that show alternative stative marking are given in (10)(a)–(e).

(10)(a) baá-li/-i   *fresh*   (d) sía-li/-i   *green*
   (b) tósa-li/-i   *white*   (e) čukú-li/-i   *black*
   (c) síki-li/-i   *red*

2.4. Adjectives derived with -i

A fourth class of stative adjectives appears to reflect an even more advanced stage of grammaticalization, one in which the stative suffix -i has become reanalyzed as part of the stem itself. These are illustrated in examples (11)(a)–(d).

(11)(a) tú'ii   *good*   (c) 'ili   *small (amount, size)*
    (b) túurui   *thick*   (d) béepani   *height*

A few stative adjectives seem to have the postposition **-tči** *on* that has become reanalyzed as part of the stem. This is illustrated in examples (12)(a) and (b).

(12)(a) 'ilít-či   *small sized*   (b) náare-tči   *same size*

Other elements that appear to have become fused into the adjective stem are the stative causative **-ti** shown in example (13)(a) and the indefinite **-ki** shown in (13)(b). Semantically these are quite distinct and, given their glosses, they seem nominal in nature.

(13)(a) čík-ti   *each, everyone*   (b) belé-ki/bée-ki   *amount*

2.5. Adjectives with an -i and -ia alternation

The final morphological quirk related to the stative marker **-i** is its alternation with **-ia** on certain postpositions and conjunctions. The corresponding long and short forms of the postpositions **-táhtia** *until* and the conjunction **kétči** *also* are given in examples (14)(a)–(b).

(14)(a) -táhti/-táhtia   *until, up to*   (b) kétči/-ketčía   *also*

3.0. The directional adverbial -i

The directional adverbial **-i** is superficially the same as the stative **-i**, but it may well come from a different historical source (cf. Langacker 1977:104). In the examples given in examples (15)(a)–(c), it means either "by" or "heading in some direction," e.g., "upwards, downwards."

(15)(a) kó'om-i   *downward*
    (b) yeéw-i   *outside*
    (c) 'áman-i   *by there*

A typical usage of the directional **-i** within the domain of the human body is given by sentence (16)(a). A typical usage within the domain of the topography is illustrated by sentence (16)(b).

(16)(a) máčam-po 'á'a siíse-k   wóki-m-meu-táhtia kó'om-i
    leg:PL   him urinate-PRF foot-PL-to-until   down-toward
    It urinated on his upper legs and all the way down to his feet.
    (b) 'únnaa   póčo'o-ku 'áman-i
    very:much woods-in   there-by
    There was very thick brush where he was going.

4.0. The adverbializer -si

Adverbs may be derived from adjectives, postpositions or verbs by the use of the suffix **-si**.[1] The examples in (17)(a)–(c) illustrate each of these possibilities. Notice also that there are long and short forms of these adverbials, the long forms having a final **-a** missing from the corresponding short forms.

(17)(a) tú'i-si/-sia   *very (much)*
    (b) béna-si/-sia   *like, similar to*
    (c) ko'oko-si/-sia   *painfully*

---

1   This suffix is another cognate that relates Yaqui to Cora.

A fairly extensive class of adjectives take the suffix **-si,** which turns them into adverbs, again with a variety of semantic results. For example, the adjective **bʷé'u** *big* becomes the adverb **bʷé'uu-si** which can be variously glossed as "big," or "largely." A typical usage is given in example (18). Some usages of these derived adverbs are functionally equivalent to the cognate object construction of English as illustrated by example (19).

(18) bʷé'uu-si yó'o-tu-k
    big-AVR elder-become-PRF
    It grew to a large size.

(19) kári-ta tósai-si yóka-k
    house-ACC white-AVR paint-PRF
    He painted the house white.

In deriving manner adverbs, the use of **-si** often signals an intensifying of the quality that the underived adjective designates or an augmenting of the process designated by the verb being modified. The usages of **tú'i-si** *good*-ADV illustrate this adverbial intensifying function clearly. In example (20) the intensifying relates to the spatial proximity expressed by the complex postpositional phrase **'a-u táhtia** *him-to-until,* which can be glossed "close to him." In example (21) the intensifying function relates to the transtive verb **'átbʷa** *to laugh at X.*

(20) tú'i-si 'á-u táhtia búite-k
    good-AVR him-to until run-PRF
    It ran up very close.

(21) tú'i-si 'á'a 'átbʷa
    good-AVR him laugh:at
    He really laughed at it.

Structurally, the derived **-si** adverbs may function in contrastive slots within a sentence with concomitant changes in the meaning of the adverb itself. Whereas in sentence (22), **tú'i-si** modifies the borrowed adjective **poloobe** (< Sp. pobre *poor*) and carries the intensifying meaning "very," in sentence (23) it occurs as a manner complement to the double verb construction **'aa ye'e** *be able to dance* and takes on the meaning "well."

(22) hunámani bibá-himáa-ri-wi yoéme 'áma hó'aa-k-an
    off:yonder cigarette-throw-NZR-to man there house-VR-PCN

    pahkó'olaa-taka-i táa tú'i-si polóobe
    festal:dancer-being-PPL but good-AVR poor
    Off yonder in "Discarded Cigarrettes," there used to live a man who was a ritual dancer for the Pascual fiesta, but he was very poor.

(23) tú'i-si káa 'áa yé'e 'íntok káa 'áa 'etého kía tené-ka kík-nee
    good-AVR NEG able dance CNJ NEG able converse only mouth-having stand-FUT
    He was not able to dance well, and he was not able to tell stories very well; he would just stand there with his tongue in his mouth.

On the other hand, in sentence (24) **tú'i-si** modifies the main verb **hikkaha** *to listen* and displays the extended meaning "with fascination," a meaning that quite naturally arises from the intensifying function of the adverb.

(24) 'áma kíkte húu'u yoéme kía 'ám 'ukúle-ka 'ám híkkaha tú'i-si
    there stand:SG that man only them like-PPL them hear good-AVR
    The man stopped and listened with fascination.

Manner adverbs may also be derived from intransitive verbs by the use of the suffix **-si,** as seen in sentence (25).

(25) hunúen 'á'a 'ée-simé-o=su hunáma'a tesó-m-po labén
    thus his think-go-when=EMP there cave-PL-in violin

    hía-wa-i 'áma hiía 'íntok 'áapa 'á-u kusí-si hiía
    sound-PSV-PPL there sound CNJ harp him-to shrill-AVR sound.
    As he was going along thinking this way, the sound of violin music came out of the cave and the loud sound of a harp.

A string of numerals marked by the suffixes **-si, -sa** (used only with "two"), and **-sia** is used to indicate the number of times an action was repeated. Sentence (26), which provides two examples of this, also illustrates the use of juxtaposition as a means of forming coordinate phrase structures.

(26) 'á-u   yepsá-ka   wóo-sa   báhi-sia   'áe-kón-i-la   kón-kón-ti-su-k.
     him-to arrive-PPL two-times three-times him-circle-STAT-ADV RDP-circle-CON-CPL-PRF
     Arriving back, the goat completely circled him two or three times.

5.0. Syntax

Yaqui adjectives are marked for a variety of roles in Yaqui syntax. This marking basically signals agreement of an adjective in case and number with the noun that it modifies.

5.1. Overview of the morphology

Adjectives agree in number and case with the substantives they modify. By this we mean that the adjectives are marked for indicating various kinds of semantic roles in Yaqui grammar. This includes the use of the suffix **-ta** for marking both direct objects and possessive relations, the use of two series of postpositions for marking locative relations and the use of the instrumental postpositions. These distinctions are reflected in both the singular and plural forms as seen in Table 12.

	Noun		Adjective	
CASES	singular	plural	singular	plural
ACC/POS	-ta	-im, -m	-'ik, -ik, k	-'im, -im, -m
LOC *in, inside*	-po	-im-po	-ku, -kuni, -kun	-im-po
LOC *on, on top of*	-tči, -t	-im-met	-ku-tči, -ku-t	-im-met
INST *by means of*	-e	-im-mea	-ku-e	-im-mea

Table 12. Case marking of nouns and adjectives.

5.2. The singular forms

The full set of morphological distinctions made in the singular are given in examples (27)–(31). In example (27) the accusative **-ta** on the noun **sewa** *flower* is matched by the accusative **-k** on the adjective **tósai** *white*. Example (28) shows a similar pattern, differing only in that the noun phrase includes a demonstrative adjective, which also appears in an accusative form **húka'a**.

(27) sewá-ta   'á'a miíka-k   tósai-k
     flower-ACC her give-PRF white-ACC
     He gave her a flower, a white one.

(28) 'áapo húka'a   wakáh-ta bíča-k   húka'a čukúi-k
     he   that:ACC cow-ACC   see-PRF that:ACC black-ACC
     He saw the cow, the black one.

The examples in (29)–(30) show the pairings of postpositions on nouns with those that appear on the modifying adjectives. In sentence (29) the postposition **-po** *in* attaches to the compound noun **sé'e-pá'aria** *sandy place*. It is matched by the postposition **-ku** *in* that attaches to the modifying adverb. In sentence (30), on the other hand, the postposition **-t** *on* attaches both to the noun **kúta** *log* and the adjective **námaka** *hard* which modifies **kúta**. In this case, however, the adjective carries the postposition **-ku** *in* which serves as the base for attaching **-t**.

(29) sé'e-pá'aria-po   bʷéka-ku 'á'a téa-k
     sand-outside-in wide-in   it   find-PRF
     He found it in a wide sandy space.

(30) kúta-t   námaka-ku-t yéhte-k
     log-on   hard-CON-on sit-PRF
     She sat on a hard log.

Example (31) shows the use of the singular form of the instrumental on both the noun and postpositional phrase whose object is a demonstrative adjective marked with **-le** that refers to **téta** *stone*.

(31) téta-e   'á'a béeba-k hunále-béna-ku-e
stone-INST it hit-PRF that-like-CON-INST
He hit him with a rock like that one.

In the singular, the Accusative/Possessive affix for the adjective is different from that used with the noun as seen in sentence (32). In the plural, however, they are the same as illustrated by sentence (33).

(32) Hóan-ta   waása húka'a   bʷé'uu-k
John-ACC field   that:ACC big-ACC
John's big field

(33) bempo-'im   karí-m   húme'e   tósai-m
they-ACC:PL house-PL those:ACC:PL white-ACC:PL
their white houses

Adjectives take other suffixes which are not normally used with either noun or verb classes. These will be described below. Following the locative postposition **-ku** *in*, the adjectives take many of the same postpositions as the nouns.

5.3. Reduplication of adjectives

The reduplication of adjectives is a productive process in Yaqui. It commonly indicates the plurality of the entity being described. In addition, it often signals an intensified state or quality. The examples in (34) and (35) show reduplication marking plural on adjectives that modify possessed objects.

(34) yán-t-em   hoká-a   náka-há'abʷa-i-ka
be:quiet-CON-you:PL sit:PL-PPL ear-stand:PL-PPL-PPL

híkkaha rú-rumu pusé-ka   née bit-čú-nee.
hear   RDP-open eye-having me see-CPL-FUT
Sit still listening to me with your ears perked up, and watch me carefully with wide open eyes.

(35) kú-kúma-laa   'ém   teén-e   hí'obe-k   húni'i sé'ebo'i tén-po   kibák-te
RDP-shut-AVR you:PL mouth-have mistake-PRF even   fly   mouth-in enter-VR:FUT
Keep your mouths tightly closed; otherwise, if you are not careful, a fly will get into your mouth.

The order for adjectives in construction with nouns depends on the function of the Adjective + Noun combination in the larger discourse. Frequently the adjective precedes the noun it modifies but in our collected text material there are many cases, especially in the accusative case, in which the adjective follows the noun. The order of current use seems to permit one of two alternative constructions, i.e., in tightly bound Noun-Adjective constructions, the adjective precedes the noun as a compounding element. In these attributive constructions, only the noun carries the marking for case and number as in example (36). In appositive constructions, however, the adjective is marked with **-k** for accusative singular as in example (37).

(36) tósai-kári-ta   bíča-k
white-house-ACC see-PRF
He saw the white house.

(37) kári-ta   bíčak   húka'a   tósai-k
house-ACC see:PRF that:ACC white-ACC
He saw the house, the white one.

Some adjectives may stand for a noun, if the noun has been introduced or identified elsewhere or its referent is contextually obvious. In sentence (38) the adjective **'uhyooí** *beautiful* is treated grammatically as though it were the head nominal in a noun phrase.

(38) bátte   si'ime húka'a   'úhyooí-k   tú'ure
nearly all   that:ACC beautiful-ACC like
Nearly everyone likes beautiful things.

Adjective Morphology 5.3.

We have found no more than two position classes for morphemes that follow adjective stems. This pattern is consistent with the nouns which the adjectives modify, since nouns rarely take more than one suffix. The most common second morpheme after noun roots is the interrogative clitic =**sa**. On adjectives, the corresponding interrogative clitic is =**su**. As seen in sentence (39), the interrogative clitics attach to postpositional bases, which are different for the noun and its corresponding adjective. The postposition -**po** attaches to the noun **sóto'i** *pot*, whereas the postposition -**ku** attaches to the adjective **čukúi** *black*.

(39) híta sóto'i-po=sa 'émpo húme'e ba'á-m tó'o-ka, húe čukúi-ku=su há'ani
thing jar-in=Q you those water-PL:ACC pour-PRF that black-in=Q maybe
Which pot did you pour the water in; was it the black one?

Sentence (40) illustrates two different kinds of compounds built from an adjective and another part of speech. In the first case, the adjective **musá'a-la** *attractive* combines with the stative verb **máči** *to appear* to yield a compound with the meaning "burlesque." In the second clause of this sentence, the adjective **bai** *cool* is compounded with the verb **iu** *to say* in a construction that links the two elements together by the connector **ti**; the compound itself is then passivized with the suffix -**wa** and is then turned into a nominal by the suffix -**me**. The nominal itself has the meaning "witty sayings." In addition, this sentence includes a third nominalization **nan-naa-mači-raa**, in which the absolutive suffix -**raa** appears to mark nominative case.

(40) sí'ime musá'ala-maáči húu'u nán-náa-mačí-raa
all attractive-appear that RDP-vulgar-appear-ABS

bái-t-íu-wa-me 'á'a kóba-po 'áu-taíte-k
cool-CON-say-PSV-NZR his head-in be-begin-PRF
All kinds of burlesque ideas and witty sayings began to occur in his head.

The postposition -**bena** *like* is used to derive adjectives from other adjectives or from noun compounds, giving a derived meaning of "being like X." In sentence (41) the adjective **tu'uri** *good* occurs in a shortened form **tu'u**. The overall construction is an equational sentence. In sentence (42) on the other hand, the adjective **yoi** *mexican* is the first element of a compound noun that is itself the object of the postposition -**bena** *like*. The entire postpositional phrase is the complement of the possessive verb consisting of an incorporated noun **híawa** *sound* and the possessive suffix -**ek**.

(41) tu'u-béna 'íi'i kari
good-like this house
This seems to be a good house.

(42) néo'okai yoi-kusiata-bena-k híawa-ek
mocking:bird mexican:flute-like-ACC sound-has
The mockingbird has a note like a flute.

Sentence (43) illustrates a discontinuous construction consisting of a nominalization in sentence initial position and a postpositional phrase consisting of a third person singular pronoun, followed by the classifier -**le**, which serves as a base for attaching the postposition -**bena**. The nominalization **alleewame** elaborates the pronoun in this construction. These characteristics are reminiscent of the pronoun-copy constructions discussed in Langacker (1977:27), which occurred in both inverted and discontinuous word orders (1977:28).

(43) 'allée-wame kaíta 'á-le-béna
be:happy-ABS nothing it-CON-like
There's nothing like happiness.

The predicative nature of most Yaqui adjectives (possibly all of them) is seen clearly in their use in descriptive equational statements such as those in examples (44) and (45), in which the entire utterance consists of an adjective and a following demonstrative pronoun.

(44) tosai huu'u
white that
That one is white.

(45) b^{w}é'u huu'u
big that
That one is big.

COMPOUNDS

1.0. Introduction

Compounds in Yaqui are formed using a variety of constituents one of which is almost always a noun, a verb, or an adjective and the other usually being a noun, a stative adjective, or a verb. The following discussion is organized according to the categories represented by the lexical items that enter into the compound. The highest level organization treats compounds as belonging to one of the major constituent categories.

2.0. Noun compounds

Noun compounds are commonly formed from pairing one noun with another. Other elements are also employed as the second member of noun compounds as will be seen below.

2.1. Noun + noun = noun

The first of the constructions that we discuss here consists of a pair of nouns which are semantically related to one another such that one noun serves as modifier and the other serves as head of the construction. Possibly these could be treated as noun phrases, but it seems more reasonable to treat them as compounds. For one, noun phrases carry only one principal pitch/stress on the head noun in contrast to compounds, which may have either one or two stresses; compounds also are partially shaped by various phonological rules that do not apply across word boundaries in noun phrases. Finally, in compounds, only the head noun takes suffixes, whereas in noun phrases, both head noun and modifiers may be marked by certain kinds of suffixation. The contrast between these two patterns is illustrated by examples (1) and (2).

(1) kúta-t námaka-ku-t yéhte-k
log-on hard-in-on sit-PRF
She sat on a hard log.

(2) páhko-ramáa-ta káte-k-a'u luúla wée
feast-arbor-ACC sit-PRF-GND straight go:SG
He went straight to the festival ramada.

Semantically, Yaqui compounds reflect several different kinds of relationships. Commonly, the relationship is metonymical, i.e., part to whole. In examples (3)–(5), the whole, which serves as the base of the relation is the first constituent in the compound, whereas the part that pertains to the whole is the second constituent. In sentence (3), for example, the region including the eyeball is the base for the eye lashes. In sentence (4) the mouth is the base for defining what the lip is. Finally, in sentence (5) the lower leg is the base for characterizing the calf muscle.

(3) tét-tebe-m púh-se'ebe-k
RDP-long-PL eye-lash-have
having very long eyelashes

(4) tú'i-si túurui-k tén-beria-k
good-ADV thick-ACC mouth-edge-have
He has a very thick upper lip.

(5) 'íntok čóbe-t 'á'a síise-k wók-oko'o-ku
CNJ buttocks-on him urinate-PRF leg-calf-in
And he urinated on his buttocks and on the calves of his legs.

The semantics of many Yaqui animate compounds is transparent. In sentence (6), for example, the first element of the compound is the name for the kind of animal designated by the compound. The second element then categorizes that animate entity along the age scale, the designated entity is a very young one. This categorizing role of the second element is further highlighted by the use of the nominalizing suffix **-laa**.

(6) masó-'aso'o-laa-ta búke-k amme
deer-baby-AVR-ACC tame-PRF they
They have made a pet of a fawn.

Frequently, one component or the other (and occasionally both) gets modified phonologically as a result of the compounding process. Notice in example (7) that the stress in **mása** shifts to the second syllable when it forms a compound with **boóa**. In addition, the long vowel of **boóa** gets shortened in the compounding process.

(7) mása *wing* + boóa *fur* > masá-bóa *feather*

Neither stress shifts nor vowel shortenings take place in forming the compound that means "corn silk" as shown in example (8).

(8) 'ábai *roasting ear* + čoóni-m *hair*-PL > 'ábai-čoóni-m *corn silk*

In forming the compound that means "oyster shell," given in example (9), the stress on the first syllable of **koóyo** *oyster* shifts to the second syllable and the long vowels in both constituents get shortened.

(9) koóyo *oyster* + beéa *bark, skin* > koyó-béa *oyster shell*

2.2. Locational noun compounds

Locational nouns may also serve as compounding elements, imposing some kind of a categorization on the whole. Typical examples are seen in examples (10)–(11). In (10) it is not clear what role the second element **kóbi'i** plays in the compound. In this case the compound may be losing its analyzability. On the other hand, the semantics of sentence (11) is transparent. In both cases however, the initial element tells what kind of physical terrain is involved.

(10) kaú-kobi'i-ku
mountain-corner-in
off there in the mountains

(11) sé'e-pá'aria-po b^{w}éka-ku 'á'a tea-k
sand-field-in big-in it find-PRF
He found it in a wide sandy place.

Locative nouns may also form part of the names of animate entities. In example (12), the nominal **aki** *pitahaya* specifies the location where a particular bird makes its habitat. In this example, the locative noun occurs in first position in the compound. The long vowels in each of the constituent lexical items also get shortened as part of the compounding process.

(12) 'aáki *pitahaya* + wiikit *bird* > 'akí-wíkit *a variety of dove*

Metaphorical relations underlie the choice of the categorizing constituent in many cases. For instance, as can be seen in example (13), the semiliquid nature of honey is the basis for selecting the nominal **ba'awa** *juice* as one constituent of the compound meaning "honey." The semantic role of **muúmu** *bee* is to specify the particular agent producing the entity labelled "juice." Taken together, the overall compound is conventionally construed as designating the honey produced by honey bees. In this compound, stress shift and vowel shortening affect **muúmu**.

(13) muúmu *bee* + bá'awa *juice, broth* > mumú-bá'awa *honey*

The meanings of particular compounds are not always predictable or computable from the meanings of their component constituents, but there is almost always a discernible cognitive basis for the resultant meaning. Thus, the compound illustrated in example (14) has a meaning which can be construed as the inference of a particular illness based on the observation of the presence of a particular watery substance, i.e., the presence of mucous implies a cold. Finally, **baá'a** undergoes stress shift and vowel shortening to appear in the compound in the form **ba'á**.

(14) baá'a *water* + čoómi-m *mucus* > ba'á-čoómi-m *a cold*

2.3. Body-part noun compounds

Body parts are often utilized in forming compounds. A clear example is the folk character name **Hikuria-wooki** "Spindlefoot." Oftentimes however, the meanings are highly unpredictable and the analyzability of the form may even be lost completely. For example, the compound **sísi'iwooki** in example (15) designates a telegraph sounder.

(15) sisi'iwoóki sisi'iwók-táka noóka
    metal   metal-being   talks
    It is metal, (and) being metal, it talks.

Since most Yaqui nouns are only two or three syllables long, it is tempting to analyze this form as a compound consisting of a form **sísi'i-** plus **woóki** *foot*. However, there is no evidence for any such analyzability to this, apparently fossilized form. A possible English analogy is the word cranberry. There is no free lexical item "cran," of course, but there certainly is a free lexical item "berry."

2.4. Abstract noun compounds

Abstract nouns may also enter into compounds, as seen in example (16). The first element is the name of the ethnic group itself, whereas the second element is a derived noun meaning "authority." The compound itself is conventionally construed as designating the people in Yaqui society who carry out official duties for the community.

(16) wá'aa hiák-ya'uraa-tu-ka'u
    DEM   Yaqui-authority-VR-former
    those who were formerly Yaqui authorities

2.5. Noun + adjective or verb

A number of noun compounds are formed by combining a stative adjective, an intransitive verb, or a transitive verb with a noun. Knowledge of cultural activities helps pinpoint what lies behind the selection of **napósa** *ashes* as one component of the compound meaning "hominy." Briefly, dry, shelled corn was soaked and boiled in lye water, the lye itself being derived from the ashes. The final CV of **napósa** is syncopated under compounding in example (17), whereas the long vowel of **baáki** gets shortened.

(17) napósa *ashes* + baák-i *cooked, stew* > napó-báki *hominy*

A perceived similarity in either shape or function (or both) lies behind the selection of constituents of compounds such as that illustrated in example 18. The second element **puusi-m** *eyes* is one constituent of the part-whole relationship "the eyes of the hand," which is conventionally understood to designate the fingers. This compound includes an additional suffix **-ia**, which can be glossed as "having the quality of X."

(18) máma-m *hand*-PL + pus-ia *having quality of eyes* > mám-pus-ia-m *fingers*.

The compound meaning "lightning," given in example (19), is a noun + transitive verb combination with the literal meaning "the rain sticks out its tongue." This is metaphorically based on the Yaqui conceptualization of the animate nature of the forces that determine weather patterns. The final sequence **-tia** is a nominalizing suffix, which contrasts with the verbalizing suffix **-te**.

(19) yúku *rain* + bé'ok-te *to stick out tongue* > yukú-bé'ok-t-ia *lightning*

Direct object nouns and transitive verbs may also combine to form compounds such as the one in example (20) that means "quiver." The meanings of the constituents of such compounds define the purpose for which a culturally produced entity is used, i.e., a "quiver" is something that you put arrows into for transportation or storage. As in the examples above, **-ia** is a nominalizing suffix.

(20) hú'i *arrow* + tó'o-te *to put something in* > hú'i-tó'o-ria *quiver*

Compounding is utilized productively as a means for coining both proper names and place names. Many of these compounds are fully analyzable, i.e., their component morphemes are readily identifiable and the composite meaning of the compound is often computable from a knowledge of the meanings of the parts. As examples (21)–(23) show, such meanings are often quite colorful.

(21) 'inii'i habiél   hunáman yéu-sii-ka čú'u-m-mé'a-m-pá'akun   yéu-yebih-pea-ka
    this   Gabriel there   out-go-PRF dog-PL-kill-NZR-outside   out-arrive:SG-DSD-PPL
    Gabriel left that place and went out, desiring to arrive at Dog Killer Flats.

(22) hunámani bibá-hímaa-ri-wi   yoéme 'áma hó'aa-k-an
     off:yonder cigarette-throw-NZR-to man there house-VR-PCN

    pahkó'olaa-taka-i   táa tú'i-si   polóobe
    festal:dancer-being-PPL but good-AVR poor

    Off yonder in Cigarrette Butts, there used to live a man who was a ritual dancer for the Pascual fiesta, but he was very poor.

(23) wána-hák   kó'om siíka 'ábah-ta   wéeka-'apo   'áman-i
     there-somewhere down   went cottonwood-POS stand:SG-GND   by:there

    San Hosée-po kó'om-i   húčukia-u yeéwi   sík-tábutči-m-po
    San Jose-in down-ward Tamper-to outside Red-Snake-PL-in

    'ómola   ba'á-čó'oko-m-po 'áman-i
    one:side water-salty-PL-at there-by

    Off there somewhere he went down past Where the Cottonwood Stands, on downward past San Jose outside of Tamper, to one side of Red Snake on past Salty Water.

A few compounds have been formed from combinations of a postposition and a following noun. For example, the postposition **bepa** *over* in (24)(a) occurs in two compounds that are possibly loan translations from English, illustrated in examples (24)(b)–(c). The occurrence of such Postposition + Noun compounds is a small piece of evidence that Yaqui did have the inverted postpositional construction described in Langacker (1977b:97). These compounds designate "trousers" and "shirt," respectively, in contrast to "underpants" and "undershirt."

(24)(a) bepa   (b) bépa-saáwea-m   (c) bépa-súpe-m
        above   *above trouser*-PL   *above shirt*-PL

3.0. Verb compounds

Compound verbs, just as compound nouns, arise from several different kinds of combinations of grammatical elements. These combinations include Verb + Verb sequences, Noun + Verb sequences and some Verb + Suffix sequences that derive new verbs with distinct lexical meanings.

3.1. Verb + verb = verb

In Verb + Verb compounds, the semantically central verb seems to be the initial constituent in the compound, whereas the semantically perpipheral one occurs as the second member. It can be viewed as encoding a schematic process that either provides a background in terms of which to view the event or it serves to modify the semantically central verb in some way.

Compounds having one form of **siíme** as the second constituent can be glossed by the formula "to go along doing X," where X is schematic for the content of the particular verb serving as the first constituent in the compound.

(25) wike *to pull* + siíme *to go* > wik-sime/wik-saka *to go pulling* SG/PL
(26) yú'ee *to push* + siíme *to go* > yú'u-sime/saka *to go pushing* SG/PL

Compounds whose second constituent is the transitive verb **tá'aa** *to know* can be glossed by the formula "to do X thoroughly." The augmentative function of **tá'aa** is clearly seen in examples (27) and (28). Additionally, the gloss of example (29) "to know by sight" implies an augmentative function measured along a scale of degree of verifiable knowledge. Thus, one knows better what he has personally seen than what he knows merely from hearsay.

(27) súale *to believe* + tá'aa *to know* > súal-tá'aa *to really believe*
(28) hoóa *to do* + tá'aa *to know* > hóo-tá'aa *to really know how to do X*
(29) bíča *to see* + tá'aa *to know* > bit-tá'aa *to know by sight*

Adverbial notions are clearly central to the formation of most Verb + Verb compounds. Yet a number of these have become highly enough lexicalized that it is no longer clear how to distinguish what is central semantically from what is peripheral. Thus, in example (30) does one "show respect lovingly" or does he "love respectfully?" Example (31), however, suggests that certain compounds do have the adverbial in first position. This particular compound appears to be a reduced form of a complex sentence in which **'étbʷa** was the manner complement of the matrix verb **yá'a** *to do*.

(30) nake *to love* + yó'ore *to respect* > nák-yó'ore *to lovingly respect*

(31) 'étbʷa *to steal* + yáa-/ya'a *to do* > 'étbʷá-yaa *to do secretly*

The feeling of the fear of death and the physical discomfort and erratic motion associated with it illustrate well the experiential basis of semantic structure, but the centrality of "jumping" and the peripheral status of "fear of death" is questionable in the Yaqui compound that means "nervous." Pragmatically, **-muúke/-kókko** *to die* SG/PL function as superlatives, analogous to the English word "die." Thus, the compound given in example (32) is the functional equivalent of the English metaphor "to be scared to death."

(32) túbuk-ta *to jump over* + muúke/kókko *to die* SG/PL > tubuh-múke *to be very nervous*

Finally, the verb **himaa** *to throw away* has an extended meaning of "to stop doing X" in the compound that means "to wean," given in (33).

(33) čé'e/čí'i *to nurse* + himmaa *to throw away* > či'i-himmaa *to wean*

3.2. Noun + verb = verb

The nouns employed in Noun + Verb compounds may serve in various semantic roles. In example (34), the word **bó'oo** *road* is a straightforward object of perception and serves as the direct object of the following constituent, the verb **bíča** *to see*. In example (35) **čoóni-m** *hair* marks the direct object of **poóna** *to pull*. Part of the meaning of this compound is that the speaker knows that the activity of hair pulling takes place within the context of violent social interactions (usually between women).

(34) boó'o *road* + bíča *to see* > bó'o-bíča *to wait for X* (lit.: *watching the road*)

(35) čoóni-m *hair*-PL + poóna *to pull* > čón-poóna *to pull hairs* (lit.: *fighting*)

Abstract nouns also appear in the direct object role as the first constituent in Noun + Verb compounds. The gloss of example (36) shows, however, that the subsequent lexicalization and acquisition of meaning is not predictable from the meanings of **tekil** *work* and **máka** *to give*. Thus the compound **tékil-máka** does not mean "to give someone work," but rather "to commission someone to do X" or "to make someone responsible for X." Similarly, the compound **hiapsi-temae** given in example (37) does not mean just to ask oneself something in private, but implies an inner discussion with oneself resulting in a decision to embark on a different pattern of behavior with respect to some issue.

(36) tékil *work* + máka *to give* > tékil-máka *to commission, make responsible*

(37) hiapsi *life/soul* + temae *to question* > hiapsi-temáe *to repent*

There are also a few compounds that consist of a subject noun and an intransitive verb. In example (38) the intransitive verb **wéče** *to fall* is used in the extended sense of "to appear suddenly." The subject noun **táhi** *fire* is also used in an extended sense, based on the transfer of heat from one domain to another, i.e., the effect of fever in a person's body is perceived as being "heat" and the source of the fever effect is likened to a fire that causes heat.

(38) táhi *fire* + wéče *to fall* > táhi-wéče *to have a fever*

3.3. Aspectual verb compounds

One class of Verb + Verb compounds shows a consistent semantic relationship between Verb1 and Verb2 such that Verb1 designates the manner of the action and Verb2 designates something about the motion of the subject. These compounds can be called "aspectual compounds," and consist of a transportation verb plus a motion verb. The motion verb places salience on some aspect of the path that the subject of the sentence traverses in carrying out the intended activity. The aspect of the path may be either the beginning point, the end point, or some intermediate point. Conceivably, the entire path could also be subsumed in the construal of the particular event. It is also clear that the particular tense/aspect of the motion verb is related to the particular construal of the scene that is appropriate to each usage.

Compounds consisting of **nuk-** *to carry* plus some form of **siíme** *to go* can be glossed "to go along carrying X." However, in most usages, it approaches more closely the meaning "to carry out" or "to carry away," as seen in the usages illustrated in examples (39)–(43). In sentence (39) **nuk-sime** indicates motion away from the speaker's location, whereas in sentence (40), it indicates motion from within an enclosed area to an outside location. Finally, in sentence (41), **nuk-sime** indicates concomitant motion of a multiplex entity.

(39) 'i'an=su née 'á'a núk-sim-nee
today=EMP I it carry-go-FUT
Well, today I will take/carry it away.

(40) húnak béha kóa-po yéu 'á'a núk-sáha-k
then well corral-in out it carry-go:PL-PRF
Then they carried it out of the corral.

(41) kúta-bankó-m-mak lopola 'á'a núk-wéiyaa hunáman-tahtia
wood-seat-PL-with beside her carry-go there-until
He carried her alongside the wooden benches up to there.

Compounds formed with **tó'o** *to leave something somewhere* and a following appropriate form of **siíme** *to go* can be glossed "to leave something somewhere and go on elsewhere without it." A reflexive version, which can be glossed "they parted company" is given in sentence (42). The prototypical meaning of leaving an inanimate object off at a particular location is illustrated by sentence (43).

(42) čúbala náu-katé-ka 'émo-tó'o-sáha-k
moment together-go-PPL RFL-leave-go-PRF
After traveling together for a while, they left one another.

(43) 'ón-ta pú'ak-ta-nee béa-m 'áme-u tó'o-si-sime
salt-ACC load-VR-FUT skin-PL them-to leave-RDP-go
He loads up the salt and leaves the skins with them.

Frequently the entity that is left alone is another human being, as illustrated in examples (44) and (45). The different verbs used in combination with **to'o-** such as "run" or "stand up" indicate that there are various ways in which someone can be left alone. Other usages of **to'o-** plus a verb are metaphorical, as seen in example (46) in which the death of one spouse is the cause of the other one being alone.

(44) si'ime née tó'o-tét-te-nee
all me leave-RDP-run-FUT
Everyone runs away from me.

(45) húnak béha 'áapo 'ám tó'o-kikte-k
then well he them left-stand-PRF
Well, then he stood up and left them.

(46) 'a'a to'o-muúku-k
he left-die:SG-PRF
He died, leaving her alone.

The stem **su'u** apparently occurs only with the verb **tóha** *to take, to leave (something somewhere)*. To begin, the verb **toha** invokes a conceptual scene involving the separation of some person moving away from the object he was transporting physically or over which he had some other kind of control. Compounds formed with the stem **su'u** *to release* and the stem **toha** *to leave* seem to always imply that someone allow something to happen that leads to some kind of separation. Commonly, these compounds fit the formula: S_x permits S_y to go.

The subscripts in this formula suggest that the subject of **su'u** is not identical to the subject of **toha**. This is a major contrast to the **to'o-siíme** compounds discussed above, in which the subject of **to'o** is identical to the subject of **siíme**. In sentence (47), for example, the subject of **wée** *to go* in the second clause is the direct object of **sú'u-tóha** in the first clause. Likewise, in sentence (48) the one who orders

162

the release is subject of **sú'u-tóhi-tébo,** wheras the ones who are going to leave are the direct object of this complex interaction.

(47) 'áke-'em 'á'a sú'u-tóha 'elá'apo wée-nee
you-IMP it leave-leave no:matter go-FUT
Turn it loose; it doesn't matter if it goes away.

(48) tómi-ta mabéta-ka 'ám sú'u-tóhi-tébo-k
money-ACC receive-PPL them leave-leave-order-PRF
Having received the money, he ordered them released.

On the other hand, the subject of the compund **sú'u-tóha** may well also be the leaver of **sú'u,** as illustrated in the metaphorical expression given in sentence (49).

(49) 'émpo hunáka'a bo'o-ta sú'u-tóha-k-o káa-máči-ku-n yebíh-nee
you that:ACC road-ACC leave-leave-PRF-if not-light-to arrive:SG-FUT
If you abandon that road, you will arrive into the darkness.

The adjective **tú'u-** *good* serves as the initial compounding element with a very limited number of verbs. In example (50) the compound consisting of **tú'u-** and **noóka** *talk* means "to speak soothingly." In example (51) the compound consisting of **tu'u-** and the possessive verb **hiaps-ek** *to have life* really means "to be good-hearted."

(50) 'á'a 'áe-ka'u 'á-u tú'u-noóka   (51) hunáa'a túa tú'u-hiaps-ek
his mother-deceased him-to good-talk   that indeed good-life-have
His mother (now deceased) spoke soothingly to him. *That person is good-hearted.*

3.4. Verb + suffix = verb

A few verbs take verbal suffixes to produce a different verb. For example, the transitive perception verb **bíča** *to see* combines with the suffix **-su** *totally, completely* to form a new perception verb **bit-ču,** which is conventionally construed as meaning "to stare." This usage is illustrated in sentence (52).

(52) čóki-híssaa-m=te bít-nee bʷéere pusé-ka 'ám bítču-nee
star-spray-PL=we see-FUT large eye-have them stare-FUT
We will see the comet; we'll stare at it with wide eyes.

The verb **bíča** also combines with **-tua** *to cause to,* to derive the compound verb **bittua,** which conventionally means "to send something" as in sentence (53).

(53) 'á'a hubía-wa bʷá'a-m-ta wasá-u bíttua-k
his wife-POS eat-NZR-ACC field-to send-PRF
His wife sent food out to the field.

As we discuss in POSTPOSITIONS, pp. 201–202 and elsewhere, **bíča** is an extremely versatile morpheme and its usages show many different stages and processes of grammaticalization. For example, although the conventionally the most established meaning of **bittua** is "to send something," in certain contexts the literal meaning "to cause to see something" may be unambiguously expressed as in sentence (54).

(54) 'á'a pusí-m hítto-ka húči bít-tua-wa-k
his eye-PL treat-PPL again see-CAU-PSV-PRF
By treating his eyes, he was enabled to see again.

All these possibilities for combining elements with **bíča,** lead us to the following conventions for citing the examples in this grammar sketch:

bíttua *to send something*   bítču *to stare at*
bít-tua *to cause to see*   bít-ču *to finish seeing*

A fourth example of a derived verb involving a verb stem and a suffix is the widely employed **tebo** *to command.* In this case the causative **-tua** plays a role to derive the compound verb **tebótua** which means "to greet," as illustrated in sentence (55).

(55) 'á'a tebótua-su-ka 'áa-mak 'etého-taite-k
    him greet-CPL-PPL him-with talk-begin-PRF
    Having greeted him, he began to visit with him.

A slightly different slant on the scene of greeting someone is reflected by the combination of **tebo** with the verbalizing suffix **-te.** In this case, the resulting compound verb can be glossed as "to send greetings" as seen in sentence (56).

(56) 'áman=te té-tebo-te
    there=we RDP-greet-VR
    We send our greetings out there.

POSSESSIVE CONSTRUCTIONS

1.0. Introduction

Possession in Yaqui is marked in a variety of ways in several distinct domains of the grammar. This includes a set of possessive pronouns that distinguish between singular and plural number for first, second, and third person possessors. In addition this paradigm includes a third person singular specific possessor suffix **-wa**, an interesting morphological parallel to the Pimic and Corachol languages (cf. Langacker 1977:86). Specified third person singular possessors, i.e., those identified by specific lexical items and constructions are marked with the accusative suffix **-ta**. Yaqui **-wa** plays a particular disambiguating role which we discuss below. Finally, possession in Yaqui is also indicated by a variety of main verbs and pronominal and verbal suffixes in other kinds of constructions. All these patterns structure the possessive relation in distinct ways which we discuss in this section.

2.0. Morphology

In this section we describe the distinctions signalled by possessive markers on nominals. These include the possessive clitics, the specified possessor suffix **-wa** and the emphatic possessive suffixes.

2.1. The possessive clitics

The paradigmatic forms given in below summarize the contrastive clitics that Yaqui employs in marking the person and number of the possessor.

'ín	*my*	'itóm	*our*
'ém	*your:SG*	'enčím	*your:PL*
á'a	*his*	bém	*their*
'á'a X-wa	*specific possessor*		

Usages of these possessive clitics are illustrated by examples (1)–(8). Notice that the head of the possessive noun phrase is the object which is possessed. Both inanimate entities, either discrete as illustrated in (1)(a), or mass as in example (1)(b), as well as kin relations, as in examples (1)(c)–(d), can be viewed as being possessed entities.

(1)(a) 'ín tómi   *my money*   (d) 'á'a kuná-wa   *her husband*
   (b) 'ém kári   *your:SG house*   (e) 'á'a tómi-wa   *his money*
   (c) 'á'a hubía-wa   *his wife*

Possessed nominal forms may carry additional marking beyond the possessive clitics. The possessed noun suffix **-ka'u**, conventionally designates the possessed relation as being deceased, as illustrated in example (2). This suffix actually represents the bimorphemic sequence **-k-a'u** perfective gerund, but we treat it as a single morpheme in its usages with kinship terms (cf. also NOUN INFLECTION, p. 136).

(2) 'itóm 'áe-ka'u
    our   mother-deceased
    our now deceased mother

Multiplex animate and mass nouns are marked with the plural suffix **-im,** as illustrated in examples (3)–(4).

(3) 'enčím wakás-im   *your:PL cows*
(4) bém waása-m   *their fields*

2.2. Marking of the specified possessor

A specified possessor nominal in possessive phrases is marked by the accusative suffix **-ta** in the singular as in example (5), and by the accusative plural **-im/-m** for multiple possessors as in example (6).

(5) Hóan-ta kári
John-ACC house
John's house

(6) húme'e tóri-m toósa-m
these rat-PL nest-PL
these rats' nests

A nominalized clause that designates the possessor of the possessed entity is also marked with the accusative suffix **-ta.** In example (7) for instance, the possessed entity is **waása** *field* whereas the possessor is **'áma hó'aa-k-am** *the one who lives over there*. In example (8) the possessed entity is **kári** *house* with the possessor again being "the one who lives over there." In these two cases, Yaqui **-ta** functions in almost the same way as the possessor "-s" in the English expression the "King of England's crown."

(7) húka'a 'áma hó'aa-k-am-ta waása
that:ACC there house-have-NZR-ACC field
the field of the person who lives there

(8) húu'u 'áma hó'aa-k-am-ta kári
that there house-have-NZR-ACC house
the house of the man who lives there

2.3. The possessor suffix -wa

The noun suffixes **-ta** and **-im**, which mark singular and plural respectively, are used for marking both direct objects and possessed objects, generally without any confusion of the two categories. The distinction is often reinforced by the noun/verb distinction. Examples (9) and (10) are typical.

(9) Hóan-ta huúbi
John-POS wife
John's wife

(10) Hóan-ta bíča-k
John-ACC see-PRF
He saw John.

Although Yaqui has one set of pronouns for marking possession and another set for marking direct objects, the third person singular form in both sets is identical, i.e., **'á'a** as in examples (11) and (12).

(11) 'á'a waákas
his cow
his cow

(12) 'á'a bíča-k
him see-PRF
He saw him.

This morphological overlap (which is actually due to semantic extension) sets up the possibility for ambiguity in certain contexts. Thus the usage of the third person singular possessive suffix **-wa** is of special interest. It is frequently added to the possessed object, e.g., **'á'a hubía-wa** *his wife*, **'á'a kári-wa** *his house*, and **'á'a číba-wa-m** *his goats*. It may also be used with possessed subject nouns as in example (13) or object nouns as in (14).[1]

(13) 'á'a hubía-wa wasá-u siíka
his wife-POS field-to go:PRF
His wife went to the field.

(14) 'á'a hubía-wa-ta núk-siíka
his wife-POS-ACC carry-go:PRF
He took his wife with him.

The use of specificative **-wa** would help disambiguate a sentence such as (15) in which **'á'a kári-ta** *his house*-ACC could refer to either the subject of the sentence or to some other third person.

(15) 'á'a kári-ta táttabe-k
his house-ACC break-PRF
He tore his house down.

On the other hand, the use of the suffix **-wa** in example (16) signals overtly that the subject of the sentence is the possessor of the house that was torn down.

---

1 In Arizona Yaqui, one may hear the forms **'in-kari-wa** or **nim-kari-wa** both meaning "my house" and **'em-kariwa** "your house." (Eloise Jelinek, personal communication).

(16) 'á'a kári-wa-ta   táttabe-k
    his house-SPEC-ACC break-PRF
    He tore his own house down.

In short, the specified third person singular possessor suffix **-wa** is one of the ways that Yaqui has to signal the concept "one's own." Examples given later in this section show other devices that Yaqui employs to signal this distinction.

It is interesting to compare contemporary Yaqui data with the discussion of **-wa** given by Buelna 1891 in Item 60. He states the following:

> Esta partícula **ua** es generalísima. Añádese á nombres, pronombres, adverbios, preposiciones y conjunciones: unos dicen que denota posesión de la cosa significada por el nombre á quien se añade; otros que es partícula de respeto; sea lo que fuere, lo cierto es, que dicha partícula es muy usada en todas las partes de la oración que no son verbo, y le da más énfasis á lo significado de aquella parte de la oracion á que se junta, y su uso más frequente es, cuando se habla con más energía: **inoporiua** *yo mismo*: **ahariua** *aquel propio*: **iminiua** *aqui en este lugar*: **amaniua** *allá mismo*: **achaiua** *padre*: **aiua** *madre*: **hubiua** *mujer casada*. Esta partícula sigue la condición de la parte de oración á que se junta. Si es nombre declinable, se declina por la primera declinacion, v.g. **atzaiua**, genitivo **atzaiuata**; **hubiua**, genitivo **hubiuata**; **cunaua**, genitivo **cunauata**. Si es adverbio, preposición ó conjunción, no se declina, *v.g.* **siutisiua** *rasgadamente*, **cocosiua** *dolorosamente*: el significado de este **ua** consta más claro de la partícula siguiente. (Buelna 1891:21, Item 60.)[2]

Dedrick finds no examples of the Possessive **-wa** being used with anything other than the third person singular possessor. In its disambiguating role, it does reinforce the salience of the notion of possession and is more likely to be used in serious and deliberate conversation. Even more, several of the particular possessed forms that Buelna cites are apparently no longer used. This suggests that contemporary Yaqui has narrowed its use of **-wa** considerably since the time of Buelna and his associates. Finally, some of the uses of **-ua** that Buelna cites probably reflect a distinct morpheme or two. It is difficult to conceive what the word **síu-ti-si-wa** would mean if the **-wa** on **síu-ti-si** *tearingly* were the possessor suffix **-wa**. On the other hand, this meaning is quite naturally related to the meaning of Passive **-wa**.

2.4. The emphatic possessive suffixes

The suffixes **-'ik** (SG) and **-'im** (PL) are used with the nominative personal pronouns making them into emphatic adjectives of possession. The subject pronouns **'ínepo** *I,* **'áapo** *he,* and **bémpo** *they* may take the Accusative/Possessive suffix **-ik** (SG), as in examples (17)–(18), or its plural counterpart **-im**, as in example (19), to highlight the possession relationship. The suffix may be used either along with the suffix **-wa** or apart from it.

(17) 'ínepo-'ik tómi-wa   (18) 'áapo-'ik yáa-k-a'u
    I-POS   money-POS   he-POS   do-PRF-GND
    my very own money   *his very own doing*

---

[2] "The particle **-wa** is maximally general in its usages. You can add it to nouns, pronouns, adverbs, prepositions and conjunctions: some say that it denotes the possession of a specific object designated by the noun to which it is added; others say that it is an honorific particle; be that as it may, what is certain is that this very particle is frequently used on all the constituents of a sentence that are not verbs, and it places emphasis on the meaning of that constituent of the sentence to which it is attached, and its most frequent usage is when it is spoken with the greatest intensity: **inoporiua** *I myself*, **ahuariua** *that very one*, **iminihua** *here in this place*, **amaniua** *right there in that place*, **achaiua** *father*, **aihua** *mother*, **hubiua** *married woman*. This particle takes on the categorization of the constituent of the sentence to which it is attached. If the constituent is a declinable noun, it is declined according to the first declension, e.g. **atzaihua**, genitive **atzaihuata**; **hubiua**, genitive **hubiuata**; **cunaua**, genitive **cunauata**. If the constituent is an adverb, preposition or conjunction, it is not declined, e.g. **siutisiua** *tearingly*, **cocosiua** *sickly*: the meaning of this **ua** is clarified by that of the following particle." (Buelna 1891:21, Item 60.)

(19) bémpo-'im waása
   they-POS field
   their very own field

Examples (16)–(18) suggest that the suffixes **-'ik** and **-'im** should occur with the full paradigm of independent subject pronouns. This would result in the paradigm given below of emphatic possessive pronouns. However, the starred forms do not occur in our data.

'ínepo-'ik	*my own*	*'itépo-'im	*our own*
*'émpo-'ik	*your own*	*'emé-'im	*your:PL own*
'áapo-'ik	*his own, her own, its own*	bempó-'im	*their own.*

Given the discovery of first person singular forms during translation, it is quite obvious that **-'ik** is not restricted to third person singular, as example (20) shows.

(20) 'ínepo-'ik 'in híapsi
   I-POS my heart
   my very own life

A third way that Yaqui has for conveying the notion "one's own" is by the use of the adverbial **túa** *indeed, verily* as illustrated in example (21). This usage applies to all persons of possessor, both singular and plural.

(21) túa 'ín kari
   indeed my house
   my very own house

Sentence (22) also shows an adjective functioning as a nominal marked as accusative, i.e., **tá'abwi-k** can be glossed as "a different one-ACC" and is conventionally construed in this context as designating a woman.

(22) 'á'a kuná-wa tá'ab^w i-k núk-siíka
   her husband-POS different-ACC carry-go
   Her husband went away with another woman.

The possessive **-wa** may be used with both concrete possessed nouns, as illustrated in example (23), and with abstract ones, as illustrated in examples (24) and (25).

(23) 'á'a tékil-wa
   his work-POS
   his work

(24) 'á'a híaps-i-wa-ta nénka-k
   his life-ABS-POS-ACC sell-PRF
   He sacrificed his own life.

(25) 'á'a 'úhyoria-wa
   his beauty-POS
   its beauty

Regarding third person singular, in the text about **Mása'asai,** Castro used two different constructions with the **-wa** suffix. In sentence (26) the possessed noun **'ábači-wa** *someone's brother* is head of a discontinous construction with the proximal demonstrative **'íi'i** *this*. The identification of who the brother is is effected through a verbal construction in which the brother's name is the complement of the verb stem **-'itea** *to be named*. In sentence (27) the possessed noun is followed by the personal name in a Noun Phrase + Appositive construction. The possessed noun also is marked by the third person singular possessive pronoun **'á'a.**

(26) 'íi'i 'íntok 'ábači-wa hikúria-wóki-'itea
   this and brother-POS Spindle-foot-named
   And this girl's older brother was named Spindlefoot.

(27) 'á'a 'ábači-wa Hikúriawoki póčo'o-kun kíbake-k
   her brother-POS Spindle-foot woods-to enter-PRF
   Her (own) brother, Spindlefoot, went into the woods.

3.0. Syntax

As we have already seen from previous examples, in possessive phrases, the possessor noun is marked by the accusative suffix **-ta**. This use of the accusative to mark possession is widespread in Uto-Aztecan languages (cf. Langacker 1977:84, 90). Sentence (28) is a typical example.

(28) 'iníi'i yóo-pahkóolaa-ta etého-i
 this enchanted-festal:dancer-ACC relate-PPL
 This is the story about the Enchanted Feaster.

3.1. The possessive verbal suffix -ek

Since we have already discussed the possessive suffix **-ek** in BE/HAVE/DO pp. 74–75, we simply provide here a few examples to illustrate further this device for conveying the possessive notion. As illustrated in sentence (29), this option entails suffixing **-ek** to an incorporated noun in a verbal possessive construction.

(29) 'aháa n-áčai 'ó'olaa tú'i-si n-ám yí'i-pea
 aha my-father ancient good-AVR I-them dance-DSD
 táa née káa-tú'ii-m wók-ek
 CNJ I NEG-good-PL foot-have
 Aha, my revered Father, how I wish I could dance to that music, but I just don't have good legs.

The suffix **-ka** is commonly used with incorporated body part nouns and count nouns to express the idea that "X has Y" (cf. BE/HAVE/DO, pp. 72–74). The extended example (30) contains several occurrences of this, also illustrating a variety of morphemic shapes, for in addition to the form **-ka**, we also see **-aka** and **-k**.

(30) húnen 'á'a 'éa-o=su hunáma'a téh-po yóo-čibá'ato tósai-ka
 thus his think-when=EMP there cave-in enchanted-goat white-being

 čukúi-ka tána-la b^{W}ási-aka káa 'awá-ka kía tét-tébe-m náka-k
 black-being curve-ADJ tail-having NEG horn-have only RDP-long-PL ear-have

 tét-tébe-m púh-sé'ebe-k bátte b^{W}íia-u núki-m hímse-ka 'á-u yéu-búite
 RDP-long-PL eye-lash-have nearly ground-to reach-PL beard-have him-to out-run
 As he was going along with these thoughts, a black and white enchanted goat, hornless, with his tail curved over his back, with long ears, very long eyelashes, and a beard that reached nearly to the ground, came running out toward him.

Sentence (31) seems curious because there is no accusative marker on the word **číba'ato**. This lack of marking indicates that a different construction is involved here and not the prototypical Possessor Noun-Possessed Object construction. In particular, **číba'ato-sih** *goat-urine* is a noun compound. Note that the word **sih** *urine* is one element of a Noun-Noun serving as an adverb which modifies the verb **húba-ka** *having the smell of*.[3]

(31) 'íi'i 'íntok yoéme čibá'ato-síh-hubá-ka siíka
 this CNJ man goat-urine-smell-PPL go:PRF
 Well, this man went on, smelling of goat urine.

3.2. Possessive marking on relative clauses

Both Yaqui relative clauses and certain adverbial clauses are also marked with possessor clitics that are preposed to the clause. These clitics mark the person and number of the subject of the relative clause or the adverbial clause. Thus, the clitic **'á'a** designates the third person singular subject of **wéye'-e-beleki** *to*

---

[3] The incorporated root form **sih** displays the result of a pair of morphophonemic rules that shortens a stem vowel and turns the grooved fricative s into a post-velar fricative **h**. This is clear when one compares the incorporated form with the related free verb and nominal forms, **siíse** *to urinate* and **'siísi** *urine*.

go everywhere in the first clause of sentence (32) and the second occurrence of it marks the third person singular subject of **bíča-u 'úhyooli** *seeing beautiful things*.

(32) hunáma naáte-ka 'á'a wéye-'e-beléki sí'ime húu'u 'á'a bíča-u 'úhyooli
there begin-PPL his go-EV-everywhere all that his see-GND beautiful
But, beginning right then, and for the whole trip, everything that he saw was beautiful.

Certain Noun-Noun compounds are of the form Possessor Noun-Possessed Object. Sentence (33) gives a typical example.

(33) páhko-ramáa-ta kátek-a'u lúula-wée
feast-arbor-POS sit-GND straight-go:SG
He went straight to the feast ramada.

3.3. Structuring the domain of possession

Although Yaqui does not have a well defined morphological system for classifying the categories of potentially possessed objects, it does have several verbs meaning "have" that are used in possessive constructions in addition to the different patterns of suffixation on the possessed nouns which we have already discussed. The structuring of the semantic domain of possession is also shown by way of certain kinds of appositive constructions that include a possessor clitic or prefix followed by members of a small set of classifier nouns such as "pet," "child," or "possession."

Generally speaking, the verbs **híp^wee** *to have* and **'áttea** *to own* take concrete objects as their complements, that is, one may have or own a cow or a house, but not happiness. The verb **bíča** *to see* has the extended meaning of "to experience," and one experiences happiness. Likewise, one does not "have life" but rather "lives."

In short, **híp^wee** tends to put the center of attention on the possession of a discrete and tangible object. However, it is rather schematic in the way it refers to the possessed object. Thus it takes as its complement a verb marked with either a third person singular object pronoun, an indefinite pronoun, or a quantifier, as in sentence (34). As another variation, a following possessive clause may be employed to further specify what the particular possessive relationship is, as seen by the use of **b^wía-k** *to have land*, in sentence (35).

(34) 'ín 'á-e 'á'a hínu-ne-'u húni'i née káa híp^wee
my it-with it buy-FUT-GND even I not have
And I don't have anything to buy it with, either.

(35) yú'in=ne híta híp^wee yú'in=ne b^wía-k
much=I things have much=I land-have
I have lots of things and I have lots of land.

The schematicity of the possessed item in the meaning of **híp^wee** and the human capacity to construe abstract ideas as discrete entities allows it to also designate abstract concepts such as "ideas," as in example (36).

(36) 'ín kóba-po 'á'a híp^wee
my head-in it have
I have it in my head.

The notion of ownership of tangible items is expressed through the term **'áttea** "possession," a word that seems to function either as a noun or as a verb. As a verb it may occur as: **'áttea-n** *used to own it*, **'áttea-k** *own it*, **'áttea-nee** *will own it*. Used as a noun it frequently designates one's clothing, as: **in-'áttea** *my clothing*; **'átteaari** *clothing*. But it does not require an overt definite noun for its complement. As a verb, however, it has tenses and does require the accompaniment of the suffix **-k** *to have* in the present imperfect as illustrated in sentence (37), or the use of **-n** in the past continuative or **-nee** in the future, as seen in sentence (38).

170

(37) 'í'an=té náu   'á'a 'áttea-k
    now=we together it   own-IMPRF
    Now we own it together.

(38) 'émpo-la hunúka'a 'áttea-nee kaábe 'é-mak   'á'a 'áttea-nee
    you-only that:ACC own-FUT no:one you-with it   own-FUT
    You alone possess it. No one else will possess it with you.

On the other hand, the suffix **-ek** when used as a verbalizer meaning "to have," may be used with either concrete nouns like **wakás-ek** *have a cow* or with abstract nouns like **'útte'a** *strength* as in **'útte'a-k** *to have strength, be strong*. Speakers do not follow these rules consistently, however, and some conform their patterns to that of Spanish.

In concepts involving relationaships, a noun with suffix **-ek** is most commonly used. This verbal construction is commonly used instead of indicating possession via possessive noun phrases. It is used quite prominently for indicating kinship relations such as those specified by examples (39)–(41).

(39) húu'u Hóan 'á'a maára-k
    that John her daughter-have
    She is John's daughter.

(40) 'áapo 'á'a yoém-ia-k
    he him child-NZR-POS
    He is his child.

(41) beétu 'á'a huúb-ek
    Bert her wife-POS
    She is Bert's wife.

The **-ek** and its allomorph **-k** also are used to indicate the ties between a person and the land where he/she works and lives, as in examples (42)–(43).

(42) háu-sa   hó'aa-k   húu'u 'ém 'ásoa ... húu'u=su
    where-INTERR house-have that your child ... that=EMP

    'ém maára   wáa'a=su 'ém 'uúsi
    your daughter that=EMP your boy
    Where does your child live? ...your daughter? your other boy?

(43) bémpo 'á'a wasá-k-an
    they   it field-have-PCN
    It used to be their field.

The notion of ownership of a domestic animal is indicated by the verb **búke** *to make a pet of*. The nominalized form **búki** *a pet*, is one of several terms that have been borrowed into local Spanish where it is used to refer to any small child.

(44) masó-'aso'o-laa-ta   búke-k=amme
    deer-baby-AVR-ACC pet-VR=they
    They have made a pet of a fawn.

POSTPOSITIONS

1.0. Introduction

Yaqui postpositions can generally be categorized as free or bound. Some can be classified as free postpositions because other parts of speech may intervene between the postpositional object and the postposition with which it forms a construction. On the other hand, there is another set of postpositions which do not enjoy this freedom of occurrence. Nonetheless, some of these do correspond to free lexical items, i.e., the bound postpositions in some cases represent the grammaticalized versions of certain positional or perceptual verbs.

As a further complication, some postpositions act as free ones in certain contexts and as bound ones in other contexts. For example, **-po** *inside* and **-ku** *in* only occur as bound postpositions, whereas others, such as **-béna** *like* seem to occur as bound morphemes in some contexts and as free in others. In some cases we do not have enough examples to be sure whether a given postposition is bound, free, or variably bound.

Semantically, the postpositions encode a wide range of spatial, temporal, and associative meanings. The bound ones all attach directly to their nominal and pronominal objects. As the data in this section amply illustrate, other classes of constituents also serve as objects for postpositions with varied semantic effects. Finally, as subsequent data will show, Yaqui has both morphemically complex postpositions as well as strings of two or more postpositions.

For purposes of presentation, we group the Yaqui postpositions into three overlapping classes grouped by both semantic and morphological distinctives. They include: the spatials, the associatives, and the **-be** postpositions. The inventory of postpositions is given below in Table 13.

The spatials		The associatives		The -be postpositions	
-u/-wi	*toward, to*	-e/-mea	*with* (INSTRUMENT)	-beas/-was	*near, beside*
-po	*in, inside*	-mak/-é	*with* (ACCOMPANIMENT)	-bépa	*over, above*
-ku	*in, on* (LOC)	-naápo	*near, close*	-be-tuk/-tuk	*under, beneath*
-étči	*on top, on*	-nasuk (PL)	*between, in the midst of*	-be-tana/-tana	*beside, at one side of*
hika	*on top of*			-be-wit-či	*simultaneously, parallel*
-táhtia	*until* (TEMPORAL)			-betčí'ibo	*for* (BENEFACTIVE)
				-béna	*like* (SIMULFACTIVE)
				-bíča	*site, location*

Table 13. Yaqui postpositions

The full set of pronominal bases marked for singular and plural of first, second, and third persons are employed as objects of the postpositions. The basic pronominal set is given in Table 14.

Person	Singular	Plural
1	né-	'itó-
2	'é-	'emó-
3	'á-	'áme-

Table 14. Pronominal objects of postpositions

The range of grammatical elements that may serve as objects of the postpositions includes personal pronouns, count nouns, locative nouns, demonstrative pronouns, demonstrative adverbs, manner adverbs, temporal adverbs, nominalizations, adjectives, and question words.

In the idiomatic expression given in example (1), a first person singular pronoun serves as the object of the postposition **-t** *on*. In example (2) the object of the postposition is the directional adverb **ama** *backwards*, whereas a locative noun **hékka** *shade* serves as object of the postposition **-u** *to* in example (3). Finally, sentence (4) provides an instance in which a derived temporal adverb serves as the object of the postposition **-po** *in*.

> (1) yoí   né-t   kópte
>   non:Yaqui me-on forget
>   *The non-Yaqui is jealous of me.* (an idiom)
>
> (2) hobé'eso 'awá-m   amá-u-bíča bi'i-ti-laa
>   ram   horn-PL back-to-site twist-PPL-PPL
>   *Rams' horns are twisted backwards.*
>
> (3) hékka-u n=á'a tóha-k
>   shade-to I=him bring-PRF
>   *I took it to him to the shade.*
>
> (4) 'iníi'i yoéme ké'esam-ria-po   née 'á'a tá'aa-o
>   this   person first:time-ABS-in I   him know-when
>   *when I first knew this man*

A question word may also serve as a postpositional base as in example (5). Note also the predicative use of the negative particle **'é'e.**

> (5) háčín-po húni'i 'é'e
>   how-in   even   no
>   *The answer is "No," regardless.*

The question marker **=sa** can attach to a postposition, as in examples (6) and (7).

> (6) háčin-po=sa   yéu-tóm-tí-nee   'ó'oo-láa-tu-k-o
>   how-in=INTERR   out-stomach-FUT   old-PPL-VR-PRF-if
>   *In what way can he be born if he is old?*
>
> (7) 'íi'i boó'o hakún-bíčáa=sa   wée
>   this road where-site=INTERR   go
>   *Where does this road go?*

A postpositional phrase may also take the manner adverb **'ínen** as its object, as illustrated in example (8).

> (8) 'ínen-po béha ču'ú-ta-u   hiía-k
>   thus-in well dog-POS-to say-PRF
>   *"In this manner," he said to the dog.*

Singular nominal objects of the postposition are marked with the accusative suffix **-ta,** as illustrated by sentence (9). The nominals in (9)–(10) are both animate nouns. Example (10) also shows the accusative **-ta** serving as a base for attaching a following postposition.

> (9) 'usí-ta   pú'ak-te-ka ... hitébii-ta-u   lúula   wée
>   child-ACC   carry-VR-PPL   doctor-POS-to   straight go
>   *He took the child straight to a "healer."*
>
> (10) hobé'eso-ta-u lúula   wée
>   ram-POS-to   straight go
>   *He went straight to the ram.*

Additional syllables and segments also serve as postpositional bases for attaching a postposition to its object. These were discussed in PHONOLOGY p. 32–33. We present a few examples of these here for the readers' convenience. One connector is the morpheme **-be,** illustrated in examples (11) and (12). Notice that both nouns serving as objects of the postposition designate classes of people in the domains of the workplace or the home.

> (11) bambró'osio 'á'a tekó-be-u   bočá-m   'a'áwa-k
>   Ambrosio   his boss-CON-to   shoe-PL ask-PRF
>   *Ambrosio asked his boss for shoes.*
>
> (12) 'ín malá-be-u   né wáate
>   my mother-CON-to   I remember
>   *I remember (to) my mother.*

Postpositions 1.0.

The plural morpheme **-m,** on locative nouns such as those seen in sentences (13)–(14), also serves as a connector for a postposition.

(13) wasá-m-me-u   né weáma-n
     field-PL-CON-to I walk-PCN
     I was walking to the fields.

(14) ba'á-čó'oko-me-u-héela káa-mékka-tahtia-bíča
     water-salty-CON-to-near not-far-up:to-site of
     It was near Salty Waters, not far from there.

The object of a postposition may also be complex, consisting of an entire noun phrase or nominalized clause. For example, the postpositional base of **-u** *to* is a noun phrase consisting of an attributive demonstrative pronoun marked as plural and a plural human noun that is head of the construction.

(15) kúčú-ta húme'e 'o'íwi-m-me-u hi-hínu-n
     fish-ACC those man-PL-CON-to RDP-buy-PCN
     He was going to buy a fish from those men.

Another complex object of the postposition consists of an adverbial demonstrative plus a following manner adverb as seen in sentence (16). The entire postpostional phrase functions as a temporal adverb.

(16) 'í'an láuti-po hunúm hák 'á'a teéka
     now quick-in there somewhere it lay:flat
     For now, put it there somewhere.

In noun phrases that consist of a Demonstrative Pronoun + Nominal Bases, a copy of the postposition occurs on both constituents. Thus in sentence (17), the instrumental postposition **-e** occurs on both the demonstrative **hunú** *that one* and the head noun **matú** *charcoal*. It also occurs with the third person singular object pronoun in immediate preverbal position. This postpositional phrase refers to the full postpositional phrase in initial position of the first clause of this doublet. This is one way that Yaqui has for creating inverted and discontinuous pronoun copy constructions.

(17) hunú-e matú-e hí'iboa mun-bakí-m 'a-e b^{w}á'a-b^{w}ása
     that-INST coal-INST cook bean-stew-PL it-INST RDP-cook
     They cook with that charcoal; they cook beans with it.

In attributive adjective constructions that serve as complex postpositional objects, both the noun and the adjective that modifies it serve as multiple objects for the same postposition. This is illustrated by example (18) in which **-po** *in* is used.

(18) 'ilí kúta-kahón-im-po 'ilitčí-m-po
     small wood-box-PL-in very:small-PL-in
     in small wood boxes, in very small ones

Like a number of other Uto-Aztecan languages, Yaqui has complex postpositions, consisting of two or more simple postpositions (cf. Langacker 1977:94). For example, the postposition **-bíča** is commonly the second member of complex postpositions. This is seen in example (19), in which it combines with a preceding postposition **-t** *on*. It may also come first, however, as in example (20) in which it follows the postposition **-ku** *in* and is itself followed by **-u** *to*.

(19) 'omó-t-bíčaa
     elsewhere-on-site
     to some other place

(20) káuwis 'íntok póčo'o-kun-bíča-u búite-k
     fox and woods-to-site-to run-PRF
     and the fox ran to the woods

In the following sections we discuss in more detail the general characteristics, both morphological and semantic, of each of the postpositions of Yaqui; beginning with the simple spatials, continuing on with the associatives, and ending with the **be-** postpositions.

2.0. The simple spatials

In the following six sections, we discuss the morphemically simple spatial postpositions. These include **-u/-wi** *toward*, **-po** *inside*, **-ku** *in*, **-étči** *on top*, **hika** *on top of,* and **-táhita** *until*.

2.1. The goal-oriented -u/-wi

When it designates location within three dimensional space, the forms **-u** and **-wi** can be glossed as "to" or "toward," having either a static locational sense or a directional one. Sentences (21) and (22) illustrate the locational use.

(21) tú'u-wa-ta   yáa-ka-me   Lióh-ta   hó'a-wi 'á'a bít-nee
     good-NZR-ACC do-PPL-NZR God-POS   house-to it   see-FUT
     A person who does good will see God's house.

(22) hunáma'a 'áme-u káa-mékka ... b^{w}é'u báu-ba'á-m   mánek
     there   them-to not-far ... big   lake-water-PL lay
     There, not far from them, was a big lake.

In its directional usages, this suffix places its focus on the destination point of some conceived path as seen in sentences (23)–(25). In sentence (23) for instance, the addressee's position at the time of hearing the utterance is the destination.

(23) húči=nee 'iním-wain   'án-nee 'emó-wi
     again=I here-about be-FUT you:PL-to
     I will come back here to you.

(24) bawé-u weče-k   kanóa-po yehté-ka   siíka
     sea-to fall-PRF boat-in   sit-PPL   went
     He went to sea; he boarded a boat and sailed away.

(25) wasá-m-me-u   né weáma-n
     field-PL-CON-to   I   walk-PCN.
     I was walking to the field.

The directional aspect of the meaning "toward" implies a path schema and this allows Yaqui to construe the relevant location as either the source point or as the goal point on a physical or metaphorical path.

(26) 'é-u   n=á'a nénki-nee
     you-to   I=it   sell-FUT
     I will sell it to you.

(27) né=wi   'a'a hínu
     me=to   it   buy
     Buy it from me.

(28) wasá-m-me-u   né weáma-n.
     field-PL-CON-to   I   walk-PCN.
     I was walking to the field.

Within the domain of human interactions, **-u** often has the extended meaning "for X," "because of X," "in order to do X," as illustrated by example (29).

(29) tékil né-u   'aáyu-k
     work   me-to   be-PRF
     There is work for me.

(30) nók-hía-wa-ta   née 'íno mahtá-bae   'á-u   né
     word-sound-NZR-ACC   I   RFL   teach-DSD   it-to I
     hoí-wa-bae   húnak káa né-u   'obiači-nee
     accustom-PSV-DSD   then   not me-to   difficult-FUT
     I want to teach myself sounds of words, become accustomed to them, then the work won't be hard for me.

This postposition has become grammaticalized as a marker of the indirect object. The six forms of the pronominal base to which **-u** attaches are given in Table 15. As can easily be seen, the singular pronominal forms that serve as the object for the longer allomorh **-wi** show up with a lengthened vowel.

Postpositions 2.1.

	Person	Singular	Plural
-u allomorph	1	né-u	'itó-u
	2	'é-u	'emó-u
	3	'á-u	'áme-u
-wi allomorph	1	neé-wi	'itó-wi
	2	'ée-wi	'emó-wi
	3		'áme-wi

Table 15. Pronominal bases with -u/-wi

The following are examples of the use of **-u** to mark indirect objects. In example (31) **-u** has a second person singular pronominal object, whereas in example (32) it takes a third person singular object.

(31) tuká=ne káa 'é-u wáate-k
yesterday=I not you-to remember-PRF
I did not remember (to) you yesterday.

(32) née bó'o-bíča-'a-ti 'á-u hiía
me lay-see-EV-CON him-to say
"Wait for me," he said to him.

A variety of grammatical elements serve as objects of the postposition **-u** and reflect several different marking strategies. In example (33) the object of the postposition is a kinship term **'itóm 'áe** *our mother* which is followed by the morpheme **be-** to which the postposition attaches. This is a clear reflection of a reanalyzed inverted pronoun copy construction similar to the construction cited in Johnson (1943). In example (34), on the other hand, the object of the postposition is the incorporated human object pronoun **yée**, which is marked by the verbalizer **-te** (cf. INCORPORATION, p. 272). A personal or human noun is marked with the accusative **-ta** as a base for attaching **-wi** as in example (35).

(33) 'itóm 'áe-be-u noóka-k
our mother-CON-to speak-PRF
He spoke to our mother.

(34) 'iníi'i naámu tásia-ta yé-te-u nu-nú'upa
this cloud cough-ACC people-CON-to RDP-bring
This cloudiness brings coughs to people.

(35) hí'ohte-ta 'áma tóha-k kobanáo-ta-wi
writing-ACC there take-PRF governor-ACC-to
He took a letter to the governor there.

Examples (36) and (37) illustrate temporal usages of **-u**. In each example the allomorph **-wi** takes as its object the temporal noun **tukáaria** *night*. In example (37) the use of **-či** *at* to signal the starting point of a temporal path contrasts with the use of **-wi** to signal the end point of that temporal path.

(36) tukáaria-wi 'ín bó'o-te-'epo-táhtia
night-to my lay-VR-GND-until
at night, until I go to bed

(37) 'itóm 'áčai-be-u n=am nók-ria-sime číkti ta'á-po taéwai-či
our father-CON-to I=them speak-APL-go every day-in daylight-in
tukáaria-wi 'ín bó'o-te-'epo-táhtia
night-to my lay-VR-GND-until
I pray to God for them daily from morning till night.

A purely static locative usage of this suffix can be glossed as "at the side of," and this is illustrated in (38). The use of **-wi** to designate the end point of a path is illustrated in sentence (39).

(38) hái=sa 'émpo súkau-bae táhi-m-me-wi
how=INTERR you warm-DSD fire-PL-CON-to
Do you want to warm yourself by the fire?

2.2. The internally bound -po "in"

The bound postposition **-po** can be glossed as "in" or "inside of." It indicates location in either time or three dimensional space, and just like the other postpositions, **-po** may follow the accusative singular **-ta** and the accusative plural **-im** when they attach to nominal bases. It also has a number of salient extended and figurative meanings. Examples (40)–(44) illustrate **-po** referring to locations in physical space.

(39) hékka-u n='a tóha-k
shade-to I=him take-PRF
I took him to the shade.

(40) yóo-'ánia-po   tútu'uli
enchanted-world-in beautiful
It is beautiful in Enchanted Land.

(41) tečóa-po čítoh-te-k
mud-in   slip-VR-PRF
He slipped in the mud.

(42) baá'a búite téta-hakía-po
water run rock-gully-in
The water flows in the rocky gully.

(43) 'áapo 'iním b^{w}ía-po weám-su-k
he   here land-in walk-CPL-PRF
He walked here on earth.

(44) kát b^{w}ía-po yéehte
not dirt-in sit
Don't sit in the dirt.

The area designated by **-po** in physical space can be a highly restricted one in its expanse, as illustrated in example (45).

(45) 'iíyim kéka n-abóli   wittí-po
here   stand my-granddad line-on
Stand here, grandpappy, on the line.

The notion of containment is particularly salient to certain kinds of entities such as a watermelon or a pot, i.e., relatively small discrete entities with a definite "inside" area. The use of the perfective **-ka** in example (46) reflects the fact that the speaker is describing a state, and not a process.

(46) báčia sákobai-po   'aáyu-k
seed watermelon-in be-PRF
Seeds are in the watermelon.

Body parts, both external and internal, are also construed as areas of containment. Examples (47)–(50) illustrate usages of **-po** to indicate locations inside the head in sentence (47), in the foot in (48), at the external ear in (49), and on the scruff of the neck and on the back in (50).

(47) 'ín kóba-po balí 'ée-ria   'aúka-n b^{w}íkáa 'áu-sú'ulika ín híapsi-po 'aúka-n
my head-in cool think-ABS be-PCN song RFL-exclusive my heart-in be-PCN
There used to be fresh thoughts in my head; there used to be nothing but songs in my heart.

(48) kó'om-čépte-ka né wók-po nasón-tu-k
down-jump-PPL I foot-in damage-VR-PRF
Jumping down, I hurt my foot.

(49) 'omée-tí 'á-u hiía láauti naká-po
man-CON him-to say slowly ear-in
"Man," he said, whispering in his ear.

(50) b^{w}ía-k=ne ho'ó-či 'íntok bí'a-m-po
dirt-have=I back-on and back:of:neck-PL-on
I have dirt on my back and on the back of my neck.

In the usage given in (51), **-po** is used in the sense of accompaniment.

(51) 'í'an sí'ime lú'u-te-k   heká-po siíka
     now all   end-VR-PRF wind-in went
     Now all has ended, it went away in the wind.

The postposition **-po** may also refer to an area of containment at the beginning point on a path that was followed by the participants in an event.

(52) kát=im   saáwea-ka   wíča-po   yéu-ténne-k
     not=they trousers-having   thorns-in out-run:PL-PRF
     They ran out of the thorn bushes without trousers.

Meteorological conditions are distributed throughout an area and the particular condition may thus be identified with the area of containment designated by **-po** as in sentence (53). This allows the location to be stated in terms of the extant condition. It also allows for certain extensions into time, differentially focusing on the span of time involved in an event, as seen in sentences (54) and (55), or focusing on a particular point within that expanse, as illustrated by (56).

(53) yúku-po wée-ka né kómona-k
     rain-in go-PPL I wet-PRF
     Walking in the rain, I got wet.

(54) bo'ó-hóa-ka   senú ta'á-po 'áman yebíh-nee
     road-make-PPL   one day-in there arrive-FUT
     Walking, he will get there in one day. (idiom, walking, traveling, etc.)

(55) ta'á-po
     sun-in
     during daylight

(56) tukáa-po yépsa-k
     night-in arrive-PRF
     He arrived in the night.

The time period designated by **-po** may be defined within more abstract domains than the cycle of the sun, moon and weather. In particular, both the agricultural cycle, illustrated in sentence (57), and the cycle of life itself are viewed as areas of containment, as are more abstract events such as that referred to by sentence (58).

(57) 'ét-po   yumá-'i   (58) súal-po   yuma-'i
     plant-in achieve-PPL   believe-in achieve-PPL
     It is time to plant.   *It is time to believe.*

Both social interactions and physical conditions are also construable as areas of containment that **-po** can designate. Note (59) and (60).

(59) tékil-po hióko-t   'an-sú-ka,   tómi-ta   'ilíiki-k   maá-čuk-ta
     work-in misery-in be-CPL-PPL   money-ACC little-ACC hand-clutch-VR
     After working so miserably, he gets only a small amount of money.

(60) 'óbe-ra   né-t   wéče-n,   táa táta-búhtia-po yéu-siíka
     lazy-ABS   me-on fall-PCN but sweat-in   out-went
     I was feeling lazy, but in sweating it went away.

Some usages of **-po** figure as part of a metaphor, as in the Yaqui expression that means "to fool someone" in example (61).

(61) púh-po yée-baí-tá'aa
     eye-in people-cool-know
     In their own sight he fools people (i.e., a prestidigitator).

2.3. The areal -ku "in, on"

The Yaqui postposition **-ku** is one of the links that Yaqui retains with Nahuatl and with Corachol. It is a very general locative, with a number of different senses related to the idea of "in" or "on." Technically, **-ku** is a locative adjectival postposition and corresponds to the noun suffix **-po** *in*. (See ADJECTIVE MORPHOLOGY, pp. 153–154.).

To begin, note the semantic contrast between the locational phrase involving **-ku,** given in example (62), and the nominalization involving **-ria,** given in example (63).

(62) póčo'o-ku
woods-in
in the woods

(63) póčo'o-ria
wood-ABS
woods

Examples (64)–(65) illustrate typical usages of **-ku**. In sentence (64) **-ku** designates a location on the back of the human body. In sentence (65) **-ku** designates a region in the middle of a container, i.e., a cup.

(64) ho'ó-t ná-nana'-á-ku 'á'a béeba-k
back-on RDP-middle-EV-in it hit-PRF
He hit it in the middle of the back.

(65) tasá-ta nú'u-ka čukúi-ba'á-ta nóah-núki-ku 'ambrósio-ta-u 'á'a tóha-k
cup-ACC take-PPL black-water-ACC half-fill-in Ambrosio-ACC-to it bring-PRF
Taking a cup and filling it half full of coffee, she brought it to Ambrose.

Extended usages of **-ku** are also common. In sentence (66) **-ku** designates position within a particular portion of the day–night cycle. In (67) **-ku** is used in the domain of physical space, designating position within a restricted expanse along a roadway. In sentence (68) on the other hand, **-ku** attaches to an adjective construed as a noun and designates position within the scale of relative economic status.

(66) bʷía-muú'u bʷía-wóho-'o-ku hó'aa-k káa-mačí-ku tú'isi híapsa
dirt-owl dirt-hole-EV-in house-have not-light-in well lives
The screech owl lives in a hole in the ground. It has no trouble seeing in the dark.

(67) hunáma hák=sabéna-ku há'ani túa bo'ó-ta
there where=INTERR:like-in perhaps indeed road-POS
ná'ulai-ku láautia 'á'a wéye-o=su
narrow-in slowly his go-when=EMP
well, perhaps somewhere there, where the road was really narrow, as he was going along very slowly

(68) puéplo-m tú'ii-ku híapsi-bae-ka-i
people-ACC good-in live-DSD-PPL-PPL
because the people want to live in prosperity, etc.

In sentence (69) the first occurrence of **-ku** takes as its object a reduplicated adjective and the entire postpositional phrase is the locative complement of the reduplicated causative verb, but it is construed as an abstract location in the domain of the human psychology, i.e., "to be in an evil frame of mind." The second use of **-ku** is as the first of two postpositons in sequence. In this case, **-ku** is bleached of a lot of its meaning and is serving as a connector element between the quantifier **sí'ime** and the second postposition **-tči.**

(69) húh-hú'ena-ku 'ám kík-kíma-tua 'álewanči híu-si-sime sí'ime-ku-tči púeplom-po
RDP-evil-in them RDP-put:in-CAU extremely sound-RDP-go all-CON-in people-in
He is causing the people to do evil; (he) is saying too much everywhere among the people.

The form **béna** occurs as a base for **-ku** in the constructions shown in sentences (70) and (71). The meaning of the postpositional phrase in (70) suggests that the postpositional use of **-béna** has its own source in a predicate adjective (cf. ADJECTIVE MORPHOLOGY, p. 155).

(70) 'ílen béna-ku née yéu-tóm-te-k
 thus like-in I out-stomach-VR-PRF
 I was born in a place something like this.

(71) 'ámman hák=sabéna-ku 'á'a nánke-k
 way:off:there where=INTERR:like-in him meet-PRF
 He met him way off there somewhere.

In many cases, an echo-vowel occurs between **-ku** and the noun that serves as its object (cf. PHONOLOGY, p. 28-29). The examples in (72)-(74) show echo vowels of the shapes **i**, **e**, and **o**, respectively.

(72) bawé-t kó'om-bíča kaáte sibá-kobi-'i-ku 'áman 'á'a núk-siŕka
 river-on down-site go:PL cliff-corner-EV-in by:there her carry-go
 He took her on past the corner of the cliff.

(73) húa-m-násu-ku kúta-pe-petče-'e-ku yéu-réhte
 wood-PL-middle-in trees-RDP-area-EV-in out-go:PL
 They went through the thickets, through a wooded area.

(74) hú'upa-sóo-'o-ku sebíi-po 'ámani káa 'áa 'áma réhti-mači-ku
 mesquite-thicket-EV-in cactus-in by:there not able there go-seem-in
 They went through the mesquite thicket, through the cactus, where it seemed impassable.

As we have already observed in (69), sometimes **-ku** appears to be largely bleached of its meaning and to have taken on the function of a connective as the base for attaching a following postposition. In examples (75)-(78) **-ku** serves as a base for attaching allomorphs of the postposition **-étči**. In sentence (75) it attaches to a nominalized verb, in (76) to an adjective, and in (77) and (78) to a quantifier.

(75) wáa'a taéwai-t téuwaa-ri-ku-tči
 that day-on say-PPL-CON-on
 On that day that it had been said that it would happen.

(76) bátčain tá'ab^{W}í-ku-t 'ée-'éan
 before different-CON-on think-SJV
 He would really like to think about something else.

(77) siŕka sí'ime-ku-t láuti wée-sime-ka-i
 went all-CON-on fast go-go-PPL-PPL
 He left, quickly going to all (the places) everywhere

(78) 'iníi'i sí'ime-ku-t hú'uneiyaa-wa-k
 this all-CON-on know-PSV-PRF
 This was known everywhere.

2.4. The proximal contact -étči "on"

The postposition **-étči** actually has four morphological shapes: **-étči**, **-ét**, **-tči**, and **-t**. It means variously "in," "on," or "at" when it is used to designate strictly spatial relations. Beyond this, however, it has a number of figurative usages in both temporal and spatial domains. What factors determine which variant is actually used in a given instance is not clear to us. The longer form **-étči** appears to be used in deliberate speech whereas the shorter form **-ét** is selected by particular stems. However, there are cases where either form may occur with a given postpositional object, e.g., the demonstrative **hunáa'a** will figure in postpositional phrases of the form **huná-et** or **huná-etči**.

When **-'étči** takes as its object a personal pronoun, it has the shortened form **-t**. Examples (79)-(82) illustrate its use with second person singular, third person singular, first person plural, and third person plural pronouns, in that order.

(79) hitá=sabéna-k 'é-t nók-nee
 thing=INTERR:like-ACC you-on talk-FUT
 They will say something-like about you.

(80) 'áe-t ča-čaáe
him-on RDP-yell
yell at him

(82) 'áme-t ča-čaáe
them-on RDP-yell
yell at them

(81) hiák-nokí 'áu-sú'uli 'itó-t 'aáyu-k
Yaqui-word RFL-only us-on be-PRF
We spoke only Yaqui.

The shortened form **-t** also attaches to nominals followed by the connector **-be-**, as illustrated in sentences (83) and (84). Both of these examples also illustrate the reanalyzed inverted pronoun copy construction.

(83) 'itóm 'áčai-be-t 'éa-ka híapsa
our father-CON-on think-PPL live
They live depending on the Lord.

(84) káa Lióh-ta 'usía-be-t híaps-e-k
not God-POS son-CON-on live-VR-PRF
He was not diligent regarding God's Son.

At least formerly, phonological conditions in part determined the morphemic shapes of **-'étči**. Numerous examples suggest that one phonological context for using the shortened form of **-'étči** is nonfinal, but post-stressed position within a phonological phrase.

(85) sí'ime-m-bépa-t 'á'a weám-nee-'u
all-PL-above-on his walk-FUT-GND
that he would walk on top of all things

(87) 'ánia-t né weáma
world-on I walk
I travel the world.

(86) wéte'epo-im ye-té-t tapuna
gnat-PL people-VR-on full
Gnats cover people.

(88) senú b^wásia-t 'á'a wíiki
one tail-on it pulls
One person pulled him by the tail.

Nominals and nominalizations of various sorts, marked with the plural **-me** often are the context for the short version **-t,** as examples (90) and (91) testify.

(89) hí'osia-t n=á'a hí'oh-te
paper-on I=it write-VR
I write it on paper.

(91) sí'ime hó'aa-raa-m-me-t siíka
all house-ABS-NZR-PL-on went
He went to all the houses.

(90) yoém 'ó'aa burú-me-t kúta pú'ak-te
yaqui old:man donkey-PL-on wood load-VR
An old man loads wood on the donkeys.

The short form **-t** also occurs as the coda of a high-toned syllable in some cases as seen in sentence (92). The second person singular and first person plural object pronouns, as seen in sentences (79) and (81) above, are one class of grammatical elements that fit this context. Sentences (93) and (94) are additional examples of this. In .sentence (94) **-t** takes a verbalized noun as its object and stress shifts from the incorporated object to the verbalizing suffix.

(92) yokó ... bo'ó-t hápte-nee
tomorrow ... road-on stand:PL-FUT
Tomorrow they will start to travel.

(94) wéte'epo-im ye-té-t
gnat-PL people-VR-on full
Gnats cover people.

(93) 'é-t té noóka-n tápuna
you-on we speak-PCN
We were talking about you.

Multiple occurrences of **-étči** in a single sentence are reasonably common. One pattern shows that the first occurrence of **-étči** takes an adverbial demonstrative as its object, whereas the second occurrence takes a locative noun as its object. Functionally, the locative noun specifies in greater detail the locational information anticipated by the adverbial demonstrative of the first postpositional phrase, as seen in example (95). Both instances of **-étči** can be considered to be phrase final and thus the semi-reduced form **-tči** is used.

(95) haísa híu-wa húe-tči pá'aria-tči
     how   say-PSV there-on outside-on
     what is being said, over there, out in the open spaces

As is true with the usages of other Yaqui postpositions, **-t** is used in the temporal domain also as is seen in sentence (96), where it attaches to the temporal noun **wásuktia** *year*. Its use in sentence (97) assimilates the time period to the time of speaking. On the other hand, the time period indicated by the **-t** postpositional phrase in that sentence is viewed as being an extended one. This construal is effected by the use of the reciprocal adverb **naa-búhtia** *throughout its extent*. Finally, the postpositional phrase with **-t** in sentence (98) anchors the the conceptualized event to the starting point of a temporal path.

(96) 'iní-a   wásuktia-t kaíta   tebáa-tu-nee
     this-ACC year-on   nothing hunger-VR-FUT
     There will be no hunger this year.

(97) taéwai-t náa-búuhtia nók-nássua
     day-on   RCP-through word-fight
     They argue all day.

(98) 'iní-a   taéwai-t naáte-ka sí'ime 'enčí   nák-nee
     this-ACC day-on   begin-PPL all   you:ACC love-FUT
     Beginning today everyone will love you.

The psychological verb **hú'unea** in its intransitive form, often takes a Noun + **-t** as its indirect complement, i.e., "to know about X," as seen in (99). In contrast, the transitive form **hú'uneiyaa** means "to know X." In short, the intransitive form with the postpositional phrase is used to increase the epistemic distance between the subject of the verb and the object of knowledge.

(99) 'iní-a   lútu'uria-t káa hú'unea
     this-ACC truth-on   not know
     He does not know about this truth.

The accusative **-ta** is used with proper names as a base for attaching **-t**. Examples (100) and (101) are typical.

(100) Hóan-ta-t   čá-čae-k   (101) sésar-ta-t   noóka
      John-ACC-on RDP-call-PRF   Caesar-ACC-on speak
      They yelled to John.   *They talk against Caesar.*

Postpositional phrases involving **-et** in combination with certain verbs have become lexicalized, leading to nonpredictable meanings in the psychological domain, signalling psychological states such as envy, diligence, and trust as illustrated in examples (102)–(104).

(102) -et + kópte   *to forget* > *to be envious of*
(103) -et + híapse   *heart*   > *be diligent*
(104) -et + 'éa   *to think*   > *to trust in*

2.5. The positional hika- "the top of"

The postposition **hika-t/-u** can can be variously glossed as "the top of," "at the top of X," "on top," "up," and "upward," among other things. It is semantically antonymous to the directional adverb **kó'om-** *down* and is unusual in its patterning. In certain of its usages it behaves like a postposition, whereas in other contexts it appears to be an adverb and as such participates in adverbial constructions which function as objects of the postposition. On the other hand, its tendency to be a free form, its status as base in construction with the postpositions **-t** *on*, **-u** *to, toward*, and its semantic value in compounds such as **hiká-pa'aku** *flat plateau* suggests that it may have originally been a body part meaning "the top of X." This is reinforced by examples (1) and (2), each of which has a pair of postpositional phrases involving **-t**. The object of the first occurrence of **-t** is a noun, the object of the second occurrence is **hiká-**. In example (1) the understood location of the walking is on the topside of the wire. In example (2) the location of the sitting is in the upper reaches of a mezquite tree.

(1) sisí'iwooki-t hiká-t wéye-n
    metal-on   top-on go-PCN
    He walked on the wire.

(2) hú'upa-t   hiká-t kátek
    mesquite-on up-on located
    He is located high up in a mesquite tree.

The usage of **hiká-** that most closely matches the prototypical Uto-Aztecan postpositional construction is one in which the nominal serving as object of the postposition is not marked with the postposition **-t**, but immediately precedes **hiká-**, which is marked with **-t** as in example (3).

(3) 'ín tótoe-ka-'u   hú'upa   hiká-t bó'e
    my rooster-former mesquite top-on sleep
    A rooster I used to have, slept up in the mesquite tree.

Particular usages of **hiká-** offer additional examples to show that Yaqui retains the central syntactic patterns of Uto-Aztecan constructions spelled out in Langacker (1977:95ff.). In sentence (4) **hiká-** is the second member of a compound in which the first member **kári** *house* is the whole to which the part **hiká-** pertains. The entire compound is also object of the postposition **-t** *on*.

(4) téku   kári-hika-t   káteka kíssos-so'o-ti   hiía
    squirrel house-top-on   seated "kíssosso'o"-CON say
    The squirrel on top of the house went "kissosso'o."

In sentence (5) the part-whole relationship between a mezquite tree and its top is again seen in which the nominal designating the whole is preposed to **hiká-**, which designates the part. Both the nominal and **hiká-** are marked with the postposition **-t**. Similarly in sentence (6) the compound noun **karíl-bo'ó** *railroad track* is marked with **-t** and **hiká-**, which designates its upper, visually and tactile surface, is also marked with **-t**.

(5) 'ínepo 'íntok hú'upa-t   hiká-t káte-ka 'ám   bítču
    I   and   mesquite-on top-on sit-PPL them stare:at
    I watched them, sitting up in the mesquite tree.

(6) karétiia-ta karíl-bo'ó-t   hiká-t yéča-'a-tua-wa-k
    cart-ACC   train-road-on top-on put-EV-CAU-PSV-PRF
    The cart was put on the railroad.

An inverted discontinuous construction is also possible in which, for example, the nominal object of the postposition occurs sentence initally and is separated from the postposition **hiká-** by the direct object of the clause. Sentence (7) is a typical example.

(7) burú-hámut-ta-či   maría hiká-t yéča-'a-wa-k
    donkey-female-ACC-on Mary top-on put-EV-PSV-PRF
    Mary was put on (top of) the donkey.

In sentence (8) **hiká-** appears to be the object of the postposition **-t** *on* and is used in conjunction with **bétuk-u** *under* to specify both the orientation and the extent of a piece of work being applied to something.

(8) hiká-t 'á'a naáte 'ía-mak   bétuk-u 'á'a yumá-'a-ria-nee
    top-on it   start this-with under-in it   achieve-EV-APL-FUT
    Start at the top and with this it (you) will complete it at the bottom.

A different construction is involved in (9), but one which illustrates the role of **hiká-** to mark the relevant part of a specific whole, in this case a body of water. Notice that the word **baá'a** *water* is itself the object of a postposition **-bépa** *over*. This suggests that **hiká-t** is in apposition to the postpositional phrase **ba'á-bepa**. Likewise in sentence (10), the compound **hiká-pá'aku** *high plateau* represents a further elaboration on the postpositional phrase **káuwi-m-met** *in the mountains*.

(9) hunáa'a taplá-kári ba'á-bepa hiká-t čá'a-si   sime-'e-téa
    that   plank-house water-over top-on float-AVR go-EV-QUO
    They say that wooden house went floating on top of the water.

(10) bʷéere miná-m-po káuwi-m-met   hiká-pá'a-ku   hó'aa-k   minéo-m
     big   mine-PL-in mountain-PL-on up-open:space-in house-have miner-PL
     The miners live in the mines in the high places in the mountains.

The contrastive postpositional phrases (11) and (12) offer complementary views on a single scene and thus provide additional evidence that **hika-,** historically at least, may have been a body part with the meaning "its top."

(11) hiká-u-bíca   (12) hiká-t-tana
     up-to-site   up-on-from
     upward   *from above*

On the other hand, the usages in (13) and (14) suggest further that **hiká-** is fundamentally an adverb meaning "high up." It is very clear from example (13) that **wikía-m** is the direct object of the clause and is not the object of any postposition. In other words, the sentence does not mean "Bareas put X on top of the cable." Likewise, there is no nominal entity whatsoever which functions as the object of the seemingly complex postposition **hiká-u** in sentence (14). Thus, **hiká-** in certain contexts is clearly an adverb in a set with the constrastive **kó'om** down.

(13) baréas ... wikía-m hiká-t čáya
     baréas   wire-PL up-on stretch
     Bareas put up the cable.

(14) 'áma ne yéu-sií-ka kía 'ánia-ta nú'u-ka masa-tú-ka=ne hiká-u
     there I out-go-PRF only world-ACC take-PPL wing-VR-PPL=I up-to

     né čá'a-tu-k   hák-un   káa 'ín ténku-ka-'apo
     I suspend-VR-PRF   where-to not my dream-PRF-GND
     I left there, I just took to the world, I sprouted wings and took to the air to places that I had never dreamed of.

2.6. The limiter -táhtia "until"

The limiting postposition **-táhtia** *until* is the past participial form of the verb **táhta/-te** *to touch, to hit, to reach, to bump into,* which has both transitive and intransitive forms. These usages are illustrated in sentences (15) and (16).

(15) húme bʷéere kaárom 'amé-bétuk yéu-rehté-ka   káa
     those big:PL wagons them-under out-walk:PL-PPL not

     'áme-u táh-táhte bʷé'ituk 'im tú'isi tet-tébe
     them-to RDP-touch because they very RDP-tall
     The big wagons that went underneath them (whale rib arch) did not even touch them because they were so tall.

(16) bém táho'ori-wa papló-ta táh-ta-wa-ka-me
     their cloth-POS Paul-ACC touch-VR-PSV-PPL-NZR
     their cloth that had touched Paul

As a nominalized verb phrase **-tahtia** has come to be conventionalized as a postpositional phrase with the meaning "up to, until." It does have spatial usages, as seen from example (17).

(17) 'itépo 'ténni-nee 'a-u-táhtia
     we run:PL-FUT him-to-until
     We will run to where he is.

The typical usages of **-táhtia** represent a metaphorical mapping from the spatial domain to the temporal domain. The spatial model is one in which an entity is being tracked along a path of movement toward some other entity and the tracking continues up to the point at which contact is established. The temporal model then, tracks the passage of an entity from one point in time to another, which is construed as the time at which an event is either completed or realized.

One interesting observation about the spatial usages of **-táhtia** is that when it takes a pronominal object, it is always in combination with the postposition **-u** *toward*, which precedes it as illustrated in Table 16.

Person	Singular	Plural
1	né-u-táhtia	'itó-u-táhtia
2	'é'u-táhtia	'emó-u-táhtia
3	'á-u-táhtia	'áme-u-táhtia

Table 16. Pronominal objects with -táhtia

The basically verbal nature of the postposition **-táhtia** is reflected in the kinds of postpositional objects that it takes. In contrast to the usual choice of nouns and pronouns, **-táhtia** calls on nominalized verbs or gerunds as its most typical object. This is seen clearly in examples (18) and (19).

(18) híba   hi-kó'a   waébas-im   lú'ute-'epo-táhtia
     always IZR-chew guayabas-PL end-GND-until
     He kept chewing until the guayabas were all gone.

(19) hunúen ne weáma-k búsan wásukti-am yumá-'apo-táhtia húnak ne yéu-síka
     thus   I walk-PRF six   years-PL   reach-GND-until then I out-went
     That is what I did for six years, then I left.

Commonly, the salient end point of the temporal path is the point in time of the speech-act. This is signalled by the use of the adverbial demonstrative **'í'an** *now* as the object of **-táhtia** in example (20). The distal adverbial demonstrative **hunáma** *there* signals the end point of temporal progression in the past as illustrated by (21), which also draws on a reduced form of **-tahtia**.

(20) 'í'an-táhtia   (21) hunáma-táhti baké'o-tú-k,
     now-until   there-until cowboy-be-VR:PRF
     until now   *And that was the end of the cowboy.*

In summary, the end point in time signalled by **-táhtia** may also be either in the present, the future, or the past. The particular temporal point is signalled by the verbal suffixes in the clause containing the postpositional phrase with **-táhtia** or by the demonstrative adverb that is the object of **-táhtia**. A time of speaking endpoint is conveyed by sentence (22), whereas future endpoints are conveyed in sentences (23) and (24). Finally, a past tense endpoint is signalled by sentence (25).

(22) húnak né yéu-sika 'í'an-táhtia
     then I out-went now-until
     Then I left, until now.

(23) 'ím te bó'o-bít-nee   kó'om 'á'a simé-'u-táhtia
     here we road-see-FUT down its go:SG-GND-until
     We will wait here until it goes down.

(24) 'ím 'enčí   'ané-o 'itóm yáha-'apo-táhtia
     here you:ACC be-íf our   come:PL-GND-until
     if you are here until our arrival

(25) 'íi'i yoéme híba pócho'o-ku weáma madéero-tu-ka'u-ta   yéu-mačía-o-'otáhtia
     this Yaqui always woods-in walk Madero -VR-deceased-ACC out-appear-CON-until
     The Yaquis just lived in the woods until the time of Madero.

3.0. The associative postpositions

In the category of the associative postpositions, we group the instrumental **-e/-mea,** the commitative **-make-/mak,** the reflexive **násuk,** and the reciprocal **náare.** All these reflect intrinsic bipolar relations that may be either asymmetric, as in the case of the instrumental, or symmetric, as in the case of the commitative.

3.1. The instrumental -e (SG)/-mea (PL)

The Yaqui instrumental is curious in that it has suppletive forms for singular versus plural object of the postposition. It generally means "with" in the instrumental sense or "by means of." Typical of Yaqui postpositions, however, it occurs with a broad range of postpositional objects, including both concrete and abstract nouns as well as pronouns, demonstratives, and adverbs. Finally, the instrumental has its own extended, idiomatic meanings.

3.1.1. The singular -e

The singular form **-e** is commonly used with concrete nominal objects. As examples (26) and (27) show, complex objects of the postposition consisting of a Demonstrative + Noun have a copy of the postposition on both the demonstrative and the object nominal.

(26) hunú-e matú-e hí'ib-oa mún-bakí-m 'a-e bʷá'a-bʷása
that-INST charcoal-INST eat-make bean-stew-PL it-INST RDP-cook
She uses that charcoal for cooking; she cooks bean stew with it.

(27) 'inía-e 'itóm tekil-a-e 'itépo 'itó-'anía
this-INST our work-CON-INST we RFL-help
With this our work, we help ourselves (i.e., make our living).

Both the singular and plural forms also take abstract nouns as their objects. Thus the instrumental **-e** is very frequently used with nominalizations marked with the possessed participializer **-'u**, illustrated by sentence (28). A typical example of the plural **-mea** with an abstract nominal object is given in sentence (29).

(28) káa-tú'ii-k 'enčím hoá-'u-e Lióh-ta baí-tá'aa-nee-ti ée-nee
not-good-ACC your do-GND-INST God-ACC "deceive"-FUT-CON thing-FUT
You think that you can deceive God with your evil doings.

(29) tú'u-nokí-m-béna-m-mea 'enčím baí-tá'aa-naa-'a-betčí'ibo
good-word-PL-like-PL-INST you:PL cool-know-FUT:PSV-EV-for(deceive)
that you should not be deceived by means of what seem to be good words

A particularly interesting idiomatic usage of the instrumental is seen in its use with the suppletive stem meaning "to die" given in example (30). It is a striking way of indicating an advanced state of thirst and is functionally almost identical to the English "I'm dying of thirst."

(30) ba'á-e muúke/kókko
water-INST die:SG:SJV/die:PL:SJV
to be very thirsty

Body parts serve as instruments, as sentences (31) and (32) illustrate. Some usages however, are nonprototypical ones. In sentence (33) for example, the use of **-e** with **kóbe** *head* indicates the manner in which a baby was born.

(31) yeká-e 'á'a húh-hu'ubʷa
nose-INST it RDP-smell
He smells it with the nose.

(32) máa-m-mea náu 'ám yéča
hand-PL-INST together them put
He puts them together with his hands.

(33) kóba-e yéu-kíkte-k
head-INST out-stand:SG:SJV-PRF
The baby was born head-first.

In example (34) the instrumental is used in a metaphorical sense, i.e., to say that people use their heads to stand on is a graphic way to describe extreme hilarity in which people are bent double with laughter.

(34) yoém-raa kóba-e hápte-ka-i ... 'aáče
person-NZR head-INST stand:PL-PPL-PPL laugh
The people laughed "standing on their heads."

Speech content is also treated as an abstract instrument. One can use his own words against his own self as expressed in example (35), or he/she can use words deceitfully as in example (36).

(35) 'áu nók-béhe'e nok-í-e
RFL word-oppose word-NZR-INST
He argues against himself with words.

(36) káa 'áa-nokí-'iči-m-mea
not able-word-DIM-PL-INST
not by means of lies

Certain usages show that the instrumental can actually designate a causative source (cf. Radden 1985). In the usage illustrated by example (37), the instrumental takes a third person singular object. In example (38), on the other hand, the object of the postposition is a nominalized clause which is the reason for which a person was unable to talk.

(37) 'á-e 'eó'o-ti-'ea
it-INST nausea-CON-think
He was nauseated by means of it.

(38) bʷan-í-m-mea káa noóka-k
cry-NZR-PL-INST not talk-PRF
He could not talk for crying.

The instrumental postposition may attach to an indefinite pronoun in a construction in which the lexical item that designates the actual instrument is incorporated into the verb, as in example (39).

(39) káita-e mó'iti-máči
nothing-INST plow-appear
There is nothing with which to plow.

3.1.2. The plural -mea

The instrumental plural form **-mea** is possibly derived historically from the bimorphemic sequence ***-mi-a**, in which ***-mi** was a plural demonstrative pronoun and the **-a** was an accusative marker (cf. Langacker 1977c:99; Casad 1992:64). A prototypical usage of the instrumental plural is given in sentence (40).

(40) téta-m-mea wikítči-m ma-máa-su
stone-PL-INST bird-PL RDP-stone-CMP
He killed birds with rocks.

A small set of body part nouns in Yaqui are conventionally construed as plurals (cf. Wierzbicka 1985; 1988). The following examples draw on the instrumental use of the hands as illustrated in sentence (41), the feet in sentence (42), and the teeth in (43).

(41) máam-mea náu 'ám yéča
hands-INST together them place
He put them together with his hands.

(42) wokí-m-mea bʷiá-ta wít-ta-k
foot-PL-INST ground-ACC line-VR-PRF
(He) made a line on the ground with his feet (foot).

(43) haíbu tám-ek 'ám-mea 'au-'íi'aa
now tooth-have them-INST RFL-DSD
He has teeth now. He is a rascal with them (i.e., *he bites*).

One usage of the instrumental plural relates to the use of a nickname, very much in the tenor of the English phrase "he goes by X." In this case however, the object of the postposition is a third person plural pronoun.

(44) káa 'ám téa-k 'ám-mea téuwaa-wa
not them name-have them-INST call-PSV
That is not his name; he is just called with that nickname.

Sentence (45) illustrates another kind of nonprototypical instrument. In this case, there is a material, but noncausative source that the instrumental plural **-mea** takes as its object.

(45) ba'á-m-mea   tápuni
     water-PL-INST full
     It is full of water.

The instrumental plural also demonstrates causative uses as clearly seen by example (46).

(46) wo'ó-m   huébena, 'ám-mea   née káa kočo-k
     mosquito-PL many   them-INST I   not sleep-PRF
     There were many mosquitoes. I could not sleep because of them.

In example (47) a postpositional phrase with instrumental **-mea** is used to indicate the mode of motion.

(47) wokí-m-mea
     foot-PL-INST
     to travel afoot

The object of the instrumental may be an abstract entity and display considerable morphological complexity. In example (48) the object of the postposition is a possessive phrase in which the head noun is marked with the accusative **-ta** and the possessed entity is a nominalization marked for plural. The object of the postposition in example (49) is a compound noun marked for plural followed by the postposition **-bena** *like,* also marked for plural.

(48) Lioh-ta   'útte'a-la-m-mea
     God-POS   strong-NZR-PL-INST
     by means of God's power

(49) tú'u-nóki-m-béna-m-mea   'enčím bai-ta'aa-naa-'a-betčí'ibo
     good-word-PL-like-PL-INST   you:PL cool-know-FUT:PSV-EV-for(deceive)
     that you should be deceived by what seem to be good words

3.2. The accompaniment -make/-mak

The postposition **-make** *with* along with its shorter form **-mak,** is used to mean "with" in the sense of accompaniment in both the literal and figurative sense. However, its meaning is becoming blurred probably due to the influence of Spanish. It is sometimes used where the instrumental **-e/-mea** would ordinarily be expected. Given the propensity for Yaqui (and Uto-Aztecan, in general) to form complex postpositions by stringing them together, it is quite possible that Yaqui **-make** represents the combination of **-mak** "with:ACC" and **-e** "INST:SG." The formation of this complex postposition was followed by the loss of analyzability into two distinct morphemes. This same process, of course, has occurred in other domains of Yaqui grammar.

The pronominal bases that **-make** takes are given in Table 17.

Person	Singular	Plural
1	ne-mák	'itó-mak
2	'ee-mák	'emó-mak
3	'aa-mák	'áme-mak

Table 17. Pronominal bases with -make

The prototypical usage of **-make** involves two distinct entities jointly involved in carrying out some activity. Typical joint activities include fighting, as in sentence (50), and talking in sentence (51). The grammatical structuring, however, is asymmetric: one of the entities is subject of the sentence, whereas the other is the object of the postposition. In sentence (50) the subject is unspecified, and there are actually two postpositional phrases that refer to a single entity, the Yaqui nation. The first postpositional phrase takes a demonstrative pronoun for its object and draws on the short form **-mak.** The second one calls on the longer form **-make** which is discontinuous from the first and elaborates on it by overtly specifying the Yaqui Nation. Sentence (51) has an overt first person singular subject that is paired with a possessed noun, also marked for first person singular.

(50) túa námaka-si 'inía-mak nássua-k hiáki-ta-make
    truly hard-AVR this-with fight-PRF yaqui-POS-with
    They fought hard with this nation (i.e., *with the Yaquis*).

(51) 'ín halá'i-mak né 'etého
    my friend-with I talk
    I am talking with my friend.

The two distinct forms of **-make** may also be used in the plural. The longer form is used in sentence (52), whereas the shorter one is used in (53).

(52) húme kúču-m sebóra-kát-ti-m-make mantéka-po wat-tá-wa-k
    those fish-PL onion-cut-PPL-PL-with grease-in throw-VR-PSV-PRF
    The fish, mixed with chopped onions, was put into the (hot) grease.

(53) wikítči-m tótoi-m-mak kuú-te-k
    bird-PL chicken-PL-with mix-VR-PRF
    Birds were mixed in with the chickens.

The blurring of the categories INSTRUMENT and COMMITATIVE is shown in (54) in which **-mak** is used in an extended instrumental sense based on the location of the speaker's emotions. The purely locative sense of **-mak** is illustrated by (55) in which **-mak** is part of a place name.

(54) túa 'ín híapsi-mak née 'á'a náke   (55) kúta-bankó-mak lópola 'á'a núk-wéeya
    indeed my heart-with I her love   wood-seat-with alongside her take-carry
    I love her with all my heart.   *He took her alongside "Wood-Seat."*

Concerning **-mak**, Buelna makes the following observations:

> Esta preposisión se junta con los pronombres en ablativo y con nombres en nominativo: significan, junto con, ... v.g., *con harina*, **tusimaque**; *lo revolverás con harina*, **tusimaque acucutianaque**; *lo comí con maiz*, **bacimaque ne abuaca**; *contigo iré*, **emomaquenesimnaque**. Adviértanse dos cosas. Primero que en medio de la oración pierde el **que**, ó lo convierte en **c**, v.g., *irás conmigo* **inoma** ó **inomac simnaque**. Segundo: que algunos le dan casi oblicuo de ablativo, v.g., **bachitamaque**, *con maíz*; pero este no es pulido lenguaje. (Buelna 1891:101, Item 299).[1]

3.3. The proximative -náapo

The postposition **-náapo** *near* appears to be a compound consisting of **-naa** (*PUA REFL)? + **-po** *in*. The pronominal bases occurring with **-náapo** are the following:

Person	Singular	Plural
1	née-náapo	'itó-náapo
2	'ée-náapo	'émo-náapo
3	'áe-náapo	'áme-náapo

Table 18. Pronominal bases with náapo

In its basic usages **-náapo** expresses the idea of close proximity within physical three dimensional space as in examples (56)–(58).

---

1 "This preposition combines with pronouns in the ablative case and with nouns in the nominative: they mean, "together with," e.g., "with flour" **tusimaque,** *you will mix it together with flour* **tusimaque a cucutianaque**;: *I ate it with corn,* **bacimaque ne abuaca**; *I will go with you,* **emomaquenesimnaque**. Take notice of two things. First that in the middle of the sentence it loses the **que**, or it converts it into **c**, e.g., *you will go with me* **inoma** ó **inomac simnaque**. Second: some people use it as an oblique ablative, e.g. **bachitamaque,** *with corn;* but this is not a standard usage." (Buelna 1891:101, Item 299).

(56) muúku-k bahkó'am-naápo kó'oko-i-m-meu tóhi-wa-k
 die-PRF Bacum-near "Chile"-NZR-PL-to take-PSV-PRF
 He died near Bacum; he was brought to Cocorit.

(57) hinté-ka táhi-náapo bo'o-te-k
 blanket-PPL fire-near lie-VR-PRF
 Covering himself, he lay down near the fire.

(58) húm 'á'a kóba-naápo bʷé'u 'áakame káte-k
 there his head-near big rattlesnake locate-PRF
 There near his head was a big rattlesnake.

In example (59) **náapo** occurs as a free postposition in a discontinous construction in which the complex postpositional object is in sentence initial position. Alternatively, one could say that the entire locative adverbial clause is the object of the postposition **náapo**. Notice that the subject of this clause is marked for the accusative.

(59) bʷé'uu ba'á-ta yepsá-'a naápo
 big water-ACC arrive-EV near
 near the place where the big water is (i.e., *ocean*)

3.4. The reflexive -násuk "middle"

The postposition **-násuk** usually occurs as a bound form, but it occasionally occurs as either a free postposition or as a derived nominal designating the central region of a discrete entity, e.g., the midriff of the human body as in example (60). Examples (61) and (62) give additional evidence for the schematic meaning of "in the middle of X." In (61) the free form is used to refer to a single discrete entity whose position is central to some unspecified region, whereas in (62) the central location is regarded as highly specific through both the use of the augmentative adverb **-tua** and the directional suffix **-i** on the sequence of postpositions itself.

(60) 'á'a násuk-láa-po
 it middle-AVR-in
 in its middle

(62) túa násu-ku-n-i
 indeed middle-in-?-DIR
 in the very middle

(61) senú-k násuk bó'o-ka-m-ta 'emé'e bít-nee
 one-ACC middle lie-PPL-PL-ACC you:PL see-FUT
 You will see one lying in the middle.

In other contexts **-násuk** can be glossed as "half" or "middle" in either a literal or figurative sense. In sentence (63) **násuk** is used with the adverbial demonstrative **'áman** to signify that a loaf of bread was broken into two approximately equal size parts. On the other hand when used to single out one individual from a collective group of the same kind, **-násuk** can be glossed "among X" as illustrated by sentence 64.

(63) páan-im násuk 'áman hám-ta-k
 bread-PL:ACC middle there break-VR-PRF
 He broke the loaf of bread in half.

(64) hunáa'a, bú'uu-ráa-ta-násuk-u wéye-n
 that:one much-ABS-POS-among-in go:SG-PCN
 He was there going in the midst of the multitude.

The preposition **-násuk** is also restricted to taking plurals for its pronominal base. This suggests that the initial syllable **-na** is a second reflex of the Proto-Uto-Aztecan reciprocal pronoun ***-na** to be found in Yaqui postpositions (cf. Langacker 1977:47). The pronominal objects that occur with **-násuk** are given in Table 19.

'itó-násuk	*among-us*
'emó-násuk	*among-you*
'áme-násuk	*among-them*

Table 19. **Pronominal bases of násuk**

Typical usages of **-násuk** are given in examples (65)–(67). In (65) **-násuk** takes a first person plural object and in (66) it takes a derived nominal marked for the plural. In (67) **násuk** appears as a bound form with a locative noun as its subject.

(65) hunáa'a 'itó-násuk yoém-tu-k-ame
that(one) us-among person-VR-PRF-NZR
the one who became a human being among us

(66) kóko-la-m-násuk bó'o-ka yéhte-k
dead:PL-NZR-PL-among lie-PPL stand-PRF
Having lain among the dead, He arose.

(67) hunáman háksa káu-násuk-u, bʷé'u pá'aria-po 'a'a weáma-o
there somewhere mountain-amid-in big open:space-in his walk-when
when he was walking there somewhere in a big plain between the mountains

As one might expect, extensions of **násuk** into the temporal domain designate the halfway point of sections within the time cycle. In example (68) **násuk** designates the midpoint of the night cycle, whereas in example (69) it designates an indefinite expanse of time within the cycle of months.

(68) tukáa-ria 'áma násuk wée-'epo-táhtia
night-ABS there middle go-GND-until
until midnight

(69) 'enéro-ta-násuk wé-o, 'á'abo nói-ti-nee
January-POS-between go-when over:here come-PPL-FUT
When January is half gone, he will come here.

Commonly **-násuk** is also followed by a second postposition, **-ku** *in*. This pair of postpositions has coalesced into a conventionalized usage in which the morphemic **-kk-** cluster from the original ***-násuk-ku** has become simplified. This gives us a morphemic sequence which we segment as **násu-ku** *middle-in*. These pairs also occur in the regular ordered constructions as seen in examples (70) and (71) as well as in inverted ones as exemplified by example (72).

(70) hunáman háksa káu-násu-ku bʷé'u pá'aria-po 'á'a weáma-o
there somewhere mountain-mid-in big open:space-in his walk-when
when he was walking there somewhere in a big plain between the the mountains

(71) 'ínepo 'enčím 'inímin bíttua lobó-m-násu-ku
I you:PL here send wolf-PL-mid-in
I will send you among wolves.

(72) hiókot 'itóm 'itó bíča-'a-násu-ku
misery our RFL see-EV-mid-in
amidst our sufferings

Násuk can also have the meaning "between" as illustrated by both of its free form uses exemplified in example (73).

(73) 'á-u yáha-k násuk 'á'a bʷíse-k, násuk 'á'a
it-to arrive:PL-PRF middle it grab-PRF middle it

bʷíse-ka, na-náu-wit 'á'a 'áak-ta-k
grab-PPL RDP-together-beside it butt-VR-PRF
They got to him, catching him between them. They butted him simultaneously, having caught him in the middle between them.

Certain usages of **násuk** also illustrate its application to more abstract concepts such as the domain of the dead of humanity illustrated in (74) and that of physical and psychological circumstances given in example (75).

(74) hunáa'a 'itó-násuk yoém tú-ka-me kóko-la-m násuk bó'o-ka yéhte-k
that:one us-among person be-PPL-NZR dead-PPL-PL among lay-PPL arise-PRF
The one who became a man here among us, arose from among the dead.

(75) 'itépo hiókot itóm 'itó bíča-'a-násuk-u húni'i 'emó-u wáate
we miserable our RFL see-EV-among-in even you-to remember
We remember you even in the midst of our sufferings here.

4.0. The -be postpositions

A number of the Yaqui postpositions begin with the syllable **be**. Langacker shows that this **be** represents the reanalysis of the Proto-Uto-Aztecan third person singular pronoun *pɨ (Langacker 1977a; 1977b:93). Its synchronic status in Yaqui is ambiguous. As soon as Dedrick began to analyze Yaqui postpositions, it seemed obvious to him that **be** was a morpheme but with the material he initially had at hand, it was not easy to determine what it meant or how it functioned.

Of the 18 postpositions **-be** did not occur with **-po, -ku, -naápo, -e/-mea, -mak/e, -táhtia,** or **-bíča.** It did occur with **-u/-wi, -etči/-et, -tána,** and **-wit**. The remaining forms present problems. While **-beas** seems to be derived from an older sequence **be-was**, the present form **-beas** itself is not reducible and is probably monomorphemic in its own right. The remaining forms, **-bépa, -béna,** and **-betčí'ibo** are also not further analyzable into distinct morphemes.

4.1. The spatial -beas/-beasi

The postposition **-beas,** with its shorter form **-beah** and its longer form **-beasi,** signals various spatial relations that can be subsumed under the general category label "located in the general proximity of." In particular usages it can be glossed "near," as in sentence (1). Often it can be glossed more specifically as "beside" or "alongside of" as in sentence (2).

(1) hú'upa-ta-béas-i n=á'a 'éu-su-ria-k
mesquite-POS-by-DIR I=it hide-CPL-APL-PRF
I hid it near the mesquite tree.

(2) huúri née-béas móbe-la bó'o-ka-n
badger me-front face-up lay-PPL-PCN
A badger was lying face up, alongside of me.

Some of the spatial usages of **-beas** involve a clear notion of orientation with respect to the speaker and the entity that is the object of attention. The meaning "in front of" illustrated by the usage of **-beas** given in sentence (3), implies a canonical position for viewing entities and a canonical direction of movement of the viewer along a conceptual path. Entities both located on that path and in the visual field of the viewer are construed as being "out in front of X."

(3) bayéena 'óta-m 'amé-béah to'o-ka-n
whale bone-PL them-front lie-PPL-PCN
Whale bones were in front of them.

The "in front of" sense of **-beas** is the basis for its metaphorical meaning of "oppose" or "challenge" illustrated in sentence (4).

(4) kaábe née-béas-i kíkte
no-one me-front-DIR stand
No one opposes me.

Another meaning of **-beas** is "the other side of X." Sentences (5) and (6) exemplify this usage.

(5) húu'u káuwis ču'u-ta-béas-i wéye-n
    that fox   dog-ACC-by-DIR go-PCN
    The fox was walking on the other side of the dog.

(6) bʷé'u káu-ta-béas-i
    big   mountain-POS-by-DIR
    on the other side of the big mountain

The temporal usages of **-beas** highlight the notion of prior time with respect to some event. In these usages **-beas** can be glossed as "before" or "until" as seen in sentences (7) and (8).

(7) 'áme-beás-i   né híta bʷása-'a-bae
    them-front-DIR I thing cook-EV-DSD
    I want to cook something before they get here.

(8) 'ím né tawá-nee   ée-béasi
    here I remain-FUT you-front
    I'll wait here till you come.

Buelna cites many illustrations of usages of -beas with pronouns. He describes them in the following terms:

> **Veuatzi.** Esta preposición se junta con pronombres en el ablativo, con nombres sustantivos rige caso oblicuo, ora sea de acusativo, ora de ablativo.
>
> Primero: significa lo mismo que "de," *v.g., de,* **aieveuatzi**; *olvídeme de él,* **aieveuat ne coptec,** ó **aieveriah ne coptec.**
>
> Segundo: significa "lo que decimos," "al encuentro," "salirle al encuentro," *v.g., le saldré al encuentro,* **aieveuat nesimnaque**; *sentaréme á donde ha de llegar, esto es, á experarle al encuentro,* **aieveuat ne iehnaque.**
>
> Tercero: significa "lo que decimos detrás de," *v.g., detrás de una mata,* **chucta veuatzi**; *me acosté detrás de una mata,* **chuctaveuat ne voca.**
>
> Cuatro: significa "junto," *v.g., ponte junto á mi,* **inoveuat e ueie.**
>
> Adviértase, que alguna vez se suele componer con la preposición **ui** antepuesta: *me olvidé de tí,* **emou veuatne coptec.** (Buelna 1891:102, Item 302)[2]
>
> (En todos los casos dichos, el autor pone **veuas** por **veuat**; quizá así se pronuncia esa preposición sincopado.).[3]

4.2. The positional -bépa "over"

The postposition **-bepa** occurs with a wide range of meanings centered on the notion "over" or "above." In addition, it has more grammaticalized usages in which it functions as one constituent within a comparative construction to signal the idea "more than," much in the spirit of English Adjective + **-er** constructions illustrated by words such as "richer" and "poorer" (cf. COMPARATIVE CONSTRUCTIONS, pp. 110–112). Yaqui **-bépa** also occurs as the first element in a few compounds such as **bépa-saáwaam** [over-pant:PL] *trousers,* **bépa-súpem** [over-shirt] *coat.*

As a locative it is used in both literal and figurative senses. In its strictly locative uses, **-bépa** can be glossed variously as "over," "above," "on top of," or "at the top." The idea of "on the top of" (a

---

2 "**Veuatzi.** This preposition is joined to pronouns in the ablative case, with substantive nouns it invokes the oblique case or it may be the accusative case or the ablative.
    First: It means the same thing as [Spanish] "de," *cf. de,* **aieveuatzi**; *I forgot about him,* **aieveuat ne coptec** or **aieveriah ne coptec.**
    Second: It means what we mean by the expression "upon encountering X," to leave upon encountering him, cf. *I left when I encountered him,* **aieveuat nesimnaque**; *I will sit down at the place to which one has to come, that is, to wait for the encounter,* **aieveuat ne iehnaque.**
    Third: It means what we mean by the expression "in back of X," cf. *behind a bush,* **chucta veuatzi**; *I laid down behind a bush* **chuctaveuat ne voca.**
    Fourth: It means "together with," cf. *Put it right next to me,* **inoveuat e ueie.**
    Notice: That once it combines with the preposition **ui** preposed to it: *I forgot about you,* **emou veuatne coptec**". (Buelna 1891:102, Item 302)

3 In all the cases cited above, the author replaces **veuas** with **veuat.** Perhaps this preposition is pronounced with syncopation.

surface) is illustrated in sentence (9), whereas the meaning "at the top of X" is given in sentence (10). Both the directional use of **hiká** *top* and its metonymic use are also illustrated in sentence (10).

(9) hunáa'a tápla-kári ba'á-bépa hiká-t čá'a-si-síme
that plank-house water-above top-on float-RDP-go:SG
The boat went floating on top of the water.

(10) hiká-u bi-bítču húm-bépa kári-hiká-t-bépa
top-to RDP-stare there-above house-top-on-above
He stared upwards at the top of the house.

A common extended usage of **-bépa** is to express the notion of superior status in social relations, as expressed by example (11).

(11) si'ime-m-bépa-t 'á'a weám-nee-'u
all-PL-over-on his walk-FUT-GND
He will excel above all the rest.

4.3. The positional betuk/-tuk "underneath"

The postposition **-tuk** along with its longer form **bétuk** can be glossed as "underneath." This postposition provides several shreds of evidence for both the historical and present status of **be-**.

For example, **bétuk** is used as the first element in certain compounds that designate items of underclothing as illustrated in examples (12) and (13). On the one hand these Yaqui forms very likely are calques from English "undershirt" and "underpants." Nonetheless, if we assume that **be-** can be segmented in these two compounds and that it represents some sort of pronoun, then we are left with a pattern that closely fits the Uto-Aztecan pronoun copy construction in its inverted order (cf. Langacker 1977:96).

(12) bétuk-súpe-m   (13) bétuk-sáawea-m
under-shirt-PL   under-pants-PL
undershirt   *underpants*

Yaqui shows limited semantic contrasts between **bétuk** and **-túk**. To begin, the short form **-tuk** is used with both singular and plural object pronouns as exemplified by examples (14) and (15). However, both **-tuk** and **betuk** are used with plural object nouns as a comparison of example (15) with (16) demonstrates. Since the pronominal base is the same in both sentences, the difference in meaning can plausibly be attributed to the presence of the syllable **-be,** a faint trace of the Proto-Uto-Aztecan pronoun **pɨ* mentioned earlier. One additional wrinkle however, is the extra vowel **-u** on the plural forms. We tentatively identify it as an additional postposition **-u** *in*. This could be related to the postposition **-'u** discussed in VERB MORPHOLOGY, pp. 142–143 (cf. **basó-'u** *to go to cut grass*). In turn, this **-u** may well contrast paradigmatically with the directional **-i** *towards* (cf. ADVERBIAL DEMONSTRATIVES, p. 214).

(14) 'áe-tuk   (15) 'áme-tuk   (16) 'áme-bétuk-u
it-under   them-under   them-under-in
under it   *under them*   *beneath/under them*

The longer form **-bétuk-u** is most commonly used with concrete nouns marked either with the accusative singular **-ta,** as in examples (17) and (18), or with the plural **-im**, as in (19) and (20).

(17) huyá-ta-bétuk-u   (19) kaáma-m-bétuk-u
trees-ACC-under-in   bed-PL-under-in
under the tree   *under the beds*

(18) sibá-ta-bétuk-u   (20) hámut-čóni-m bʷía-ta-bétuk-im kaá mo-móye
cliff-ACC-under-in   woman-hair-PL ground-ACC-under-they not RDP-decay
under the cliff   *Woman's hair does not decay under the ground.*

I have found no metaphorical uses of this postposition in examples gleaned from spontaneously narrated text. On the other hand, from a passage translated by Castro (circ. 1943) comes the metaphorical use of **-bétuk** given in sentence (21).

(21) 'iníi'i páplo Liós nésau-ta-bétuk   'áu híp^{w}ee
     this Paul God command-ACC-under RFL has
     This Paul has himself under God's command.

The expression translated as "under God's command" is probably not natural Yaqui but would be understood by the analogy with Spanish, i.e., this usage represents a calque.

Examples (22) and (23) show clearly the role that Yaqui **-bétuk** plays in both discontinuous and inverted pronoun copy constructions. In example (22) the pronoun copy **'ame** *them* is the object of the postposition **-bétuk** in a postpositional phrase that follows the subject noun **baké'o** *cowboy* (< Sp. *vaquero*). The noun that elaborates the object of the postposition is in sentence initial position and is followed by the subject of the sentence. In sentence (23) the postposition **-tuk** takes a third person plural pronominal object which is elaborated by the reduced adverbial clause which follows **-tuk**.

(22) hí'ito-m ... baké'o 'áme-bétuk kópana-n
     Hi'ito-tree-PL cowboy them-under nap-PCN
     A cowboy was resting under the Hi'ito tree.

(23) bát-naáta-ka 'áme-tuk hó'aa-ka-n
     first-begin-PPL them-under house-have-PCN
     At the first, he was living below where those other people lived.

In certain contexts, **-bétuk** means "underneath" as seen in sentence (24), in which the plural subject pronoun attaches to **-bétuk**.

(24) b^{w}ía-ta-bétuk=im káa mo-móye
     dirt-POS-under=they not RDP-rot
     They do not rot underneath the ground.

Postpositions also enter into adverbial phrase constructions in which they provide a more specific orientation to the meaning of the adverbial demonstrative that precedes them. In sentence (25) for example, the object of the postposition **bétuk** is **húm** *there*. This adverbial is elaborated by the sentence final postpositional phrase **mésa-ta bétuk** *under the table*.

(25) káa húm bétuk kátek há'ani mésa-ta bétuk
     not there under located maybe table-POS under
     Is not that it under there, under the table?

4.4. The source-oriented bétana/-tana

The bound postposition **-tana** alternates with the free postposition **bé-tana** and can be variously glossed as "at one side of," "from," and "regarding." The strictly locative meaning "at one side of" is clearly seen in the usages of **-tana** in example (26).

(26) kaáčin=té waé=tána 'aáne 'ía-tána=te tawá-nee
     no:way=we that=side be this-side=we remain-FUT
     There's no way we can get to the other side; we'll have to remain on this side.

Within the domain of the human body, **-tana** can designate the side of the face or head as is evidenced by sentence (27). Metaphorical usages of **-tana** include references to conceptual space as in sentence (28).

(27) wépul-ka-tána tósai-m puús-ek
     one-being-side white-PL eye-have
     He has a white eye on one side.

(28) wáka'a hú'enak 'emó-tána 'áu-ka-m-ta 'ómo-la bé'aa-k
that:ACC evil:ACC you-from be-PPL-NZR-ACC one:side-ABS lack-PRF
He put to one side the evil that was in you.

Example (29) shows the role of Yaqui **-tana** as one member in a string of postpositions in a complex phrase. In these usages, **-tana** has a clear directional meaning in which its object (which is either a directional itself or another postposition) signals the beginning point of the directed path.

(29) sí'ime-ku-t napé-kóni-la hikát-tána 'íntok bétuk-tána
all-in-on around-circle-ABS up-from and under-from
all around, everywhere, upward and downward

When it takes the adverbial **yeu** *outside* as its object, **-tana** refers to the perceptually accessible outer surface of a discrete entity, such as a watermelon, as illustrated in example (30).

(30) sákobai bʷá-si yéu-tána síari wáhiwa sikíi
watermelon ripe-PPL out-side green inside red
When watermelon is ripe, outside it is green and inside it is red.

In its temporal use **-tana** can be glossed "from a particular point in time." The temporal adverb **kétwoo** *early* specifies the point in time referred to by **-tana** in example (31).

(31) kétwóo-tána púči'ilai-ta hía-o
early-from Puchi'ilai: bird-POS sound-when
In the morning when the Puchi'ilai bird sings.

Yaqui **-tana** like all the other postpositions attaches to a variety of complex bases. In sentences (32) and (33) the object of the postposition consists of a locative subordinate clause.

(32) ba'á-bé'e-ka-tána
water-scatter-PPL-from
the different places where water is[4]

(33) wóh-naíki puéplo-m-bé'e-ka-tána náah-nu-nu'ubʷia
twice-four town-PL-scatter-PPL-from around-RDP-carry
He was carried around to the eight towns.

Within the domain of societal and personal relations, **-tana** designates the particular or group under discussion. The typical object of the postposition in such cases is a personal pronoun, as illustrated by sentences (34) and (35).

(34) 'itépo=té 'áe-tána tehtíiko-m
we=we him-side witness-PL
We are his witnesses.

(35) táa wáa'a née-tána 'éa-me 'áma yolé-'e-nee
but that me-side think-NZR there escape-EV-FUT
But the one who trusts me will escape there.

The notion of origin or the starting point on a spatial or temporal path is salient to many of literal and figurative uses of **betana** *from*. Examples (36)–(39) show particular locations that are the points of origin that **-tana** designates including distinct sectors of a country as in (36), topographical regions as in (37) and (38), and extraterrestrial locations in (39).

(36) 'í'i-bo née wée teháh bétana
this-from I come Texas from
I come from this direction, from Texas.

---

4 The appropriate translation of this word in this context is "scattered, dispersed." The only word that I know of that might be related to it is **bé'ee**, meaning "to lack." The semantics seem anomalous, however, and we may actually have homonyms here.

(37) wasá-m bétana né yepsa-k
　　 field-PL -from I arrive-PRF
　　 I came from the fields.

(38) póčo'o-ria bétana wée
　　 woods-ABS from come
　　 He comes from the woods.

(39) téeka bétana 'ánkeles 'á-u kó'om-yépsa-k
　　 sky from angel him-to down-arrived-PRF
　　 An angel from heaven came down to him.

The source that **-tana** designates may be a communicative source as suggested by sentence (40).

(40) 'emó-u n-á'a téuwaa-mačí 'enčím 'á'a hú'uneiyaa-nee-'epo-bétana
　　 you-to I-it tell-able your it know-FUT-GND-from
　　 I must tell you this so that you may know about it.

Yaqui also employs **-tana** as one element in the complex expression that is used to indicate cardinal directions.

(41) néh-po 'íntok ta'á-ta yéu-wée-'e-bétana sím-ne
　　 I and sun-POS out-go:SG-EV-from go-FUT
　　 And I will go to the east.

4.5. The positional -bé-wit-či "beside"

The postposition **-bé-wit-či** has two shorter forms, **-wit-či** and **-wit**. Both of these shorter forms illustrate further the former historical status of **-be** as a third person singular pronoun, with a few synchronic traces of that status retained in present day Yaqui. As examples (42) and (43) suggest, when the object of the postposition is a place name, the longer form **-béwitči** is used. In this domain, that of geographical space, **-béwit(či)** can be glossed as "alongside of."

(42) hunáman wée báhko'a-m-bewitči hú'upa soó'o-ku 'ámmani
　　 there go:SG Bacum-PL-beside mezquite thicket-in by:there
　　 He went along through the mesquite thicket, there alongside of Bacum.

(43) mó'oči-m-meu héela yáhi-nee mó'oči-m-béwit
　　 Los Mochis-PL-to nearly arrive-FUT Los Mochis-PL-beside
　　 You will come near to Los Mochis, alongside Los Mochis.

On the other hand, with either a pronominal object of the postposition or a personal name nominal, the short form **-wit** is used as illustrated by sentences (44) and (45). Example (44) also shows that in the temporal domain, **-wit** can be glossed as "at the same time." Within the domain of measures, as in example (45), **-wit** can be glossed as "the same size as."

(44) máakina kumí'ipa-bétana wée-ka 'áa-wit 'áma yépsa-k
　　 engine Cumipas-from come-PPL him-with there arrive-PRF
　　 The train from Cumipas got there at the same time that he did.

(45) hú'u réesensia 'éhteer-ta-wit wéye
　　 that Crecensia Esther-POS-with go:SG
　　 Crecensia is the same size as Esther.

4.6. The benefactive/causative/purposive -betčí'ibo

The postposition **-betčí'ibo** can be glossed "for," "because of," or "in order to" and is used with nouns, verbs, adjectives, manner adverbs, and pronouns. Both its polysemy and its specific links to events that allow other events to transpire, as well as its links to events that are the goals of purposeful acts, reflect a functional parallel between Yaqui **-betčí'ibo** and the causal prepositions of English. This does not entail, however, that we are claiming that **-betčí'ibo** is a prototypical causative of the sort defined by formal syntax. With nouns, it conveys the notion of doing something for the benefit of someone, as in examples (46)–(48).

(46) né-le-béna-si yoéme-m-betčí'ibo
     I-CON-like-AVR people-PL-for
     It is for people like me.

(47) lisénsia-ta mák-wa-k 'a'a tékil-wa-betčí'ibo
     permission-ACC give-PSV-PT his work-POS-for
     He was given permission for his work.

(48) kaíta lot-tí-a née-betčí'ibo
     nothing tire-PPL-ABS me-for
     There is no weariness for me.

Entire clauses serve as objects of **-betčí'ibo**. Notice, however, that these clauses are nominalized, as can be seen from the form of the subject pronouns that mark them, i.e., the accusative/possessed object pronouns are used to mark the subordinate clause subjects. The first person plural possessor pronoun marks the clause containing two occurrences of **-betčí'ibo**, the first of which takes a third person singular object pronoun. The second marks the verb of the subordinate clause and the use of **-betčí'ibo** in this case seems to be a kind of concord with the first usage. The usage illustrated by example (50) consists of stating the grounds for the narrator's admiration, whereas that of example (51) expresses the intended purpose of the subject of the subordinate clause.

(49) 'itóm 'áe-betčí'ibo híapsi-nee-'e-betčí'ibo
     our   him-for   live-FUT-EV-for
     so that we should live for him

(50) tú'i-si 'ám 'uttía húme'e maómeo-m 'áa 'ám tómi-haría-'a-betčí'ibo
     good-AVR them admire those acrobat-PL able them money-hunt-EV-for
     He admired the acrobats very much for the way they could make money.

(51) waté-m bém hínne'u-bae-'e-betčí'ibo
     some-PL their save-DSD-EV-for
     because they wanted to save some of them

In some cases **-betčí'ibo** signals the cause of what is expressed by the main verb. This usage is a second functional parallel to the causal usages of English prepositions discussed in Radden (1985). As examples (52)–(54) show, **-betčí'ibo** in these instances, can be glossed as "on account of," "because of," and "for."

(52) súum 'éa-ka taáwa-k bém bíča-'u-betčí'ibo
     amaze think-PPL remain-PRF their see-GND-for
     They were surprised because of what they saw.

(53) Lióh-ta-t 'á'a baí-sae   híba-po 'émo-betčí'ibo
     God-ACC-on it cool-IMP (appreciate) always-in you:PL-for
     always thankful to God because of you

(54) húka'a 'itóm čúpa'i-ka   híaps-i-'éa-'u   káa 'itóm
     that   our fulfill-PPL-PPL live-NZR-think-GND (ought to) not our
     čúpa-'i-a-ka-betčí'ibo
     fulfill-PPL-CON-PPL-for
     because we did not fulfill that which we should have fulfilled

With subordinate clauses as the object of the postposition, **-betčí'ibo** commonly serves to indicate that one activity is the purpose for which another activity was carried out, i.e., it is used as a subordinating conjunction to mark purpose clauses as seen in examples (55)–(57).

(55) kárpa-m tobók-ta-k heká-ta káa 'ám síuta-nee-'e-betčí'ibo
     tent-PL lift-VR-PRF wind-POS not them tear-FUT-EV-for
     They took up their tents so that the wind would not tear them.

(56) kári-ta réuwe-k 'áma hó'a-betčí'ibo
     house-ACC rent-PRF there live-for
     They rented a house to live in.

(57) nésau-ta nénka-k sí'ime 'áma yéu-kát-nee-'e-betčí'ibo
     order-ACC give-PRF all there out-go-FUT-EV-for
     He gave orders that everyone should leave there.

Yaqui is not restricted to using only subordinate clauses for indicating purpose, however. Commonly a manner adverb is employed as the object of the postposition **-betčí'ibo**. The entire postpositional phrase in turn marks the purpose clause, which can be construed as the complement of the manner adverb, as exemplified by sentence (58). The complex postpositional sequence consisting of **-po** and **-betčí'ibo** also takes manner adverbs as its postpositional object. This is illustrated in sentences (59) and (60). In this construction, the clause is not nominalized, but rather is characterized by a finite verb. Two different demonstrative adverbs are used in these constructions and this difference between the use of **hunúe** in sentence (58) and **inían-po** in sentences (59) and (60) is definitely contextually determined. We hypothesize that **hunúe** refers to a person or event as cause for happiness and **'inían-po** designates the consequence of something that has happened.

(58) hunúe-betčí'ibo née túa 'alléa
     that-for I indeed happy
     For that reason I am very happy.

(59) 'inían-po-betčí'ibo sí'ime 'á'a súale
     thus-in-for all him believe
     For that reason, everyone believes him.

(60) 'inían-po-betčí'ibo sí'ime 'á'a súale-me káa múk-nee
     thus-in-for all him believe-NZR not die-FUT
     For that reason all who believe in Him will not die.

When **-betčí'ibo** takes the indefinite pronoun **híta** as its object, the entire postpositional phrase can be glossed as "why," and the entire clause containing it appears to be an embedded question as seen in sentence (61).

(61) 'íntok né káa hú'unea híta-betčí'ibo 'á'a bʷán-simé-'u
     and I not know thing-for her cry-go-GND
     And I do not know why she went along crying.

Finally, as a number of the examples given in this section illustrate, an echo-vowel is inserted between **-betčí'ibo** and the final suffix of the verb in the clause serving as the postpositional object. Notice example (62).

(62) náu 'ám yumá-'a-né-'e-betčí'ibo
     together them attain-EV-FUT-EV-for
     for bringing them together

4.7. The simulfactive -béna

Although the simulfactive postposition **-béna,** meaning "like" or "similar to," along with **-bépa** *above,* was dealt with in some detail in COMPARATIVE CONSTRUCTIONS pp.105–108 and 110–116, its usages clearly relate it to the rest of the postpositions. The notion "be" is central to its meaning as is the entire schema that includes a target of comparison and a standard of comparison. Not all of these aspects need to be overtly expressed in any given use. The meaning of **-béna** in sentences (63) and (64), for example, approximates that of the English verb "seem."

(63) tú'ii-béna 'íi'i kári
good-like this house
This seems to be a good house.

(64) hunúen-tu-béna
thus-VR-like
That seems to be the way it is.

Examples (65) and (66) overtly express the standard of comparison, i.e., "straight talk" and "being youthful."

(65) wítti nók-wame kaíta 'ále-béna
straight talk-NZR nothing it-like
There is nothing like straight talk.

(66) húnak 'émpo hú'ub^wa-yó'o-tu-m-ta-béna-nee
they you just:now-grow-VR-NZR-ACC-like-FUT
Then you will be just like a youth (again).

The usage of **-béna** in example (67) includes an overt specification of both the target of the comparison and the standard according to which the comparison is being made. The standard is expressed via an incorporated postpositional phrase which has a compound noun as its object and the postpositional phrase itself is construed as a possessed object. The target of the comparison is the subject of the sentence itself.

(67) neó'okai yoí-kuksía-ta-béna-k
mockingbird mexican-flute-ACC-like-have
The mockingbird has a note like a flute.

Béna can also be adverbialized with **-si** as can be seen in sentence (68).

(68) né-le-béna-si yoéme-m-betčí'ibo
I-CON-like-AVR people-PL-for
It is for people like me.

4.8. The ubiquitous -bíča/-bičáa

The postposition **-bíča** is used to designate locations in both physical space and time. Often it signals a specific goal or location and can be glossed as "site of, location of." In both Yaqui and Mayo, **bíča** functions as a bona fide verb meaning literally "to see" and, figuratively, "to experience," as shown by examples (69)–(71).

(69) čóki-híssa-m né bíča-k
star-scattered-PL I see-PRF
I saw the comet.

(71) 'inó-nee bam-sí-bíča
RFL-I hurry-AVR-see
I am in a hurry.

(70) 'itépo hú'ena-m-po 'ito-bíča
we evil-NZR-in RFL-see
We are experiencing hard times.

The postposition **-bíča** forms the second member of several compounds. This agrees fully with the observation that it comes from a verb. Many of these compounds involve adverbial demonstratives, as in examples (72)–(74).

(72) háu-bíča
where-site
to where

(73) bína-bíča
this:way-site
coming this way

(74) wám-bíča
that:way-site
going off in that direction

Conventionalized expressions with **-bíča** involve other constituents as well. These include the reciprocal adjective **nau** *together* with the resultant meaning "face to face" as in example (75), and the quantitative adverb **húči** *again* with the meaning "once again," as seen in examples (76).

(75) náu-bíča
together-site
face to face

(76) húči-bíča
again-site
once again (returns)

There is even a reduplicated version of **-bíča** which reinforces the goal oriented aspect of its meaning in example (77).

(77) bíča-u-bíča
site-to-site
going forward, ahead, progressing.

This orientation to a goal as a part of the meaning of **-bíča** is clear simply from the meanings of the constructions in which it takes personal pronouns as its postpositional object. The entire set is presented in Table 20. Notice that in each case, the postposition **-u** *toward* attaches to the object pronoun and together with it serves as the object of **-bíča**.

Person	Singular	Plural
1	né-u-bíča	'itó-u-bíča
2	'é-u-bíča	'émo-u-bíča
3	'á-u-bíča	'áme-u-bíča

Table 20. Personal pronominal objects with -bíča

In its usage as a postposition, **bíča** is commonly the final member of complex postpositional phrases. For example, the complex postpositional phrase consisting of a Nominal + **-u** followed by **-bíča** is conventionally taken to indicate movement toward the site or location of some event or situation. Sentences (78)–(80) are typical examples.

(78) 'iním yéu-sií-ka   wasá-m-me-u-bíča
here   out-go-PRF   field-PL-?-to-site
He left here and went to the fields.

(79) 'ií'i boó'o mehiko-u-bíča   wée
this road   Mexico:City-to-site go
This road goes to Mexico City.

(80) húči sím-nee 'á'a bʷía-raa-u-bíča
again go-FUT his land-ABS-to-site
He will return to his country again.

Complex adverbial constructions often involve **-bíča** as the second member. In such constructions, **-bíča** functions as the anchor point for the locational relationship communicated by the entire construction. The combinations are all clearly distinct semantically. Thus, **'amá-u-bíča** *back-to-site* in example (81) means "backwards," **'ám-bíča** *that-site* in example (82) means "in that direction," and **'omó-t-bíča** "elsewhere-on-site" means "somewhere else" as seen in example (83).

(81) hobé'eso 'awá-m 'amá-u-bíča bí'i-ti-laa
ram   horn-PL back-to-site twist-PPL-PPL
A ram's horns are twisted backwards.

(82) yoéme búsani-ka 'ám-bíča kaáte
man   six-being that-site go:PL
Six men are going away in that direction.

(83) kát 'omó-t-bíča   sí-sime
not elsewhere-on-site RDP-go
Don't you go off somewhere else.

DEMONSTRATIVES

1.0. Introduction

Morphologically and semantically, Yaqui demonstratives display considerable complexity. They can be arranged in an array of paradigmatic sets that are related to one another based on how they display distinct contrasts within different semantic domains.

2.0. The paradigmatic sets

In this section and in section 3.0. we distinguish and describe several paradigmatic sets of demonstratives that function in Yaqui grammar. The first we consider to be the basic set. The other sets introduce additional complexities in their own ways. They consist of the pausal singular forms, the plural forms, the nominative and accusative plural forms, and proximal **-ni-** with the contrastive **-nu-** and **-na-** forms.

2.1. The basic demonstratives

The first set of demonstratives that we present here is considerd to be the basic one in that these forms appear to reflect three degrees of distance relative to the speaker, i.e., speaker's location versus the point of his attention directed at something slightly removed from his actual vantage point versus the point distally removed from both speaker and hearer. In addition, in their singular forms they are marked for either nominative or accusative case. Finally, the nominative forms of the basic demonstrative set are characterized by a long vowel that is shortened in the corresponding accusative forms as shown in Table 21. Functionally, Yaqui demonstratives often serve as definite articles.

	Nominative	Accusative	
Proximal	'íi	'íka	*this one right here*
Medial	húu	húka	*that there (neutral)*
Distal	wáa	wáka	*that one off yonder*

Table 21. Singular demonstratives

2.2. The pausal singular forms

A second morphological set of demonstrative forms is derived by inserting a glottal stop following the word final vowel and then reduplicating that vowel in a new word final position. Typologically, this is reminiscent of the pausal forms of Cora and Hopi (cf. Casad 1984:181–182). The idea of being in a specific area as opposed to being in a non-specific area also seems to be part of the semantic distinctions signalled by this set of Yaqui demonstratives. This is another disinction sometimes found in Uto-Aztecan demonstrative systems (cf. Langacker 1977:99).

Proximal	'íi'i	'íka'a	*this one right here*
Medial	húu'u	húka'a	*that one right there*
Distal	wáa'a	wáka'a	*that over there*

Table 22. Singular pausal demonstratives

A nominative usage of the proximal singular demonstrative **'íi'i** *this one* is given in (1)(a), where **'íi'i** is part of the fronted noun phrase in a WH- question. The use of **'íi'i** as a subject nominal is seen in (1)(b).

(1)(a) 'íi'i boó'o hakún-bíčáa=sa wée
      this road where-site=INTERR go
      Where does this road go?

(b) 'íi'i bátte tú'ii-k hí'ohte
    this nearly good-ACC write
    This (boy) nearly writes well.

2.3. The plural forms

The conventionalized neutralization of nominative versus accusative case marking on plural nouns in Yaqui carries over to the demonstratives, as the forms in Table 23 show.

	Nominative/Accusative
Proximal	'íme'e
Medial	húme'e
Distal	wáme'e

Table 23. Plural demonstratives

A typical usage of the proximal accusative plural **'íme'e** is illustrated in example (2).

(2) kaíta 'íntok bʷá'e 'íme'e híba
nothing and eat these only
He does not eat anything else, only these.

This proximal form has a reduced variant, **'íme**, when it occurs sentence initially and in an attributive position. This is exemplified in sentences (3) and (4).

(3) 'íme=san náka-m súka-sió'o-te
these=EXP ear-PL hot-pain-VR
These ears of mine burn painfully.

(4) 'íme 'o'ówi-m sú-súa-k-ame 'ínen hiía
these man-PL RDP-wise-PRF-NZR thus say
This is what the wise men say.

The proximal specific demonstrative **'iníme'e**, with the added morpheme **-ni** (see 3.0) also has a reduced variant of the shape **'iníme** in similar environments, as seen in sentences (5) and (6).

(5) 'iníme wakás-im nénki-baa-wa
these cow-PL sell-DSD-PSV
These cows are for sale.

(6) bémpo 'iníme'e kúču-m tú'i-si tú'ure
they these:ACC fish-PL good-AVR like
They like these fish very much.

2.4. Nominative versus accusative plural

The sentences (3)–(6) above illustrate clearly the often noted neutralization of the contrast between the nominative and the accusative in the plural. Reinforcing this point, note that the proximal specific **'íme'e** marks the plural subject in sentence (7) and the plural direct object in sentence (8).

(7) tú'isi=m 'o'óbe 'íme'e 'ili yoéme-m
very=they lazy these little person-PL
These little folks are surely very lazy.

(8) 'áapo humák 'íme'e hí'osia-m wáata-nee
he maybe these paper-PL want-FUT
He will probably want these papers.

Likewise, the distal specific **húme'e** marks the plural subject in sentence (9), the plural direct object in sentence (10), and the plural oblique object in sentence (11).

(9) húme'e wóki-m=sán káa bétte-si bo'ó-hoóa huná-e-mak 'áman yépsa-k
those foot-PL=EXP NEG heavy-AVR road-make that-CON-with there arrive-PRF
And his lightfooted legs finished the trip.

(10) 'ám ne-nénka húme'e máh-béa-m
them RDP-sell those deer-skin-PL
He sells deer skins.

(11) čúkula   béha húme'e hímsi-m-mea sí'ime púhba-t 'á'a číke
     afterward well those beard-PL-INST all   face-on him sweep
     Afterward it brushed all his face with its beard.

Finally, the remote specific plural demonstrative **hunáme'e** marks subject in sentences (12) and (13) and direct object in sentence (14).

(12) bakótči-m 'áma réhte hunáme'e kurúes-im-tea
     snake-PL there go:PL those   Kurues-PL-called
     There are snakes there; they are called "Kurues."

(13) tú'i-si-m   tómi-ta   koóba hunáme'e maómeo-m
     good-AVR-PL money-ACC earn those   acrobat-PL
     Those acrobats really earned a lot of money.

(14) hunáme'e baá'a-m   hé'e-ka tú'i-si bíssat-ču-k
     those   water-PL:ACC drink-PPL good-AVR vomit-CPL-PRF
     Having drunk that water, he really vomited.

3.0. Singular nominal demonstratives

An additional set of demonstrative forms includes a medial syllable of the form **ni** in the proximal forms and **nu** and **na** in the non-proximal forms. The morphological pattern suggests the nominative non-proximal forms **huna** and **hunu**, but as free forms, they do not occur in our data. The entire series of contrasts between **ni, na** and **nu** does occur, however, as components of more morphologically complex forms, including those given in examples (12)–(14).

	Nominative	Accusative
Proximal	'iníi'i	'iníka'a
Distal	húnúu'u	hunúka'a
Distal	hunáa'a	hunáka'a

Table 24. Singular nominal demonstratives

Typical examples of these demonstratives are given in examples (15) and (16).

(15) 'iníi'i muúku-k bahkó'a-m naápo tinahéa-'a-téa-'apo muúku-k
     this   die-PRF Bacum-PL near Tinajera-EV-named-in die-PRF
     This man died near Bacum at a place called Tinajera.

(16) hunáa'a baákot 'ém ko'oko-si yáa-k-a'u
     that   snake your pain-AVR do-PRF-GND
     the snake that you hurt

Example (15) illustrates the use of the proximal form **'iníi'i**, whereas example (16) draws on the contrastive distal nominative form **hunáa'a**. Yaqui apparently makes a clear distinction between distal entities that are completely off the stage, as in (16), and distal entities that are nonetheless still within the range of one's vision. For this latter situation, Yaqui employs **hunúu'u** as illustrated in examples (17) and (18).

(17) hunúu'u   yoém 'ó'aa híba   kék-ke'e-we
     that:visible man old   always RDP-chop:wood-go
     That old man always cuts wood.

(18) bátkomo ba'á-te-ta   née hí'i-sae hunúu'u póttia-ta yú'ee
     batamote water-VR-ACC me drink-IMP that   bloat-ACC overcome
     He told me to drink Batamote tea; it relieves bloatedness.

3.1. Use as postpositional bases

Yaqui also has two series of demonstrative forms that serve as postpositional bases in which they are formed by adding a postpositional **-e** (instrumental?) to a basic demonstrative form. As is the case for all the sets of demonstratives given thus far, the postpositional base demonstratives reflect the variously calibrated distance orientation widespread in Uto-Aztecan (cf. Casad 1984:181–182; Langacker 1977:99). The first series of postpostional base demonstrative employs the singular forms of the basic set and the postpositional **-e**.

Proximal	'íe-
Medial	húe-
Distal	wáe-

Table 25. Demonstrative postpositional objects I

The second set of demonstratives that serve as postpositional objects includes a second syllable of the form **ni, na** or **nu**, i.e., the series that is shown in Table 24. The contrast between demonstratives with a **na** versus **nu** syllable is reminiscent of the Huichol prefixal distinction between **na-** *this side of a line at right angles to the speaker's line of sight* and **nu-** *on the far side of a line at right angles to the speaker's line of sight* (cf. Grimes 1964:90) The vowels involved in the morphemic contrast appear to be oriented oppositely from the vowels of the Huichol morphemic contrast, but the interesting thing is that both Yaqui and Huichol register the contrast which can be linked to the model of a speaker, the speaker's line of sight, and a line out in front of the speaker that crosses his/her line of sight at right angles. Finally, changes in morpheme member position within a paradigm are not particularly problematic.

Proximal	'iníe-	*this one here*
This side	hunúe-	*that one right there*
That side	hunáe-	*that one over there*

Table 26. Demonstrative postpositional objects II

The grammaticalization of the **-na** and **-nu** contrast in Yaqui shows an extension of the spatial usages into the domain of psychology. In example (19) the specific demonstrative **hunúe-** is the object of the postposition **-betčí'ibo** and refers to a particular reason for the speaker's expressed happiness. In example (20) the distal **hunáe-** is the object of the instrumental postposition and refers back to the sentence initial noun phrase **húme'e woki-m** *those feet*.

(19) hunú-e-betčí'ibo née túa   'alléa
     that-INST-for   I   indeed happy
     For that reason I am very happy.

(20) húme'e wóki-m-sán káa bétte-si bo'ó-hoóa huná-e-mak 'aman yépsa-k
     those foot-PL-EXP NEG heavy-AVR road-make that-CON-with there arrive-PRF
     And his lightfooted legs finished the trip.

3.2. The source of the -e forms

The following three sentences suggest strongly that the **-e** on the postpositional demonstratives does find its source in the instrumental postposition **-e.** Sentence (21) shows the use of **-e** as a transparent instrumental postposition attached to a body part noun as its object. In sentences (22) and (23) the demonstrative form marked with **-e** is in construction with a following concrete noun and a possessed abstract noun, respectively, in a complex object of the postposition. Since modifiers in Yaqui are marked to agree in case with the head of the phrase they occur in, it is quite natural to construe the **-e** in these two demonstratives as being the instrumental postposition.

(21) yéka-e   húh-hu'ubʷa
     nose-INST RDP-smell
     He smells it with his nose.

(22) hunú-e   matú-e   hí'i-boa mún-bakí-m 'a-e   bʷá'a-bʷása
     that-INST charcoal-INST eat-make bean-stew it-INST RDP-cook
     She uses that charcoal for cooking: she cooks bean stew with it.

(23) 'inía-e   'itóm tekil-a-e   'itépo 'itó-'anía
     this-INST   our   work-CON-INST   we   RFL-help
     With this our work, we help ourselves.

Typical examples of the demonstratives with **-e** that are used as objects of the postposition are given in sentences (24) and (25). The proximal **'íe** and the distal **waé** are exemplified here.

(24) 'íe nokí-t   née káa hú'unea
     this word-on I   not know
     I don't know the meaning of this word.

(25) kááčin=té   waé-tána 'aáne, 'ía-tána=te   tawá-nee
     no:way=we that-from be   this-from=we   remain-FUT
     There's no way we can get to the other side, we'll have to stay on this side.

Certain usages of the demonstratives appear to retain the use of an accusative marker -a, as seen in (26).

(26) 'iní-a   taéwai-t naáte-ka sí'ime 'enčí   nák-nee
     this-ACC day-on   begin-PPL all   you-ACC love-FUT
     Beginning today everyone will love you.

A few usages of the demonstratives carry a final **-m,** which must reflect the accusative plural **-me** in a reduced form. Example (27) is typical.

(27) 'áapo hunámem-met 'éa
     he   those-on   think
     He trusts in those.

Some demonstrative forms serve as postpositional bases without any trace of accusative marking at all. This is true both for cases in which the demonstrative serves as the postpositional object itself, as in example (28), and for cases in which it is simply one component in a complex object of the postposition, illustrated by example (29).

(28) 'í'i-bo   née wée teháh-bétana
     this-from I   come Texas-from
     I come from this direction, from Texas.

(29) hiká-t 'á'a naáte 'ía-mak   bétu-ku 'á'a yumá-'a-ria-nee
     top-on it   start this-with under-in it   achieve-EV-APL-FUT
     Start at the top and with this you will complete it at the bottom.

Finally, the demonstratives also have extended usages in which they designate locations in the temporal domain. The contrastive use of **hunáme'e** and **wáa'a** is possibly related to the relative remoteness of the events being described to the time of speaking.

(30) hunáme'e taéwai-m-metči káa-hé'ee-me   yá'ut-tu-k
     those   day-PL-in   NEG-drink-NZR chief-VR-PRF
     Cajeme was chief in those days.

(31) wáa'a taéwai-t téuwaa-ri-ku-tči
     that day-on   say-PPL-CON-on
     On that day that it had been said (that it would happen).

4.0. Syntax

In this section we discuss the demonstratives of Yaqui as they are used in context, both at the sentence level and at discourse level.

4.1. Demonstratives and sentence types

Demonstratives participate in a number of distinct phrasal types and grammatical constructions. Most commonly they function as a type of determiner in noun phrases of the form Determiner + Noun. Example (32) illustrates the highlighted nominative form **hunáa'a** in construction with subject nouns.

(32) heéwi 'áčai-t-iia   hunáa'a pahkó'olaa káa 'áa yé'ee-me
     yes   sir-CON-say that   festal:dancer NEG able dance-NZR
     moró-ta-wi   bibá-m   mabét-ču-ka-i
     Moor-ACC-to cigarette-PL receive-CPL-PPL-PPL
     "Yes sir!" the festal dancer who was not able to dance said to the Moor who contracted him, as he received the cigarettes.

A demonstrative may serve as the head of a noun phrase in its own right. Examples (33)–(34) show topicalized demonstratives in subject position.

(33) hunáa'a 'íntok bibá-hímmari-u   yéu-siíka béha
     that:one CNJ   cigarette-discarded-to out-went well
     bo'ó-t wée kó'oko'i-m-meu luúla.
     road-on go Cocorit-PL-to straight
     Well, the man left Cigarrette Butts and took the road straight to Chile Peppers.

(34) hunáa'a túa   tú'u-hiaps-ek
     that   indeed good-life-have
     That person is good-hearted.

Demonstratives may also mark headless relative clauses, i.e., those not introduced by a specific nominal form. Example (35) shows demonstrative **húka'a** marking a headless object relative clause. Example (36), on the other hand, illustrates the use of **huna'a** to mark a headless subject relative clause.

(35) 'á'a hí'oh-te-'e   húka'a 'ém bít-tua-wa-k-a'u-ta
     it   write-VR-you that:ACC your see-CAU-PSV-PRF-GND-ACC
     Write what you see.

(36) hunúm lú'ute-k hunáa'a káa 'áa yé'ee-me   káa 'áa 'etého-me.
     there end-PRF that   NEG able dance-NZR NEG able talk-NZR
     That's where the man who was not able to dance and not able to tell stories wound up.

Demonstratives precede the head noun when they appear as modifiers in noun phrases. The singular distal demonstrative form **huú'u** is commonly used as a modifier in subject noun phrases, whereas the proximal demonstrative form **'íka'a** is used in direct object noun phrases, as seen in example (37).

(37) 'iká'a   né-sau-ta   nénka-k   sí'ime-m 'áma yéu-kát-ne-'e-betčí'ibo
     this:ACC IZR-order-ACC deliver-PRF all-PL   there out-go-FUT-EV-for
     He gave this order so that all would go out of there.

As the following examples illustrate, such subject noun phrases may come in distinct positions within a sentence. The normal Subject-Object-Verb order, seen in examples (38) and (39), calls attention to the goat's action, whereas the inverted order in example (40) highlights the psychological effect that the experience has on the man.

(38) húu'u čibá'ato héno-m-po   'áe-t mámma-ka 'á'a
     that goat   shoulder-PL-on it-on hand-PPL him
     té'eb^{w}a-táite-k pusí-m-po yéka-po tén-po
     lick-begin-PRF eye-PL-in nose-in mouth-in
     The goat put its forelegs on the man's shoulders and began to lick him in his eyes, his nose, and his mouth.

(39) húnak 'íntok húu'u čibá'ato 'á-u   nótte-k
     then CNJ   that goat   him-to return-PRF
     Then the goat came back to him.

(40) 'áma kíkte   húu'u yoéme kía 'ám 'ukúle-ka 'ám híkkaha tú'i-si
     there stand:SG that man   only them like-PPL them hear   good-AVR
     The man stopped and listened with fascination.

Demonstratives also occur in discontinuous constructions with the nominals that they designate. In example (41) the demonstrative **húme'e** is fronted by the topic pivot **'íntok** *and*. It modifies the plural noun **taáka-m** *fruit* which follows **'íntok**.

(41) húme 'íntok taáka-m yóh-ti-taite-k
those and fruit-PL fall-CON-begin-PRF
And the fruit began to fall from the trees.

As noted earlier, demonstratives are marked for both singular and plural and are used in numerous roles in Yaqui grammar. In example (42) a plural demonstrative **húme'e** is used as an attributive in a subject noun phrase, whereas a distal form **huná-e** is used as the object of the accompaniment postposition **mak**.

(42) húme'e wóki-m-san káa bétte-si bó'o-hoóa huná-e-mak 'aman yépsa-k
those foot-PL-EXP NEG heavy-AVR road-abide that-CON-with there arrive-PRF
And his lightfooted legs finished the trip.

Demonstratives may also serve as modifiers in various kinds of phrasal constructions. The accusative form **hunaka'a** in sentence (43) modifies the nominal **wepu'ula** *one* which is also marked in the accusative and functions as the head of the phrase. In sentence (44) the nominative singular **hunáa'a** qualifies the subject noun **yoéme** *man*.

(43) sí'ime 'áma mátču-k hunáka'a wépu'ulai-k 'áma 'átb^{W}a-ka mátču-k
all there dawn-PRF that:ACC one-ACC there laugh:at-PPL dawn-PRF
Everyone was still wide awake when morning came, all laughing at that one man when dawn came.

(44) béha túa 'átb^{W}a-wa hunáa'a yoéme
well indeed laugh:at-PSV that man
Well, that man was really a riot.

Quantifiers may occur in the same noun phrase along with a demonstrative and an attributive adjective in that order. In (45) the demonstrative used is the specific, distal plural **wáme'e**.

(45) sí'ime wáme'e 'ilí 'uúsi-m kée woói wásuk-te-me
all those little child-PL not:yet two year-VR-NZR
all the little children who were not yet two years old

The demonstrative form **'inía** appears to help mark contrastive focus in sentence (46).

(46) née hiókoe káa=ne túa 'áa 'etého 'ó'oben táa 'inía
me excuse NEG=I indeed able converse although but this

'etého-i-mak ne yéu-tóm-te-ka 'emó-u 'a'a téuwaa-k
tell-PPL-with I out-stomach-VR-PPL you:PL-to it tell-PRF
Excuse me, although I am not able to tell stories very well, yet having been born with this story, I tell it to you.

Yaqui employs both the nominative and accusative forms of demonstratives in comparative constructions. The target of the comparison is marked with the nominative form, as seen in examples (47)–(49), and the standard of the comparison is marked in the accusative. There are a variety of constructions marking the standard of comparison. The postpositional object form **hunáe** is used with **-bépa** in example (47). The demonstrative may also function as a determiner in the noun phrase that is the object of the postposition as seen in example (48). Finally, in example (49) the accusative form **hunáka'a** serves as the object of the postposition.

(47) 'iníi'i hunáe-bépa tú'ii
this that-above good
This is better than that.

(48) 'ii'i kári   hunáe kári-ta-bépa   čé'a b^wé'u
    this house that   house-POS-above more big
    This house is bigger than that house.

(49) 'iníi'i hunáka'a-bépa čé'a káa-tú'ii
    this   that:ACC-above more not-good
    This is worse than that.

4.2. Demonstratives in discourse

Demonstratives are used in subtle ways in discourse. The topicalized non-proximal pausal form **hunáa'a** is used in sentence (50) below, taken from a Yaqui folktale.

(50) heéwi 'áčai-t-iia   hunáa'a pahkó'olaa   káa 'áa yé'ee-me
    yes   sir-CON-say that   festal:dancer NEG able dance-NZR

    moró-ta-wi   bibá-m   mabét-ču-ka-i
    Moor-ACC-to cigarette-PL receive-CPL-PPL-PPL
    "Yes sir!" the festal dancer who was not able to dance said to the Moor who contracted him, as he received the cigarettes.

From the same folktale, the distal form **wáa'a** is used within a direct quotation in sentence (51), showing that the demonstratives within a single discourse may reflect two different levels of organization, i.e., the spatial relationships signalled by the narrator as clues to orient his hearers in contrast to the spatial relationships signalled by quoted speakers for orienting their addressees who are also participants in the narrative.

(51) heéwi 'áčali-m 'á'abo=su 'áu wée-'et-ia wáa'a pahkó'olaa báhi taéwai-ta wéye-o
    yes   sir-PL here=HL RFL go-CON-say that festal:dancer three day-POS go-when
    Yes, sirs, the festal dancer said he'd come here in three days.

The context of discourse structure clearly relates to the usage of demonstratives as heads of noun phrases. When the antecedent is known or has already been introduced in the text of some story, some demonstratives and quantifiers function as full noun phrases as in sentences (52) and (53).

(52) 'iníi'i sí'ime-ku-t hú'uneiyaa-wa-k
    this   all-CON-on know-PSV-PRF
    This was known everywhere.

(53) hunáka'a 'enčím 'itó-t ta'aa-ne-'e-betčí'ibo
    that:ACC your us-on know-FUT-EV-for
    So that you might know this about us.

More neutral forms of the demonstratives are used to refer to persons who have already been "on stage" in the text. Thus, the nominative form **húu'u** is used as the determiner for the subject noun phrase in example (54) in which the salient character is taking his leave of the scene in question.

(54) heéwi 'áčai 'enčí   te bó'o-bít-nee-t-iia   húu'u
    yes   sir you:ACC we lay-see-FUT-CON-say that

    moóro siká-a-ri   siká=ne Liós-e'ém-čanía-bu
    Moor go:SG-PPL-PPL went=I God-you-hello-HRT:PL
    "Yes sir, we will wait for you," said the Moor, as he was taking his leave, "Goodbye, I'm going now."

Noun phrases with the neutral nominative form of the demonstrative occur post-verbally at the end of episodes in narrative texts, as in sentences (55) and (56). This latter sentence illustrates a conjoined multiplex subject in which the conjoined subjects are linked by the use of the postposition **-mak** *with*.

(55) 'á'a sís-sís-su-ka   siíka   tesó-u lúula pólak-ti-síme   húu'u čibá'ato
     him RDP-urinate-CPL-PPL go:PAST cave-to straight oblique-CON-go:SG that goat
     Having finished urinating on him, the goat went straight back to the cave, loping sideways.

(56) húnen=su tesó-po lú'u-te-k   húu'u labén híawa-i
     thus=EMP cave-to end-VR-PRF   that violin sound-PPL

   'áapa čibá'ato-mak náu   lú'u-te-k
   harpa goat-with   together end-VR-PRF
   The violin music in the cave thus ended and the harp music and the goat all ended together right there.

Finally, the proximal demonstrative form **'iní'i** is conventionally used as one means for closing off a narrative text. The form of this conventional expression is seen in example (57).

(57) 'iníi'i híba
     this   only
     This is it.

ADVERBIAL DEMONSTRATIVES

1.0. Introduction

The demonstrative pronouns of Yaqui, discussed in the previous chapter of this grammar, designate persons or entities that are located in various ways with respect to the speaker and the hearer. In this section, we discuss the adverbial demonstratives. These designate the locations within which given entities interact or locations within which particular states and relations exist. Both classes of grammatical morphemes thus overlap in their morphological structures as well as in their meanings. This overlap also carries over into the set of deictic manner adverbs.

2.0. The semantic parameters

The relevant semantic parameters that figure in the usages of Yaqui adverbial demonstratives include, first of all, the relative distance between the speaker and the entity that the adverbial demonstrative designates. Secondly, it includes the degree of specificity that the speaker attaches to the referent. The third semantic parameter is the directionality of the movement of the characters in the event vis-à-vis the speaker's conceived vantage point.

2.1. The distance parameter

The basic overlap between demonstrative pronouns and adverbial demonstratives in Yaqui consists of marking the relative distance between a speaker and the entity that he has in mind, if not in sight. Yaqui, like several other Uto-Aztecan languages, employs a threefold distinction of relative distance. These degrees of distance can be labelled proximal, medial, and distal, with proximal locations being those closest to the speaker and distal locations being those farthest away from the speaker. Medial locations are those in between, usually within eyeshot of the speaker, and often being those points of intense focal attention.

Category	PROXIMAL	MEDIAL	DISTAL
	i	u	a
Demonstrative pronoun	'íi'i	húu'u	wáa'a
	'íme'e	húme'e	wáme'e
Adverbial demonstrative	'ím	húm	'áman
	'ími'i	húmu'u	'ámman
			hunáman
Manner adverb	'ínen	húnen	hunálen
		'iníen	hunúen

Table 27. Categories of Yaqui deictics

Morphologically, the distance distinctions are marked in demonstrative pronouns, adverbial demonstratives and manner adverbs by the vocalic nucleii **i**, **u**, and **a**, respectively. These morphological and semantic distinctions are all summarized in Table 27.

2.2. Degrees of specificity

The demonstrative adverbial forms are distinguished along other lines also, including the relative degree of specificity that is attached to a particular location. Thus, the locative form **'ím** means "here" in a relatively general sense, whereas its pausal counterpart **'ími'i** can be glossed as "right here." The difference in usage between the two forms can be stated as follows: the neutral form is **'ím** and the speaker ordinarily uses it unless something special requires him to specifically signal to the hearer the specific location to which he is referring. For example, if the speaker is instructing someone to set something down, usually he would express himself as in example (1) without employing any accompanying gestures for the hearer's aid. However, under special circumstances (perhaps exasperation with his helper's inability to discern the desired location), he would both point out the place precisely for the hearer and use the pausal form **'ími'i**, as in example (2).

(1) 'ím 'á'a yéča
here it put
Put it here.

(2) 'ími'i 'á'a yéča
here:specific it put
Put it right here (where I am pointing).

As a second example, the neutral form **'ím** would be used by the speaker in making a matter of fact comment about someone's location at a previous point in time as illustrated by example (3). This locational information, however, might be quite surprising to the addressee, who would, in turn, both register his surprise and seek a confirmation of that information by the use of the pausal form **'ími'i**, as in example (4).

(3) hú'u Hoan 'ím 'a'áne-n tuúka
that John here be-PCN yesterday
John was here yesterday.

(4) 'ími'i
here:specific
You mean, right here?

2.3. The directional forms with -i

Beyond these basic forms discussed above, Yaqui employs an almost bewildering array of morphemically related but more complex forms. For example, the adverbial demonstrative forms **'áman, 'ámman, hunáman** all occur with a suffix **-i**, which, in certain contexts, has a clear directional meaning. This suffix also occurs with each of the manner adverbial forms, but its meaning in such cases is not clear and it may be related historically to the stative **-i** rather than to the directional **-i**.

3.0. Usages in given situations

The rhetorical ends that the speaker has in mind determines the choice of which form to use in a particular situation. Particular factors that enter into such choices are explainable in terms of information gleaned from a number of domains: for example, adverbial demonstrative forms ending in V'V are more likely to occur in phrase final or sentence final position than they are to occur sentence initially. Many of the forms are also morphemically complex, built up from combining one identifiable morpheme with another.

3.1. The proximal forms

The proximal form **'ím** often designates the speaker's location at the time of the speech-act as in sentence (5). It may also anchor a conceived pathway whose origin is construed as the speaker's location, as in sentences (6) and (7).

(5) 'ím né 'usí-hamut-ta haríu-si-sime
here I child-woman-ACC hunt-RDP-go
I am here looking for a little girl.

(7) 'ím lúula wée-nee
here straight go:SG-FUT
Go straight this way.

(6) 'énč=a'a mák-nee, 'ím 'énči 'ané-o
you=it give-FUT here you:ACC be-if
I will give it to you, if you are here at that time.

The proximal form **'ími'i** is used to indicate an even more precise region anchored to the speaker's position at the time of the speech-act, as in sentences (8) and (9).

(8) 'ími'i 'á'a bít-nee
here:specific it see-FUT
You will see it right here.

(9) 'ími'i 'á'a yéča húka'a pú'ato
here:specific it place that:ACC plate
Put that plate right here.

The proximal form **'iním** prototypically designates the speaker's location at the time of his speech-act as in example (10). It may also refer to a specific area tied to the speaker's location, but one of indefinite extension throughout the physical terrain as in (11). This same adverbial demonstrative is used in the even more abstract domain of discourse space to anchor one statement to another specific one as exemplified by example (12).

(10) 'émpo káa hú'uneiyaa-n 'iním 'ín ané-'u
you not know-PCN here my be-GND
Didn't you know that I was here?

(11) 'iním híak-bʷía-po né hó'aa-k
here Yaqui-land-in I home-have
I live here in Yaqui land.

(12) 'iním 'aáyu-k húu'u lútu'uria
here be-PRF that truth
Here you have the truth.

All the adverbial demonstrative forms ending in **-mi'i** are the most specific ones in terms of the locations that they designate. In example (13) the proximal form **'iními'i** designates metaphorically the earth upon which we live.

(13) ínimi'i bʷan-bʷía-po
here cry-ground-in
here, in this valley of tears

The proximal sets of demonstrative pronouns, adverbial demonstratives and the manner adverbs all have more complex forms derived by prefixing to them the morpheme **'iiy-** *precisely*. In all cases, the semantic result is to signal a high degree of specificity to the identity of the person, entity, location, or manner of activity under discussion. The basic contrast among these derived forms is given in Table 28.

Demonstrative pronoun	'iiy-íi'i	*precisely this one*
Adverbial demonstrative	'iiy-ími'i	*precisely here*
Manner adverb	'iiy-ínien-i	*precisely this way*

Table 28. Proximal deictics

In its use with the demonstrative pronouns, **'iiy-** can be used to signal precision with respect to both singular and plural entities, which may further be construed as subjects, objects or possessors. Examples (14) and (15) illustrate these points. In (14) **'iíy-** is seen as a part of a more complex nominative plural demonstrative **'iíyime'e**, whereas the accusative form of **'iíy-** in its demonstrative use is illustrated by example (15).

(14) 'iíy-ime'e čé'a tú'u-híapse-k-an
precisely:this-these more good-heart-have-PCN
These particular people were more noble hearted.

(15) 'in hála'i 'iíy-ika'a 'úhbʷán-ta née yá'a-ria
my friend precisely:this-ACC favor-ACC me do-APL
My friend, do precisely this favor for me.

Sentence (16) illustrates the strictly locative usage of **'iíy-** in its combination with the adverbial demonstrative **'imi'i**; the resulting form can be glossed as "right here at this precise location."

(16) 'iíy-imi'i kéka wít-ti-po
precisely-here stand line-ACC-on
Stand precisely on the line.

A more extended version of **'iíy-** is given in sentence (17) in which it combines with the manner adverb **'ilen** *thus*. The resulting combination can be glossed "precisely in this manner."

(17) 'iíy-ilen-po suma'a-naa 'íka'a wikósa-ta 'áttea-k-ame
precisely-thus-in tie-FUT:PSV this:ACC belt-ACC own-PRF-NZR
The owner of this belt will be tied up precisely in this way.

The locative adverb **'iíyimi'i** *precisely right here* is the most specific of the various proximal adverbial demonstrative forms. It is bimorphemic and illustrates nicely the principle that ideas that go together are also placed together linguistically. This is called Behagel's law and its importance is increasingly being recognized by linguists (cf. Haiman 1985:106, 238; Langacker 1987:361). To make things more precise, morphemes combine with one another because they overlap with one another semantically. However, the overlap is partial, since each one has a unique contribution to make to the overall construction.

In the case in point, our adverbial demonstrative **'iíyimi'i** consists of the preposed specificative **'iíy-** and a following proximal adverbial demonstrative **-ími'i** "right here." Taken together, the locative meaning "precisely here" of **'iíy-** reinforces the meaning "here" of **-mi'i** to result in a complex form which can be glossed as "right here in this precise location." The particular entity whose location is designated by **'iíy-** is not specified at all in the composite meaning of the adverbial **'iíyimi'i**. This backgrounding of reference to a discrete entity allows the Yaqui speaker to apply **'iíy-** to even more abstract entities.

The distal form **húm** is also used to designate a specific location, as in examples (18) and (19).

(18) húm né káa wéama-n
there I NEG walk-PCN
I was not walking there.

(19) yoéme húm tekípanoa
person there work
A man is working there.

3.2. The -n- forms

The adverbial forms that contain an intervocalic nasal **-n-** show semantic contrasts that correlate with the quality of the following vowel, which may be either **u** or **a** (cf. also DEMONSTRATIVES, p. 205). In sentence (20) the use of **-nu-** correlates with a location that is at the endpoint of a path from an unspecified location distal to one that is an "onstage" location for the purposes of the speaker. These **-nu-** locations are ones that are usually within the field of vision of the speaker as in sentence (21).

(20) hámut hunúm b^wána-ka yépsa-k
woman there:specific cry-PPL arrive-PRF
A woman arrived there crying.

(21) hunúm-uni 'á'a teéka
there-indefinite it put
Put it down there somewhere.

The medial distance form **húmu'u** designates specific locations that are generally within the speaker's field of vision as in sentence (22).

(22) húmu'u káa wéama há'ani hú'u Hóan
there:specific NEG walk perhaps that John
Isn't that John walking yonder?

The medial distance **hunúmu'u** relates to a line that runs at right angles to the speaker's line of sight and divides the speaker's visual field into two distinct areas, one at the speaker's side of that boundary line, the other at the far side of that boundary line. In sentence (23) the location of a road that the speaker is looking at is construed as extending along this boundary line.

(23) 'ém boó'o hunúmu'u bó'o-ka
your road there:at:perifery lay-PPL
That's your road, right over there.

The distal form **hunáma** can be glossed as "toward there" or "further away." In sentence (24) it is used to signal motion from a distal location toward some other location even further removed from the speaker's initial reference point. The destination at the river can be viewed as being in an area outside the area between the speaker's location and the conceived distal location said to be the initial location of the person in motion.

(24) hunáma 'íntok bát^we-u kó'om-siíka
there and river-to down-go:PAST
And from there he went down to the river.

The related form **hunáma'a** can designate a location completely out of sight, which again is compatible with the notion of the speaker's field of vision being a bounded area, with the possibility of defining locations of conceived entities as being either within this area or outside of it. In sentence (25) in connection with the indefinite locative **háksa** *somewhere*, it designates a specific distal location.

(25) hunáma'a háksa hakía-po káte-ka 'ám bʷá'e
there:distal somewhere creek-in sit-PPL them eat
Sitting down somewhere there in a creek, he ate them.

The distal form **hunámani**, exemplified in sentence (26), is another way that Yaqui has for marking out of sight, distal locations. The final vowel of this form is probably the directional suffix **-i**.

(26) hunámani wáh-bʷía-po tekipánoa
there:yonder field-land-in work
He is working off yonder in the field.

4.0. The wa- forms

Yaqui has another complete series of adverbial demonstratives which are built on the morpheme **wa-** in combination with other following morphemes. In example (27) **waé** *there* serves as the object of the postposition **-tána** *side*. The stressed **é** is likely the postpositional base referred to in DEMONSTRATIVES pp. 205–207. This analysis leaves us with the morpheme **wa-**, which may be glossed as "beyond the boundary line." Topographic features such as rivers provide natural boundary lines and barriers in terms of which usages such as those in example (27) are based.

(27) kaáčin=te waé-tána 'an-née
no:way-we there-side be-FUT
There's no way we can get to the other side.

The adverbial demonstrative **wá'am** can be glossed as "by there" or "past there" as in examples (28) and (29). In its strictly locative usages as in example (30), it can be glossed "off yonder."

(28) húme'e né-t wá'am káte-me káa né-u te-tébo-te
these:NOM me-at beyond go:PL-NZR NEG me-to RDP-greet-VR
Those who go past me do not greet me.

(29) né-t wá'am nát-čá'a-ka kaáte
me-on past row-suspend-PPL go:PL
One after another, they go on past me.

(30) siíka táa káa wá'am 'á'a tékil e-u-bíča
go:SG:PAST but NEG off:there it work it-to-site
He left, but he did not go off yonder to his work.

This adverbial demonstrative also has several extended usages in combination with other adverbials. In example (31) it combines with **hunáma** to mean "properly." This seems to suggest that the meaning of **hunáma** is defined in respect to an abstract bounded area and **wá'am** designates the area of indefinite extension outside that area. If we can assume that the speaker's perspective is from the middle of the bounded area, then we could reasonably see how **hunáma** designates the boundary of the entire area of appropriate behavior centered on the speaker.

(31) hunáma'a-wá'am 'á'a hóo-nee-'e-tea-ka téhwaa-ri
there-past it do-FUT-EV-QUO-PPL tell-PPL
I was told that he would do it properly.

The sequence **káa-hak-wá'am** is conventionally used with the verb meaning "to see" to mean "not be disorderly," as illustrated by example (32), or "carelessly" as in example (33).

(32) húu'u píhkan káa-hak-wá'am bít-naa
DEM bishop NEG-somewhere-pass:over see-FUT:PSV
The bishop must not be disorderly.

(33) hú'u 'iníka'a tékia-k-ame káa hák-wá'am bít-naa
that this:ACC work-have-NZR NEG somewhere-NZR see-FUT:PSV
The person who has this work must not be seen acting carelessly.

Two more adverbial demonstrative forms related to **wá'am** are **wá'ami**, given in example (34) and **wána** illustrated in (35). The form **wá'ami** can be glossed as "off yonder" or "by there," deriving its directional meaning from the suffix **-i** *toward, following a path*.

(34) haí=sa 'a-'án-wa wá'ami
how=Q RDP-be-PSV off:there
How are things going off yonder?

(35) wána=te pá'aku 'á'a kečá-'a-nee 'itépo=te 'íntok náu-hinkó'ola-rók-nee
there=we outside him stand-EV-FUT we=we and together-race-QUO-FUT
We will stand him off yonder, and we will say that we are going to run a race.

5.0. The 'áma series of adverbs

The complexity of the adverbial demonstrative system of Yaqui is shown further by its use of another morphological series of forms built on the basic root **'áma**. The set is given here in Table 29.

Proximal	'áma	*there (within eyeshot)*
Medial	'áman	*right there*
Distal	'ámani	*off there further away*
Maximal distal	'ámmani	*way off yonder*

Table 29. Series of ama- adverbs

A given usage of a Yaqui adverbial demonstrative obviously involves more than simply specifying the distance between the speaker's location and the location where the narrated events unfold. In sentence (36), for example, the first reference to the location of Gabriel Sparrow's path is made by the form **'ámani**, which refers back to the locations specified by the two postpositional phrases that begin the sentence and can be glossed as "passing by there." The second adverbial demonstrative **'áma** is found in the subordinate locative clause and can be glossed as "there where." The third adverbial demonstrative **'áman** is in the sentence final independent clause. It takes in the entire scene as its scope, giving a global perspective on the location and can be glossed "there off yonder." The point to be noted here is that all three adverbial demonstratives refer to the same location in the conceived space within which the events of the folktale unfold.

(36) 'akí-sóo'o-ku sebíi-po 'áman-i káa 'áa 'áma réh-ti-mačí-ku 'áman wée
pitahaya-thicket-in cactus-in there-by not able there walk-PPL-appear-in there go
He went through the pitahaya thickets and chollas, places that didn't seem passable.

In many contexts, such as that of example (37), **'áman** designates the addressee's location.

(37) néhpo=su 'áman 'emó-u yéu-yebíh-nee
I=EMP there you:PL-to out-arrive-FUT
I will come there to you.

In examples (38) and (39) **'áman** refers back to a specific location previously mentioned in a conversation, one well established in the awareness of the interlocutors in the speech situation.

(38) 'é'e né káa 'áman wée-bae
no I not there go-DSD
No, I don't plan to go there.

(39) 'enčí 'áman weáma-o ne 'enčí bíča-k
you:ACC there walk-when I you:ACC see-PRF
I saw you when you were walking there.

The location that **'áman** refers to may be overtly expressed in a sentence such as (40).

(40) wáaria-bétana 'é-u bíttua-wa-k néhpo 'áman=e'e nói-ti-sae-wa ne-mák wée-nee
guard-from you-to send-PSV-PRF I there-you go-PPL-IMP-PSV me-with go-FUT
I have been sent from the "guardia"; you are ordered to go there, you will go with me.

The adverbial **'ámmani** can be glossed "way off yonder." The geminate **-mm-** can be construed as a kind of reduplication which intensifies the degree of distance involved. This implies a fourfold distinction along the distance scale, the maximum that appears to be found in the Uto-Aztecan languages (cf. Langacker 1977:104). In short, **'ammani** *way off yonder* signals the most distal of all the locational relationships encoded in Yaqui. In the second clause of sentence (41), the adverbial demonstrative **'áma** refers back to **'ámmani** of the first clause.

(41) káa-te-k   'ámman-i 'intok hunúen káa-te-ka,   'áma hó'aa-k
     house-make-PRF there-DIR and   thus   house-VR-PPL there live-PRF
     He built a house way off yonder, and so having built it, he lived there.

Adverbial demonstratives are often elaborated by other kinds of adverbial clauses that immediately follow them in a sentence. In (42) the adverbial **hunáma'a** is elaborated by the postpositional phrase **'áme-u káa mékka** *not far from them*.

(42) hunáma'a 'áme-u káa-mékka b^wé'u báu-ba'á-k   mánek
     there   them-to not-far   big lake-water-ACC lay
     There not far from/to them was a lake.

Adverbial demonstratives can also serve as postpositional bases, as in example (43), in which the adverbial demonstrative **hunáman** refers to a specific location which is the end point of the discourse participant's path.

(43) kúta-bankó-m-mak lópola 'á'a núk-wéiyaa hunáman-táhtia
     wood-seat-PL-with beside it   carry-go   there-until
     He carried it alongside the wooden benches up to there.

The adverbial **hunáman** designates specific locations known to both the speaker and the addressee. Specific locations are not necessarily those within the visual field of the interlocutors of the speech situation nor do they need to be identified overtly within the domain of the sentence in which **hunáman** is used, for example, see sentence (44), although they may well be spelled out overtly, as is done in sentence (45).

(44) hunáman 'émpo téhwaa-tu-nee hitása 'ém hóo-nee-'u
     there   you   tell-VR-FUT   what   your do-FUT-GND
     There, you will be told what you are to do.

(45) hunáka'a hí'osia-ta hunáman 'á'a b^wíh-wa-ka-'apo,   'á'a 'ú'aa-wa-k
     that:ACC paper-ACC there   his seize-PSV-PPL-GND him take-away-PSV-PRF
     The paper was taken away from him, there in the place where he was seized.

The directional counterpart **hunámani** may be elaborated by a specific place name as in example (46).

(46) hunámani bibá-himáa-ri-wi   yoéme 'áma
     off:yonder cigarette-throw-NZR-to man   there

     hó'aa-k-an   pahkó'olaa-taka-i táa tú'i-si polóobe
     house-VR-PCN festal:dancer-PPL but good-AVR poor
     Off yonder in Discarded Cigarettes, there used to live a man who was a ritual dancer for the Pascual fiesta, but he was very poor.

Specific locations may also be elaborated by an overt locative noun, a locative phrase, or even a locative adverbial clause. In example (47) the location designated by **húm** was also within the eyeshot of both speaker and hearer, i.e., Castro and Dedrick.

(47) húm makó'očin-ta   wéek-a'u   b^wé'u hó'aa-raa-tu-ka-n
     there guamuchil-POS stand-GND big   house-AZR-VR-PPL-PCN
     There, where the guamuchil tree is standing, used to be a big town.

The adverbial **hunáma'a** designates a nonspecific location, i.e., the exact location is either not known to either speaker or hearer, or the specifics of the location are not relevant to interlocutors. The nonspecificness of the location is spelled out overtly by the adverbial modifier **háksa** *somewhere* as in example (48).

(48) hunáma'a háksa baká-túu'u-ku tó'e
there somewhere carrizo-thicket-in lie:down:PL
They slept there somewhere in a carrizo thicket.

6.0. The adverbial 'omó-tči "off to one side"

The locative adverb **'omó** occurs in our data only in combination with the postposition **-tči/-t**, which is glossed variously as "in," "on," or "at" and with the verbalizing suffix **-la**. In construction with **-tči/-t**, it conveys the meaning "somewhere else" as in example (49). In its usage with **-la**, it means "off to one side" in a metaphorical sense as in example (50). The shift of tone placement on **'omó** correlates with its distinct class membership in these two sentences. The form with the high tone on the second syllable is a a body part nominal object of a postposition. The form with the high tone on the first syllable is a derived adverb.

(49) 'omó-t 'á'a tóha
one:side-to it take
Take it off somewhere else.

(50) húka'a nésau-ta 'ómo-la tawáa-k
that:ACC law-ACC one:side-VR leave-PRF
He disregarded the law.

7.0. The manner adverbs

Yaqui employs a variety of manner adverbs that can each be glossed "thus" but whose usage is determined by many of the same concepts that lie behind the usage of the adverbial demonstratives, e.g., the notions of distance and boundary limits. The basic distance, directional and manner distinctions are reflected in the forms given in Table 30.

Proximal	'ínen	*this way*	'iníen-i	*here*
Distal	húnen	*that way* *in this way*	hunúen-i	*there* *in that way*
Maximal Distal	hunálen	*that way*	hunáleni	*there (way) over there* *in that other way*

Table 30. Deictic manner adverbs

With regard to these manner adverbs, the distinction between **'ínen, húnen, 'iníen, hunúen,** and **hunálen** is a delightful example of how aspects of the speech-act situation take on sufficient salience that they get overtly coded onto language. Yaqui has at least six ways to express the notion "thus" and they reflect the degree of distance between the interlocutors in the speech situation and the particular interaction in focus. The proximal form of "thus" can be glossed as "just as I am doing it here." The medial form of "thus" can be glossed as "just as that person right over there is doing it," and the distal form can be glossed as "just as that person off yonder does it."

Among the locative adverbs is the form **'ámani,** which retains some of the distal indefinite locational meaning and has acquired the implicational meaning "just as you like," as illustrated by example (51). The use of **'ínen** as a quotative procomplement is shown by example (52), and the use of **húnen** as the complement of a mental-act verb is illustrated in (53).

(51) 'ém 'a'a wáata-'apo 'ámani
your it want-GND there
the way you want it or *just the way you want it*

(52) 'ínen 'éa-n yé-'a-kéča-'a-bae-n
thus think-PCN out-him-stand:SG-EV-DSD-PCN
This is what he was thinking; he was wanting to release him.

(53) 'éme'e 'íntok káa húnen 'éa-k
you:PL and not thus think-PRF
But that was not your will.

Manner adverbs can function as the entire complement of psychological predicates as in sentence (54) in which **béna** is used as the main verb of the sentence. The most frequent psychological predicate that takes a manner adverb as its complement is **'ea** *to think"* as in example (55).

(54) hunúen-tu-béna
thus-VR-like
It seems like it is that way.

(55) húnen 'á'a 'éa-o=su hunáma'a téh-po yóo-čibá'ato tósai-ka čukúi-ka
thus his think-when=EMP there cave-in enchanted-goat white-being black-being

tána-la b^{w}ási-a-ka, káa 'awá-ka, kía tét-tebé-m náka-k tét-tebé-m
curve-ADJ tail-CON-having NEG horn-having only RDP-long-PL ear-having RDP-long-PL

púh-séebe-k bátte b^{w}iía-u núki-m himsé-ka 'á-u yéu-búite
eye-lash-having nearly ground-to reach-PL beard-having him-to out-run
As he was going along with these thoughts, a black and white enchanted goat, hornless, with his tail curved over his back, with long ears, very long eyelashes, and a beard that reached nearly to the ground, came running out toward him.

Manner adverbs in Yaqui are not restricted to only designating interactions located somewhere within physical or conceived space, but they can also clearly designate discrete objects. The contrast between these two functions is illustrated by sentences (56) and (57). In both cases a proximal form of the manner adverb serves as object of the postposition **béna** *like*; however, the form of the manner adverb is slightly different in each case and the postposition is also marked differently. In sentence (56) the manner adverb is **'inílen** and **béna** is marked with a second postposition **-ku**. This suggests that the final **-n** of **'inilen** is a reflex of the Proto-Uto-Aztecan ***-na** *place of*. The gloss of sentence (56) reinforces the fact that we are speaking of a location in physical space when we use **'inílen**. On the other hand, in sentence (57) the speaker used the form **'iníle** and marked the postposition with the accusative suffix **-k,** clearly indicating that he was talking about a discrete object, a construal fully consonant with the prototypical meaning of **wáata** *to want*.

(56) 'inílen-béna-ku née yéu-tómte-k
thus-like-in I out-born-PRF
I was born in a place like this place.

(57) 'iníle-béna-k né wáata
this-like-ACC I want
I want one like this.

A similar contrast is seen in the usage of the manner adverb **hunúen** in sentence (58) and the accusative form of the demonstrative **hunú** in sentence (59). As the glosses suggest, the manner adverb designates the speaker's presumptuousness in his interaction with someone else in a given speech-act, whereas **hunú-ka** designates the actual content of the speech-act, i.e., the words that the speaker actually used.

(58) 'émpo kaábe-ta hiníle hunúen 'á-u híu-nee-ka-i
you none-ACC fear thus him-to say-FUT-PPL-PPL
Aren't you afraid of anyone, talking to him like that?

(59) 'émpo káa 'á'a hiníle hunú-ka 'á-u teuwaa-nee-ka-i
you not him fear that-ACC him-to say-FUT-PPL-PPL
Aren't you afraid of him, having said that to him?.

The manner adverb **húnen** serves as an appropriate conclusion marker, making reference backwards to the stated unexpected result of something. In sentence (60) Castro used it to explain why he left a good paying job on the railroad and took up another job with the circus.

(60) húmak húnen čúp-ia-tu-ka-n
perhaps thus fulfill-NZR-VR-PPL-PCN
Perhaps it was so destined (for me).

A highly marked anaphoric conclusion marker consists of the manner adverb **'inílen** as one constituent in construction with the verbalizing element **tu** and the perfective suffix **-k,** all of which jointly serves as a sentence initial adverbial subordinate clause that anchors the main clause that follows it to previous clauses in the discourse which served to state the grounds for the conclusion. Sentence (61) is a typical example of this construction.

(61) 'inílen-tu-k   káa-wótti   'emé'e
     thus-VR-PRF   not-agitated you:PL
     Therefore you should be calm.

A demonstrative adverb may occur in construction with a postposition to carry out a pronominal function in a sentence. In example (62) the manner adverb **'inen** *thus* is the base for attaching the postposition **-po** *in*. The composite structure serves as an anticipatory reference to quoted material.

(62) 'ínen-po béha ču'ú-ta-u   hiía-k
     thus-in   well dog-CON-to   say-PRF
     He talked to the dog in this way.

8.0. Temporal adverbs

Temporal adverbs are also related to the demonstratives and to the adverbial demonstratives in various ways. They express a number of ideas such as "today," "now," and "then." Two forms of **'í'an** *here* are used in sentences (63) and (64) as temporal adverbs, whereas **húnak** *then* is used as a temporal adverb in sentence (65).

(63) 'í'an=su   née 'á'a núk-sim-nee
     today=EXP I   it   carry-go-FUT
     Well, today I will take/carry it away.

(64) 'í'ani né túa   kaíta   hóo-máči
     today I indeed nothing do-ABS
     There is absolutely nothing for me to do today.

(65) húnak béha kóa-po   yéu 'á'a núk-sáha-k
     then   well corral-in   out it   carry-go:PL-PRF
     Then they carried it out of the corral.

Temporal concepts are also commonly expressed through quantifier phrases that are composed of a numeral and a temporal noun root that together serve as the object of a postposition, as seen in sentence (66).

(66) báhi   taéwa-ta 'á'abo 'áu   yebíh-ne-'et-iía
     three day-POS   here   RFL   arrive-FUT-CON-say
     When three days are past, he says that he will be here.

QUANTIFIERS

1.0. Introduction

Quantifiers are a special class of modifiers that indicate how many occurrences of an entity are involved in an interaction or participate in a complex relation. They also indicate degrees of extension within particular domains such as those of three dimensional physical space and time. In both Quantifier + Noun constructions and in discontinuous constructions in Yaqui they take number and case markings of the sort used with adjectives which agree with the number and case markings on the nouns that they modify. There are also syntactic restrictions on the usages of quantifiers, and the nature of their semantics reflects itself in interesting ways in Yaqui grammar.

2.0. The inventory

Table 31 presents a listing of all the morphemically simple quantifiers except for the numerals, which are described in NUMERALS, pp. 229–233 of this grammar.

seénu	*one*
huébena	*much, many (usually people)*
bú'uu	*much, many (usually things)*
sí'ime	*all (people or things)*
haíki	*a quantity of people or things*
waáte	*some, others*
násuk	*half*
nóas	*half (full)*

Table 31. Morphemically simple quantifiers

3.0. Some semantic properties

Although quantifiers are not nouns per sè, characteristics of some quantifiers such as **sí'ime** *all* and **waáte** *some* seem to straddle both noun and quantifier categories. The other quantifiers also do this occasionally. But most generally these occur in discontinuous phrases where the noun has already been introduced.

The meanings of quantifier phrases may be further modified by using the negative particle **káa** *no, not*, the adjective **'ilí** *little*, or the adverb **bátte** *nearly* for specifying a finer precision of quantity. Some of these combinations are given in Table 32.

The negatives		The adjective 'íli		The adverbial bátte	
káa huébena	*not many*	'ilí huébena	*quite a few*	bátte sí'ime	*nearly all*
káa bú'uu	*not much*	'ilí bú'uu	*quite a bit*	bátte násuk	*nearly half*
káa sí'ime	*not all*	'ilí haíki	*a few*	bátte nóas	*nearly half (full)*
káa haíki	*not much*				

Table 32. Morphemically complex quantifiers

The quantifiers, both simple and morphemically complex, can be freely substituted in almost any kind of sentence that would call for the use of a quantifier. For example, sentences (1) and (2) show the contrast between **káa huébena** and **'íli huébena.**

(1) káa huébena haámuči-m 'áma tekipánoa-n
    not many   woman-PL   there work-PCN
    Not many women were working there.

(2) 'ilí huébena haámuči-m 'áma tekipanoa-n
    little many woman-PL   there work-PCN
    Quite a few women were working there.

223

The concept of fractions of a whole is difficult to express in Yaqui. There appear to be no terms that directly encode precise concepts such as "one-third," "two-fifths" and so on. Yaqui does employ two words to express the idea of "one half." These are **násuk** *middle, center, among* and **nóas** *half (full?)*. When **násuk** is modified by the adverbial demonstrative **'áman** *there* it means "half," as illustrated by sentence (3), where **násuk** precedes **'áman**.

(3) páan-im   násuk-'áman 'ám hám-ta-ka   'ám kúča'a-yaa-k
    bread-PL:ACC half-there them break-VR-PPL them spoon-make-PRF
    Breaking the bun in half, he used it as a spoon.

The opposite word order also occurs, as can be seen in example (4), in which **násuk** is more tightly bound to the noun **wásuktia** *year* with which it serves as object of the postpositional sequence **-meu-táahtia** *to-until*.

(4) 'áman násuk-wásuktia-m-meu-táhtia
    there half-year-PL-to-until
    up to half a year

Finally, a slightly different version of the formula for expressing the idea of "one half" is given in example (5). In this case, there is a short form of the adverbial demonstrative **'áma** followed by an inverted postpositional phrase composed of **násuk** and its object **taéwai** *day* marked with the accusative singular **-ta**.

(5) báhi   taéwai-m 'íntok 'áma násuk taéwai-ta
    three day-PL and   there half day-ACC
    three and a half days

The form **nóas** can be glossed as "half (full?)." In example (6) it is further specified by a following postpositional phrase which takes an adverbial **núki** as its object.

(6) tasá-ta   nú'u-ka   ba'á-čukúi-ta   nóas núki-ku 'á-u   'á'a tóha-k
    cup-ACC take-PPL water-black-ACC half up:to-in him-to it take-PRF
    Taking the cup half full of coffee, she brought it to him.

4.0. Use as modifiers

Quantifiers normally precede the nouns they modify, as shown by sentences (7) and (8). The quantifier **huébena** modifies a plural subject noun in sentence (7). In (8), **sí'ime** performs an analogous function.

(7) huébena haámuči-m 'áma tekipánoa-n   (8) sí'ime 'óuwo waáke
    many   woman-PL there work-PCN   all   plant dry
    Many women were working there.   *All the plants are drying out.*

In sentence (9) **waáte** is used in the sense of "some." Examples of this usage are uncommon.

(9) yokó   'iním 'áe-ku waté 'o'ówi-m 'á'abo yáhi-nee
    tomorrow here time-in some man-PL over:here arrive:PL-FUT
    At this time tomorrow, some men are coming over here.

Both a quantifier and a demonstrative may occur together as joint modifiers of the head noun in a noun phrase. As shown by sentence (10), the quantifier precedes the demonstrative in such phrases. Some of these combinations seem to be partitive in nature, as suggested by sentence (11).

(10) sí'ime húme'e wó'i-m   kía-k   tú'ure
     all   those coyote-PL delicious-ACC like
     All coyotes like what is delicious.

(11) sí'ime 'iníme'e be-béa-'u
     all   these   RDP-skin-VR
     He skins all of these.

Quantifiers such as **sí'ime** and **huébena** are implicitly plural, and thus do not ordinarily carry marking for nominative and accusative singular, as suggested by examples (12) and (13).

(12) káa sí'ime wikítči-m 'áa   'á'a mamáto
    not all   bird-PL be:able it imitate
    Not all birds can imitate it.

(13) húebena húya-m há'ab^we-ka-'apo né hó'aa-k
    many   tree-PL stand:PL-PPL-in I house-have
    I live where there are a lot of trees (standing).

Quantifiers can also be modifiers of incorporated nouns. In sentence (14), for example, the quantifier **buu'ú** *much* modifies the incorporated body part noun **čoóni** *hair* that is part of a verbal possessive construction

(14) bu'ú-m   čoóne-k
    much-PL:ACC hair-VR
    He has a lot of hair.

When a mass noun is construed as a locally defined or well-bounded entity, even it can be construed as a discrete entity. In this case, an implicitly plural quantifier may also be construed as a discrete entity and become eligible for marking with the accusative singular **-ta**. In sentence (15) the quantifier **huébena** occurs with an indefinite pronoun and illustrates the usual construal of an implicitly plural quantifier without any particular suffixal marking. In sentence (16), on the other hand, **sí'ime** designates the totality of one's possessions and the speaker conceives of this as a well-defined quantity which is subject to certain kinds of manipulations. Thus the quantifier is also construed in this way and is given a unitary meaning equivalent to one, which allows it to be treated grammatically as a discrete noun. Thus it gets marked with the accusative singular noun suffix **-ta**.

(15) huébena híta 'áma 'aáyu-k
    many   thing there be-PRF
    There are a lot of things there.

(16) sí'ime-ta húka'a 'ín híp^wee-'u-ta násuk-'áman né á'a ná'ikim-te-nee
    all-ACC that:ACC my have-GND-ACC half-there I it divide-VR-FUT
    I will divide everything I own in half.

The quantifiers **haíki** and **bú'uu** are used as modifiers in temporal phrases in examples (17) and (18). The role of **haíki** as modifier in a noun phrase is given in example (19).

(17) haíki   taéwa-ta wée-o   (19) haíki   muní-m=sa   'émpo wáata
    quantity day-ACC go-when   quantity bean-PL=INTERR you want
    after a few days had gone by   *How many beans do you want?*

(18) bú'uu tukáa-ria-m-po náa-búuh-ti
    many night-ABS-PL-in about-through-PPL
    through many nights

As modifiers, some of the quantifiers may also function as adverbs as illustrated by example (20).

(20) húebena naámu
    much   cloud
    It is very cloudy.

5.0. Nominal properties

Quantifiers, are similar to the demonstratives in that they display certain nominal-like characteristics. For one, quantifiers can serve as the head noun in noun phrases all by themselves. In this case they show nominative or accusative marking just like prototypical nouns. In example (21) the quantifier **sí'ime** *all* is marked with the plural suffix **-m** and functions as a plural subject, whereas in examples (22) and (23) it is marked with the accusative singular **-ta** and serves as the direct object. Finally, in example (24) **sí'ime** is again marked with the plural **-m**, but here it serves as the direct object of the clause.

(21) sí'ime-m ko-kóba-su-ka muúku-k
 all-PL RDP-gain-CPL-PPL die-PRF
 He died, having surpassed all the rest.

(22) sí'ime-ta né 'áttea-k
 all-ACC I own-PRF
 I own everything.

(23) née 'á'a béhe'e-tua-k sí'ime-ta
 I him pay-CAU-PRF all-ACC
 I paid him, all (of it).

(24) 'áapo sí'ime-m yó'ore
 he all-PL:ACC respect
 He respects everybody.

Examples (25)–(28) are typical of the usages of **waáte** as a noun. In examples (25) and (26) it functions as the subject of a sentence.

(25) waté né-mak sáha-k
 others me-with go:PL-PRF
 The others went with me.

(26) waté 'íntok hí'i-bʷéhe kúta-m hápte-ne-'e-po
 some and IZR-dig pole-PL:POS stand-FUT-EV-GND
 Others were digging (holes) where the poles were to be erected.

Examples (27) and (28) show the use of **waáte** as a direct object and an oblique object of the postposition **-mak** *with*.

(27) yokó-ne húči waté-m hí'oh-te-nee
 tomorrow-I again others-PL:ACC write-VR-FUT
 I will write some more of them tomorrow.

(28) waté-m-mak née tawáa-k
 others-PL:ACC-with me leave-PRF
 They left me with the others.

As examples (29 and (30) illustrate, Yaqui also uses quantifiers as pronouns in very much the same way that English uses the word "one" or Spanish uses "uno." As these examples show, Yaqui quantifiers often serve anaphorically in the grammar as both subjects, as in example (29), and objects as in (30).

(29) senú bʷásia-t 'á'a wíike
 one tail-on it pulls
 One person pulled him by the tail.

(30) senú-k násuk-bó'o-ka-m-ta 'emé'e bít-nee
 one-ACC middle-lie-PPL-PL-ACC you:PL see-FUT
 You will see one lying in the middle.

The preponderance of examples of **waáte** found in texts display its use as a kind of pronoun. In almost all cases the antecedent noun has been introduced and is referred to but not repeated. Examples (31) and (32), taken from a text, illustrate these points. In sentence (31) the antecedent is **húme'e híakim** *those Yaquis*. The two uses of **waáte** are partitive. The first instance can be rendered "some of them" and the second instance can be rendered "others of them." Both clearly refer back to this sentence initial noun phrase.

(31) húme'e híaki-m 'áma náu kón-ta-wa-ka béha waté béha 'áma yéu-ténne-k
 those Yaqui-PL there together surround-VR-PSV-PPL well some well there out-run:PL-PRF

 waté 'íntok 'áma kóko-k haámuči-m húni'i kóko-k 'íntok 'uúsi-m
 some and there die:PL-PRF woman-PL even die:PL-PRF and child-PL
 The Yaquis, having been surrounded there, some ran away, others died there, even women and children died.

The antecedent of both usages of **waáte** in sentence (32) is the first person plural subject clitic found on both the predicative use of the complex quantifier **'ilí huébena** *quite a few* and on the conjunction **taa** *but*. The first two instances of waáte can be rendered as "some of us" and the third instance can be rendered "others of us."

(32) 'ilí huébena=te táa=te ná'ikim-tu-k wá'am-bíča waté sáha-k,
    little many=we but=we divide-VR-PRF yonder-site some go:PL-PRF

    waté péesio-u-bíča sáha-k waté 'íntok húm 'asiénda-m-po kiímu-k
    some Hermosillo-to-site go:PL-PRF some and there farm-PL-in enter:PL-PRF
    There were quite a few of us, but we divided up, some went off yonder, some went to Hermosillo, others went out to the farms.

In sentence (33) the complex quantifier **'ilí haíki** functions as the head of a noun phrase. Note that in context this refers to Yaquis previously introduced.

(33) 'ilí haíki-ka wóki-m-mea sáha-k
    small amount-PPL foot-PL-INST go:PL-PRF
    A few of them went on foot.

Quantifiers normally precede the nouns that they modify in noun phrases. As example (34) shows, such quantifier-noun phrases may serve as obliques, i.e., as marking locatives.

(34) sí'ime hó'a-ra-m-met siíka
    all house-AZR-PL-on went
    He went to all the homes/villages.

Quantifiers such as **sí'ime** also can serve as the objects of a postposition. In sentence (35) **sí'ime** is the object of the postposition **-mak** *with*. It is object of the postpositional sequence **ku-t** *in, on* in sentence (36) and the object of the postposition **-bépa** *above* in sentence (37).

(35) hunák=ne sí'ime-m-mak 'áa 'etého-nee
    then=I all-PL-with be:able talk-FUT
    Then I will be able to talk with everybody.

(37) čé'a tú'ii sí'ime-m-bépa tú'ii-ka
    more good all-PL:ACC-above good-PPL
    This is better, it is the best of all

(36) bʷé'ituk=ne sí'ime-ku-t hú'unee-nee
    because=I all-in-on know-FUT
    because I will know about everything

6.0. Predicative usages of quantifiers

Another characteristic of Yaqui quantifiers is that they also have predicate usages. In example (38) **bú'uu** is the predicate in a complement clause and is marked for a first person plural subject. Predicate usages of quantifiers also appear in appositive constructions.

(38) bésa='e hú'unea bú'uu=te
    well=you know many=we
    Well, you know that there are many of us.

The quantifier **húebena** may take the verbalizing suffix **-ka** in its predicative usages. Sentence (39) is a typical example of this usage.

(39) 'ín kóba-po huebena-ka 'aúk-an tú'u-wa
    my head-in much-PPL be-PCN good-NZR
    There used to be a lot in my head, goodness.

Discontinuous constructions are very common. This allows the speaker of Yaqui to highlight one part or another of the quantifier phrase. In example (40) a topicalized subject **téputč-im** is quantified by the quantifier **bú'uu** *many* which serves as the predicate in an appositive adverbial clause. On the other hand, the quantifier may follow the head noun in a single clause but still be discontinouous from it. In sentence (41), for example, the quantifier is separated from a plural noun by a subject clitic.

(40) téputč-im 'ín súpe-m-po 'aáne tú'isi-m bú'uu
    flea-PL my shirt-PL-in be very-PL many
    There are fleas in my shirt, lots of them.

227

(41) hípeta-m   né bú'uu-m   yá'a-bae
     mat-PL:ACC I many-PL:ACC make-DSD
     I want to make a lot of mats.

Quantifiers may enter into derivational processes of various sorts. In sentence (42) the quantifier **bú'uu** takes the suffix **-si** and thus functions as an adverb.

(42) bú'uu-si   né hákun   tóhi-ri
     much-AVR I somewhere take-PPL
     Many times I have been taken to different places.

Quantifiers may also become incorporated in verbal constructions. In sentence (43) **bú'uu** takes the causative suffix **-ria**, forming a verb meaning "to multiply," i.e., "to become numerous."

(43) 'émpo 'á'a bú'uu-ria-nee
     you   it   much-VR-FUT
     You will make it multiply.

Sentences (44) and (45) illustrate clearly the use of the quantifier **sep** as an intensive temporal adverb meaning "immediately." In both cases, **sep** occurs in sentence initial position. Note that in sentence (45) **sep** itself is the base for attaching the emphatic particle =**su**.

(44) sép   bibá   'á-u   tó'o-sáka-'a-wa-k
     at:once cigarrettes him-to leave-go:PL-EV-PSV-PRF
     Right away, the contractual cigarrettes were left with him.

(45) sép=su   sóoni-m   'á-u   bébi-a-k
     at:once=EMP music-PL him-to hit-PSV-PRF
     At once his dance music began.

NUMERALS

1.0. Introduction

Numerals are a special case of the quantifiers, as evidenced by the many parallels they show in their syntactic and morphological patterning, as well as by their semantic characteristics. The numerals from one to ten in Yaqui are still relatively well known and are used with some degree of frequency. However, as of the present, we have not made any kind of frequency count of the numerals in order to be able to give any accurate figures.[1]

2.0. The cardinal numbers

The cardinal numerical system is relatively straightforward, although, as can be seen in Table 33, the inventory from one to ten shows some interesting compounds of its own.

seénu, wépul	*one*	búsani	*six*
woói	*two*	wóo-búsani	*seven*
báhi	*three*	wóh-naíki	*eight*
naíki	*four*	bátani	*nine*
mámni	*five*	wóh-mámni	*ten*

Table 33. Basic cardinal numbers

The numbers from one to six and nine appear to be basic. The numbers seven, eight, and ten are built on a base **wóo** (or its alternate form **wóh-**) *two* which is preposed to the basic number forms **búsani** *six*, **naíki** *four* and **mámni** *five*, respectively. The formation for eight and ten is straightforward, whereas that for seven seems odd, since there seems to be no rational meaning to **woo-**, unless it might mean "second six." However, if you have a system without any zero so that counting at birth starts at one and if you overlap the second cycle of a base of six so that the start of the second cycle is also at six, then six plus two does calculate out to seven. Note that the employment of overlapping cycles in MesoAmerican counting systems is now well documented (Terrence Kaufman, Catalina, AZ lecture, February, 1989). The problem with this account, however, is that no overlapping occurs in forming the Yaqui words for the higher numbers such as **báhi-takáa** *sixty*, for example.

2.1. "One" is more than "one"

As another complication, Yaqui employs three different forms, all of which mean "one." These are **seénu**, **wépul** and **wépu'ulai**. (Yaqui has neither a definite nor an indefinite article as such.) The demonstrative pronoun **huú'u** *that one* very frequently functions as the definite article. The numerals **seénu** and **wépul**, along with the derived form **wépu'ulai** also seem to serve as indefinite articles that designate an unspecified person or thing. This is especially clear in the following usages of **seénu**. In sentences (1) and (2) **senú** designates an indefinite subject. In sentence (3) it designates an unspecified direct object.

(1) 'áman senú weáma 'ála hunáa'a tú'i-si 'áuwi
there one walk:SG indeed that:one good-AVR fat
One is going along over yonder and that one is really fat.

(2) senú sí'ime-ta 'á'u-nee b^wá'a-m-ta híta huni'i
one all-ACC ask-FUT eat-NZR-ACC thing even
A person may ask for anything, food, anything whatsoever.

---

[1] Studies have been made on the aboriginal counting systems of the Indian languages of America, and Dedrick has contributed data on the Yaqui system to some of these, though he has not yet seen the results.

(3) tuká=ne   'íntok senú-k   bemúča-k
    last:night=I CNJ one-ACC whip-PRF
    And I whipped someone last night.

The schematic meaning of **senú** fits it especially for a role in making pronominal reference back to a previously specified participant in discourse. Thus it may enter into correlative partitive constructions in which its first usage may signal "the one" and its second usage in a complex sentence may refer to "the other." In sentence (4) both usages of **senú** refer back to the sentence initial quantified participial **woí-ka** *being two*.

(4) woí-ka   náu   katé-'e-tea-n   senú há'ani wó'i-itea   senú 'íntok káuwis
    two-being   together go:PL-EV-QUO-PCN   one perhaps coyote-QUO   one CNJ   fox
    It is said that the two were travelling together; one perhaps was a coyote, the other was a fox.

In short, these data show that Yaqui **seénu** is not a protypical number word, but rather has become grammaticalized to serve as an indefinite pronoun that signals an indefinite unitary entity, either as subject, object or a unitary subset of associated plural entities.

2.2. Wépul is only "one"

In clear contrast to **seénu**, the notion of "one" in the set of cardinal numbers used for counting is salient to the meaning of **wépul** and its derived form **wépu'ulai**. In sentence (5) **wépu'ulai** signals the quantity of "one" discrete entity from among a set of such entities. The accusative form is given in examples (6) and (7). The partitive notion of selecting one, and only one, out of a larger set is also illustrated by the usage of the accusative **wépu'ulai-k** in sentence (6).

(5) wépu'ulai-ka híba bé'ee
    one-being   only lack
    Only one is missing.

(6) wépu'ulai-k 'á'a téhwaa-k   hunáka'a káa 'á'a bʷá'a-sae
    one-ACC   her show-PRF   that:one NEG it   eat-IMP
    He showed her one of them and commanded her not to eat it.

(7) 'itépo náu   we-wéri-'i-tea   wépu'ulai-k té naú   'áčae-k
    we   together RDP-kin-EV-QUO   one-ACC   we together father-have
    We are all kin to one another, they say; we all have one and the same father.

The usages of **wépul** in other kinds of constructions reinforce the notion that "one" in the sense of counting items is salient to its meaning. As observed with nouns, **wépul** means "one and only one," whereas in adverbial phrases that indicate the number of repetitions of the entity produced in a given event, or repetitions of the event itself, **wépu'ulai** is marked with the accusative plural **-m** and specifically signals the fact that the entity was produced only once. This is illustrated in sentence (8).

(8) wépu'ulai-m pí'olai-m   čá-čae-k
    one-ACC:PL thin-ACC:PL RDP-scream-PRF
    He gave a single shrill scream.

Adverbial phrases formed by suffixing the adverbial suffix **-si** to **wépul** as exemplified in example (9), highlight the single occurrence of some event per se. This example also contrasts with (8) and suggests that the form **wépu'ulai** used in that example is a nominalized version of the basic numeral **wépul**.

(9) 'iníi'i wépul-si híba hóo-wa
    this   one-AVR only do-PSV
    This is done only once.

In its role as object of a postposition, **wépul** again illustrates its meaning of "one" as opposed to "more than one." The usage in sentence (10), for example, is based on the fact that most people have two functioning eyes.

(10) wépul-ka-tána tósai-m puúse-k
one-being-from white-ACC:PL eye-have
On one side she had a white eye.

Finally, the distributive usage of **wépul** is marked by gemination of the first vowel of its nominalized form as observed in sentences (11) and (12) and, as one might expect, its meaning is "one by one." It can be marked for either singular or plural as these two examples also show.

(11) táa wée'-e-pulai-ka 'á'a yáa-k-a'u béhe'e-wa-ta mabét-nee
but GM-EV-one-being his do-PRF-GND pay-NZR-ACC receive-FUT
But each one will receive the salary for what he did.

(12) hunáa'a=san wée-'e-pulai-m béhe'e-tua-nee
that:one=EXP GM-EV-one-PL:ACC pay-CAU-FUT
He will pay each and every one. or *He will pay them one by one.*

2.3. The compound number terms

Numbers with values between ten and twenty are formed by means of an appended phrase that consists of the adverbial **'áma** followed by one of the numbers whose values range from one to nine as illustrated by the forms given in Table 34.

wóh-mámni 'áma wépu'ulai	*eleven*
wóh-mámni 'áma woói	*twelve*
wóh-mámni 'áma báhi	*thirteen*
wóh-mámni 'áma naíki	*fourteen*
wóh-mámni 'áma mámni	*fifteen*
wóh-mámni 'áma búsani	*sixteen*
wóh-mámni 'áma wóo-búsani	*seventeen*
wóh-mámni 'áma wóh-naíki	*eighteen*
wóh-mámni 'áma bátani	*nineteen*

Table 34. Compound numbers–the teens

One of the most obvious facts about the Yaqui numeral system is that originally the vigesimal rather than the decimal system was used, and that the number of fingers, plus the toes, were the basis for the count of twenty, coded as **takáa** *one body*. Higher numbers are obtained by using the adjoined phrase cited above that consists of the adverbial **'áma** + Number. Multiples of twenty are calculated by preposing a cardinal number to the word **takáa**, resulting in combinations such as **bahi takáa** *three bodies* = 60. Select forms from 20 to 100 are given in Table 35.

senú-takáa (one body)	*twenty*	20
senú-takáa 'áma wépu'ulai	*twenty-one*	21
senú-takáa 'áma wóh-mámni	*thirty*	30
woí-takáa	*forty*	40
woí-takáa 'áma wóh-mámni	*fifty*	50
báhi-takáa	*sixty*	60
báhi-takáa 'áma wóh-mámni	*seventy*	70
naíki-takáa	*eighty*	80
naíki-takáa 'áma wóh-mámni	*ninety*	90
mámni-takáa	*one hundred*	100

Table 35. Vigesimal number system

SONORA YAQUI LANGUAGE STRUCTURES

The unwieldiness of the system for indicating numbers greater than ten has made it a bit impractical for general usage, and due to the relative simplicity of the Spanish numerical system, many younger Yaquis probably use the Spanish numerical system throughout, or they use combinations of Yaqui basic terms with Spanish higher category terms to form a blended number combination. For example, numbers with values that are multiples of one hundred or one thousand are formed by analogy with the Spanish counting system, as the examples in (13)(a) and (13)(b) suggest.

(13)(a) báhi síento = 300 < Sp. trescientos
(b) mámni míil = 5000 < Sp. cinco mil

2.4. The ordinal numbers

Yaqui does not seem to have an ordinal number system as such. A term **bat** *in front, forward* is used to carry the idea of "first" (in line or in authority). For the succeeding ordinal numbers, the closest approximation of an ordinal system is to use the expression **'inía-mak woí(kai)** *with this* + NUM-*being*, as seen in example (14).

(14) húu'u 'ín hí'oh-te-'u   'inía-mak woói-kai
     that my paper-VR-GND this-with two-being
     what I have written, with this being two (i.e., *my second letter*)

3.0. Derived forms

Yaqui employs the adverbial suffix **-si** attached to number words to form a complete series of verbal modifiers with the meaning "X times." In complex numeric phrases, the adverbial suffix attaches to the very last word in the phrase, much the same way as the English possessive "-'s" attaches to complex noun phrases in such examples as the "King of England's hat" or the "Queen of England's consort." The most commonly used forms are given in Table 36.

wépul-si	*once*
woó-sa	*twice*
báhi-si	*thrice*
naíki-si	*four times*
mámni-si	*five times*
búsani-si	*six times*
wóo-búsani-si	*seven times*
wóh-naíki-si	*eight times*
bátani-si	*nine times*
wóh-mámni-si	*ten times*
wóh-mámni 'áma wépu'ulai-si	*eleven times*

Table 36. Derived adverbs—"X times"

The notion "each" is conveyed in Yaqui by the derived form **wée'-e-pulai-m** as in example (12), given earlier. In addition, the quantifier **číkti** *all, total* may also be used in the sense of "each" or "every," as seen in example (15).

(15) bémpo číkti wásuktia-po té'opo-u sáha-k
     they each year-in   temple-to go:PL-PRF
     They went to the temple every year.

Distributive usages of the numbers are derived by either lengthening the vowel of the initial syllable, as in example (16), or by reduplicating the first syllable of the number word and using the derived form in conjunction with the reciprocal pronoun **-náu** *together*, as in example (17).

(16) táa wée'-e-pulai-ka   'á'a yáa-k-a'u   béhe'e-wa-ta mabét-nee
     but GM-EV-one-being his do-PRF-GND pay-NZR-ACC receive-FUT
     But each one will receive the salary for what he did.

(17) hunáme'e ba-báhi-ka-nau   'áma ya-yáha-n
     those   RDP-three-being-together there RDP-arrive:PL-PCN
     They were coming in three by threes.

4.0. Syntax of the numeral constructions

Just like quantifiers in general, numbers precede the nouns they modify in noun phrases. In sentence (18) **báhi** *three* modifies a personal noun in a noun phrase that functions as the subject of an adverbial locative clause. In sentence (19) **wóh-naiki** *eight* modifies the reified locative noun of the subject noun phrase of the main clause. In sentence (20) **naíki** *four* modifies the animate noun in the subject noun phrase.

(18) 'áman yéu-kéča-'a-wa-k   báhi pahkó'a-m haíbu súma'i-taka 'áma yé'ee-n
     there out-stand:SG-EV-PSV-PRF three feaster-PL now tied-being there dance-PCN
     He was taken to where he was to perform, where three tied Pascal Dancers were already dancing.

(19) wóh-naíki puéplo náu   yáha-ka   'á'a pahkó-ria-k
     two-four town   together arrive:PL-PPL him feast-APL-PRF
     All the eight towns, coming together, participated in the burial ceremonies for him.

(20) naíki wakás-im wasá-u kiímu-k
     four cow-PL   field-to enter:PL-PRF
     Four cows got into the field.

Number phrases precede the nouns they modify regardless of their complexity. In example (21) a complex number **woí-takáa** *40* precedes a noun which serves as the object of a postposition. The number apparently does not take accusative marking in this case.

(21) woí-takáa wásuktia-m-po 'áma né-sau-pea-n
     two-body year-PL-in   there UNSPEC-command-DSD-PCN
     He wanted to rule there for 40 years.

Number can be used as heads of noun phrases and take the appropriate case marking, depending upon their role in the sentence. As example (22) shows, accusative is marked by **-k** on number words

(22) sí'ime 'áma mátču-k   hunáka'a wépu'ulai-k 'áma 'átbʷa-ka   mátču-k
     all   there dawn-PRF that:ACC one-ACC   there laugh:at-PPL dawn-PRF
     Everyone was still wide awake when morning came, all laughing at that one man when dawn came.

A Number + Noun Phrase can be further modified by a preceding quantifier. In example (23) the quantifier **sí'ime** *all* serves to emphasize the totality of the Yaqui population subsumed under the number phrase "eight towns:"

(23) béha sí'ime wóh-naíki puéplo-m bée'eka-tana
     well all   two-four town-PL scattered-from

     náah-   nu-nú'ubʷi-a   'á'a muké-'e-po-táhtia
     everywhere RDP-invite-PSV his die-EV-GND-until
     Well, he was invited throughout all the eight Yaqui towns from then until he died.

The numbers occur in a variety of verbalized forms with **-ka** and **-taka**. They may also appear in construction with **tu** *to be* as in example (24).

(24) mámni-m-tu-ka-n   húme'e 'áma yáha-k-ame
     five-PL-VR-PPL-PCN   those there arrive:PL-PRF-NZR
     There were five of them, those who arrived there.

ADJECTIVE CONSTRUCTIONS

1.0. Introduction

This section deals with a class of words that are difficult to classify because at times they act like stative verbs and in other contexts they function as participials. They also often modify other words. As another peculiarity, some of the members of this class require suffixes which seem to have no function except as marking them as members of this class. We have already discussed these properties of adjectives in ADJECTIVE MORPHOLOGY pp. 146–152, so we will not go into any detail regarding the morphology and the semantics of adjectives here. In this section of the grammar, we mainly discuss the adjectives as they are used both attributively, i.e., as nominal adjuncts, and predicatively. For all practical purposes, the traditional category names serve here. We simply refer to them as adjectives and adverbs.

2.0. Form

A number of adjectives only occur with a final **-i** vowel. This may well reflect the Proto-Uto-Aztecan nominalizing suffix ***-i,** which has extended into the domain of aspect and may have even become reanalyzed as a part of the stem (cf. Langacker 1977:63–68). As the examples in Table 37 show, there are actually three classes of -i final adjectives, those with **-i** as the stem final segment, those with the suffix **-li,** and those with the suffix sequence **-la-i** (cf. ADJECTIVE MORPHOLOGY, pp. 147-148). The examples in row three of Table 37 illustrate adjectives ending in the suffix **-la,** which provides a bit of evidence for analyzing the **-lai** sequence in the adjectives of row four as a bimorphemic one.

-i	túuru-i	*thick*	'il-i	*small*
-li	tutú'u-li	*pretty*	baá-li	*fresh*
	'ámma'a-li	*precisely*		
-la	bemé-la	*new*	musá'a-la	*funny*
	kówi-la	*curled up*	'átta-la	*face down*
-la-i	tápsio-la-i	*thin*	ná'u-la-i	*narrow*

Table 37. **Adjectives with final -i**

Adjectives can be reduplicated to indicate plural number of the noun being modified. In example (1) the reduplicated adjective modifies the inherently multiplex bodypart noun which is an incorporated noun in a possessive verbal construction. The reduplicated adjective in example (2) illustrates the use of the negative with an adjective to form antonyms, i.e., a tender morsel comes from a young chicken rather than from an old rooster.

(1) tét-tébe-m   púh-sé'ebe-k
RDP-long-PL eye-lash-having
having long eyelashes

(2) káa mo-móli-m
NEG RDP-mature-PL
tender ones

3.0. Syntax

Adjectives ordinarily precede the items they modify when they function as attributives. Frequently in this position they form compounds with the nouns that they modify. In such cases, the adjective does not carry any case or number marking of its own, as shown in examples (3) and (4).

(3) tósai kári-m
white house-PL
white houses

(4) hunúen yéu-siíka pahkó ramáa-ta yéča-'a-su-a-k-o pahkó'a-m
thus out-went feast shed-ACC placed-EV-CPL-PSV-PRF-when feaster-PL

náu béep-su-a-k-o pahkó béha naáte-k
together hit-CPL-PSV-PRF-when feast well begin-PRF

That's the way it came out; when the feast shelter had been put up and the other festal dancers had come together, the feast started.

3.1. Strings of attributive adjectives

Yaqui may distribute a string of attributive adjectives throughout a sequence of conjoined clauses, each of which describe a distinct characteristic of the same entity, as is the case in example (5).

(5) húu'u pahkó'olaa 'íntok 'á'a 'átbʷa-táite-k káa 'awá-k-am-ta bíča-ka roóbo
that festival:man CNJ him laugh-begin-PRF NEG horn-have-NZR-ACC see-PPL round

kóba-k-am-ta bíča-ka-i 'íntok tánala a'a bʷásia-ka-'a-betči'ibo
head-have-NZR-ACC see-PPL-PPL CNJ curved his tail-having-EV-for

And that Pascal dancer began to laugh at it, just seeing the hornless, round head, and seeing the way it had its tail curved up over its back.

Yaqui permits strings of predicate adjectives that modify a possessor noun as illustrated in example (6).

(6) húnen 'á'a 'éa-o=su hunáma'a téh-po yóo-čibá'ato tósai-ka čukúi-ka
thus his think-when=EMP there cave-in enchanted-goat white-be black-be

tána-la bʷási-a-ka káa 'awá-ka kía tét-tebé-m náka-k tét-tebé-m
curve-ADJ tail-CON-have NEG horn-having only RDP-long-PL ear-having RDP-long-PL

púh-sé'ebe-k bátte bʷiía-u-núki-m hímse-ka 'á-u yéu-búite
eye-lash-having nearly ground-to-reach-PL beard-having him-to out-run

As he was going along with these thoughts, a black and white enchanted goat, hornless, with his tail curved over his back, with long ears, very long eyelashes, and a beard that reached nearly to the ground, came running out toward him.

An attributive adjective plus a noun phrase may take a demonstrative as its initial constituent as is the case in example (7). This gives us a noun phrase of the form Demonstrative + Atttributive Adjective + Noun.

(7) húu'u bʷé'u kúta
that big wood
that big log

3.2. Functioning as heads of noun phrases

Adjectives can function as the heads of noun phrases, in which role they can be marked as either nominative or accusative. In the accusative, they are marked with the suffix -k as in examples (8) and (9)

(8) wó'i-m kía-k tú'ure   (9) 'á'a kuná-wa tá'abʷi-k núk-siíka
coyote-PL delicious-ACC like   her husband-POS different-ACC carry-go
Coyotes like delicious (food).   *Her husband went away with another woman.*

3.3. Accusative marking on adjectives

The multiple accusative marking in Yaqui serves to maintain categorial distinctions in the grammar. In sentence (10) there are three adjectives that modify an abstract noun **'éeria** *thought* incorporated into the verb, and treated as a possessed object by the verbalizing suffix **-k** and a verb **nooka** *to speak* respectively. All of these are marked by the accusative suffix **-k,** rather than the accusative **-ta**. This suggests strongly that the adjectives marked with **-k** are more like verbs in nature than they are like nouns. Nevertheless, they also have noun-like properties since two of the adjectives, **kó'oko** *painful* and **bétte** *heavy*, function as coordinate adjuncts to the verb **nooka** in example (10). This shows that the marking on Yaqui adjectives serves for more than simply indicating agreement, although of course, it does that (cf. Jelinek and Escalante 1989:422–426).

(10) 'émpo hú'ena-k 'éeria-k kó'oko-k 'íntok bétte-k noóka
you evil-ACC thought-have painful-ACC and heavy-ACC speak
You have evil thoughts and speak painful and heavy words (i.e., *disagreeable speech*).

Example (11) shows the joint usage of the accusative **-ta** and its counterpart **-k** in a single object noun phrase. Note that in this sentence, the word order is reversed from the usual Adjective + Noun configuration. This can be construed as a kind of appositive construction in which the adjective carries out the role of a predicate.

(11) tómi-ta 'ilíiki-k maáčuk-ta-ka
money-ACC little-ACC grasp-VR-PPL
and receiving just a tiny bit of money

A second appositive construction is seen in sentence (12) in which the adjective **'iilitči-m** *very small-PL* is marked for plural and modifies the Plural Adjective + Noun combination **'ili kauwi-m** *small hill-PL*.

(12) yú'in čúuba 'á'a wéye-o=su 'ilí káu-pé-pétče-'e-ku 'áman 'á'a
much time:span his go-when=EMP small mountain-RDP-vale-EV-in there his

wéye-o=su 'ilí káuwi-m 'iilítči-m póo-póoh-ti-hoká-'a-po
go-when=EMP small hill-PL very:small-PL RDP-scatter-CON-be-EV-GND

'í'ibo ta'á-ta 'áman wéče-'e-bétana
from sun-POS there fall-EV-from
After he had gone on for a good bit of time and as he was going through a small mountain pass, there were lots of very small peaks scattered about, off toward the west.

3.4. Objects and possessors

Attributive adjectives in Yaqui show clearly the mixing of the categories of direct object and possession in the ways that adjectives are marked in particular contexts. In the if clause of example (13), the adjective **yumá** *enough* is marked with the accusative form **-'ik** and refers to the incorporated noun **tóm** *money* to which is suffixed the possessor **-ek** *to have*. Given that when **-'ik** attaches to pronouns it means "X's very own," it seems clear that its usage in this example is the bridge between indicating ownership or control over some entity and the transitive notion of applying effective force to something. This transitive idea also is in examples (14) and (15) in which the name of the physical object that results from cooking is not overtly realized lexically. This latter pattern in accusative marking is paralleled by the accusative marker **-k** on the quantifier in example (15).

(13) né-u 'á'a 'á'awa yumá-'ik tóm-ek-o
me-to it ask enough-ACC money-have-if
Ask me for it, if you have enough money.

(14) tú'i-si née káka-k bʷá'a-bʷasa
good-AVR I sweet-ACC RDP-cook
I make very sweet candy.

(15) bʷé'ituk huébena-k 'ée-síme
because much-ACC think-go
because he was going along thinking about a lot of things

The conventional merging of nominative and accusative marking on plural nouns, which carries over to the set of demonstrative and quantifier forms in Yaqui, also reflects itself in the case marking of plural forms of attributive adjectives. The plural marker, of course, is the ubiquitous suffix **-m**. Plural adjectives, however, are often also reduplicated as in example (16).

(16) taáwe tótoi-'asó'o-la-m   káa mo-móli-m   híba tú'ure
     hawk chicken-born-ABS-PL:ACC not RDP-mature-PL:ACC only like
     The hawk only likes tender young chickens.

In example (17) the possessed object is an incorporated compound noun which is marked by the verbalizing possession suffix **-k**. The adjective **tosái** *white* is marked by **-m** and possibly could be glossed as a schematic noun phrase meaning "white ones."

(17) tú'isi yó'o-we   haíbu tosái-m   čáo-boa-k
     very old-go:SG now white-ACC:PL chin-hair-has
     He is very old, he now has white whiskers.

Further illustrating the point that the marking of plural adjectives parallels that for plural nouns is shown clearly in sentences such as (18) in which a plural kinship noun, which is reduplicated, is accompanied by an attributive number that is discontinuous from the head noun.

(18) bawé b^{w}íkola-ku-t wéye-ka-i woói-m náu wé-weri-m bíča-k
     sea edge-CON-on go-PPL-PPL two-PL:ACC together RDP-kin-PL:ACC see-PRF
     As he was going along the seashore, he saw two brothers.

3.5. In discontinuous constructions

As illustrated by sentence (18) adjectives can occur in discontinuous constructions with the nouns they modify. In example (19) the head noun marked in the accusative occurs in sentence initial position, separated from the adjective which follows it by the subject clitic.

(19) ču'ú-ta   né b^{w}é'uu-k nún-nu'ub^{w}a-n
     dog-ACC I big-ACC RDP-carry-PCN
     I was carrying a big dog.

As mentioned above, adjectives can become part of a compound consisting of both the adjective and the noun that it modifies, as, for example, the adjective **kúta** *wooden* does in example (20). This example also shows that when an Adjective + Noun construction serves as the object of a postposition, the attributive adjective agrees not only in number with the head noun, but also in oblique marking with the postposition.

(20) kúta-kahón-im-po 'iílitč-im-po
     wood-box-PL-in very:small-PL-in
     in the very tiny wooden boxes

Yaqui forms some antonyms by simply negating the positive form of an adjective, as in (21)(a)–(b).

(21)(a) tú'ii   (b) káa-tú'ii
     good   *not-good* (i.e., *bad*)

3.6. Degrees of comparison

Adjectives mark three degrees of comparison, i.e., positive, comparative, and superlative. In this section we are basically concerned with constructions involving adjectives expressed in the positive degree. Comparatives and superlatives are illustrated here and discussed in considerably more detail in COMPARATIVE CONSTRUCTIONS, pp. 105–116.

The positive degree is that expressed by the normal basic form of the adjective. It simply signals the fact that a particular quality or state of affairs exists, as **b^{w}é'u** *big* does in example (22).

(22) b^{w}é'u kári
     big house
     big house

The comparative degree of an adjective is expressed by means of a construction that preposes the adverbial **čé'a** *more* to an Attributive Adjective + Noun Phrase as shown in example (23).

(23) čé'a bʷé'u kári
　　 more big　house
　　 a bigger house

The superlative degree is signalled by the quantifier **sí'ime,** marked for the appropriate number for the accusative. This quantifier is the object of the postposition **-bepa** *above*. The resulting postpositional phrase is followed by the comparative **čé'a** and the particular Attributive Adjective + Noun Phrase, as seen in example (24).

(24) sí'ime-m-bépa čé'a bʷé'u kári
　　 all-PL-above more big house
　　 the biggest house of all

The lack of equality between two states is indicated by the use of the adverbial **čé'a** plus an adjective for indicating positive inequality, as exemplified by example (25). Likewise, **čé'a** plus the antonym of some adjective is used for specifying a negative inequality as in example (26).

(25) čé'a tú'ii　　　　　　(26) čé'a káa tu'i
　　 more good　　　　　　　more not good
　　 better　　　　　　　　 *worse*

Adverbs also can be placed on a three point scale of degree. In the positive degree, adverbs precede the verbs they modify as shown by example (27).

(27) tú'isi tekipanoa
　　 well　work
　　 work well

The comparative degree of an adverb patterns like the comparative degree of the adjective. It is simply preceded by the comparative degree adverb **čé'a** *more,* as illustrated in example (28).

(28) čé'a tú'isi tekipánoa
　　 more well work
　　 work better

The Quantifier + **-bépa** + **čé'a** construction then, is also used to designate the superlative degree of the adverb that modifies a verb as in example (29).

(29) sí'ime-m-bépa čé'a tú'isi tekipánoa
　　 all-PL- above　more well work
　　 ...work the best of all

3.7. Adjectives and adverbs

Predicate adjectives may be preceded by adverbs. In sentence (30), the adjective **tútu'uli** *pretty* is preceded by the adverb **tú'isi** *very*, which itself is derived from the adjective **tú'i** *good* by means of the suffix **-si**.

(30) tú'isi tútu'uli hámut-tu-k-an-téa
　　 very pretty　woman-VR-PRF-PCN-QUO
　　 It is said that she was a very beautiful woman.

Nonderived adjectives may also serve as modifiers of verbs, i.e., as adverbs. as shown by the use of **lúula** *straight* in example (31).

(31) 'á'a sís-sís-su-ka　　siíka tesó-u lúula polák-ti-sime　　　húu'u čibá'ato
　　 him RDP-urinate-PPL go:PRF cave-to straight oblique-CON-go:SG that　goat
　　 Having finished urinating on him, that goat went straight back to the cave, loping sideways.

DEFINITE PRONOUNS

1.0. Introduction

Yaqui definite pronouns distinguish three numbers of persons, both singular and plural. Gender is not germane to the Yaqui pronominal system. The definite pronouns assume a wide range of forms in order to carry out a number of functions in the grammar. These include the grammatical roles of subject, direct object, reflexive object, possessor and object of the postposition. They also display a wide range of morphological structures, appearing as free, independent pronouns, as clitics or as one or more sets of bound forms. Finally, there are even combinations of these pronouns. Given the copious examples found in preceding sections of this grammar, we present here only summaries of the pronoun sets and a few examples for each.

2.0. The nominative forms

The nominative forms consist of two sets of independent subject pronouns, a set of subject clitics and a set of emphatic reflexive pronouns.

2.1. The independent forms

The first set of nominative forms consists of the independent subject pronouns, given in Table 38.

Person	Singular	Plural
1	'ínepo	'itépo
2	'émpo	'emé'e
3	'áapo	bémpo

Table 38. Independent subject pronouns

Examples (1)–(3) illustrate the use of the second person singular subject pronoun **'émpo**, the third person singular **'aápo**, and the second person plural **'emé'e** respectively.

(1) 'iním 'émpo wée 'ín hápči 'émpo humák hunáa'a hú'ub^{w}a 'ín 'á-u nokáʻu
    here you come my sir you perhaps that just-now my him-to talking
    Is that you coming here, my Lord? Perhaps you are the one to whom I was just talking.

(2) 'áapo 'áma 'amé-mak sáha-k
    he there them-with go:PL-PRF
    He went there with them.

(3) 'emé'e 'íntok ketúni 'á'a téuwaa-nee
    you:PL and still it tell-FUT
    And you will continue telling it.

The second set of nominative forms are reduced variants of the independent subject pronouns. The reduction consists in the loss of the final root vowel. These reduced forms, given in Table 39, combine with direct object pronouns and with adverbial forms.

Person	Singular	Plural
1	'ínep-	'itép-
2	'émp-	'emé-
3	'áap-	bémp-

Table 39. Reduced independent subject pronouns

The third person singular reduced independent subject pronoun combines with a third person singular object clitic in example (4). Sentence (5) then, pairs a first person plural subject pronoun with a third person plural direct object clitic.

(4) 'áap='a'a bíča-k (5) 'itep=am hínu-k
    he=it   see-PRF   we=them buy-PRF
    He saw it.   *We bought them.*

2.2. The subject clitics

A third set of nominative forms consists of a set of subject clitics. These have shorter and longer forms depending on the phonological shape of the stem to which they attach. As can be seen from Table 40, third person singular is umarked in this series of subject pronouns.

Person	Singular	Plural
1	=ne	=té
2	=é'e-	='em
3		=mme

Table 40. Subject clitics

The use of the first person singular subject clitic is exemplified in sentence (6), whereas the use of the first person plural subject clitic is given in sentence (7).

(6) haí=sa   ne túa   'áme-u 'ané-ka 'ám 'át-tua-nee
    how=INTERR I indeed them-to do-PPL them laugh-CAU-FUT
    What can I do to make them laugh?

(7) heéwi 'áčai 'enči=te   bó'o-bít-nee-t-iia   húu'u moóro siká-a-ri :
    yes   sir you:ACC=we lay-see-FUT-CON-say that Moor go:SG-PPL-PPL
    "Yes Sir, we'll wait for you," said that Moor, as he was taking his leave.

The second person singular form **-é'e** shortens to **-'é** in unstressed syllables following a vowel final stem as in example (8). The third person plural form shortens to **-m** in that same context as shown in example (9).

(8) hái=sa='e   'émo bíča   (9) tú'isi=m   'o'óbe 'íme'e 'ili yoéme-m
    how=Q=you RFL see   very=they lazy   these little person-PL
    How are you doing?   *These little folks are surely very lazy.*

Subject clitics commonly occur following the first word in a sentence. These are postposed to intransitive verbs, as in example (10), and to manner adverbs, as in example (11).

(10) siká=ne   (11) tú'uli-s=e'e   'áa hí'ohte
     go=I   pretty-ADV=you able write
     I am going now.   *You can write beautifully.*

The first person singular, first person plural, and third person plural forms are preceded by an epenthetic vowel **-a** when cliticized to certain consonant final forms as seen in (12)–(14). This epenthetic vowel is what we labelled an "echo vowel" in PHONOLOGY, pp. 28–29.

(12) sáhak-a=te   (13) há'amu-k-a=te   (14) yáha-k-a=mme
     go-EV=we   climb-PRF-EV=we   arrive-PRF-EV=they
     We are going now.   *We climbed up.*   *They arrived.*

2.3. Subject clitic sequences

The first and second person singular and plural clitics will also attach to the set of free form pronouns above forming subject clitic sequences. These sequences include the first person singular **'ínepo=ne**, the second person singular **'émpo='e**, the first plural **'itépo=te**, and the second person plural **'emé='em**.

A typical example of such a subject clitic sequence involving the second person singular is given in example (15).

(15) 'émpo='e káa 'áman wée'-éan
you=you not there go-ought
You ought not go there.

2.4. Subject pronoun + -ik and -im

The independent subject pronouns enter into Pronoun + Suffix sequences with the accusative singular suffix **-ik** and its plural counterpart **-im**. This sequence is used to mark both direct object as well as possessor. The second person singular and the first and second person plural forms are not attested in our data, but are most certainly possible semantically.

Person	Singular	Plural
1	'inepo-'ik	*'itépo-'im
2	*'émpo-'ik	*'emé-'em
3	'áapo-'ik	bempó-'im

Table 41. Accusative/possessor pronouns

Examples of these are seen in sentences (16)–(21). Sentence (16) illustrates two usages of the third person singular object pronoun. In the first clause it functions as the direct object, in the second clause it occurs as the the subject of a nominalized clause. Sentence (17) illustrates a simple sentence in which the clitic sequence **'áapo-ik** marks the subject of the sentence, but the main verb is actually a gerund and the entire complement of **'útte'a** *it is necessary* is actually a nominalized clause.

(16) 'itépo 'áapo-'ik náke 'áapo-'ik čé'a bát 'itom 'á'a náke-ka-'a-betčí'ibo
we he-ACC love he-POS more first us his love-PPL-EV-for
We love him because he loved us first!

(17) 'útte'a 'áapo-'ik nésau-nee-'u
necessary he-POS command-FUT-GND
It is necessary that he be in command.

The connection between the accusative and possessive usages of these clitic sequences is seen clearly in examples (18)–(21). In example (18) the clitic sequence **bempó-'im** marks the possessor of the cattle mentioned in the sentence. In example (19) the subject of the sentence is marked by the first singular **'ínepo-'ik** and the third singular **'áapo-'ik** in the second clause designates the possessor of the hands that the speaker mentions.

(18) túa bempó-'im wakás-im 'ám b^wá'a-ka
truly they-POS:PL cow-PL them eat-PRF
It was indeed their cattle that ate them.

(19) 'ínepo-'ik híapsi 'íntok sí'ime-ta húka'a 'áapo-'ik mám-po 'ín sú'u-tóhi-ri
I-POS life and all-ACC that:ACC he-POS hand-in my release-leave-PPL
My life and everything I have released into his hands.

The contrast between the marking of subjects of nominalized clause and direct objects in declarative clause is shown clearly by the usages of the third plural **bémpo-im** in examples (20) and (21).

(20) bémpo-'im wáata-'u   (21) 'áapo túa bempó-'im bíča-k
they-POS want-GND   he truly they-ACC see-PRF
what they want   *He truly saw them.*

3.0. The emphatic reflexive subject pronouns

A third morphemically complex pronominal set, the emphatic reflexive subject pronouns is formed by suffixing the adverbial **-la/-ela** *only, alone* to the independent subject pronouns.

Person	Singular	Plural
1	'ínepo-la	'itépo-la
2	'émpo-la	'emépo-la
3	'áapo-la	bémpo-la

Table 42. Emphatic reflexives pronouns

A first person plural usage is illustrated in example (22).

(22) 'itépo-la 'áma tawa-ba-bae-k
we-alone there remain-RDP-DSD-PT
We stayed there by ourselves.

A second set of emphatic subject pronouns is formed by suffixing **-la** to the reduced subject pronouns. In all such cases, the suffix **-la** surfaces in its vowel initial form **-ela**. These shorter forms are equivalent in meaning to the longer ones and a more detailed study is needed in order to distinguish them semantically. The paradigm with **-ela** is as follows:

Person	Singular	Plural
1	'ínep-ela	'itóp-ela
2	'émp-ela	'emép-ela
3	'áap-ela	bémp-ela

Table 43. Reduced reflexive pronouns

Example (23) illustrates the use of the third person singular reduced reflexive **'áap-ela** in which it signals the fact that the subject did something all by him/herself.

(23) 'áap-ela 'ám koóba-k
he-alone them win-PRF
He beat them all by himself.

The use of the first person plural reduced reflexive **'itóp-ela** is illustrated by example (24).

(24) 'itóp-ela 'ím hoóka
we-alone here sit:PL
We are here all by ourselves.

The suffix -'ik also serves as a base for attaching certain postpositions, as illustrated by sentences (25) and (26).

(25) 'áapo-'ik-ut 'aáyu-k húu'u lútu'uria
he-ACC-on be-PRF that truth
The truth is in him.

(26) 'íka'a té híp^{w}ee, 'áapo-'ik-bétana
this:ACC we have he-POS-from
We have this from him.

Mayo also has corresponding morphemes -'**orik** (sg), -'**orim** (pl). These forms are used for emphasis. They illustrate in a particularly striking way, the extension of the Accusative marker to also mark the Possessor relation, a pattern common to Uto-Aztecan. In less marked forms, the regular accusative set or possessive set is used (cf. POSSESSIVE CONSTRUCTIONS, p.166–167).

4.0. Direct object pronouns

The complexities of Yaqui case markers are further seen in the sets of morphemes that are used to mark the related functions of direct object, indirect object, possessor and object of the postposition.

To begin, Yaqui has a series of independent object pronouns as well as a series of direct object clitics. In contrast to the marking for subjects, third person singular is marked in the clitic sequence. The independent direct object pronouns are as follows:

Definite Pronouns 5.0.

Person	Singular	Plural
1	née	itóm
2	'enčí	'enčím
3	'á'a	'ám

Table 44. Independent direct object pronouns

Examples (27) and (28) illustrate a variety of direct object pronouns. In example (27) a second person singular independent direct object pronoun follows a sentence initial first person singular independent subject pronoun. Sentence (28) contains a string of subordinate clauses with first person singular subject, indirect object and direct object pronouns, respectively. In addition, an indirect object construction with a second person plural pronominal object occurs in sentence initial position.

(27) 'ínepo 'enčí bó'o-bít-nee
    I   you   await-FUT
    I will wait for you.

(28) 'emó-u 'á'a téuwaa-k 'emé'e 'íntok née muk-sú-k   húni'i ketúni 'á'a
    you-to it tell-PRF you:PL CNJ   I   die-CPL-PRF even still it

    téuwaa-nee híba 'ém túa   né-u   wáati=née   káa-báe-ka húni'i
    tell-FUT   always you indeed me-to remember=me   NEG-DSD-PPL even

    née híkkahi-su-me née híkkahi-su-ka-me née tá'aa-k-ame
    me hear-CPL-NZR me hear-CPL-PPL-NZR me know-PRF-NZR
    I have told it to you, and even after I am dead you will go on telling it, and in that way you will be remembering me, even though you didn't intend to, those who are hearing me now, those who have heard me, and those who know me.

An unmarked third person singular subject and a third person singular object pronoun are seen in example (29). Third person singular subject and third person plural object pronouns occur in that order in example (30).

(29) 'á'a béeba-k   (30) 'áapo 'ám bíča-k
    it   hit-PRF   he   them see-PRF
    He hit it.   *He saw them.*

The second set of direct object markers is the set of clitic pronouns, given in Table 45.

Person	Singular	Plural
1	née	'itóm
2	'e'em	'enčím
3	'á'a	'ám

Table 45. Direct object clitics

The use of third person singular direct object **'á'a** is shown in sentence (31), whereas the second person singular **e'em** is given in the second clause of sentence (32). The use of the third person plural direct object **'ám** is illustrated in (33).

(31) tú'i-si   'á'a 'átbʷa   (33) 'ám yi'i-pea
    good-ADV   him laugh:at   them dance-DSD
    He really laughed at it.   *What an urge he had for dancing to that music!*

(32) siká=ne Liós 'e'ém-čania-bu
    went=I God you-help-HRT:PL
    Goodbye, I'm going now.

5.0. Possessive pronouns

The paradigm of possessive pronouns is highly reminiscent of that given in Table 45 for the direct object pronouns, but only the the first and second person plural and one of the third person singular forms are

245

are identical to the direct object pronouns, as can be seen from Table 46. Note also that the third person singular possessor is indicated by two forms, one designating a specific possessor and the other a nonspecific one. The nonspecific possessor marker is actually a suffix. This is another trait that links Yaqui to other Pimic languages and to Cora and Huichol (cf. Langacker 1977:86).

Person	Singular	Plural
1	'ín	'itóm
2	'ém	'enčím
3	'á'a (SPEC)	bém
	-wa (UNSPEC)	

Table 46. Possessive pronominal clitics

Several of the possessive pronouns are illustrated by examples (34)–(36). A second person singular clitic **'ém** is used in sentence (34), whereas a first person plural is employed in sentence (35). Finally, a use of the second person plural **'enčím** is given in sentence (36).

(34) hái=sa   káa 'á'a wáata há'ani húka'a 'ém mó'obe'i-ta
     how=INTERR not it want perhaps that:ACC your hat-ACC
     Don't you want your hat?

(35) 'itóm wakás-im tíiko-m-po kiímu-k
     our   cow-PL   wheat-PL-in enter-PL-PRF
     Our cows got into the wheatfield.

(36) tú'isi beméla húu'u 'enčím kaáro
     very new   that   your:PL car
     Your car is very new.

6.0. Reflexive pronouns

The set of Yaqui reflexive pronouns is presented in Table 47.

Person	Singular	Plural
1	'íno	'itó
2	'émp	'emó
3	'áu	'emó

Table 47. Reflexive pronouns[1]

The following examples illustrate typical usages of the reflexive pronouns. The third singular **au** is used in example (37), the first person plural **'itó** in example (38), and the third person plural **'emó** in example (39).

(37) hunáma béha 'áu kó'okoi-su-ka 'áu 'íne'e-te-k
     there well RFL sick-CPL-PPL RFL feel-VR-PRF
     Well, after having fallen sick, she recovered.

(38) húči=té   'itó bít-nee
     again=we RFL see-FUT
     We'll see each other again sometime.

(39) haámuči-m nássua-n   tú'isi 'emó čón-póna-n
     woman-PL fight-PCN very   RFL hair-pull-PCN
     Some women were fighting, they really pulled out each others' hair.

---

[1] The form **'emo** is also used for second person singular possessor in Arizona Yaqui.
(Eloise Jelinek, personal communication)

7.0. Pronominal objects of postpositions

The set of pronouns that serve as objects for the full set of postpositions (described under POSTPOSITIONS, pp. 173–175) is given in Table 48. The forms with **-le** only occur with the postposition **béna** *like*.

Person	Singular	Plural
1	né-, néle-	'itó-, 'itóle-
2	'ée, 'éle-	'emó-, 'emóle-
3	'áa-, 'áe-, 'ále-	'áme-

Table 48. Postpositional object pronouns

Examples (40)–(44) illustrate typical usages of the pronominal object of the postposition. A shortened form of the second person singular is given in examples (40) and (41).

(40) tuúka té 'é-t noóka-n táa káa hú'ena-si
yesterday we you-on speak-PCN but not bad-AVR
Yesterday we were talking about you, but it wasn't bad.

(41) heéwi liós 'e'ém-čiókoe liós 'e-mák wée-nee
yes God you-merciful God you-with go-FUT
OK, goodbye, God bless you; God go with you.

The third person singular pronominal object of the postposition is exemplified in example (42); the use of a first person plural is illustrated by sentence (43), and a second person plural is used in example (44).

(42) húu'u trén 'áa-wit 'áma yépsa-k
that train him-with there arrive-PRF
The train got there the same time he did.

(43) yúku 'á'abo 'itó-u wéye
rain over:here us-to come
The rain is coming over to us.

(44) haísa kaábe há'ani 'emó-násuk hunáka'a 'áa hoá-me
how nobody perhaps you-PL-among that-ACC able do-NZR
Is there no one among you who can do that?

The postposition **-u** *to* is conventionally used with a direct object pronoun to indicate the indirect object. Example (45) illustrates a first person singular indirect object, whereas (46) shows a second person singular indirect object. A third person singular indirect object is seen in the nominalized clause of the quotative sentence (47).

(45) bʷé'ituk 'o'ów-im kaábe né-u noóka
because man-PL nobody me-to speak
because no man speaks to me

(46) 'inía-beléki-k 'emó-u téuwaa-k 'áčali-m
this-amount-ACC you-to tell-PRF sir-PL
Sirs, this little amount I have told you.

(47) 'iním 'émpo wée 'émpo humák hunáa'a hú'ubʷa 'ín 'á-u noká-'u
here you come you perhaps that just:now my him-to speak-GND
Is that you coming here, perhaps you are the one I was just talking to?

INDEFINITE PRONOUNS, OBLIQUES, and ADVERBS

1.0. Introduction

In this chapter we summarize the various lexical items that Yaqui employs as indefinite pronouns and illustrate the kinds of grammatical constructions in which they are used. On a clear morphological basis, we divide them into positive and negative indefinite pronouns. It will also be clear that, morphologically, the positive indefinites are closely related the the WH-words (cf. QUESTIONS, pp. 90–96), another common pattern in Uto-Aztecan (cf. Langacker 1977:110) and in many other language families as well. We also treat in this section other kinds of indefinite lexical items such as locatives and adverbs of manner, time, and quantity because they are morphologically and syntactically parallel to the indefinite pronouns in a variety of ways.

2.0. Positive indefinites

The set of positive indefinite pronouns in Yaqui includes **hábe** *who* and **híta** *what*. In addition, Yaqui employs the quantifying terms **senú** *one* and **waáte** *several* to indicate singular and plural indefinites. Finally, **hák** *where* to indicate an indefinite location, **haíbeu** for an indefinite period of time, and **haíki** for an indefinite quantity.

Yaqui uses the quantifier **senú** as an indefinite pronoun in very much the same way that English uses the word "one" or Spanish uses "uno." A pair of typical usages are shown in sentences (1) and (2). As these examples indicate, Yaqui **senú** often serves anaphorically in the grammar as either a subject, as in sentence (1), or as an object, as illustrated in sentence (2).

(1) senú b^{w}ásia-t 'á'a wíike
    one tail-on it pulls
    One person pulled him by the tail.

(2) senú-k násuk-bó'o-ka-m-ta 'emé'e bít-nee
    one-ACC middle-lie-PPL-PL-ACC you:PL see-FUT
    You will see one lying in the middle.

The preponderance of examples of **waáte** found in texts show that it is employed as a kind of pronoun. In almost all cases the antecedent noun has been introduced earlier in the text and is referred to, but is not repeated. Example (3), taken from a text, illustrates these points. In this sentence the antecedent is **húme'e híakim** *those Yaquis*. The two uses of **waáte** are partitive. The first instance can be rendered "some of them" and the second instance can be rendered "others of them." Both clearly refer back to this sentence initial noun phrase. A more detailed description of the usage of **senú** is given in NUMERALS, pp. 229–230 and the use of **waáte** is discussed in QUANTIFIERS, pp. 224–227.

(3) húme'e híaki-m 'áma náu kón-ta-wa-ka béha waté béha 'áma yéu-ténne-k
    those Yaqui-PL there together surround-VR-PSV-PPL well some well there out-run:PL-PRF

    waté 'íntok 'áma kóko-k, haámuči-m húni'i kóko-k, 'íntok 'uúsi-m
    some and there die:PL-PRF woman-PL even die:PL-PRF and child-PL
    The Yaquis, having been surrounded there, some ran away, others died there, even women and children died.

Yaqui expresses the notion "any," as in "anyone, anything, anywhere," and "anytime" by adding **húni'i** *even* to the indefinite pronouns **hábe** and **híta**, to give the complex indefinites **hábe húni'i** *anyone, whoever,* and **híta húni'i** *however*. Other notions such as *whoever, whatever, wherever, whenever,* and *however* are expressed by a similar combination. A common word order for an "any" construction is for the adverbial **húni'i** *even* to follow an indefinite pronoun such as **híta** *thing*. This is illustrated by sentence (4). However, **húni'i** may well be discontinous from the indefinite pronoun, as exemplified in sentence (5).

249

(4) híta   húni'i téuwaa-ka   yée-'át-tua
    thing even   say-PPL   people-laugh-CAU
    Anything he says makes people laugh.

(5) 'itóm   b^wíh-taite-k   kía   hábe   yoém-ta   húni'i = b^wan
    us   seize-begin-PRF   just any:one   person-ACC   even = EXP
    They began to seize us, just any Yaqui whosoever.

The indefinite pronoun **híta** *thing* can be marked for plural, as seen in sentence (6), which contains both the singular form **híta** in the first clause, and the plural form **híta-m** in the second one.

(6) béha híta hakú'ubo   hún-im   nu-nú'ee   kétčia hakú'ubo   híta = m   nu-nú'ee
    well thing from:where there-they   RDP-take   also   from:where   thing = PL RDP-take
    Well, they were also taking anything whatsoever from anywhere; wherever they found them, they took them.

Positive indefinite pronouns in Yaqui are frequently marked with the question marker **-sa**, but because these forms are used as relative pronouns, I transcribe them as unitary words. The function of the question marker = **sa** appears to be just a way of heightening the degree of indefiniteness associated with the pronoun, i.e., effecting the change of meaning from "something" to "whatever," for example. It may also be a reflex of the implicit embedded question that relates to the meaning of the sentence in which the **-sa** indefinite pronoun is used.

(7) 'aáki-m   hitása b^wá'a-mačí-ka   'áma   'aayú-k
    pitahaya-PL   thing   eat-seem-PPL   there be-PRF
    Pitahayas (and) all kinds of edible (fruit) are there.[1]

Sentence (8) shows an indefinite pronoun serving as the object of a postposition, which in turn is marked by the postclitic = **sa**. In this case, the semantic force of = **sa** is clearly that of augmenting the degree of indefiniteness attached to the pronominal object of the postposition.

(8) hitá-'apo = sa   bibá-ta   yáa-k
    thing-in = INDEF   cigarette-ACC   make-PRF
    In some way he made a cigarette.

The indefinite locative is **hak** *somewhere*. In sentence (9) it occurs in construction with an adverbial demonstrative **'áman** *there*, whereas in sentence (10) it cliticizes to the distal adverbial demonstrative **wána**. In both cases, the role of **hák** is to specifically attribute indefinite extension to the location within which the respective event transpires.

(9) 'áman   hák   bo'ó-ta   nasé-'epo   húme   'usí-m   hápte-k
    there   somewhere   road-POS   fork-GND   those boy-PL   stand-PRF
    There somewhere, where the road forked, the boys stopped.

(10) wána-hak   kó'om siíka   'ábah-ta   wéeka-'apo   'áman-i san hosée-po
     there-somewhere   down   went   cottonwood-POS   stand:SG-GND   by:there San Jose-in

     kó'om-i   húčukia-u   yeéwi   sík-tábutči-m-po   'ómola ba'á-čó'oko-m-po   'áman-i
     down-ward   Tamper-to   outside   Red-Snake-PL-in side   water-bitter(?)-PL-at   there-by
     Off there somewhere he went down past Where the Cottonwood Stands, on downward past San Jose outside of Tamper, to one side of Red Snake on past Salty Water.

The locative **hák** may also be marked with the question clitic = **sa**, to signal an indefinite extension of the physical locale in which an event took place. Typical of such locales are bamboo patches, as in example (11), and gulleys, as in example (12).

---

1 The shorter forms **hák** and **híta** could have been used in each of these sentences. Here we may have an instance of the influence of Spanish on Yaqui.

(11) počó'o-ku hunáma'a háksa baká-t   túu'u-ku tó'ee
    woods-in there   where carrizo-in thicket-in lie-PL
    Off in the woods, somewhere there in a carrizo thicket, they slept/lay down.

(12) hunáma háksa hakía-po kátek
    there   where arroyo-in locate-PRF
    It is there somewhere in an arroyo.

The indefinite **háksa** *somewhere* has an extended usage in the temporal domain, in which it signals occurrence of some event in indefinitely extended past time. A typical usage is exemplified in example (13).

(13) háksa   wée-ka-i   kó'oko'i-m-po b^wé'uu-si
    somewhere go-PPL-PPL chile-PL-in   big-ADV

    pahkó-baa-wa-o   'áman né-hun-wa-k.
    feast-DSD-PSV-when there UNSPEC-invite-PSV-PRF
    Well, at some time back then, when there was going to be a really colossal feast in Chile Peppers, he was invited to take part.

An addition variation on the theme of **hák**, is the form **hákwoo**, which can be glossed as "whenever." It is exemplified in sentence (14), a complex sentence which also uses an inverted combination of **kaíta huní'i** and two more uses of **kaíta**. A clear instance of **hákwoo** in construction with **huní'i** is given in sentence (15).

(14) hún-tú-k=san   káa námaka-si 'áme-t   noká-'ate-k   kía hakwóo
    even-VR-PRF=EMP not hard-AVR them-on speak-CND-PRF even whenever

    huní'i kaíta híta huní'i kaíta mák-na   kaíta 'áma 'áttea-nee
    even   nothing thing even nothing give-FUT:PSV nothing there possess-FUT

    wakás-im-po wáa'a wóh-naíki puéplo
    cow-PL-in   that two-four towns
    So it is, if we do not talk hard about this matter, we will never be given anything, will never be given anything; the people of the eight towns will never own anything there among the cattle.

(15) 'íntok kía hakwóo húni'i káa wóh-naíki puéplo 'ám mák-baa-wa   'íme'e wakás-im
    and   only when   even not twice-four town them give-DSD-PSV these cattle
    And they don't have any intention of ever giving any of these cattle to the Eight Towns.

In conjunction with a following adverbial demonstrative **wá'am**, the interrogative form **háksa** has become idiosyncratically grammaticalized into a manner adverb with the lexicalized sense of "indifferently," as illustrated in sentence (16).

(16) túa 'emó náke káa hák=sa=wá'am   'emó bíča b^wéituk-o   yoóko
    truly RFL love not where=Q=by:there RFL see indifferently because-CND tomorrow

    matčúko   hitása béna-k   'ayú-k-o   két náu   'ée-báa-nee.
    day:after:tomorrow thing like-ACC be-PRF-CND also together think-DSD-FUT
    They truly love each other and do not disregard each other because, tomorrow or the day after, if something unexpected happens, they want to be of one accord.

Some of the indefinites such as **haíki** "an amount of X" display a surprising combination of semantic characteristics. In sentence (17) the indefinite **haíki** is both reduplicated (a characteristic of adjectives) and is marked for the accusative (a characteristic of nouns and adjectives when serving as heads). Finally it is also marked with the question clitic =**sa**.

(17) húnak bésa wáa'a wakáh-raa puéplo-m bée'eka-tána ná'iki-m-te-naa
    then well that cow-AZR people-PL all:around-from divide-PL-VR-FUT:PSV
    ha-haíki-k=sa   'áme-u támačia-naa
    RDP-amount-ACC=Q them-to measure-FUT:PSV
    Then those cattle would be divided throughout the people and the amounts would be distributed among them proportionately.

3.0. Negative indefinites

Yaqui, like its Southern Uto-Aztecan relative Náhuatl, forms negative indefinite pronouns by prefixing the negative particle **kaá** to the respective forms of the positive indefinite pronouns (cf. Langacker 1977:121). This involves drawing on the forms **hábe** *someone*, **híta** *something*, **hak** *somewhere*, **hákuni** *somewhere*, **haíbu** *now* and **háčini** *somehow*. The combination of **kaá** with these indefinite bases has led to the set of contracted forms listed in Table 49.

Neg Form	NEG + X	Meaning
kaábe	< káa-hábe	*no one*
kaíta	< káa-híta	*nothing*
káak	< káa hak	*nowhere*
kaákuni	< káa-hákuni	*nowhere*
kaíbu	< káa-haibu	*never*
kaáčini	< káa-háčini	*(in) no way*

Table 49. Negative indefinites

Typical examples of the use of the indefinite **kaabe** *no one* to function as the subject in a sentence are given in sentences (18) and (19).

(18) hunáma'a naáte-ka kaábe ko-kóčo-k
    there   begin-PPL nobody RDP-sleep-PRF
    From then on, no one went to sleep.

(19) kaábe née 'áma 'ám maná-'a-sae kaábe né 'áma 'ám maná-'a-tua-k
    no:one me there them place-EV-IMP no:one me there them place-EV-CAU-PRF
    No one commanded me to put them there, no one made me put them there.

The indefinite **kaíta** may also function as the subject of a sentence, as suggested by example (20).

(20) wame'e 'íntok 'o'ówi-m yoém-yóri-m 'í'an láuti-po kaíta 'áme-u paltáar-oa
    those   and   man-PL   indian-outsider now quickly-in nothing them-to lack-VR
    But right now, these half-breeds lack nothing.

Both **kaábe** and **kaíta** are frequently used as predicates in their own right, in answer to the questions "Is X there?" and "Do you have any X?" Typical usages are given in examples (21) and (22).

(21) kaábe *X is not here.*   (22) kaíta *There is no X.*

A common predicative use of the indefinite **kaíta** is to help signal the end of a narration, as in the formulaic sentence given in (23).

(23) híba kaíta 'íntok-o hunúm čúpu-k
    only nothing CNJ-when there finish-PRF
    There is nothing else and it ends there.

The indefinites may also function as modifers in a noun phrase, as shown by the use of **kaábe** in the subject noun phrase of examples (24) and (25), and the use of **kaíta** in the direct object noun phrase in example (24).

252

(24) máa-su   'í'ani   'iním desmonte-po kaábe yoéme 'áma tekipánoa
　　 for-example right-now here clearing-in no-one Yaqui there work
　　 For example, right now, no Yaqui is working where the land is being cleared.

(25) 'iníka'a munisipal-ta   'iním hiáki-m-násuk   yehté-k-o húnak kaábe
　　 this:ACC municipal-ACC here yaqui-PL-among sit-PRF-if then no-one

　　 kobanáo-tu-nee   kaábe puéplo-tu-nee   kaábe yá'u-raa-tu-nee
　　 governor-VR-FUT no-one (elder)-VR-FUT no-one chief-AZR-VR-FUT

　　 číkti puéplo-m bélle-'e-ka-tána
　　 all town-PL scattered-EV-being-from
　　 If this municipal authority is seated here, then there will be no (Yaqui) governors, there will be no (Yaqui) civil authorities, there will be no (Yaqui) military authorities anywhere throughout the whole nation.

(26) kaíta tékil-ta mák-wa
　　 nothing work-ACC give-PSV
　　 He is given no work.

An indefinite pronoun may also be the head of of complex noun phrase serving as either subject or object. Such a noun phrase may also involve specifying some kind of a partitive relationship in which **kaíta** could be glossed as "not one out of an entire group of X entities." In sentence (27) the class of entities that **kaíta** schematically designates is a collective set of herds of cows. In sentence (28) the membership of the Yaqui nation is the basis for the partitive relationship. In sentence (29) the identical group provides the membership, but the additional specification of residence in a particular town is specified.

(27) 'inía híaki-ta-bétana kaíta tepóhti-m híp^{w}ee wáa'a wakáh-raa
　　 this yaqui-ACC-from nothing brand-PL have that cattle-AZR
　　 Not a one of them carries the brand of any Yaqui.

(28) hún-tuk=san   wáa'a hiáki kaíta   kía wépul wakáh-ta húni'i káa 'áma 'áttea-k
　　 even-VR:PRF=EMP that Yaqui nothing just one cow-ACC even not there own-PRF
　　 So that, in fact, no Yaqui owns even one head of that cattle.

(29) hunáka'a wakáh-raa-ta čúlti nénk-iwa-m-ta   wáa'a wóh-naíki puéplo
　　 that:ACC cow-AZR-ACC remote sell-PSV-NZR-ACC that eight town
　　 káa hú'uneiyaa ní kía wáme'e delegaom-tea-me   húni'i káa hú'uneiyaa
　　 not know or even those delegates-QUO-NZR even not know
　　 Not a person of the Eight Towns nor even any of those delegates knows anything about those cows being sold on the sly.

A typical use of the temporal **kaíbu** is given in example (30).

(30) 'émpo kaíbu 'ém 'ea-'u-mak yéu-wée-nee
　　 you never your think-GND-with out-go-FUT
　　 You will never succeed (lit. come-out) with your idea.

PART IV: VERB STRUCTURE

VERB STEMS

1.0. Introduction

The most neutral word order used in forming a Yaqui utterance is Subject-Object-Verb; that is, the verb complex occurs at the end of an utterance. As is typical of Uto-Aztecan languages, the verb system is the the most complex and the most difficult feature of Yaqui grammar to describe adequately. In this section and in the four that follow, we consider the Yaqui verb from several angles, both internal to the verb stem and external to it in terms of its distribution into verb phrases and its cooccurrences with other types of grammatical entities. In this section, we begin by treating one aspect of verb structure, i.e., the categorization of Yaqui verb stems and the associated morphological and semantic characteristics of these stems.[1]

A Yaqui verb stem, in its nonfinite form, is distinguishable both morphologically and semantically from the other parts of speech such as nouns, adverbs, and adjectives on several grounds. These latter may be uttered as minimal free forms, whereas the verb stem cannot normally or naturally be, because of its cognitive status. On the other hand, in both its finite and nonfinite forms, the Yaqui verb is accompanied by diagnostic constituents in its clause.

2.0. The three major verb classes

The most convenient way to define the verb classes in Yaqui is to list them under three categories: intransitive verbs, transitive verbs, and verbs which may be either transitive or intransitive. Each of these categories permits further subdivisions.

Yaqui grammar distinguishes between transitive and intransitive verbs in several ways. For one, there is a difference in the marking of clausal constituents. Thus, intransitive verbs must be accompanied by a subject noun or pronoun, whereas transitive verbs must be accompanied by both a subject and object nominal or pronoun. (In both cases, the absence of an overt subject marks third person singular.) Differences in the meanings related to patterns of reduplication also distinguish transitive verbs from intransitive ones, as do the patterns for suppletion.

However, there is also a large class of verbs in Yaqui which do not have distinct transitive/intransitive stems. Verbs that may be either transitive or intransitive are subdivided into three categories: those with stems that take the suffixes **-a/-ta** to indicate transitive and **-e/-te** to indicate intransitive, those with some kind of phonological modification to distinguish between intransitive and transitive, and those that can be either transitive or intransitive without any change whatsoever in the verb form.

2.1. Intransitive verbs

Intransitive verbs are subdivided according to the formation of the plural stem into: those with a different (suppletive) stem for the plural subject; those in which reduplication of the first syllable is used when there is a plural subject; and those which retain the same form of stem for both singular and plural subjects.

The suppletive intransitive verbs have one stem form when the subject of the sentence is singular and have a distinct one when the subject of the sentence is plural. The verb meaning "to run," for example, has the stem **búite** for singular subjects and **ténne** for plural ones.

---

[1] Verb stems may also be derived from nouns (or other parts of speech). Some derived stems display layers of derivation, where a verb may be converted into a noun and then converted back into a verb again, for example. These derivational patterns were described in VERB MORPHOLOGY, pp. 137–148.

(1)(a) 'áapo 'áman búite-k
　　　he　there　run:SG-PRF
　　　He ran there.

(b) bémpo 'áman ténne-k
　　they　there　run:PL-PRF
　　They ran there.

The verb meaning variously "to sit," "to be seated," or "to be situated" utilizes the stem form **yeésa** for singular subjects and **hoóye** for plural ones, as illustrated by sentences (2)(a) and (2)(b).

(2)(a) húu'u Hóan hiba 'im yeésa
　　　that　John always here sit:SG
　　　John always sits here.

(b) bémpo 'áman hoóye
　　they　there　sit:PL
　　They sit over there.

In passing, note that the adverbial suffixes **-se/-bo** *to go to do X* are also suppletive for the number of the subject. This likely suggests that these two suffixes were actually grammaticalized from an original intransitive suppletive pair of motion verb stems. The contrastive meanings of these two suffixes is illustrated in (3)(a) and (3)(b) by their use with the same verb stem.

(3)(a) 'áapo 'áman tekipánoa-se-k
　　　he　there　work-go:SG-PRF
　　　He went there to work.

(b) bémpo 'áman tekipánoa-bo-k
　　they　there　work-go:PL-PRF
　　They went there to work.

The pairs of stems given in Table 50 are additional examples of suppletive intransitive verbs. Many other Yaqui verbs are suppletive for number.

Singular	Plural	Meaning
wečé	wátte	*to fall*
weáma	réhte	*to walk*
wéyek	há'abʷek	*to be standing*
muúke	kóko	*to be dying*
kátek	hoóka	*to be located*

Table 50. Intransitive suppletive verb stems.

Numerous intransitive verbs reduplicate the first syllable to indicate a plural subject. Table 51 presents several of these pairs of verb stems. The usages of these verbs and others are discussed in 3.2. on pp. 263–264.

Singular	Plural	Meaning
kóče	ko-koče	*to sleep*
báhume	ba-báhume	*to swim*
'uúba	'u-'úba	*to bathe*

Table 51. Reduplicated intransitive verb stems

Another major set of intransitive verbs use the same form for singular and plural subjects. The verb **čik-tu** *to be lost, to become disoriented*, marked with the verbalizer **-tu**, is a typical example as shown by examples (4)(a) and (4)(b). Note that in this context, **-tu** has a passive meaning.

(4)(a) čik-tú-k=ane
　　　lose-VR-PRF=I
　　　I got lost.

(b) čik-tú-k=ate
　　loose-VR-PRF=we
　　We got lost.

2.2. Transitive stems

Some transitive stems are suppletive and we need to call attention to the pair, **mé'aa** and **sú'aa** *to kill*, which represents a small class of verbs in which one form of the stem is used with singular objects, and a second is used with plural objects.

A large number of transitive stems can be labelled "regular" because, other than for reduplication, they do not change their shape under different syntactic and semantic conditions. These include **čike** *to brush, to sweep*, **bʷá'ee** *to eat*, **béeba** *to hit, to drive* and **máya** *to stone*, illustrated in sentences (5)–(8).

(5) čibá'ato híms-im-mea sí'ime púhba-t 'á'a číke
    goat whiskers-PL-INST all face-on him brush
    The goat brushed all his face with his whiskers.

(6) mún-bák-ta bʷá'ee
    bean-cook(boil)-ACC eat
    He eats bean soup.

(7) wakás-im 'áme-u béeba-k
    cow-PL them-to hit(drive)-PRF
    They drove the cattle toward them.

(8) 'á'a máya 'á'a béeba húka'a bakót-ta
    it stone it hit that-ACC snake-ACC
    Stone it, hit it, that snake.

A number of transitive stems take alternate forms depending on the suffix that occurs on them. For example, the verb **yáa**, meaning "to do, to make," has the form with the long vowel when it occurs with the perfective suffix **-k**, as in sentence (9), but takes the form **yá'a** when it occurs with the future, as in sentence (10).

(9) 'á'a yáa-k   (10) 'á'a yá'a-nee
    it do-PRF   it do-FUT
    He did it.   *He will do it.*

Representative examples of transitive stem alternates are given in Table 52.

Basic	Modified	Meaning
hoóa	hoo	to make
múhe	'múhu-	to stab
'ukkúle	'úkkul-	to desire X
búke	búk-	domesticate
čóna	čón-	to beat

Table 52. Transitive verb stem alternates

It is not clear what factor determines this pairing of the verbal suffixes with particular stem forms. The realized vs. unrealized differentiation does not seem to hold across the board. While perfective **-k** and past-continuative **-n** do refer to realized events, participializer **-k** and **-o** *if/when* definitely do not.[2]

The division into a single pair of verb stem forms reflecting a consistent perfective vs. imperfective distinction also does not seem to hold. For example, the verb **'úkkule** appears to draw on both its long form and its short form when it designates an ongoing process as illustrated in examples (11) and (12).

(11) kúču-m bít-ču-ka tú'i-s=am 'úkkule-ka-i
     fish-PL see-CPL-PPL much-ADV=them desire-PPL-STAT
     Seeing the fish, he really yearned for them.

(12) húme'e čuúna-m 'úkkul-wa-tči-si 'áma tó'o-ka-n
     those fig-PL desire-PSV-on-ADV there lie:PL-PPL-PCN
     Those figs were lying there very appetizingly.

Note, however, that the form of **'úkkule** given in example (11) is a verb marked for the past imperfective, whereas the shortened form in example (12) is an adverbialized passive form. The force of the passive is sufficient to place a perfective construal on the verb form, whereas the adverbialization

---

2   Dedrick has made a quick check on the whole set of 19 Yaqui verbal suffixes. Of these, only **-k** PRF, **-n** PCN, **-ka** PPL, and **-o** *if/when* suffix to the basic free form of the verb. All the rest: **-bae, -nee, -naa, -wa, -su, -tua, -ria, -tebo, -sae, -le, -pea, -'ea, -se/-bo, -patči**, and **-amča** suffix to modified verb stems.

259

accomodates a perfectively construed entity to an imperfective view of the overall situation being described.

Some verbs like **múhe** *to shoot* may actually display three stem forms depending upon which suffix occurs with it, as illustrated in sentences (13)–(15). The form **muhe,** for example, occurs with the past continuative **-n** in sentence (13), whereas the form **muhu** occurs with the perfective **-k,** as in sentence (14) and, in sentence (15) the form **muhi** occurs with the causative suffix **-tua.**

(13) wikítč-im mu-muhe-n
bird-PL RDP-shoot-PCN
He was shooting birds.

(14) 'án=a'a múhu-k
I=it shoot-PRF
I shot it.

(15) 'áu 'á'a múhi-tua-ka-n
RFL it shoot-CAU-PPL-PCN
He was trying to shoot it.

The verb stem **hoóa** *to make* appears in its full form when followed by the past continuative **-n,** as seen in sentence (16), but shortens to **hoo-** when followed by the passive **-wa,** as in sentence (17).

(16) húme'e máh-béea-m 'ám súpe-hoóa-n
those deer-skin-PL them shirt-make-PCN
He used to make shirts out of deer-skin.

(17) b^wé'uu-si kapée-hoo-wa
big-AVR coffee-make-PSV
They are making a lot of coffee.

Sometimes the shorter form appears in a compound and/or reduplicated stem, whereas the longer form appears in the simple perfective, as is true for the stem **čóna,** illustrated in sentences (18) and (19).

(18) 'usí-ta čóna-k
child-ACC slap-PRF
He slapped the child.

(19) téni-t 'á'a čó-čón-tébo-k
mouth-on him RDP-slap-order-PRF
He commanded him to slap his mouth.

The meanings of a few verbs require the specification of both a direct and an indirect object. For example, the verb **máka** *to deliver to, to give* has this kind of a requirement on its usage. Sentences (20) and (21), for example, have first person singular subjects and second person singular indirect objects, but differ in that sentence (20) has an abstract noun for its direct object, whereas sentence (21) has a third person singular object pronoun for designating its direct object.

(20) húnen ne 'enči lútu'uria-m máka
thus I you:ACC truth-PL:ACC give
In that way I give you the truth.

(21) née 'enči 'á'a mák-nee wáka'a 'ém wáata-'u-ta
I you:ACC it:ACC give-FUT that:ACC your want-GND-ACC
I will give you that which you want.[3]

The process of suppletion is not at all productive among transitive Yaqui stems. The one known pair, however, **mé'a** and **sú'aa** does follow the well-known Uto-Aztecan pattern for using one stem form for indicating singular objects and another for plural objects. The subject usually, but not necessarily, is singular as in examples (22) and (23).

(22) 'á'a mé'aa-k húka'a bakót-ta
it:ACC kill-PRF that:ACC snake-ACC
He killed the snake.

(23) masó-m sú'a-ka 'áu 'ania
deer-PL kill-GND RFL help
He earns-his-living by killing deer.

---

[3] The remaining words: **'úkkule, búke,** and **čóna** follow the pattern described above.

2.3. Transitive/intransitive verbs

There is a relatively limited class of stems that take the suffixes **-a** or **-ta** for signalling their transitive usages and take **-e** or **-te** to mark their their intransitive usages. The forms illustrated in sentences (24)–(38) practically exhaust the inventory of such stems.

In example (24)(a), the stem form **kót-ta** illustrates a transitive usage, whereas in (24)(b) **kót-te** marks an intransitive usage of the stem that means "to break."

(24)(a) húka'a   kúta-ta   kót-ta-k   (b) kót-te-k   húu'u púentes
that:ACC pole-ACC break-TRN-PRF   break-INTR-PRF that bridge
He broke the stick/pole.   *The bridge broke.*

The pair of examples (25)(a)–(b) show a stem marked with a final **-a** vowel to signal its transitive usage, and its corresponding intransitive usage marked by a stem final **-e**. As these examples suggest, in its transitive usage, **b^{w}ása** means "to cook." In its intransitive usage, the form **b^{w}áse** means "to ripen" or "to mature."

(25)(a) wáka-bák-ta   b^{w}ás-a
meat-stew-ACC cook-TRN
She is cooking stew.

(b) minai-m   b^{w}ás-e-'e-te-k-o   mékkaa winhúba
cantelope-PL ripe-INTR-EV-VR-PRF-when far fragrant
When canteloupes are ripe, their fragrance carries a long way.

The transitive usages of the verb stem **pút-** meaning "to shoot" are marked **-ta** as illustrated in example (26)(a), whereas their reflexive and intransitive usages are marked by **-te** as shown in example (26)(b). This can also be seen in several other examples below.

(26)(a) tuúka   yoói   wó'i-ta   pút-ta-k   (b) hí'obe-ka   'áu pút-te-k
yesterday Mexican coyote-ACC shoot-TRN-PRF   mistake-PPL RFL shoot-VR-PRF
Yesterday a Mexican shot a coyote.   *He shot himself by mistake.*

In its transitive usages, the reduplicated form of **bék** means "to shave" as in example (27)(a). In its intransitive and reflexive usages, it means "to scrape" as in example (27)(b).

(27)(a) haíbu tósai-m čao-bóa-k, hámak 'ám bék-bek-ta
now white-PL chin-hair-have sometimes them RDP-shave-TRN
He now has white chin whiskers; sometimes he shaves them.

(b) kába'i kúta-t 'áu bék-te-k
horse stick-on RFL scrape-INTR-PRF
The horse scraped himself on a stick.

The meanings of transitive and intransitive pairs are usually related in transparent ways. For example, the transitive form of **kón** means "to form a circle around X" as in example (28)(a), whereas the intransitive form means "to follow a curved path" or "to go around X location" as in example (28)(b).

(28)(a) wáe-t 'á'a kón-ta húka'a bakót-ta
there-on it circle-TRN that:ACC snake-ACC
Circle the snake on the other side.

(b) mó'obači-wi yáha-ka hunáman kón-te-k sáusa-u lúula
Mo'obachi-to arrive:PL-PPL there circle-VR-PRF Sausa-to straight
Having arrived to Mó'obaci, they went around it, straight to Sausa.

Among the transitive vs. intransitive relations signalled by the **-ta** vs. **-te** morphemic contrast is the prototypical relationship between an active and a passive sentence, as seen in examples (29)(a) and (b), in which **pú'ak-ta** means "to load X" and **pú'ak-te** means "be loaded."

(29)(a) tóoke-m-po híta pú'ak-ta-nee 'ón-ta pú'ak-ta-nee 'á'a nénkí-betčí'ibo
truck-PL-in thing load-TRN-FUT salt-ACC load-TRN-FUT it sell-for
They will load things on trucks; they will load salt to sell it.

(b) híak-bat^wé-po báči-pú'ak-te-ka hunáman 'á'a tó-tóha-n
Yaqui-river-in grain-load-INTR-PPL there it RDP-take-PCN
The grain was loaded from the Yaqui river territory and was taken there.

Some additional verbs that illustrate this same morphological contrast include the verbs **nót-ta/-te** *to return* and **noí-ta/-te** *to go away to X*. Both verbs, however, are almost exclusively used in their intransitive forms. Examples of transitive usages of these two verbs in our files are scarce. Whereas we have numerous examples of their usage with the intransitive **-te,** Dedrick has only occasionally overheard expressions like that given in sentence (30).

(30) lipró-ta 'á-u nót-ta-k
book-ACC him-to return-TRN-PRF
He returned the book to him.

Sentences (31) and (32) give typical intransitive usages of the verb **nói-te**, which means "to go to a distal location," and its rare transitive counterpart, given in sentence (33) means "to send X back to a distal location."

(31) 'áman 'ém nói-te nót-te-ka née téhwa-nee
there you-PL go-INTR return-INTR-PPL me tell-FUT
You go there, and when you come back, tell me.

(32) húbena wásuktia-m wéye né 'ím nói-te-ka-i
many year-PL go I here go-INTR-PPL-PPL
Many years have passed since I (first) came here.

(33) 'á'a b^wía-raa-u 'á'a noí-ta-k
his land-ABS-to him send-TRN-PRF
He sent him back to his own country.

The transitive form **bíak-ta,** illustrated in sentence (34), means "to rotate X" or "to turn X over." Its intransitive counterpart, given in sentence (35), means "to roll over."

(34) b^wicía-p-am bíak-ta-ka 'ám b^wá'e
smoke-in-them turn-TRN-PPL them eat
After having rotated them in the smoke, he eats them.

(35) báhi-si báh-po bíak-te-k
three-AVR grass-in turn-INTR-PRF
He rolled over in the grass three times.

The transitive usage of **tubúk-ta** means "to jump over X" as seen in sentence (36). The intransitive counterpart exemplified in sentence (37) means "to jump up."

(36) 'áme-pat wée-taite-ka kanál-ta tubúk-ta-k
them-front go-begin-PPL canal-ACC jump-TRN-PRF
Going ahead of them, he jumped over the canal.

(37) masó 'áman túbuk-te-k
deer there jump-INTR-PRF
A deer jumped up over there.

The only examples that we have for the transitive verb **čépta** and its intransitive counterpart **čépte** *to jump* are the intransitive forms which can be glosses as "to jump up," as in (38)(a) or "to leap up," as in (38)(b).

(38)(a) masó 'ámman čép-te-k
deer way:off jump-INTR-PRF
Upon leaping up, he stood firmly.

(b) hiká-u čép-ti-pat kútti kíkte-k
upward-to leap-INTR-upon firmly stand-PRF
A deer jumped up way off yonder.

3.0. Phonologically modified forms

Yaqui verb stems are modified in a variety of ways phonologically in the different contexts in which they are used. In the following section we summarize the most salient categories of these stem modifications. As the data will show, there is often a semantic motivation for these phonological changes.

3.1. Transitivity changing suffixes

Some stems undergo a modification in their shape when they take suffixes that change their transitivity status. For example, the intransitive verb stem **'éa** means "to think" or "to wish," as in example (39)(a). It has **'eiyaa** *to judge, to think, to esteem* as its derived transitive form as illustrated in sentence (39)(b).

(39)(a) née húnen 'éa
I thus wish
That is how I think.

(b) tú'isi n=a'a 'éiyaa
much I=him esteem
I esteem him very much.

A second pair of derived forms, the intransitive **hú'unea** and the transitive **hú'uneiyaa** are given in (40)(a)–(b). These have meanings "to know" and "to be informed," respectively.

(40)(a) 'emé'e hú'un-ea 'iníá-e 'itóm 'ito 'anía-'apo
you:PL know-INTR this-INST our RFL help-GND
You know that we earn our living this way.

(b) néhpo két húnen 'á'a hú'un-eiyaa
I also thus it:ACC know-TRN
I also know it that way.

A few stems show differential pitch placement for transitive vs. intransitive pairs. For example, compare **taáwa** *to stay somewhere, to remain* in sentences (41)(a) and (b) with **tawáa** *to leave something, to cause to remain* in sentence (41)(c).

(41)(a) 'áman taáwa-k
there stay-PRF
He stayed there.

(c) wate-m-mak née tawáa-k
other-PL-with me leave-PRF
He left me with the others.

(b) kaita 'áma taáwa-k
nothing there stay-PRF
There was nothing, nothing left.

Other examples in Yaqui have the same form for both intransitive and transitive usages. A typical example is the perception verb **biča** *to see*, exemplified in (42).

(42)(a) áapo tú'i-si biča
he well sees
He sees well.

(b) 'áapo tú'i-si 'á'a biča-k
he well it see-PRF
He saw it well/clearly.

3.2. Reduplication

Generally, the reduplication of Yaqui stems serves one of at least three functions: to indicate multiple occurrences of an entity, i.e., plural subjects and objects; to signal repeated occurrences of an event; or to attribute intensity to an event or process.[4] The contrast between the simple past form **miíka-k** *to give*-PRF and its reduplicated counterpart illustrates well the repetitive use of reduplication.

(43)(a) tómi-ta 'a'a miíka-k
money-ACC him give-PRF
He gave him money.

(b) 'ábaim 'am mi-mík-sime
roasting-ears them RDP-give-go
She went on giving roasting ears to them.

The contrast between sentences (44)(a) and (b) shows the use of reduplication to mark the plurality of subjects of an intransitive verb. In sentence (44)(c), on the other hand, reduplication is used to mark the habitual nature of a regularly recurring event.

---

4 In general, reduplication indicates plurality or repetition of the action indicated by transitive verbs and plurality of subject for the intransitive verbs. However, since the suppletive forms of the intransitive verb already indicate singular or plural subject, for these the meaning indicates repetition of the action as with transitive verbs.

(44)(a) húu'u hoán kári-po   kóče
       that John house-in sleep
       John is sleeping in the house.

   (b) ketúni ko-kóče   húme'e maoméeo-m
       still RDP-sleep those acrobat-PL
       The acrobats were still sleeping.

   (c) 'áma bó'e húu'u Hóan híba 'áma bo-bó'e
       there lies that John always there RDP-lies
       That's where John sleeps, he always sleeps there.[5]

The two occurrences of reduplication in example (45) illustrate the intensifying function of reduplication with a psychological verb in one case and its marking of a plural object of a transitive verb in the other.

(45) kía 'itóm bái-tát-ta'aa   káa-tú'ii wíko'i 'ám-mea   yée
     only us fresh-RDP-know (deceive) not-good rifle them-INST people

     sús-su'a-su-i-'i-tea
     RDP-kill-CPL-PPL-EV-say
     It was nothing but a big deception. They said, "Rifles are not good, people get killed with them."

In example (46) the two cases of reduplication indicate a plurality of passive subject.

(46) húnen té béha kía ná'iki-m bí-bíttua-hapte-ak 'enemíigo-ta té mu-múhi-saí-wa
     thus we well only divide-PL RDP-send-begin-PSV enemy-ACC   we RDP-shoot-IMP-PSV
     Thus we began to be sent everywhere. We were commanded to shoot the enemy.

Reduplication is common in onomatopoetic expressions as an iconic reflection of the repetitiveness of the event. In example (47) the repeated firing of cannons in battle is described by the reduplicated form **wása-wásak**.

(47) b^wíčia híba káu-po   béha b^wít-wása-wásak-ti   'aáne húme'e kanyóon-im
     smoke only mountain-on well smoke-"wasa-wasak"-CON doing those cannon-PL
     The mountain was covered with a haze of smoke; the cannons were going "wása-wásak" as they spouted smoke from their muzzles.

Reduplication is also used with constituents other than verbs and adjectives. As examples (48) and (49) clearly illustrate, adverbs and postpositions may also be reduplicated to indicate the plurality of individuals involved in a situation.

(48) 'íntok bankó-m-be-béna ča-čáka-'a-ku   náu-bíča   hoóka
     and   bench-PL-RDP-like RDP-sideways-EV-in together-site located:PL
     And they were on each side, facing each other like chairs lined up.

(49) sí'ime wáa'a káa ba-bámse-m-ta-betčí'ibo
     all   that not RDP-hurry-NZR-ACC-for
     for everyone who is not really in a hurry

Finally, incorporated nouns may be reduplicated, as example (50) nicely shows.

(50) nát-bépa   ka-káa-te-wa
     vertical-above RDP-house-INTR-PSV
     Houses are being built one above the other.

---

5 There are analogous forms for plural subject, **tó'e, to-tó'e** meaning "to go to bed:PL."

3.3. Vowel and consonant gemination

Vowel and consonant gemination is limited and selective, and several distinct derivational processes overlap in producing the present surface forms. Scarcity of examples makes it difficult to formulate precise rules. In the examples of gemination of consonants and vowels that Dedrick has collected to date, either the habituality or the prolongation of the activity seems to be invoked by the speaker.

Reduplication and gemination may both figure in the overall pattern of stem phenomena relating to individual verb stems such as **wíke** *to pull*. The basic transitive form means "to pull." The reduplicated form highlights the repetition of the action of pulling as illustrated by example (51)(b) and the geminated form highlights the extension of the activity throughout time, as in example (51)(c).

(51)(a) wíke *pull* (b) wi-wíke *pull repeatedly* (c) wíike *pull continuously*

The same pattern is observed for certain intransitive verbs such as **yépsa** *to arrive*, which has an additional singular form **yebíh** and a suppletive plural form **yáha**.

(52)(a) ye-yépsa (SG) *arrive repeatedly* (c) yéepsa (SG) *arrive continually*
(b) ya-yáha (PL) *arrive repeatedly* (d) yaáha (PL) *arrive continually*

There are often at least two possible ways of reduplicating a stem and the question of which stems take which manner of reduplication is not fully predictable. Thus, the verb meaning "to receive" does not reduplicate the initial CV of the stem **mabéta** but rather it reduplicates the initial CVC, resulting in a geminate **bb**. The reduplicated form itself designates habitual action, a meaning that relates to both repeated action and to the extension of an event through time.

(53)(a) mabéta *receive* (b) *ma-mábeta (no examples) (c) mábbeta *receive habitually*

On the other hand, the verb stem **bʷá'e** *to eat* utilizes both kinds of reduplication to signal graphically distinct semantic construals of eating habits. Example (54)(a) signals the simple imperfective view that someone is in the process of eating. In contrast, example (54)(b) pictures the eating as a repetitive process or an ongoing series of identical events. Finally, the last example in the set places our attention on the great quantities of food our subject consumes.

(54)(a) hi'ibʷa'a (b) bʷa-bʷá'e (c) bʷáb-bʷa'e
He is eating. *He always eats.* *He is a real glutton.*

Sets of forms such as: **taáwa** (*intransitive*) *to remain*, and **tawáa** (*transitive*) *to cause to remain*, and **siíka** *went*, **sikáa** *having gone* are unique and do not represent any active process that I can identify, although they may represent a distinction between imperfective and perfective stem forms.

Forms as: **bʷi'i-bʷise** *repeatedly grab* from **bʷíse** *to grab* and **hií-'ibʷa** *to eat*:INTR, **hi-hí'ibʷa** *eat repeatedly* or *many eating* from **bʷá'e** *to eat*:TRN reflect the echo-vowel process described under morphophonemics (cf. PHONOLOGY, pp. 28–29).

3.4. CVC reduplication and consonant gemination

An important reduplication process in Yaqui reduplicates with a CVC closed syllable. The reduplicated syllable carries high pitch and is closed by a copy of the initial consonant of the verb in question. This process is represented graphically for three differently shaped verb stems in Table 53.

Base		Reduplication
cv [+str] cv	>	cv [+str] c-cvcv
cvv [+str] cv	>	cv [+str] c-cvcv
cv [+str] vcv	>	cv [+str] c-cvvcv

Table 53. Closed syllable reduplication pattern

This type of reduplication signals the intensity with which some action is being carried out or the intenseness of some quality or state of affairs being indicated by a verb or an adjective. Morphologically, this reduplication process also gives rise to long consonants, illustrating that consonant gemination has become partly grammaticalized in Yaqui, as can be seen by comparing the glosses for the forms given below. (Note that the letters (a)–(c) refer to the patterns in Table 53 above.)

(55)(a) Single Subject kóče   *sleep*
       Plural Subject   ko-kóče   *sleep*
       Intense   kók-koče *be exceedingly sleepy*
   (b) Single Subject   noóka   *talk*
       Plural Subject   no-nóka   *talk repeatedly*
       Intense   nón-noka *talk too much*
       Single Subject   teébe   *tall*
       Plural Subject   te-tébe   *tall*
       Intense   tét-tebe *exceedingly tall*
   (c) Single Subject   náako   *drunk*
       Plural Subject   na-náako *repeatedly drunk*
       Intense   nán-naako *exceedingly drunk*

The stem **yó'o-** indicates a variety of related concepts such as "growth", "maturity," and "respectability" and can be reduplicated several ways. The kinds of reduplicated forms currently used are given in Table 54. A consideration of the meanings associated with the distinct forms shows both general patterns and specific lexicalization. There are actually three different forms of reduplication associated with marking of plural subjects. However, one of the three forms also involves the use of the derivational suffix **-raa** that turns the predicate adjective into a nominalization. Gemination of different vowels of the stem then allows Yaqui to derive a second nominalization. These forms and their meanings are summarized in Table 54.

Grammar	Form	Meaning
Singular	yó'o-we	*is mature, grown*
Plural	yo-yó'o-we	*are mature*
Adverb	yóy-yo'o-we	*exceedingly respectable*
Derived	yoó'o-we	*the elders, ancestors*
Derived noun	yo'óo-raa	*authorities*

Table 54. Reduplicated forms of yó'o

It is not always easy to differentiate repeated activity from habitual or prolonged activity. Context and the meanings of the forms used all figure in trying to determine the particular usage of a reduplicated form. The following examples from different texts are a fair sampling of the types of reduplication referred to here. There may well be several forms of reduplication used in a single sentence.

Example (56) shows three usages of reduplication, the first two express the notion of prolonged duration, and the other one expresses the notion of repetitive events.

(56) báhi ta'á-po húu'u páhko káa lú'u-lú'u-te   páhko lú'u-ti-síme-o
     three day-in that   feast not RDP-end-INTR   feast end-CON-go-when

láau-láautia batό'o-raa sáka-'a-sáka
RDP-slowly people-ABS RDP-EV-go:PL
The feast did not end for three days. As the feast began to draw to a close, groups of people began leaving at odd intervals (i.e., slowly began going away).

Example (57) shows the use of reduplication to indicate the simultaneous shared participation in a set of events by a multiplicity of individuals.

(57) ketúni ko-kóče húme'e maromeeo-m ko-kót-búsa-ka 'emó
still RDP-sleep those acrobat-PL RDP-sleep-awake-PPL RFL

bítču púh-báhi-la-m-taka bu-búsa
stare face-swell-PPL-PL-PPL RDP-awaken
The acrobats were still sleeping. When they finally awoke from their sleep, they stared at one another. They had awakened with their faces swollen.

The use of reduplication to signal repetitive action is clearly illustrated by example (58), in which a person is handing out a discrete object to a multiplicity of people one at a time.

(58) wée-'e-pu-la-im yéu-wíike-ka yée 'ám mí-mík-síme
GM-EV-one-PPL-PL out-GM:pull-PPL people them RDP-give-go
She went pulling the roasting ears out one by one and giving them to each of the people.

The next four sentences that we discuss illustrate reduplicated forms that mark intensity of state or activity. In (59) **bíb-bitču** means "to stare at intently." In (60) the adverb **bátte** *nearly* is reduplicated to drive home the point of how close things came to really being a tragedy. The second reduplicated form in this sentence signals the multiplicity of joint malefactors.

(59) hunáme'e pusí-m-mea 'itóm 'usí-la bíb-bit-ču
those eye-PL-INST our boy-DIM RDP-look-CPL
She stared intently at our lad with those eyes.

(60) hunáme'e bát-bátte 'á'a me-mé'a
those RDP-nearly him RDP-kill
Those people very nearly murdered him.

The "intensity" signalled by the reduplicated form in (61) may well be the strength of the speaker's doubt that orders can even be carried out.

(61) 'áapo-ik né-sau-mak yéu-yúy-yuma-'a-te-k-o
he-POS IZR-order-with out-RDP-attain-EV-INTR-PRF-CND
if one can really carry out his command

Reduplication indicating the extension of a process throughout time can also be employed in the domain of conceived time, i.e., time relating to conceived situations that never did arise. This is indicated by the use of the counterfactual past continuative suffix **-n** in example (62).

(62) kúču-ta né 'áman hi-hínu-n táa káa né-u nénk-i-wa-k
fish-ACC I there RDP-buy-PCN but not me-to sell-PPL-PSV-PRF
I really planned to buy a fish there, but it wasn't sold to me.

(63) 'áman 'itóm b^{w}í'i-b^{w}íse kútti 'itóm b^{w}í'i-b^{w}íse
there us RDP-seize firmly us RDP-seize
They captured every last one of us there; we were firmly held prisoners.

Example (64) illustrates a reduplicated verb **táh-táh-te,** which indicates multiple, but identical involvement of a multiplicity of subjects in the event and a reduplicated adjective **tét-tebe,** which indicates augmented height.

(64) baké'o-m 'áme-bétuk yéu-reh-té-ka káa 'áme-u
cowboy-PL them-under out-go-INTR-PPL not them-to

táh-táh-te b^{w}é'ituk-'ím tú'isi tét-tebe
RDP-touch-VR because-they very RDP-tall
The cowboys riding under them could not come near to touching them because they were so tall.

INCORPORATION

1.0. Introduction

In this section we consider a class of phenomena that are highly grammaticalized and form a part of complex verb stems in Yaqui, but are not clearly compounds in the sense described earlier in COMPOUNDS, pp. 160–164. Semantically, these items are adverb-like, but have not become suffixes, as is often the case in Uto-Aztecan, (cf. Langacker 1977:133). For the most part, they have nominal, adverbial and postpositional sources.

The items, **báa-** *now*, **bát-** *first*, **náas-** *all around*, **nát-** *on top of*, **náu-** *together*, **yée-** *people*, and **yeu-** *out* represent a small class of elements that have become incorporated into particular verb stems. In some cases their grammatical source is obvious because there are other constructions in which they occur separately from the verb, e.g., although they commonly prefix to intransitive verbs, in some contexts, pronouns may be inserted between them and transitive verbs.

2.0. The manner adverbial báa-

The manner adverbial **báa-** can be variously glossed as "at once," "once for all," or "right now." The first two examples illustrate its use as a free adverbial. In sentence (1) it occurs preceding an indefinite pronoun that is also in preverbal position. In sentence (2) it occurs sentence initially and serves as the base for attaching following subject and direct object clitics.

(1) bámse=ne báa híta nú'u-bae-ka-i
hurry=I now something get-DSD-PPL-PPL
I'm in a hurry right now because I urgently need something.

(2) báa=t=a'a čúpa-'a-ne 'á'a čúpa-ka kópti-nee
now=we=it finish-EV-FUT it finish-PPL forget-FUT
We will finish it at once and having finished it, will forget it.

Examples (3) and (4) illustrate the use of **báa** as an incorporated element in construction with intransitive verbs. In example (3) its use relates to the time of speaking, whereas in example (4) its use represents an extension into the domain of human affairs. In particular, it encodes the attaching of an augmented degree of importance to a useful item.

(3) lóttilaa-taka=né wée báa-yúm-hó'e-pea
tired-being=I come now-rest-DSD
I am very tired, I want to rest right away.

(4) hittoa káa báa-tá'aru-mači
medicine not once-lose-seem
The medicine should by no means ever be lost.

3.0. The adverbial bát-

The adverbial **bát** *in front of, first, former* has both locative and temporal usages as suggested by its glosses. Its locative use with the meaning "in front of" or "ahead of" is illustrated in sentence (5). Two related temporal usages are given in sentences (6) and (7). In sentence (6) **bat-** is used in the sense of being first in a temporally ordered sequence which is anchored to the time of speaking. On the other hand, in sentence (7) the anchor point for the temporally ordered sequence is a point in time past, in particular, the time when the speaker was a child.

(5) 'inia beléki-k né bát 'émo-u téuwaa
this:ACC amount-ACC I first you-to tell
I am telling you this amount first.

(6) hunáme'e bát-kaáte
those   first-go:PL
Those people are going ahead.

(7) bát-naáte-ka   née káa yó'ó-taka-i
first-begin-PPL I   not old-being-PPL
back in the beginning when I was young

4.0. The locative náas-

The manner adverbial **náas-** has a number of related meanings based on the spatial concepts "all around" and "here and there." It has the extended meaning "to go around doing X." It also has an allomorph **náa-**. This proclitic is undoubtedly related to the verb **naáse** *to turn (to the right or left), to fork (as a road), to separate.* Example (8) shows the use of **náas** as a free adverbial in preverbal position separated from the main verb of the clause it is in by a direct object clitic.

(8) 'áa'a hiókole-ka náas   'á'a nu-núp-taite-k
her pity-PPL   around her RDP-take-began-PRF
Feeling sorry for her, he began taking her around to different places.

When **náas** becomes incorporated into a verb, the final **-s** gets softened to **-h**, as seen in the following examples which illustrate the use of **náah** as an adverbial incorporated into an intransitive verb complex. In usages such as that of example (9), **náah-** designates localized motion and can be glossed as "all around in the participant's immediate location." Its directional usage, given in example (10), can be glossed as "heading off in all directions."

(9) tú'i-si   tú'i t-iáa-ka   náah-čepte, 'álléaka-i
good-AVR good CON-say-PPL around-jump happy-PPL
"That's real good," he said, jumping around with joy.

(10) náah-bit-ču
around-see-CPL (i.e., stare at)
looking intently in all directions

Sentence (11) illustrates a habitual usage of **náah-** in which the custom of going from village to village at given intervals is designated. In sentence (12) a more restricted view of a habitual pattern is illustrated. In this case it designates one's manner of deportment.

(11) 'áa-mak náah-réhti-nee   wóh-naiki puéplo-m bée'eka-tána
him-with around-walk:PL-FUT twice-four town-PL locations-from
They would go around to the scattered eight pueblos with him.

(12) 'émpo két yó'o-ri-sia-či-si   náah-kúak-te
you also old-PPL-ABS-on-AVR around-turn-VR
You also go around respectably.

Another instance of localized motion is given in sentence (13). In this case **náah-** relates to the motion of a manipulated object within the confines of a cooking pot. On the other hand, abstract motion is involved in the usage of **náah-** exemplified by sentence (14). This usage consists of implied motion driven by a negative force dynamic agent.

(13) sebóra wát-ta-wa-ka   haaréki náah-kúak-ta-wa-k
onion throw-VR-PSV-PPL frequently around-turn-VR-psv-PRF
The onions were thrown in and frequently stirred around.

(14) puéplo-ta   náa-b^{w}áa-b^{w}áa-ta-ka-i
people-ACC around-RDP-perturb-VR-PPL-PPL
perturbing the people

5.0. The adverbial nát-

The locative manner adverb **nát-** can be glossed by such phrases as "things piled on top of each other," "things touching one another," or "things lined up one after another." Most likely **nát-** represents a coalescence of the old Uto-Aztecan reflexive ***naa** and the Yaqui postposition **-t** *on*. This is suggested by its status as a free grammatical element in a sentence. In examples (15) and (16) **nát** is separated from the main verb in its clause by a following direct object clitic.

(15) tékwa-ta béak-ta-ka nát 'á'a wát-ta-ka 'á'a núk-sime
meat-ACC slice-VR-PPL top it pile-VR-PPL it carry-go
Slicing the meat and putting it in a pile, he took it away.

(16) kárpa-m tá-tabe-k nát 'am tót-ta-ka nát
tent-PL RDP-take:down-PRF top them pile-TRN-PPL top

'ám hoá-ka tú'ulí-si nát 'ám suma-k
them make-PPL pretty-AVR top them tie-PRF
They took down the tents, folding them together, piling them on top of one another, they tied them together neatly.

Two superficially quite distinct meanings of **nát** are illustrated by examples (17) and (18). The difference, however, can be accounted for by the meanings of the two verbs with which **nát-** incorporates. The idea of "suspend," for example, implies a slender extended entity such as a rope hanging down from a rafter, whereas the use of **nát-** implies an image of a succession of discrete entities that occupy the succession of points distributed along a path. In example (18) the use of the verb meaning "to group" implies a localized meaning to be attached to **nát**.

(17) né-t wá'am nát-ča'a-ka kaáte
me-on by over-suspend-PPL go:PL
The people go by me one by one in single file.

(18) si'ime wáa'a púeplo súum-'éa-ka 'áme-u nát-móčak-te-k
all that people amaze-think-PPL them-to top-group-INTR-PRF
In amazement, all the people gathered/crowded together to them.

Example (19) shows an interesting use of **nát** in which it occurs first as the object of the postposition **-bepa** *over* and then again as a postposition in construction with **nát-bepa**. The entire construction means "over and over again" and may possibly be construed as a kind of reduplicated adverbial, in which the reduplication is iconic of the complex conceptualization itself.

(19) bésa='e hú'unea, háiki-si wečia-po-sa nát-bépa-nát 'aáyu-k
well=you know how:many-AVR fall-in-Q over-above-over be-PRF
You well know how many times, over and over again, it happened.

6.0. The reciprocal náu-

The reciprocal incorporated adverbial of manner **náu** illustrates a second variation based on the combination of ***naa** and a postposition. In this case, it combines with **-u** *to, toward*. It can often be glossed as "together" or "in a group." Its original status as a free adverbial is retained in its use as a base for direct object clitics of transitive verbs, as exemplified by sentences (20) and (21).

(20) nau=te bit-ču-su-k
together=we see-CPL-CPL-PRF
We have now finished seeing each other (completely).

(21) woi-ka náu-katé-'e-tea-n
two-be together-go:PL-EV-QUO-PCN
They say that these two were once traveling together.

As examples (22) and (23) suggest, the incorporation of **náu** is not limited to just prototypical intransitive verbs. In sentence (22) **náu** occurs in construction with the transitive stem **toha** *to bring*, which has for its direct object the sentence initial nominal marked for accusative **tómi-ta**. In sentence (23) **náu** serves as object of the postposition **-biča** *site* and partially specifies the location for the activity specified by the intransitivized verb **hi'oh-te** *to write*. The postpositional phrase **náu-bíča** itself can be glossed as "both sides."

(22) tómi-ta   né náu-tóha-k
money-ACC I   together-bring-PRF
I got money together.

(23) nau-biča   ne 'ae-t hi'oh-te-k
together-site I   it-on paper-VR-PRF
I wrote on both sides of it.

The use of **náu** as a free morpheme is illustrated by sentence (24) in which it serves as a base for attaching the first person plural subject clitic. Example (24) also shows an object noun **nabó** *cactus fruit* which is incorporated into a verbal construction that pairs it with the postposition **-u** *to, toward*. The postposition has taken on the purposive meaning "go to do X." As we have already noted, this is an interesting tie to a Cora construction with the prefix **uu-** and a following noun, described in Casad 1982.

(24) náu=te   nabó-'u-nee
together=we cactus:fruit-go:to:get-FUT
We will go gather cactus fruit together.

Sentence (25) illustrates the incorporated form of **náu-** as opposed to the free form shown in example (24). Here the subject of the sentence is the quantifier **sí'ime** *all* and **náu** attaches to the plural motion verb stem **sáha** *to go*.

(25) sí'ime náu-sáha-k
all   together-go:PL-PRF
They all went away together.

The use of **náu-** to signal joint involvement in a single event by a multiplicity of participants is illustrated by examples (26)–(28). The precise specification of how many participants are jointly involved is indicated by the numeral marked with the accusative as in example (28).

(26) 'íiyilen   té náu-hiía-n
thus:precisely we together-sound-PCN
This is exactly what we said together.

(28) wépu'ulai-k té náu   'áčae-k
one-ACC   we together father-have
We jointly have the same father.

(27) hobé'eso-m náu-rúkte-k   náu-etého-taite-k
ram-PL   together-approach-PRF together-talk-begin-PRF
The rams came together and began to talk together.

7.0. The incorporated unspecified human object yee-

Yaqui retains traces of markings for unspecified objects at various points in its grammar. One of these is found in the use of **yee-** to indicate unspecified animate objects, conventionally construed to designate people in general. The corresponding Mayo form is **yore-,** also meaning "relating to people in general." Historically, this object marker is probably derived from **yoéme** or **yoréme** *person*. In simple verbal constructions such as those in sentences (29)–(32), **yee-** designates direct object entities. The subject of these constructions are typically human as seen in sentences (29)–(30). An unmarked subject is conventionally understood as being human, or at least personal, as suggested by example (30).

(29) 'áapo kía yée-mahtá-bae
he   just people-teach-DSD
He just wants to teach people.

(30) yée-yó'ore
people-respect
He respects people.

Animate nonhuman entities can also be the subject of verbs that take **yee-** as sentences (31) and (32) demonstrate. In the first of these the subject is a cat, whereas in the other it is a dog.

(31) miísi yée-súke'
cat   people-scratch
A cat scratches people.

(32) ču'ú yee-buúe
dog people-scold
A dog growls at people.

Occasionally, **yee** is still used as a free form. In example (33) **yee** occurs in sentence initial position, immediately preceding the matrix verb **'aa** *be able to do X*, but it is actually the direct object of the embedded compound verb **bai-tat-ta'aa** *to deceive*. The semantic role of the entity being designated by **yee** is variable. Whereas in simple sentences **yee-** marks direct objects, in causatives **yee** marks the subject of the caused event as suggested by examples (34) and (35).

(33) yée   'áa   bai-tát-ta'áa
     people able   cool-RDP-know
     He is a deceiver.

(35) tú'ii bo'ó-t   yée-puh-te-tua-me
     good road-on people-eye-VR-CAU-NZR
     the one who causes people to recognize the good road

(34) híta   téuwaa-ka húni'i yée-'át-tua-nee
     thing   say-PPL   even   people-laugh-CAU-FUT
     Anything he says makes people laugh.

Finally, in sentence (36) **yee** is the incorporated object of the applicative verb, and applicative suffix **-ria** is actually a malefactive. This sentence could equally well be translated as "They eat a lot of things to the detriment of people."[1]

(36) 'únna=m   hita   yée-bʷá-bʷá'a-ria
     much=they   thing   people-RDP-eat-APL
     They eat a lot of people's things.

To close on a morphological note, when followed by an object pronoun, **yee-** contracts to **ye-**, as in the example below.

(37) yée   'am   máka ——> yé'am-máka
     people them   give
     He gives them to people.

8.0. The locative adverbial yéeu-/yéu-

The incorporated locative adverbial **yéeu-** and its alternative **yéu** *outside, in an open space* is a reduced form of the free adverbial **yeéwi** *in the outside, open spaces*. It is used both literally and idiomatically. In its usages, **yéu-** is probably the most productive of any of the Yaqui morphemes that have been incorporated into verb stems.

The use of **yéu** as a free adverbial is seen in example (38). Here a third person singular pronoun intervenes between **yéu** and the motion verb **pu'a** *to choose*.

(38) néhpo yéu 'á'a pu'a-k
     I   out it   choose-PRF
     I chose it.

Frequently **yéu-** specifies the destination of a path or scale as it does in example (39) where it signals the endpoint of the physical extension of an unspecified entity. In example (40) it signals the starting point of Gabriel Sparrow's trip in the first clause where it incorporates with the motion verb **siíka** *to go*:SG SUBJ. It signals the end point of that trip in the second clause where it combines with the goal oriented verb **yebíh** *to arrive*.

(39) 'inim yéu-yúu-yúma'
     here   out-RDP-reach
     It gets this far.

(40) 'inii'i habiél   hunáman yéu-sii-ka   čú'um-mé'am-pá'a-kun   yéu-yebih-pea-ka
     this   Gabriel there   out-go-PRF   dog-killer-prairie-in-toward out-arrive-DSD-PPL
     Gabriel left that place and went out desiring to arrive at Dog Killer Place.

In examples (41) and (42) the endpoint of a path is also signaled by **yéu-** by incorporation with the verbs **yépsa** *to arrive* and **not-** *to return*. The multiple highlighting of the end point of the path is striking

---

1 We are indebted to Eloise Jelinek for this particular analysis.

in sentence (41), where it is specified by a proximal adverbial demonstrative and a postpositional phrase with **u-** *toward* in addition to the two components of the verb complex itself.

(41) 'inim née 'emó-u yéu-yépsa-k
here I you-to out-arrive-PRF
I have come out here to you.

(42) hunúen tu'isi kaa-mačia-k yéu-nót-te-k kaita téa-ka-i
thus very not-light-ACC out-return-INTR-PRF nothing find-PPL-PPL
So it was that he returned way after dark not having found anything.

Other extended usages of **yéu-** signal the highlighting of a single entity from among a group of similar entities. Thus it is used with verbs such as **ná'ateho** *to accuse* in sentence (43) and **pu'a** *to choose* illustrated earlier in sentence (38).

(43) hunáa'a ba'akot 'á'a yá'u-raa-u 'enči yéu-ná'ateho-k
that snake his chief-ABS-to you:ACC out-accuse-PRF
That snake accused you to his authorities.

The locative **yéu-** also combines with two distinct verbs to express from two different perspectives the act of being born. In example (44) **yéu-** represents the end of motion along a path from the mother's womb into the open. In example (45) it represents the static location of the newborn child after birth.

(44) yéu-tóm-te   (45) yéu-kík-te
out-stomach-VR   out-stand-VR
to be born   *to be born*

Related to one of the perspectives that Yaqui takes on the process of being born, more generally **yéu-kík-te** signifies transition into a different state. The particular destination may be signalled by a postpositional phrase, as in example (46).

(46) čúuba-tu-k tékil-po yéu-kík-te-nee
moment-be-PRF work-in out-stand-VR-FUT
You'll be off work shortly.

Another extended usage of **yéu-** with the motion verb "to go" is quite common across languages. Metaphorically speaking, for an event to occur is for it to go out into the open. A pair of conventionalized Yaqui expressions that illustrate this are given in sentences (47) and (48). The first of these signals a general outcome of some series of events. The second predicts no success from the result of someone's mental effort.

(47) hunúen yéu-sii-ka
thus out-go-PRF
It came out/happened that way.

(48) 'émpo kaíbu 'ém 'éa-'u-mak yéu-wée-nee
you never your think-GND-with out-go-FUT
Your idea will never work.

Temporal usages of **yéu-** are also common. Sentences (49) and (50) show the use of **yéu-** as part of the way to talk about the day cycle.

(49) čikti-ta'á-po héela yéu-matčú-'u-béleki
every-sun-in nearly out-dawn-EV-amount
almost every day at dawn

(50) ta'á-ta yéu-wée-'e-bétana
sun-POS out-go-EV-from
from the east

Both **yee-** and **yéu-** contract to **yé'-** before certain pronouns. This creates a potential ambiguity with the incorporated unspecified human object marker, which also reduces to **ye'-** under certain conditions. The meanings of the other constituents in the local environment are usually sufficient for enabling the Yaqui speaker to remove the ambiguity. Sentence (51) shows the reduced form of **yéu,** whereas (52) gives us an instance of the reduced form of **yee**.

(51) té'opo-po yeéwi yé-'a wíke-k
temple-in outside out-him drag-PT
They dragged him outside of the temple.

(52) hunáka'a hoóa kía yé-'a-naké-'e-betcí'ibo
that do just people-his-love-EV-for
He does that just because he loves people.

SYNTACTIC MARKING

1.0. Introduction

This section presents an overview of the devices which Yaqui employs to mark the interactions between verbs and nominals that participate in major syntactic processes, largely those that involve major clausal constituents. This includes the marking of subjects and objects in simple clauses, as well as their marking in certain complex sentences, i.e., causatives and applicatives.

2.0. Pronominal marking

As already discussed in DEFINITE PRONOUNS, p. 241, Yaqui makes a three-way distinction of persons, as well as the distinction between singular and plural number for both subjects and objects. As is common in Uto-Aztecan, third person singular subject is often unmarked. Thus there is no subject marker in either sentence (1) or (2).

(1) sí'ime hó'a-ra-m-met siíka
all house-AZR-PL-on went
He went to all the homes/villages.

(2) káa-mantéka-ka-me bʷá'ee
not-lard-have-NZR eat
He eats the ones without grease.

2.1. Subject marking

Subjects may be marked by independent pronouns. In addition, both subjects and objects are commonly marked by clitics in Yaqui. Generally, if the subject is marked by an independent pronoun, there is no clitic subject marker in the sentence as example (3) suggests.

(3) néhpo=su 'áman 'emó-u yéu-yebíh-nee báhi taéwai-ta wée-o
I=EMP there you-to out-arrive-FUT three day-ACC go-when
I will indeed come over there to you in three days!

In simple clauses, subject markers precede object markers in the left to right order within the clause. Example (4) below shows this for clitic subject and object markers. Sentences (5) and (6) show this for a quantifier serving as the subject noun phrase and for a clitic marking third singular direct object.

(4) 'án=a'a téa-k
I=it find-PRF
I found it.

(5) sí'ime 'á'a wáata
all him want
Everyone wanted him.

(6) sí'ime 'á'a nákke
all him love
They all loved him.

In both independent and dependent clauses, overt subject nominals tend to occur in clause initial position, whereas object nominals occur closer to the verb. Sentence (7), for example, contains three clauses, each of which demonstrates a preverbal subject noun phrase. The initial dependent adverbial clause contains a possessed locative noun as passive subject. The second adverbial clause is introduced by a plural human noun, and the main clause has a nominalization **páhko** *feast* as its clause initial subject. Subsequent examples will show that this order can be reversed under a variety of circumstances (cf. BASIC SENTENCE STRUCTURE, pp. 43–45).

(7) hunúen yéu-siíka páhko ramaá-ta yáča-'a-su-a-k-o
thus out-went feast shed-POS placed-EV-CPL-PSV-PRF-when

pahkó'a-m náu béep-su-a-k-o páhko béha naáte-k
feaster-PL together hit-CPL-PSV-PRF-when feast well begin-PRF
That's the way it came out; when the feast shelter had been put up and the other festal dancers had come together, the feast started.

The word order in which subject precedes the object holds for both independent and dependent clauses, as seen in the next two examples. In sentence (8) the third person plural subject clitic **=m** attaches to the sentence initial adverb, which is itself marked with the emphatic clitic **-su.** This is followed by the indefinite pronoun marked for accusative with **-ta.** In the main clause of sentence (9) the third person singular subject is left unmarked and the direct object, consisting of **sí'ime** *all* marked for accusative, is in clause initial position. The neutral order of subject and object, however, is given in the quotative clause that follows. Here the subject is the first person independent pronoun **néhpo** and the direct object is signalled by **waká'a bato'ooraa-ta** *those baptized ones.*

(8) béha=su=m   kaábe-ta   yó'ore-ka 'ám 'á'a yáa-ka-i
    well=EMP=they   no:one-ACC respect-PRF they it   do-PPL-PPL
    Well, they did it because they don't respect anyone.

(9) sí'ime-ta yá'a-pea-ka 'éan 'ó'obek hái=sa túa   néhpo
    all-ACC do-DSD-PPL   SJV   although how=Q indeed I

    'áu-ka   wáka'a   bató'oo-raa-ta   'allée-tua-nee.
    I do-PPL that:ACC baptize-ABS-ACC   happy-CAU-FUT
    He really had a deep desire to do everything, saying, How can I possibly make (those) people happy?

Subject clitics may be discontinuous from the verb of the clause whose subject they are, as illustrated in sentences (10) and (11). The first of these examples shows a reflexive particle occurring between the subject and object particles, and the next, example (11), illustrates a procomplement occurring there. In both cases, the object particle immediately precedes the verb. This may suggest that subject particles developed later in the history of Yaqui than the object particles (cf. Langacker 1977:137). Also in example (11) the second person singular subject pronoun **'émpo** is followed by both a manner procomplement and a third person singular direct object clitic. In example (12) the first person singular subject clitic **née** is followed by a postpositional phrase **'ae-t** *it-on.*

(10) búsan mét-po   té náu   'á'a 'áttea-laa
     six   month-in we together it   own-PPL
     We have owned it together for six months.

(11) hunúen-tu-k=san   'émpo 'inían 'á'a yá'a-nee
     thus-VR-PRF=EXP   you   thus   it   do-FUT
     Since it is that way, you will do it thus.

(12) 'í'i=b^wan sísi'iwooki née 'ae-t mám-te-k   haíbu nók-nee
     this=EXP iron   I   it-on hand-VR-PRF now   speak-FUT
     This particular piece of metal (telegraph key), if I put my hand on it, will talk.

The subject clitic seems to act as a topic pivot for fronted direct object nominals, as example (13) suggests, that is, the subject clitic's position is the anchorpoint for determining what the initial position is for preposing a topicalized nominal.

(13) hiák-nók-ta   né hí'ohte-n waté-k   née tá'aa
     yaqui-word-ACC   I write-PCN some-ACC I   know
     I was writing down Yaqui words; I (already) know some.

2.2. Object marking

Yaqui marks both direct and indirect objects, but does not always distinguish them morphologically. Indirect objects may be marked by the accusative suffix **-ta** as in example (14), or by the directional postposition **-wi/-u.**

(14) heéwi 'áčai-t-iía hunáa'a pahkó'olaa káa 'áa yé'ee-me   moró-ta-wi
     yes   sir-CON-say that   festal:dancer NEG able dance-NZR Moor-ACC-to

     bibá-m   mabét-ču-ka-i
     cigarette-PL receive-CPL-PPL-PPL
     "Yes sir!" the festal dancer who was not able to dance said to the Moor who contracted him, as he received the cigarrettes.

278

The accusative marker **-ta** has a number of usages in which it marks other than prototypical direct objects, motivated at least in part by its extension to mark the genitive relation. In the following example, it is used to mark the fact that the expanse of time is limited to a certain quantity, i.e., three days. The expression **bahi taéwa-ta** really means "at the end of three days."

(15) báhi   taéwa-ta 'á'abo 'áu yebíh-ne-'e-t-iía
     three day-POS here   RFL arrive-FUT-EV-CON-say
     When three days are past, he will be here.

Accusative **-ta** also marks position in logical space. In example (16) **-ta** marks specific entities that represent one end of a comparison scale for which the covert subject of the sentence represents the other.

(16) kabá'i-ta   wée-la-'apo hí'i-bʷa-k   boéh-ta wée-la-'apo hé'e-ka
     horse-POS   go-PPL-GND IZR-eat-PRF   ox-POS go-PPL-GND drink-PRF
     He ate like a horse and drank like an ox.

The directional **-u** can be used for marking indirect objects, and it also marks the location in space occupied by a patient nominal. Both usages are illustrated in the following example.

(17) čibá'ato 'á-u   yepsá-ka   'á-u   téne-la   kíkte-k
     goat   him-to arrive-PPL him-to upright-ADV   stand:SG-PRF
     Upon arriving to where the man was, the goat stood up on its hind legs right in front of him.

Yaqui, in harmony with Mayo, draws on a small set of verbs such as **maka** *to give* and **mahta** *to teach* to encode double objects. Such double objects are more common in more morphologically-complex verbs.

In particular, causative and applicative verb constructions typically allow two objects to be specified; often one of them is encoded as a free nominal marked in the accusative, whereas the other is marked with the object clitic. Both may be marked by clitics, however. In example (18) the first person singular subject pronoun **née** designates the passive subject of the causative sentence whereas the third person singular object pronoun **'á'a** designates the object of the verb **hariu** *to hunt*. A clear distinction between the direct object and the benefactee roles is illustrated in example (19). Now the direct object is in sentence initial position and the direct object clitic, which designates the benefactee, is in immediate preverbal position.

(18) mékkaa-bétana née 'á'abo   'á'a haríu-tua-wa
     far:away-from I   over:here him hunt-CAU-PSV
     I am sent over here, from far away, to find him.

(19) tabú-ta   'á'a mé'e-ria-ka, 'á'a kuhá'abʷa-k
     rabbit-ACC her kill-APL-PPL it   broil:spit:on-PRF
     Having killed a rabbit for her, he broiled it.

2.3. Unspecified object marking

Yaqui retains traces of unspecified object marking via the incorporated unspecified human object marker **yée** discussed earlier (cf. INCORPORATION, pp. 272–273) and two prefixes, the inanimate **hi'i** and the human **ne-**.

2.3.1. Inanimate unspecified hi'i-

The inanimate unspecified marker **hi'i-** and its reduced form **hi-** are the most productive of the unspecified object markers that Yaqui employs. It generally indicates that someone is performing some kind of action on things in general. A common effect of its use with transitive verbs is to lower the degree of transitivity inherent to the composite verb. Thus in many contexts it carries out the role of an intransitivizer. This prefix is probably a reduced form of the Proto-Uto-Aztecan indefinite pronoun ***hita** *a thing* (cf. Langacker 1977:120).

The following sets of sentences illustrate the contrast between protypical transitive usages of several Yaqui verbs and their corresponding usages with the unspecified object marker **hi-**. To begin, the stem **čó'ila** means "to rope X" in its transitive usages. With **hi-**, it means "to be roping, to be lassoing."

(20) kába'i máhhai-m-ta   né čó'ila-k
horse scare-NZR-ACC I rope-PRF
I roped a wild horse.

(21) waká-kóau ne weáma-n b^wé'uu-si hi-čó'ilaa-wa kába'i-m
cow-pen I walk-PCN big-AVR IZR-rope-PSV horse-PL
I was out in the cow-pen; roping was going on in a big way.

The stem **béeba**, in its transitive usages, means "to strike X" or "to hit X."

(22) 'á'a béeba 'á'a béeba húka'a   bakót-ta   kát 'á'a sím-tua
it hit it hit that:ACC snake-ACC NEG it go-CAU
Hit it! Hit that snake. Don't let it get away.

(23) póči-e   kúta-e   hí-bép-síme-n
short-INST stick-INST IZR-hit-go-PCN
He went along, striking out with a short stick.

In its transitive usages, the stem **kó'a/kó'o-** means "to chew on X." In its intransitive usages with **hi-**, this stem carries the meaning "to masticate, to chew."

(24) yoi-sána-ta   kó'a-síme-n
Mexican-cane-ACC chew-go-PCN
He was going along chewing sugar cane.

(25) mékka-'a-ria-t wéye-ka hi-kó'o-sime
far-EV-ABS-on go-GND IZR-chew-go
He went along chewing (roasting ears) off in the distance.

(26) bóa-yáhu-yáhu-ti   hi-kó'a
wool-RDP-ripple-CON IZR-chew
The hair on his back ripples in rhythm as he chews his cud.

The transitive usage of **čoóna** carries the meaning "to strike someone" or "to slap someone."

(27) tení-t   'á'a čó-čón-tébo-k
mouth-on him RDP-slap-IMP-PRF
He commanded him to hit him in the mouth.

The nominalized form, meaning "a slap," also employs the unspecified object prefix **hi-**.

(28) Liós 'é-t   'á'a nót-ta-nee   'inika'a hi-čón-ta
God you-on it return-VR-FUT this-ACC IZR-slap-ACC
God will pay you back for this slap.

The transitive form of the stem **čiike** can be glossed as "to brush something," as in example (29). In its intransitive usages with **hi-**, it designates sweeping in general, as exemplified in example (30).

(29) hímsim-mea sí'ime púhba-t 'á'a číke
beard-INST all face-on him brush
He brushed all his face with his chin-whiskers.

(30) 'á'a hubía-wa kári-po hí-čike-n
his wife-POS house-in IZR-sweep-PCN
His wife was sweeping in the house.

The transitive usage of **b^wá'e** means "to eat X," whereas its intransitive counterpart **hi'i-b^wá** can be glossed as "to be in the process of eating."

(31) kúču-bák-ta   né   b^wá'a-ka
     fish-stew-ACC I   eat-PRF
     I ate some fish stew.

(32) 'á'a hó'a-u   siíka   hí'i-b^wá-betčí'ibo
     his house-to go:PRF   IZR-eat-for
     He went to his house to eat.

The causative form **hi'i-b^wá-tua** means "to feed X." Sentence (33) provides a typical example.

(33) 'á'a hi'i-b^wá-tua-k
     him   IZR-eat-CAU-PRF
     He fed him.

The intransitive form of **má'ake** *to chop X* means simply "to chop," as illustrated in example (34).

(34) née 'áa   hi-má'ako tép^wa-m-mea
     I   able IZR-chop axe-ACC:PL-INST
     I am able to chop with an ax.

In sentence (34) the role of **-m-**, the accusative plural, is to function as the base for attaching a postposition. Examples (35) and (36) show that the result of passivization of a verb places **hi'i-** in the role of unspecified subject.

(35) kába'i mám-kót-ti   hi-bép-wa-k
     horse   leg-break-AVR   IZR-hit-PSV-PRF
     A horse's leg was broken from being hit.

The transitive verb **ná'ikia** means "to separate" or "to divide." In its intransitive usages with **hi-**, it means "it counts to X quantity."

(36) senú-takáa   hi-ná'ikai-wa-'apo
     one-body   IZR-divide-PSV-GND
     In numerals, it is twenty.

2.3.2 Unspecified animate subject or object né-

The unspecified object marker **né-** is used with regard to people or living things. It has a very limited distribution. In our files **sáuwe** *to command, to order,* **ha'as** *to follow,* and **hun** *to invite* are the only transitive verbs we have identified with certainty that use this prefix.

The transitive verb **sáuwe** means variously "to command," "to order," or "to do something." In its intransitive form with **né-**, it means "to rule" or "to govern," as illustrated by sentence (37). The nominalized counterpart with **né-** means "orders." A typical use is illustrated in sentence (38).

(37) woi-takáa wásuktia-m-po 'áma né-sau-pea-n
     two body   year-PL-in   there IZR-order-DSD-PCN
     He was wanting to rule there for forty years.

(38) bo'ó-t   hapté-ka   né-sáu-ta   yáa-k
     road-on stand-PPL   IZR-order-ACC   do-PRF
     Taking to the road, they carried out the orders.

Example (39) shows the verb **sauwe** taking a reflexive object. In this case it does not carry the prefix **né-**. This morphological contrast strongly suggests that **né-** retains synchronic status as an unspecified object marker, albeit one that has largely fallen into disuse.

(39) née-káa yá'u-ra-k   ínepo 'íno sáuwe
     I-not   chief-ABS-have   I   RFL order
     I am under no one's authority, I govern myself.

The transitive verb **ha'ase** means "to follow X." In its use with **né-**, it takes on the generalized meaning "to track animals," as illustrated in sentence (40).

(40) née 'áa né-h-ha'ase
     I able IZR-RDP-follow
     I am able to track (animals).

The following example shows a passive form of the transitive verb stem **hun-** *to invite*, which may be cognate with Guarijío **uhúla-ni** *to send him, to give him an order*, Tarahumara **hu-rá** *to send*, and the Eudeve **hurán** *to send* (cf. Miller 1988:89, no. **hu-13**). There is both semantic motivation and historical phonological motivation that justifies relating these forms to Yaqui **hun.** In addition, Mayo has the attested form **né-hune** *to invite* (Larry Hagberg, personal communication). The passivization of this stem, marked with the unspecified object marker **né-**, shows how an unspecified object marker can come to have the meaning of "unspecified subject." (cf Langacker 1977b:46)

(41) kó'okoi-m-po bʷé'úu-si páhkó-baa-wa-o   'áman né-hun-wa-k
     Cocorit-PL-in big-AVR feast-DSD-PSV-when there IZR-invite-PSV-PRF
     When there was going to be a big feast in Cocorit, he was invited there.

The prefix **ná-(t-),** which seems to carry out the same function of intransitivizing sentences as does **né-**, is unique in that it occurs only with the verb **temáe** *to ask, to question someone*.

Examples (42)–(43) illustrate both transitive and intransitive usages of the verb **temáe.** Its usage, however, with **nát-** implies an unspecified object as being associated with the verb. In sentence (42) the reduplicated form **te-temáe** takes a third person plural direct object, and illustrates two characteristics of transitive verbs. Sentence (43) gives both an intransitive use with **nát-** in the first "because" clause and a transitive use with an indefinite pronominal direct object in the very next clause. Notice that the meaning of **náttemáe** is "to ask."

(42) hái=sa 'emé'e 'á'a mabéta-k-ti   'ám te-temáe
     how=Q you:PL it receive-PRF-CON them RDP-ask
     "Did you receive it?" he asked them.

(43) kán=nee hú'unea-k bʷé'ituk né káa ná-t-temáe-k
     not=I know-PRF because I not IZR-CON-ask-PRF
     kaábe-ta   temáe-k táa ne 'í'an hú'unea
     no:one-ACC ask-PRF but I now know
     I didn't know, because I didn't ask. I didn't ask anyone but I now know (anyway).

In its basic form, **temáe** has a ditransitive meaning "to ask someone for something." The **-t-** on **ná(t)-** must be phonologically determined because this prefix cannot be the same as **na-t-** *one on top of another*, described on p. 271. Note that, in this sentence the meaning of **temáe** with **nát-** is "to pry into some private matter." In short, this form of the unspecified object marker represents the case in which the stem initial consonant **t-** becomes geminated because it occurs in post-tonic position.

(44) kaábe-ta-u   né suúa 'íntok née káa ná-t-témae
     no:one-CON-to I bother and I not IZR-CON-ask
     I don't bother anyone, and I don't pry.

In its passive form, **temáe** has the meaning "to be interrogated," as seen in sentence (45). In addition, the passive suffix **-wa** ablauts the stem final vowel of **temáe** to **i**.

(45) mó'el yéhte-k hunáma béha temái-wa
     Mó'el sit-PRF there well ask-PSV
     Mó'el sat down; he was interrogated there.

The verb **temáe** also has the extended meanings of "to repent" or "to search one's soul." These latter meanings, illustrated in sentences (46) and (47), may be post-conquest developments.

(46) sí'ime 'ánia-či 'émo temái-nee bʷé'ituk té téhwaa-ri
     all world-in RFL ask-FUT because we advise-PPL
     People in all the world are to repent, because we are ordered to.

(47) sí'ime-m 'emo-'am híapsi-temái-ne-'e-bétana Lióh-ta-u   'ám nók-ria-nee
     all-PL RFL-them heart-repent-FUT-EV-from God-CON-to them speak-APL-FUT
     We must pray to God that everyone will repent.

3.0. The passive -wa

The final device that Yaqui uses for encoding unspecified clausal entities is the suffix **-wa,** which marks passive subjects. As Escalante has so convincingly shown in his recent paper (Escalante 1990), Yaqui does not allow for an agent phrase in this sentence type. Several reasons, both typological and functional account for this.

To begin, sentences (48) and (49) illustrate simple passive independent clauses with third person singular subjects. Both of these clauses are also marked with the perfective **-k**.

(48) hunáma 'é'eria-wa-k   (49) nák-wa-k
     there   guard-PSV-PRF   love-PSV-PRF
     He was buried there.   *He was loved.*

Yaqui uses the passive **-wa** productively. If anything, Yaqui uses the passive more frequently than English does. Generally, Yaqui passives are functionally equivalent to the corresponding English constructions. The two usages in sentence (50) are typical. The first instance has a first person singular passive subject and illustrates a perfective use of the passive. The second instance is an imperfective use with a second person singular subject.

(50) wáaria-bétana né 'é-u bíttua-wa-k   'áman='e'e nói-ti-sai-wa
     guard-from   I you-to send-PSV-PRF there=you go-CON-IMP-PSV
     I have been sent to you from the Council; you are ordered to go there.

Succinct chains of passive clauses are common in Yaqui narrative discourse.

(51) hú'upa-u   sumá-'a-wa-k   yokória-po mé'e-wa-k   bʷé'uu-si páhko-wa-k
     mesquite-to tie-EV-PSV-PRF morrow-on kill-PSV-PRF big-AVR feast-PSV-PRF
     It was tied to a mesquite tree; the following day it was butchered and they had a very big feast.

(52) yépsa-ka   tebóte-k   yóopna-wa-k   mabét-wa-k   kúta-t yéča-'a-wa-k
     arrive-PPL greet-PRF answer-PSV-PRF receive-PSV-PRF log-on put-EV-PSV-PRF
     Upon arriving he greeted them, was answered, received inside and was given a block on which to sit.

Some usages of the passive are difficult to translate into English. This is especially true for impersonal constructions such as that illustrated by example (53). The most accurate rendering of this sentence seems to be "There is work going on there."

(53) 'áman tekipánoa-wa
     there work-PSV
     They are working there.

4.0. Number agreement

Yaqui verbs agree with their subjects and objects in both person and number. Third person singular subject is unmarked. Paradigms and illustrative sentences for this are given in DEFINITE PRONOUNS, pp. 258–265. In addition, some intransitive verbs reduplicate for plural subjects. Others employ a suppletive stem to mark a plural subject (see VERB STEMS, pp. 257–258).

5.0. Subordination

The perfective participle suffix **-ka** marks subordinate clauses designating events that are temporally prior to the event referred to by the verb of the main clause in a sentence. Thus in sentence (54), the fire is lit before the coffee can be made, and in sentence (55) the people from the eight Yaqui towns had to congregate together before they could hold the burial ceremonies for the enchanted Paschal Dancer.

SONORA YAQUI LANGUAGE STRUCTURES

> (54) náya-ka kápe hoóa 'inii'i=b^wan maria flooreh-tea
> fire-PPL coffee make this=EXP   Maria Flores-called
> *Lighting a fire, she made coffee. This particular woman was called Maria Flores.*
>
> (55) wóh-naíki puéplo náu   yáha-ka   'á'a pahkó-ria-k
> two-four town   together arrive:PL-PPL him feast-APL-PRF
> *All the eight towns, coming together, participated in the burial ceremonies for him.*

The suffix **-o** is another way that Yaqui indicates subordination. As example (56) shows, as well as several of those already given above, **-o** used as a temporal subordinator means "when." Other usages of **-o** are discussed in ADVERBIAL CLAUSES, pp. 388-395.

> (57) yú'in čúuba 'á'a wéye-o=su   'ilí káu-pé-pétče-'e-ku   'áman 'á'a
> much time his go-when=EMP small mountain-RDP-vale-EV-in there his
>
> wéye-o=su   'ilí káuwi-m 'iilítči-m póo-póoh-ti-hoká-'apo   'í'ibo ta'á-ta
> go-when=EMP small hill-PL small-PL RDP-scatter-CON-be-GND from sun-POS
>
> 'áman wéče-'e-bétana
> there fall-EV-from
> *After he had gone on for a good bit of time and as he was going through a small mountain pass, there were lots of very small peaks scattered about, off toward the west.*

6.0. Causative suffixes

In this section we illustrate some of the usages of two Yaqui suffixes that group together semantically within the domain of causation. Although these two suffixes are distinct semantically in that the one **-tua** can be glossed "to cause to be," "to make," and the other **-ria** can be glossed as "to do in the behalf of someone," both of them relate to the same general domain and both can be construed as complex categories that overlap in certain ways (cf. Langacker 1977b:144; Tuggy 1981; 1988).

6.1. The causative suffix -tua

Yaqui causatives illustrate the common point that causatives range over a wide area of meaning, starting from the prototypical meaning of "to make" on through the inchoative "to cause to become" on to the applicative "to put" or "to apply X to Y." As we have noted earlier, in VERB MORPHOLOGY, p. 143, the causative verbal suffix **-tua** *to cause to,* is sometimes also used to verbalize a noun, with the meaning "to cause to have," "to put on," or whatever the noun and the context suggest.

In its most concrete sense, **-tua** can be glossed "to make something out of X," as illustrated in example (1).

> (1) píisaa-m   saáwea-tua-wa-k
> blanket-PL:ACC trouser-CAU-PSV-PRF
> *He was dressed in trousers formed out of a blanket.*

Many of the usages of **-tua** can be glossed as "to bring about some change of state X." The particular state is highly, possibly infinitely, variable. Among them are physical states of being, such as being able to walk, suggested by example (2), and more immaterial states as life itself, as illustrated in example (3). Verbs of perception such as **hikkahi** *to hear* may also be marked with **-tua** to signal the causation of the perception as shown in example (4).

> (2) 'itóm 'á'a weám-tua-ka-'apo-béna-si
> our him walk-CAU-PPL-GND-like-ADV
> *as if we had caused him to be able to walk*
>
> (3) 'emé'e 'á'a mé'aa-k wáka'a yée-híapsi-túa-m-ta
> you:PL him kill-PRF that:ACC people-life-CAU-NOM-ACC
> *You killed the one who causes people to live.*

284

(4) káa nanáu-mačí-k née híkkahi-tua-síme
   not alike-appear-ACC me hear-CAU-goes
   He causes me to hear a lot of different kinds of things.

The use of **-tua** also takes in cases of caused meteorological events, as seen in example (5). Notice also that because **-tua** suffixes directly to the verb stem it can be followed by a variety of suffixes and clitics.

(5) Liós yúk-tua-bae-'e-te-k   yúk-tua-nee   káa yúk-tua-bae-'e-te-k
   God rain-CAU-DSD-EV-VR-CND rain-CAU-FUT not rain-CAU-DSD-EV-VR-CND

   húni'i káa yúk-tua-nee
   even not rain-CAU-FUT
   If God wants it to rain, He'll make it rain; if He doesn't want it to rain, He won't cause it to rain.

The reflexive comes into play with mental events. The entire causative construction built on the stem **tá'aa** *to know* can be paraphrased as "to make up one's own mind about something." This usage is illustrated by sentence (6).

(6) b^wé'ituk né kaíta 'íno tá'aa-tua-bae-k   táa Krihto-ta kuus-et mé'e-wa-k-a'u
   because I nothing RFL know-CAU-DSD-PRF but Christ-ACC cross-on kill-PSV-PRF-GND
   But I determined not to know anything but Christ crucified.

A slightly different view of causative-force dynamics (cf. Talmy 1985) is seen in usages of **-tua** that imply the exertion of some force over a period of time. The negative **káa** in example (7) actually comes under the scope of the causative in this sentence, even though morphologically it is not as closely tied to the verb as the causative suffix **-tua**. Another way of saying this is that everything to the left of **-tua** in a sentence falls within its scope. On the other hand, the imperative sentence in (8) draws on the strong negative **kát**, which has its scope over everything to the right of it, and **-tua** has its scope only over the verb stem and the reflexive clitic that precede the stem.

(7) bátte   káa 'ám ko-kót-tua-k   (8) kát 'émo tíu-tua
   nearly not them RDP-sleep-CAU-PRF   not RFL shame-CAU
   They nearly kept them from sleeping.   *Don't be ashamed.*

With induced states the scope of **-tua** includes everything that precedes it in the sentence as seen in example (9). Notice that the subject of the caused event is marked by the third person singular direct object marker **'á'a**, which immediately precedes the verb stem in both clauses of (9). The object of the caused event is marked by the first person singular direct object **'ito** in the first clause and by the negative indefinite pronoun in the second clause.

(9) káa 'itó 'á'a yó'ori-tua-ka   kaíta 'á'a máhhai-tua
   not us him respect-CAU-PPL nothing him fear-CAU
   causing him not to respect us and (causing him) not to fear anything

Succeeding suffixes can have **-tua** in their scope, as can be seen in sentence (10), where the left to right order of the lexical items in the English translation practically reverses the right to left ordering scope relation of the morphemes in this sentence.

(10) 'ám bít-tá'aa-tua-tebo-bae-n
    them see-know-CAU-IMP-DSD-PCN
    He was wanting to give a command to cause [others] to know them by sight.

Usages of **-tua** to mean "to put X on Y" show that the meaning of the causative morpheme **-tua** may grade into the field of meanings associated with the applicative morpheme **-ria.** In other words, causative and applicative do not constitute rigidly separate categories. A fairly concrete applicative use of **-tua** is shown in example (11), where it designates the placing of a tangible entity on the physical surface of another discrete physical entity. More precisely **-tua** suffixes to the nominal **sewa** *flower*. The composite meaning is "to put flowers on X." This then is a clear case in which the notion of causative overlaps with that of the applicative. In example (12) the use of **-tua** with the incorporated noun **wikóh** *belt* designates the act of putting a piece of apparel on a person.

(11) kat=é'em hí'osia-ta nee sewá-tua
 not=you:PL paper-ACC me flower-CAU
 Don't put paper flowers on me.

(12) kat=é'em wi'í-ta née wikóh-tua
 not=you-PL fiber-ACC me belt-CAU
 Don't put a fiber belt on me.

The nouns to which **-tua** suffixes may assume a variety of semantic roles. On the one hand, the noun may be a patient which undergoes some potential change of state, as in example (13) below **wok-tua** *to give good feet to X*. On the other hand, in example (14) **-tua** suffixes to the incorporated noun **'óno** *salt*, which is the instrument with which the event is carried out.

(13) 'áčai tú'ii-m née wók-tua
 sir good-PL:ACC me foot-CAU
 Sir, give me good feet.

(14) wakáh-ta 'ón-tua-ka 'á'a núk-siika
 meat-ACC salt-CAU-PPL it take-go:PRF
 Salting the meat, he took it away.

Yaqui marks the subjects of caused events in the accusative case as illustrated in sentence (15), as it also does for the objects of caused events in sentence (16).

(15) 'íntok 'áe-t 'éa-ka kaíta 'á'a máhhai-tua
 and him-on think-PPL nothing him fear-CAU
 And trusting in him, he causes him not to fear anything.

(16) wáka'a ..bém bo'ó-hóo-ria-'u-ta 'émpo há'ani 'ám
 that:ACC their road-make-NOM-GND-ACC you perhaps them

sú'u-tóhi-tua-bae-'e-tea
release-leave-CAU-DSD-EV-QUO
It is said that you are wanting to make them leave their customs.

In certain usages, the combination of **-tua** and the verb it suffixes to means "to make someone do X." Example (17) is typical of this usage.

(17) kaábe né 'áma 'ám mána-'a-tua-k
 no:one me there them place-EV-CAU-PRF
 No one made me place them there.

With motion verbs, the use of **-tua** acquires the meanings such as "to send X away," as in example (18) or "to send X to do Y" as in (19).

(18) kaábe 'a'a sím-tua-k
 no:one him go-CAU-PRF
 no one sent him away

(19) mékkaa-bétana née 'a'abo 'a'a haríu-tua-wa
 far:away-from I over:here him search-CAU-PSV
 I am sent over here, from far away, to find him.

In other usages, **-tua** carries the sense of permission or allowance to do X. In these instances it can be glossed "let X do Y." Typical examples of this usage with motion verbs are given in examples (20) and (21).

(20) káa 'á'a ha-háse-k kía-la'a sím-túa-k
 not it RDP-chase-PRF only-it go-CAU-PRF
 He didn't chase after it, he just let it go away.

(21) bémpo káa 'áman 'á'a kibák-tua-k
 they not there him enter-CAU-PRF
 They wouldn't let him enter there.

Certain usages are highly ambiguous and may be understood in either the permissive sense, the obligating sense, or the inchoative sense, as the various glosses for sentence (22) suggest.

(22) káa 'itóm 'á'a yó'ori-tua
    not us him worship-CAU
    He doesn't let/make/cause us to worship him/it.

The usage of **-tua** in example (23) can be labelled the instigative usage, implying the idea of provoking a negative result. In sentence (24) on the other hand, the causative meaning seems to be bleached of a lot of its causative force, partly because of the meaning of the verb stem itself. A clear implication of this sentence is a negative one: the attempt was not successful.

(23) 'íntok née káa née 'ám kí'i-tua-pea
    and I not me them bite-CAU-DSD
    And I surely don't want to cause them to bite me either.

(24) káuwih-ta 'áu bít-le-ka 'áu 'á'a múhi-tua-ka-n
    fox-ACC RFL see-think-PPL RFL it shoot-CAU-PPL-PCN
    And thinking that he saw a fox, he was trying to shoot it.

Particular usages of **-tua** imply the volitional giving of something to someone, as illustrated in example (25).

(25) híttah-ha túa néhpo 'enčí b^wá'a-tua-nee
    what-INTERR indeed I you:ACC eat-CAU-FUT
    What in the world can I give you to eat.

6.2. Derivational usages of -tua

Yaqui causatives, as is true of causatives in general, induce a number of idiosyncratic semantic changes in the stems that they affix to. For example, the combination of the motion verb **wee-** *to go* plus **-tua** in construction with the accusative form **'eteho-ta** *talk* and an indirect object postpositional phrase means "to carry on good conversation." This is shown by sentence (26).

(26) tú'ii 'etého-ta né-u wée-tua-síme
    good talk-ACC me-to go-CAU-go:SG
    He carries on a good conversation with me.

The causative expression **ténni-tua** *run*:PL-CAU in construction with **taéwai-m** *days* can be literally glossed as "to make the days run," but it actually means "to waste time," as exemplified by sentence (27) or "to pass the time idly, as in sentence (28).

(27) káa kia taéwai-m ténni-tua-nee
    not just day-PL run:PL-CAU-FUT
    Don't waste the days.

(28) 'ilí haíki taéwai-m saka-'a-tua-su-ka siíka
    little how:many day-PL go:PL-EV-CAU-CMP-PPL went
    After whiling away a few days, he left.

Some verbs allow both the causative **-tua** and the applicative **-ria** to co-occur. This results in verb forms such as **síok-tua-ria** *to make someone sad*, as illustrated by sentence (29).

(29) 'ín híapsi 'ém née síok-tua-ria
    my heart you me sad-CAU-APL
    You make me to be sad at heart.

Frequently, however, the notion of an induced psychological state is handled by the use of **-tua** all by itself, as is suggested by sentence (30).

(30) haísa né 'aú-ka yoém-raa-ta 'allée-tua-nee 'át-tua-nee
    how I do-PPL people-ABS-ACC happy-CAU-FUT laugh-CAU-FUT
    What can I do to make the people happy, to make them laugh?

Certain usages of **-tua** carry the meaning of "have" or "be in psychological state X" as in sentence (31). In this usage of **-tua,** the force dynamic notion implicit to this meaning of **-tua** is backgrounded to the induced state.

(31) ʼemo ʼómti-tua-ka ʼínen hiʼa
RFL anger-CAU-PPL thus say
They say that because they're angry.

The unpredictable semantics of causative constructions is nicely illustrated by the causative verb **bít-tua** which literally means "to cause to see," but in its conventional usage it is taken to mean "to send something." This particular meaning represents the grammaticalization of an implication, i.e., if someone sends you something, it comes into your presence and you therefore see it. Sentence (32) provides a typical instance of this usage.

(32) ʼiním-wáin bít-tua-ri-ʼi-tea
here-about see-CAU-PPL-EV-say
You are sent here they say.

The causative form of the schematic verb **aáne** *to do* seems to be idiomatic for prostitutes or loose women in the expression **hámut ʼán-tua-ri**, given in example (33).

(33) ʼhámut ʼán-tua-ri-m-mak
woman do-CAU-PPL-PL-with
with bad women

Another use of the causative form of **ʼaáne** can be glossed as "cause to have X," where X is some nominal that designates a particular condition, i.e., misery, as in example (34).

(34) wáme hiókot ʼenčím ʼán-tua-me
those misery you-PL be-CAU-NZR
those who cause you to suffer

The causative form of the verb **béheʼe** *to oppose X* does not mean "to put someone at odds with X," but rather "to pay for X in retribution," as suggested by example (35).

(35) ʼáʼa béheʼe-tua-nee
it oppose-CAU-FUT
He will pay for it.

Abstract nouns can be verbalized with the suffix **-te** and the resulting combination can then take the causative **-tua.** In example (36) the apparent resultant meaning is "to cause X to have breath." Actually, the conventional meaning is "to bring back to life."

(36) kóko-la-m-nasuk   ʼáʼa híabih-te-tua-ka-me
die:PL-PPL-PL-among him breath-VR-CAU-PPL-NZR
the one who caused him to be raised back to life

In combinations with an adverb, the causative **-tua** seems to carry the meaning of "have" or "become" as suggested by example (37).

(37) ʼemó=ʼem bamíh-tua
RFL=you:PL hurry-CAU
hurry up

In the domain of naming, the causative can combine with the nominal **tea** *name*. The resulting combination can be glossed "to give X a name," as example (38) illustrates. In the domain of general activities, the causative **-tua** takes on a more neutral meaning of "do," as seen in example (39).

(38) ʼáʼa téa-túa-k
him name-CAU-PRF
He named him.

(39) ʼe-mák ʼáʼa wée-tua
you-with it go-CAU
do it with you (idiom: lo sigo contigo)

A number of usages show the transparent causative meaning "make X do something," as in examples (40) and (41).

(40) 'á'a bʷán-tua
him cry-CAU
cause him to cry

(41) hí'osia-ta nók-tua-nee
paper-ACC talk-CAU-FUT
will cause paper to talk

With reflexives, the causative construction may have the meaning "to make oneself like X." In example (42), the adverbial **hákwoo** means "a long time ago" and the causative **-tua** suffixes to a Spanish loan word.

(42) hákwoo=nee baké'o-m 'ino mamáto-tua-n
when=I cowboy-PL RFL imitate-CAU-PCN
A long time ago, I tried to imitate a cowboy. or
A long time ago I pretended that I was a cowboy.

The unpredictabilty of causative phenomena is again seen clearly in example (43) in which the causative **-tua** has within its scope both the verb stem that precedes it and the adverbial suffix that follows it.

(43) 'a'a čai-tua-sime
him yell-CAU-go-SG
He causes him to go yelling. or *He goes causing him to yell.*

Were the right to left ordering of scope relations to be determinative, then we should expect the form ***čai-sime-tua** for the meaning "he causes him to go around yelling," but that is not what we get here. On the other hand, the Verb1-X-Verb2 schema that runs throughout Yaqui, and Southern Uto-Aztecan in general, is precisely what gives us the actually observed morphological order. The anomaly of scope relations in this example and the role of the bi-verb schema suggests that **-tua** itself is a reanalyzed sequence of Proto-Southern Uto-Aztecan ***tu** *to be* and a following imperfective participle **-a**. Such an analysis jibes perfectly well with Hale's Apodosis Condition and his observation that the first verb in such constructions is marked for the imperfective (Hale 1959:303)

6.3. The applicative suffix -ria

The applicative suffix **-ria** in its prototypical sense, means "to do something on behalf of someone." Prototypical usages are illustrated in examples (44)–(47). In example (44) the activity is directed to a single person, whereas in sentence (45) it is directed toward a class of people.

(44) tabú-ta 'á'a mé'e-ria-ka, 'á'a kuhá'abʷa-k
rabbit-ACC her kill-APL-PPL it broil:spit:on-PRF
Having killed a rabbit for her, he broiled it.

(45) táhka-reo-po ne weáma-n há'iyeo-m hí'i-boo-ria-n
tortilla-AGT-in I walk-PCN mescalero-PL IZR-cook-APL-PCN
I used to be a tortilla maker; I cooked for the agave cookers.

That which is done for someone may be very general, as suggested by the use of **-ria** in sentence (46) or it may be an expressed command, as in sentence (47).

(46) senú wéye-m-ta née yá'a-ria 'ém 'áa híta hoá-'apo 'amani
one go-NZR-ACC me do-APL your able thing do-GND there
Do something for me that is within your expertise.

(47) wáka'a 'ém nésauwi né 'enčí 'á'a yá'a-ria-nee
that:ACC your command I you:ACC it do-APL-FUT
I will do your command for you.

In its most concrete usages, **-ria** signals the providing of a distinct entity for someone else's use or consumption, as illustrated in examples (48)–(50). Here the distinct entities are coffee in example (48), food in general in (49) and bread in (50).

(48) čukúi-ba'á-ta   'á'a bʷása-'a-ria-k
    black-water-ACC him cook-EV-APL-PRF
    She cooked coffee for him.

(49) láuti   bʷá'a-m-ta   'á'a haríu-ria-se
    quickly eat-NZR-ACC him search-APL-go
    He went to look for food for him right away.

(50) woói páan-im   mesá-u 'á'a mána-'a-ría-ka 'á-u   čaaé
    two   breads-PL table-on him lay-EV-APL-PPL him-to call
    Having put two pieces of bread on the table for him, she called him.

In more abstract senses, **-ria** can signal verbal activity that is undertaken in behalf of someone else, as illustrated by examples (51) and (52).

(51) née lioh-ta-u   'enčím bʷán-ria   (52) 'iníi'i sép   'á'a hewí-te-ria-k
    I   God-CON-to you-PL cry-APL   this at:once him yes-VR-APL-PRF
    I pray to God for you.   *This fellow said "yes" on his behalf, at once.*

The applicative activity can be reflexive, i.e., one can do something on his/her own behalf as seen in examples (53)–(55).

(53) tú'ii mó'obe'e-ta 'áu hínu-ria-k   (55) 'enčím bó'o-hóo-ria-su-k-a'u
    good hat-ACC   RFL buy-APL-PRF   your   road-do-APL-CMP-PRF-GND
    He bought himself a good hat.   *That project which you did for yourselves.*

(54) káa 'áa 'áu nók-ria
    not able RFL talk-APL
    He is not able to speak on his own behalf.

The idea of retribution, for good or for evil, is frequently conveyed by the applicative form of verbs such as **hoóa** *to do*. Examples (56) and (57) illustrate this usage. Sentence (56) presents a conventional way of saying "thank you" and may well be a calque from Spanish. It literally means God will make it good for you.

(56) Liós 'enčí   'á'a tú'u-yá'a-ria-nee
    God you-ACC it   good-make-APL-FUT
    God will repay you. (Thanks)

(57) lútu'uria-m   hípʷee-me tú'u-wa-ta   yá'a-ria-naa
    truth-PL:ACC have-NZR good-NOM-ACC do-APL-FUT:PSV
    Justice will be done for the one who is in the right.

In some cases, the applicative seems to have become lexicalized as part of the stem and its benefactive force gets backgrounded as in the Yaqui verb **mám-tóh-te-ria** *to give X a hand*, given in a passive form in (58).

(58) kó'om-čepté-ka tú'isi mám-tóh-te-ria-wa-k
    down-jump-PPL very   hand-clap-VR-APL-PSV-PRF
    When he jumped down, he was vigorously applauded.

Some uses of **-ria** are privative in nature rather than benefactive. Thus, rats eat peoples' things, rather than leave good things with people, as illustrated in example (59). The use of the applicative with the verb stem **wíu-ta** *to destroy*, as exemplified in example (60), is also a clear privative use.

(59) tóri-m 'únnaa   híta yee-bʷá-bʷa'a-ria
    rat-PL very:much thing people-RDP-eat-APL
    Rats sure eat a lot of people's things.

(60) 'enčí-m takáa-wa 'enčím wiu-ta-ria-nee-m-ta   kat='e'em 'ám   mahhae
    your-PL body-ABS you:PL destroy-VR-APL-FUT-NZR-ACC not=you them be:afraid
    Don't be afraid of those who destroy your bodies.

We have mentioned the usage of the suffix **-ria** as a nominalizer in the section NOUN MORPHOLOGY, page 126. Here, as in many other cases, whether one construes a morpheme as being one suffix with different usages, or whether he considers each usage to require one to consider the distinct usages as being homophonous forms may be difficult to resolve. Example (61) illustrates this point. It has two instances of **-ria,** the first on the temporal noun "night" and the second on the verb "attain."

(61) hunúen báhi tukáa-ria-m yumá-'a-ria-wa-k
thus three night-NZR-PL attain-EV-APL-PSV-PRF
In that way they spent three nights.

Ordinarily, the patient of the applicative verb is human, or at least, animate, However, as example (62) shows, an inanimate entity, such as a pole, may also function as patient of the applicative verb.

(62) kúta-t hiká-t sumá-'a-ria-ka-n
pole-on high-on tie-EV-APL-PPL-PCN
It was tied to a pole way up high.

An attenuated use of **-ria** shows it serving to mark indirect objects. In example (63) the patient of the applicative verb turns out to be the passive subject of the sentence. The sentence itself can be glossed "he was æpermissioned' on his own behalf." In example (64) the patient of the applicative verb **etého-ria** *to speak to X* is marked by the first person direct object pronoun.

(63) hunáman lisénsia-ria-wa-k
there permission-APL-PSV-PRF
He was given permission there.

(64) káa túa 'á'a 'álléa'u-ti-hiá-ka née 'etého-ria 'á'a hi-muča-k-t-iia
not indeed his happiness-CON-say-PPL me relate-APL, him UNSPEC-bury-PRF-CON-say
He conversed with me, telling me that he was not very happy. "We buried her," he said.

In certain usages, the applicative suffix **-ria** seems to be used in a nearly prototypical causative sense of bringing about some change in the current state of affairs. In example (65) **-ria** is used in combination with a quantifying adjective and the change itself consists in multiplying the number of sheep in a flock. In example (66) the change consists of an increase in understanding of religious matters. In example (67) the growth is that of a planted seed, but the seed is a metaphorical one.

(65) 'amabútti ne 'ám bú'uu-ria-k
exceedingly I them much-APL-PRF
I caused them (sheep) to increase exceedingly.

(66) Liós yée-yó'o-tu-ria-m-ta
God people-grow-VR-APL-NZR-ACC
God who gives people growth

(67) Liós 'á'a yó'o-tu-ria
God it grow-VR-APL
God causes it to grow.

INFLECTIONAL AND DERIVATIONAL AFFIXATION

1.0. Introduction

In this chapter we describe the usages of a variety of suffixes that mark both oblique relations of constituents to verbs and a number of volitional, modal, and tense/aspect notions. The oblique relations are marked by grammaticalized versions of the suppletive verb **-sime** (SG)/**-saka** (PL) *to go,* and the purposive **-se** (SG)/**-bo** (PL) *to go to do X*. Volitional notions are encoded by the following suffixes: desiderative **-bae**, heightened desiderative **-pea**, and indirect desiderative **-'íi'aa**. The modal suffixes of Yaqui include: subjunctive **-'ea-n**, past subjunctive **-ka + -'ea/-'ee + -n**, and presumptive **-le**. There are only two suffixes that we treat as tense markers: future **-nee** and future passive **-naa**. The tense/aspect markers include: perfective **-k**, imperfective participle **-ka**, remote stative **-i**, and past continuative **-n**. Aspect, marked by the suppletive forms in Yaqui, includes: inceptive aspect **-taite** (SG) and **-hapte** (PL), cessative aspect **-yaate**, and completive aspect **-su**. The final affix that we discuss in this section is the verbalizing **-oa,** which may possibly be a borrowing from Spanish mediated by Nahuatl.

2.0. Adverbial affixation

In this section, we discuss two pairs of adverbial suffixes which represent the grammaticalized versions of two pairs of motion verbs that in their main verb usages are suppletive for singular versus plural subject. The first pair consists of **-sime** and **-saka**.

2.1 The adverbials -sime (SG)/-saka (PL)

Yaqui encodes one pair of adverbial notions onto verbs by means of the suppletive auxiliaries **-sime** (SG) and **-saka** (PL) *to go.* Yaqui grammar preserves both a main verb usage and an auxiliary usage for this pair of morphemes. The intransitive verb **síme/sáka** *to go, be in motion* is a bona fide verb and is used in any apppropriate circumstance in which the concept of going is to be expressed. The main verb usages of **síme/sáka** are illustrated by examples (1)–(3). A variety of morphophonemic processes affect the shapes of these two morphemes. As shown by example (1), **-sime** shortens to **-sim** when followed by the future suffix **-nee**. An echo vowel appears when suffixing the passive **-wa** to the plural form **-saka,** as in example (2), or in its reduplicated form, illustrated by example (3).

(1) yokó=ne   pótam-meu sím-nee
tomorrow=I Potam-to   go-FUT
I am going to Potam tomorrow.

(2) páhko-u sáka-'a-wa
feast-to go:PL-EV-PSV
They are going to the feast.

(3) láau-láautia yoém-raa sáka-'a-saka
RDP-slowly people-AZR go:PL-EV-go:PL
Slowly the people were leaving in groups.

Most commonly, **-sime** and **-saka** occur as the second member of complex verb constructions, lending an aspectual meaning to the entire structure. One typical auxiliary usage is illustrated in example (4). Semantically, the auxiliary usage of **-síme/-sáka** highlights the duration of the ongoing process designated by the main verb.

(4) sí'ime hunáa'a lú'uti-sime
all   that   end-go
All that matters is coming to an end. or
All that matters is passing out of style.

The particular orientation of movement with respect to a speaker's location is not clearly specified by the semantics of **-síme** and **-sáka**. While the default value may be considered to be motion away from the speaker's vantagepoint, as in example (5), the semantics of particular adverbials may impose a specific orientation on the motion implicit in the meaning of **-síme** and **-sáka**. Notice the semantic contrast between the following two examples.

(5) 'áe-t yéh-síme 'á'a čái-túa-síme
    it-on sit-go it yell-CAU-go
    He is going along sitting in the cab; he is going along making it whistle.

(6) trén 'á'abo   híu-síme
    train this:direction sound-go
    The train is coming this way whistling.

In its highly productive grammaticalized usages as an auxiliary element **-síme** has both literal and figurative senses. These senses all highlight the ongoing nature of the process that is designated by the verb which **-sime** modifies. This constrasts clearly with the usages of the suffixes **-se** (SG)/**-bo** (PL) *to go*, which are discussed below. In sentence (7), for example, **-síme** highlights abstract motion at the beginning point of a process.

(7) 'ínepo 'ilí hú'unee-síme
    I   little know-go
    I am beginning to understand a little bit. or *I am making a little progress at learning.*

In sentence (8) **-síme** modifies two usages of the main verb **-wée**, which is related to two alternate versions of a single scene in which one person is following another person. The usage of distinct postpositional phrases shows how the speaker can put contrastive highlighting on the most salient entity in each of the two conjoined clauses.

(8) 'áapo ne-pát   wée-síme née 'íntok 'ae-t čá'aka wée-síme
    he   me-before go-go   I   and   him-on follow go-go
    He is going ahead of me, and I am going along following him.

In certain auxiliary usages, **-síme/-sáka** retains its meaning of physical motion within three-dimensional space.

(9) hitá=sa   'émpo hóo-si-síme
    what=INTERR   you   do-RDP-go
    What are you going around doing?

In its auxiliary usage, **-síme/-sáka** may itself undergo reduplication as in example (10).

(10) húme'e 'áme-mak 'emó tú'uri-sa-saka-me
     those them-with RFL enjoy-RDP-go:PL-NZR
     Those who go (are) enjoying themselves with those others.

Ordinarily **-sáka** is used in its basic form to indicate that the process involves a multiplex participant, as in examples (11)–(12).

(11) wée'epula-im   'á'a tékil-ta béhe'e-wa-ta mabét-sáka-nee
     one:by:one-PL his work-ACC value-POS-ACC receive-go:PL-FUT
     Individually they will be paid according to the value of their work.

(12) táa waté ne-pát   lú'u-ti-sáka
     but others me-before end-CON-go-PL
     But some are dying ahead of me.

Complex sentences often employ a string of clauses, each of whose main verbs has the same subject and may be marked with a form of the auxiliary that agrees in number with the subject of the clause, as in examples (13)–(14).

(13) nát-čá'aka   čá'a-sáka   'emó wík-sáka
     order-suspend   suspend-go RFL pull-go:PL
     They go one after another, tied together, they go pulling one another.

(14) 'usí-m   'íntok 'áe-t   čá'a-ka   ténni-sáka   'íntok čái-saka
     child-PL and him-on hang-PPL run:PL-go:PL and   yell-go:PL

  músiko-m   'íntok báa-hó'o-ti   hí-pon-sáka
  musician-PL and blare-noise-AVR IZR-hit-go:PL
  The children went running and yelling after him. The musicians were going along playing blaring music.

2.2. The andatives -se (SG)/-bo (PL)

The pair of directional andative suffixes **-se** (SG) and **-bo** (PL) is probably related to both the singular form of the suppletive intransitive verb **sime** *to go* and the word **bo'o** *road*, which may well be the nominalization of an older plural form of the verb "to go;" cf. Cora **-hu'u** *to go* (plural subject). In contrast to the suffixes **-sime/-saka**, discussed above, **-se** and **-bo** indicate that the implied motion is undertaken for the purpose of carrying out the action indicated by the verb that **-se** or **-bo** is suffixed to. In short, this motion suffix contributes a purposeful perspective to the scene associated with the sentence in which it is used as in sentences (15) and (16). In contrast to **-sime** and **-saka** which highlight the ongoing process of the activity being described, **-se** and **-bo** present the activity either as a bounded whole or as on ongoing state of affairs. Examples (15) and (16) illustrate this, and the key to the construal is found in the presence or absence of the perfective **-k**.

(15) hitá=sa   'émpo 'áman nú'u-se-k   (16) mótčik-ta née nú'u-se
     what=INTERR you there get-go-PRF   turtle-ACC I   get-go
     What are you going there to get?   *I am going to get a turtle.*

Whereas sentences (15) and (16) are typically understood as designating future events, examples (17)–(21) designate past tense situations. The clause with the verb marked by **-se** or **-bo** can still be construed either imperfectively, as in examples (17) and (18), or perfectively, as in examples (19) and (20).

(17) láuti   b^{w}á'a-m-ta   'á'a haríu-ria-se
     quickly eat-NZR-ACC him search-APL-go
     He went quickly to look for food for him.

(18) weró-ta 'áman 'anía-se
     güero there help-go
     He went there to help Güero.

(19) hó'a-raa-m-met   weámi-'i-se-k
     house-AZR-PL-on walk-EV-go-PRF
     He went for the purpose of visiting the villages.

(20) tebó-te-i-ta   né 'á-u tóhi-'í-se-k
     greet-VR-NZR-ACC I   him-to bring-EV-go-PRF
     I went to take greetings to him.

(21) yéu-siňka wasá-m-meu-bíča híta nénki-se-ka-i
     out-went fields-to-site   thing sell-go-PPL-PPL
     He went out to the fields to sell his wares.

In sentences (22)–(24) note that the default value of **-se** *go to do X* has been overridden to mean "come to do X." This represents the grammaticalization of an implicature; i.e., since "I" am now talking to "you" obviously I have come here to you from somewhere. Sentence (24) could be either "come" or "go" depending on context.

(22) lútu'uria-ta né 'enčí   makí-'i-se-k
     truth-ACC I you:ACC give-EV-go-PRF
     I have come to give you the facts.

(23) 'etéhoi né 'emó-u téuwaa-se-k
 story I you:PL-to tell-go-PRF
 I have come to tell you a story.

(24) kítti-'u-se-k = ane
 masa-VR-go-PRF = I
 I have come to get masa.[1]

The usages of the plural andative **-bo** illustrate the same points made above regarding the singular **-se**. Sentences (25)–(26) refer to future events, whereas sentences (27)–(28) speak of past tense events.

(25) yéu-bit-bo = te
 play-see-go = we
 We are going to see the game.

(26) hán = te hi'i-b^wá-bo
 HRT = we IZR-eat-go:PL
 Let's go eat.

(27) 'áman = té 'á'a bít-bo-k
 there = we him see-go-PRF
 We went there to see him.

(28) kúpte-o ta'á-ta 'aman wéčí-se-o tábero-m heká-'a-wi yáhi-bo-k
 evening-when sun-POS there fall-go-when Tabero-PL wind-EV-to arrive:PL-go-PRF
 In the evening as the sun was setting, they were coming into Tabero's Wind.

3.0. Volitional notions

Volitional notions are encoded by the suffixes **-bae** desiderative, **-pea** heightened desiderative, and **-'íi'aa** indirect desiderative.

3.1. The desiderative -bae

The desiderative verbal suffix **-bae** *to wish to* is used very productively in Yaqui. It is obviously a grammaticalized version of the main verb **báe,** and can still be used as a verb by itself. As a main verb it can even take itself for a suffix, as in example (29). In this case, it gets modified to the form **-baa.** It is likely that a reduplication pattern in conjunction with the the common verb-verb compound construction, as illustrated in example (30), sanctioned the development of the suffixal usage.

(29) báe-ka húni'i née káa báa-bae-k
 wish-PPL even I not wish-wish-PRF
 Even though I wanted to, I didn't want to want to.

(30) híba káa súka-báe 'ii'i taéwai
 always not warm-DSD this day
 This day still doesn't want to get warm.

Supporting this point of view is that one clear instance of a reduplicated form of this suffix often occurs, i.e., **-ba-bae,** as exemplified in example (31).

(31) 'enríkes nótti-bá-bae-k
 Enriquez return-RDP-want-PRF
 Enriquez really wanted to return.

In addition to its potential for reduplicating, an additional piece of evidence that the desiderative suffix **-bae** has grammaticalized from a free verb is seen in its common usage with the meaning "want to do X" in Verb1-Verb2 constructions. Typical glosses for such Verb + **-bae** constructions include "want to hear" as in example (32), "want to visit" as in example (33), and "want to live" as in (34).

---

1 Spanish **masa** = tortilla dough

296

(32) 'émpo káa née hikkahi-bae-ka káa née híkkaha
    you not me hear-DSD-PPL not me hear
    You don't hear me, because you don't want to hear me.

(34) káa né 'íntok híaps-i-bae
    not I and live-PPL-DSD
    I don't want to live any longer.

Although the concept of wish or desire is very evident and prominent to many of its usages, in the early years Dedrick's language associates more frequently gave him the future concept as its equivalent. This extension from a verb of "want" to a marker of the future aspect is attested for other Uto-Aztecan languages (Burton Bascom, personal communication). The notion of "intentionality" is also highly salient to many of its usages.

(35) wiča'arakia-m né yá-'a-bae   (36) wáka'a=ne   núnu-bae
    slingshot   I make-EV-DSD   that:one-ACC=I invite-DSD
    I am going to make a slingshot.   *I am going to invite him.*

Although **-bae** is basically a desiderative, in its grammaticalized usages it serves as often as not as a future tense marker.

(37) Liós yúk-tua-báe-'e-te-k   yúk-tua-nee
    God rain-CAU-DSD-EV-VR-PRF:CND rain-CAU-FUT
    If God wants to make it rain, He will make it rain.

(38) puéplo-ta-u=ne   nók-bae-ka-'ea
    people-ACC-to=I talk-DSD-PPL-think
    I would like to speak to the people.

With motion verbs, **-bae** takes on the meaning "go to do X" as in examples (39)–(40).

(39) wáa'a wéye-me hí'i-bʷa-báe-ka wéye   (40) 'áme-mak=ne wée-bae
    that go-NZR eat-DSD-PPL   go   them-with=I go-DSD
    The one in motion is looking for food.   *I am going with them.*

Examples (41) and (42), which are used when taking leave of someone, show the contrastive use of stems for the suppletive verb meaning "go" in construction with **-bae**. Note also the change of subject clitics.

(41) sím-bae=ne   (42) sáka-'a-bae=te
    go-DSD=I   go:PL-EV-DSD=we
    I am going now.   *We are going now.*

When followed by the passive suffix **-wa**, **-bae** has an alternate form **-baa**. Thus this morphemic alternation affects both main verb and suffixal usages of **-bae**.

(43) hái=sa   téa-tua-baa-wa
    how=INTERR name-CAU-DSD-PSV
    What is he/she going to be named?

The suffix **-bae** is intrinsically imperfective in its semantics, i.e., it presents a situation as being in process, as in examples (44)–(45). In sentence (44) something was on the verge of being sold, whereas in example (45) the duration of the process in view is entirely in the future.

(44) nénki-baa-wa-ka   táa híu-po-su   lú'ute-k-téa
    sell-DSD-PSV-PPL but taste-in-EMP end-PRF-say
    It was to have been sold, but the people ate it all up just sampling it.

(45) 'enčím bai-tá'aa-baa-nee-me
    you:PL "deceive"-DSD-FUT-NZR
    those who will be wanting to deceive you

On the other hand, in both sentences (46) and (47) the time of the durative process overlaps with the time of speaking.

(46) péuti-baa-wa
butcher-DSD-PSV
They are going to butcher.

(47) sáka-'a-baa-wa
go:PL-EV-DSD-PSV
They want to go. or
They are preparing to go.

As suggested by examples (44)–(47), the imperfective construal of **-bae** is not confined to simple present, past, or future tense situations. It fits perfectly well with more complex tense/aspect schemas also. This includes backgrounded events that serve as the ground for locating perfectively construed events as in sentence (48). It also can serve as the background for locating an unrealized perfective event as in sentence (49).

(48) háksa wée-kai kó'okoim-po b^wé'uu-si páhko-baa-wa-o 'áman néhun-wa-k
where go-PPL Cocorit-in big-AVR feast-DSD-PSV-when there invite-PSV-PRF
Once when they were going to have a big feast in Cocorit, he was invited there.

(49) 'í'an senú hákun-biča bíttua-baa-wa-'a-te-k-o segúuro-po wée-baa-nee
now one somewhere-site send-DSD-PSV-EV-VR-PRF-if secure-in go-DSD-FUT
Nowadays, if someone is to be sent somewhere, he will want to go securely.

3.2. The heightened desiderative -pea

The desiderative suffix **-pea** has additional allomorphs of the shape **-pée** and **-pé'ea**, respectively. Semantically, it indicates an emotional desire on the part of the speaker that is stronger than the desire that the speaker feels when he uses **-bae.** It can frequently be glossed by phrases such as "to want to, to wish to, to yearn for, to long after, to desire to." This suffix derives from combining the postposition **-po** *in* with the verb **'ea** *to think, to feel*. It has become fused into a single unit as shown by the fact that native speakers reject a form like ***yéu-po-'ea** *play-in-think*, insisting that it should be **yéu-pea** *play*-DSD with the meaning "He desires very much to play." By inserting an additional morpheme, the original form from which **-pea** was grammaticalized can be restored and is accepted. For example, Dedrick has observed instances of **yéu-po hiba 'éa** *play-in only think,* meaning "He only thinks about playing," or "All he wants to do is play." Typical usages of **-pea** with the verbs of main clauses are given in examples (50)–(52).

(50) ká=ne 'íntok pócˇo'o-ku hó'a-pea
not=I and woods-in live-DSD
I do not want to live in the woods any longer.

(51) lótti-laa-taka né wée báa-yúm-hó'e-pea
tire-PPL-being I come at:once-rest-make-DSD
I come really tired, I want to rest at once.

(52) sí'ime=te tekipánoa-pea
all=we work-DSD
We all desire to work.

Subordinate and nominalized clauses show the kinds of suffix strings that may attach to **-pea,** which itself always attaches to a verb stem. In sentence (53) **-pea** is followed by the participial string **-ka-i** in a subordinate adverbial clause, whereas in sentence (54) it is followed by the gerundial **-'u.**

(53) 'útte'a wéye mo'oči-m-meu yebíh-pea-ka-i
strong go Los Mochis-to arrive-DSD-PPL-PPL
He went as fast as he could because he really wanted to get to Los Mochis.

(54) née hú'unea sí'ime-m 'enčím tekipánoa-pea-'u
I know all-ACC your:PL work-DSD-PPL
I know that you all desire to work.

Inflectional and Derivational Affixation 3.3.

The intensified emotional implication of **-pea** in some instances has been lexicalized in particular ways with given verbs. Thus, with the stem **bʷá'e,** the addition of **-pea** *to want very much to eat* comes to have the conventionalized meaning of "to be starving," as in sentence (55).

(55) kía te hí'i-bʷa-pea-ka 'ím hoóka
only we IZR-eat-DSD-PPL here seated
We're just sitting here starving.

The scope of **-pea** includes everything that precedes it up to the subject pronoun in the clause in which it occurs. Thus in sentence (56), **-pea** has within its scope the causative verb and the direct object clitic in **'ám kí'i-tua** *them bite*-CAU.

(56) kée née ké'e 'íntok née káa née 'ám kí'i-tua-pea
not:yet me bite and I not me them bite-CAU-DSD
They have not yet bitten me, and I have no desire to cause them to bite me.

The strong emotion attached to the use of **-pea** is reflected in its compatibility with situations being viewed imperfectively. In short, a certain time lapse is usually associated with strong emotional responses. Thus both examples (57) and (58) are understood as reflecting past durative situations. Note that there is no past tense or participial marking in sentence (58).

(57) sí'ime-ta yá'a-pea-ka-'ea-n 'ó'obek
all-ACC do-DSD-PPL-think-PCN although
though he was wishing that he could do everything

(58) kát=im 'o-'óbe húme'e maoméeo-m 'o'oben táa=m káa páp-pea
not=they RDP-lazy those acrobat-PL though but=they not work-DSD
It wasn't that the acrobats were lazy, they just didn't feel like working.

Morphologically, **-pea** parallels **-bae** in that it has an allomorph with a long vowel when it is followed by the passive suffix **wa-,** as in example (59).

(59) húme'e sirkéeo-m bítču-pee-wa-n
those circus:men-PL stare-DSD-PSV-PCN
They really wanted to see the circus performers.

A kind of reduplication also applies to **-pea,** as in example (60). This particular sequence appears to preserve the **-'ea** *seem* verb stem that is part of the polymorphemic source for the grammaticalized nonreduplicated version **-pea**.

(60) káa 'á'a yóopna-k bʷé'ituk bʷán-pe'ea-k
not him answer-PRF because cry-RDP-DSD-PRF
She didn't answer him because she could hardly keep from crying.

3.3. The indirect desiderative **'íi'aa**

The indirect desiderative **'íi'aa** comes from the main verb **híia** *to say*. All of its usages are based on what somebody says. The desiderative notion on the part of some speaker is implied semantically. This seems to be a unique morpheme in which the subject desires that some, usually, different (non-coreferent) subject carry out the action indicated by the verb to which **-'íi'aa** is affixed and over which it holds its scope. The subject of the overall sentence in which **-íi'aa** is used may be either the speaker or someone reported by others. Nominals and pronouns designating these entities are in the nominative case in declarative sentences. In the passive form **-'íi'aa-wa,** the subjects are not specified. The nominals and pronouns indicating the subjects of the clauses serving as complements to **-íi'aa** are always marked in the accusative.

The non-coreferent subject (NCRS) may be persons, things, or circumstances. These are marked in the accusative case, being treated as objects of **-'íi'aa**. Direct objects of transitive verbs are also in the accusative case. In a simple transitive verb sentence in which only pronouns are used, the following order of constituents is rigid: Subject:NOM + Non-coreferent subject:ACC + Object:ACC + Verb-IN:DSD. This schema represents the prototypical -**íi'aa** construction, which is exemplified in sentence (61).

    (61) 'áapo   'enčí   'á'a   bép-'íi'aa
         he:NOM you:ACC him:ACC hit-IN:DSD
         He wants you to hit him.

In sentence (62) the subject of the sentence is the one desiring an action, whereas the direct object of **'íi'aa**, i.e., **itom** *us* is the subject of **nénki** *to sell*. The pronoun **'áme** that immediately precedes **nénki** refers to horses, the direct object of "sell."

    (62) hunáme'e   'íme'e kába'i-m 'itóm 'áme-u 'am nénki-'íi'aa
         those:people these horse-PL us   them-to them sell-IN:DSD
         Those people want us to sell these horses to them.

In sentence (63) the speaker is the subject of the clause embedded to -**íi'aa**, whereas the addressee is the subject of the entire sentence.

    (63) 'émpo b^wá'a-m-ta   káa nee b^wáa-'íi'aa
         you   eat(food)-NZR-ACC not me eat-IN:DSD
         You don't want me to eat food.

In examples (64) and (65) the speaker is subject of the entire sentence, the addressee is subject of the embedded clause, and the direct object of the embedded clause is an embedded question.

    (64) túa   ne 'enčím   'á'a hu'unéiyaa-'íi'aa haísa maísi=nee 'obísi 'ín 'íno bíča-'apo
         truly I   you:ACC it   know-IN:DSD   how manner=I busy my RFL see-GND
         I really want you to know how busy I am.
    (65) túa   née 'enčím   'á'a hú'unéiyaa-'íi'aa
         indeed I   you:PL:ACC it know-IN:DSD
         I want very much that you know it.

The foregoing examples suggest that the subject of the clause embedded to -**íi'aa** is always marked in the accusative. Examples (66)–(68) reinforce this observation.

    (66) Lióh-ta   híapsi 'enčím   bít-'íi'aa-ka-i
         God-ACC spirit   you:PL:ACC see-IN:DSD-PPL-PPL
         He wants you to receive/experience God's spirit.
    (67) tú'u-lútu'uria-ta 'enčím   hú'uneiyaa-íi'aa
         good-truth-ACC you:PL:ACC know-IN:DSD
         He wants you to know the good truth.
    (68) káa tá'ab^wi-si   wée-m-ta   'ám máhta-'íi'a-ka-i
         not different-AVR go-NZR-ACC them teach-IN:DSD-PPL-PPL
         because he doesn't want him to teach them something different

Whereas the speaker may well be the subject of the embedding verb -**íi'aa,** as in example (69), he cannot simultaneously be the subject of the clause that is the complement of -**íi'aa.** Thus this sentence must mean "I don't want them to bite me!" and cannot be understood as meaning "I don't want to bite them." The latter idea is expressed in Yaqui by sentence (70) in which there is only a single first person singular clitic, the third person plural object clitic attaches to a preceding negative particle and the verb itself is marked with -**bae,** and not with -**íi'aa.**

(69) 'íntok née káa née 'ám kíi-'íi'aa
and I not me them bite-IN:DSD
And I don't want them to bite me.[2]

(70) née ká='am kí'i-bae
I not=them bite-DSD
I do not want to bite them.

Even when the complement clause contains an intransitive verb, the subject of that clause embedded to **-'íi'aa** is still marked in the accusative as seen by the first person accusative **'enčí** in example (71), the third person singular accusative demonstrative pronoun **waká'a** in example (72), and the accusative plural **sí'ime-m** in example (73).

(71) 'epéesiom-po né 'enčí tawá-'íi'aa-ka-i
Ephesus-in I you:ACC stay-IN:DSD-PPL-PRP
because I was wanting you to stay at Ephesus

(72) 'emé'e 'á'a jú'uneiyaa wáka'a káa yéu-'á'a-mačía-'íi'aa-m-ta
you:PL him know that:one:ACC not out-him-appear-DSD:AGT-NZR-ACC
You know the one who doesn't want him to appear.

(73) sí'ime-m tekipanoa-'íi'aa
all-PL:ACC work-IN:DSD
He wants everyone to work.

Examples (74) and (75) are ambiguous and the meaning is determined by the context. Each sentence may be understood either transitively or intransitively. This arises as a result of **wee-** being the contracted form for both **wéye** *to go* and **wéiyaa-** *to take, to carry*.

(74) 'a-u 'úhb^wana 'áman 'á'a wée-'íi'aa-ka-i
him-to beg there him take-IN:DSD-PPL-REMOTE
He begged him, wanting him to take him there. or
He begged him, wanting him to go there.

(75) hámbróosio-ta-u 'uhb^wána, 'áman 'á'a wée-'íi'aa-ka-i
Ambrosio-CON-to beg there him go-IN:DSD-PPL
She begged Ambrosio, wanting him to go there. or
She begged Ambrosio, wanting him to take her there.

(76) hika-u mámma čaí-wa-m-ta čá'a-tu-'íi'aa-ka-i
high-to hand yell-PSV-NZR-ACC cease-VR-IN:DSD-PPL-REMOTE
He raised his hand wanting the yelling to cease.

The desiree may indeed be both the speaker of the sentence and the subject of the clause that is the complement of **'íi'aa** as in sentence (77).

(77) sí'ime-m=ne wepu'ulai-béna-si né bít-'íi'aa
all-ACC=I one-like-AVR I see-IN:DSD
I want to see all of you being like one person.

The specific activity that is desired by the speaker may be either a state, encoded as an intransitive verb, or a process, encoded as a transitive verb. Example (78) illustrates both. The first clause suffixes **-'íi'aa** to the stative verb **tawá**, which is the background for carrying out the desired process of the second clause, in which the verb **né-sau** *to order someone* comes within the scope of the second occurrence of **-íi'aa** in the sentence. This latter occurrence is the reduced version **-iá-**, which follows a sequence of an echo-vowel and the connector **-ti-**. In example (79), the unreduced form follows the verbalizer **-tu** in a clear example of its use as a main verb. Note that the verb preceding **-tu** is part of a nominalization.

---

2   In Arizona Yaqui, an alternate order of subject and object clitics is possible.
    kaa 'ám née kíi-'íi'aa
    NEG S O V-V
    This construction has the very same meaning as that given in example (69). (Eloise Jelinek, personal communication.)

(78) 'áman né 'enčí   tawá-'íi'aa-ka-i   waté-m-met 'enčí   nésau-nee-'et-iá-ka-i
     there I   you:ACC stay-IN:DSD-PPL-PPL other-PL-on you:ACC order-FUT-CON-say-PPL-PPL
     I wanted you to stay there, saying that you should take charge of the others.

(79) sí'ime-m   hínne'u-i-m-tú-'íi'aa
     all-PL:ACC save-PPL-PL-VR-IN:DSD
     He wants everyone to be saved.

Yaqui makes frequent uses of passive forms. Usually the passive form mildly highlights the verbal or object part of the communication, but it also may be used (as in several of the following examples) when the speaker/subject feels it more discreet not to specify the subject. Yaqui does not normally use third person plural forms as oblique passives.

The passive form **-'íi'aa-wa** is used in an impersonal way; the speaker, for one reason or another, chooses to leave unspecified who the subject of **-ii'aa** is. In such cases, the subject of the clause embedded to **-'íi'aa** is marked in the nominative, rather than in the accusative. Thus the second person plural subject pronoun form **'em** is used in example (80) instead of the accusative form **'énči** used above in sentence (78).

(80) hunam-mea=sa='em   tú'u-wa-m-po   yó'o-tu-'íi'aa-wa
     those-INST=QUO=you:PL good-NZR-PL-in grow-VR-DSD:AGT-PSV
     It is desired that you grow by means of them.

There seems to be considerable sensitiveness among Yaquis in matters that they consider might offend. Undoubtedly the use of the passive form is one way to avoid specifically naming a person or persons. But the Yaquis seem to use the passive form with considerable frequency, so that it may be used either just for the purpose of being vague, or simply as a variation in style. Sentences (81)–(83) were taken from Sebastian Gonzales's autobiographical text. Sentence (81) was in answer to a question. Again note the use of the first person plural subject pronoun **té**. Sentences (82) and (83) put Sebastian in the embarrassing position of having been hired to kill his own people.

(81) té kókko-'íi'aa-wa
     we die-IN:DSD-PSV
     It was desired that we die.

(82) húme'e yoéme-me-'eb^wan té 'ám-mea   sú'a-'íi'aa-wa-ka
     those yaqui-PL-well   we them-INST kill-IN:DSD-PSV-PPL

     'ám ma-mák-wa   húme'e wíko'i-m
     them RDP-give-PSV those rifle-PL
     We were given rifles (because) it was desired that we kill Yaquis with them.

(83) 'ínepo 'ám 'anía-ka nássua-'íi'aa-wa
     I   them help-PPL fight-IN:DSD-PSV
     It was desired that I fight on their behalf.

The entire **-'íi'aa** construction can itself be embedded in a complex sentence by suffixing to it either of the two gerundive suffixes **-'u**, as in example (84), and **-'apo**, as in sentence (85).

(84) táa húu'u Lióh-ta 'á'a hóo-'íi'aa-'u   'áman wée-ka tú'ii-k   hoá-me
     but the:one God-POS him do-IN:DSD-GND there (manner) go-PPL good-ACC do-NZR
     but the one who does the good that God wants him to do

(85) 'áapo'ik hái=sa   'á'a čúp-'íi'a-'apo   'áman hunúen yéu-sií-ka
     his   how=PRO it finish-IN:DSD-GND there (manner) thus   out-go-PRF
     That's the way it came out, the way he wanted it to come out.

There is also an idiomatic usage of the suffix **-'íi'aa** in which the reflexive pronouns (**'íno, 'émo, 'áu, 'itó, 'emó**) are prefixed to **-'íi'aa**. The entire construction means either "to be mean" or "to intend to do harm." For example, in speaking of her baby a mother used sentence (86). The reflexive may also be used to refer to a mean dog, as in sentence (87).

302

(86) tám-ek 'ám-mea 'áu-'íi'aa
teeth-has them-with RFL-IN:DSD (be mean)
He has teeth, he is really mean (bites) with them.

(87) húu'u čú'u 'áu-'íi'aa
that dog RFL-IN:DSD (be mean)
That dog is mean.

Examples (86) and (87) are interesting because they suggest that **-'íi'aa** retains a main verb usage, albeit one that does not seem obviously related to the notion of expressing a desire for someone to do something. A possible suggestion comes from the observation that the Cora expression meaning "he is angry" is the word **nʸú'ukami'i**, which literally means "he wants to speak," but carries the negative implication that the angry one is not saying anything and that you can determine the dangerous state of affairs by simply looking at the one in question. This would account for the other meaning of the reflexive **-'íi'aa** construction, i.e., "X intends to do harm."

It is also interesting to compare the semantics of **-'íi'aa** with that of imperative sentences. Both imperatives and **-'íi'aa** relate to a conceptual scene in which two participants asymmetrically interact within the speech-act setting such that one person is attempting to determine what another person should do. In imperatives, the initiator of the speech-act is usually not co-referential with the intended initiator of the intended action. With **-'íi'aa**, on the other hand, the desiree is prototypically not co-referential with the initiator of the intended action. For imperatives, the speaker's expressed concern may range in force from a hint (kind of a desiderative) to a life-and-death command. On the other hand, **-'íi'aa** is basically an indirect desiderative; the desiree may be epistemically distinct from active participants in the speech situation and **-'íi'aa** cannot be used in a direct command. Thus, **-'íi'aa** is in clear illocutionary contrast with **-sae** and **-tebo**, which can be used for making commands.[3]

Examples (88)–(91) present a four-way contrast in meaning between the active **-'íi'aa**, the imperative **-sae**, the command form **-tebo**, and the passive **-'íi'aa-wa**. Note that neither **-sae** nor **-tebo** can be used in the place of **-'íi'aa** in sentences such as (91) (unless the speaker were to refer to God —or perhaps to a "rainmaker") whereas **-'íi'aa** can be used freely.

(88) bémpo 'áman 'enčí noíti-'íi'aa
they there you:ACC go-IN:DSD
They want you to go there.

(89) bémpo 'áman 'enčí noíti-sae
they there you:ACC go-IMP
They command you to go there.

(90) hú'u hóan 'á'a yá'a-tebo-k
that John it do-IMP-PRF
John ordered him to do it.

(91) yúk-'íi'aa-wa
rain-IN:DSD-PSV
It is desired that it rain.

4.0. The modal suffixes

Yaqui modal suffixes are grammaticalized versions of mental act verbs meaning "to think" or "to presume." They may occur as single suffixes or they may be part of more complex suffix sequences.

4.1. The subjunctive mode -'ea-n

The intransitive verb **'éa** *to think, to desire, to intend to, to plan to,* has also become grammaticalized as a very productive suffix for marking subjunctive mode. Its usage as a main verb is illustrated in sentence (1), whereas its modal suffixal usage is exemplified in sentence (2).

(1) kaíta=su=ne 'éa
nothing=CTX=I think
I don't have any opinion.

(2) 'áman mabét-ču-'ee-wa-n
there receive-CPL-think-PSV-PCN
He ought to have been well received there.

When followed by the past continuative suffix **-n**, **'ea** is almost always equal to the English subjunctive auxiliaries: "would, should/ought to." It should be noted here that **-'éa** may be followed by

---

[3] Imperatives can also be used in inner speech; for example, in situations in which someone is talking to himself, trying to work up nerve to do something that he/she feels is unpleasant such as getting out of bed in spite of one's lazy feelings.

the perfective **-k,** or by the future/potential **-nee,** i.e., **'éa-k** and **-'ee-nee,** but in these instances is more apt to refer to what was thought, or might be thought. The usage of **'ea** with the emphatic/focus suffix **-su** is treated elsewhere (cf. PARTICLES and CLITICS, pp. 47–51). The suffix **-pea,** also discussed in section 3.2. of this chapter, is derived from the suffix **-po** + **-'éa,** and is sometimes expressed as **-pe'ea.** This verb also has **'éiyaa** as its transitive form.[4]

Typical usages of **-'éa** with the past continuative **-n** are illustrated by sentences (3)–(7). Notice that the clause in which **-'éa-n** occurs is the ground for the statement being made in the conditional clause, which is typically marked with either the conditional suffix **-o** or with the morphemically complex **-'e-te-k-o** EV-VR-PRF-CND. The order of protasis and apodosis clauses is also flexible in Yaqui as a comparison of sentence (3) with sentences (4) and (5) shows.

(3) tú'ii-'éa-n   te kaa ho'ó-t 'am pú'ak-ta-ne-'e-te-k-o
good-SJV-PCN we not back-on them carry-VR-FUT-EV-VR-PRF-CND
It would be good if we didn't have to carry it/them on our backs.

(4) 'ála, 'ínepo tóme-k-o   pahkóa-u nee wée-'ea-n
indeed I   money-have-CND feast-to I go-SJV-PCN
If I had money, I would go to the party.

(5) káa née 'ú'ute buíte-o née b^{w}íh-'ea-n
not I strong run-CND me grab-SJV-PCN
If I had not run so fast, he would have grabbed me.

The conditional suffix **-o** sometimes does not even appear in the protasis clause, as illustrated by sentences (6) and (7).

(6) hunúka'a báh-ta   'áa b^{w}á'a-tu nehpo 'á'a b^{w}áa-'ea-n
that:ACC grass-ACC able eat-be I   it eat-SJV-PCN
If that grass were edible, I would eat it.

(7) tépa-bát tút-tut-ti   'á'a ta'aa-'ea-n[5]
"oh-that" RDP-tight-PPL it know-SJV-PCN
Oh, that he might know it well.

Although the clause with **-'ea-n** may occur as the first clause of a conditional sentence, as in sentence (8), statistically the preference seems to be to put it in the sentence final position, as seen in sentence (9).

(8) mékkaa=te kék-ke'ewe   tú'ii-'éa-n   te káa ho'ó-t 'ám wéyaa-'a-te-k-o
far:away=we RDP-cut:wood good-SJV-PCN we not back-on them carry-EV-VR-PRF-if
We have to go far away to cut stove wood, it surely would be nice if we didn't have to carry it home on our backs.

(9) b^{w}é'ituk 'iníka'a tá'aa-'a-te-k-o   kát=ím kríhto-ta
because this:ACC know-EV-VR-PRF-if not=they Christ-ACC
kúus-et sekola po-pón-'ea-n
cross-on stretched RDP-nail-SJV-PCN
Because if they had known this, they would not have nailed Christ stretched out on a cross.

As a main verb, **-'éa** has an allomorph of the shape **'ee.** Both main verb and suffixal usages are found in a single complex verb construction in the second clause of sentences (10) and (11). The lengthened vowel allomorph allows the distinction between verb and suffix to be maintained.

(10) hunúen-po-béha mah-tí-la-m-taka-i   káa hú'ena-k 'ée-sáka-'ea-n
thus-in-well teach-PPL-NZR-PL-being-PPL not evil-ACC think-go:PL-SJV-PCN (SUBJ)
Since you have been taught in this way, you shouldn't go (around) thinking evil (things).

---

4 It is probably because Spanish has to use the subjunctive form to express this kind of desiderative that Johnson analyzed it as a subjunctive (cf. Johnson 1962:42).

5 Castro also gave "Ojala" as one of the meanings of **tepa-bat.**

(11) bát-čaín   tá'ab^wi-ku-t   hita 'ée-'ea-n
    first-anyway   different-in-on   thing   think-SJV-PCN
    Perhaps he might still be thinking about something else.

The suffixal form also has an allomorph **'ee** when it precedes the future suffix **-nee**. The contrast between its allomorphic shapes is seen clearly in the following two sentences. The unaltered form is given in example (12) and the lengthened, harmonized form is given in example (13).

(12) 'áapo náa-búuhti wée-bae-ka-'ea-n
    he   on-through   go-DSD-PPL-SJV-PCN
    He had been intending to go on through.

(13) bú'uu-raa-ta   'aúk-a'u   kibák-bae-ka-'ee-nee
    much-NZR-POS   be-GND   enter:SG-DSD-PPL-SJV-FUT
    He might want to enter into the multitude.

A few suffixal usages with the past continuative **-n** appear to retain the verbal meaning "to think." This usage is likely the link between the main verb and suffixal usages of **-'ea**.

(14) 'áapo 'íntok náa-búuh-ti   wée-bae-ka-'ea-n
    he   and   on-through-AVR   go-DSD-PPL-SJV-PCN
    And he had been thinking of going on past there.

4.2. The past subjunctive -ka + -'ea-n

The past subjunctive usages of **-'ea-n** are preceded by the participial suffix **-ka**. The meaning of **-'ea-n** in these constructions seems to be that of indicating remote possibility. Thus in example (15), the use of **-'ea-n** implies the subject's inability to do a lot of things.

(15) huébena-k 'ée-sime sí'ime-ta yá'a-pea-ka-'ea-n   ó'obe-k
    much-ACC   think-go   all-ACC   do-DSD-PPL-SJV-PCN   although-ACC
    He was going along thinking about a lot of things, he was wishing he could do everything.

In cases such as example (16) the use of **-'ea-n** indicates a perceived strong intentionality, in this case intentionality with a distinct evil end.

(16) hú'ena-k 'ía híaki-ta-u   wée-tua-k 'á'a tehál-bae-ka-'ea-n
    evil-ACC this yaqui-ACC-to go-CAU-PRF him   destroy-DSD-PPL-SJV-PCN
    The Yaqui were badly abused, they were wanting to annihilate them.

The intent implied by the use of the past subjunctive **-'ea-n**, however, is not necessarily "bad." In example (17) it merely reflects strong emotional desire for something.

(17) čé'ewa=su búiti-síme bwé'ituk karíl-ta ku-kúh-híkkaha-k   'a'a bwíh-bae-ka-'ea-n
    more=EMP   run-go   because   train-ACC RDP-whistle-hear-PRF   it   grab-DSD-PPL-SJV-PCN
    He ran even harder, he had heard the train whistle and he was wanting to catch it.

4.3. The presumptive -le

Yaqui expresses another modal idea by the use of the presumptive suffix **-le**, which can be glossed as "to think to be." Straightforward examples are given in (18) and (19).

(18) 'emó habé-le-ka   tá'ab^wi-m-mak   kúak-te
    RFL   someone-think-PPL   different-PL-with   turn-VR
    They go around with others because they think they are somebody.

(19) híta áu   tá'aa-le-me
    thing RFL know-presume-NZR
    one who thinks he knows things

In its prototypical sense of "to think to be X," **-le** suffixes to both nominalizations, as illustrated in example (20), and indefinite pronouns, as in example (21).

(20) tú'u-waa-le
good-NZR-think
to think to be good

(21) hábe-le
someone-think
to think to be someone

Part of the meaning of **-le** involves the idea of "contrary to the expected state of affairs." This is shown in sentence (22) in which **-le** is used with the verb **'áawe** *to know how to do X* in the first clause, but the presupposition that it carries is denied by the use of the negative **kaa** in conjunction with **'áawe** in the second clause.

(22) senú két 'áu 'áawe-le-nee   káa húni'i 'áawe-ka-i
one also RFL know:how-presume-FUT not even know:how-PPL-PPL
A person might think he was competent even when he wasn't really competent at all.

The particular kind of thinking implied by the use of **-le** is considered to be socially inappropriate to some extent, i.e., "X is putting on airs about Y." Thus the person being described in example (23) is putting on airs of having been offended, when in actuality there has been no offense.

(23) híta 'emó huíwa-le-ka   réhte-me
thing RFL feel-think-PPL go:PL-NZR
people who go around thinking that they are offended

The notion "to be able to do something" is also a part of the meaning of **-le,** as is the related notion of "to be doing something." These two construals, plus the ideas of "contrary to the expected state of affairs" and "socially inappropriate" are what distinguishes **-le** so clearly from **-ea-n,** which we discussed above. Both construals can be associated with a single sentence, as in the following examples. In sentence (24) the actual state of affairs is that the subject is not eating a ram. The implication of sentence (25) is that the people are not really good after all.

(24) hobé'eso-ta 'áu b^{w}á'a-mači-le-ka-i
ram-ACC RFL eat-appear-think-PPL-PPL
He was thinking that he would be eating a ram.
He was now thinking of himself as eating that ram.

(25) 'emé'e túa   'emó tú'u-waa-le
you:PL indeed RFL good-VR-think
You(PL) really think that you are good people.

The perceived lack of conformity to an expected state of affairs is clearly part of the meaning of **-le** in example (26). As is usual with polysemous morphemes, not all of the particular meanings are realized in any given context. There is no obvious social norm, for example, involved in the usage of **-le** in that instance, whereas there certainly is in both usages of **-le** in sentence (27). Finally, in sentence (28) the implication is that the people will not find what is good for them.

(26) káa 'á'a hunáa'a-tu-ka káa 'á'a mačí-le-ka-i
not him that-VR-PPL   not him seem-think-PPL-PPL
because it didn't seem to them that that one was really the one

(27) híta 'émo huíwa-le-ka   réhte-me 'íntok emó habé-le-ka
thing RFL offended-think-PPL go-NZR and RFL someone-think-PPL

tát-tá'ab^{w}i-mak   kúakte
RDP-different-with turn
People who go around thinking that they are offended and because they have a high opinion of themselves, they turn to others.

(28) tú'u-wa-ta   'áma 'emó téu-mači-le-ka-i
good-NZR-ACC there RFL find-seem-think-PPL-PPL
Because they think that they will find there that which is good for them.

In example (29) the clause with -le has been nominalized by the use of the active nominalizer **-me**. In example (30) the entire expression consisting of the indefinite pronoun and -le is nomininalized as evidenced by the suffix **-me** which attaches to the modal **-le**.

(29) híta 'áu tá'aa-le-me
thing RFL know-think-NZR
one who thinks he knows things

(30) 'emo habe-le-me
RFL someone-think-NZR
those who think they are great

5.0. The tense markers

As is typical for other Uto-Aztecan languages (cf. Langacker 1977b:151), Yaqui shows little indication of suffixes that mark pure tense. Instead, the usual situation is for the tense markers to display a range of meanings that include aspectual values and distinct epistemic states.

The matter of whether an action or a condition is situated in the past, present, or future depends more heavily upon the total context of utterances in which these tense/aspect suffixes, **-bae**, **-nee**, **-naa**, and **-k**, are used than it does upon the meanings of the suffixes themselves, although the idea of tense is not entirely lacking in them.

5.1. The future tense marker -nee

The future tense takes in a variety of potentially occurring states and events, which may or may not be linked to a high degree of purposefulness or intentionality on the part of a specific agent. As the discussion of the following examples will illustrate, several other factors also partly determine the usages of **-nee**. To begin, intentionality is clearly a salient aspect of the meaning of **-nee** in examples (31)–(33).

(31) lúula yéh-te-'u-táhtia bó'o-bít-nee táa čukúi-ba'a-ta kaíta-nee
straight set-VR-GND-until road-see-FUT but black-water-ACC nothing-be
He may wait till noon, but there won't be any coffee.

(32) kaíbu=nee 'íntok 'á'a sú'u-tóhi-nee 'éla'apo=su=nee 'áa-mak 'ó'o-múk-nee
never=I and it alone-leave-FUT no:matter=EMP=I it-with old-die-FUT
I'll never stop drinking it, even though I die of old age because of it.

(33) yá'uraa-ta té bít-nee hunáa'a 'itóm híkkahi-nee
authority-ACC we see-FUT those us hear-FUT
We will see the authorities; they will hear us.

On the other hand, intentionality is not a salient aspect of the meanings of **-nee** in examples (34) and (35). Instead, the expectation of a change of state is what is behind these latter two usages of the future marker **-nee**.

(34) kát kapée hé'ée čukúi-s=e'e 'áu-nee
not coffee drink black-AVR=you be-FUT
Don't drink coffee, it will make you turn black.

(35) kó'om kúak-te-'u-bíča čé'a sébe-nee
down turn-VR-GND-site more cold-FUT
It's going to get colder toward evening.

Sometimes **-nee** is used to indicate slight possibility, potentiality or a reduced intentionality. In cases such as example (36) it can be glossed by the English modal "may."

(36) née hiókoli-nee-m-ta téu-nee hunáa'a habésa=ne híapsi-tua-nee
me pity-FUT-NZR-ACC find-FUT that-one whoever=me life-CAU-FUT
I may find someone who will pity me; that person will "restore" me.

The future is also sometimes used to express customary activities on the part of someone, as in examples (37) and (38), or conventional wisdom about particular causes and results, as in example (39).

(37) 'áe   yoká-'a-nee   hí'osia-ta   nók-tua-nee
     it-with paint-EV-FUT paper-ACC   talk-CAU-FUT
     He will paint with it; he will make paper talk.

(38) burú-m-met   yéh-sím-nee kaíbu wokí-m-mea wée-nee
     donkey-PL-on sit-go-FUT   never foot-PL-on go-FUT
     He rides on donkeys and will never go on foot.

(39) 'áu bamíh-tua-me   láuti múk-nee-'e-tea
     RFL hurry-CAU-NZR   soon die-FUT-EV-QUO
     It is said that one who hurries will die soon.

Some usages even approach the notion of conditionality as in example (40), or encapsulate a modal notion such as "should X happen" as in example (41), or even "can do X" as illustrated by example (42).

(40) 'á'a woíta 'éla'apo wée-nee
     it   untie no:matter go-FUT
     Untie it; it doesn't matter if it goes away.

(41) seénu káa-tú'ii-k-mak   wée-nee-'e-te-k   'áap-ela wée-'e-te-k   čé'a tú'ii
     one   not-good-ACC-with   go-FUT-EV-VR-PRF:CND he-alone go-EV-VR-PRF:CND more good
     It is better that one travel alone than that he should travel with a bad companion.

(42) née ka='ám   tú'ure 'ó'oben táa haísa 'án-nee
     I   not=them like   though but how   be-FUT
     I don't like them, but what can be done about it?

The verb to which **-nee** suffixes may well describe an ongoing situation, with the future in the speaker's mind actually consisting of a conceived contrary to fact state of affairs, as in example (43).

(43) tú'ii-ean té káa hoo'ó-t 'ám pú'ak-ta-nee-'e-tek-o
     good-SJV we not back-on them carry-VR-FUT-EV-PRF-CND
     It would be good if we didn't have to carry it on our backs.

Other usages of **-nee** are associated with the notion of strong probability, as illustrated in example (44) or almost certainty, at least as perceived by the speaker, as illustrated by example (45). Example (46) reflects expressed strong intent by the speaker.

(44) kaábe 'enčím   'á'a 'ú'aa-nee
     no:one you:PL:ACC it take:away-FUT
     No one will take it way from you.

(45) 'í'an=te   'á'a nók-su-nee
     today=we it   read-CMP-FUT
     We will finish reading it today.

(46) néhpo 'enčí   'á'a yá'a-ria-nee 'é-u   'á'a wéiyaa-nee nótti-patči
     I   you:ACC it   make-APL-FUT you-to it   bring-FUT return-upon
     I will make it for you and will bring it to you upon my return.

Related to the role of **-nee** to mark customary events and conditions is the speaker's usage of **-nee** to simply describe a future plan of action.

(47) wána=te pá'aku 'á'a kečá-'a-nee,   'itépo=te 'íntok náu-hinko'ola-rok-nee
     there=we outside him stand-EV-FUT we=we   and   together-race-QUO-FUT
     We will stand him off yonder, and we will say that we are going to run a race.

A second predictive usage of **-nee** reflects the speaker's statement of expectations based on his/her perception of an ongoing situation.

(48) ketúni bínwaa yúk-ne-m-ta-béna   hewí
     still long   rain-FUT-NZR-ACC-like yes
     It sure looks like it's going to rain for a long time yet, doesn't it?

(49) 'enčím   bái-ta'aa-baa-nee-me
     you:PL:ACC cool-know:(deceive)-DSD-FUT-NZR
     the ones who will want to deceive you

A few usages show a more grammaticalized version of **-nee** in which it serves to relate a temporally following event to a preceding one which is causally related to it in that the actuality of the preceding event either permits or blocks the carrying out of the potentially occuring following event, as in example (50).

(50) 'ín 'á-e   'á'a hínu-nee-'u   húni'i née káa hip^wee
     my it-with it buy-FUT-PPL even I   not have
     And I don't have anything to buy it with either.

(51) káa=née 'á'a tá'aa táa née 'á'a tá'aa-nee-ka   huné'ela
     not=I   it   know but I   it   know-FUT-PPL   alone
     I don't know it, but I am going to learn it.

5.2. The future passive -naa

For all practical purposes, the future passive suffix **-naa** is used in many of the same ways as **-nee** except that it is in the passive form. It is therefore used in sentences in which an instigative agent is back-grounded and the affected entity is highlighted.

The prototypical usage of **-naa** pairs the notion of temporal futurity relative to the time of speaking with that of a highlighted patient nominal, as illustrated by sentence (52). This example illustrates the point that Escalante has recently made, that in Yaqui passive sentences, there is no overt passive subject (Escalante 1991).

(52) hunáa'a tú'u-wa-ta   yá'a-ria-naa
     that-one good-NZR-ACC   make-APL-FUT:PSV
     That one will be justified.

It is commonly said that passives in Amerindian languages are only used when it is already obvious from the context who the agent is.[6] Sentence (53) illustrates this point nicely, since both clauses are marked with the future tense marker. The initial clause, however, has an overt agent nominal and has its main verb marked with **-nee**. This sets up the context for the second clause. The verb of the second clause is marked with the passive **-naa**.

(53) híta   téuwaa-ka yée-'át-tua-nee   háhhaana hía-ka 'atb^wá-naa
     thing   say-PPL   people-laugh-CAU-FUT ridiculous say-PPL laugh-FUT:PSV
     Anything he says makes people laugh; there will be laughter at the ridiculous things he says.

As illustrated by sentences (54)–(56) the highlighted entity (passive subject) is realized grammatically in a variety of ways. These include the use of a demonstrative pronoun in sentence (54), a second person singular subject clitic in (55), and a noun in (56).

(54) hunáa'a   húni'i kaíta-'apo bít-naa   két-čan   humák wiutá-naa
     that:thing even nothing-in see-FUT:PSV also-EXP perhaps destroy-FUT:PSV
     That thing is going to be considered useless; perhaps it will even be destroyed.

(55) 'iním naáte-ka-i   haibu=s=e'e   wáatia-náa
     here begin-PPL-PPL   now=EMP=you   love-FUT:PSV
     Beginning here, you will now be loved.

(56) yoéme hákun   bít-tua-naa   mékkaa hák   húni'i
     people anywhere see-CAU-FUT:PSV far   where even
     Yaquis will be sent anywhere, even very far away.

---

6   This is a point made strongly by Artemisa Echegoyen when describing to Casad the use of passives in Otomí (personal communication).

Oftentimes, a clause whose main verb is marked with **-naa** will have no overt patient or object nominal, as in sentence (57). Thus, impersonal sentences in Yaqui are often marked with the passive future **-naa**.

(57) hí'osia-t kéča-'a-naa
paper-on put-EV-FUT:PSV
It will be put on paper.

The use of **-naa** on verbs in purpose clauses and conditional clauses reinforces the points made above that the Yaqui future tense does much more than indicate pure temporal futurity. In sentence (58), for example, both usages of **-naa** point to hypothetical situations.

(58) bʷé'ituk néhpo sumá-'a-naa-ka 'íntok káa sumá-'a-naa-ka huní'i
because I bound-EV-FUT:PSV-PPL and not bound-EV-FUT:PSV-PPL even
Because, whether I am to be bound, or not to be bound...

Passive clauses marked with **-naa** also serve as complex postpositional objects with the purposive postposition **-betčí'ibo** *for* as in examples (59) and (60). An echo-vowel is inserted between the suffix **-naa** and the postposition in these sentences.

(59) 'áman hí'oh-te-k húme'e waté-m-mewi tú'isi 'á'a mabét-naa-'a-betčí'ibo
there write-VR-PRF those other-PL-to well his receive-FUT:PSV-EV-for
They wrote to the others there, that he might be well received.

(60) 'á'a yó'ore-ka híapsi-náa-'a-betčí'ibo
him respect-PPL live-FUT:PSV-EV-for
that (they) should live worshipping him

6.0. The tense/aspect marking

Yaqui employs a wide variety of suffixes and suffix combinations to mark the kinds of tense and aspect distinctions it makes. These include the distinction between perfective and imperfective states, present versus past continuative, simple past versus remote past, and inceptive versus terminative aspect.

6.1. The perfective aspect suffix -k

This is probably the most frequently used suffix of any. In its prototypical usage, it seems to indicate that the action is viewed as an undifferentiated whole, or as a happening at a point in time, rather than as an unfolding process or a continuation which would be indicated by an unmarked form of the verb. For example, when an older brother asked the narrator (in an autobiographical text) **hitása 'émpo 'áman nú'u-se-k** *What are you going to do over there?* or. *What are you going to get over there?* the narrator was still on his way and the event was still in the future.

Due to the overwhelming numbers of occurrences of this suffix and the need for a wider context to really understand its meaning, we provide here only a limited number of illustrations. The perfective suffix has the predominate shape **-k,** and is often word-final, as in examples (1)–(5). There are no semantic restrictions on the kinds of verbs that can take **-k**. In example (1), for instance, the first two usages of **-k** are with intransitive verbs that designate the process of decay, used metaphorically here. The third usage is with a derived verb.

(1) 'ín 'éeriam moí-su-k 'ín híapsi moóyo-k sí'ime lú'u-te-k heká-po sií-ka
my thoughts decay-CMP-PRF my life decay-PRF all end-VR-PRF wind-in go-PRF
My thoughts are decayed, my life is decayed, everything has ended, it has "gone with the wind."

In sentences (2) and (3) perfective **-k** occurs with the intransitive stems **taáwa** *to remain* and **'aáyu** *to happen.*

(2) kaíta-'apo taáwa-k
nothing-in remain-PRF
It came to nothing.

(3) haí=sa 'émpo 'aáyu-k
how=Q you be-PRF
What happened to you?

Causative and applicative verbs can also be marked with perfective **-k** as seen in sentences (4) and (5).

(4) sawá-yóh-te-k
leaf-shed-VR-PRF
It has shed its leaves.

(5) hiáki 'á'a múhu-k 'á'a ró'i-te-k
yaqui him shoot-PRF him cripple-VR-PRF
A Yaqui shot him; he crippled him.

A very limited number of verbs take **-ka** as an allomorph of this suffix **-k**. This sets up the imperfective-perfective contrast in the forms of certain verb stems. These contrasts are shown in Table 55.

Imperfective	Perfective	Meaning
hé'ee	hé'e-ka	*to drink*
čé'ee	čé'e-ka	*to nurse*
bé'ee	bé'ee-ka	*to lack*
né'ee	né'e-ka	*to fly*
b^wá'ee	b^wá'a-ka	*to eat*
siíme	sií-ka	*to go:SG*

Table 55. Imperfective stems versus perfective -ka

Note that the suffix **-ka** is used as a perfective only when attached directly to the stem in this set of verbs as in sentences (6)–(8). In sentence (6) both the imperfective **-ka** and the perfective **-ka** are seen. The imperfective one occurs on the stem of the verb **téa** *to find* in the first clause, whereas the perfective **-ka** occurs on the verb **hé'e** *to drink* in the second clause.

(6) hakía-po ba'á-m téa-ka 'áma sép=im hobó'o-hé'e-ka
arroyo-in water-PL find-PPL there at:once=they full-drink-PRF
Finding water in an arroyo, right away they drank to their fill there.

Another clue as to which **-ka** is used in a given sentence is usually found in the overall meaning of the sentence as illustrated in examples (7) and (8).

(7) húu'u wiíkit 'ám-bíca mékka né'e-ka
that bird there-site far:away fly-PRF
The bird flew far away in that direction.

(8) hunáma'a wáka-bák-ta b^wá'a-ka
there meat-stew-ACC eat-PRF
He ate beef stew there.

If other morphemes follow the stem, the regular perfective **-k** is used. In sentence (9), for example, **-k** suffixes to the desiderative **-bae**.

(9) ba'á-m hí'i-bae-k
water-PL drink-DSD-PRF
He wanted to drink water.

Both allomorphs of the perfective occur in sentence (10). In the first clause **-k** suffixes to the reduplicated stem of **siíme** *to go*, whereas **-ka** suffixes to the verbal compound **yeu-sií-** in the second clause.

(10) hunúen=né weám-si-sime-k búsan wásuktia-m yumá-'apo-táhtia húnak né yéu-sií-ka
thus=I walk-RDP-go-PRF six year-PL attain-NZR-until then I out-go-PRF
That is what I did for six years, then I left.

As suggested in Table 55, there are very few verbs that mark the imperfective versus perfective distinction in this manner. Yaqui has an imperfective participle suffix **-ka** that is homophonous with this perfective allomorph of **-k** and is also used quite productively. See section 6.2. of this chapter for a discussion of that suffix.[7] A clear example of the use of the imperfective participle **-ka** is given in example (11). Here **-ka** suffixes to the passive **-wa** in the main verb of an impersonal sentence.

(11) sí'ime táewa-ta yí'i-wa-ka kúp-te-k
all day-ACC dance-PSV-PPL eve-VR-PRF
There was dancing all day long until evening came.

Frequently, complex sentences contain strings of clauses whose main verbs are marked with the perfective **-k** as in examples (12) and (13).

(12) tú'isi káa-mačia-k yéu-nót-te-k kaíta téa-ka-i
very not-light-PRF out-return-VR-PRF nothing find-PPL-PPL
It was very dark when he returned, not having found anything.

(13) ba'á-nu'ú-ta 'étapo-k, ba'á-m á'a hí'i-tua-k
water-carry-ACC open-PRF water-ACC:PL him drink-CAU-PRF
He opened his canteen and gave him a drink of water.

The perfective may also mark realized purpose clauses as in example (14).

(14) tebó-te-i-ta né 'a-u tóhi-'i-se-k
greet-VR-NZR-ACC I her-to bring-EV-come-PRF
I have come to bring her greetings.

The suffix **-k** is sometimes also used in conditional-type utterances. In sentences (15) and (16) the phrases **'á'a béeba-k húni'i** and **yeté-t wéče-k** are understood as conditionals rather than as perfectives. Technically they should be: **'á'a béeba-k-o húni'i** and **yeté-t wéče-k-o**. But the usage of the perfective as a conditional is not uncommon.

(15) kat=a'a béeba 'á'a béeba-k húni'i túa 'á'a mé'e-nee
not=it hit it hit-PRF even truly it kill-FUT
Don't hit it, (but if) you hit it, be sure you really kill it.

(16) hiák-bíba hunáa'a két yée-na-náson-te ye-te-t wéče-k
yaqui-tobacco that also people-RDP-damage-VR people-CON-on fall-PRF

hák-húni'i takáa-po 'á-et wéče-k hunáma-béha héok-ti-nee
where-even body-on it-on fall-PRF that-well blister-VR-FUT
That also damages/hexes people if it falls on a person anywhere; if it falls on his body, it will raise a blister (like being burned).

Examples (17)–(18) reinforce the suggestion of (15) and (16) that in the conditional sentence usage of perfective **-k,** the conditional clause occurs before the result clause.

(17) 'áman hák 'in hubí-ta bíča-'a-te-k láut='á'a yebíh-sau-nee
there where my wife-ACC see-EV-VR-PRF quickly=her arrive-IMP-FUT
If you see my wife anywhere, tell her to come home quickly.

(18) naamuku-k kaábe-ta tiu-nee
drunk-PRF no:one-ACC shame-FUT
If a person is drunk, he isn't ashamed in front of anyone.

6.2. The imperfective participle -ka

The imperfective participle **-ka** serves both to highlight the durativeness cohering to particular situations as well as to background the entire situation to another one expressed in the main clause of a sentence.

---

7 In addition to this homophonous pair, there is a suffix **-ka** which means "have" (cf. BE/HAVE/DO, pp. 65–66) and finally, an accusative suffix **-ka**. The possessive suffix **-ka** attaches to nouns and is therefore easily distinguished from the perfective suffix.
(i) sambayo bʷásia-ka née wóm-ta-k
fluffy tail-having me scare-VR-PRF
A fluffy tailed thing frightened me.

Thus it functions as a sort of subordinator and often is functionally equivalent to English "-ing" and Spanish "-ando, -iendo." In sentences (19) and (20) it acts as a verbalizer as well.

(19) bóosa-po mamá-ka kaita téa-k
pocket-in hand-PPL nothing find-PRF
Putting his hands in his pocket, he didn't find anything.

(20) kó'om-koba-ka 'á-u lúkti-sime
down-head-PPL him-to approach-go:SG
Lowering his head, he approached him.

In certain cases, **-ka** appears to conjoin clauses. In the following example, although there may be a logical progression between learning and helping, there is no clear subordinate relation between the two clauses that can be gleaned from Castro's translation of it into Spanish. The progression is, however, reflected in the order of the clauses in the sentence. Likewise, the logical progression between building a house and living there is iconically reflected in the word order in sentence (22), but is not reflected in Castro's translation.[8]

(21) 'á'a tá'aa-ka 'á-e 'íno 'anía-báe
it know-PPL it-with RFL help-DSD
I want to know it and help myself with it.

(22) kári-te-ka 'áma hó'aa-k
house-VR-PPL there house-VR
He built a house and lives there.

Other usages of **-ka** suggest a subordinator role for it in clauses which are the ground for the main clause, i.e., the subordinate clause expresses the particular activity which is carried out in order to effect a given result which is expressed by the main clause.

(23) hióko-t=ne 'ane-ka hí'i-bʷá
misery-in=I be-PPL IZR-eat
I go through misery (just to make enough) to be able to eat.[9]

(24) tebé-i boó'o 'ála bínwa bó'o-hóa-ka 'ámman yebíh-nee
long-NZR road indeed long road-make-PPL there arrive-FUT
But if the road is long, you have to travel a lot to arrive.[9]

In sentence (25) two temporal expressions delineate the temporal framework within which the subject carried out his activities, i.e., he worked. The sentence initial temporal places the entire event in a day prior to the speaker's recounting of it, whereas the sentence final temporal, marked with the perfective **-k**, marks the end of the activity on that day. The use of the imperfective **-ka** on the verb **tekpanoa** backgrounds the activity to the temporal endpoint, i.e., his work ended in the evening. Once again, word order in a Yaqui clause reflects iconically the speaker's choice in what to highlight and what to put into background in framing his statements. The particular tense/aspect markers he employs are crucial indicators of these choices.

(25) tuká=ne tekípanoa-ka kúpte-k
yesterday=I work-PPL evening-VR:PRF
Yesterday, I worked until the evening.

The **-ka** in sentence (25) is the participle suffix. The sentence can also be translated "I was still working when it got dark." In contrast, **tekipánoa** also takes the **-k** suffix for conveying the perfective meaning, i.e., **tekipánoa-k** *he worked.*

The particular tense that is appropriate for rendering a clause subordinated by **-ka** is derived from the particular tense/aspect marking of the main clause. In sentences (26)–(28) the main verb in each sentence

---

8 Castro glossed these two examples as follows: (a) "aprender y ayudarme con ello."
(b) "Hizo una casa, alli vive"
9 Castro was very idiomatic in his translations of the sentences in this last section of illustrations, which we appreciated very much. We provide here Castro's equivalents in Spanish for sentences (23)–(24).
(23) Me sacrifico para comer.
(24) Pero si es camino largo, tengas que caminar mucho para llegar.

final clause carries the perfective **-k** in its use as a marker of simple past tense. Each of the preceding clauses is marked for anterior time with the imperfective **-ka**.

(26) 'an=a'a tút-tu'uru-ka kaá=ne 'íno yúu'u-k
I=it RDP-like-PPL not=I myself push-PRF
I liked it so much I couldn't control myself.

(27) né háksa wée-ka wi'í-po nók-taite-k sutú-m-mea 'á'a poná-ka 'á'a nók-tua
I where go-PPL wire-on talk-begin-PRF finger-PL-with it pound-PPL it talk-CAU
Somewhere there, I began to talk on wire; I pounded it with my fingers and made it talk.

(28) čúbala náu katé-ka=su 'émo tó'o-saha-k
short:time together go-PPL=EMP RFL leave-go:PL-PRF
After traveling together for a short time, they separated.

A complex sentence may include a string of juxtaposed clauses, each marked with the imperfective participle **-ka** as illustrated by sentence (29).

(29) húu'u káuwis káa wóm-te-ka kó'om-kóba-ka 'á-u lúkti-síme
that fox not afraid-VR-PPL down-head-PPL him-to approach-go
The fox was unafraid; it lowered his head and approached him.

The imperfective **-ka** may occur suffixed to the main verb of the final clause in these complex sentences under certain conditions. In example (30) **-ka** is followed by the past continuative **-n** in the second clause. In this sentence the use of the past continuative backgrounds a past imperfective situation, i.e., "was thinking" to the other which is simultaneous to it, "was trying to shoot." The past continuative **-n** marks the highlighted event.

(30) 'amú-reo kauwíh-ta 'áu bít-le-ka 'áu 'á'a múhi-tua-ka-n
hunt-NZR fox-ACC RFL see-think-PPL RFL it shoot-CAU-PPL-PCN
The hunter, thinking that he saw a fox, was trying to shoot it.

The use of the participle **-ka** to mark anteriority of action in "when" clauses is seen very clearly for cases in which the subordinated clause is expressed as a negative, i.e., in contrary to fact clauses.

(31) kée née kuná-ka naáte-ka hunúka nu-nú'ub^{w}á-n
not:yet me husband-PPL begin-PPL that RDP-own-PCN
She already owned that before she married me.

(32) kó'om=ne čépte-ka wók-po nasón-tu-k
down=I jump-PPL foot-in damage-VR-PRF
Jumping down, I hurt my foot.

Some of these sentences are systematically ambiguous between temporal construals and causal ones. Thus sentence (32) can mean either "When I jumped down, I hurt my foot," or "Because of jumping down, I hurt my foot."

The imperfectivity in the meaning of **-ka** allows it also to be applied to situations other than those in the past, as well as to express simultaneity of action as in sentence (33) which contrasts clearly with the anterior action of sentence (34).

(33) téku kári hiká-t káte-ka kíssoso'o-ti hiía čápala máma-ka húnen híia
squirrel house top-on sit-PPL kissoso'o-CON says clasp hand-PPL thus says
A squirrel is on top of the house going "kissoso'o;" he says that with his hands clasped.

(34) 'á'a mé'aa-ka mantéka-ta=ne yáa-k
it kill-PPL lard-ACC=I make-PRF
After killing it, I made lard.

A complex sentence may contain a string of subordinate clauses marked by **-ka** as seen in example (35).

(35) 'ín tóto-ek-a'u hú'upa-t bó'e búsa-ka ku-kús-su-ka
my rooster-have-GND mesquite-on sleep awake-PPL RDP-crow-CPL-PPL

ko'om-čepté-ka ba'a-u lúula búite
down-jump-PPL water-to straight run

A rooster I used to own slept up in a mesquite; when he'd wake, he'd crow, then jump down and run straight to the water.

The participial **-ka** also serves to mark oblique clauses expressing the notion of means.

(36) bʷíčia-m bʷá'ee-ka híapsa
worm-PL eat-PPL lives
It lives by eating worms.

A negative subordinate clause marked by **-ka** may also be construed as the purpose for which some action is avoided as in example (37). The construction consisting of **'ea** *to think*, and imperfective participle **-ka** is construed to mean "rather than" and the clause itself expresses an implied negative as suggested by example (38).

(37) káa née híkkahi-bae-ka káa née híkkaha
not me hear-DSD-PPL not me hear
You don't understand me because you don't want to understand.

(38) 'em takáa kóp-'éa-'a-ka=su
your body lose-think-EV-PPL=EMP
rather than lose your body

Some uses of the imperfective also signal habitual or customary action as illustrated in examples (39) and (40).

(39) 'aráo-e 'á'a topák-ta-ka 'á'a ná-nawi-te-ka tú'uli-s=a'a
plow-with it turn:over-VR-PPL it RDP-same-VR-PPL pretty-AVR=it

banyá-ka 'áma mó'i-te-ka báči-ta 'áma wó'o-ta-nee
irrigate-PPL there plow-VR-PPL seed-ACC there throw-VR-FUT

With the plow I break it up, then I level it; after having irrigated it well, I plow it and sow the seed there.

(40) 'emé'e tú'isi hú'unea 'emó-nasuk 'ané-ka 'emo-betčí'ibo tú'ii-k
you:PL well know you-among be-PPL RFL-for good-ACC

wáata-ka haí-sa tú'i-si itóm híapsa-k-a'u
want-PPL how-PRO good-AVR our live-PRF-NZR

You yourselves know very well how we lived among you, wanting that which was for your good.

6.3. The remote stative -i (-ka + -i)

The remote stative suffix **-i** reinforces the notion of anteriority to the present speech situation of the situation designated by the subordinate clause of complex sentences. It suffixes to the imperfective participle **-ka,** discussed above, and is often paired with another clause whose main verb is marked by the suffixal sequence of imperfective **-ka** and the past continuative **-n** as in example (41). As we mentioned earlier, **-n** marks the highlighted clause in the sentence, whereas **-i** marks the background in sentences such as (41). The force of **-ka** is to impose a notion of duration on the situation designated by the subordinate clause, whereas the sequence **-tu-ka-n** establishes the basic anteriority of the entire sentence to the time of the speech-act.[10]

(41) néhpo káa-yó'ó-ta-ka-i   kapyéo-tu-ka-n
     I   not-old-VR-PPL-STAT shepherd-VR-PPL-PCN
     Because of being young, I used to be a shepherd.

The use of **-i** is not restricted to past tense situations, however. In example (42) it is used to mark a contingent possibility linked to future results stated in the sentence final clause.

(42) láau-láauti tú'u-híapsi-m-mea   'á'a mámmate-ka-i 'á'a téu-nee
     RDP-slowly good-heart-PL-INST it   note-PPL-STAT it   find-FUT
     If you search for it diligently, with a good heart, you will find it.

In a quotative situation, the remote stative helps ground the past tense speech-act in a broader context. In example (43) the background consists in an explanation of why the speaker said what he did. In example (44) the background is an indirect account of the content speech-act itself, whereas the highlighted clause classifies the type of speech-act, i.e., an urgent and emotional request. In sentence (45) the material that is backgrounded is used to bring the speaker physically onto the scene of the event.

(43) 'émpo 'ála   'omo-t-bíčaa   húmak wée-ka tiía
     you   indeed one:side-on-site perhaps go-PPL say

     huu'u čéema káa 'á'a yoém-'éíyaa-ka-i
     that Cheema not him person-esteem-PPL-STAT
     "You are probably going somewhere else," said Cheema, not trusting him.

(44) 'ambróosio-ta-u 'úhbʷána 'áman 'á'a wée-sae-ka-i
     Ambrose-ACC-to beg   there him take-IMP-PPL-STAT
     He pleaded with Ambrose, asking him to take him there.

(45) sírko hán=sa 'ím hák   kátek-ti   nát-temai   hó'aa-raa-po yepsá-ka-i
     circus how=Q here somewhere located-CON UNSPEC-ask house-ABS-in arrive-PPL-STAT
     Upon arriving in town he asked, "There is not a circus anywhere around here, is there?"

The relational nature of **-i** is seen clearly in both example (46) and (47). The relation is that of simple anteriority in time. In both sentences, the temporally anterior clause is in sentence final position.

(46) hunáme béha 'ée-béas hoóte-k   'emó hiák-yáa-ka-i
     those   then you-front stand:PL-PRF RFL yaqui-make-PPL-STAT
     Those are the ones who stood in front of you, having made themselves into Yaquis.

(47) tú'i-si   káa-mačía-k   yéu-nótte-k   kaíta téa-ka-i
     good-AVR not-light-PRF out-return-PRF nothing find-PPL-STAT
     He returned long after darkness, not having found anything.

The stative suffix **-i** is also used in questions that designate hypothetical situations, i.e., situations that are epistemically distant from the actual speech situation.

---

10 This sequence is also observed for the homophonous possessive suffix **-ka**.
    hapá'ači 'áman yéu-siíka tawé-masas-m hissaa-ka-i   'íntok tebe-m lansa-ka-i   sikíi-k
    Apache there out-go   hawk-feather-PL headdress-have-STAT and long-PL spear-having-STAT red-ACC

    puhba-ka-i   tét-tébe-m   repá-ka-i   'íntok yú'in koká-ka   'áman yeu-buite-k
    face-have-STAT RDP-long-PL earrings-having-STAT and   much necklace-having there out-ran-PRF
    An Apache Indian ran out there, he was wearing a hawk-feather headdress, he had a long spear, a red face, long earrings, and lots of beads (around his neck).

(48) hakwóo=sa   humák lú'u-ti-nee-ka-i   kaíbu
     where(when):go=INTERR perhaps end-VR-FUT-PPL-STAT never

   lú'u-ti-nee b^wé'ituk híba 'é-'ét-wa
   end-VR-FUT because always RPD-plant-PSV
   When would it ever run out; it will never run out because it is always being planted.

(49) sákobai-m   momói káka-si b^wáh-nee-ka-i
     watermelon-PL mature sweet-ly ripe-FUT-PPL-STAT
     The watermelons are mature, so that they can ripen sweetly.[11]

The remote stative **-i** can also be used on the main verb of simple sentences. In this case, the speech-act itself is the ground on which the anterior temporal relation is based as in examples (50)–(52).

(50) 'í'an báhi taéwai yúk-yáate-ka-i
     now three day rain-stop-PPL-STAT
     This is the third day since it stopped raining.

(51) húebena wásuktia wéye 'ím née noi-te-ka-i
     many year go here I arrive-VR-PPL-STAT
     Many years have gone by since I came here.

(52) húme=sán b^wára-m kía bóa ya-yahú-i-ka   á-'áuwi-ka-i
     those=EXP sheep-PL only wool RDP-ripple-PPL-PPL RDP-fat-PPL-STAT
     Those particular sheep were wool-rippling fat.

Both purpose and result clauses are often marked with stative **-i**. Again these clauses are in second-sentential position and may even be followed by a "because" clause.

(53) 'ínepo 'íntok kibáke-k kári-wi b^wá'a-m-ta haríu-se-ka-i b^wé'ituk ne tébaure
     I and enter-PRF house-to food-NZR-ACC hunt-go-PPL-STAT because I hungry
     I went into the house looking for food because I was hungry.

(54) kétwóo naáte-ka heéka sápa wéče-ka-i 'í'an sebe-heéka
     early begin-PPL wind ice fall-PPL-STAT now cold-wind
     The wind began blowing early; it is freezing. The wind is cold today.

A clause marked with **-i** may itself express the reason for a particular stated event as in example (55).

(55) húnen hiía 'á'a mé'e-tébo-bae-ka-i
     thus say him kill-IMP-DSD-PPL-STAT
     He said that because he was wanting to command to kill him.

In example (56) the entire sentence is located at a time prior to the speech-act, but the clause marked with **-ka-i** is simultaneous temporally to the first clause.

(56) túa ne káa 'é-u wáate-k hunáman weáma-ka-i
     truly I not you-to remember-PRF off:there walk-PPL-STAT
     I sure didn't think about you while I was walking off yonder.

In sentence (57) the suffix **-i** designates a state that no longer exists. The force of the negative **-kaa** is to divorce the former state from present reality, whereas the participle **-ka** imposes a duration on the extension of the former state. In sentences (58) and (59) **-i** marks an adverbial clause temporally simultaneous to the event signalled by the main clause.

---

11 Castro: "Sandias sasónas para madurarse dulces."

(57) 'émpo káa 'ili-yó'o-ta-ka-i
you   not little-old-VR-PPL-STAT
You are not young any more.[12]

(58) 'émpo kaábe-ta hiníle hunúen 'á-u híu-nee-ka-i
you none-ACC fear thus him-to say-FUT-PPL-STAT
Aren't you afraid of anyone, talking to him like that?[12]

(59) 'émpo káa 'á'a hiníle hunúka 'á-u teuwaa-nee-ka-i
you not him fear that:ACC him-to say-FUT-PPL-STAT
Aren't you afraid of him, having said that to him?

6.4. The past continuative -n

The suffix **-n** may be the only genuine tense marker in Yaqui. Buelna calls it "pretérito imperfecto" and refers to it in contrast to the "perfecto" and "pluscuamperfecto" in the following passage: "... porque el pretérito imperfecto lo acaban los Tehuecos en **t**, los Yaquis en **n**, y los Mayos en **i**. El perfecto lo acaban todos en **c** [=**-k**]. El pluscuamperfecto los Tehuecos en **cat**, los Yaquis en **can**, y los Mayos en **cai**." (Buelna 1891:61)[13]

There is no contemporary data available on the Tehueco language, but the Yaquis and Mayos still use the **-n/-i** endings for this tense. As for the **cai/can** to which Buelna refers in the above passage, I treat it as a polymorphemic sequence consisting of the participial suffix **-ka** in construction with **-n**. The past continuative **-n** also combines with the subjunctive mode marker **-'ea** and several other suffixes as we will soon see.

In all the examples we have noted, **-n** seems to be a general past continuative that is used in many contexts. The past durative may well be used in a main clause, as in examples (60) and (61), but its usages in more complex sentences are more common.

(60) kan=nee yú'in wásuktia-ka-n
not=I   many year-VR-PCN
I was not very old.

(61) kúta-t bakóče hiká-t súma-'a-ria-ka-n
pole-on snake high-on tie-EV-APL-PPL-PCN
A snake was tied high on the pole.

Commonly, the past continuative usages of Yaqui can be glossed as "used to do X" or "used to be X" as examples (62)–(63) illustrate. In sentence (64) it can be glossed "used to be known as X."

(62) 'áme-tuk hó'aa-ka-n
them-under house-having-PCN
He used to live under them (trees).

(63) néhpo kapyéo-tu-ka-n túa=ne mékkaa yéepsa-n yú'in née kabáa-ka-n
I   shepherd-be-PPL-PCN really=I far arrive-PCN many I goats-having-PCN
I used to be a shepherd; I used to take them really far away; I had a lot of goats.

(64) 'á'a habói-wa iníe tea-m-mea tá'ee-wa-n
his grandfather-POS this name-ACC:PL-INST know-PSV-PCN
His grandfather used to be known by this name.

In sentences such as (65) the past durative presents the event of the main clause as an ongoing process in past time. The process mentioned in the first clause of the sentence, whose main verb is marked with the imperfective participle **-ka**, sets the stage for the use of the past continuative **-n** in the second clause.

---

12 Castro was very idiomatic in his translations of the sentences in this last section of illustrations, which we appreciated very much. We provide here Castro's equivalents in Spanish for sentences (57)–(58).
   (57) Tan grande que estás.
   (58) No temes a nadie para decirle así?
13 "because the Tehuecos end the imperfective preterite with a **-t**, the Yaquis with an **-n** and the Mayos in an **-i**. All of them end the perfect with a **-c** [=**-k**]. The Tehuecos end the past perfect with **-cat**, the Yaquis with **-can** and the Mayos with **-cai**." (Buelna 1891:61)

(65) káuwih-ta bít-le-ka   'á-u   'á'a múhi-tua-ka-n
     fox-ACC see-think-PPL him-to it   shoot-CAU-PPL-PCN
     Thinking he saw a fox, he was trying to shoot it.

The past continuative can be used in both clauses of a complex sentence. In this usage, both clauses are temporally simultaneous, although one may still be the background against which the event described in the other clause is being located. The second clause in example (66) is a juxtaposed purpose clause. In example (67) the second clause is in apposition to the first one.

(66) tuká=ne   'ín hálla'i bíči-'i-se-ka-n   'áa-mak=ne 'etého-bae-n
     yesterday=I my friend see-EV-go-PPL-PCN him-with=I talk-DSD-PCN
     Yesterday I went to see my friend; I was wanting to talk with him.

(67) néhpo kápyeo-tu-ka-n   yú'in né kabáa-ka-n
     I   shepherd-VR-PPL-PCN many I goat-VR-PCN
     I used to be a shepherd; I had a lot of goats.

The following three sentences, which were given by Castro, represent three alternatives for expressing the notion of having resided at the speaker's locality. All three use the past durative, although the usage in sentence (68) seems perfective in nature. The usage in sentences (69) and (70) can be glossed by the English present perfect "have been." All these examples are similar in that they link a durative state to the time of the speech-act itself. The notion of extension into anterior time is explicitly lexicalized in the form of the adverbial expression, which enhances the salience of the imperfectivity of the past durative **-n**.

(68) bínwa-tu-k=né   'ím nóite-ka-n   (70) binwa-tu-k=ne   'im 'aáne-n
     long:time-VR-PRF=I here come-PPL-PCN   long-VR-PRF=I have be-PCN
     I came here a long time ago.   *I have been here a long time.*

(69) binwa-tu-k=ne   'im káteka-n
     long-VR-PRF=I here be:located-PCN
     I have been located here a long time.

Often the surrounding circumstances of a past durative event are left unexpressed, as in examples (71) and (72).

(71) súpe-m-po=ne   b^{w}íse-ka-n
     shirt-PL-on=me grab-PPL-PCN
     He was hanging on to my shirt.

(72) b^{w}é'u yá'ut-tu-ka-n   sí'ime-ta né-sauwe-n
     big   chief-VR-PPL-PCN all-ACC IZR-command-PCN
     He was a big chief, he ruled everything. or *He used to be a big chief, he ruled everything.*

Different lexicalizations of the passive notion are shown clearly in the following two examples. Example (73) is glossed as a passive sentence, but there is no passive morpheme involved. The "passiveness" probably comes from the presence of the verbalizer **tu-**, which can also be glossed as "be." The use of the past continuative **-ka** + **-n** imposes the tense change on **tu-**. On the other hand, the passive morpheme is used in example (74). In this case the imperfective participle **-ka** does not occur with **-n**, which argues for the independent morphemic status of both **-ka** and **-n**.

(73) puéeta-u tóhi-tu-ka-n   (74) pueeta-u to-tohi-wa-n
     door-to take-VR-PPL-PCN   door-to RDP-take-PSV-PCN
     He was taken to the door.   *He was brought to the door.*

Temporal words marked with the perfective **-k** may also serve as the context in which a past durative condition is situated as example (75) suggests.

(75) tutúkabia-k   sebé-a-ka-n
     last:night-PRF cold-CON-PPL-PCN
     It was cold last night.

An interesting combination of perfectives and imperfectives combine in example (76) to highlight a completed event. In this example results of a change of state are presented as persisting throughout a span of time in the past.

(76) múk-su-ka-n
     die-CPL-PPL-PCN
     He was completely dead. or *He had died.*

Although **-n** most frequently co-occurs with the imperfective participle **-ka,** it also co-occurs with a number of other suffixes. In examples (77)–(78) it suffixes to the subjunctive **-'ea**.

(77) sí'ime-ta yá'a-pea-ka-'ea-n   'ó'obe-k
     all-ACC do-DSD-PPL-SJV-PCN though-PRF
     although he was wanting to do everything

(78) híaki-m tehál-bae-ka-'ea-n
     yaqui-PL destroy-DSD-PPL-SJV-PCN
     He was wanting to annihilate the Yaquis.

The past continuative also suffixes to the desiderative **-bae** as in examples (79) and (80).

(79) 'áapo 'iním méhiko-po né-sau-bae-n
     he   here Mexico-in IZR-rule-DSD-PCN
     He was wanting to rule here in Mexico.

(80) 'aa-mak né 'etého-bae-n
     him-with I talk-DSD-PCN
     I was wanting to talk with him.

It can even suffix to a regular verb stem, as in examples (81) and (82), or to a verbalizer such as **-te** as illustrated by example (83).

(81) 'áapo 'íntok tú'i-si   'am-mea tómi-yó'o-n
     he   and   good-AVR them-INST money-earn-PCN
     And he was earning a lot of money with them.

(82) haámutči-m né 'átbʷá-su-k   náu   'ím nássua-n
     woman-PL I laugh-CMP-PRF together they fight-PCN
     I laughed at some women; they were fighting.

(83) haíbu kó'om-kúak-te-n
     now   down-turn-VR-PCN
     It was now getting on toward evening.

As the preponderance of the examples given earlier show, **-n** most commonly suffixes to the imperfective participle **-ka** as in example (84).

(84) ín kóba-po huébena-ka 'áu-ka-n
     my head-in much-be   be-PPL-PCN
     There used to be a lot in my head

Finally, **-n** suffixes to the passive **-wa** as in example (85).

(85) sí'ime tékil bétte-a-ka-n   'íntok kaíta kobá-'a-wa-n
     all   work heavy-VR-PPL-PCN and   nothing earn-EV-PSV-PCN
     All work was difficult, and you earned nothing for it.

7.0. Aspectual marking

Aspectual marking in Yaqui can be divided into three categories: inceptive, cessative and completive. We present in the following sections data to illustrate these distinctions.

7.1. The inceptive aspect

Yaqui draws on a variety of lexical items for indicating inceptive aspect. Most commonly, it uses the suppletive pair **-taite** (SG) and **-hapte** (PL) in general to mean "to begin doing X." I have found **-taite** used only as a bound form, occurring with both singular and plural verbs. The verb form **hápte** *to stand up*:Plural Subject is often used idiomatically to mean "to begin" or "commence doing something," as will be seen below. In Sebahti's texts, **hápte** is only used with animate subjects, whereas he used **taite** only with inanimate subjects. He has one instance in which the verb **naáte** *to begin, to commence* is used as a bound form. This most likely originated as part of a verb-verb compound.

On several occasions, Dedrick's first language associate gave him the form **-táhitia** for **-taite**. This is most likely an older form of speech. Examples (1)–(2) give instances of this older form. In addition example (2) shows that Yaqui employs a second verb **naáte** meaning "to begin" as an inceptive aspect marker in verb-verb compounds.

(1) wáme'e yukatáan-e-u   tóhi-tu-ka-'u-m   húči 'ímwain yéu-tóhi-tahitia-k
    those Yucatan-CON-to bring-VR-PPL-GND-PL again hereabout out-bring-begin-PRF
    Those who had been taken to Yucatan once again began arriving back here.

(2) karíl-bo'ó-ta   hóo-naáte-wa-o   b^{w}ía-ró'ak-te-ta
    train-road-ACC make-begin-PSV-when dirt-mound-VR-ACC

    hóo-tahitia-k-o   ringo-m-meu 'áu takéa-k
    make-begin-PRF-when   "gringo"-PL-to RFL hire-PRF
    When the railroad was beginning to be built, when they were putting up the roadbed, he hired himself to the gringos.

The following examples present typical instances of these aspectual markers. They all fit common Uto-Aztecan patterns of forming aspectual systems from verb-verb compounds. The main verb origin of the aspect markers in Yaqui is clearly seen in that both of the suppletive variants of the verb meaning "to begin" are used as aspect markers. Typical usages of the singular form **-taite** are given in (3)–(10). Commonly, **-taite** is used in the perfective, as seen in examples (3)–(7), as well as in many of the other examples cited in this section. Subordinate temporal clauses usually precede the clause containing the inceptive aspect marker as sentences (3)–(5) illustrate.

(3) née 'á'a sóba-o=san   kabá'i hubá-taíte-k
    I   it broil-when=EXP horse smell-begin-PRF
    Well, when I was broiling it, it began to smell like horse meat.

(4) takó-ta   siú-ta-ka   'á'a híhho'o-táite-k
    palm-ACC tear-VR-PPL it weave-begin-PRF
    Ripping the palm leaves, she began to weave them.

(5) húu'u toóro 'ám   bíča-ka kóba-wíuti-taíte-k
    that bull them see-PPL head-weave-begin-PRF
    Seeing them, the bull began to weave his head around.

Adverbials are often fronted in these clauses as examples (6) and (7) show.

(6) sép=née hi-pik-táite-k   (7) sép   báh-ta   b^{w}á'a-táite-k
    at:once=I IZR-squeeze-begin-PRF   at:once grass-ACC eat-begin-PRF
    I began to milk at once.   *He began to eat grass at once.*

Yaqui also uses **-taite** in a number of unexpected ways. Certain usages would seem to call for the use of the plural **hápte** because they seem to imply that plural subjects are involved in the particular situations that they designate. Nonetheless, the singular **-taite** is selected for use as the inceptive aspect marker. Although this might seem arbitrary, there is a quite reasonable semantic basis for this. To begin, certain kinds of collective entities can be construed as singular subjects, for example, fruit, as in example (8).

(8) húme'e 'íntok taáka-m yóhti-taite-k
    those and   fruit-PL fall:PL-begin-PRF
    And the fruit began to fall.

Some usages of **-taite** suggest that the number of the direct object may in some cases be more important than the number of the subject. Thus, in the first clause of example (9) the plural demonstrative **hunáme'e** *those* is the subject and **taite** is still used as the aspect marker. Likewise, in example (10) the subject of the second clause is plural, but the singular **-taite** is nonetheless used as the aspect marker.

Notice, however, that the subject of that clause is actually reciprocal, i.e., a multiplex subject does something jointly so that only one collective group is engaging in the activity.

(9) hunáme'e béha née máhta-taite-k   née háksa wéeka nók-taíte-k
    those   well me teach-begin-PRF I   where going speak-begin-PRF
    They began to teach me, and somewhere along there I began to talk.

(10) sekka'ana kíkte-ka   nau-bo'o-hoo-táite-k
     other:side stand-PPL together-road-make-begin-PRF
     He changed sides with him, and they began traveling together.

Finally, **-taite** can be used to refer to the inception of existence of a category of entities, as in example (11).

(11) hunáma naáte-ka   kabá'im 'áu-taite-k
     there begin-PPL horses be-begin-PRF
     At that point, horses began to exist.

Generally, **hápte** *to begin* (PL) is used for indicating that a plurality of discrete entities are jointly involved in initiating some kind of activity. The main verb use of **hápte** *to stand* (PL) is attested by example (12).

(12) mékka-'am hapté-su-k-o   'amé-t ča-čae-k
     far-they stand:PL-CMP-PRF-when them-on RDP-yell-PRF
     When they had stood far away, he yelled at them.

A typical example of the aspectual use of **hápte** is given in examples (13)–(15). Note that all these usages have plural subjects. As example (13) shows the plural subject may be overtly mentioned in a preceding clause without being repeated in the clause in which **hápte** itself occurs.

(13) roéto moína kaahé'em-ta kári-ta   táya-k húnak béha nássua-hápte-k
     Loreto Molina Cajeme-POS house-ACC burn-PRF then well fight-stand-PRF
     Loreto Molina burned Cajeme's house; well, that's when they began to fight.

(14) húme'e yoém-léepeo-m née bíno-hí'i-tua-hápte-k   ne-mák náah-kát-hápte-k
     those yaqui-trash-PL me liquor-drink-CAU-stand-PRF me-with around-go-stand-PRF
     Those Yaqui "low-lifers" began to make me drink liquor; they began to go around with me.

(15) húme'e hurásim té'opo-po yéeu-hápte-k
     those "Jews" church-in play-stand-PRF
     The "Jews" began to play in the church building.[14]

7.2. The cessative aspect -yaáte

The verb **yaáte,** meaning "to cease" or "to stop," is another main verb which has become grammaticalized as the aspectual member in verb-verb compounds. For example, its main verb use is illustrated by sentences (16) and (17).

(16) yaáte-k=ate   (17) ču'ú 'íntok čái-yaáte-k   'á'a nók-híkkaha-ka-i
     finish-PRF=we   dog and   yell-stop-PRF him talk-hear-PPL-STAT
     We have now finished.   *The dog stopped barking when he heard him talking.*

The cessative aspect usage of **-yaáte** is exemplified by examples (18)–(20). Notice that this verb takes both singular and plural, as well as animate and inanimate subjects in contrast to **taite** and **hápte** discussed above. A singular subject is illustrated in example (18), whereas plural subjects are exemplified by examples (19) and (20)

(18) yí'i-yáate-ka   béha 'ámeu 'etého-taite-k
     dance-stop-PRF   well them-to talk-begin-PRF
     Having stopped dancing, he began talking to them.

---

14 In this example, the term "Jews" designates the members of a Yaqui ceremonial society.

(19) 'iníka'a nássua-yáate-k-o   wáme'e yukatáan-e-u   tóhi-tu-ka'u-m
    this:ACC fight-stop-PRF-when those   Yucatan-CON-to take-VR-former-NZR

   'inímwain   yeu-tóhi-tahitia-k
   around:here out-bring-begin-PRF
   When they had finished fighting, those who had been taken to Yucatan began arriving back in these parts.

(20) húme 'íntok-o sóntaom bíča-ka Papló-ta bép-yaáte-k
    those and-when soldiers see-PPL Paul-ACC beat-stop-PRF
    When they saw the soldiers, they stopped beating Paul.

Finally, a meteorological noun, extended into the temporal domain, is treated as a plural subject of **-yaáte** in example (21).

(21) 'í'an báhi taéwai yúk-yáate-ka-i
    now three day   rain-stop-PPL-PRP
    It is now three days since it stopped raining.

7.3. The completive aspect marker -su

The completive aspect marker **-su** probably derives historically from the Proto-Uto-Aztecan verb ***su** *to finish* (cf. Langacker 1977b:155) It has clearly related cognate forms in both Cora and Huichol (cf. Casad 1984:355-6; 363; Grimes 1964:94). As an aspect marker, **-su** intensifies the completing of an event and can oftentimes be rendered by such phrases as "to really do something" or "to finish something totally" as in examples (22) and (23). With intransitive verbs, it signals the complete end of a particular state of affairs as in example (24). Other usages relate to a more semantically neutral "to bring something to an end" as in sentence (25).

(22) yoéme-m né 'átb^{w}á-su-k
    man-PL I laugh:at-CPL-PRF
    I really laughed at some men.

(23) 'emé'e 'ám kobá-'a-su-laa
    you:PL them conquer-EV-CPL-PPL
    You have completely conquered them.

(24) táa wáme'e háibu sáka-'a-su-nee
    but those now go:PL-EV-CPL-FUT
    But they will be completely gone by now.

(25) 'í'an té 'á'a nók-su-nee
    now we it read-CPL-FUT
    Today, we will finish reading it.

The completive suffix **-su** occurs only within the verb complex and is to be distinguished from the postclitic =**su** emphatic that attaches to various parts of speech or phrases. It does appear in nominalizations, however, as shown in example (26).

(26) née híkkahi-su-me née híkkai-su-ka-me, née ta'aa-me
    me hear-CPL-NZR me hear-CPL-PPL-NZR me know-NZR
    the ones who hear me (completely), the ones who heard me, the ones who know me

When completive **-su** is followed by the passive **-wa**, the resulting configuration is **-sua**, as in example (27).

(27) 'í'an 'ábe čúkta-su-a
    now nearly cut-CPL-PSV
    It is now nearly all cut down.

In many of its usages, **-su** marks simple past as in examples (28)–(30). These three examples are semantically complementary with **-su** and the following suffixes, which in these examples are **-ka** PPL, **-ka'u** PRF-GND, and **-k** PRF. In each case **-su** holds its scope over the verb to which it suffixes and construes the event that the verb designates as simply occurring. The suffixes and suffix sequences that follow **-su** hold their scope over the entire clause and present that clause as being anterior in time to either the event encoded into the second clause, as in examples (28) and (30), or as anterior to the time of speaking as in example (29).

(28) béha 'ám wáča-'a-su-ka bíi-bíi-ta-su-k
    well them dry-EV-CPL-PPL RDP-twist-VR-CPL-PRF
    When he had finished drying them, he twisted them.

(29) 'enčím haíbu mabét-ču-k-a'u
    your:PL now receive-CPL-PRF-GND
    what you have already received

(30) baká-čúkti-sú-k 'íntok hékkaa-po káte-ka yúmhó'e
    carrizo-cut-CPL-PRF and shade-in sit-PPL rest
    When he had finished cutting the carrizo, he sat in the shade and rested.

The completive **-su** may be used in subordinate clauses, as well as in main clauses. A pair of occurrences of **-su** in subordinate gerundial clauses is shown in examples (31) and (32).

(31) tekú-ta há-ha-su-ka 'á'a bʷíse-k
    squirrel-ACC RDP-chase-CPL-PPL it catch-PRF
    Having chased a squirrel, he caught it.

(32) 'á'a bʷá-'a-su-ka káa 'áu tú-tu'u-ru-k
    it eat-EV-CPL-PPL not RFL RDP-good-VR-PRF
    After he finished eating it, it made him sick.

Completive **-su** is commonly used in adverbial temporal clauses. In sentence (33) **-su** is used in a temporal clause marked by the suffix **-o** *when*. In the next sentence it is used in a temporal adverbial clause marked with the perfective **-k**, and in example (35) it is used in an adverbial clause marked with the imperfective participle **-ka**.

(33) 'ém bo'ó-u kíkte-nee yúm-ho'e-su-k-o
    your road-to stand-FUT attain(?)-rest-CPL-PRF-when
    You can resume your journey after you have finished resting.

(34) ta'á-ta 'áman wét-ču-k kaa híta yuúma
    sun-POS there fall-CPL-PRF not thing attain
    When the sun had set, he still had not gotten anything.

(35) hunáman nássua-su-ka húči húya-u wát-te-k
    there fight-CPL-PPL again woods-to fall-VR-PRF
    When they had finished fighting there, they fled to the woods again.

One specific indication of the intensifying role of **-su** is seen in the lexicalization of the verb **-biča** *to see* in combination with completive **-su** to result in the tight-knit construction **-bitču** which has the resultant meaning "to stare at X," as shown by example (36). In sentence (37) a second occurrence of **-su** is allowed, showing that the first occurrence has probably been reanalyzed as part of the stem.

(36) kóba-'a-su-a-ka ... mékkaa káteka náah-bitču-nee
    win-EV-CPL-PSV-PPL far:away stand around-stare:at-FUT
    Having been beaten he stood far away and stared around.

(37) náu te bítču-su-k
    together we stare:at-CPL-PRF
    We have now met again.

The following pair of sentences illustrates graphically the intensifier function of **-su**. The neutral form of the warning simply uses the future **-nee** as in sentence (38). The more severe form of that warning employs **-su** along with **-nee** shown in sentence (39).

(38) née 'enčí bép-nee
    I you:ACC hit-FUT
    I will whip you.

(39) née 'enčí   bép-su-nee
    I   you:ACC beat-CPL-FUT
    I will really give you a whipping.[15]

Finally, as previous examples have also suggested, completive **-su** is frequently followed by the perfective suffix **-k**. This is illustrated by sentences (40)–(41).

(40) 'emó=m   čón-pón-su-k   'emó=m   súpe-síu-síuti-wíik-su-k
    RFL=they hair-pull-CPL-PRF   RFL=they shirt-RDP-tear-pull-CPL-PRF
    They pulled each other's hair out and tore each other's blouses.

(41) 'enčí=née yebíh-su-k-t-ea-n
    you:ACC=I arrive-CPL-PRF-CON-think-PCN
    I was thinking that you had already arrived.

7.4. The suffix -oa

Yaqui has a suffix **-oa** that, apparently, occurs only (or at least predominately) on loanwords, and in particular, on borrowed Spanish verbs. Yaqui undoubtedly borrowed from Aztec terms like **tekipán-oa** *to work* (Seri: **ktikpan**; O'odham: **čikpan**), **hítt-oa** *to heal*, **híihh-oa** *to weave*, **táhkai** (**tlaškatl**) *tortilla*, **hípetam** (**petátl**) *mats*, and many others.

Because of its phonological shape and the productivity in Yaqui of processes that form compound verbs, it seems plausible to assume that this suffix derives from **hoóa** *to do, to make*. It is not clear that this is the whole story, however.

Dedrick has not found any reference to **-oa** as a verbalizer in Buelna. In pp. 127-199 of his "Vocabulario," in the Spanish to Cáhita section, he provides the entries: "Curar enfermedad." **Ahitoa**. (1891:153). "Trabajar." **Tequipanoa huame**. "Trabajo." **Tequipanoa**." p. 194. And in pp. 203-232 of the "Diccionario" of this work, in the section Cáhita to Spanish he cites "Hitoa.- Curar." and he even cites the verb form "**Hoa**.- Hacer." 1891:213.

The curious thing about **-oa** is that it is restricted to occurring with the infinitive form of verbs borrowed from Spanish. Within language families there are both cognates and borrowings. Yaqui **-oa** is a verbalizing suffix which was and still is productive for making borrowings from Spanish. The problem has to do with whether or not certain terms were "mediated" through Aztec. On the surface it would seem that there was never sufficient contact between the Aztecs and the Yaqui to allow for such a process to occur.

To begin, Cortez arrived in Tenochtitlan in August 1519. The Spaniards established their rule there and used the Aztecs and Aztec language for some of the administration of their government (Karttunan 1984:1). But there seems to be little evidence that there was any contact with the Yaquis during that time. In 1525 Nuño Beltran de Guzmán left Mexico City with soldiers, cavalry and Spanish colonists to establish colonies and claim territory along the west coast of Mexico. He arrived as far as Culiacan by 1529, and in 1533 sent Diego de Guzmán to conquer the Yaquis. Diego de Guzmán crossed the Yaqui River and engaged in a fierce combat with the Yaquis, which he claims to have won. But he returned to Culiacan, and later both Nuño and Diego de Guzmán returned to Mexico City, the settlement at Culiacan being the farthest north they had established a colony (Spicer 1981:46).

There doesn't seem to have been any further activity in the northwest until the 1590's when Capitán Diego Martínes de Hurdaide in "1599 como interino por ausencia del capitán D. Alonzo Diaz" extended "el círculo de las conquistas españolas" (Buelna p. LII). Hurdaide made repeated but unsuccessful attempts to subjugate the Yaquis.

Later the Yaquis voluntarily "surrendered" and asked that Jesuit priests (but no Spanish colonists) be sent to them. In 1617, Andrés Perez de Ribas and Tomás Basilio were sent to them and the Jesuits continued there until the expulsion of all their Society from New Spain in 1767. Given the above

---

15 The perfective form **nee 'enči bepsu-k** *I you beat*-CPL-PRF reinforces the point that we make here since it can be glossed as "I really beat you up." (Eloise Jelinek, personal communication)

circumstances, it makes one wonder how terms like **pipiáar-oa** *to lend/borrow,* **pasiyál-oa** *to stroll around* and other of the earlier borrowings could have been "mediated" through Aztec. It seems more probable to me that these terms were introduced during the time of the Jesuits' occupation of 1617 to 1767 when Spanish and "Cáhita" were spoken. There are some other factors, moreover, that we need to cite.

There is ample record that Nahuatl was used as an administrative language throughout New Spain in the earlier part of the colonial period. And Aztec speaking assistants were among them. Spicer notes, for example, that in 1609, Diego de Hurdaide sent in some "Christian Indians" to help secure the capture of two Ocoroni leaders (1981:47). It seems quite likely that the Jesuits themselves also drew on "Christian Indians" to accompany them on their trips. These are the ones who may well have been the source of the borrowing into Yaqui of many Spanish verbs that had first been borrowed into Nahuatl, an entire class of which were modified by means of the Nahuatl suffix **-oa** (cf. Karttunnen 1984:11). These borrowings subsequently found their way into a number of other indigenous languages, including Yaqui.

The infinitive forms of a number of Spanish verbs were adapted early on into Yaqui. Note that the earlier borrowings show more phonological modification than recent borrowings. This infinitive form was adopted into Yaqui with the suffix **-oa,** a process that was well developed by the end of the 17th century, (Karttunnen 1984:4). This led to a number of forms that we now find in the Yaqui lexicon, e.g., example (42)(a)–(d).

(42)(a)	pipiar (Sp: fiar)	+ -oa >	pipiáaroa	*to lend*
(b)	pasíyal (Sp: pasear)	+ -oa >	pasiyáaloa	*to go walking*
(c)	pensar	+ -oa >	pensaároa	*to think*
(d)	cantar	+ -oa >	cantaróa	*to sing*

In addition, although Yaqui has terms for "to visit" and "to think," occasionally these will be considered not quite precise enough and they use **'á'abo né 'enci bisitaaroa-sek** "I have come over here to visit you," and **hunuen né pensaaroa** "That's what I think." Although these expressions are used somewhat "tongue-in cheek," the morpheme **-oa** is currently productive.

To conclude, some of these Yaqui forms actually represent Spanish words that were first borrowed into Aztec outside of the Yaqui-Mayo homeland and were subsequently borrowed into Yaqui. In short, these borrowings actually were mediated through Nahuatl (cf. Karttunnen 1984:1-4; Casad 1988:90). The Yaqui word **tekipánoa** is one small piece of evidence for this account: there is no native Spanish word **tekipán**, but there certainly is a Nahuatl one, as well as a Nahuatl nominal **tékil** *forced labor.*

OVERALL VERB STRUCTURE

1.0. Introduction

In this section we summarize the range of grammatical patterns exhibited by the Yaqui verb. We bring together here data related to a number of topics that were treated in detail in distinct chapters of this grammar such as BE/HAVE/DO, VERB MORPHOLOGY, VERB COMPOUNDS and POSSESSIVES. The patterns that we summarize here include constructions whose internal tightness ranges along a gradient from the loosely associated, involving clitics of various kinds, to the highly integrated constructions with sequences of prefixes and suffixes. This overview also includes a summary of the position classes of morphological elements that enter into these verbal constructions and describes the more obvious ordering relationships that occur among them in Yaqui verb structures.

2.0. The grammaticalization path

Studies such as Heine and Reh 1984 and Traugott and Heine 1991 lay out for us an entire field of research about processes that we can call grammaticalization. This term refers to a wide range of processes by which free lexical items undergo semantic and morphological change to take on a variety of roles as grammatical functors. In this chapter we summarize the kinds of lexical elements that have become incorporated or closely attached to verb stems.

2.1. Compound verbs

As discussed in COMPOUNDS, p.157–164, compounding of various parts of speech is very common in Yaqui and opens the door for the grammaticalization of many lexical items. With respect to the verbs, we have observed four patterns of constituent combination. These are summarized in Table 56.:

Verb + Verb = Verb
Noun + Verb = Verb
Verb + Suffix = Verb
Suffix + Suffix = Verb

Table 56. Compound verb constituency

Each of the constituent type combinations of Table 56 has its own further complexities. Thus, Verb + Verb compounds often employ one of a small set of manner verbs as the initial verb in the compound (cf. COMPOUNDS, pp. 154–155). These are summarized in Table 57.

núk-	*to take, to carry*
tó'o-	*to leave, go away from*
sú'u-	*to release,*
tú'u-	*to do well*

Table 57. Manner verbs in compounds

Examples (1)–(3) illustrate **nuk-** *to take, to carry.*

(1) 'í'an=su   né 'á'a núk-sím-nee
 today=EXP I it carry-go:SG-FUT
 Well, today I will take it away with me.

(2) húnak béha kóa-po yéu 'á'a núk-sáha-k
 then well pen-in out it carry-go:PL-PRF
 Well, then they took it out of the cow-pen.

(3) kúta-bankó-m-mak lópola 'á'a núk-wéiyaa hunáman-táhtia
 wood-chair-PL-with beside her carry-carry there-until
 He took her past Wooden Benches, that far only.

Examples (4)–(6) illustrate typical usages of **tó'o-** *to leave, go away from*.

(4) čúbala náu-katé-ka 'émo tó'o-sáha-k
short:time together-go:PL-PPL RFL leave-go:PL-PRF
After travelling together for a while, they separated.

(5) 'ón-ta pú'ak-ta-nee béa-m 'áme-u tó'o-si-síme
salt-ACC load-VR-FUT skin-PL:ACC them-to leave-RDP-go:SG
He loads up with salt and goes, leaving the skins with them.

(6) sí'ime née tó'o-tét-ten-nee
all me leave-RDP-run:PL-FUT
Everyone will run away from me.

The verb **sú'u-** *to release* forms compounds only with **tóha** *to carry, to take, to deposit* as illustrated in sentences (7)–(9).

(7) 'áke'em 'á'a sú'u-tóha 'éla'apo wée-nee
you:PL:IMP it release-place no:matter go:SG-FUT
Turn it loose, it doesn't matter if it goes away.

(8) tómi-ta mabéta-ka 'ám sú'u-tóhi-tébo-k
money-ACC receive-PPL them release-place-IMP-PRF
Having received the money, he ordered that they be released.

(9) 'émpo hunaka'a bo'ó-ta sú'u-tóha-k-o káa-mačí-kun yebíh-nee
you that:ACC road-ACC release-place-PRF-if not-light-in arrive:SG-FUT
If you abandon that road, you'll come out in the darkness.

The adjective **tú'u-** *good, legal* commonly forms compounds with a number of different stems. In these compounds **tú'u** serves as an adverb to modify the meaning of the following verb.

(10) 'á'a 'áe-k-a'u 'á-u tú'u-noóka
his mother-PRF-GND him-to good-talk
His (now deceased) mother spoke soothingly to him.

(11) hunáa'a hámut túa tú'u-híaps-ek
that woman truly good-heart-have
She was a very good-hearted woman.

Various kinds of verbs also function to modify the meanings of psychological verbs and motion verbs that are the second member of Verb-Verb compounds (cf., COMPOUNDS, pp. 160–161). Many of the meanings are transparently related to the verbs that enter into the compound. Thus in example (12) the adverb **yó'ore** expresses the manner of a psychological concept showing love, whereas in examples (13)–(16) the second verb designates a kind of physical activity that accompanies the main activity expressed in the first verb of the compound. In example (17) the second verb expresses the general capacity that permits one to exercise the particular activity designated by the schematic verb **hoóa**. On the other hand, in example (18) the the second stem in the compound, the verb **hímmaa** *to throw away*, is a graphic way of designating the cessation of the activity designated by the first verb **če'e**, which appears here in an ablauted form **či'i**. The compound in example (19) is a graphic way to describe an unpleasant psychological state, combining verbs which designate a physical activity and a feeling of extreme distress, respectively.

(12) náke + yó'ore > nák-yó'ore
love *to respect* *to lovingly respect*

(13) wíke + síme > wík-síme
pull *to go:SG/PL* *to go pulling*

(14) 'étbʷa + yáa > 'étbʷa-yáa
steal *to do* *to do secretly*

(15) yú'u	+	sáka	>	yú'u-sáka
to push		*to go:PL*		*to go pushing:PL*
(16) hoóa	+	tá'aa	>	hóo-tá'aa
to do		*to know*		*to know how to do*
(17) bíča	+	tá'aa	>	bít-tá'aa
to see		*to know*		*to know by sight = to recognize*
(18) čí'i[1]	+	hímmaa	>	čí'i-hímmaa
nurse		*to throw away*		*to wean*
(19) tubúk-ta	+	kokko	>	tubúh-kókko
jump over		*to die:PL*		*to be very nervous*

The second verb compound pattern in Table 56 is Noun + Verb = Verb. Typical examples of this kind of compound are given in examples (20)–(23).

(20) táhi	+	wéče	>	táhi-wéče
fire		*to fall*		*to have a fever*
(21) híapsi	+	temáe	>	híapsi-temáe
soul		*to question*		*to repent life*
(22) čoóni	+	poóna	>	čón-póna
hair		*to pull*		*to pull someone's hair*
(23) tékil	+	máka	>	tékil-máka
work		*to give*		*to give a task = to commission*

The third compound pattern consists of Verb + Suffix = Verb. The suffix in this case has become grammaticalized. For example, the verb **bíča** *to see* will take the completive suffixes **-su/-ču** and the causative suffix **-tua** to form verbs with specialized meanings. Thus, to look at something intently is to stare at it, and to cause someone to see something implies sending it to him or her.

(24) bíča	+	-su/-ču	>	bít-ču
to see		*completive*		*to stare at*
(25) bíča-	+	-tua	>	bít-tua
to see		*causative*		*to send something*

The fourth pattern is one that consists of a pair of suffixes in a compound of the form Suffix + Suffix = Verb. The verbal source of **-tebo** *to order, to command* is shown clearly in its usage with the verbalizer suffix **-te** or the causative suffix **-tua**. This results in the transitive and intransitive forms of the verb meaning "to greet," **tebótua** *to greet someone* (TRN) and **tebóte** *to send one's greetings* (INTR).

(26) 'áman né tebóte
 there I greet
 I send my greetings out there.

(27) sí'ime-m né 'áman tebótua
 all-PL:ACC I there greet
 I send my greetings to everyone out there.

2.2. Derivational suffixes

A variety of suffixes are used to turn nouns, adjectives and adverbs, among other things, into verbs. Several of these have a variety of morphological shapes that are at least partially determined by morphophonemic rules. For ease in presentation, they are listed in Table 58 as a single form, e.g., as **-ek** rather than as **-'Vek/-ek/-k**.

---

[1] This is an ablauted form of the stem **če'e** *to nurse*.

-ek	to have, to own	-tea	to name,
-te	to do, to make	-tua	to cause to be,
-tu	to become, to be transformed	-oa	VR (Spanish loans)
-'u	to go to do		

Table 58. Yaqui verbalizing suffixes

As evidenced from Table 58, a wide variety of semantic effects can be obtained depending on the particular incorpororated element and the derivational suffix with which it combines. Examples of the possessive **-ek** are given in sentences (28) and (29). A more complete description of the usages of this suffix is given in BE/HAVE/DO, pp. 74–75.

(28) tú'i-si tú'ii-k kár-ek
good-AVR good-ACC house-have
He has a very good house.

(29) sawá-yóh-te-k káa náppat hékkaa-k
leaf-fall-VR-PRF not any:more shade-have
It shed its leaves; it doesn't make shade anymore.

Note that the examples in (28) and (29) lack a specified possessor. This type of construction is used more frequently than those that mark specific possessors with possessive pronouns, and which are illustrated in examples (30) and (31).

(30) 'áapo 'á'a kár-ek
he it house-have
It is his house.

(31) haí=sa 'émpo simó-'o-tea-m-ta hápč-ek?
how=INTERR you Simon-EV-name-NZR-ACC father-have
Is a man named Simon your father?

The verbalizing suffix **-ek** also has a participial form **-ka**. Some illustrations of its usage are given in examples (32) and (33).

(32) bóosa-po mamá-ka kaíta téa-k
pocket-in hand-PPL nothing find-PRF
Inserting his hand into his pocket, he found nothing.

(33) kó'om-kóba-ka 'á-u lúk-ti-síme
down-head-PPL him-to approach-PPL-go:SG
Lowering his head, he approached him.

Examples of **-te** are given in sentences (34)–(39). Note that this verbalizing **-te** is used only with incorporated nouns and adjectives, and should not be confused with the **-te** of the paradigmatic verbal transitivity **-ta/-te/-ti** set.

(34) yéu-tóm-te
out-stomach-VR
to be born

(35) kía woói-m wásuk-te-k híba
just two-PL:ACC year-VR-PRF only
It only lasted two years.

(36) née 'áa wók-te
I able foot-VR
I can track animals.

Some usages of **-te** are applicative in nature, signaling that a particular activity is specifically directed to someone for his/her benefit, as suggested by the derived verbs in sentences (37)–(39). As sentence (37) suggests, the activity can be reflexive.

(37) káa-te-k 'ámmani 'íntok hunúen káa-te-ka 'áma hó'aa-k
house-VR-PRF off:yonder and thus house-VR-PPL there live-PRF
He built a house way off yonder, and so having built it, he lived there.

(38) nóolia-ma-ti hiía 'á-u mám-te-patči
hurry-HRT-CON say him-to hand-VR-upon
"Hurry then," he said, as he extended his hand to him.

(39) súpe-m-po kóba-te
shirt-PL-in head-VR
He put on a shirt.

Verbalizing **-te** is also used with some adjectives to form special verbs as **tú'u-te** *to fix, to repair*.

(40) bankó-m tú'u-te
    chair-PL good-VR
    He fixes chairs.

(41) hunáa'a 'óo'ou masó-bea-m bʷálko-te
    that   man   deer-skin-PL soft-VR
    That man tans deer skins.

(42) 'iníi'i 'uúsi 'íntok sép   'á'a hewí-te-ria-k
    this   boy and   at:once him yes-VR-APL-PRF
    And this boy immediately affirmed it.[2]

The verbalizer **-tu** has additional usages in which it can simply be glossed as "be." Examples (43) and (44) illustrate this usage.

(43) kía 'á'a hábe-tu-k   húni'i 'íntok kía 'á'a híta-tu-k   húni'i
    just it who-VR-PRF even   and   just it thing-VR-PRF even
    no matter who or what it is

(44) mámni wásuktia-m-po páah-tu-k
    five year-PL-in   peace-VR-PRF
    There was peace for five years.

Clear examples of the developmental meaning of **-tu**, i.e., "to become X" or "to get into X state" are given in examples (45) and (46).

(45) pá'aku káa-tú'ii tóokoa-tu-ne-mme.
    outside not-good dust-VR-FUT-they
    Outside is not good; they will get dusty.

(46) 'émpo haíbu híaki-tu-su-k
    you   now Yaqui-VR-CPL-PRF
    You have now completely become a Yaqui.

Names of the days of the week have been adopted from Spanish but require the addition of the suffixes **-tu** and **-k**.

(47) lunéh-tu-k   yépsa-k   máateh-tu-k   siíka
    Monday-VR-PRF arrive-PRF Tuesday-VR-PRF went
    He came Monday and left Tuesday.

Some adverbials and procomplements may also take **-tu**.

(48) čúubaa-tu-k-o   (49) 'inílen-tu-k   káa-wótti   'emé'e
    moment-VR-PRF-when   thus-VR-PRF not-alarmed you:PL
    after a moment had passed   *For this reason, don't be alarmed.*

There is a special construction in which **-tu** is used with a verb that follows the auxiliary **'áa** *to be able to* to give the overall concept of "able to be done, possible."

(50) 'áa hóo-tu   (52) káa 'áa 'á-u   nók-tu
    able do-VR   not able him-to speak-VR
    It can be done.   *You can't talk to him.*

(51) 'áa bít-tu   (53) hunáa'a 'uúsi 'áa sáu-tu
    able see-VR   that   child able order-VR
    It is visible.   *That child does what he is told to.*

---

2 Note the locational contrast signalled by the demonstrative pronouns **hunáa'a** and **iníi'i** in examples (41) and (42).

A limited number of nouns may take the verbalizing suffix **-'u,** which imparts an intentive meaning to the derived verb. Examples of this are the following:

(54) basó-'u-k čibá-m-betči'ibo
grass-VR-PRF goat-PL-for
He went to get grass for the goats.

(55) maáso-m be-béa-'u
deer-PL:ACC RDP-skin-VR
He skins deer.

One of the most productive of all the derivational suffixes is the appelative **-tea.** Typical examples of this are given in sentences (56) and (57).

(56) kopáal-im-tea-m-ta 'á'a miíka-k
copal-PL-VR-NZR-ACC him give-PRF
They gave him something called copal.

(57) mátilde-'e-tea-m-ta né haíwa
Matilde-EV-VR-NZR-ACC I seek
I am looking for someone named Matilde.

Sentences (58)–(59) illustrate common usages of the causative suffix **-tua** to signal the physical application of an entity to someone. The typical result is a kind of possessive sentence in which the constructional meaning can be glossed as "cause X to have Y." A more abstract version is given in sentence (60).

(58) 'á'a súpe-tua-k
him shirt-VR-PRF
They put a shirt on him.

(59) kát=e'em wi'í-ta née wikóh-tua
not=you:PL string-ACC me belt-VR
Don't put a cord belt on me.

(60) 'áčai tú'ii-m née wók-tua
sir good-PL:ACC me foot-VR
Lord, cause me to have good feet.

The suffix **-oa** is used with Spanish loan infinitives. It possibly derives from the verb **hoóa** *to do, to make.* But the examples given in sentences (61) and (62) are old borrowings from Spanish that may well have come into Yaqui from Nahuatl, since Spanish verbs borrowed into Nahuatl in their infinitive forms were usually modified with the Nahuatl formative **-oa** (cf. the discussion in INFLECTIONAL AND DERIVATIONAL AFFIXATION, pp. 325–326).

(61) tómi-ta née pi-piáar-oa
money-ACC me RDP-loan-VR
Lend me some money.

(62) tuká=te pótam-po pasíyaal-oa-k
yesterday=we Potem-in outing-VR-PRF
Yesterday we went for an outing in Potam.

2.3 The adverbials forming compounds

A number of adverbial elements have been grammaticalized in two ways. For one, they frequently serve as the first member in verbal compounds. In other contexts, they may alternatively be classified as proclitics (cf. INCORPORATION, pp. 256–262).

báa-	*once for all, right now*	náu-	*together*
bát-	*first, in front*	yée-	*people*
náas-	*all around*	yéeu/yéu-	*outside*
nát-	*one on top of the another, one after another*		

Table 59. Adverbials as compounding elements

The example of **báa-** *once for all* given in sentence (63) shows its extended meaning of "right now."

(63) lót-ti-laa-taka ne wée báa-yúmhó'e-pea
tire-PPL-PPL-being I go right:now-rest-DSD
I'm really tired; I wish I could rest right now.

In sentence (64) this same adverbial shows its role as a base for attaching subject and object clitics. Its usage in sentence (65) is that of heightened importance.

(64) báa=t=a'a čúpa-'a-ne   'á'a čúpa-ka   kóp-ti-nee
     now=we=it finish-EV-FUT   it   finish-PPL forget-PPL-FUT
     Let's finish it right now and having finished, forget it.

(65) híttoa   káa báa-tá'aru-máči
     medicine not now-lose-seem
     The medicine should by no means be lost.

The usages of **bát-** *first, in front of* in examples (66)–(67) show its role of specifying the lead point in a time sequence.

(66) hunáme'e bát-kaáte   (67) 'inía   beléki-k   né bát-'emó-u téuwaa
     those   first-go:PL   this:ACC amount-ACC   I first-you-to tell
     Those go first.   *I tell you this amount first.*

Sentences (68)–(71) illustrate the usages of **náas-** *all around, here and there*. The first four of these sentences show a variety of its spatial meanings, and the last, example (72), speaks of a kind of customary deportment on the part of the subject of the sentence.

(68) túa-su   tú'ii-t-iá-ka   náah-čépte   'állea-ka-i
     very-EXP good-CON-say-PPL   around-jump   happy-PPL-PPL
     "Very good indeed," he said jumping all around with joy.

(69) náah-bít-ču
     around-look-CMP
     He looked intently in all directions.

(70) 'áa-mak   náah-réh-ti-nee   puéplo-m bée'e-ka-tána
     him-with around-walk:PL-PPL-FUT   town-PL   scatter-PPL-from
     They would go around to all the scattered villages with him.

(71) 'á'a hióko-le-ka   náas='a'a   nu-núp-taíte-k
     her pity-VR-PPL   all:around=her RDP-take-begin-PRF
     Feeling sorry for her, he began to take her all around.

(72) 'émpo két yó'o-ri-sia-či-si   náah-kuák-te
     you   also old-AJR-AVR-in-AVR   around-turn-VR
     You also go around respectably.

The adverbial **nát-** *in succession, one on top of the other* is illustrated by examples (73)–(75).

(73) kárpa-m tá-tábe-k   nát='am   tót-ta-ka   nát='am hoá-ka tú'uli-si
     tent-PL RDP-lower-PRF   pile=them throw-VR-PPL   pile=them do-PPL pretty-AVR

     nát='am   súma-k
     pile=them tie-PRF
     They took down the tents, folded them, placed them one on top of the other, and tied them into a neat bundle.

(74) né-t-wá'am   nát-čá'a-ka   kaáte
     me-on-past   succession-suspend-PPL go:PL
     They go past me one after the other in succession.

(75) bésa-'e   hú'unea haíki-si   wéčia-po=sa   nát-bépa-nat 'aáyu-k
     well=you know   how:many-AVR   fall-in=Q   pile-over-pile be-PRF
     Well, you know how many times over and over this happened.

Sentences (76)–(80) illustrate typical usages of the incorporated adverbial **nau-** *together*.

(76) woí-ka náu-katé-'e-tea-n
     two-VR together-go:PL-EV-QUO-PCN
     It used to be said that two were travelling together.

333

(77) náu=te   bít-ču-su-k
     together=we   see-CPL-CPL-PRF
     We have had a real good visit together.

(78) náu-bíča   né 'áe-t   hí'oh-te-k
     together-site I it-on   write-VR-PRF
     I wrote on both sides of it.

(79) náu=te   nabó-'u-nee
     together=we   cactus:fruit-VR-FUT
     We will go gather cactus fruit together.

(80) hobé'eso-m náu-rúk-te-k   náu-'etého-taíte-k
     ram-PL   together-near-VR-PRF together-talk-begin-PRF
     The rams came near to each other and began to talk together.

Examples of the incorporated unspecified human object marker **yée-** *people* are given in sentences (81)–(84).

(81) 'áapo kía yée-máhta-bae
     he   just people-teach-DSD
     He just wants to teach people.

(82) miísi yée-súke
     cat   people-scratch
     A cat scratches people.

(83) ču'ú yée-búue
     dog people-scold
     A dog growls at people.

(84) tóri-m 'únnaa-m híta yée-b^wa-b^wá-'aria
     rat-PL much-PL thing people-RDP-eat-APL
     Rats eat up a lot of people's things.

The morpheme **yéeu/yéu-** *outside* has an extremely wide range of usage. The sentences in (85)–(91) are typical. Sentences (85) and (86) illustrate its spatial usages.

(85) ta'á-ta   yéu-wée-'ebetana
     sun-POS   out-come-from
     from where the sun rises

(86) 'iním té 'emó-u   yéu-yáha-k
     here we you:PL-to out-arrive:PL-PRF
     We have come over here to you.

In sentence (87) it indicates a location distinct from that of the speaker's location.

(87) čúuba-tu-k   tékil-po té yéu-kík-te-nee
     moment-VR-PRF   work-in we out-stand:PL-VR-FUT
     We'll get off work shortly.

A number of the usages of this adverbial are metaphorical, with **yéu-** indicating such diverse concepts as a successful outcome, illustrated in sentence (88), or the pressing of charges against someone, as in sentence (89)

(88) 'émpo kaíbu 'ém 'éa-'u-mak   yéu-wée-nee
     you   never your think-GND-with out-go:SG-FUT
     Your idea will never work.

(89) hunáa'a baákot 'á'a yá'u-raa-u   'énčí   yéu-ná'ateho-k
     that   snake its chief-ABS-to you:ACC out-accuse-PRF
     That snake accused you to its authorities.

Examples (90) and (91) illustrate specialized usages of **yéu-** related to making a selection from an unspecified mass in example (90) and the appearance of a new born child in example (91).

(90) néhpo yéu='a'a pú'a-k
     I   out=it   choose-PRF
     I chose it.

(91) yéu-tóm-te-k
     out-stomach-VR-PRF
     It was born.

3.0. The transitivity classes

Yaqui verbs can be broadly classified along a transitivity parameter that is defined partly in terms of morphology and syntax and partly along semantic lines. In short, verbs in this language generally fall into three major classes: transitive verbs, intransitive verbs, and multitransitive verbs, with multitransitives being those that participate in morphological processes that allow them to function as either transitive, intransitive, or stative verbs.

3.1. Intransitive verbs

As discussed in VERB STEMS, pp. 257–258, intransitive verbs can be categorized according to the three ways the stem relates to the marking of subjects. Some intransitive stems are suppletive for singular versus plural subjects, others are reduplicated in order to indicate that the subject is plural, and finally, there is a large set of verb stems that remain constant regardless of the number of the subject.

A pair of examples with suppletive stems are **búite** (SG)/**ténne** (PL) *to run* shown in example (1)(a)–(b) and **yeésa** (SG)/**hoóye** (PL) *to sit* in example (2)(a)–(b).

(1)(a) 'áapo 'áman búite-k
    he   there run:SG-PRF
    He ran there.

(b) bémpo 'áman ténne-k
    they there run:PL-PRF
    They ran there.

(2)(a) húu'u Hóan híba 'ím yeésa
    that John always here sit:SG
    John always sits here.

(b) bémpo 'áman hoóye
    they there sit:PL
    They sit there.

A pair of examples that reduplicate their stems are **kóče** (SG)/**ko-kóče** (PL) *to sleep*, illustrated in examples (3)(a)–(b), and **'uúba** (SG)/**'u-'úba** (PL) *to bathe* in examples (4)(a)–(b).

(3)(a) 'áapo kári-po bó'o-ka kóče
    he house-in lie-PPL sleep
    He is lying down asleep in the house.

(b) tú'i-si ko-kóčo-k húme'e maoméo-m
    good-AVR RDP-sleep-PRF those acrobat-PL
    Those acrobats slept soundly.

(4)(a) 'uúsi bát^{w}e-po 'uúba
    boy river-in bathe
    The boy is bathing in the river.

(b) 'ú-'uba=mme
    RDP-bathe=they
    They are bathing.

Sentences (5)(a)–(b) exemplify stem forms that remain constant whether used with singular or plural subjects. In this pair of sentences, the subjects are marked by first person singular and first person plural postclitics, respectively.

(5)(a) čík-tu-k=ane
    disorient-VR-PRF=I
    I got lost.

(b) čík-tu-k=ate
    disorient-VR-PRF=we
    We got lost.

3.2. Transitive verbs

Yaqui transitive stems are also categorized according to morphological, syntactic, and semantic characteristics. There is a large class of transitive verbs that use the same stem form regardless of the number of the direct object. In addition, there is also a class of stems that can take a double object, i.e., these can have an overt direct object as well as an overt indirect object. Finally, there is a small class of transitive verbs that have suppletive stems with one stem for singular direct objects, and another distinct form for plural direct objects. (There is also a set of multi-transitive stems which take distinct morphological markings to distinguish their intransitive and transitive usages. These will be discussed in the next section, multi-transitive stems.)

Examples of regular transitive stems include **číke** *to brush*, **b^{w}á'e** *to eat*, **máya** *to stone*, and **béeba** *to hit*. Typical usages are given in sentences (6)–(9).

(6) čibá'ato hímsi-m-mea sí'ime púhba-t 'á'a číke
    goat whisker-PL-INST all face-on him brush
    The goat brushed all his face with his whiskers.

(7) mún-bák-ta b^{w}á'ee
    bean-cooked-ACC eat
    He is eating bean soup.

(8) wakás-im 'áme-u béeba-k
   cow-PL them-to hit-PRF
   They drove the cattle toward them.

(9) 'á'a máya 'á'a béeba húka'a bakót-ta
   him stone him hit   that:ACC snake-ACC
   Stone that snake, hit it!

Other verbs of this class are described in some detail in VERB STEMS, pp. 258–260.

Examples of transitive stems that are suppletive for singular and plural objects include **mé'aa** (SG)/**sú'aa** (PL) *to kill* as in examples (10)(a)–(b), **hímmaa** (SG)/**wó'ota** (PL) *to throw* as in examples (11)(a)–(b), and **kibátča** (SG)/**kiíma** (PL) *to put into* in examples (12)(a)–(b).

(10)(a) 'á'a mé'aa-k húka'a bakót-ta   (b) masó-m   sú'a-ka   'áu 'anía
      it kill-PRF that:ACC snake-ACC   deer-PL:ACC kill:PL-PPL RFL help
      He killed the snake.   *He earns his living by killing deer.*

(11)(a) téta-ta   mékkaa himmaa-k   (b) haíti-ba'á-m   'áma wó'o-ta-k
      stone-ACC far:away throw-PRF   dirty-water-PL:ACC there throw:out-VR-PRF
      He threw the stone far away.   *She threw out the dirty water there.*

(12)(a) 'ilí 'usí-ta   kári-u 'á'a kibátča-k   (b) húme'e kabáa-m=ne   kóa-u   kiíma-k
      little child-ACC house-to him put:in-PRF   those goat-PL:ACC=I pen-to put:in-PRF
      She put the little child in the house.   *I put the goats in the goat pen.*

Examples of double object transitive stems include **máka** *to give*, **miíka** *to give (a gift)*, **máhta** *to teach*. Illustrative usages are given in examples (13)–(16). In (13), a second person singular personal pronoun **'enči** marks the indirect object, whereas the abstract noun **lútu'uria** *truth*, marked for the accusative plural designates the direct object. In example (14) the indirect object is signalled by the third person singular **'á'a** and the direct object is marked with a Demonstrative + Accusative Noun Phrase.

(13) hunúen né 'enčí lútu'uria-m máka   (14) 'áapo-'ik 'á'a máka-k húka'a lípro-ta
    thus   I you:ACC truth-PL:ACC give   he-ACC   it   give-PRF that:ACC book-ACC
    In that way I give you the truth.   *He gave him the book.*

A first person object pronoun **née** indicates indirect object in example (15), whereas the direct object is marked by the sentence initial accusative noun **ba'á-ta** *water*. Reflexive pronouns also function in double object constructions in Yaqui as shown by example (16) which employs the first person singular reflexive pronoun **'íno**. The direct object in this sentence is marked by the abstract compound nominal, itself marked with the accusative suffix **-ta**.

(15) ba'á-ta·   née miíka   (16) 'í'an=ne nók-hía-wa-i-ta   'íno máhta-bae
    water-ACC me give   today=I word-sound-VR-NZR-ACC RFL teach-DSD
    Give me a drink of water.   *Today I am going to teach myself the sounds of words.*

3.3. Multi-transitive stems

Multi-transitive verbs have both transitive and intransitive usages. They can be divided into four subclasses based on how they relate to certain morphological processes. The first set of stems takes its transitivity marking from one of a set of suffixes of the form **-ta/-te/-ti** which correlate with transitive, intransitive, and participial usages, respectively. The second set is marked with **-a** for transitive verbs, **-e** for intransitive verbs, and **-i** for stative verbs. The third set is very limited and distinguishes its transitive and intransitive forms by the use of suprasegmentals and other phonological distinctions. The fourth class, those whose stems remain constant regardless of transitivity value, is rather extensive.

Examples of the **-ta/-te/-ti** class include **kót-** *to break* and **nót-** *to return*. The transitive and intransitive counterparts are often related in straightforward ways semantically. Thus, the transitive form **kót-ta** means "X breaks Y," as illustrated by example (17)(a) whereas its intransitive counterpart means "X breaks," as illustrated in example (17)(b). Its participial counterpart **kót-ti** means "X is broken, as shown by example (17)(c).

(17)(a) húka'a   kúta-ta   kót-ta-k
       that:ACC stick-ACC break-TRN-PRF
       He broke the stick.

   (b) húu'u púentes kót-te-k
       that bridge break-INTR-PRF
       The bridge broke.

   (c) kót-ti   húu'u sóto'i
       break-PPL that   clay:pot
       The clay pot is broken.

The participialized form **kót-ti** may also serve as an adjective as in sentence (18).

(18) sóto'i-ta   kót-ti-ta   'áma bíča-k
     clay:pot-ACC break-PPL-ACC there see-PRF
     He saw a broken clay pot there.

More frequently **-ti/-i** forms are used as connecting elements that allow additional morphemes to be brought into the complex verb word.

(19)(a) 'áma taáwa-k   kót-ti-la-taka-i
        there remain-PRF break-PPL-PPL-be-PPL
        It remained there broken.

   (b) húu'u pú'ato láuti   kót-ti-nee
       that plate quickly break-PPL-FUT
       That plate is going to break soon.

Similarly, the transitive **nót-ta** means "X returns Y," as seen in sentence (20)(a) where it refers to someone's returning a horse to its owner. The intransitive **nót-te**, on the other hand, means "X returns to Y location," as illustrated by example (20)(b).

(20)(a) 'á-e   'án-su-ka   kabá'i-ta 'á-u   nót-ta-k
        it-INST be-CMP-PPL horse-ACC him-to return-TRN-PPL
        When he finished with the horse, he returned it to him.

   (b) tekipánoa-su-ka   'á'a hó'a-u   nót-te-k
       work-CMP-PPL   his house-to return-INTR-PPL
       Having finished working, he returned home.

A second, but related, class of multi-transitive verbs shows characteristic vowel alternations of **-a/-e/-i**. These also indicate the transitive-intransitive-stative trichotomy. For example, the transitive form of the verb meaning "to cook" is **b^{w}ása**, as illustrated by sentence (21)(a)–(b); its intransitive counterpart, meaning "to mature on the vine" is **b^{w}áse**, as shown by sentence (21)(c)–(d).

(21)(a) haámutči-m wáka-bák-ta   b^{w}á'a-b^{w}ás-a
        woman-PL meat-cook-ACC RDP-cook-TRN
        The women are cooking beef stew.

   (b) wáka-bák-ta   'á'a b^{w}ás-a-'a-ria-k
       meat-stew-ACC him cook-TRN-EV-APL-PRF
       She cooked beef stew for him.

   (c) mínai-m 'ábe   b^{w}áse
       melon-PL nearly ripe-INTR
       The melons are nearly ripe.

   (d) minai-m   b^{w}ás-e-'e-te-k-o   mékkaa wínhuba
       canteloupe-PL ripe-INTR-EV-VR-PRF-if far:away fragrant
       When canteloupes are ripe, their fragrance carries a long way.

The stative form **b^{w}ási** can be used as an adverb with the extended metaphorical meaning of "maturely" in the psychological sense, as evidenced by sentence (22).

(22) b^{w}ás-i-si   'á'a yóopna-k
     mature-PPL-AVR him answer-PRF
     He answered him maturely.

A third class of multi-transitive stems consists of those modified phonologically in certain ways to distinguish between intransitive and transitive forms. Some of these distinctions may reflect formerly productive morphological differences. Others involve differential suprasegmental configurations.

Examples of this class of multi-transitives include the mental-act verb **'éa** *to think*, with its transitive counterpart **'éiyaa** *to esteem*, exemplified in sentences (23)(a)–(b).

(23)(a) née két húnen 'éa
       I also thus think
       That's what I think too.

(b) sí'ime tú'i-si   'á'a 'éiyaa-n
     all good-AVR him esteem-PCN
     Everyone esteemed him highly.

Morphologically similar is the pair **hú'unea** *to know about X* with its transitive counterpart **hú'uneiyaa** *to know X*, given in sentences (24)(a)–(b).

(24)(a) 'emé'e hú'unea 'inía-e 'itóm 'itó 'anía-'apo
       you:PL know:INTR this-INST our RFL help-GND
       You know that by means of this we earn our living.

(b) néhpo két hunúen 'á'a hú'uneiyaa
     I also thus it know:TRN
     I also know it that way.

Yaqui can also exploit suprasegmental distinctions for indicating morphological and syntactic category differences. A good example is the existential verb **taáwa** *to remain*, given in example (25)(a), with its transitive causal counterpart **tawáa** *to cause to stay* in example (25)(b).

(25)(a) 'áman taáwa-k
       there stay-PRF
       He stayed there.

(b) bémpo húme'e waté-m-mak 'áma 'á'a tawáa-k
     they those other-PL-with there him leave-PRF
     They left him there with the others.

The final subcategory of multitransitive verbs in Yaqui consists of those that employ the same morphological shape for both transitive and intransitive usages. Examples of this class include the perception verbs **bíča** *to see* and **híkkaha** *to hear, to understand*. Both of these verbs seem basically to be transitive in which case they highlight the object of the perception. They are also sometimes used intransitively, in which case their use highlights the act of perception. For example, in sentence (26)(a) the question is directed at one's ability for visual perception, whereas example (26)(b) names the object that was perceived visually.

(26)(a) hái=sa káa bíča há'ani
       how=INTERR not see maybe
       Can't you see?

(b) 'í'an kétwoo né bakót-ta bíča-k
     today early I snake-ACC see-PRF
     I saw a snake early this morning.

Likewise, the intransitive use of **híkkaha** in sentence (27)(a) focuses on the subject's lack of ability for aural perception, whereas its corresponding transitive use in sentence (27)(b) spells out the entities who were not perceived aurally.

(27)(a) 'áapo káa híkkaha
       he not hear
       He cannot hear.

(b) 'itépo ká='am híkkaha-k
     we not=them hear-PRF
     We didn't hear them.

3.4. Prefixes and proclitics

Compounding processes have also been the door for further grammaticalization of erstwhile lexical items into prefixes and proclitics. There are two bona fide prefixes and seven proclitics in Yaqui. Some of the prefixes have very limited usage, but the proclitics are widely used. The prefixed morphemes are both markers for unspecified nominal entities. As discussed previously in NONDISTINCT ARGUMENT PHENOMENA, pp. 80–83, Yaqui has two unspecified object prefixes. These are **hi-/hí'i-** used to indicate an inanimate object and **ne-/na-** used to refer to a human object.

The unspecified inanimate prefix **hí'i-** is widely used in the Yaqui verb. Here we cite a few representative examples. The basic verbs used in these sentences are all transitive: **čó'ilaa** *to rope* *something,* **béeba** *to hit something,* **kó'a/kó'o-** *to chew something,* **čoóna** *to hit something,* **číke** *to sweep something.*

(28) wáka-kóa-u né weáma-n b^wé'uu-si hí-čó'ilaa-wa
cow-pen-to I walk-PCN big-AVR UNSPEC-rope-PSV
I was out in the cow-pen; roping was going on in a big way.

(29) kába'i mám-kót-ti hí-bép-wa-k
horse foot-break-PPL UNSPEC-hit-PSV-PRF
A horse's leg was broken from being hit.

(30) mékka-'a-ria-t wéye-ka hí-kó'o-sime
far:away-EV-NZR-on go:SG-PPL UNSPEC-chew-go
He continued chewing as he went along off in the distance.

(31) Lios 'é-t 'á'a nót-ta-nee 'íka'a hí-čón-ta
God you-on it return-VR-FUT this:SG:ACC UNSPEC-slap-ACC
God will pay you back for this slap.

(32) 'ákkoo kári-po wáhiwa hi-číke
older:sister house-in inside UNSPEC-sweep
Our older sister is in the house sweeping.

The unspecified human object marker **ne-** is used infrequently, and in some cases appears to have been reanalyzed as part of the verb stem. The verbs used in the examples are the transitive stems: **sáuwe/sáu-** *to command,* **haáse** *to follow,* and **húnu(?)/hún-** *to invite.*

(33) woi-takáa wásukti-m-po 'áma né-sau-pea-n
two-body year-PL-in there UNSPEC-command-DSD-PCN
He was wanting to rule there for forty years.

(34) née 'áa né-h-há'ase
I able UNSPEC-RDP-track
I know how to track.

(35) b^wé'uu-si páhko-baa-wa-o 'áma né-hún-wa-k
big-AVR feast-DSD-PSV-when there UNSPEC-invite-PSV-PRF
When there was going to be a big feast, he was invited there.

The allomorph **na-** is used only with the verb **temáe** *to ask.*

(36) né káa hú'unea b^wé'ituk né káa ná-t-temáe-k
I not know because I not UNSPEC-RDP-ask-PRF
I don't know, because I didn't ask.

4.0. The verbal suffixes and their class ordering

The suffix system of Yaqui verbs is very complex, consisting of at least 32 morphemes that may be suffixed to verbs. There seem to be at least nine class positions after the verb stem in which they may occur, with a maximum of four or five suffixes occuring on any particular stem. The suffixes may be divided into four general classes, the first of which we designate as auxiliary-verb or modal suffixes, partly because they represent the grammaticalized versions of modal verbs.

These suffixes not only modify the meanings of the verbs to which they attach, but, along with the derivational suffixes discussed in section 2.2 of this chapter, they verbalize nouns, adjectives, or adverbs. Semantically, these suffixes relate to the domains of causation, of the emotions, of perception, and of the speech-act. Reference to all these domains invokes usages that can be based on both static and processual predicates. The inventory of these suffixes is summarized in Table 60.

-tua	to cause to	-le	to think, to be able to
-ria	to...on the behalf of	-roka	to say that...
-sae	to order to...	-'íi'aa	to want X to...
-tebo	to order, to cause to	-'éa-n	may, might do
-bae	to wish to, to want to	-maáči	to seem to
-pea	to yearn to		

Table 60. Modal suffixes

The Yaqui verb shares an important suffixal relation to several other Uto-Aztecan verbs in its employment of a pair of adverbial suffixes that convey the meanings "coming" and "going" to the verbs with which they are used. Their main verb source is indicated by their suppletive forms for singular versus plural subjects. These are displayed in Table 61.

-se	Intentive:SG	-síme	Andative:SG
-bo	Intentive:PL	-sáka	Andative:PL

Table 61. Adverbial suffixes

The Yaqui verb is marked by a number of different tense/aspect suffixes also. These signal distinct perspectives on the event described by the verb. Semantically, they include notions such as the inception or cessation of activity or the completeness with which the activity is carried out. Other distinctions include either durative (imperfective) or punctiliar (perfective) construals of the action. Other suffixes invoke conceived time relative to the speaker's time of speaking and may present the conceived time as either anterior or posterior to the time of the speech-act. The inventory of tense/aspect markers in Yaqui is shown in Table 62.

-su	to completely...	-k	Perfective
-taite	to begin to...	-n	Past Continuative
-yaáte	to cease to...	-ka	Imperfective Participle
-wa	Passive	-taka	Imperfective Simultaneous
-nee	Future, Potential	-a'u	Remote Imperfective
-naa	Future Passive	-'u	Gerundive

Table 62. Tense/aspect suffixes

The final grouping of suffixes, given in Table 63, consists of a set of subordinating suffixes. Semantically, these signal notions of contemporaneous time and the conditional or hypothetical status of stated events. Some of these obviously arise from postpositions.

-o	if, when
-patči	at the time of
-amča	as if
-apo	nominalizing suffix

Table 63. Subordinating suffixes

5.0. The suffix position classes

Although many of the suffix sequences of Yaqui can be readily described, a number of factors must be taken into account in doing so. For one, there appear to be three overlapping sets of suffixes based on the morphological class of particular verbs. Many verbs take suffixes on the bare stem. For these, suffixal order is easier to plot. A substantial number of other verbs take verbalizing suffixes of the canonical shape CV. There are four of these: **-tu**, **-ta**, **-te**, and **-ti**. Suffix order with these is also generally straightforward. Finally, there are three vocalic formatives **-'a**, **-'e**, and **-i**, which appear to occur in various suffix positions.

Beyond these considerations is the fact that several of the suffixes themselves are mutually exclusive (or very nearly so) in their occurrences, but appear to be bases for attaching other sets of suffixes. Finally, the suffix position for a given suffix cannot be simply stated as the occupancy of a single slot within the overall position class framework, but rather must be stated in terms of a range of positions within which it may occur under specific circumstances (for an analogous description of the problems in determining affix order, cf. Grimes 1964:23).

For example, if a given suffix occurs next to the verb stem, it is said to occupy suffix position one. If it also occurs word finally following a string of three other suffixes, it is said to occupy suffix position four. A plausible statement of its distributional range is that it variously occupies suffix positions one to four, since further data would likely show it to be preceded by only one suffix in certain cases and by two suffixes on other contexts. In this summary, we attempt to state only the most obvious of these positional variants.

The chart in Table 64 displays the basic position class relationships that are attested to occur among the Yaqui verbal suffixes as compiled from all of the examples contained in this work. The evidence supporting these orderings is given in subsequent paragraphs that list the preceding and following suffixal contexts for each morpheme. In addition, we mention problematic or alternative suffix orders. Down the left side of the table we list the extrametric anchoring contexts to which the suffix position class number is calculated. These include Stem, Echo-vowel (EV), and Verbalizers (-ti, -te, -ta, and -tu).

S T E M	1	2	3	4	5	6	7	8	9
	-tua -ria	-tebo -sae	-su	-bae	-wa -sime	-ka	-i -tea	-'ea	-n -nee
EV		-pea	-naa -mači	-le	-saka		-k		-o -a'u
-ti -te -ta -tu	-'íi'aa -taite -yaate -roka -taka					-bo -se		-amča	-'u -apo -patči

Table 64. Yaqui suffix position class order

Following the verb stem, these suffixes tend to occur in the same order as listed in Table 64, each modifying the complex ahead of it. More than one auxilary-verb type may be used in a given construction. Some of these are also verbs or verbalizers in their own right. The ordering relationships displayed by the chart above are supported by the following observed co-occurrences.

On quasi-morphological grounds, the descriptive statements are divided into three sections. The first section details the first and second position suffixes, whereas the following section treats the intermediate position suffixes. The third section presents the final position suffixes.

5.1. First and second position suffixes

The first and second position suffixes include the causative **-tua**, the applicative **-ria**, the indirect quotative **-'íi'aa**, the inceptive **-taite**, the cessative **-yaate**, the quotative **-roka**, the participializer **-taka**, and the imperative **-tebo**. (The modal **-mači**, the strong desiderative **-pea**, and the participializer **-le** are also considered to be first and second position suffixes, but due to problematic orderings will be discussed in the following section.)

The causative **-tua** and the applicative **-ria** both occur immediately following verb stems. In addition they may occur in either order, as shown in examples (1) and (2). Thus it is simplest to call them first and second position suffixes, with the proviso that, if only one of them occurs with the verb, it will invariably occupy first position.

(1) háisaaka 'emé'e bʷáana 'íntok híapsi-ta   née siók-tua-ria
    why   you:PL cry   CNJ   heart-ACC me sad-CAU-APL
    Why do you all cry and make my heart sad for me?

(2) 'útte'a-po tékil-ta 'áu 'á'a hóo-ria-tua-k
    force-in work-ACC RFL him do-APL-CAU-PRF
    He forced him to do the work for him.

The causative **-tua** is followed immediately by the imperative **-sae** and **-tebo,** the desideratives **-pea** and **-bae,** the imperfective **-ka,** the perfective **-k,** the future **-nee,** and the past continuative **-n.**

(3) 'íntok né káa né 'ám kí'i-tua-pea húni'i
    CNJ   I not me them bite-CAU-DSD even
    And I don't intend to let them bite me, either.

Examples (4)–(6) illustrate the use of causative **-tua** with transitive verbs.

(4) née mékka-bétana 'á'a haríu-tua-wa-k
    I   far:away-from him search-CAU-PSV-PRF
    I was sent here from far away to look for him.

(5) 'émpo há'ani 'ám sú'u-tóhi-tua-bae-'e-tea
    you maybe them release-put-CAU-DSD-EV-QUO
    They say that maybe you are trying to make them stop that.

(6) kaábe né 'áma 'ám maná'a-tua-k
    no:one me there them place-CAU-PRF
    No one made me put them there.

With intransitive verbs **-tua** becomes a transitivizer, as shown by examples (7) and (8).

(7) kát 'á'a si-sím-tua   wánna'abo 'á'a kón-ta
    don't it RDP-go:SG-CAU other:side it   circle-VR
    Don't let it get away; block it from the other side.

(8) bátte káa 'ám ko-kót-tua-k
    nearly not them RDP-sleep-CAU-PRF
    They almost kept them from sleeping.

(9) 'itóm 'á'a weám-tua-ka-'apo-béna-si
    our   him walk:SG-CAU-PPL-GND-like-AVR
    as if we had caused him to walk

(10) bémpo káa 'áman 'á'a kibák-tua-k
     they not there him enter:SG-CAU-PRF
     They wouldn't let him go in there.

(11) káa kía taéwai-m ténni-tua-nee
     not just day-PL:ACC run:PL-CAU-FUT
     Don't just waste time.

The applicative **-ria** is immediately followed by the imperative **-sai** in example (12), the imperfective **-ka** in example (13), the passive **-wa** in (15), and by the perfective **-k** in (17) and (18). It can also be followed by the indirect desiderative **-'ii'aa,** the future suffixes **-nee** and **-naa,** the andatives **-se** and **-sime,** and in some contexts by the causative **-tua.**

(12) 'áapo 'á'a yá'a-ria-sai-wa-k
     he   him do-APL-IMP-PSV-PRF
     He was ordered to do it for him.

(13) tabú-ta   'á'a mé'e-ria-ka 'á'a kúhha'abʷa-k
     rabbit-ACC her kill-APL-PRF it   broil-PRF
     Having killed a rabbit for her, he broiled it.

(14) née lióh-ta-u   'enčím bʷán-ria
     I   God-CON-to   you:PL cry-APL
     I pray to God for you.

(15) kó'om-čép-te-ka   tú'isi   mám-tóh-te-ria-wa-k
     down-jump-VR-PPL   very   hand-clap-VR-APL-PSV-PRF
     When he jumped down, he was applauded vigorously.

(16) tóri-m 'únnaa   híta-yée-bʷá-bʷa'a-ria
     rat-PL very:much   thing-people-RDP-eat-APL
     Rats eat an awful lot of people's things.

(17) tú'ii mó'obe-ta 'áu   hínu-ria-k
     good hat-ACC   RFL   buy-APL-PRF
     He bought himself a good hat.

(18) čukúi-ba'a-ta   'á'a   bʷása-'a-ria-k
     black-water-ACC   him   cook-EV-APL-PRF
     She cooked coffee for him.

In sentences (19) and (20) **-ria** becomes a kind of a causative, illustrating a common trait of Uto-Aztecan in which the categories causative and applicative overlap.

(19) hunáman lisénsia-ria-wa-k   (20) 'enčím bó'o-hóo-ria-su-k-a'u
     there   license-APL-PSV-PRF   your:PL road-make-APL-CMP-PRF-GND
     They were given a license (to work) there.   *that which you did*

The indirect desiderative **-'íi'aa** occurs in first position following both transitive and intransitive verbs. In certain cases it follows the verbalizing suffix **-tu**. It is followed only by the participial **-ka** and the passive **-wa** in our data.

(21) 'áapo tú'u-lútu'uria-ta 'enčim   hú'uneeya-'íi'aa
     he   good-truth-ACC   you:PL:ACC know-IN:DSD
     He wants all of you to know the real truth.

(22) 'émpo bʷá'a-m-ta   káa née bʷá'a-'íi'aa
     you   eat-NZR-ACC   not me eat-IN:DSD
     You don't want me to eat any food.

(23) sí'ime-m   tekipánoa-'íi'aa
     all-PL:ACC   work-IN:DSD
     He wants everyone to work.

(24) hó'aa-po=te 'enčí   tawá-'íi'aa
     house-in=we you:SG:ACC stay-IN:DSD
     We want you to stay at home.

(25) hunám-mea-sa='em   tú'u-wam-po   yó'o-tu-'íi'aa-wa
     those-INST-CON=you good-NZR-in   grow-VR-IN:DSD-PSV
     It is desired that you mature in goodness by means of those things.

(26) híka-u   mámmaa   čaí-wam-ta   čá'a-tu-'íi'aa-ka-i
     upward-to   hand   yell-NZR-ACC   cease-VR-IN:DSD-PPL-PPL
     He held up his hands because he wanted the yelling to cease.

Both the inceptive **-taite** and the cessative **-yaate** invariably occur immediately following a verb stem. The examples contained in our data appear to show these two suffixes being followed almost exclusively by the perfective **-k,** but this may simply be a limitation of the data as suggested by sentence (29).[3]

---

3   It is purely accidental that the examples entered in our files for the morphemes **-taite** and **-yaáte** are only followed by the perfective **-k** and the participial **-ka** . Either of these suffixes may take any of the total set of verbal suffixes with which it is conceptually compatible.

(27) húnak taáka-m yóhti-taite-k
    then fruit-PL fall-INC-PRF
    Then the fruit began to fall.

(28) čú'u 'íntok čaaí-yaáte-k   'á'a noka-m-ta   híkkaha-ka-i
    dog CNJ   bark-STOP-PRF him speak-NZR-ACC hear-PPL-PPL
    And the dog stopped barking when he heard him speak.

As far as tense/aspect is concerned, sentence (27) could equally well have been expressed as (29) in which the future **-nee** follows the inceptive =**táite**, whose final vowel is ablauted to **-i**.

(29) bʷáh-su-k   'ála   yóhti-táiti-nee
    ripe-CPL-PRF indeed fall:PL-INC-FUT
    However, when they are ripe, they will begin to fall.

What seems to be a relatively recent innovation in the Yaqui tense/aspect system is the usage of the verb **hapte** *to stand up*:PL as an inceptive. This seems to be used where humans are involved and **-taite** is used where animals or things are concerned. Illustrating usages of the inceptive **hápte**, Sebahti's text provides the examples shown in sentence (30).

(30) kó'om lúula té 'ám mu-múhi-hápti-nee   si mu-múhi-hápte-a-k-o
    down straight we them RDP-shoot-INC-FUT if RDP-shoot-INC-PSV-PRF-if
    We will begin to shoot straight down at them if they begin to shoot at us.

The cessative **-yaáte** may also be used as seen in sentence (31).

(31) 'ám nók-nássua-yáati-'ii'aa-ka-i   pá'akun 'ám bíttua-k
    them word-fight-STOP-IN:DSD-PPL-PPL outside them send-PRF
    Wanting them to stop arguing, he sent them outside.

The preference, however, seems to be to use **-yaáte** in the perfective aspect as suggested by sentence (32).

(32) 'iním nássua-yáate-k-o   húme'e waté húci nótte-k
    here fight-STOP-PRF-when those   others again return-PRF
    When the fighting stopped (in the Yaqui area), the others (from Yucatan) began to return.

The quotative suffix **-roka** derives from a main verb usage. It typically follows directly after the stem that is its complement. It may also follow the stativizing participial suffix **-ti**, which in other contexts serves as a subordinator. It is followed in our data only by the future **-nee** and the past continuative **-n**. In certain construactions, **-roka** is tightly bound to the preceding verb stem by an echo vowel, as can be seen in sentence (36).

(33) 'á'abo   'itó-u noí-ti-roka
    over:here us-to come-PPL-QUO
    He says that he is coming over here to visit us.

(34) 'itépo 'íntok náu   hínko'o-laa-rók-nee
    we   and   together race-PPL-QUO-FUT
    And we will say that we are going to run a race.

(35) bémpo náabúuh-ti-a   kát-róka-n
    they on:through-PPL-PPL go:PL-QUO-PCN
    They said that they were going on through.

(36) 'é=wi=m   nói-ti-róka 'úhbʷán-ta 'ém mám-po yečá-'a-roka
    you=to=they go-PPL-QUO plea-ACC your hand-in place-EV-QUO
    They said that they were coming to you; they said that they had a request to place in your hands.

The stative participle **-taka** reflects a fusion of the sequence of the verbalizer **-ta** and the imperfective **-ka**. It invariably occurs in first position following the stem to which it attaches, and appears to be followed only by the stative suffix **-i**.

(37) bát-naáte-ka née káa yó'o-taka-i
first-begin-PPL I not old-being-PPL
in earlier times, when I was young

This suffix may be used with nouns, pronouns, and adverbs as well as with verbs. Examples (38)–(40) show the use of **-taka** with nouns.

(38) hunáa'a=san kóba-taka sí'ime-m nésauwe-me
that:one=EXP head-PPL all-PL:ACC command-NZR
That one, being the head, rules over everyone.

(39) sisí'iwok-taka noóka
iron-PPL speak
Even though it is iron (telegraph key), it talks.

(40) 'áma hó'aa-k-an pahko'olaa-taka-i
there house-have-PCN festal:dancer-PPL-PPL
He used to live there because he was a festal dancer.

Example (41) shows the use of **-taka** with a pronoun. This has the effect of turning the pronoun into an emphatic personal pronoun.

(41) 'émpo-taka húni'i lú'u-ti-nee
you-PPL even end-PPL-FUT
Even you yourself will come to an end.

Example (42) and (43) illustrate **-taka** used with adjectives:

(42) bʷé'ituk néhpo túa-taka húnen 'emó-u hiía
because I indeed-PPL thus you:PL-to say
Because I tell you with certainty that it is so.

(43) 'íntok sí'ime-taka húni'i
and all-PPL even
and everything as well

It also serves as the second constituent in compound verbs, usually being attached to either the connector **-ti-** or the participial **-la.** This is its most frequent use.

(44) lót-ti-laa-taka ne wée
tire-PPL-PPL-PPL I go
I am going along very tired.

(45) bʷaáro-m senú mačúk-ti-taka mámni sentaabo-m
purslane-PL:ACC one grasp-PPL-PPL five cent-PL
One bunch of purslane costs five cents.

(46) kúta-pú'ato-m báksia-taka mo-móbelaa-čá'aka
wood-plate-PL:ACC wash-PPL RDP-face:down-suspended
The wooden plates were washed and lying face down.

(47) baákot kó'oko-si 'aú-la-taka húya-u kibáke-k
snake pain-AVR be-PPL-PPL woods-to enter:SG-PRF
The wounded snake entered the woods.

The imperative **-tebo** usually occurs immediately after the stem in position one. However, if the causative **-tua** is present, it occurs in position one and **-tebo** in position two. The suffixes that attach directly to **-tebo** include the completive **-su,** the desiderative **-bae,** the imperfective **-ka,** and the perfective **-k.**

(48) 'íntok sí'ime-m 'áu 'ám bít-tebo-su-ka čúkula
CNJ all-PL:ACC RFL them see-IMP-CPL-PPL after
And after he had caused all of them to see him...

(49) 'ám bít-tá'aa-tua-tébo-bae-n
 them see-know-CAU-IMP-DSD-PCN
 He was wanting to command him to come to know them by sight.

Examples (50)–(52) give common usages of **-tebo** IMP/CAU.

(50) 'asuka-ta tu-túh-tebo-ka dulse-ta yáa-k
 sugar-ACC RDP-grind-IMP-PPL candy-ACC make-PRF
 Ordering them to grind sugar, he made candy.

(51) tómi-ta mabéta-ka 'am sú'u-tóhi-tebo-k
 money-ACC receive-PPL them release-place-IMP-PRF
 Having received money he ordered that they be released.

(52) 'au yó'o-ri-tebo
 RFL respect-PPL-IMP
 He causes himself to be respected.

5.2. Problematic orderings near the stem

Three other suffixes arfe considered to be first and second position suffixes even though they do not occupy either of those places in Table 64. They are the strong desiderative **-pea**, the modal **-mači**, and the suffix **-le**. The strong desiderative **-pea**, which expresses a bit more intense degree of yearning than **-bae**, may be preceded by either a verb stem or by the causitive **-tua**. It is followed by the completive **-su**, the passive **-wa**, the imperfective **-ka**, the past continuative **-n**, or the gerundial **-'u**.

(53) ká=ne 'íntok póčo'o-ku hó'a-pea
 not=I and woods-in home-DSD
 I don't want to live in the woods any longer.

(54) lót-ti-laa-taka né wée báa-yúmho'e-pea
 tire-PPL-PPL-being I come at:once-rest-DSD
 I'm coming really tired; I yearn to rest once for all.

(55) sí'ime=te tekipánoa-pea
 all=we work-DSD
 We all have a desire to work.

(56) kée née ké'e 'íntok née káa née 'ám kí'i-tua-pea
 not:yet me bite and I not me them bite-CAU-DSD
 They haven't bitten me yet, and I have no desire to cause them to bite me.

(57) húme'e sirkeeo-m bítču-pee-wa-n
 those circus:men-PL stare-DSD-PSV-PCN
 They really wanted to see the circus performers.

(58) káa 'á'a yóopna-k bʷé'ituk bʷán-pe'ea-k
 not him answer-PRF because cry-DSD-PRF
 She didn't answer him because she wanted to cry.

(59) 'útte'a wéye mo'oči-m-meu yebíh-pea-ka-i
 strong go Los Mochis-to arrive-DSD-PPL-PPL
 He went as fast as he could because he really wanted to get to Los Mochis.

The modal **-mači** usally occurs in first position following a verb. It has wide spectrum of meanings including "seem to be, appear to be." Basically **maáči** denotes "light, visibility." It may also follow one of the verbalizing suffixes **-ta** or **-ti** and the connector vowel **-'a**. It may be followed by the participle **-le** as in example (60), by the imperfective participle **-ka** as in example (61), or by the perfective **-k**.

(60) hobé'eso-ta 'áu bʷá'a-mači-le-ka
 ram-ACC RFL eat-seem-think-PPL
 because he was going along thinking that he was going to eat a ram

(61) tú'u-wa-ta   'áma 'emo   téu-máči-le-ka-i
     good-NOM-ACC there yourselves find-"able"-PRE-PPL-PPL
     because you thought that you would find what was good for you there...

Another pair of problematic orderings are seen in the instances in which **maáči** follows completive **-su**. In example (62) it may be functioning as a main verb. In (63) it follows the verbalizer **-tu** and is in turn followed by the presumptive suffix **-le** and a pair of participial suffixes. Finally, in example (64) it precedes the verbalizer **-tu** and, as in (62), it may also be serving as a main verb.

(62) bát^wee b^wé'uu-'u-tea ká-ak   yéu-baa-su-maáči
     river big-CON-QUO   no-where   out-cross-CMP-appear
     They say that the river is up; apparently there is no place to cross it.

(63) túa   káa 'á'a hunáa'a-tu-mačí-le-ka-i
     truly not him that-VR-appear-PRE-PPL-PPL
     He truly did not think that he was the one. or
     He truly did not think that it appeared to be him.

(64) húu'u káa yéu 'á'a mačí-a-tua-me
     that not out him appear-VR-CAU-NZR
     the one who causes him not to appear

The suffix **-le** occurs immediately following verb stems. Often it also follows the suffix **-mači**, and thus can be considered a first and second position suffix. Its form with a long vowel also follows the completive **-su**.

(65) híta 'áu tá'aa-le-me
     thing RFL know-PRE-NZR
     one who thinks he knows a lot

(66) senú két 'áu 'áawe-le-nee   káa húni'i 'áawe-ka-i
     one also RFL be:able-PRE-FUT   not even be:able-PPL-PPL
     One may also think that he is capable, when he really isn't capable.

(67) káuwih-ta 'áu bít-le-ka
     fox-ACC   RFL see-PRE-PPL
     thinking that he saw a fox

5.3. The intermediate position suffixes

The intermediate position suffixes include the completive **-su**, the imperative **-sae**, the future passive **-naa**, the desiderative **-bae**, the passive **-wa**, the andatives **-sime** and **-saka**, the imperfective **-ka**, the future **-nee**, the adverbials **-se** and **-bo**, the stative **-i**, the perfective **-k**, the subjunctive **-'ea**, and the appelative **-tea**.

The completive suffix **-su** marks a pair of tense/aspect differences that clearly contrast with the usages of the perfective **-k**. Whereas the perfective **-k** marks simple past in such forms as **'á'a čuk-ta-k** *he cut it*, the usage of **-su** adds to that construal the notion of completeness. Thus, **'á'a čúk-ta-su-k** can be glossed as either "he completely cut it" or as "he finished cutting it."

Completive **-su** must be considered a first to third position suffix. It most commonly follows verb stems in first suffix position, but it also follows the causative suffix **-tua**, the imperative **-tebo**, and the desiderative **-pea**. The suffixes that may follow **-su** include the desiderative **-bae**, the passive **-wa**, the stative **-i**, the imperfective **-ka**, the subjunctive **-'ea** (= **-'ee**), and the perfective **-k**.

(1) báat   'án-su-baa-wa   (2) 'enči   née bép-su-nee
    once:for:all be-CPL-DSD-PSV   you:SG:ACC I   hit-CPL-FUT
    It is desired that this be finished   *I'll clobber you.*
    once and for all.

A pair of problematic orderings involving **-su** is seen in its preceding both the modal **-maáči** and the applicative **-ria** in a few instances.

The imperative **-sae/-sai** follows verb stems, the verbalizing suffixes **-te** with transitive verbs, and **-ti** with intransitive verbs, an echo-vowel, and the applicative **-ria**. It often occurs word finally, but may also be followed by the imperfective **-ka** and by the passive suffix **-wa**.

(3) 'áapo 'enčí née haríu-sae 'á-u='e'e hí'oh-te-sai-wa
he you me hunt-IMP him-to=you write-VR-IMP-PSV
He asked me to find you; he wants you to write to him.

(4) 'enči ne 'ám 'é'e-ria-sae
you:ACC me them guard-APL-IMP
I ask you to guard them for me.

(5) kaábe née 'áma 'ám maná-'a-sae
no:one me there them place-EV-IMP
No one ordered me to put them there.

(6) 'áman='e'e nói-ti-sai-wa
there=you go:SG-CON-IMP-PSV
You are ordered to go there.

(7) 'ili haíki ta'á-po 'áma='a tawá-sae-ka 'á-u 'úhbʷana-k
few amount day-in there=him stay-IMP-PPL him-to plead-PRF
They begged him to stay there for a few days.

(8) 'áman née tekipánoa-sai-wa-t-iia húu'u
there I work-IMP-PSV-CON-say that(boy)
"I was ordered to go work there," said the boy.

The desiderative **-bae** may occur immediately following the verb stem, as shown by example (9). In other contexts it follows the imperative **-tebo** (as mentioned previously) and the applicative **-ria**. It is followed by the andative **-sime** in example (10), and in other contexts below by the passive **-wa,** the imperfective **-ka,** the perfective **-k,** and the past continuative **-n**.

(9) híba káa sebe-bae 'íi'i taéwai
just not cold-DSD this day
Today just doesn't want to get cold.

(10) 'íno=ne bám-si-bíča 'emó-u hí'ohte-báa-síme-ka
RFL=I hurry-ADV-see you:PL write-DSD-go:SG-PPL
I am pressuring myself because of wanting to proceed with this letter to you.

As a suffix **-bae** means "to wish to, to want to." In the following example, **bae** is used as a verb meaning "to want to." This example, which was given to Dedrick by Castro, is the only instance he has noted of this type of usage.

(11) báe-ka húni'i káa bá-bae-k
wish-PPL even not RDP-wish-PRF
Although he wanted to, he didn't want to want to.

The desiderative **-bae** is frequently used to indicate the future tense. The absence of any other overt tense marking usually indicates that the action is concurrent with the time of the narration. This is one of the most frequently occurring of all the suffixes.

(12) 'émpo káa=née híkkahi-bae-ka káa=née híkkaha
you not=me hear-DSD-PPL not=me hear
You don't hear me because you don't want to.

(13) 'áa-mak=ne 'etého-bae-n
him-with=I visit-DSD-PCN
I was wanting to talk with him.

(14) wáa'a wéye-me hí'i-b^wá-bae-ka wéye
　　 that　go-NZR　IZR-eat-DSD-PPL　go
　　 The one who is moving is in motion because he is searching for food.

(15) káa=né 'íntok híaps-i-bae
　　 not=I　and　live-PPL-DSD
　　 I don't want to live any longer.

(16) sáka-'a-bae=te
　　 go:PL-EV-DSD=we
　　 We are going now.

(17) Liós yúk-tua-bae-'e-te-k　yúk-tua-nee
　　 God　rain-CAU-DSD-EV-VR-PRF:if　rain-CAU-FUT
　　 If God wants it to rain, he will cause it to rain.

(18) haí=sa téa-tua-báa-wa
　　 how=Q　name-CAU-DSD-PSV
　　 What are they going to name him/her?

The passive **-wa** follows the causative **-tua** in sentences (19) and (20). It can also follow the applicative **-ria** and the verbalizers **-tu, -ta,** and **-te**. It may also occur as early as position one after the stem. Other suffixes that precede it include the desiderative **-sae/-sai**, the desiderative **-bae**, the connective **-'a**, the completive **-su**, and the indirect desiderative **-ii'aa**. It is immediately followed by the imperfective **-ka**, the perfective **-k**, the past continuative **-n**, and the temporal/conditional **-o**.

(19) káa-tú'ii-k　kóba-ka　wée-nee hák　'o-'ómti-tua-wa-k-o
　　 NEG-good-ACC　head-have　go-FUT　where　RDP-anger-CAU-PSV-PRF-CND
　　 A person is not apt to use his head if he has been made angry.

(20) mékkaa-bétana née 'á'abo　'á'a　haríu-tua-wa
　　 far:away-from　I　over:here　him　search-CAU-PSV
　　 I am sent over here, from far away, to find him.

(21) náu té hínko'olaa-rók-nee
　　 together we race-QUO-FUT
　　 We will say that we are going to run a race.

(22) hunám-mea 'emé'e yó'o-tu-'íi'aa-wa
　　 those-INST　you:PL　grow-VR-IN:DSD-PSV
　　 It is desired that you grow by means of those things.

The singular andative **-sime** occurs immediately following verbs stems as well as following the verbalizer **-ti**, the causative **-tua**, the applicative **-ria**, and the passive **-ri**. Immediately following suffixes include the imperfective **-ka**, the past continuative **-n**, and the conditional **-o**. It also occurs word finally. The plural andative **-saka** occurs only immediately following a verb stem in our data and it is also followed only by the subjunctive **-'ea** and the future **-nee**.

(23) 'á'a čái-tua-síme
　　 him yell-CAU-go:SG
　　 He causes him to go around yelling

(24) haámuč-im 'áe-t　čá'aka b^wán-saka
　　 woman-PL him-on follow cry-go:PL
　　 The women followed him crying.

The imperfective **-ka** in distinct verb words directly follows verb stems, the verbalizers **-ta** and **-tu**, the indirect desiderative **-'íi'aa**, the desiderative **-bae**, the strong desiderative **-pea**, the participial **-le**, the completive **-su**, the passive **-ri**, the applicative **-ria**, the passive **-wa**, the cessative **-yaate**, and the andatives **-sime** and **-saka**. It also occurs word finally.

(25) masó-m sú'a-ka 'áu 'anía
　　 deer-PL:ACC kill:PL-PPL RFL help
　　 He earns his living by killing deer.

(26) 'á-e   'án-su-ka   kabá'i-ta   'á-u   nót-ta-k
     it-INST be-CMP-PPL horse-ACC him-to return-VR-PPL
     When he finished with the horse, he returned it to him.

(27) muúku-k   bʷíčia-tu-ka-i
     die-PRF   worm-VR-PPL-PPL
     He died as a result of having become wormy.

(28) tékwa-ta   béak-ta-ka   náta'a-wát-ta-ka   'á'a   núk-siíme
     meat-ACC slice-VR-PPL pile:it-throw-VR-PPL it   take-go:SG
     Having sliced the meat and laying it in a pile, he takes it away.

(29) 'ilí   haíki   taéwai-m saka-'a-tua-su-ka   siíka
     little how:many day-PL   go:PL-EV-CAU-CMP-PPL went
     After whiling away a few days, he left.

(30) 'emo 'ómti-tua-ka   'ínen hiía
     RFL anger-CAU-PPL thus say
     They say that because they're angry.

Although the imperfective **-ka** frequently occurs in word final position, it is also commonly followed by suffixes such as the stative **-i**, the gerundial **-'u**, the perfective **-k**, the past continuative **-n**, the subjunctive **-'ea**, and the gerundial **-apo**.

(31) múk-su-ka-n
     die-CPL-PPL-PCN
     He was completely dead. or *He had died.*

(32) 'á'a wók-hahá-tebo-ka-i   húnen hiía 'á'a mé'e-tebo-bae-ka-i
     him foot-follow-IMP-PPL-PPL thus say him kill-IMP-DSD-PPL-PPL
     He said that because he was commanding him to trail him because he was wanting to command him to kill him.

(33) 'ínepo 'á'a bíča-k naámukia-tu-k-o   wečía-tu-ka-n
     I   him see-PRF drunk-VR-PRF-when fallen-VR-PPL-PCN
     I saw him when he was drunk; he had fallen down.

(34) híaki-m   tehál-bae-ka-'ea-n
     yaqui-PL destroy-DSD-PPL-SJV-PCN
     He was wanting to annihilate the Yaquis.

The future **-nee**, and its passive form **-naa**, indicate that the action of the verb will or may take place. Future **-nee** may also be immediately preceded by the simulfactive suffix **-le**. Although the future suffix **-nee** may occur as early as in position one, it most frequently occurs in word final position following such suffixes as the causative **-tua**, the applicative **-ria**, the quotative **-roka**, the desiderative **-bae**, the completive **-su**, the andatives **-sime** and **-sáka** (> **čáka**), the presumptive **le-**, the verbalizing suffixes **-te**, **-ti**, and **-tu**, and the subjunctive **-'ea**. In non-final positions, it is followed by the imperfective **-ka**, the gerundial **-'u**, the appelative **-'etea**, and the conditional complex **-'e-te-k-o** EV-VR-PRF-CND.

(35) bó'o-bít-nee táa čukúi ba'á-ta   kaíta-nee
     lay-see-FUT but black water-ACC nothing-FUT
     He may wait for it, but there won't be any coffee.

(36) senú 'áu 'áawe-le-nee   káa húni'i 'áawe-ka-i
     one RFL know:how-PRE-FUT NEG even know:how-PPL-PPL
     A person may think that he knows how to do it, when he really does not know how.

(37) wée'epulai-m 'á'a tékil-ta   béhe'e-wa-ta   mabét-čáka-nee
     one:by:one-PL his work-POSS worth-NZR-ACC receive-go:PL-FUT
     Everyone will go on receiving the worth of his work.

The suffix **-naa** is the passive form of future active **-nee**. It may be preceded immediately by a verb stem, an echo-vowel **-a**, the causative **-tua**, or the applicative **-ria**. When it occurs on the verb of a relative clause, it may be followed by the gerundial postposition **-'u**. Typical examples of the usages of the suffix **-naa** are given in examples (38)–(40).

(38) hunáa'a tú'u-wa-ta yá'a-ria-naa
    that (one) good-ABS-ACC do-APL-FUT:PSV
    Justice will be done on that person's behalf.

(39) ha-hána hiá-ka 'átbʷa-naa
    RDP-absurd say-PPL laugh:at-FUT:PSV
    He will be laughed at for talking absurdly.[4]

(40) hunáe taéwai-tči áe-t 'á'a yó'o-ri-naa-'u
    that day-on it-on his revere-VR-FUT:PSV-GND
    On that day he will be respected.

The adverbial suffixes **-bo** and **-se** are followed only by the perfective **-k** and by the temporal suffix **-o** in our data. [In examples (43) and (47) **-se** is followed by the imperfective participial **-ka**, and in example (46), by the temporal suffix **-o**. Preceding contexts include verb stems, the applicative **-ria**, the stative **-i**, and the gerundial **-'u**, which appears to be another anomalous ordering.

(41) láuti bʷá'a-m-ta 'á'a haríu-ria-se
    quickly eat-NZR-ACC him search-APL-go:SG
    He went to look for food for him right away.

(42) tebó-te-i-ta né 'á-u tóhi-'í-se-k
    greet-VR-NZR-ACC I him-to bring-EV-go:SG-PRF
    I went to take greetings to him.

(43) yéu-siŋka wasá-m-meu-bíča híta nénki-se-ka-i
    out-went field-PL-to-site thing sell-go:SG-PPL-STAT
    He went out to the field to sell his wares.

(44) hán=te hi'i-bʷá-bo
    HRT=we IZR-eat-go:PL
    Let's go eat.

(45) 'áman=té 'á'a bít-bo-k
    there=we him see-go:PL-PRF
    We went there to see him.

(46) kúpte-o ta'á-ta 'aman wéčí-se-o tábero-m
    evening-when sun-POS there fall-go:SG-when Tabero-PL
    heká-'a-wi yáhi-bo-k
    wind-EV-to arrive:PL-go:PL-PRF
    In the evening as the sun was setting, they were coming into Tabero's Wind.

(47) 'ínepo 'íntok kibáke-k kári-wi bʷá'a-m-ta
    I and enter-PRF house-to food-NZR-ACC
    haríu-se-ka-i bʷé'ituk ne tébaure
    hunt-go:SG-PPL-STAT because I hungry
    I went into the house looking for food because I was hungry.

The suffix **-i** immediately follows certain verb stems. In addition, it follows the imperfective participle **-taka**, the cessative **-yaate**, the passive **-ri**, the completive **-su**, and the imperfective **-ka**. In turn, it is immediately followed by the andative **-se**, the subjunctive **-'ea**, and the appelative **-tea**.

---

4   Castro translated this example: "Diciendo miles de cosas para que la gente se ría."

The verbal suffix **-i** frequently follows the participializing suffix **-ka**. But whereas **-ka** is often used as a subordinator, **-ka-i** generally signals the end of the phrase.[5]

(48) hakwóo-sa humák lú'u-ti-nee-ka-i   kaíbu lú'u-ti-nee b^wé'ituk híba 'é-'ét-wa
when-Q   perhaps end-VR-FUT-PPL-STAT never end-VR-FUT because always RPD-plant-PSV
When would it ever run out; it will never run out because it is always being planted.

(49) 'í'an báhi taéwai yúk-yáate-ka-i
now three day   rain-stop-PPL-STAT
This is the third day since it rained.[6]

The perfective **-k** indicates that the action is considered as a bounded whole and not as an ongoing process. It usually also marks past time, but not always. The perfective **-k** most commonly occurs in word final suffix postion. However, it can be followed by the conditional **-o** and the gerundial **-a'u**. It is preceded by almost all of the other suffixes in particular verb words.

(50) 'ín 'éeriam moí-su-k   'ín híapsi moóyo-k sí'ime lú'u-te-k   heká-po sií-ka
my thoughts decay-CMP-PRF my life decay-PRF all   end-VR-PRF wind-in go-PRF
My thoughts are decayed, my life is decayed, everything has ended, it has "gone with the wind."

(51) kaíta-'apo taáwa-k
nothing-in remain-PRF
It came to nothing.

(52) hunúen=né weám-si-sime-k   búsan wásuktia-m yumá-'apo-táhtia húnak né yéu-siíka
thus=I   walk-RDP-go-PRF six years   attain-NZR-until then I out-go
That is what I did for six years, then I left.

(53) tebó-te-i-ta   né 'a-u tóhi-'i-se-k
greet-VR-NZR-ACC I her-to bring-EV-come-PRF
I have come to bring her greetings.

(54) čúbala   náu katé-ka=su   'émo tó'o-saha-k
short:time together go-PPL=EMP RFL leave-go:PL-PRF
After traveling together for a short time, they separated.

The subjunctive **-'ea**, in its suffixal usages, follows the imperfective **-ka**. In turn it may be followed by the future **-nee**, the past continuative **-n**, or the gerundial **-'u**. It also occurs in word final position.

(55) puéplo-ta-u=ne nók-báe-ka-'ea
people-ACC-to=I talk-DSD-PPL-think
I would like to speak to the people.

(56) sí'ime=ta yá'a-pea-ka-'ea-n   'ó'obek
all=ACC do-DSD-PPL-think-PCN although
though he was wishing that he could do everything

(57) née tóme-k-o   páhko-u née wée-'éa-n
I money-have-if feast-to I go-SJV-PCN
If I had money, I would go to the feast.

---

5   This **-i** may be an alternate form of the past participializer **-ri**; e.g.: **yá'a-ri** *done*, **kí'i-ri** *bitten, a bite*, or it may be a different suffix in its own right. Examples: **kó'om** *down*; **kó'om-i** *downward*; **hiabíh-te-i** *resurrected*; **béhe'e-wai-i** *(its) value*; **'ésso-i** *hidden*; **'etého-i** *conversation, a story*; **'etého-su-i** *related completely*; **tebó-te-i** *a greeting* (See Example (53), p. 376.) We have generally glossed **-i** as PPL. Apparently, we have two or three homophonous morphemes **-i**.

6   Spanish translation: ...despues de que terminó la lluvia.

5.4. The final position suffixes

The final position suffixes include the past continuative **-n**, the conditional **-o**, the conditional complex **-'e-te-k-o**, the gerundial **-'u**, the gerundial **-'Vpo**, the counter expectation **-amča**, and the sequential **-patči**.

Regarding tense, only the past continuative marker **-n** specifically indicates the time at which the action occurred. This suffix occurs in word final position and follows a wide variety of suffixes, including the verbalizer **-te**, the quotative **-roka**, the desiderative **-bae**, the strong desiderative **-pea**, the passive **-wa**, the imperfective **-ka**, the appelative **-tea**, and the subjunctive **-'ea**.

(58) lolá-ta 'asóa-m 'iníka'a 'ábači-róka-n
    Lola-POS child-PL this:one:ACC brother-VR-PCN
    Lola's children used to call this man "brother."

The temporal/conditional suffix **-o** is similarly restricted to word final position, but follows a wide range of other suffixes, as well as immediately following verb stems.

(59) 'állee-sáka kúpte-o ta'á-ta 'áman wéču-k-o táberom-me-wi
    happy-go:PL eve-when sun-POS there fall-go-when Taberom-CON-to

    yáha-k ta'á-ta 'áman wét-ču-k-o
    arrive:PL-PRF sun-POS there fall-CMP-PRF-when
    They were traveling along happily as the sun was setting, and arrived at Taberom after sunset.

(60) káa 'enčím sáha-k-o yokó=ne páan-im káa bʷá'a-nee
    not you:PL go:PL-PRF-if tomorrow=I bread-PL:ACC not eat-FUT
    If you people don't leave, I won't have any bread to eat tomorrow.

(61) káa née 'ú'ute búite-o née bʷíh-'ea-n
    not I strong run-if me grab-think-PCN
    If I had not run fast, he would have grabbed me.

(62) 'óri-tu-k-o 1864 'á'a wéeya-o hunúm háku'u
    this-VR-PRF-when 1864 it go-when there somewhere
    This happened during 1864, there somewhere.

The conditional complex **-'e-te-k-o** occurs only word finally, following the desiderative **-bae**, the passive **-wa**, and the future **-nee**.

(63) senú hákun-bíča bíttua-baa-wa-'a-te-k-o segúuro-po wée-baa-nee
    one where-site send-DSD-PSV-EV-VR-PRF-if secure-in go-DSD-FUT
    If someone is to be sent somewhere, he will want to go with expense money.

(64) tú'ii-'éa-n té káa ho'ó-t 'am pú'ak-ta-nee-'e-te-k-o
    good-think-PCN (SJV) we not back-on them carry-VR-FUT-EV-VR-PRF-CND
    It would be good if we didn't have to carry them on our backs.

The gerundial **-a'u** usually occurs in word final position but may be followed by the accusative singular **-ta** or the accusative plural **-m**. It marks both relative and adverbial clauses, contributing the idea of a terminated state in past time. The usage of **-V'u** and **-'Vpo** is almost identical.

(65) wáme'e hó'aa-raa-m-tu-k-a'u-m kaíta-tu-k
    those house-ABS-PL-VR-PRF-GND-PL nothing-VR-PRF
    What had been the houses there, disappeared.

(66) wáa'a ró'i-tu-la-tu-k-a'u kúpti kíkte-k
    that cripple-VR-PPL-VR-PRF-GND quickly stand:SG-PRF
    The one who had been crippled, stood up quickly.

(67) wáa'a hámut-tu-k-a'u   wakáh-tu-k
     that woman-VR-PRF-GND cow-VR-PRF
     The one who had been a woman, was turned into a cow.

The gerundial suffix **-'u** may occur as early as in the first suffix position after the verb stem, but it is invariably in word final position in all contexts in which it occurs. It is also preceded by the indirect desiderative **-'íi'aa**, the strong desiderative **-pea**, the andative **-sime**, the subjunctive **-'ea**, and the imperfective **-ka**. It is likely that the gerundial **-a'u**, discussed above, finds its morphological source in the sequence of the imperfective **-ka** and this suffix.

(68) née hú'unea sí'ime-m 'enčím tekipánoa-pea-'u
     I   know   all-ACC your:PL work-DSD-GND
     I know that you all desire to work.

The gerundial **-apo** may follow a verb stem directly. In our data it is also directly preceded by the passive **-wa**, the participial **-le**, the imperfective **-ka**, and the future **-nee**. In all of these contexts, **-apo** occupies word final position.

The most common usage of **-'u** and **-'Vpo** is in possessed gerundial constructions to produce relative phrases. There is not a great deal of difference in their meanings and sometimes they may be used interchangeably.

(69) 'áman tekipánoa-n búsan wásuktia-m yumá-'apo-táhtia.
     there work-PCN   six   year-PL:POS reach-GND-until
     He worked there until he had completed six years.

(70) kaábe-m   tá'aa-'apo 'áman číbeh-te-k
     no:one-PL:POS know-GND   there scatter-VR-PRF
     No one knows where they scattered to.

(71) 'iním 'akí-ta   káteka-'apo béha páah-ta nú'u-ka
     here pitahaya-POS located-GND well peace-ACC take-PRF
     They accepted peace here in Where the Pitahaya is Located.

Where required, however, the postpositional locative concepts of "toward" **-'u** and "in" **-'Vpo** may be included.

(72) ba'á-ta   kó'om-siká-'u' née wée-bae
     water-POS down-go-GND   I   go-DSD
     I am going to Water's Going Down Place.

(73) 'áapo ba'á-ta   kó'om siká-'apo tekipánoa
     he   water-POS down go-GND   work
     He works in Water's Going Down Place.

The suffix **-amča** is a word final suffix that, in our data, occurs only following the perfective **-k**.

(74) kía hunáman bi-bítču-tebo-k-amča   'aáyu-k
     just there RDP-see-IMP-PRF-CTX   be-PRF
     I was just staring up there, as if I had been ordered to do so.

(75) heká-po hiká-t yé'e-mča 'aáne
     wind-in high-on dance-CTX do
     He performed as if he were dancing on air up there.

The sequential mode postposition **pat/patči** is also word final.

(76) 'iníka'a tebó-tua-pat   waté-m   nát-temae
     this:ACC greet-CAU-upon other-PL UNSPEC-ask
     As soon as he had greeted them, he asked about the others.

Overall Verb Structure 5.4.

(77) nóolia-ma-ti-ia   húu'u hosé maría 'á-u   mám-te-patči
     hurry-HRT-CON-say that Joe Mary him-to hand-VR-upon
     "Well, hurry then," said Jose María as he extended his hand to him.

(78) totói   'o'wia ku-kuh-pat   kó'om čépte-k
     chicken male RDP-crow-upon down jump-PRF
     After he crowed, the rooster jumped down.

PART V: COMPLEX SENTENCES

COORDINATION

1.0. Introduction

Yaqui employs a variety of devices and combinations of those devices to mark coordinate sentence and phrase structures in discourse. These include a pair of coordinating conjunctions and the adversative conjunction **taa** *but*. In addition, Yaqui frequently juxtaposes conjuncts that are of the same syntactic pattern. It can even place ordinarily juxaposed phrases into a discontinous construction. In some of these cases, it is difficult to say whether the construction is a coordinate one or a subordinate one.

2.0. Coordinating conjunctions

Yaqui draws on three primary constructions for encoding coordinate linguistic structures at various levels from the phrase to the sentence. These include the use of the introducer **'íntok,** the use of simple juxtaposition, and the use of the postposition **-mak** *with*.

2.1. The introducer **'íntok**

The most commonly used coordinating conjunction in Yaqui is **'íntok** *and*. It is used for simple concatenation of clauses in complex sentences like those in examples (1)–(3), in which it occurs as the introducer to the second conjunct.

(1) tú'-si   káa 'áa yé'ee 'íntok káa 'áa 'etého   kía tené-ka   kík-nee
    good-AVR NEG able dance CNJ   NEG able converse only mouth-having stand-FUT
    He was not able to dance well, and he was not able to tell stories very well; he would just stand there with his tongue in his mouth.

(2) néhpo=ne káa 'áa   yé'ee 'íntok ne káa 'áa 'etého
    I=I   NEG able dance CNJ   I NEG able converse
    kía né tiwé-ka   'áma kík-nee
    only I shame-PPL there stand:SG-FUT
    I can't dance and I can't tell stories; I just stand there embarrassed.

(3) hunúen 'á'a 'eé-síme-o=su   hunáma'a tesó-m-po labén hiá-wa-i
    thus   his think-go-when=EMP there   cave-PL-in violin sound-PSV-PPL
    'áma hiía 'íntok 'áapa 'á-u   kusí-si hiía
    there sound CNJ   harp him-to shrill-ADV sound
    As he was going along thinking this way, the sound of violin music came out of the cave and the loud sound of a harp.

The conjunction **'íntok** may conjoin a string of clauses as in example (4), where it is used twice to form a sentence with three coordinate clauses.

(4) húči 'áe-kóni-la   sik-áa ho'ó-t   'íntok 'á'a siíse-k
    again him-circle-ADV go-PPL back-on CNJ   him urinate-PRF
    'íntok čobé-t 'á'a siíse-k   wok-óko'o-ku
    CNJ   butt-on him urinate-PRF leg-calf-on
    And having gone around him, it also urinated on his back and urinated on his buttocks and on the calves of his legs.

Commonly, the conjunction **'íntok** serves as the anchorpoint for preposing topicalized nouns. In such cases **'íntok** occurs in second position in the sentence initial clause as illustrated by sentence (5).

SONORA YAQUI LANGUAGE STRUCTURES

(5) húu'u pahkó'olaa 'íntok 'á'a 'átbʷa-táite-k káa 'awá-k-am-ta bíča-ka róobo
that festival:man CNJ him laugh-begin-PRF NEG horn-have-NZR-ACC see-PPL round

kóba-k-am-ta bíča-ka-i 'íntok tána-la 'a'a bʷásia-ka-'a-betčí'ibo
head-have-NZR-ACC see-PPL-PPL CNJ curve-ADV his tail-having-EV-for

And that Pascal dancer began to laugh at it, just seeing the hornless, round head, and seeing the way it had its tail curved up over its back.

Complex postpositional phrases may also be conjoined. Example (6) includes a string of four such phrases, with **'íntok** conjoining the third and fourth phrases.

(6) sí'ime-ku-t napé-kónila hiká-t-tána 'íntok betúk-tána
all-in-at close-around up-on-side and under-side

everywhere, all around, above and below

Adverbials may also be fronted to initial position in the sentence. The conjunction **'íntok** also serves as pivot for these fronted constituents. In sentence (7) a temporal adverb has been fronted to sentence initial position for purposes of foregrounding the last event in a temporal sequence of events. This forms a clear contrast with the use of the participial **-ka** to background an initial clause which is temporally overlapping with the duration of the event related by the second clause, as in sentence (8).

(7) húnak 'íntok húu'u čibá'ato 'á-u nótte-k
then CNJ that goat him-to return-PRF

Then the goat came back to him.

(8) čibá'ato 'á-u yepsá-ka 'á-u téne-la kíkte-k
goat him-to arrive-PPL him-to upright-ADV stand:SG-PERF

Upon arriving to where the man was, the goat stood up on its hind legs.

The conjunction **'íntok** also serves as the base for attaching the conditional suffix **-o** as seen in sentence (9). In this case, **'íntok** itself conjoins two clauses that are discourse closers, and the subordinating suffix **-o** apparently adds a temporal specification to the discourse closer as a whole. In any event, this sentence illustrates a formulaic use of the conditional and provides a case in which the dividing line between subordination and coordination gets blurred.

(9) híba kaíta 'íntok-o hunúm čúpu-k
only nothing CNJ-when there finish-PRF

There is nothing else and it ends there.

2.2. Juxtaposed conjuncts

Yaqui commonly indicates the syntactic equivalence of a pair of grammatical units by simply juxtaposing them. These conjuncts may be either clausal or phrasal, as the following examples amply illustrate. When the juxtaposition involves a pair of clauses, usually the order of those clauses mirrors the temporal sequence in which the related events were carried out in the objective scene, as it does in sentence (10).

(10) moró béha 'áman yépsa-k kó'oko'i-m-mewi páhko-m-mewi lútu'uria-m nénka-k
Moor well there arrive-PRF chile-PL-to:PL feast-NZR-to:PL truth-PL deliver-PRF

The Moor got back to the ones in Chile Peppers who were giving the fiesta and gave them his report.

Sentence (11) nicely illustrates the use of juxaposition on two distinct levels of grammatical organization. At the clause level, the clauses meaning "he put his forelegs on his shoulders" and "he began licking him" are simply juxtaposed to indicate immediate temporal succession. At the other level, three postpositional phrases are simply strung together to indicate the full range of body locations which were affected by the licking.

(11) húu'u čibá'ato henó-m-po   'áe-t   mámma-ka 'a'a
     that goat   shoulder-PL-on him-on hand-PPL him
     té'eb^wa-táite-k   pusí-m-po yéka-po tén-po
     lick-begin-PRF   eye-PL-on nose-in mouth-in
     The goat put its forelegs on the man's shoulders and began to lick him in his eyes, his nose and his mouth.

Subordinate temporal clauses may also be juxtaposed to indicate their joint subordination to the main clause in a sentence. Sentence (12) shows two such juxtaposed temporal clauses, marked by the suffix **-o**. Both of these clauses are subordinate to the main clause occurring at the end of the sentence.

(12) hunúen yeu-siíka páhko ramaá-ta yéča'-a-su-a-k-o   pahkó'a-m
     thus   out-went feast shed-ACC placed-EV-CPL-PSV-PRF-when   feaster-PL
     nau   béep-su-a-k-o   páhko-beha naáte-k
     together hit-CPL-PSV-PRF-when feast-well begin-PRF
     That's the way it came out; when the feast shelter had been put up and the other festal dancers had come together, the feast started.

Yaqui allows discontinuity between postpositional phrases serving as conjuncts. In both sentence (13) and (14) one postpositional phrase occurs preverbally, whereas the other occurs following the main verb. Notice, moreover, that the postpositional phrase following the verb is modified by an adverb in both cases, suggesting a kind of extraposition of a complex phrasal unit.

(13) 'íntok kóba-méhe'e-ku   'a'a té'eb^wa-k   náka-m-po číkti
     CNJ   head-forehead-in   him lick-PRF   ear-PL-in all
     And it licked him in the forehead and all over his ears.
(14) mačám-po 'a'a siíse-k   wóki-m-meu-táhtia kó'om-i
     leg:PL   him urinate-PRF   foot-PL-to-until down-toward
     It urinated on his upper legs and all the way down to his feet.

Sentence (15) illustrates another case in which it is hard to distinguish between subordination and coordination. There are three clauses in this sentence. On the one hand, it is plausible to describe the structure of this sentence by saying that here we have the juxtaposition of two subordinate clauses which are in turn juxtaposed to the sentence final independent clause. On the other hand, the sentence initial clause, which is temporally prior to the second clause, may also be subordinate to it.

(15) 'á'a či-čík-su-ka   kó'om-čépte-ka siíka   wóh-mámni   wa'ák-ti-po
     him RDP-sweep-CPL-PPL   down-jump-PPL go:PAST two-unit:hand(?) step-PPL-in
     After it had finished brushing his face, it jumped down and went away about ten paces.

Adverbials may also be conjoined in Yaqui. Sentence (16) illustrates the juxtaposition of two adverbials built on number words to form an "X or Y" construction. We have been perplexed not to have found a native term for "or," even to the point of wondering if there is actually a form that we have overlooked. This situation is fairly common in Uto-Aztecan, however (cf. Langacker 1977b:161).

In sentence (16) the usage of the juxtaposed construction **wóo-sa báhi-sia** seems to suggest the meaning "two or three times." At best the use of juxtaposition is ambiguous since it is used for a variety of functions.

(16) 'á-u   yepsá-ka   woó-sa   báhi-sia 'a'a kón-i-la   kón-kón-ti-su-k
     him-to arrive-PPL two-AVR three-AVR him circle-STAT-PPL   RDP-circle-CON-CMP-PRF
     Arriving back, the goat completely circled him two or three times.

Two juxtaposed nominalizations that elaborate a sentence initial noun phrase whose head is the quantifier **sí'ime** *all*, are illustrated in sentence (17).

SONORA YAQUI LANGUAGE STRUCTURES

    (17) sí'ime musá'ala-maáči   húu'u nán-náa-mačí-raa
          all   attractive-appear that   RDP-laugh-appear-ABS

        baí-t-iu-wa-me   'á'a kóba-po 'aú-táite-k.
        cool-CON-say-PSV-NZR his head-in be-begin-PRF
        All kinds of burlesque ideas and witty sayings began to occur in his head.

In sentence (18) we observe two juxtaposed main clauses both backgrounded by a single participial clause. Two clauses are also juxtaposed in sentence (19). In this case however, although both are translated as coordinate main clauses, the second one is marked by the participial **-ka,** and not by the perfective **-k.** Both juxtaposed clauses may be marked by perfective **-k,** as in sentence (20).

    (18) 'áman yepsá-ka mabét-wa-k   sép   hí'i-bʷa-túa-wa-k
         there arrive-PPL receive-PSV-PRF at:once UNSPEC-eat-CAU-PSV-PRF
        Arriving there, he was received and was fed at once.

    (19) kába'i-ta   wée-la-'apo hí'i-bʷa-k   boéh-ta wée-la-'apo hé'e-ka
         horse-POS go-PPL-GND UNSPEC-eat-PRF ox-POS go-PPL-GND drink-PRF
        He ate like a horse and drank like an ox.

    (20) hunáma béha sép   supé-yéča-'a-wa-k   píisaa-m saáwea-tua-wa-k
         there   well at:once shirt-take:off-EV-PSV-PRF blanket-PL trouser-CAU-PSV-PRF
        Then right there, his shirt was taken off and a blanket was made into trousers for his legs.

Conjoining may also involve two juxtaposed complement clauses. In sentence (21) the juxtaposed clauses meaning "they mocked him" and "they laughed at him raucously" can both be construed as joint complements of the verb **'áayu** *to be* of the sentence initial clause.

    (21) 'áma 'aáyu-k-ti-m   'á'a hiáawa-ka báaho'o-ti   'aáče
         there be-PRF-CON-PL him mock-PPL raucous-CON laugh
        It was there that they mocked him and laughed raucously at him.

Likewise, main clauses may be juxtaposed. In sentence (22) the quantifier **sí'ime yoem-raa** *all the people* marks the subject of both of the juxtaposed main clauses.

    (22) 'ám 'át-tua   sí'ime yoém-raa kóba-e
         them laugh-CAU all   people-ABS head-INST

        háapte-ka-i   'átta-la   wát-wát-te-ka 'aáče
        stand:PL-PPL-PPL face-down RDP-pile-VR-PPL laugh
        He made them laugh; all the people were standing on their heads and rolling over one another with laughter.

Relative clauses may also be juxtaposed. In sentence (23) the quantifier **hunáa'a** *that one* serves as the head for both of the following relative clauses. Both this sentence and the previous one illustrate the use of quantifiers to signal overtly the identity of the subjects of conjoined clauses.

    (23) hunúm lú'ute-k hunáa'a káa   'áa yé'ee-me   káa 'áa 'etého-me
         there end-PRF that   NEG able dance-NZR NEG able talk-NZR
        That's where the man who was not able to dance, and not able to tell stories, wound up.

Juxtaposed relative clauses may also be linked semantically by the identity of the direct object of the verbs that they employ. The example in sentence (24) shows three such relative clauses in a string.

(24) 'émo-u 'á'a téuwaa-k 'emé'e 'íntok née muk-sú-k   húni'i ketúni
you-to it tell-PRF you CNJ I die-CMP-PRF even still

'á'a téuwaa-nee híba   'ém túa né-u wáati-nee   kaá-bae-ka
it tell-FUT always you indeed me-to remember-FUT NEG-DSD-PPL

húni'i née híkkahi-su-me   née híkkahi-sú-ka-me   née tá'aa-k-ame
even me hear-CMP-NZR me hear-CMP-PPL-NZR me know-PRF-NZR

I have told it to you, and even after I am dead you will go on telling it, and in that way you will be remembering me, even though you didn't intend to, those who are hearing me now, those who have heard me, and those who know me.

2.3. Marked with postposition -mak

The second conjunct in a pair of conjoined noun phrases may be marked by the postposition **-mak** *with*, as in example (25).

(25) húnen=su tesó-po lú'u-te-k   húu'u labén híawa-i
thus=EMP cave-to end-VR-PRF that violin sound-PPL

'áapa čiba'áto-mak nau   lu'u-te-k
harp goat-with together end-VR-PRF

The violin music in the cave thus ended and the harp music and the goat all ended together right there.

3.0. Adversative sentences

The conjunction **taa** can be glossed "but" and serves to mark adversative sentences. In sentence (26) the use of **taa** signals the unexpected state of poverty that surrounds a person who has an otherwise prestigious position in the society.

(26) hunámani bibá-hímaa-ri-wi   yoéme 'áma hó'aa-k-an
off:yonder cigarette-throw-NZR-to man there house-VR-PCN

páhko'olaa-taka-i   táa tú'i-si   polóobe
festal:dancer-being-PPL but very-ADV poor

Off yonder in Discarded Cigarrettes, there used to live a man who was a ritual dancer for the Pascual fiesta, but he was very poor.

In sentence (27) the speaker contrasts his desire to carry out a highly desirable religious role with his utter inability to do so.

(27) 'aháa n-áčai   'ó'olaa tú'i-si   n=ám yi'í-pea   táa nee káa-tú'ii-m   wók-ek
aha my-father ancient good-ADV I=them dance-DSD CNJ I NEG-good-PL foot-have

Aha, my revered Father, how I wish I could dance to that music, but I just don't have good legs.

The adversative **taa** can also be used as a disclaimer. In sentence (28) for example, the speaker is downgrading his own ability as a story teller, in probable contradistinction to his reputation.

(28) née hiókoe káa ne túa   'áa 'etého 'ó'oben táa 'inía
me excuse NEG I indeed able converse although but this

'etého-i-mak ne yéu-tóm-te-ka   'emó-u 'á'a téuwaa
tell-PPL-with I out-stomach-VR-PPL you:PL-to it tell

Excuse me, although I am not able to tell stories very well, yet having been born with this story, I tell it.

In some contexts, the force of **taa** is that of surprise at an unexpected result. The use of the emphatic clitic =**su** in the same clause reinforces the idea of an unexpected result, as in sentence (29) in which the speaker recalls his consternation at confusing a coyote with a deer.

(29) masó-ta   née 'aámu-n   táa née hí'obe-ka   wo'i-ta=su=ne   me'aa-k
     deer-ACC I   hunt-PCN but I mistake-PPL coyote-ACC=EMP=I kill-PRF
     I was hunting a deer, but I made a mistake; it was a coyote I killed.

Finally, a more neutral version of **taa** is used to relate the statement of a problem that the speaker encountered to the solution for that problem which is stated in the adversative clause of sentence (30). The problem was the onset of a feeling of debility; the solution was to get rid of that feeling by taking a treatment in a sweathouse.

(30) 'óbera   né-t   weče-n   táa táta-buhtia-po   yéu-siíka
     laziness me-on   fall-PCN but hot-sweat-in   out-went
     Laziness fell on me, but in sweating it went away.

Adversative sentences of the form "this" or "that" and "either this" or "either that" are marked by the borrowed Spanish conjunction **'oo** (<Spanish **o**), as in sentences (31)–(32). The conjuncts consist of a variety of grammatical classes. In sentence (31) the conjuncts are demonstratives serving as direct objects, whereas in sentence (32) temporal adverbs are conjoined.

(31) 'iníka'a   'émpo wáata 'óo hunáka'a há'ani
     this:ACC   you   want or that:ACC maybe
     Do you want this one or that one?

(32) 'í'an 'óo yoóko   'áu yebíh-nee-t-iia-n   húu'u kóbanao
     today or tomorrow RFL arrive:SG-FUT-CON-say-PCN   that governor
     The governor says that he will come either today or tomorrow.

The word **húnak** *at that time, then* may also serve as a sequential conjunction. It occurs in both simple and complex forms. Its use in its simple form is illustrated in sentences (33) and (34). In (35) it occurs with the expletive clitic **-san**.

(33) wéte'epo-'im yeká-po kík-kímu   húnak kóba wánti-nee
     gnat-PL   nose-in RDP-enter   then head hurt-FUT
     Gnats get in one's nose, then the head will ache.

(34) hunáka'a tékil-ta   né čúpu-k   húnak né tá'ab^{w}i-k   naáte-k
     that:ACC work-ACC I finish-PRF   then I different-PRF   begin-PRF
     I finished that job, then I started a different one.

(35) bái-tá'aa-wa-ka-i   'ó-'ómte-k   húnak=san hú'ena-k yá'a-sae-k
     deceive-PSV-PPL-PPL   RDP-anger-PRF   then=EXP evil-ACC do-IMP-PRF
     Having been deceived, he became angry, so then he commanded that an evil thing be done.

COMPLEMENT CLAUSES

1.0. Introduction

In this chapter we discuss the various kinds of clauses that serve as subjects or objects of sentences with the exception of relative clauses, which we discuss in the following chapter. In particular, we group the complement types according to the semantics of the verbs that govern them and show the contrast between main verb usages and more grammaticalized usages of the governing verbs.

2.0. The governing verbs and position of the complement

In general terms, the kinds of complements we discuss here are all governed by verbs of mental activity or capacity. These verbs include the capacitative **'áa**, which means variously "to be able to do X," "to know how to do X," and "to be competent for X." The mental activity verb **'ea** *to think* and its extensions, various forms of the speech-act verb **híia** *to speak,* and several other speech-act verbs, and onomatopoetic verbs are additional examples of verbs that govern the kinds of complements that we treat below.

2.1. The capacitative **'áa**

The auxiliary verb **'áa** (**'ára** in Mayo) is the phonologically reduced form of the main verb **'áawe** *to know how to do X, to be able to do X*. It is highly grammaticalized in that it does not take any of the verbal suffixes, and the attendant categories of past or future tense, or conditional mode, among others, are marked on the verb that serves as its complement The peculiarities of this auxiliary may point to an original status as an adverbial meaning "well" in a typological parallel to Cora.[1]

Examples (1)–(2) illustrate main verb usages of **'áawe**. In sentence (1) **'áawe** occurs with only a preceding adverbial. In sentence (2) it occurs with a first person singular independent pronoun. This verb is used only in the context of a discussion in which someone's ability to perform some kind of work or activity is in view, as can be seen in examples (1)–(2). In these usages, it is more like a prototypical intransitive verb than like a transitive one.

(1) 'ábe 'áawe
    nearly know:how
    He nearly knows how to do it.

(2) néhpo 'áawe
    I   know:how
    I know how to do it.

More complex sentences involving the main verb use of **'áawe** are also attested. In example (3) it occurs in each one of the four juxtaposed clauses, the first three of which are independent clauses. In its main verb usage, **'áawe** is marked with various tense and aspect suffixes. Here it is followed by the suffix sequence **-le-nee** PPL-FUT in the third clause and by **-ka-i** PPL-STAT in the fourth clause.

(3) 'ínepo 'á-u 'áawe   kaábe né-le-béna-si   'á-u 'áawe
    I   it-to know:how no:one I-CON-like-ADV   it-to know:how

    sénu két 'á-u 'áawe-le-nee   káa húni'i 'áawe-ka-i
    one also it-to know:how-PPL-FUT   NEG even   know:how-PPL-STAT
    I can do that; there is no one who is able to do it as well as I can; a person might think that he could do it when he really could not do it at all.

Sentences with **'áawe** as a main verb clearly differ in structure and meaning from those with the reduced auxiliary **'aa**. The differences include both the suffixes that are permitted to occur with these stems as well as the kind of conjuncts that they take and the placement of those conjuncts. As example (4) illustrates, the main verb **'áawe** takes adverbial and pronominal adjuncts in pre-verbal position.

---

1 O'odham clearly builds "able" sentences on an adverb meaning "well" (Eloise Jelinek, personal communication).

(4) 'émpo 'iníka'a tékil-ta 'enčí hóo-ria-m-ta wáata-'a-te-k-o hunáa'a 'áma
you this:ACC work-ACC you do-APL-NZR-ACC want-EV-VB-PRF-if that:one there

'aáwe
know:how

If you want someone there to do this work for you, that man there knows how to do it.

In its auxiliary uses, the reduced form **'áa** takes a following verbal complement in a kind of complex verbal construction. Any suffixation that is involved affects the verb that serves as the conjunct of **'áa**. The direct object of the conjunct verb occurs preceding the conjunct of **'áa** in example (5), which is a strong suggestion that we have a matrix verb as nucleus of this bi-clausal construction.

(5) née 'áa 'á'a hoóa-n
I able it do-PCN
I was able to do it.

The postverbal position of the complement of **'aa** is seen twice in the conjoined sentence given in example (6).

(6) tú'i-si káa 'áa yé'ee 'íntok káa 'áa 'etého kía tené-ka kík-nee
very-ADJ NEG able dance CNJ NEG able converse only mouth-having stand-FUT
He was not able to dance well, and he was not able to tell stories very well; he would just stand there with his tongue in his mouth.

Capacitative **'áa** governs complements containing both transitive and intransitive verbs, as exemplified by examples (7) and (8). Notice also that the clause in which **'áa** is used in sentence (8) is also the subordinate clause of a contrary to fact conditional sentence.

(7) kílima'ičhia-ka=ne ká=nee 'áa kíkte
numb-PRF=I NEG=I able stand
My leg is asleep, I can't stand.

(8) hunáka'a báh-ta 'áa b^{w}á'a-tu-k-o néhpo 'á'a b^{w}áa-'ea-n
that:ACC grass-ACC able eat-be-PRF-CND I it eat-CND-PCN
If that grass were edible, I would eat it.

As discussed earlier in connection with the verbalizing suffix **-tu** (cf., VERB MORPHOLOGY, p. 140), **'aa** is also used in a special construction with a following verb. The construction as a whole means that something is "do-able," as shown by sentences (9) and (10).

(9) káa 'áa sáu-tu
not able command-be
He is disobedient. or *He is not able to be commanded.*

Adverbial modifiers to the complement of **'aa** may occur in preverbal position in the main clause as can be observed in sentence (10).

(10) káa 'emó čó'ila-k b^{w}é'ituk=im náako-la-m táa=m tu'i-si 'áa
not RFL rope-PRF because=they be:drunk-NZR-PL but=they good-AVR able

ká-kaba-'e
RDP-horse-VR
They didn't rope each other because they were drunk, but they were expert riders.

The auxiliary **'áa** can occur between its complement verb and the direct object of that complement verb. In sentence (11) both the subject and object nominals occur in preverbal complex position in the main clause. In sentence (12) the complex subject nominal precedes **'aa**, whereas the direct object clitic follows it.

(11) čólloi   kúta-ta   'áa   wóhok-ta
     woodpecker wood-ACC able pierce-VR:TRN
     The woodpecker can make holes in a pole.

(12) kusía-ta-béna-k   hía-wa-ek   káa sí'ime wikítči-m 'áa 'á'a mamáto
     flute-POS-like-ACC sound-NOM-have not all bird-PL able it imitate
     It (mockingbird) has a note like a flute; not all birds can imitate it.

Sentence (13) nicely illustrates the distinction between the simple version of **'áawe** and the fully inflected verb that it governs. Indirect object postpositional phrases may also occur between **'aa** and the verb that it governs, as illustrated in sentence (14).

(13) 'ínepo 'áma bó'o-ka káa 'áa kíkte-ka-i   tamú-láa-tu-ka-n
     I there lie-PPL not able stand-PPL-STAT dizzy-NZR-VR-PPL-PCN
     I was lying there because I wasn't able to get up; I was knocked out.

(14) káa nee 'áa 'emó-u noóka-k   híabih-te-i-m-béna-si-a
     not I able you-to speak-PRF life-VR-NZR-PL-like-AVR-PPL
     I wasn't able to speak to you like regenerated people.

2.2. The mental activity verb **'éa**

The mental activity verb **'éa** can be variously glossed as "to think," "to wish," "to feel," and "to make a judgement," among other meanings. All of these meanings draw on ostensibly intransitive forms of this verb, which has the alternate form **'ee**. This verb can also be nominalized in several ways. Finally, Yaqui has the corresponding pair of transitive stems **'éiyaa** and **'éeyaa** which are also polysemous and can be glossed variously as "to esteem X," "to love X" or "to think highly of X." The transitive form is mostly restricted to usage as a main verb.

The intransitive form, **'ea, 'ee-**, on the other hand, is used as a main verb, as a matrix verb, and as a tightly bound verbal suffix in several different types of constructions. In what follows, we illustrate its usages as a main verb, as a matrix verb, and as a type of subjunctive marker in contrary to fact propositions, and in "instead of" and "rather than" types of constructions. We also illustrate its role as a modal reinforcer with desideratives or with meanings such as "intend to do X" or "plan to do X." The matrix verb also has the idiomatic meanings of "to trust in X" or "to depend on X" when it occurs in construction with a proper noun that serves as object of the postposition **-t** *on*.

Sentence (15) illustrates its main verb use in the sense of "to think" or "to hold an opinion of X." The use there of the negative indefinite pronoun **kaíta** *nothing* suggests that **'ea** is not a prototypical intransitive verb, but rather is a verb that, semantically speaking, has an internal object that can be elaborated in a variety of ways. This is also suggested by the fact that the manner procomplement **húnen** *thus* can be used with **'ea** as example (16) shows. The use of the procomplement then leads to the construction of a complex sentence with a sentential complement following **'éa** as suggested by sentence (17).

(15) kaíta=su=ne   'éa
     nothing=CTX=I think
     I don't have any opinion.

(16) 'éme'e 'íntok káa húnen 'éa-k
     you:PL and not thus think-PRF
     But that was not your will.

(17) 'ínen 'éa-n   yé-'a-kéča-'a-bae-n
     thus think-PCN out-him-put:SG-EV-DSD-PCN
     This is what he was thinking; he was wanting to release him.

As a main verb, **'éa** has second meaning which can be characterized as "X is willing for Y." This meaning is illustrated in example (18).

(18) Lióh-ta   húnen   'éa-o
     God-POS   thus   will-if
     if it is God's will

In its nominalized form, **'éa** is marked with the gerundial **-'u,** and comes to mean "X's will." The identity of X is effected through a proper noun or nominalization marked with the accusative **-ta** as can be seen in example (19).

(19) táa 'á'a híkkahi-nee   yá'ut-ta   'éa-'u
     but it hear(obey)-FUT   chief-POS   will-GND
     But you must obey the authorities' will (wishes).

A second kind of nominalization of **-'éa** is formed with the ubiquituous **-me** suffix. Its use is illustrated in sentence (20). The difference between the two nominalizations is that **'éa-'u** designates an abstract quality "what the authorities want," whereas **'éa-m** designates the human entity who desires something. The use of **'éa** in sentence (20) also illustrates its meaning of "X trusts in Y," which is partly derivative of the preverbal postpositional phrase **lióh-ta-t** God-ACC-on. As sentence (21) shows, trust can also be placed in abstractions and the results of one's own efforts.

(20) húu'u lióh-ta-t   'éa-me   'allée-wa-m-ta   bít-nee
     that God-ACC-on trust-NZR joy-PASS-NZR-ACC   see-FUT
     The person who trusts in God will enjoy happiness.

(21) 'ín tékil-et hiba né 'éa b^{w}é'ituk-ne káa tekipánoa-k-o káa hí'i-b^{w}á-nee
     my work-on only I rely because-I   not work-PRF-if   not IZR-eat-FUT
     I only trust in my work, because if I don't work, I don't eat.

Noun incorporation, which operates so widely in Yaqui grammar, gives us another way of structuring the scene in which someone uses the verb **'éa** and its related form **'éiyaa** to express the notion of trust in someone. There are two conventionalized constructions in which **'ea** means "to believe in" or "to trust in a person." In these constructions, the nominal **yoéme** *person* is incorporated into a complex verb stem with **-'éa**. These two constructions are functional equivalents of some of the foregoing with the only difference that they are restricted to referring to people or supernatural beings.[2]

(22) Hóan-ta-t   né yoém-'éa-n   (23) Lióh-ta   né yoém-'éiyaa
     John-ACC-on   I person-think-PCN   God-ACC   I person-think
     I had been trusting in John.   *I am trusting God.*

A third main verb version of **'éa** can be viewed as as a semantic extension of the volitional version illustrated above in examples (18) and (19). In sentence (24) the use of **'éa** in conjunction with the desiderative form of **ya'a** *to do* expresses strong desire on the part of the subject of the sentence to achieve a particular result.

(24) yá'a-péa-ka 'éa-n 'ó'obek haí-sa   túa   néhpo 'aú-ka wáka'a bató'oo-raa-ta
     do-DSD-PPL SJV   although how-INTERR indeed I   do-PPL that:ACC baptize-ABS-ACC

     'allée-tua-nee.
     happy-CAU-FUT
     He really had a deep desire, saying, "How can I possibly make people happy?"

---

2 In addition to all the detail in this section, **'éa** and **'éiyaa** find a role in the complex verb stems **hú'unea, hú'uneiyaa** that mean "to know."
   (i) haíbu=ne 'áe-t hú'unea
       now=I   it-on know
       I already know about it.
   (ii) 'á'abo né 'enčím   hú'uneiyaa-se-k
        over:here I you:PL:ACC know-come-PRF
        I came over here to know how you folks are.

Complement clauses 2.2.

As a main verb, **'éa** can also be passivized. In this case it also appears in the phonologically modified form **'ée,** as exemplified in sentence (25). Note also that in this example, the sentential complement precedes the main verb **'éa**. (The passive form of **'éa-** also has an extended meaning of "to experience an emotion.")

(25) húči náu   tekipánoa-baa-wa-ka 'ée-wa
     again together work-DSD-PSV-PPL think-PSV
     It was thought that they would be working together again.

The modified form **'ée** occurs in a variety of other morphemic contexts. In example (26) it precedes the auxiliary motion verb **-sime** *to go*:SG. In this sentence, **éa** clearly functions as a transitive verb. It takes as its complement a quantifier marked with the accusative **-k**.

(26) b^{w}é'ituk huébena-k 'ée-sime
     because   much-ACC   think-go
     because he was going along, thinking of many things

In summary, the **'ée** main verb forms occur when followed by specific suffixes; these include the desiderative **-pee/-pea** as in example (27), the passive **-wa** as in the abstract nominalization **'éewačime** *faith* in example (28), and **-sime** *go*:SG illustrated above in example (26).

(27) hábé-ta-t   húni'i 'itóm 'ée-pee-su-ka-'apo
     someone-CON-on even   our   trust-DSD-CPL-PRF-GND
     when we were yearning to trust in anyone whomsoever

(28) 'á'e téa-wa-m   'íntok 'áme-t   'ée-wa-či-me   'útte'a-m   'á'a máka-k
     his name-POS-PL   and   them-on trust-PSV-AVR-NZR   strength-PL him give-PRF
     His name, and faith in his name, gave him strength.

Another occurrence of the **'ée** form as main verb is seen when it is followed by its grammaticalized subjunctive counterpart **-'éa,** illustrated in sentence (29). This is highly reminiscent of the main verb **bae** *to want* which gets modified to **baa** when it is followed by its grammaticalized counterpart desiderative **-bae** (cf. INFLECTIONAL AND DERIVATIONAL AFFIXATION, p. 296–298).

(29) bát-čain tá'ab^{w}i-ku-t   híta   'ée-'éa-n
     maybe   different-CON-on   thing think-SJV-PCN
     Then maybe he would be thinking about something else.

The verb **'éa** also takes complements marked with the subordinator **-ti**. Such complements precede the verb and can be as simple as a singular word. In sentence (30) **'éa** takes a string of two such adverbial complements. Note that **-ti** suffixes to each of these adverbial complements of **-ea**.

(30) suá-ti   'éa,   'obí-ti   'éa
     fret-AVR   think busy-AVR   think
     He felt frustrated and under pressure.

Examples such as (31) below in which the subject clitic precedes the verb **'ea**, reinforces the observation made on sentence (30) above that the connective **-ti-** at least formerly followed the protosis condition described in Hale (1983:304,310), i.e., it was in certain contexts a word final suffix, that ultimately derived from the Proto-Uto-Aztecan absolutive ***-tu**. A pair of sentential complements linked to **'éa** by **-ti-** are illustrated in example (31) and (32).

(31) 'émpo 'á'a yá'a-nee-ti=ne   'ea
     you   it   do-FUT-CON=I   think
     I think that you will do it.

(32) humák húni'i 'áme-násuk   téu-naa-ti   'éa   'áapo
     maybe even   them-among   find-FUT:PSV-CON   think he
     He thinks that perhaps he may be found among them.

In certain contexts, the connector **-ti-** is linked to the complement of **'éa** by an echo-vowel.

(33) 'á'a máhhae túa   'á'a hapá'ači-'i-ti-'ea-ka-i
     him fear   really him Apache-EV-CON-think-PPL-PPL
     They were afraid of him; they thought he really was an Apache.

In some cases, the connector -ti- reduces to -t-. As example (34) shows this often the case when it follows an echo-vowel. In these instances, the sequence -ti + -'ea may contract to -t-ea with the meaning of "he thinks." This contraction should not be confused with the quotative -tea *he says*.

(34) 'itóm híapsi-m yolé-'e-ne-'e-t-ea-ka-i
     our life-PL rescue-EV-FUT-EV-CON-think-PPL-ABS
     because we thought that our lives would be saved

The tightly bound suffixal variants of -'**éa** provide subtle clues as to those aspects of its meaning that relate to their particular grammaticalized usages. In combination with the past continuative suffix that attaches to it and the conditional -**o** in a preceding or following clause, '**éa** takes on a counterfactual meaning approximating the English "would be X" or "would do X." In these constructions, the role of the past continuative -**n** is an iconic registration of the epistemic distance between the actual situation and the counterfactual or hypothetical one.

(35) 'iníka'a tá'aa-'a-te-k-o   kát=im   kríhto-ta   kúus-et sékola
     this:ACC know-EV-VR-PRF-CND not=they Christ-ACC cross-on stretched:out

     po-pón-'ea-n
     RDP-nail-SJV-PCN
     If they had known this, they would not have nailed Christ on the cross.

(36) mékkaa=te kék-ke'e-we   tú'ii-'ea-n te káa
     far:away=we RDP-get:wood-VR   good-SJV-PCN we not

     ho'ó-t 'ám pú'ak-ta-ne-'e-te-k-o
     back-on them carry-VR-FUT-EV-VR-CND
     We have to go a long way for wood; it would be good if we didn't have to carry it on our backs.

A clear bit of evidence for the relatively great epistemic distance from reality of the situation designated by -'**éa-n** is the negative polarity between the statements and their implicatures in these examples. For example, the positively stated "if" -clause in sentence (35) is paralleled by the negative implication that the subjects did not really know something crucial. The negatively stated conclusion of (35) is paralleled by the positive implication that the subjects had in fact nailed Christ to the cross. Likewise, in sentence (36) the negatively stated "if" clause has the implication that the subjects are in fact carrying firewood on their backs and the conditional clause carries the negative implication that the actual situation is not good.

(37) kóko-k-ame   káa hi-híabih-te-o=su   húnak=su kríhto húni'i káa híabih-te-'ea-n
     die:PL-PRF-NZR not RDP-rise-VR-if=CTX then=CTX Christ even   not rise-VR-SJV-PCN
     If the dead do not resurrect, then neither would Christ be resurrected.

(38) née tóm-ek-o   páhko-a-u   né wée-'ea-n
     I   money-have-if feast-CON-to   I go-SJV-PCN
     If I had money, I would go to the fiesta.

Similarly, the negative "if" clause in sentence (37) carries the implication that the dead do indeed rise again, whereas the conditional clause with -'**éa-n** implies that Chirst has been resurrected from the dead. Finally, the implication of the "if" clause in sentence (38) is that the speaker has no money and the implication of the -'**éa-n** clause is that he will not go to the fiesta.

Other combinations of suffixes with -'**éa-n** are used to signal closer epistemic distance to reality between the hypothetical situation and the actual one. This is particularly true for combinations of -'**éa** with the imperfective participial **-ka** and the counter expectation particle **=su**. This morphemic sequence links to **'éa** via an echo-vowel.

(39) čé'e-wan=su   tú'ii   wáa'a híta   yée-mík-ame   'á'a mabét-'ea-'a-ka=su
     more-VR=CTX   good   that thing people-give-NZR   it   receive-SJV-EV-PPL=CTX
     It is better to give than to receive.

(40) 'e-t   'áu-ka-m-ta   tá'aru-k tú'ii-nee káa sí'ime 'ém takáa kóp-'ea-'a-ka=su
     you-on be-PPL-NZR-ACC   lose-PRF good-FUT   not all   your body lose-SJV-EV-PPL=CTX
     It is better to lose a member than to lose the whole body.

The implications of the clauses in sentences (39) and (40) is that the situations the speaker is describing do in fact occur, at least potentially. This conclusion is reinforced by the use of an indicative declarative clause as one member of an "instead" sentence in example (41). The assertion of the **'éa** clause in this sentence is that the people did not believe someone.

(41) 'iníme'e 'íntok 'á'a súal-'éa-'aka=su   hú'ena-si híu-taite-k
     these   and   him believe-SJV-PPL=CTX   evil-AVR say-begin-PRF
     And these (men), instead of believing in him, began to say evil things.

The way the pieces fit together differentially can lead to quite different meanings. Note, for example, the opposite ordering of **'ea** with respect to the gerundial **'apo** in examples (42) and (43). The difference between these two sentences appears to be that the **'éa** clause in sentence (42) is construed as designating a location, whereas the **'ea** clause of sentence (43) designates a person.

(42) té'opo-m-po   Lióh-ta   'án-'ea-'apo=su   kúta moóno-m   'aáyu-k
     temple-PL-in God-POS   be-SJV-GND=CTX   wood doll-PL   be-PRF
     In the temples, in the place where God ought to have been, there were wooden idols.

(43) 'áapo 'á'a téuwaa-nee-ka-i   'enčím-tu-ka-'apo-'éa-'u
     he   it   tell-FUT-PPL-PPL   you:PL-VR-PPL-GND-SJV-PCN
     He will be the one who says it, instead of its (actually) being you (who says it).

The last usage of the suffix **-'éa** that we discuss here is its usage with the desiderative **-bae**. Curiously, as the examples (44)–(48) show, the pairing of these two suffixes is in construction with the imperfective participle **-ka**. Semantically, there is an overlap in the meaning of **-'ea** with that of **-bae**. This is suggested by the usage we described earlier in this section, i.e., example (29).

One basis for the overlap is clear from examples (44) and (45), namely, that this modal use of **-'éa** is appropriate for describing both future events, as illustrated in example (44), as well as past ones, as seen in example (45).

(44) yoém-raa-ta-u   née nók-bae-ka-'éa   née 'á-et hióko-i-nee
     person-ABS-POS-to   I   speak-DSD-PPL-DSD   me it-on pity-PPL-FUT
     With your permission, I'd like to speak to the people.

(45) 'áapo bú'uu-raa-ta   'ané-'epo kibák-bae-ka-'éa-n
     he   many-ABS-POS   be-GND   enter:SG-DSD-PPL-DSD-PCN
     He was wanting to enter into where the crowd was.

Sentences (46) and (47) show a usages of **-bae** and **-'éa** in sentences that are functional equivalents. Both express the speaker's desire to attend a future social event.

(46) páhko-ta ne bít-bae   (47) pahkó-ta=ne bít-po 'éa[3]
     feast-ACC I see-DSD   feast-ACC=I see-in think
     I want to go to (see) the feast.   *I am thinking about going to the feast.*

---

[3] This example is interesting because it illustrates the kind of context within which the grammaticalization of the strong desiderative **-pea** took place, i.e., **-po** + **-'éa** > **-péa**.

Statistically, the usages of modal **-'éa** with the past continuative **-n** are much more frequent than the usages with potential aspect. What ties both potential future and past continuative together in these usages with **-'éa** is the implication that the expressed desire has not yet been met by the conceived temporal reference point of the event in question. Thus in example (48) the implication is that the subject was not able to do everything, whereas the implication of example (49) is that the subjects had not yet succeeded in transmitting some message. Finally, the implication of example (50) is that the subject had not yet caught the train because it had not quite arrived.

(48) sí'ime-ta yá'a-pea-ka-'éa-n
all-ACC do-DSD-PPL-DSD-PCN
He was wishing that he could do everything.

(49) hunáka'a nók-ta yéu-yumá-'a-ria-bae-ka-'éa-n
that:ACC word-ACC out-reach-EV-APL-DSD-PPL-DSD-PCN
They were wanting to fulfill (carry out) that message.

(50) karíl-ta ku-kúh-híkkaha-k 'á'a b^{W}íh-bae-ka-'éa-n
train-ACC RDP-whistle-hear-PRF it grab-DSD-PPL-DSD-PCN
He heard the train whistling, and he was wanting to catch it.

2.3. The speech act verb hiía

The speech act verb **hiía** has grammaticalized in a variety of ways in Yaqui grammar, showing copious use of both a free form and several variants of reduced forms that in some cases have coalesced with other grammatical elements. As examples (51) and (52) show, the complement of the free verb **hiía** precedes it in a sentence. In fact, the complement of **hiía** may be discontinuous from it, with a constituent such as the indirect object immediately preceding the matrix verb, as is true for both of these sentences.

(51) čúbala née bó'o-bíča-ti wó'i-ta-u hiía
moment me wait-for-CON coyote-ACC-to say
"Wait for me a moment," he said to the coyote.

(52) 'íli máo-nóka húsai-m hiíms-ek-ti 'a-u hiía
little Mayo-talk brown-PL beard-has-CON him-to say
"He speaks a little Mayo and has a brown beard," he said to him.

The reduced form **-iá** is often used as a marker of indirect discourse. As is the case for the main verb, the complement of **-iá** precedes it in word order within the sentence, as in example (53).

(53) káa 'ám Liós-im-t-iá-ka kaábe-ta 'ám yó'ori-sae
not them God-PL-CON-say-PPL no:one-ACC them worship-IMP
He says they are not gods and commands not to worship them.

2.4. Other speech act verbs

Several other speech act verbs occur in Yaqui. These include **'uhb^{W}ána** *to implore, to beg*, **téuwaa** *to tell*, **nóoka** *to speak X language,* and **te'e** *to tell*. As sentence (54) suggests, the complement of **'uhb^{W}ána** follows it in word order.

(54) 'áme-u 'uhb^{W}ána-k 'áma tawá-bae-ka 'au tekipanoa-bae-'e-ti-iia-ka
them-to beg-PRF there remain-DSD-PPL RFL work-DSD-EV-CON-say-PPL

'áma yéu hí'i-b^{W}á-bae-'e-ti-iia
there out IZR-eat-DSD-EV-CON-say
He begged them that he might stay there; he said that he was looking for work and that he wanted to stay and to eat there.

The complement of the applicative form of **eteho** *to tell* occurs preverbally in the normal position for prototypical direct objects. Sentence (55) is a typical example of this.

Complement clauses 2.5.

(55) káa túa 'á'a 'alléa-'u née 'etého-ria-k
    not truly his happy-GND me tell-APL-PRF
    He told me he was a bit sad.

The verb **téuwaa** functions in some contexts as a ditransitive verb, taking pronominal subjects, indirect objects and direct objects. All of these roles are realized overtly in sentence (56).

(56) 'áapo káa ne-u 'á'a téuwaa tá'ab^wí-ka né-u 'á'a téuwaa
    he not me-to it tell different-being me-to it tell
    It wasn't he who told me, it was somebody else.

The complements of both **téuwaa** and **te'e** precede these verbs in word order. The connective **-ti** also appears as the terminal element in their complements.

(57) saáwa-m b^wía-laábos-im-ti téuwaa-wa bái-t-iu-po
    salla-PL dirt-nail-PL-CON call-PSV cool-CON-say-in
    The Sallas are jokingly called dirt-nails.

(58) néhpo n=á'a saíra-k-ti té'e-ka húu'u kuču-reo
    I I=him brother-have-CON say-PRF that fisher-AGT
    "He is my brother," said the fisherman.

(59) 'áa tú'u-kun 'émpo 'á'a tá'aa-ti húči té'e-ka
    ah good-then you him know-CON again say-PRF
    "Well, good, so you know him," he said again.

With a highly marked topicalized noun in sentence initial position, the complement clause of **te'e** may be placed at the end of the sentence.

(60) mása'asai 'íntok 'á'a téa-ka 'ínen té'e-ka 'iním 'émpo wée 'ín-hápči
    S. M.Flower and him see-PPL thus say-PPL here you go my-father
    And, S. M. Flower, noticing him, said: "Is that you, my father?"

2.5. Onomatopoetic complements

A number of different verbs may take complements utilizing onomatopoetic forms in conjunction with reduplication processes. These onomatopoetic expressions commonly reflect sounds of various kinds, such as slurping water or coffee. A wide range of personal action verbs govern these complements, which are almost invariably marked with the connective **-ti** in complement final position. As sentence (61) suggests, the typical reduplication pattern is to employ two occurrences of the onomatopoetic syllable. In this case, there are three such onomatopoetic complements, i.e., **hóo-hóo** *to slurp,* **póm-pom** *to drink,* and **sun-sun** *to shuffle the feet.*

(61) čúkui ba'á-ta hóo-hóo-ti póm-pom-ta tasá-ta
    black water-ACC RDP-slurp-CON RDP-drink-VR cup-ACC

    wá'am b^wíse-ka 'im-biča sun-sun-ti wee
    there grab-PPL here-site RDP-shuffle-CON go
    He slurped his coffee and went shuffling off in that direction.

The reduplication of these complements is an iconic reflective of the repetitive nature of the physical acts themselves. Sentence (62) is a striking example of this iconicity with its four repetitions of the onomatopoetic syllable **ró'o**.

(62) čúkula boés-im wee-la-'apo ró'o-ró'o-ró'o-ró'o-ti hé'e
    later ox-PL go-manner-in RDP-RPR-RDP-glug-CON drink
    And afterwards he drinks sounding like oxen when they swallow.

Some onomatopoetic complement structures appear to involve compounding, as evidenced by examples (63) and (64), although it is not always obvious what the source of the individual elements is. In example (63) the compound **baá-ho'o-** consists of a compound of the form **baá,** whose meaning is indeterminate and may well be onomatopoetic in its own right. The second element is an onomatopoetic syllable representing loud laughter. The complement itself can be glossed as "raucous laughter." The onset of the racket described in the onomatopoetic complement of sentence (64) is reflected in the opening syllable **ká-** and the repetitiveness of that racket is reflected in the reduplicated portion **-ya-ya'a**.

    (63) číbu-ra   'áma 'aáyu-k-ti-m   'á'a hiaawa-ka baá-ho'o-ti   'aače
         bitter-ABS there is-PRF-CON-they his mock-PPL baá-ho:ho-CON laugh
         They mocked him saying, here comes a "bitter pill" and laughed at him raucously.

    (64) páhko naáte-k   b^{w}é'uu-si káyaya'a-ti   híu-wa
         feast begin-PRF big-ADV racket:RDP-CON sound-PSV
         The celebration began; there was a lot of racket.

3.0. Marking of complements

The clauses that serve as complements of Yaqui verbs show a wide range in morphological properties from the sentential end of the spectrum to the nominal end. Some complements are fully sentential, i.e., they share all of the semantic and morphological characteristics of an independent sentence. Others consist of strings of lexical items that are almost like independent sentences but yet have restrictions on their subject marking and tense/aspect marking that make them partially resemble possessed nouns or postpositional phrases. At the nominal end of the spectrum are clauses that are marked by nominalizations and single proper names.

    The nominalization in example (65), formed with **-wame,** serves as the subject complement of the negated predicate **tú'ii** *good*. In this example, the complement follows the negated predicate adjective.

    (65) káa-tú'ii   yée-sú'a-wame
         not-good people-kill-NZR
         Murder is bad.

The subject complement of **kaa tú'ii** may also precede it in the normal preverbal subject position as sentence (66) suggests.

    (66) kókko-wame káa-tú'íi b^{w}án-máči
         die:PL-NZR not-good cry-CAU
         Death is not good; it makes one cry.

    In the middle of the verbal to nominal scale is the quotative complement of an applicative form of a verb of saying, illustrated in sentence (67). This clause is marked with a third person singular object marker **'á'a**, which is also used in Yaqui to mark third person singular possessors. The second noun-like characteristic of this clause is the gerundial suffix **-'u** which occurs in clause final position. Sentence (68) contains an object complement clause which is marked by both a first person possessor clitic that immediately precedes the verb **'ane.** In addition, the verb is marked by the gerundial **-'u**.

    (67) káa túa   'á'a 'alléa-'u   née 'etého-ria-k
         not truly his happy-GND me tell-APL-PRF
         He told me he was a bit sad.

    (68) 'émpo káa   hú'une-iyaa-n   'iním 'ín 'ané-'u
         you NEG know-TRN-PCN here my be-GND
         Did you not know that I was here?

    The ubiquitous **mači** *to appear, to cause to appear* also takes complements that are marked with a possessor clitic in preverbal position and by the gerundial suffix **-'u** on the verb of the complement clause. In sentence (69) the possessor clitic is the second person plural **'enčí-m.**

    (69) 'itó-u yé-'a-mačí-a-k   'enčí-m 'a'a hoá-'u
         us-to out-it-appear-CON-PRF your-PL its do-GND
         He revealed to us that you did it.

3.1. The existential 'aáne "be, do"

The existential **'aáne** takes a variety of complement types that range throughout the entire nominal-sentential spectrum. At the nominal end of the spectrum, the shortened form of **'án** "be" occurs as the base of a postposition and takes as its complement a second postpositional phrase that functions as a subordinate adverbial clause. This is illustrated by sentence (70).

(70) hióko-t   'án-po=ne híapsa
     misery-at be-in=I   live
     I am barely able to survive.

Existential **'aáne** "be" also takes more sentential like complements. In example (71) the complement clause is marked with the accusative pronoun **'am** *them* but the verb form itself is finite; there is no gerundial marking to deverbalize it.

(71) haí=sa   ne túa   'áme-u 'ané-ka 'ám 'át-tua-nee
     how=INTERR I indeed them-to do-PPL them laugh-CAU-FUT
     What can I do to make them laugh?

3.2. The quotative -tea

The quotative **-tea** takes a wide range of complements from single proper nouns to entire sentences. With proper nouns it typically means "X is named Y." As is common for complements in Yaqui, the complement of **-tea** precedes it in the word order within the sentence. Sentence (72) is a typical example of its use.

(72) 'áapo hóan-tea
     he   John-be:named
     His name is John.

With vowel final forms as the last section of the complement, an echo-vowel links the complement to **-tea,** as can be observed in sentences (73) and (74).

(73) 'usí-hámut-ta   ne haríu-si-síme matílde-'e-téa-m-ta
     child-woman-ACC   I hunt-RDP-go   Matilde-EV-name-NZR-ACC
     I am looking for a girl named Matilde.

Sentence (74) presents a grammaticalized version of **-tea,** in which it serves as a quotative particle. This usage, in which we can gloss **-tea** as "so they say," represents an extension from its uses illustrated above, in which it can be glossed "X is named Y."

(74) 'áu bamíh-tua-me   láuti muk-née-'e-tea
     RFL hurry-CAU-NZR   soon die-FUT-EV-QUO
     They say that one who hurries will die soon.

3.3. The imperfective participial -ka

A very common process for marking subordinate clauses in Yaqui is the use of the imperfective participial **-ka.** These subordinate constructions often play an adverbial role in the sentences they occur in. The tense/aspect value that attaches to the subordinate clause apparently derives from the tense/aspect value of the main verb in the matrix clause. Thus in example (75) **-ka** designates a time period that is contemporaneous with the future form **yáhi-nee** *will arrive.*

(75) yoóko   yoéme búsani-ka 'á'abo   'é-u   yáhi-nee
     tomorrow men   six-being this:way you-to arrive-FUT
     Tomorrow six men will come over here to you.

Likewise, in example (76) the particular time reference of **-ka** is contemporaneous with the present repetitive/habitual form **ho-hóa.**

SONORA YAQUI LANGUAGE STRUCTURES

(76) hunáa'a búite-m-ta-béna-ka   noká-m-ta   ho-hóa
     that   run-NOM-ACC-like-being word-NOM-ACC RDP-make
     That pen, being like a running thing, makes words.

Finally, the time reference of **-ka** is contemporaneous to the past tense event **yuúma-k** *to reach* in example (77).

(77) nokí káa-tú'ii-ka   néu   yuúma-k
     word not-good-being me-to reach-PRF
     I received some bad news.

Adverbial subordinate clauses may also be marked by a postposition such as **'apo** *in* that takes a verb and its complement as its base, as in sentence (78). The temporal complement in this case consists of a free adverbial **yoóko** *tomorrow* and the quantifier **báhi** *three* marked for plural.

(78) yoóko   báhi-m   hiá-'apo yoéme búsani-ka 'á'abo   yáhi-nee
     tomorrow three-PL sound-in man   six-being this:way   arrive-FUT
     Tomorrow at three o'clock, six men will come here to you.

The suffix **-ka** used in sentences (75)–(78) is widely used to form participialized modifiers with the general meaning "being X," as the glosses of those sentences suggest. This suffix also attaches to verbs. Thus, sentence (78) could be expanded by adding a participialized verb marked with **-ka** preceding the main verb as in sentence (79).[4]

(79) yoóko   yoéme búsani-ka 'á'abo   'é-u   čaáe-ka   yáhi-nee
     tomorrow men   six-being this-way   you-to call-PPL arrive-FUT
     Tomorrow six men will come over here calling for you.

4.0. Embedded questions

Syntactically, embedded questions are a type of complement clause (Langacker 1977:172) and ordinarily follow their matrix clause. As is common in other Uto-Aztecan languages, embedded questions in Yaqui reflect both a finite versus non-finite clause distinction and the functional split between Yes/No questions and WH-questions. In the case of finite clauses, the Yaqui embedded question has the same form that it would have were it used as an independent clause in a direct question. Finite clause structure appears to be restricted to embedded WH-questions. Finally, embedded questions may function as either subjects or objects.

Semantically, embedded questions reflect the expression of one's thoughts to himself or the backgrounding of a speaker's role in forming particular thoughts, i.e., they may represent one kind of indirect quotation. Thus, mental-act verbs are most commonly used as the matrix verbs in this type of sentence.

4.1. Embedded Yes/No questions

Embedded Yes/No questions in Yaqui frequently function as the means for conveying indirect quotation, although they are not restricted to such a role. Generally the main verb of an embedded Yes/No question is marked with the gerundial suffix **-'apo**, whereas the subject nominal is marked by a possessive form, as in sentence (80). Other postpositions may also be used to mark the main verb of embedded Yes/No questions. These include **-betana** *from, regarding,* as in sentence (81) and **-t** *on, about* as in sentence (82). Notice also that examples (80) and (81) utilize the speech-act verb **-náttemae** *to ask* as the main verb, whereas example (82) calls on the mental-act verb **hú'uneeya**. Finally, in all three examples, the embedded Yes/No question precedes its matrix verb, a pattern consistent with other complement types already discussed.

---

4   It would be useful to compare the usage of Rio Fuerte speakers with that of the Rio Mayo speakers in respect to the noun **yoeme**. The Rio Fuerte speakers are in the area that was occupied by the people called "Tehueco" by Buelna. The Mayo form **yoréme** may still be used with the possessive **su**.

(80) yumá-'ik   bém   tóm-ek-a-'apo   hú'unee-bae-ka witti   'áme-u   náttemae-k
    enough-ACC their money-have-EV-GND know-DSD-PPL straight them-to ask-PRF
    Wanting to know whether they had enough money, he asked them directly.

(81) 'áapo-'ik 'á'a wáata-'u-bétana 'á-u   nát-temae-k
    he-ACC   it want-GND-from him-to ask-UNSPEC-PRF
    He asked him if he wanted it.

(82) Pótam-po bém 'ané-'u-t   hú'unee-bae-ka 'áman 'ám haríu-se-k
    Potam-in their be-GND-on know-DSD-PPL there them search-go:to-PRF
    Wanting to know if they were in Potam, he went there to look for them.

Embedded questions will often have a particle or word in them that can be glossed "whether" or "if." However, as evidenced by examples (80)–(82), Yaqui employs no such morphemes. Instead the gerundial **-'apo** and the postpositions **-betana** and **-t** are the functional equivalents with their own particular semantic contributions to the whole. Taken together with the possessive marking in the embedded question clauses to which they pertain, one could gloss them as "their having enough money," "regarding his wanting it" and "about their being in Potam," respectively. Impressionistically, Yes/No embedded questions are less frequently encountered than embedded WH-questions.

4.2. Embedded WH-clauses

Embedded WH-clauses in Yaqui are very different structurally from embedded Yes/No question clauses. For one, the embedded clause occurs following the matrix verb. In addition, the embedded clause itself is virtually identical to the form of an independent WH-question. In sentence (83) the embedded clause begins with the WH-word **haisa** *how*. Also, the matrix verb is one of mental activity, in particular, the verb **ya'a** *to do,* expressed in the strong desiderative form, which is in turn embedded in the subjunctive **'ean**.

(83)(a) sí'ime-ta yá'a-pea-ka 'éan 'ó'obek haí=sa   túa   néhpo
      all-ACC do-DSD-PPL SJV although how=Q indeed I

      'aú-ka wáka'a bató'oo-raa-ta   'allée-taú-nee
      do-PPL that:ACC baptize-(people)-ABS-ACC happy-CAU-FUT
      He really had a deep desire, saying, "How can I possibly make people happy?"

   (b) haí=sa   ne túa   'amé-u 'áne-ka 'ám 'át-tua-nee
      how=Q I indeed them-to do-PPL them laugh-CAU-FUT
      What can I do to make them laugh?

The matrix verb for an embedded WH-question may well be complex in its own right. In sentence (84) the matrix verb **hu'unéiyaa** is itself embedded in the indirect desiderative **-'íi'aa**.

(84) túa ne énčím   'á'a hu'unéiyaa-'íi'aa haísa maísi=nee 'obísi 'aáne
    truly I you:PL:ACC it know-IN:DSD   how manner=I busy be
    I really want you to know how busy I am.

Specific mental-act verbs serve as the matrix for embedded WH-questions just as they do for the embedded Yes/No questions discussed above. A typical example, with the verb **hú'unea**, is given in example (85). Its transitive counterpart was already given above in example (84).

(85) 'emé'e hú'unea haíki-si   wečía-po nát-bépa   'aáyu-k
    you:PL know how:many-AVR fallen-in together-above be-PRF
    You all know how many times it happened.

Embedded questions may be marked by a complex question marker consisting of a WH-word and a postposition. In example (86) the WH-word **híta** *something* serves as object of the postposition **betčí'ibo** *for*. The entire postpositional phrase is construed as meaning "why."

377

(86) 'intok né káa hú'unea híta-betčí'ibo 'á'a bʷán-simé-'u
    and   I   not know thing-for   her cry-go-GND
    And I do not know why she went along crying.

The postposition **bíča** *site* takes **hákun** *where* as its object and is in turn marked by the interrogative suffix **-sa** for introducing an embedded question whose verb is nominalized, having its subject marked by a third person plural possessive clitic and carrying the gerundive suffix **a'u** in example (87).

(87) kán=nee hú'unea hákun-bíčaa=sa bém sáha-k-a'u
    not=I   know where-site=Q their go:PL-PRF-GND
    I don't know which way they went.

Embedded questions serving as subjects of the sentence appear to be restricted to functioning as the complements of passive verbs as in sentence (88). A suggestion that such clauses actually are treated as syntactic subjects is seen from example (89) in which the embedded question is fronted to its matrix verb, much like a topicalized nominal would be.

(88) káa hú'unee-wa híta-taewai-t 'á'a yebíh-nee-ú
    NEG know-PSV thing-day-on his arrive-FUT-GND
    It is not known when he will arrive.

(89) 'á'a yaá-k-a'u   káa bít-wa
    his do-PRF-GND NEG see-PSV
    What he did was not seen.

Embedded questions employ virtually the entire range of indefinite pronouns that participate in WH-questions. An embedded quantity WH-question is given in example (90).

(90) haíki taéwai-m bém 'áma tawá-bae-'u-t   káa hú'unee-wa
    QNT day-PL their there remain-DSD-GND-on NEG know-PSV
    It is not known how long they will stay there.

RELATIVE CLAUSES

1.0. Introduction

Relative clauses serve to modify a noun or pronoun in a sentence and consist of subordinate clauses that refer to that noun. They specify certain information about it, information that may either be essential to understanding who the designated entity is, or non essential, merely specifying in further detail some class of information about that noun. The modified noun itself is often called the head of the relative clause. A relative clause that specifies essential information is a restrictive relative clause, whereas one that specifies nonessential information is called a nonrestrictive relative clause (Langacker 1977b:176).

Yaqui relative clauses function as subjects, direct objects and oblique objects. The following section, for expository purposes, is organized according to these categories.

2.0. Subject relative clauses

Subject relative clauses often occur in preverbal position in the sentence as illustrated by examples (1)–(3). In examples (1) and (2) the head noun occurs in first position and the clausal head consists of a Demonstrative + Noun sequence. The relative clause itself is introduced by another demonstrative that cross references to the head noun.

2.1. Kinds of subject relative clauses

Sentences (1) and (2) also illustrate distinct kinds of subject relative clauses, i.e., the relative clause in sentence (1) refers to the subject of a transitive sentence, whereas the relative clause in sentence (2) cross-references to the subject of an equative sentence. This difference correlates with a difference in the form of the demonstrative that Yaqui employs in the respective head noun phrases. Finally, the topicalized demonstrative may either precede or follow the head noun. In sentence (2) the head noun **hóan** precedes the demonstrative in a kind of equative construction that is elaborated by the relative clause that follows. In sentence (3), on the other hand, the demonstrative **hunáa'a** is actually the head of a subject nominalized clause whose nominalized core is built up from a verb **búite** *to run* plus the agentive nominalizer **-m**. This nominalization is marked for the accusative and serves as the object of the postposition.

(1) húu'u 'uúsi húu'u tá-tabúh-te-me   ba'á-po 'áu himma-k
    that boy that RDP-sweat-VR-NZR water-in RFL throw-PRF
    That boy who was sweating threw himself into the water.

(2) Hóan hunáa'a húu'u 'á'a yáa-k-ame
    John that   that it   do-PRF-NZR
    John is the one who did it.

(3) hunáa'a búite-m-ta-béna-ka   noká-m-ta-ho-hóa
    that   run-NOM-ACC-like-PPL word-NOM-ACC-RDP-make
    That pen, being like a running thing, makes words.

A subject relative clause may also be extraposed to follow the main verb in a discontinuous construction. Thus, in example (4) the head of the relative clause is a topicalized demonstrative serving the role of a full nominal. The rest of the relative clause is discontinuous from it, following the main verb **kibáke-k** *he entered*. It is introduced by a reduced form of the demonstrative. Notice that there is no possession marking in this subject relative clause.

(4) hunáa'a 'áman kibáke-k   húu'u čé'a bát 'áma yepsá-k-a'u
    that:one there enter-PRF that more first there arrive-PRF-GND
    That one who had gotten there first then entered.

On the other hand, the subject of the entire sentence may be identical to the subject of the relative clause. In such cases, there may be multiple subject marking, i.e., both a sentence initial subject pronoun and a subject clitic on the adverb occur in addition to the regular subject marking for the relative clause in example (5).

(5) 'émpo kaíbu='ee 'ém 'éa-'ú-mak yéu-wée-nee
you never=you your think-GND-with out-go-FUT
What YOU think will never work out.

2.2. Formation of subject relative clauses

A common way of forming relative clauses is to employ a verb nominalized by the agentive participle **-me** as examples (1) and (2) showed. In example (6) the nominalization **wéye-me** *the one who is coming* is marked by the accusative/possessive suffix **-ta** even though the one it designates is the subject of the transitive verb **wáata** *to want*. The sentence initial demonstrative, marked for the accusative, also cross-references to the nominalization. The overall accusative marking paired with the matrix verb **hu'unéa** suggests a layering of subordinate clauses, i.e., example (6) has an embedded question with a subject relative clause inside of it.

(6) húka'a 'á'abo wéye-m-ta wáata-'u-t ne hu'unéa
that:ACC over:here come-NZR-POS want-GND-on I know
I know what the one who is coming over here wants.

Some subject relatives are marked for polarity, i.e., Yaqui allows negative relative clauses with the nominalizer **-me**. In cases like the one that follows in example (7), the overt noun phrase head includes a demonstrative pronoun that is in the nominative case. This precludes the marking of the relative clause with a subject possessor clitic because a nonreflexive nominal is, by definition, either a subject or an object, but not both.

(7) heéwi 'áčai-t-iia hunáa'a pahkó'olaa káa 'áa
yes sir-CON-say that festal:dancer NEG able

yé'ee-me moró-ta-wi bibá-m mabét-ču-ka-i.
dance-NZR Moor-ACC-to cigarette-PL receive-CPL-PPL-PPL
"Yes sir!" the festal dancer who was not able to dance said to the Moor who contracted him, as he received the cigarettes.

An additional set of subject relatives is formed by use of the past participials **-i, -ia,** and **-ri,** as well as by the perfect participial **-laa** and its shortened form **-la**. All of these suffixes have several usages. These include the functions of an imperfective participle in construction with verb stems, predicate adjectives, attributive adjectives, and as a past passive participle.

For example, the contrast between a transitive applicative form of a verb and the stative participial form of that verb is illustrated by the applicative and stative forms in examples (8)(a) and (b). This same stative **-i** figures in the compound of (8)(c).

(8)(a) baák-e   (b) háibu baák-i   (c) waka-bák-i
     to cook   *it is now cooked*   *beef stew*

Similarly, the use of the suffix **-ia** in a main verb is shown in example (9)(a) and contrasts with its use as a stative in a subject participial phrase in example (9)(b)

(9)(a) weč-ía húu'u kúta   (b) kúta weč-ia 'áma bó'o-ka
fall-PPL that wood   wood fall-PPL there lie-PPL
The trunk has fallen.   *There is a fallen trunk there.*

The passive participle use of **-ri** is illustrated by sentence (10)(a). The contrastive relative clause use is illustrated in sentence (10)(b). The relative clause status of the construction within the copula sentence is partly signalled by the accusative suffix **-ta** on the subject of the relative clause. The naturalness with which this sentence can be translated as "This was Cajeme's doing" suggests that it is not a prototypical relative clause, however.

(10)(a) kapée hallépana yá'a-ri   (b) káa-hé'ee-m-ta   yá'a-ri 'iníi'i hunáa'a
       coffee at:once   make-PPL   not-drink-NOM-POS(a name) do-GND this   that
       The coffee was made at once.   *This is what Cajeme did.*

2.3. A historical note on relative clauses

Of the past participials, the suffixes **-ia** and **-ria** have not been found in possessed constructions. The former is apparently restricted to subject relatives, whereas the latter occurs only in object relatives, a feature that goes back to Proto-Uto-Aztecan (Langacker 1977b:181). This may be a possible argument that **-í** is an absolutive suffix, as is **-rí**. Since Yaqui has lost both those **t**'s that served as the absolutive suffix (Langacker 1977a:95), it is likely that **-i** and **-ri** are related morphologically. In line with this, note that the authors of ARTE have identified as members of a single class the suffixes **-i, -ia, -ri, -iria,** and **-ria** (and a suffix **-ye** = ?) calling them all "nominalizers." "Hay nombres sustantivos en **i** o **ri** que se forman de verbos, añadiendo la **i** o **ri** ... Cuales verbos hayan de tener el **i** solamente, y cuales el **ri**, es difícil saber por reglas: el uso lo enseñara." (Buelna 1891:14 Item 37)[1]

Buelna makes a similar statement on p. 15 regarding the suffixes **-iria, -ria** and **-ia**. "Tambien se forman los sustantivos de la misma significación que los pasivos ... poniendo ... una de estas tres partículas **iria, ria** ó **ia** ... **buite** huirse, **buitiria** el fugitivo: de **ténne** huirse muchos, **ténniria** los fugitivos. La misma dificultad padecen, para saberse cuáles toman unas partículas y cuales otras." (1891:15, Item 39)[2]

Buelna deals rather extensively with the formation of relative clauses on pages 16 through 19 and on pages 50 and 51. He notes, for example, the role of the nominalizer **-me** with an accusatively marked nominal as follows: "... La fe con que se cree en Dios, **Diosta sualuame**:" (Buelna 1891:16 Item 43).[3]

He also notes the use of a derivational active participle **-ye**. "Estos son los participios... añadiendo al verbo... esta partícula **ye**, se forma un nombre, ... significa la acción, ó el termino de ella... amado... sueño... **'ín eriaye, 'ín cotzeye**.... Discípulo de Cristo: **Jesucristota noctehoaye**: tu amado **em eriaye**." (Buelna 1891:16 Items 44, 45).[4]

Abstract nouns, or verbal substantives, are generally derived from verbs with **-me**. "Hay otros verbales sustantivos, que significan el termino abstracto.... Estos son los participios en **me**, v.g., **buauame, hiuame** ...la comida, la bebida; ... " (Buelna 1891:16,17 Item 46).[5]

Buelna notes three ways for forming relative clauses in Cáhita: "**El que, la que,** lo dicen por uno de tres modos. Primero: por el participio, v.g., el que vino, **iepsacame** ...Segundo: por el verbal en **ye**, v.g., el que mandaste azotar, **emvebtevoye**...Tercero: por el verbal in **i** ó **ri**, v.g., lo que compraste, **em hinuri**: lo que repartiste, **em hinenqui**." (Buelna 1891:50,51 Item 157.)[6]

Relative clause formation involving the use of possessed participials is well documented in Buelna. Of the the particles and suffixes mentioned by Buelna above, Yaqui currently employs all except the **-ye**

---

[1] There are substantive nouns ending in **i** or **ri** which are derived from verbs by adding the **i** or **ri**. ... It is difficult to formulate a rule that would tell which verbs have only the **i** or only the **ri**, the usages themselves determine it. (Buelna 1891:14, Item 37).

[2] Also, substantives are derived that have the same meaning as the passives ... by adding one of these three particles **iria, ria,** or **ia** ... **buíte** *to flee,* **buitiria** *the fugitive,* from **ténne** *to flee* PL, **ténneria** *the fugitives.* The same difficulty presents itself here: how one can tell which stems take which particles and which ones take the others. (Buelna 1891:15, Item 39).

[3] The faith by which one believes in God, **Diosta sualame**. (Buelna 1891:16).

[4] These are the participles ... adding them to the verb ... this particle **ye** is used for forming an abstract noun, ... it designates an action or the completion of an action ... beloved **'ín eriave**, asleep **'ín cotzeye**. Disciple of Christ: **Jesucristota noctehoaye**; your beloved **em eriaye**. (Buelna 1891:16, Items 44, 45).

[5] There are other verbal nouns which designate the abstract term. ... These are the participials which end in **-me,** e.g., **buauame, hiuame** *the food, the drink.* (Buelna 1891:16,17).

[6] He who, she who, they express this in one of three ways. First: by means of the participial suffix, e.g., the one who came, **iepsacame** ... Second, by the verb suffixed with **-ye**, ev.g., the one whom you commanded to be whipped **emvebtevoye**... Third: by the verbal ending in **i** or **ri**, e.g., that which you bought **em hinuri**; that which you handed out **em hinenqui** (Buelna 1891:50–51, Item 157).

suffix. According to current usage, the gerundizers **-'u/-'Vwi** and **-'Vpo** could be used appropriately in all the **-ye** examples that Buelna lists.

In examples (11)–(12), the suffixes **-i** and **-ri** are employed as nominalizers to derive the forms that serve as possessed abstract nouns.

(11) 'ín 'etého-i súa-wa 'i-e Lióh-ta-t 'enčím hú'unee-'ii'aa-ka-i
my talk-GND wise-PSV-NOM-INST God-CON-on you:PL:ACC know-IN:DSD-PPL-PPL
What I said was with wisdom, because I wanted you to know about God.

(12) bém yá'a-ri tú'i-si 'úttia-wa
their do-GND good-AVR applaud-PSV
What they did was really applauded.

3.0. Object relative clauses

An object relative clause is one in which the head noun which is being relativized functions as the direct object within the subordinate clause that modifies it. Notice that the subject of the relative clause is marked by a possessor clitic and may be distinct from the subject of the sentence in which it occurs. In the following example, the subject noun phrase of the sentence designates the same entity that functions as the direct object of the subordinate clause, i.e., the snake.

(13) hunáa'a baákot 'ém kó'oko-si yáa-k-a'u 'enčí ná'ateho-k
that snake your pain-ADV make-PRF-GND you:ACC accuse-PRF
The snake that you hurt accused you.

3.1. The morphology of object relative clauses

The nuclear component of the Yaqui object relative clause is a verb marked by a gerundial suffix. It is also marked by a possessor clitic in preverbal position. The pattern for this type of relative clause is summarized below.

REL CL = Head + POS CLITIC + Verb + GND

Relative clauses of this type are marked by different sets of possessive morphemes. Yaqui relative clauses are thus at the nominal end of the spectrum. The paradigm of possessive clitics that mark the subjects of relative clauses is given in Table 65.

'ín	*my*	'itóm'	*our*
'ém	*your* (SG)	'enčím	*your* (PL)
'á'a +-wa	*his/hers/its*	bém	*their*

Table 65. Subjects of relative clauses as possessors

Example (14) shows a discontinuous construction in which the head of the clause is a noun phrase of the form Demonstrative + Noun and the relative clause is placed between the demonstrative and the head noun. The relative clause itself consists of a nominalized form of the verb meaning "to live there." The derived possessed nominal **hó'aa-ka-me** *the one having a house* is marked by the accusative case suffix **-ta**. The accusative demonstrative **huká'a** refers to that one who is also the owner of the field.

(14) húka'a 'áma hó'aa-ka-m-ta waása
that:ACC there house-having-NOM-POS field
the field of the person who lives there

The verbal core of the relative clause may be marked by any one of several forms of participial and gerundive suffixes. This is another way in which relative clauses are located at the nominal end of the spectrum. These participials may appear with, or without, an intervening connector element inserted by the echo-vowel rule. The relevant forms are **-a'u**, **-'u**, **-wi**, and **-po**.

The gerundizing suffixes **-'u/-'Vwi** and **-'Vpo** are obviously related to the noun postpositions **-u/-wi** *to, toward* and **-po** *in, inside*. Note examples (15)(a) and (15)(b).

(15)(a) kári-u/kári-wi   *to the house*
    (b) kári-po   *in the house*

These suffixes are used almost exclusively in possessed constructions to form relative clauses very similar to the English expression "This was John's doing." Although English can employ a functionally equivalent cleft expression such as "This is what John did," Yaqui has only the possessed gerund in its grammar. Typical examples are (16) and (17). The relative clauses of these sentence have second person singular subjects. Note that the relative clause in (16) is syntactically the subject of the main clause, whereas the one in (17) is the direct object of the main clause of the sentence in which it appears.

(16) 'áma wéye húu'u 'óo'ou 'ém bít-bae-'u
    there go that man your see-DSD-GND
    There goes the man that you want to see.

(17) 'án=a'a yá'a-nee 'ém 'á'a wáata-'apo 'ámani
    I=it make-FUT your it want-GND there
    I'll make it any way that you want it.

The meanings "movement toward" or "static location at" that are clearly relevant to the postpositional usages of **-'u** and **-'apo** as often as not are bleached of their locative meanings when they occur in relative clauses. Nevertheless, they may be retained as part of the meaning of the gerundive forms used in relative clauses, as is clear from sentences (18) and (19) in which the possessed gerundial clause is actually a conventionalized place name. The directional usage of the place name in sentence (18) is marked with **-'u**, whereas the static locational usage in sentence (19) is marked with **-apo**.

(1) ba'á-ta kó'om-sika-'u née wée-bae
    water-POS down-go:SG-GND I go:SG-DSD
    I am going to Where the Water Goes Down.

(19) ba'á-ta kó'om-sika-'apo hó'áa-k
    water-POS down-go:SG-GND house-have
    He lives in Where the Water Goes Down.

3.2. Regarding relative pronouns

It should be observed that, technically speaking, Yaqui does not have a distinct set of relative pronouns that corresponds to the set of interrogative pronouns that we discussed earlier, i.e., **habé=sa** *Who?*, **hitá=sa** *What?*, **hakún=sa** *Where?* Rather, these same indefinite pronoun forms are put to use in forming indefinite relative clauses as shown by sentence (20). Notice, however, that the usage of the interrogative pronouns for relative pronouns is a relatively recent innovation.

(20) 'án=a'a yá'a-nee 'ém haísa 'á'a wáata-'apo 'ámani
    I=it make-FUT your how it want-GND there
    I'll make it the way that you want it.

In addition to having heads that participate in nominative-accusative marking, and having verbs that serve as postpositional bases, relative clauses can be marked for tense and aspect. The temporal distinction made by the examples of object relatives thus shows another way that Yaqui relative clauses display both nominal and verbal properties.

(21) húu'u tékil 'ém hoá-'u
    that work your do-GND
    the work that you are doing

(22) húu'u tékil 'ém hoa-k-a'u
    that work your do-PRF-GND
    the work that you did
    the work that you had done

The nominalizing suffix **-laa** may also participate in the formation of object relatives. Again, the difference between an object relative and a nominalization is minimal, the verb form itself being a nominalization.

(23) híba 'á'a wée-tua wáka'a ne-sau-ta 'ém mabét-laa
always it go-CAU that:ACC INTR-command-ACC your receive-GND
Always carry out the commands that you have received.

(24) 'ém né-sau-laa-po bemé-la wée-me hóo-wa
your INTR-order-GND-in new-GND go-NZR do-PSV
Under (in) your government (what you have commanded), new things are accomplished.

(25) Lióh-ta 'útte'e-laa-m-mea 'á-u hénno-te
God-POS be:strong-GND-PL-INST it-to shoulder-VR
He undertakes it by means of God's power.

The suffix **-laa/-la** seems to function mostly as a nominalizer as in example (26) or as a perfect participializer in finite clauses as in example (27).

(26) húka'a čiktu-la-ta 'á'a téa-'apo-táhtia 'á'a haríu-nee
that-ACC lose-PPL-ACC his find-GND-until his search:for-FUT
He will search for the lost one till he finds it.

(27) née kée 'á'a bít-laa
I not:yet him see-PPL
I have not yet seen him.

4.0. Oblique relative clauses

Oblique relative clauses are formed by adding certain postpositions to the verb. In theory, any of the postpositions would seem to be proper candidates for forming oblique relative clauses. In daily usage, the most frequently occurring postpositions that Yaqui draws on for forming oblique relative clauses are **-e** INST:SG, **-mea** INST:PL, otherwise glossed as "with" or "by means of" and **-etči** *in, at*.

Yaqui also draws on a variety of other, less commonly used postpositions for building up oblique relative clauses. In the following examples we observe the use of **táhtia** *until* in example (28), **-t** and **-tči** *on* in example (29), and **-betana** *from* in example (30).

(28) 'á'a muké-'epo-táhtia yó'o-ri-wa-k
his die-GND-until respect-PPL-PSV-PRF
He was respected until he died.

(29) hunáe taéwai-t 'áapo-'ik 'á'abo nót-ti-nee-'u-tči
that day-on he-POS over:here return-PPL-FUT-GND-on
on that day when he returns

(30) senú-k 'ečá-k-a'u-bétana senú híba hunáka'a 'áma hí-čúpa-nee
one-POS plant-PRF-GND-from one only that:ACC there IZR-complete(harvest)-FUT
From what one plants, that only will he harvest.

Another kind of oblique relative clause is formed by employing the instrumental postposition **-e** *with* in conjunction with the proper accusative form of the clitic as in example (31).

(31) hunúen 'á'a téuwaa-'u-e 'ám nók-ko-kóba-ka-i
thus his say-GND-INST:SG them word-RDP-win-PPL-PPL
Thus, by means of what he was saying, he out-argued them all.

Object relatives with a full nominal head are marked with the accusative suffix **-ta** (see example (10)(b), p. 363). The suffix itself occurs as the last element in the relative clause. This again shows the nominal-like nature of Yaqui relative clauses since many of the bases that **-ta** attaches to are nominals derived from verbs by either the active nominalizer **-me** as used in examples (32)–(33), the gerund **-'a'u** used in example (34) or the postposition **-'apo** used in (35).[7]

---

7 This is a point at which Yaqui diverges from its more southern neighbors, Cora and Huichol, in which a significantly higher degree of verbal properties attach to relative clauses.

(32) behák   né bakót-ta   bobók-ta   bʷá'e-m-ta   né bíčak
     moment:ago I snake-ACC frog-ACC   eat-NZR-ACC   I saw
     Just a while ago, I saw a snake eating a frog.

(33) 'á'a súale-k   húka'a   káa-tú'ii-k   bó'o-hóo-ria-m-ta-su
     him believe-PRF that:ACC not-good-ACC lay-do-APL-NZR-ACC-EXP
     They believed the one who did wrong.

(34) bémpo 'usí-ta kó'om-wéče-k-a'u-ta   híapsa-m-ta   tóbok-ta-k
     they boy-ACC down-fall-PRF-GND-ACC   live-NZR-ACC   lifted-VR-PRF
     They lifted up alive the boy who had fallen.

(35) Sonóora-ta mám-po   wéče-ka-'apo
     Sonora-POS hand-in   fall-PRF-GND
     The fall/conquest of Sonora.

5.0. Headless relative clauses

As we have seen from numerous examples in this section of the grammar, the head of a relative clause may be either a simple noun or a complex noun phrase. Yaqui also employs headless relative clauses, that is, relative clauses that have no overt noun head. Such clauses, however, usually have a demonstrative form that functions as the clausal head. The relative clause in example (36) is marked for the accusative case. The verb in this relative clause is marked with the gerundial **-ri**. The accompanying possessive pronoun **bem** *their* signals the subject of the relative clause.

(36) wáka'a   bém tá'aru-ri
     that:ACC their lose-GND
     what they lost

ADVERBIAL CLAUSES

1.0. Introduction

Semantically, adverbial clauses in Yaqui express a wide range of locative, temporal, and abstract concepts. In clear contrast to relative clauses, which highlight discrete entities, adverbial clauses highlight locations in space, time, or abstract domains of various sorts. The markers that Yaqui employs include suffixes on nouns as well as on verbs and postpositions.

2.0. Two kinds of adverbial clauses

The adverbial clauses of Yaqui discourse can be broadly categorized as locative adverbial clauses and temporal adverbial clauses. The temporal adverbial clauses reflect several kinds of temporal relations between the event related by the main clause and the backgrounded temporal clause.

2.1. Locative adverbial clauses

Locative adverbial clauses can often be considered to convey the notion "there where X occurs" as one part of their meaning. In Yaqui such clauses may be marked with an adverbial demonstrative pronoun that is further elaborated by a subordinate clause marked with the accusative/possessive suffix **-ta** and is thus on the nominal end of the noun-verb spectrum. In example (1) the verb of the subordinate clause is also marked with the postposition **-wi** *to*. This is an additional indication that adverbial relative clauses are on the nominal end of the spectrum. Finally, note that the adverbial demonstrative **'áman** is discontinuous from the subordinate clause.

(1) 'áman hó'a-k b^{w}ía-ta b^{w}éhi-wa-'a-wi
    there home-has dirt-POS dig-PSV-EV-to
    He lives there where they are digging dirt.

In the minimal adverbial relative illustrated by example (2), no adverbial demonstrative occurs, but the subject noun **ba'á** *water* is marked with the accusative/possessive suffix **-ta,** as also seen in (1) above, and the verb is marked by the gerundial suffix **-'Vpo**, which in this case implies the locative concepts "in," "place," or "location," all of which reflect its grammatical source in the postposition **-po** *in*.

(2) ba'á-ta kó'om-siká-'a-po
    water-POS down-go-EV-in
    where the water goes down

In example (3) the subject of the adverbial relative, marked as usual by the accusative/possessive suffix **-ta,** occurs sentence initially as a topicalized constituent, followed by the adverbial demonstrative **'áma** *there* and the rest of the adverbial relative clause. The postposition **-bétana** *from* marks the subordinate verb in this construction, which designates a physical location.

(3) ta'á-ta 'áma yéu-wee-'e-bétana
    sun-POS there out-go-EV-from
    from where the sun comes out (i.e., *east*)

Yaqui can string together in a single sentence several "where" clauses as in example (4). This sentence also shows a verb-verb compound that serves as an attributive adjective that is discontinuous from the noun that it modifies.

(4) 'áman yéu-kéča-'a-wa-k   báhi pahkó'a-m haíbu súma'i-taka 'áma yé'ee-'apo
    there out-stand:SG-EV-PSV-PRF three feaster-PL now tied-being   there dance-GND:place
    He was taken to where he was to perform, where three tied Pascal Dancers were already dancing.

387

2.2. Temporal clauses

The marking of a temporal adverbial relative is very much like the locational one, showing accusative/possessive marking on the subject noun and the presence of an adverbial demonstrative. Again, the verb is marked with a suffix, but in this case it is the temporal/conditional suffix **-o**, which can be glossed "when." In sentence (5) the temporal suffix **-o** is followed by the emphatic clitic =**su,** which highlights the content of the temporal clause.

(5) ta'á-ta sík-čin-ti 'áma wéč-o=su
sun-POS red-cotton-ADV there fall-when=EMP
as the sun was setting like red cotton

Yaqui adverbial clauses mark a number of distinct temporal relations including those of anteriority, simultaneity, and future potential. Yaqui employs a variety of devices for marking these relations. These grammatical elements include tense/aspect suffixes, postpositions, and the conditional suffix **-o**.

"When" clauses tend to occur as the first clause in the sentence and are often marked by the participial **-ka**. Sentences (6)–(9) are typical examples. Often the relation signalled by a temporal clause marked by **-ka** can be glossed as "having done X, then Y happened," as is the case in sentence (6).

(6) wóh-naíki puéplo náu yáha-ka 'á'a pahkó-ria-k
two-four town together arrive:PL-PPL him feast-APL-PRF
All the eight towns, coming together, participated in the burial ceremonies for him.

The relation between the adverbial **-ka** clause and the main clause can be temporally overlapping and the sentence itself is not restricted to only designate potentially occurring situations, as is clear from sentence (7).

(7) 'iníka=ne hú'uneiyaa-ka túa 'alléa
this=I:ACC know-PPL indeed happy
Knowing this makes me very happy.

In general, the adverbial clause marked by **-ka** is imperfective in aspect and provides the conceptual background to the main clause whose verb is in the perfective aspect as in sentence (8) and (9).

(8) kóko-la-m-násuk bó'o-ka yéhte-k
die:PL-PPL-PL-among lie-PPL stand-PRF
He arose from among the dead.

(9) 1740-po kalíhto, nássua-ka kobá-'a-wa-k 'ótám-káu-po
1740-in Calixto fight-PPL gain-EV-PSV-PRF bone-mount-in
When Calixto fought in 1740, he was beaten at Bones Mountain.

In sentence (10) a subordinate "when" clause is marked by the simple perfective form of the verb. In addition, this sentence illustrates a sequence of a demonstrative and a quantifier which together form a modifier-head construction.

(10) sí'ime 'áma mátču-k hunáka'a wépu'ulai-k 'áma 'átbʷa-ka mátču-k
all there dawn-PRF that:ACC one-ACC there laugh:at-PPL dawn-PRF
Everyone was still wide awake when morning came, all laughing at that one man when dawn came.

In sentences (11) and (12) the subordinate adverbial clauses are temporally simultaneous to the main clauses, and the verbs of those main clauses are marked for completive aspect. This usage shows that the overall event is being construed as a bounded whole and that the temporal location of the subordinate clause is being calculated against the successive stages of the process designated by the verb in the main clause.

(11) 'áapo 'íntok yánti   wée-ka   'ám bít-ču
     he   CNJ   motionless stand-PPL them see-CPL
     But he just stood there quietly, staring at them.

(12) kat-é'em   wa'ák-ti-ka   née=bít-ču
     NEG-you:PL   mouth:open-CON-PPL   me=see-CPL
     Don't gape while you are looking at me.

2.3. A "while" clause marking simultaneity

The role of the imperfective **-ka** to plot the succession of states internal to a backgrounded process against the development of a process encoded by a main clause verb has already been mentioned with respect to the usages of **-ka** in examples (6)–(9) above. It is further seen clearly from the gloss of example (13).

(13) kát=e'e   té'ite-ka   'áman yebíh-nee
     not=you stumble-PPL   there arrive-FUT
     May you arrive there without stumbling (while you are on the way).

Generally, as suggested by example (13), manner adverbial clauses mark the simultaneity of a backgrounded ongoing process. Example (14) also shows this. The main verb, as in sentences (11)–(12), is marked with the completive **-su**, here realized phonetically as **-ču** (see PHONOLOGY, p. 30).

(14) wáa'a 'íntok yoéme káa 'áa yé'ee-me   hunáma wée-ka   'á'a bít-ču
     that CNJ   man   NEG able dance-NZR there stand:SG him see-CPL
     Well, the man that couldn't dance stood there staring at it.

Whereas manner adverbial clauses are consistently marked as imperfective, the range of subordinate verb types is essentially open. In sentence (15) an instrument noun-verb compound serves as the verb of the manner adverbial clause.

(15) 'íi'i 'íntok yoéme čibá'ato síh-hubá-ka   siíka
     this CNJ   man   goat   urine-smell-PPL   go:PAST
     Well, this man went on, stinking of goat urine.

Posture verbs commonly function as the nucleus in adverbial clauses as in examples (16) and (17).

(16) pahkó'ola yánti   wée-ka   'á'a bó'o-bíča
     feast:person motionless stand-PPL him lay-see
     The Pascal Dancer stood still waiting for it.

(17) 'á-u   kíkte-ka   'áman 'á'a bít-ču
     him-to stand:SG-PPL   there him see-CPL
     It stood off there staring at him.

The postposition **-patči** also functions to mark temporal adverbial clauses. In its various usages, it can be assigned meanings such as "upon," "at the time of," and "immediately after." Sentence (18) gives a common example.

(18) 'ín tótoi 'o'ów-ia   kukúh-patči kó'om-čépte-k
     my chicken male-PPL crow-upon   down-jump-PRF
     As soon as my rooster crowed, he jumped down.

The temporal relation signaled by **-patči** is often that of immediate anteriority as sentence (18) suggests. The temporal proximity of the two events being related may be so close that the use of **-patči** may even grade into that of marking simultaneity as its uses in sentences (19) and (20) suggest. These examples also illustrate a main verb use of **tíia** and the use of the hortatory suffix **-bu**.

(19) Liós 'é'em čanía-bú tíia wáa'a yo'o-tu-i   kíkte-patči
     God you:ACC help-HRT says that old:man-VR-PPL stand-upon
     "Hello," said the old man, upon standing before him.

(20) nóolia-ma t-iía 'á-u mámte-patči
 hurry-HRT says him-to hand-VR-upon
 "Well, hurry then," he said, as he extended his hand to him.

The use of **nau** *together* in combination with the verb **yáhi** *to arrive* in example (21) highlights the temporal contiguity of the events being related by the speaker. Here the end point in the development of the backgounded event is linked to the realization of the future event referred to by the verb of the main clause.

(21) 'íntok té tenni-nee 'a-u-táhtia náu-yáhi-patči náu té 'á'a 'aak-ta-nee
 and we run-FUT him-to-until together-arrive-upon together we him butt-CAUS-FUT
 And we will run to where he is, and upon arriving together, we will butt him together (between us).

In sentence (22) **-patči** is used with a verb whose activity is viewed as a future potential one. The use of the future suffix **-nee** on the main verb places the entire scene into a future time setting. This statement is also true for sentence (21), given above.

(22) 'é-u n='a'a wéiyaa-nee nótti-patči
 you:to I=it bring-FUT return-upon
 I will bring it to you upon my return.

The glosses of sentences (23)–(25) below reinforce the foregoing comments about the close temporal sucession of the events related by the adverbial clauses marked by **patči** and the main clauses that they modify. One way to account for this is in terms of Lakoff's Spatialization of Form Hypothesis, i.e., the postpositional usages of **-patči** imply spatial contact between a grounding entity that is used to locate within the spatial setting the entity highlighted in the relation being signalled by **-patči.** This entails that, in the mapping from the spatial domain to the temporal domain, the notion of spatial contact between a pair of discrete entities extends to apply to conceived temporal contact between a pair of events (cf. Lakoff 1991).

(23) 'íka'a tebó-tua-patči watém 'á-u nát-temae
 this:ACC greet-CAU-upon others him-to UNSPEC-ask
 As soon as he had greeted him, he asked about his (distant) friends/relatives.

(24) heéwi-t-iu-patči kíkte-k
 yes-CON-say-upon stood-PRF
 Immediately upon saying yes, he stood up.

(25) hikáu-čépti-patči tútti kíkte-k
 up-jump-upon well stood-PRF
 As soon as he jumped up, he stood firm.

Temporal anteriority can be signalled by other means in Yaqui, also. As suggested by examples (6) and (8), given earlier, a temporally antecedent subordinate clause is often marked by the participial suffix **-ka.** Sentence (26) illustrates the adverbial use of **sép** *at once* in the main clause as an adverb meaning "immediately."

(26) 'áman yepsá-ka mabét-wa-k sép hí'i-b^{w}a-tua-wa-k
 there arrive-PPL receive-PSV-PRF at:once IZR-eat-CAU-PSV-PRF
 Arriving there, he was received and was fed at once.

In example (27) the sentence initial quantifier is marked for plural accusative. Reduplication on the verb in the subordinate clause marks plural direct object. The subordinate clause itself is temporally antecedent to the time of the main clause. Antecedent time, in this case, is marked on the subordinate verb by both the completive **-su** and the participial suffix **-ka.**

(27) sí'ime-m ko-kobá-su-ka muúku-k
 all-PL RDP-gain-CPL-PPL die-PRF
 He died, having surpassed all the rest.

An "after" clause may also be marked by both the completive **-su** and the participial **-ka,** as in sentence (28). The sentence final clause is an adverbial clause measuring the extent of the distance covered.

(28) 'á'a či-čík-su-ka   kó'om-čepté-ka siíka   wóh-mámni wa'ák-ti-po
     him RDP-sweep-CPL-PPL down-jump-PPL go:PAST twice-five   step-PPL-in
     After it had finished brushing his face, it jumped down and went away about ten paces.

Sentence (29) illustrates the point that Yaqui also uses juxtaposition for indicating the immediate sequencing of one event following another, i.e., the two juxtaposed passive clauses are grammatically coordinate, but iconically sequenced in line with the normal temporal succession of events.

(29) hunáma béha sép   supé-yéča-'a-wa-k   piisáa-m   saaweá-tua-wa-k
     there   well at:once shirt-off-EV-PSV-PRF blanket-PL trouser-CAU-PSV-PRF
     Then right there, his shirt was taken off and a blanket was made into trousers for his legs.

3.0. Irrealis adverbial relations

Yaqui adverbial clauses in the logical domain represent common extensions from the spatial and temporal domains. This is seen in both the form of the grammatical patterns used to encode such concepts as well as in the polysemy of the various markers that Yaqui employs in these domains. The logical relations include notions such as "if," "counter expectation" and "counter factual."

3.1. Temporal "if" clauses

In Yaqui, "if" clauses are marked by the suffix **-o**. As is common in Uto-Aztecan languages, this suffix has meanings that relate to both temporal and logical space, i.e., **-o** can mean either "if" or "when." The particular meaning which is intended is ordinarily deducible from the construction in which the sequence is used.

The following examples illustrate the temporal usage of the suffix **-o**. In sentences (30)–(32) the temporal clause occurs in sentence initial position. As examples (30)–(31) also suggest, temporal clauses may also be strung together in a single sentence. Metaphorical usages of the verbs meaning "to stand" and "to hit" are illustrated in the two "when" clauses of example (30).

(30) páhko ramáa-ta   yečá-'a-su-a-k-o   pahk-ó'a-m
     feast shelter-ACC stand-EV-CMP-PSV-PRF-when feast-old:man-PL

     náu   béep-su-a-ka-o   pahko naáte-k
     together hit-CMP-PSV-PRF-when feast begin:PRF
     When the feast "ramada" was built, when the "pascolas" were brought together, the feast began.

(31) 'iníi'i yoói   karíl-bo'ó-ta hóo-naáte-wa-o
     this   non-yaqui rail-road-ACC make-begin-PSV-when

     téta hóo-tahitia-k-o   'áu takéa-k
     stone make-INC-PRF-when RFL hire-PRF
     This Mexican hired himself out, when they were beginning to build the railroad bed, when they were putting the gravel on it.

(32) naíki taéwa-ta sím-su-k-o   húči 'áma yéu-sáha-k
     four day-ACC go-CMP-PRF-when again there out-go:PL-PRF
     When four days had passed, they left there again.

The use of **-o** to mark a clause whose temporal extension is the background for situating a perfectively construed event is illustrated by sentence (33).

(33) káa-hé'ee-m-ta   két 'iním né-sauwe-o   sí'ime wáa'a
    NEG-drink-NZR-POS still here INTR-command-when all   that

    bato'o-raa   na'iki-m sáha-k
    baptized-ABS scatter-PL go:PL-PRF
    While Cajeme was still ruling here, all the people scattered.

In sentence (34) the complex adverbial demonstrative phrase **hunúm háku'u** *somewhere around there* spells out in rough detail the temporal setting to which the suffix **-o** relates the content of the adverbial clause.

(34) hunúm háku'u   'abe   née yéu-tóm-te-o   há'ani
    there somewhere nearly I   out-stomach-VR-when perhaps
    It was somewhere around that time, just before I was born.

3.2. "If" and "because" clauses

The temporal relationship between the "when" clause and the main clause sometimes parallels the relation between a causing event and a caused one as does English "when." This is true of sentence (35), for example, and the dependent adverbial clause could plausibly be glossed as either an "after" clause or a "because" one. Note that in this case, the verb of the temporal clause is perfective, whereas the predicate adjective and the intransitive verb in the main clause are both imperfective.

(35) 'á'a kunáwa sií-k-o   púh-báhiyaa-taka húni b^{w}aána
    her husband go-PRF-when face-swell-being even cry
    When her husband left her, her face was swollen from crying.

Sentence (36) as well as earlier examples, contrasts with sentence (35) in that the verb of the dependent adverbial clause is imperfective and the verb of the main clause is perfective.

(36) pá'aria-po   'á'a weáma-o-su   wó'i   pócǒ'oria-bétana wée
    open:space-in his walk-when-HL coyote woods-from   go
    While he was walking in an open space, a coyote came out of the woods.

As suggested by all the previous examples, a "when" clause is marked by the suffix **-o** which attaches to the final lexical item in the clause. The "when" clause itself, although commonly imperfective, may also be construed perfectively as it is in sentence (37).

(37) 'áman yéu-tóhi-wa-o   bató'o-raa 'á'a téa-ka   čáai-táite-k
    there out-bring-PSV-when baptize-ABS him note-PPL yell-INC-PRF

    'ála,   'í'ani hi'á'ab^{w}e čí'icibo   nú'upa-wa-k   téta'ahaao
    indeed now   look   bitter:herb bring-PSV-PRF "estafiate"
    When this man was brought out, the people, recognizing him, began to yell: "Well now, what has been brought, here, a very bitter herb, and estafiate, too!"

A "when" clause often specifies quantified time indicated by a postpositional phrase that takes a numeral phrase marked in the accusative for its object.

(38) néhpo=su 'áman 'emó-u yéu-yebíh-nee báhi taéwai-ta wée-o
    I=EMP   there you-to out-arrive-FUT three day-ACC go-when
    I will indeed come over there to you in three days.

3.3. Conditional "if" clauses

As is common for Uto-Aztecan languages (cf. Langacker 1977a:192) as well as in many other languages (cf. German and Navajo), Yaqui temporal **-o** *when*, extends semantically to come to mean "if" in the conditional sense. The next set of examples illustrates typical conditional usages of **-o**. Often the subordinate clause that **-o** marks is itself related in a more complex structure involving the relation "because," as in sentence (39).

Adverbial clauses 3.3.

(39) bʷéʼituk ne káa ʼenčím   sáha-k-o   bʷána-ka matčú-nee
     because I   not you:PL:POS go:PL-PRF-if cry-PPL   wake:up-FUT
     Because if you don't go, I'll wake up crying tomorrow.

Ordinary "if" clauses often imply a negative assumption on the part of the speaker. Thus, in sentence (40), the speaker is assuming that his addressee is in the wrong. The use of the future **-nee** in the main clause is significant here, indicating contingency, not certainty.

(40) lútuʼuria-m ʼáu-k-o   néhpo ʼenčím   híkkahi-nee
     truth:ACC   be-PRF-if I   you:PL:ACC hear-FUT
     If you were in the right, I would hear your case.

On the other hand, conditional clauses embedded to main clauses expressed in the past tense often signal contrary to fact contingencies. Thus, in sentence (41) the narrator is expressing what did not happen, leaving in the background what the hearer can assume did happen. The inference of what did happen is actually contained lexically in the initial sentence of this complex example. Note that the main clauses of the conditional sentences are all marked by the past continuative subjunctive **-ʼea-n**.

(41) táa káa née bʷíse-k   bʷéʼituk=ne túʼisi ʼúʼute búite káa née ʼúʼute búite-o nee
     but not me grab-PRF because=I very   strong run   not I   strong run-if me

     bʷíh-ʼea-n   supé-m-po nee bʷíse-ka-n   táa née máam-mea ʼáʼa béeba-k
     grab-think-PCN:SJV shirt-PL-on me grab-PPL-PCN but I   hand-INST him hit-PRF

     káa ne=ʼa béeba-k ketúni nee bʷís-si-sím-ʼea-n   híba túa   ne ʼáa-mak
     not I=him hit-PRF still me grab-RDP-go-think-PCN:SJV truly indeed I him-with

     nássua-ʼea-n
     fight-think-PCN:SJV
     But he didn't grab me, because I really ran fast. If I hadn't run so fast, he would have grabbed me; he had grabbed my shirt, but I hit him with my hand. If I hadn't knocked him off with my hand, he would probably still have a hold of me; in all probability I would have had to fight with him.

Occasionally the usage of **-o** is ambiguous between the temporal and conditional meaning. For example, the sentence in (42) can be understood either way.

(42) humák húniʼi káa báu-nee yukú-k-o
     perhaps even not leak-FUT rain-PRF-if/when
     Maybe it won't leak if/when it rains.

The conditional clause may also occur as the last clause in a complex sentence as sentence (43) illustrates.

(43) ʼínepo ʼenčí   ʼanía-nee ʼenčí húnen ʼéa-o
     I   you:SG:ACC help-FUT you   thus think-if
     I will help you, if you want (me to).

Conditional clauses may be strung together in rather lengthy sequences as in example (44).

(44) ʼitóm yáha-ʼapo-táhti   ʼím ʼenčí   ʼané-o kée   ʼenčí muké-o ʼenčí
     our   arrive:PL-GND-until here you:ACC be-if not:yet you   die-if you

     híapsa-o ʼíntok ʼiním ʼito-béas   ʼenčí ʼané-o née ʼenč=aʼa mák-nee
     live-if and   here us-front:of you be-if I   you=it   give-FUT
     By the time we come back, if you are here, if you haven't yet died, if you are still alive, and if you are here in front of us, I will give it to you.

In its temporal sense, the suffix -o is used sometimes in conjunction with **-tu-k** to indicate dates given as days and years, as in example (45) and as was discussed earlier in VERB MORPHOLOGY, pp. 140–141.

393

(45) hunáman 'á'a bʷíh-wa-ka-'apo   'á'a 'u'áa-wa-k   1887-tu-k-o
    there   his seize-PSV-PRF-GND him take-PSV-PRF 1887-VR-PRF-when
    It was taken away from him there where he was seized; that was in 1887.

The "if" clause can also occur as the final clause in a complex sentence especially if the resulting condition is topicalized, as in examples (46)–(49). The "if" clause may even imply an actual state of affairs, as it does in sentences (46) and (47).

(46) tú'ii-'éa-n   té káa ho'ó-t 'ám pú'ak-ta-nee-'e-te-k-o
    good-SJV-PCN we not back-on them carry-VR-FUT-EV-VR-PRF-if
    It would be good if we didn't have to carry them on our backs.

(47) mínai-m   mékkaa win-húba bʷásé-'e-te-k-o
    canteloupes far   fragrant ripe-EV-VR-PRF-if/when
    Canteloupes are fragrant for a long distance away if they are ripe.

Likewise, the "if" clause may imply a hypothesized or possible state of affairs as is suggested by sentences (48) and (49).

(48) haísa=nee híu-nee   'íka'a   téuwaa-bae-'e-te-k-o
    how=I   sound-FUT this:ACC say-DSD-CON-VR-PRF-if
    What do I say, if I want to say this?

(49) né-u 'á'a 'á'awa 'á-u yumá'ik tóme-ka-'a-te-k-o
    me-to it   ask   it-to enough money-have-CON-VR-PRF-if
    Ask me for it, if you have enough money (to buy it).

Sequences of "if" clauses in a single sentence may be conjoined by the coordinating conjunction **'intok** as illustrated by sentence (50).

(50) senú táta-búh-ti-nee   hewí tekipánoa-'a-te-k-o   'íntok bo'ó-hoá-'a-te-k-o
    one hot-sweat-VR-FUT yes work-EV-VR-PRF-if/when and   road-make-EV-VR-PRF-if/when
    A person sweats a lot, doesn't he, when/if he works and when/if he travels.

4.0. "Without" clauses

Another type of adverbial clause in Yaqui expresses the concept of engaging in one activity without engaging in some other one either simultaneously or previously. Such "without" clauses may be marked by a sentence initial negative that has scope over a subordinate clause marked by the participial **-ka** as in example (51). The excluded event of the adverbial clause is backgrounded to the highlighted event of the main clause, which here is treated as an, as yet, unrealized state of affairs, marked by the future **-nee**. It may also be treated as a realized event, in which case the main verb is marked by **-ka** and the verb of the adverbial clause is marked by the participial **-ka** and the stative **-i** following it, as in example (52). Finally, the "without" clause may occur either before, as in example (51), or following the main clause as in sentence (52).

(51) kát=e'e hí'i-bʷa-ka   tó'o-nee
    not=you INTR-eat-PPL lie-FUT
    You will go to bed without eating.

The use of the perfective form **matču-k** *to dawn*-PRF is a perfective form, but the meaning of the stem itself implies a span of time which is elaborated specifically by the temporal phrase **sí'ime tukáa-ta** all night-ACC *all night long*. This usage is possibly a calque from the Spanish "madrugarse."

(52) sí'ime tukáa-ta   tekipánoa-ka mátču-k   káa kóčo-ka-i
    all   night-ACC work-PPL   dawn-PRF NEG sleep-PPL-STAT
    He worked all night without having slept.

4.1. Counterfactive clauses with -ean and -o

Contrary to fact conditional clauses may be marked by some element + **'ea-n** in the apodasis clause and by the conditional suffix **-o** in the protasis as example (53) illustrates. The clause **tú'ii-'éa-n né kía kómona-k-o** *it would have been good if I had only gotten wet* carries the implication that what actually happened was significantly more than getting wet. The remainder of this complex sentence states precisely what else did take place.

(53) yúku-po né wée-ka kómona-k tú'ii-'éa-n né kía kómona-k-o
rain-in I go-PPL get:wet-PRF good-think-PCN I only get:wet-PRF-if

táa nee kómona-ka 'íntok tečóa-po čítoh-te-ka 'attala weče-k
but I get:wet-PPL and mud-in slip-VR-PPL flat:on:back fall-PRF

Yesterday, I got wet walking in the rain; it would have been good if I had only gotten wet, but I got wet and slipped in the mud and fell flat on my back.

Sentence (54) has a negative conditional clause marked by **-o** and an apodasis clause marked by **-ea-n**. The clear implication of the negative clause is that the speaker really did run fast, whereas the implication of the result clause is that the other person did not catch him.

(54) káa nee 'ú'ute búite-o née bʷíh-'ea-n
not I strong run-if me grab-think-PCN
If I hadn't run fast, he would have grabbed me.

The conditional clause can be final to a sentence and can have the conditional marking on the verb **-ea**. In this case, the combination **-ea-o** seems to indicate a marked degree of doubt on the speaker's mind as in sentence (55).

(55) 'ínepo 'enčí 'anía-nee 'enčí húnen 'éa-o
I you:SG:ACC help-FUT you:SG:ACC thus think-if
I will help you, if you want.

Both temporal and conditional usages of **-o** can be mixed in the same Yaqui sentence. In sentence (56) this mix occurs as part of a string of concatenated **-o** clauses with the conclusion clause as the last.

(56) 'itóm yáha-'apo-táhti 'ím 'enčí 'ané-o kée 'enčí muké-o
our arrive:PL-GND-until here you:ACC be-if not:yet you die-if

'enčí híapsa-o 'íntok 'iním 'ito-béas 'enčí 'ané-o née 'enč=a'a mák-nee
you live-if and here us-front:of you be-if I you=it give-FUT

By the time we come back, if you are here, if you haven't yet died, if you are still alive, and if you are here in front of us, I will give it to you.

4.2. Simulfactive clauses

The suffix **-amča** *as if* does not occur very frequently in text material and may be going out of usage, although example (57) below is from a relatively recent autobiographical narration that Dedrick recorded. Semantically, the usage of this suffix implies a comparison between an actualized event and a conceptualized one which is the basis for the comparison. In this sentence the speaker's posture is compared to that of a person who had been commanded to look up into the sky, although no one had actually instructed him to do so. In example (58), on the other hand, the dancer engaged in optical deception to cause the observers to think that he was actually dancing on air.

(57) hunáman hikáu bítču kía hunáman bi-bit-ču-tebo-k-amča 'áayu-k
there up see:CPL only there RDP-see-CPL-IMP-PRF-as:if do-PRF
I was staring up at that place; I did it as if I had been commanded to look up there.

(58) 'áman b^wé'u sísi'iwoki-u hiká-u yepsá-ka heká-po hika-t yé'e-mča 'aáne
    there big "wire"-to up-to arrive-PPL air-in up-on dance-as-if does
    He went up high on the high wire; having gotten up there, he made as if he were dancing on the air.

Yaqui has a number of other ways to express notions such as "just as" or "just like." To begin, the connector **kía** *only* commonly marks this relation. The postposition **-béna** also is employed for this purpose. Both of these grammatical devices may be used together in a single sentence as is illustrated in sentence (59). This sentence also illustrates the use of an adjective formed with **-la**.

(59) 'áme-u kibáke-k kía 'áme-u kík-síme torómpa-ta
    them-to enter-PRF only them-to stand-go:SG top-POS

    betéa-po kóče-'e-béna-sia mú'ila kík-sime
    pan-in sleep-EV-like-AVR serene stand:SG-go
    He entered into his dance; he went into a serene routine that was like a top spinning in a pan, so rapidly that it was just as if he were standing there fast asleep.

A related adverbial notion is that of "just" or "only." The quantificational adverb **kía** marks this relationship also. It usually occurs as the second constituent in a main clause, as example (60) shows, but it may also be the first constituent in a subordinate clause as seen in (61).

(60) sóoni-m kía híkkahi-nee
    music-PL only hear-FUT
    He would just listen to the music.

(61) néhpo=ne káa 'áa yé'ee 'íntok ne káa 'áa 'etého kía ne tiwé-ka 'áma kík-nee
    I=I NEG able dance CNJ I NEG able converse only I shame-PPL there stand:SG
    I can't dance and I can't tell stories; I just stand there embarrassed.

Sentence (62) illustrates a hypothetical "as though" clause. Note also the reflexive pronoun in this sentence. It is formed by suffixing a morpheme **-la/-ela** to a reduced form of the third person free subject pronoun **aapo**.

(62) hunáa'a híba 'áapela-e-béna-si hiá-ka mátču-k
    that only he:alone-CON-like-AVR say-PPL dawn-PRF
    It was as though he were the only one who had anything to say when dawn came.

Concessive clauses, which can be marked by subordinators meaning "even though" are marked in Yaqui by the quantifying adverb **'ó'oben** as in example (63), where it occurs in clause initial position, even preceding the adversative coordinating conjunction **taa**.

(63) née hiókoe káa ne túa 'áa 'etého 'ó'oben táa 'inía 'etého-i-mak
    me excuse NEG I indeed able converse although but this tell-PPL-with

    ne yéu-tom-té-ka né 'emó-u 'á'a téuwaa
    I out-stomach-VR-PPL I you:PL-to it tell
    Excuse me, although I am not able to tell stories very well, yet having been born with this story, I tell it.

Negative concessive clauses are marked by the introducer **huní'i** with or without the following adverbial **ketúni** *still* and by a reduced negative suffix complex in clause final position. Note example (64).

(64) 'emó-u 'á'a téuwaa-k emé'e 'íntok née múk-su-k   húni'i ketúni 'á'a teúwaa-nee híba
     you-to it   tell-PRF you   CNJ   I die-CPL-PRF even still it tell-FUT always

   'em tua   ne-u wáati-nee káa-báe-ka   húni'i nee híkkahi-su-me
   you indeed me-to remember-FUT NEG-DSD-PPL even me hear-CPL-NZR

   nee híkkahi-su-ka-me   nee tá'aa-k-ame
   me hear-CPL-PPL-NZR   me know-PRF-NZR
   I have told it to you, and even after I am dead you will go on telling it, and in that way you will be remembering me, even though you didn't intend to, those who are hearing me now, those who have heard me, and those who know me.

4.3. "Because" clauses

"Because" clauses are commonly marked by the introducer **b^we'ituk** and often occur as the initial clause in a complex sentence, as illustrated by example (65). These adverbial clauses often occur preceding the main clause of the sentence as example (66) shows.

(65) b^wé'ituk haíbu kó'om-kúakte-n
     because now   down-turn-PCN
     because the sun had now sunk low

(66) b^wé'ituk wáa'a wéye-me hí'i-b^wá-bae-ka   wéye
     because that   go-NOM INTR-eat-DSD-PPL go
     Because that one is on the move, he is going around looking for food.

Sentence (66), given above, is somewhat complicated semantically. The participialized desiderative **-bae-ka** semantically is conventionally interpreted to mean "because he wants to do X." Another way of translating this sentence would be "Because the one who is on the move, he is on the move because he wants to eat (or he is looking for food)." Sentence (67) presents a similarly structured pair of "because" clauses.

(67) b^wé'ituk huébena-k 'ée-sime sí'ime-ta yá'a-pea-ka-'éa-n
     because much-ACC think-go all-ACC do-DSD-PPL-think-PCN

   'ó'obe-k   háisa túa   néhpo 'áu-ka
   though-ACC   how   indeed I   do-PPL
   Because he went thinking a lot of things, he was yearning to do everything: "What can I do?"

The heightened desiderative **-pea**, together with the participial **-ka** form an additional manner of marking "because" clauses, as illustrated by sentence (67) above and (68) below. In sentence (68) the "because" clause occurs following the main clause.

(68) 'útte'a wéye mó'oči-m-me-u   yebíh-pea-ka-i
     strong go   Los Mochis-PL-NZR-to arrive-DSD-PPL-PL
     He went as fast as he could because he was anxious to get to Los Mochis.

4.4. Manner clauses

The final type of adverbial clause that we discuss here can be called "how" clauses. Some of these are clearly morphologically related to the interrogative forms described earlier in QUESTIONS, pp. 90–96 and in COMPLEMENT CLAUSES, pp. 377–378. These are all marked by the word **haísa**. As examples (69)–(71) suggest, the final syllable **-sa** of the **haísa** employed in "how" clauses is likely the question marker **=sa** found in the other Yaqui WH-words such as **habé=sa** *Who?*, based in the indefinite personal pronoun **hábe** *person* and **haíki=sa** *how much*, based on **haíki** *an indefinite quantity*.

(69) habé=sa   'émpo bít-bae
     person=Q you   see-DSD
     Whom do you wish to see?

(70) haíki muní-m-sa 'émpo wáata
    amount bean-PL:ACC-Q you:SG want
    How many beans do you want?

(71) sí'ime-ta ya'a-pea-ka 'ean 'o'obek hai=sa tía nehpo
    all-PPL do-DSD-PPL SJV although how=INTERR indeed I

    'aú-ka waka'a bato'oo-raa-ta 'allee-túa-nee
    be-PPL that:ACC baptize-ABS-ACC happy-CAU-FUT
    He really had a deep desire, saying, "How can I possibly make people happy?"

To distinguish the adverbial clause connector usage from the interrogative usage, we conventionally cite the former as an unanalyzable whole as in sentence (72), whereas we cite the WH-form as a bi-morphemic sequence, as in example (71) above.

(72) 'á'a yá'a-nee 'ém haísa 'á'a wáata-'apo 'ámani
    it do-FUT your how it want-GND by:there
    He will do it however you want it done.

Yaqui employs other devices as well for marking manner adverbial clauses. These include the postposition **-betana** *with regard to* as shown in sentence (73), and the postposition **-t** *on, about* in combination with the manner adverbial **háčin** *manner* as in example (74).

(73) 'á'a yá'a-nee-'epo-bétana hú'unee-bae-n
    it do-FUT-GND-about know-DSD-PCN
    He wanted to know about doing it.

(74) háčin 'á'a yá'a-nee-'u-t nát-temae-k
    manner his do-FUT-GND-on IZR-ask-PRF
    He asked how to do it.

PART VI: A YAQUI TEXT

HABIEL MÓ'EL

"Gabriel Sparrow's Narrow Escape"[1]

Ambrosio Castro

(1) 'iníi'i há'ani yoéme habiél mó'el-téa-n
this perhaps person Gabriel Sparrow-called-PCN
Once upon a time there was a man named Gabriel Sparrow.

(2) méte'etóma-ka-'apo-bétuk hó'aa-ka-n
belly-have-GND-under house-having-PCN
He used to live at the foot of Méte'etomak.

(3) 'iníi'i meté'etóma-k-ame kó'oko-im-po ta'á-ta yéu-wéye-'e-bétana taáwa
this belly-have-NZR chili-PL-in(Cocorit) sun-POS out-come-EV-from remain
This mountain named Méte'etomak is located to the east of Cocorit.

(4) 'iníi'i habiél mó'el hunáman yéu-sií-ka čú'u-mé'a-m-pá'a-kun
this Gabriel Sparrow there out-go-PRF dog-kill-PL-plain-in
One day this Gabriel Sparrow left home because he wanted to go to Dog-killer-Flats.

(5) yéu-yebíh-née-ka-i. 'óta-m-káu-ta kátek-a'apo
out-arrive-FUT-PPL-STAT bone-PL-mountain-ACC located-in

'áman yéu-sií-ka. 'ilí kúta potčíi-ta mám-po mačú'ute-ka
there out-go-PRF little wood short-ACC hand-in grasp-VR-PPL
He went past Bones Mountain and he went carrying a short stick in his hand.

(6) bo'ó-hóa tebé
road-make long
It was to be a long trip.

(7) bo'ó-po wéye-k báhko'a-m-meu lúula 'ánia-ta nú'u-ka
road-in go-PRF Bacum-PL-to straight world-ACC take-PPL
He headed straight toward Bahkó'am (?).

(8) bʷéere húam-po-betuk 'áma behúk-tí-sime waté-m 'íntok túbuk-ta-síme
large trees-in-under them duck-CON-go other-PL and jump-VR-go
As he went he stooped to duck under some of the larger trees and he jumped over the smaller bushes.

(9) 'únnaa póčo'o-ku 'ámani.
very:much woods-in by:there
There was very thick brush where he was going and there was no (direct) road or path.

(10) póčo'o-ku 'obíači-ku 'ámani hiókot 'ané-ka bó'o-hóa
woods-in difficult-in by:there misery be-PPL road-make
Some of the woods were very thick and difficult to get through and it was hard going.

(11) hunúen tebé-bo'ó-po 'á-u kéča'i-ka wee
thus long-road-in him-to stand-ing go
So he went with a long, difficult trip ahead of him.

---

1 Yqui text recorded 1941 to 1944.

SONORA YAQUI LANGUAGE STRUCTURES

(12) hunáman báhkó'am bewit-či hú'upa-sóo'o-ku
there Bacum beside-in Mesquite-thicket-in
He passed to one side of Bacum, through the mesquite thickets,

(13) 'akí-sóo'o-ku sebíi-po
pitahaya-thicket-in cholla-in
through the pitahaya thickets, through the cactus thickets

(14) 'ámani káa 'áa 'áma rehtí-mačí-ku
by:there not able there go:PL-seem-in
places that seemed impossible to get through,

(15) hunáma 'áman wee wáa'a yoéme Habiél Mó'el
there by:there go that person Gabriel Sparrow
on went this man Gabriel Sparrow.

(16) túa kó'om kúakte-o=su hunáma hak=sa-béna-ku há'ani túa bo'ó-ta ná'ulai-ku
truly down turn-when=EMP there where=Q-like-in perhaps truly road-POS narrow-in
About mid afternoon, there somewhere on a very narrow path

(17) láaut-a'a wéye-o=su bakót 'áawas yéu-sií-ka
very:slowly-his go-when=EMP snake across out-go-PRF
as he was going along rather slowly, a snake crossed in front of him

(18) táa wáa'a baákot 'á'a bo'ó-t wéye
but that snake her road-on go
But the snake was just on her way somewhere.

(19) habiél 'íntok 'áu-'á'a mée-'e-túa-ka ho'ó-t nananá-'a-ku 'á'a béeba-k
Gabriel and RFL-it kill-EV-CAU-PPL back-on middle-EV-in it hit-PRF

wá-e kúta-poči-e
that-with stick-short-INST
Intending to kill the snake, Gabriel hit it in the middle of the back with the short stick he was carrying.

(20) táa káa 'á'a mé'aa-k kía kó'oko-si 'á'a yáa-k baákot
but not it kill-PRF only pain-AVR it do-PRF snake
But he didn't kill the snake; he just injured it.

(21) kó'oko-si 'áu-la-táka húya-u kibáke-k mó'el 'íntok káa 'á'a haháse-k
painful-AVR be-PPL-being woods-to enter-PRF Sparrow and not it chase-PRF

kía-la-'a sím-tua-k
only-CON-it go-CAU-PRF
The injured snake entered into the brush and Gabriel Sparrow did not chase after it, he just let it go on.

(22) yú'in čúbaa 'á'a wéye-o=su séeh-čúk-ti bʷé'u pá'aria 'á-u yéu-mačia-k
much time his go-when=EMP once-cut-CON big open:space him-to out-appear-PRF
After he had travelled along for a good bit, suddenly a large open space appeared before him.

(23) hunáma 'íntok yoéme teébe 'á'a nánki-ka wée 'á-u kíkte-k 'á'a tebótua-k
there and person tall him meet-PPL come him-to stand-PRF him greet-PRF
And there was a tall man coming to greet him. The man stood before him and greeted him:

(24) Liós 'é'em čánia 'áčali-ti 'á-u hiía
God you help sir-CON him-to say
"Good afternoon, sir," he said to him.

402

(25) Liós 'é'em čiókoe t=a'a yóopna-k húu'u mó'el
God you pity CON=him reply-PRF that Sparrow
"Good afternoon," answered Gabriel Sparrow.

(26) heéwi 'áčali tí-hiía wáa'a yoéme wáaria-bétana 'é-u bíttua-wa-k néhpo
yes sir CON-say that person Guard-from you-to send-PSV-PRF I
"Indeed, sir," said the man, "I have been sent to you from the village authorities.

(27) 'áman='e'e noiti-saí-wa ne-mák wée-nee
there=you go-command-PSV me-with come-FUT
You have been ordered to appear there; come with me."

(28) heéwi 'ačai túa=su tú'i t-iía húu'u mó'el
yes sir truly=EMP good CON-say that Sparrow
"All right, sir, good enough," said Gabriel Sparrow.

(29) náuw=im sáha-k
together=they go:PL-PRF
They went together.

(30) 'áman yepsa-ka tebóte-k
there arrive-PPL greet-PRF
When they arrived, there were the mutual greetings.

(31) yesá='e 'áčali ti-hía húu'u kóbanao yó'owe
sit=you sir CON-say that governor elder
"Sit down, sir," said the senior governor.

(32) mó'el yehte-k
Sparrow sit:SG-PRF
Gabriel Sparrow sat down.

(33) hunáma béha temái-wa
there well question-PSV
The interrogation began.

(34) heéwi 'ačal-im haísa túa yéu-sika-'apo 'émpo wáka'a hámut-ta bo'ó-t kó'oko-si
yes sir-PL why truly out-go-PPL you that:ACC woman-ACC road-on painful-AVR

yáa-k 'áčali
did sir
"Now, sir, can you give us the reason why you injured that woman on the road?"

(35) túa né kaábe-ta bo'ó-t nankí-la tebé-bó'ó-po wée-ka húni'i kaábe-ta bíča
truly I no:one-ACC road-on meet-PPL long-road-on come-PPL even nobody-ACC see
"I met absolutely no one on the road and I have come for a long distance without seeing anyone."

(36) 'émpo 'usi-hámut-ta kó'oko-si yáa-k t-iía húu'u kóbanao
you child-woman-ACC pain-AVR do-PRF CON-say that governor
"You injured a girl," the senior governor said.

(37) 'áa heéwi 'ačali né-tče='em hiókoe túa né kaábe-ta kó'oko-si yá'a-la
ah yes sir me-on=you pardon truly I nobody-ACC painful-AVR do-PPL
"Indeed, sir, I beg your pardon but I have injured absolutely no one."

(38) húnakbéha hámut 'áma kátek-ame temai-wa
then:well woman there seated-NZR question-PSV
Then the woman who was seated there was questioned.

(39) haí=sa hiía maála,
how=INTERR say lady
"What do you say, child?"

(40) káa 'iníi'i hunáa'a 'enči   kó'oko-si yáa-k-ame
     not this that   you:ACC pain-AVR do-PRF-NZR
     Is this not the one who injured you?"

(41) haná'aka hápči 'iníi'i hunáa'a 'áawah née wéye-o kúta-e   née béeba-k
     sure   sir   this   that   across I   go-when stick-INST me hit-PRF
     "He certainly is, sir. He is the one. As I was crossing in front of him, he hit me with a stick."

(42) hó 'ačai 'émpo hunáa'a-téa   t-a'u   hiía húu'u kobanao yó'owe
     ahaa sir you that-she:says CON-him:to say that governor elder
     "Well, sir, she says that you are the one," said the senior governor.

(43) mó'el   músu-la   káte-ka 'ínen hiía báhi lióh-ta téa-m-po   nétče='em hiókoe
     Sparrow serious-PPL sit-PPL thus say three gods' name-PL-in me:on=you pardon
     Gabriel Sparrow, who was now seated there with a very serious expression, said: "In the three God's names, I beg your pardon,

(44) túa   né kaábe-ta   bít-laa
     truly I nobody-ACC see-PPL
     I have seen absolutely no one,"

(45) nétče='em   hiókoe tí-húči   té'e-ka
     me:on=you pardon CON-again say-PPL
     "Pardon me," he replied again.

(46) heéwi 'áčal-im 'átt=a'a hiókoi-nee   t-iía   sí'ime wáa'a puéplo
     yes   sir-PL we=him pardon-FUT CON-say all   that people
     "Well, sirs, we will pardon him," said all the people present.

(47) hunáma béha hióko-i-wa-ka   kikte-ka 'ám
     there well pardon-STAT-PSV-PPL stand-PPL them
     Having been pardoned there, he stood up and thanked them.

(48) Lióh-bʷania-k sika=ne Liós 'é'em čanía-ti-tee-'e-ka
     God-cry-PRF go:SG=I God you help-CON-say-EV-PPL
     "Well, I guess I'll be going now. A good evening to you all."

(49) pa'a-kun-bíča   yéu-wáak-te-k   wáaria-po
     out-side-toward out-stride-VR-PRF guard-in
     Having said this, he strode toward the outside.

(50) kée   yé='a   weye-o wáa'a wáaria-tu-k-'a'u wáa'a pá'aria-tu-k-a'u
     not:yet out=his go-when that guard-VR-PRF-GND that open:space-VR-PPL-GND
     sí'ime wáme'e hó'a-raa-m-tu-ka-'um   kaíta-tú-k
     all   those village-ABS-PL-VR-PRF-GND nothing-VR-PRF
     He hadn't even gotten completely out of the assembly there, before everything disappeared, the assembled authorities, the open space, all the houses, everything.

(51) kaíta-'apo   taáwa-k
     nothing-in remain-PRF
     They just weren't there.

(52) húči-béna-si   húa-soo'o-ku   taáwa-k
     again-like-ADV wood-thicket-in remain-PRF
     It was just wooded thicket as it had been before.

(53) wáa'a póobe mó'el   humák húni'i káa máhhae-k káa 'áu wómta-k
     that poor Sparrow perhaps even not fear-PRF not RFL scare-PRF
     Poor Gabriel Sparrow, he continued his trip and seemed not to be frightened or scared.

(54) húči bó'o-hóo-táite-k   wáa'a 'ilí kúta-póči-e   húya-m bép-síme máoh-te-sime
    again road-make-begin-PRF that little stick-short-INST bush-PL hit-go weed-cut-go

    húya-m túbuk-ta-síme
    bush-PL jump-VR-go
    He went on hitting the brush with the little stick he was carrying, knocked weeds out of the way, went jumping brush

(55) bʷéere-m-bétuk behúk-ti-síme bó'o-hóo-taíte-k
    large-PL-under duck-CON-go road-make-begin-PRF
    and ducking under the larger trees, he began making his way.

(56) hunáen bo'ó-hóa-ka=su   kúpte-o   ta'á-ta 'áman sík-čín-ti wéče-o
    thus road-make-PPL=EMP evening-when sun-POS there red-cotton-CON fall-when
    Well, on he went, and in the late afternoon, as the setting sun was tinting the sky a reddish hue,

(57) batʷé-ta túbuk-ta-n wána'a ba'á-ta   kó'om-si-ka-'apo kó'om héela
    river-ACC leap-VR-PCN off:there water-POS down-go-PPL-in down nearly
    he crossed the river close to Where the Water Goes Down.

(58) hunáman yéu-sií-ka húči hú'upa-po kibáke-k
    off:there out-go-PRF again mesquite-in enter-PRF
    He came out on the other side and entered the mesquite thickets again.

(59) túa kút-sá'ite-o béha čú'u-mé'a-m-pá'a-kun yéu 'án-síme-n
    truly dark-when well dog-kill-PL-plain-in   out be-go-PCN
    Just when it was about completely dark he arrived at Dog Killer Flats.

(60) hunúen-po béha 'á'a wawái-m-me-u   yéu-yépsa-k čú'u-mé'a-m-pá'a-kun
    thus-in   well his relative-PL-CON-to out-arrived dog-kill-NZR-plain-in

    hó'aa-ka-m-mewi
    house-have-PL-to
    So it was that he came to the home of his relatives, the ones who live in Dog Killer Flats.

(61) yepsá-ka tebó-te-k yóopna-wa-k mabét-wa-k   kúta-t yéča-'a-wa-k
    arrive-PPL greet-VR-PRF answer-PSV-PRF receive-PSV-PRF wood-on put-EV-PSV-PRF
    Arriving he greeted them, was answered, and received inside, and given a wooden block to sit on.

(62) hunáma káte-ka 'áu 'etého sí'ime-ta wáka'a bo'ó-t 'á'a bíča-k-a'u
    there seat-PPL RFL relate all-ACC that:ACC road-on his see-PRF-GND

    hiókot 'á'a 'an-su-k-a'u
    misery his be-CPL-PPL-GND
    Seated there he recounted to them all the experiences of the day, what he had seen on the trip, and how difficult it had been to get there.

(63) 'ámani 'ámeu-u 'á'a téuwaa
    there them-to it tell
    He detailed it all to them.

(64) húnak-pobéha hiák-yó'o-tu-i 'á-u yéhte-ka kútanaa-po 'áu tú'u-te-ka 'ínen
    then-in:well Yaqui-old-VR-PPL him-to sit-PPL throat-in self good-VR-PPL thus

    'á-u hiía
    him-to say
    Then, when he had finished, there was a very old Yaqui man who, seating himself there and clearing his throat, said to him:

(65) héewi núhmea hunáa'a baákot 'íntok wáa'a b^wé'u pá'aria-tu-k-a'u wáa'a híak
yes relative that snake and that big plain-VR-PRF-GND that Yaqui

yá'u-raa-tú-k-a'u 'ée-béah yéhte-k-a'u sí'ime hunáa'a bakót yá'u-raa
chief-ABS-VR-PRF-GND you-near sit-PRF-GND all that snake chief-ABS
"Well, young friend, that snake, and all that big clearing, and the village and the Yaqui authorities that appeared there before you, all of that was a snake tribunal.

(66) hunáme'e 'enčí hióko-le-ka káa 'enči bép-su-k
those you:ACC pity-think-PPL not you:ACC hit-CMP-PRF
They felt sorry for you, so they did not have you whipped.

(67) hunáa'a bakót 'ém kó'oko-si yáa-k-a'u 'á'a yá'u-ra-u 'enčí yéu-ná'ateho-k
that snake your painful-AVR do-PPL-GND her chief-ABS-to you:ACC out-accuse-PRF
The snake that you injured, accused you to her authorities.

(68) hunáme béha 'ée-béah hóote-k 'emó híak-yáa-ka-i
those well you-front locate-PRF RFL Yaqui-make-PPL-STAT
These authorities appeared before you, having made themselves into Yaqui people.

(69) hunáa'a yá'u-raa hunáka'a hámut-ta nok-ria-k
that chief-ABS that:ACC woman-ACC speak-APL-PRF
Those authorities defended that woman.

(70) táa čé'a-sán 'éa-ka káa bemúča-'a-wa-k
but more-EXP think-PPL not beat-EV-PSV-PRF
But fortunately you were not beaten.

(71) 'inían-po béha 'í'an naáte-ka-i kát haíbu ta'á-po bakót-ta wéye-o
thus-in well today begin-PPL-STAT not:IMP now day-in snake-ACC go-when
So for that reason, beginning now and from now on, never hit a snake when it is on the move.

(72) kát=a'a béeba
not:IMP=it hit
Do not hit it!

(73) 'á'a béeba-k húni'i túa 'á'a mé'e-nee b^wé'ituk hunáa'a baákot káa mukú-k-o 'enčí
it hit-PRF even truly it kill-FUT because that snake not die-PRF-if you:ACC

ná'ateho-nee
accuse-FUT
If you do hit it, make sure that you kill it, because if the snake does not die it will accuse you.

(74) bo'ó-t yánti 'á'a bó'o-k-o húnak 'á'a mé'e-nee táa túa 'á'a mé'e-nee
road-on still it lie-PRF-if then it kill-FUT but truly it kill-FUT
If it is lying still in the road, then kill it but be sure that it is completely dead."

(75) wéye-m-ta kát béba b^wé'ituk wáa'a wéye-me hí'i-b^wá-bae-ka wéye
go-NZR-ACC not:IMP hit because that go-NZR INTR-eat-DSD-PPL go
"Don't kill a moving snake because the one that is on the move is looking for something to eat.

(76) wáa'a 'íntok bó'o-ka-me 'áu-ii'aa-bae bó'o-ka
that and lay-PPL-NZR RFL-IN:DSD-DSD lay-PPL
But the one that is lying still has bad intentions.

(77) 'inían-po né 'enčí lútu'uria-m máka 'ín núhmea
thus-in I you:ACC truth-ACC give my relative
That is why I am setting you straight.

(78) liós 'é'em čiókoe   'útte'esia kát   'íntok bakótč-im réhte-me béba
     thank you:PL be:merciful very:much not:IMP again snake-PL go-NZR hit

   'enčím   húči ná'ateho-nee
   you:ACC again accuse-FUT
   By God's mercies, I seriously recommend that you do not hit a moving snake again, or it will accuse you again."

(79) 'áa heéwi Liós 'é'em čiókoe   'útte'esia t-iía   húu'u mó'el   tóno-m-mea
     ah yes God you:PL be:merciful very:much CON-say that Sparrow knee-PL-with

   wée-ka-i
   stand-PPL-STAT
   "Is that true? Thank you very much," said Gabriel Sparow kneeling before the old man.

(80) húnak naáte-ka-i   'íme hiák-im   bakótč-im kat-éme   káa béba.
     then begin-PPL-STAT these yaqui-PL snake-PL moving-NZR not hit
     Beginning at that time, Yaquis do not hit moving snakes.

REFERENCES

Buelna, Eustaquio. 1891. *Arte de la lengua Cahita, por un Padre de la Compañia de Jesús*. México D.F.: Buelna.

Burnham, Jeffrey. 1988. "Mayo Suprasegmentals: Synchronic and Diachronic Considerations." In William Shipley, ed. *In Honor of Mary Haas: From the Haas Festival Conference on Native American Linguistics*: 37–51. Berlin and New York: Mouton de Gruyter.

Casad, Eugene H. 1984. "Cora." In Ronald W. Langacker, ed. *Southern Uto-Aztecan Grammatical Sketches*: 153–475. Arlington: The Summer Institute of Linguistics and the University of Texas at Arlington.

_____. 1992. "Cora Postpositions." *Leuvense Bijdragen: Leuven contributions in linguistics and philology* 81:45–70.

Crumrine, Lynn S. 1961. *The Phonology of Arizona Yaqui with Texts*. Anthropological Papers of the University of Arizona no. 5. Tucson: University of Arizona Press.

Dedrick, John. 1946. "How Jobe'eso Ro'i Got His Name." *Tlalocan* 2:163–166.

_____. 1977. "Spanish Influence on Yaqui Grammar?" *IJAL* 43.2:144–149.

_____. 1985. "Las Cartas en Yaqui de Juan 'Bandera.'" *Tlalocan* 10:119–187.

Diebold, A. Richard. 1964. "Incipient Bilingualism." In Dell Hymes, ed. *Language in Culture and Society: A Reader in Linguistics and Anthropology*: 495–508. New York, Evanston and London: Harper & Row and Tokyo: John Weatherhill, Inc.

Dozier, Edward P. 1964. "Two Examples of Linguistic Acculturation: The Yaqui of Sonora and the Tewa of New Mexico." In Dell Hymes, ed. *Language in Culture and Society: A Reader in Linguistics and Anthropology*: 509–520. New York, Evanston & London: Harper & Row and Tokyo: John Weatherhill, Inc.

Escalante, Fernando. 1990a. *Voice and Argument Structure in Yaqui*. Ph.D. dissertation, University of Arizona.

_____. 1990b. "Setting the Record Straight on Yaqui Passives." *IJAL* 56:289–292.

Evers, Larry, and Felipe S. Molina. 1987. *Yaqui Deer Songs/Maso Bwikam: A Native American Poetry*. Tucson: University of Arizona Press.

_____. 1992. *Hiakim: The Yaqui Homeland*. Special Issue of *Journal of the Southwest*: Vol. 34, No. 1.

Fábila, Alfonso. 1940. *Las Tribus Yaquis de Sonora: Su cultura y anhelada autodeterminación*. México, D.F.: Departamento de Asuntos Indígenas.

Fraenkel, Gerd. 1959. "Yaqui Phonemics." *Anthropological Linguistics* 5:7–18.

Hagberg, Larry. 1988. "Stress and Length in Mayo." In William Shipley, ed. *In Honor of Mary Haas: From the Haas Festival Conference on Native American Linguistics*: 361–375. Berlin and New York: Mouton de Gruyter.

_____. 1993. *An Autosegmenal Theory of Stress*. Ph.D. dissertation, University of Arizona

Haiman, John. 1985. *Natural Syntax: Iconicity and Erosion*. Cambridge, U.K.: Cambridge University Press.

Heath, Jeffrey. 1977. "Uto-Aztecan Morphophonemics." *IJAL* 43:27–36.

Heine, Bernd, and Mechthild Reh. 1984. *Grammaticalization and Reanalysis in African Languages*. Hamburg: Helmut Buske Verlag.

Hu-DeHart, Evelyn. 1981. *Missionaries, Miners and Indians: Spanish Contact with the Yaqui Nation of Northwestern New Spain, 1533–1820*. Tucson: University of Arizona Press.

———. 1984. *Yaqui Resistance and Survival: The Struggle for Land and Autonomy, 1821–1910*. Madison: The University of Wisconsin Press.

Jelinek, Eloise, and Fernando Escalante. 1988. "'Verbless' Possessive Sentences in Yaqui." In William Shipley, ed. *In Honor of Mary Haas: From the Haas Festival Conference on Native American Linguistics*: 411–429. Berlin, New York, and Amsterdam: Mouton de Gruyter.

Johnson, Jean B. 1940. "El Yaqui." Unpublished manuscript.

———. 1943. "A Clear Case of Linguistic Acculturation." *American Anthropologist* 45:427–434.

———. 1962. *El Idioma Yaqui*. México, D.F.: Instituto Nacional de Antropología e Historia, Departamento de Investigaciones Antropológicas.

Karttunen, Francis. 1985. *The Long-Term Effects of Spanish Language Contact on Nahuatl and Yucatecan Maya*. Austin: The University of Texas Linguistics Research Center.

Kurath, William, and Edward M. Spicer. 1947. *A Brief Introduction to Yaqui: A Native Language of Sonora*. University of Arizona Bulletin, Vol. 18: No. 1. Social Science Bulletin No. 15. Tucson: The University of Arizona.

Langacker, Ronald W. 1977a. "Syntactic Reanalysis." In Charles N. Li, ed. *Mechanisms of Syntactic Change*: 57–139. Austin: University of Texas Press.

———. 1977b. *Studies in Uto-Aztecan Grammar*, Vol. 1. *An Overview of Uto-Aztecan Grammar*. Arlington: The Summer Institute of Linguistics and the University of Texas at Arlington.

———. 1977c. "The Syntax of Postpositions in Uto-Aztecan." *IJAL* 43:11–26.

———. 1980. *Studies in Uto-Aztecan Grammar*, Vol. 2. *Aztecan Grammatical Sketches*. Arlington: The Summer Institute of Linguistics and the University of Texas at Arlington.

———. 1982. *Studies in Uto-Aztecan Grammar*, Vol. 3. *Uto-Aztecan Grammatical Sketches*. Arlington: The Summer Institute of Linguistics and the University of Texas at Arlington.

———. 1984. *Studies in Uto-Aztecan Grammar*, Vol. 4. *Southern Uto-Aztecan Grammatical Sketches*. Arlington: The Summer Institute of Linguistics and the University of Texas at Arlington.

Lindenfeld, Jacqueline. 1971. "Semantic Categorization as a Deterrent to Grammatical Borrowings: A Yaqui Example." *IJAL* 37:6–14.

———. 1973. *Yaqui Syntax*. Berkeley: University of California Press.

López, Gerardo, and José Luis Moctezuma. 1994. "Dialectología Cahita." In Gerardo López Cruz and José Luis Moctezuma Zamarrón, eds. *Estudios de Lingüística y Sociolingüística*: 221–274. Hermosillo, Sonora, México: Universidad de Sonora e Instituto Nacional de Antropología.

Martínez Fabián, Constantino. 1994. "La reduplicación en las raíces nominales del yaqui." In Gerardo López Cruz and José Luis Moctezuma Zamarrón, eds. *Estudios de Lingüística y Sociolingüística:* 157–177. Hermosillo, Sonora, México: Universidad de Sonora e Instituto Nacional de Antropología.

Miller, Wick R. 1980. "The Classification of the Uto-Aztecan Languages Based on Lexical Evidence." Paper presented to the Uto-Aztecan Historical Symposium at the 1980 Summer Linguistic Institute, University of New Mexico at Albuquerque, N.M. June 26, 1980.

____. 1991. "Agent in Passive Sentences in Yaqui and Guarijio." *IJAL* 57:519–523.

____. with Kevin Jon Hegg, Laurel Anderton, and Cindy High. 1988. *Computerized Data Base for Uto-Aztecan Cognate Sets*. Salt Lake City: University of Utah, Department of Anthropology.

Moisés, Rosalio, Jane Holden Kelly, and William Curry Holden. 1971. *The Tall Candle*. Lincoln: The University of Nebraska Press.

Radden, Günter. 1985. "Spatial Metaphors Underlying Prepositions of Causality." In Wolf Paprotté and Rene Dirven, eds. *The Ubiquity of Metaphor: Metaphor in Language and Thought*: 177–207. Current Issues in Linguistic Theory, Vol. 29. Amsterdam and Philadelphia: John Benjamins.

Savala, Refugio. 1980. *Autobiography of a Yaqui Poet*. [Edited by Kathleen M. Sands.] Tucson: The University of Arizona Press.

Spicer, Edward H. 1940. *Pascua: A Yaqui Village in Arizona*. Chicago: University of Chicago Press.

____. 1943. "Linguistic Aspects of Yaqui Acculturation." *American Anthropologist* 45:410–26.

____. 1954. "Pótam: A Yaqui Village in Sonora." *American Anthropologist* 56:4, Part 2. Memoir 77.

____. 1980. *The Yaquis: A Cultural History*. Chicago: University of Chicago Press.

____. 1981. *Cycles of Conquest: The Impact of Spain, Mexico, and the United States on the Indians of the Southwest, 1533–1960*. Tucson: The University of Arizona Press.

Traugott, Elisabeth Closs, and Bernd Heine, eds. 1991. *Approaches to Grammaticalization*. 2 vol. Amsterdam and Philadelphia: John Benjamins.

Wierzbicka, Anna. 1985. "'Oats' and 'Wheat': The Fallacy of Arbitrariness." In John Haiman, ed. *Iconicity in Syntax*: 311–342. Cambridge, U.K.: Cambridge University Press.

____. 1988. *The Semantics of Grammar*. Studies in Language Companion Series no. 18. Amsterdam and Philadelphia: John Benjamins.